A CRITICAL AND EXEGETICAL
COMMENTARY

ON THE

GOSPEL ACCORDING TO ST. JOHN

BY

ARCHBISHOP J. H. BERNARD

VOLUME II

A CRITICAL AND EXEGETICAL COMMENTARY

ON THE

GOSPEL ACCORDING TO ST. JOHN

BY THE

MOST REV. AND RIGHT HON. J. H. BERNARD, D.D.

EDITED BY THE

REV. A. H. McNEILE, D.D.

(IN TWO VOLUMES)

VOL. II

EDINBURGH

T. & T. CLARK, 38 GEORGE STREET

PRINTED IN GREAT BRITAIN BY
MORRISON AND GIBB LIMITED

FOR

T. & T. CLARK, EDINBURGH
NEW YORK: CHARLES SCRIBNER'S SONS

FIRST IMPRESSION . . . 1928
Latest Reprint 1972

VOLUME II

VIII. 12. Πάλιν οὖν αὐτοῖς ἐλάλησεν ὁ Ἰησοῦς λέγων Ἐγώ
εἰμι τὸ φῶς τοῦ κόσμου· ὁ ἀκολουθῶν μοι οὐ μὴ περιπατήσῃ ἐν τῇ

Jesus declares Himself the Light of the World (VIII. 12–20)

VIII. 12. πάλιν οὖν αὐτοῖς ἐλάλησεν ὁ Ἰησοῦς.[1] The introductory πάλιν does not fix the context of the discourse
which follows, for it is merely resumptive or indicative of the
beginning of a new section, as at v. 21 (see on 1[35]). Verses 12–20
have points of contact with c. 7 (cf. 7[28] and 8[14]), and it is possible
(although not certain; see on 7[45]) that they should be taken in
continuation of the sayings 7[28-38]. If vv. 12–20 follow directly
on 7[52], as we take them, we must suppose the words of 8[12] to be
addressed to the Pharisees, who proceed (8[13]) to find fault with
them. This, indeed, is implied in αὐτοῖς. Nevertheless, the
proclamation " I am the Light of the World " recalls such
sayings as 7[37. 38], which were addressed to all and sundry.

ἐλάλησεν λέγων, λέγων introducing the words spoken; see
on 3[11], and cf. Mt. 14[27].

ἐγώ εἰμι τὸ φῶς τοῦ κόσμου. This is one of the great " I
am's " of the Fourth Gospel, for which see Introd., p. cxviii.

Just as the word of Jesus about the Living Water (7[37. 38])
may have been suggested by the water ceremonial at the Feast
of Tabernacles, so it has been thought that the claim " I am
the Light of the World " may also have a reference to the festal
ceremonies. On the first night of the feast, there was a ceremony of lighting the four golden candlesticks in the Court of
the Women (see v. 20), and there is some evidence for the
continuance of the ceremony on other nights. This may have
provided the occasion for the words of Jesus about light
and darkness. But Philo's account of the Feast of Tabernacles would furnish an equally plausible explanation. He
says that this feast is held at the autumnal equinox, in order
that the world (κόσμος) may be full, not only by day but also
by night, of the all-beautiful light (τοῦ παγκάλου φωτός), as at
that season there is no twilight (de septen. 24). We have in
this passage a close parallel to τὸ φῶς τοῦ κόσμου, but no stress
ought to be laid upon such verbal coincidences. The passage
of Philo shows, however, that the Feast of Tabernacles suggested the idea of light to some minds.[2]

[1] For the section 7[53]–8[11], see the notes at the end of this volume on
the Pericope de Adultera.
[2] Strayer (J.T.S., 1900, p. 138) argues that the imagery was sug-

The Hebrews had thought of God as giving them light, and as being their light. "The Lord is my Light" was the confession of a Psalmist (Ps. 27[1]); "the Lord shall be thy everlasting Light" was the promise of a prophet (Isa. 60[19]). The later Rabbis applied the thought to the Messiah: "Light is the Name of Messiah," they said.[1] The vision of Deutero-Isaiah was larger, for he proclaimed that the Servant of Yahweh would be a Light to the Gentiles (Isa. 42[6] 49[6]; cf. Lk. 2[32]). But the saying ἐγώ εἰμι τὸ φῶς τοῦ κόσμου goes far beyond this, for the κόσμος (see on 1[9]) includes all created life.[2] There is no Hebraic parallel to be found for such a thought,[3] the expression of which here is thoroughly Johannine in form. See Introd., p. cxviii.

In the Prologue, the Word of God is spoken of as the Light. John the Baptist was not the Light, but he came to bear witness of the Light (1[8]), which was τὸ φῶς τὸ ἀληθινόν, lighting every man (1[9]). In the Person of Jesus, the Light came into the world (3[19]), as Jesus Himself said, ἐγὼ φῶς εἰς τὸν κόσμον ἐλήλυθα (12[46]). And so here (8[12]) and at 9[5], the majestic phrase ἐγώ εἰμι τὸ φῶς τοῦ κόσμου is put into the mouth of Jesus.

In the Sermon on the Mount, according to Mt. 5[14], Jesus said to His hearers ὑμεῖς ἐστε τὸ φῶς τοῦ κόσμου. This is apparently to say more than Paul said to his converts when he called them φωστῆρες ἐν κόσμῳ (Phil. 2[15]); and it is not certain that Mt.'s Greek rendering of our Lord's words is accurate here.[4] But if it is precise, the application of the words τὸ φῶς τοῦ κόσμου to faithful citizens of the kingdom of heaven must be wholly different from its application when Christ used it of Himself and said, "*I* am the Light of the World." This is to make an exclusive claim, such as could be made by no other speaker, although others might claim to share in the assurance of Christ that His people are, as contrasted with non-Christians, the world's light. Cf. 7[38] and the note thereupon.

gested by the Feast of Dedication or τὰ Φῶτα (10[22]), in connexion with which he puts this discourse.

[1] Lightfoot, *Hor. Hebr.*, iii. 330.

[2] This majestic claim is weakened in the form in which it appears in the *Acts of John* (§ 95): λύχνος εἰμί σοι τῷ βλέποντί με.

[3] Westcott quotes from Buxtorf a sentence from the Jerusalem Talmud (*Shabb.* c. 2) to the effect that "the first Adam was the light of the world"; but the parallelism seems to be only verbal. Indeed, the Hebrews had not any clear idea of the κόσμος as an ordered universe of being.

[4] Abbott (*Diat.* 1748; cf. 435) urges that Mt.'s report must be wrong, and that what Jesus really said was, "Ye *have* the Light of the World." But there is no evidence for this, nor would it suit the context, Mt. 5[13-16].

σκοτίᾳ, ἀλλ᾿ ἕξει τὸ φῶς τῆς ζωῆς.   13 εἶπον οὖν αὐτῷ οἱ Φαρισαῖοι

ὁ ἀκολουθῶν μοι οὐ μὴ περιπατήσῃ ἐν τῇ σκοτίᾳ. To
" follow " Jesus is to walk in the light. It is the first act of
discipleship (1³⁷), and the last precept in the Gospel enjoins it
as the essential thing (21²²). See 12²⁶. Jesus Himself is
" the Way " (14⁶).

The Hebrew verb הָלַךְ " to walk " is often used in the O.T.
figuratively of conduct in general (*e.g.* 2 Kings 20³), and is
sometimes, when used in this sense, rendered in the LXX by
περιπάτειν (*e.g.* Prov. 8²⁰, Eccles. 11⁹). This use of περιπάτειν
is found only once in the Synoptists (Mk. 7⁵; cf. Acts 21²¹),
but occurs over 30 times in Paul, and frequently in Jn. (see
12³⁵, 1 Jn. 1⁶·⁷ 2⁶·¹¹; cf. 2 Jn.⁶, 3 Jn.³·⁴). It is, in fact, a
Hebraism.

The contrast between the Two Ways, of Darkness and of
Light, is not peculiar to Jn. (cf. Barnabas, § 18), but it is
a favourite topic in his Gospel (see, for "walking" in light or
in darkness, 11⁹ 12³⁵, 1 Jn. 1⁶·⁷). Job (29³) speaks of the days
when God watched over him: " and by His light I walked
through darkness " (cf. Mic. 7⁸). This is part of the thought
in " he that followeth me shall not walk in darkness, but shall
have the light of life "; but it is less explicit. The Light of
God is the Light of Life (τὸ φῶς τῆς ζωῆς).

The *Odes of Solomon* several times express the idea of the
believer walking in the Light of Christ, *e.g.* " He set over
[His way] the footprints of His light, and I walked therein "
(vii. 17; cf. xxix. 7, xxxii. 1).

The phrase τὸ φῶς τῆς ζωῆς may mean the Light which
imparts life or illuminates life; or it may mean the Light which
issues from Life. We have seen that in 6³⁵ the primary meaning of " I am the Bread of Life " is understood by the evangelist
to be " the Bread which gives life " (6³³), but the deeper meaning of " the Living Bread " is not excluded (6⁵¹). So here
we must allow for a double suggestiveness in the phrase τὸ
φῶς τῆς ζωῆς. When we apply such concepts as ζωή, φῶς,
to God or to Christ, we cannot treat them as if we knew them
to be fundamentally distinct. They are qualities or aspects
of Absolute Being, and it is beyond our powers to define them
adequately or explain their mutual relation. In the Fourth
Gospel, Christ is the *Light*: He is also the *Life* (11²⁵ 14⁶).
Perhaps Light *is* Life, in its essence; perhaps Life, truly
understood, *is* Light. See on 1⁴, and Introd., p. cxl.

13. εἶπον οὖν αὐτῷ οἱ Φαρισαῖοι. For the " Pharisees,"
see on 7³², and cf. 1²⁴. Their objection was that the testimony
of Jesus to His own claims was not admissible, according to

Σὺ περὶ σεαυτοῦ μαρτυρεῖς· ἡ μαρτυρία σου οὐκ ἔστιν ἀληθής. 14. ἀπεκρίθη Ἰησοῦς καὶ εἶπεν αὐτοῖς Κἂν ἐγὼ μαρτυρῶ περὶ ἐμαυτοῦ, ἀληθής ἐστιν ἡ μαρτυρία μου, ὅτι οἶδα πόθεν ἦλθον καὶ ποῦ ὑπάγω· ὑμεῖς δὲ οὐκ οἴδατε πόθεν ἔρχομαι ἢ ποῦ ὑπάγω. 15. ὑμεῖς κατὰ τὴν σάρκα κρίνετε, ἐγὼ οὐ κρίνω οὐδένα. 16. καὶ ἐὰν κρίνω δὲ ἐγώ, ἡ

the rules of evidence which governed the controversies of the Rabbis (see on 5[31]). Self-witness was always suspect, and might be disregarded as being untrue.

14. The answer of Jesus κἂν ἐγὼ μαρτυρῶ περὶ ἐμαυτοῦ, ἀληθής ἐστιν ἡ μαρτυρία μου is in formal contradiction with His former admission ἐὰν ἐγὼ μαρτυρῶ περὶ ἐμαυτοῦ, ἡ μαρτυρία μου οὐκ ἔστιν ἀληθής (5[31], where see note); but there is no real contradiction, for here he takes higher ground, so to speak, than on that occasion, and claims that the Divine origin and dignity of which He is conscious justify Him in bearing witness to Himself. This is the very badge of Deity (see v. 18), although it is true that no individual man could claim it (as He had said, 5[31]). He alone could be called ὁ ἀμήν, ὁ μάρτυς ὁ πιστὸς καὶ ἀληθινός (Rev. 3[14]).

ὅτι οἶδα πόθεν ἦλθον, "because I know (with complete knowledge) whence I came," sc. at the Incarnation (cf. 1[1] 13[3] 16[28]).

καὶ ποῦ ὑπάγω, "and whither I go"; see on 7[33] for ὑπάγειν used of "going to the Father."

The words which follow, ὑμεῖς . . . ὑπάγω, do not appear to have been present in the texts known to Origen, but the omission is readily explicable by *homoioteleuton*, ὑπάγω . . . ὑπάγω.

ὑμεῖς δὲ (א om. δέ) οὐκ οἴδατε πόθεν ἔρχομαι. That is, they did not know of His heavenly origin, although (like the Jewish interlocutors of 7[28]) they may have known that He was of the family at Nazareth.

ἢ ποῦ ὑπάγω. See on 7[33].

BDNT support ἤ; the rec., with אLWΘ, has καί.

15. The Pharisees had complained that the self-witness of Jesus was unsupported and therefore untrustworthy (v. 13). In v. 14 Jesus has answered that their objection, however sound if applied to a mere man, fails in His case: they do not know His origin or His home. He now adds that their judgment is superficial because of this ignorance of His true being.

ὑμεῖς κατὰ τὴν σάρκα κρίνετε, "you judge superficially"; cf. for κατὰ τὴν σάρκα, 1 Cor. 1[26], 2 Cor. 5[16]. The Pharisees had done just what He had previously warned them not to do, when He said μὴ κρίνετε κατ᾽ ὄψιν (7[24]).

κρίσις ἡ ἐμὴ ἀληθινή ἐστιν, ὅτι μόνος οὐκ εἰμί, ἀλλ᾿ ἐγὼ καὶ ὁ πέμψας

ἐγὼ οὐ κρίνω οὐδένα. The ultimate purpose of His coming into the world was to save it, not to judge it (3¹⁷); and if an individual man would not obey His word, Jesus did not judge him *then*: the spoken word would judge him at the Last Day (12⁴⁸). At that Great Assize, the Son of Man will be the Judge (see on 3¹⁷ 5²², and Introd., p. clviii). But the saying ἐγὼ οὐ κρίνω οὐδένα refers to the action of Jesus during His public mission on earth, and not to the future judgment of the world. There is a sense in which He *did* judge, or discriminate between one man and another, during His earthly ministry (see vv. 16, 26); but ἐγὼ οὐ κρίνω οὐδένα expresses not only that this was not the *purpose* of His mission (see 3¹⁷), but that it was not His *habit*. It was a charge made against Him that He did not discriminate sufficiently, that He consorted with publicans and sinners (Mk. 2¹⁶, Lk. 15²), that He did not repel the sinful woman at the Pharisee's house (Lk. 7³⁹). Even in the case of the adulteress whose guilt was proved, when judgment must have been condemnation, He said οὐδὲ ἐγώ σε κατακρίνω [8¹¹]. His example was consonant to His own precept μὴ κρίνετε (Mt. 7¹).

This saying of Christ ἐγὼ οὐ κρίνω οὐδένα is found only in Jn., but its genuineness becomes the more apparent the more closely it is examined. It is a paradox, for it is seemingly contradicted in the next verse, but it is one of those terse, pregnant paradoxes of which the Synoptists have preserved many examples.[1]

16. For ἀληθινή (BDLTW 33) the rec. has ἀληθής (אΝΓΔ⊗). For ἀληθινός, see on 1⁹.

ἐὰν κρίνω δέ κτλ., "but if I judge, my judgment is sound," *i.e.* not merely true, but soundly based and complete. Cf. ἡ κρίσις ἡ ἐμὴ δικαία ἐστίν (5³⁰, where see note).

The judgment of Christ is not that of a single individual, for μόνος οὐκ εἰμί, ἀλλ᾿ ἐγὼ καὶ ὁ πέμψας με. Cf. vv. 26, 29, for the same thought, and again 16³² οὐκ εἰμὶ μόνος, ὅτι ὁ πατὴρ μετ᾿ ἐμοῦ ἐστίν. The consciousness of this perpetual association with the Father is explicitly claimed by the Christ of Jn.; but it is implied, too, in the bitterness of the cry " Why hast Thou forsaken me," which is recorded only by Mk. and Mt. Herein was the anguish of the Cross, as they picture it.

The general principle to which the Pharisees appealed, *sc.* that judgment, like testimony, must not depend on one individual, is well illustrated in a Jewish saying (*Pirke Aboth*, iv. 12, quoted by Westcott), " Judge not alone, for none may judge alone save One."

[1] Cf. Introd., p. cx.

I*

με. 17. καὶ ἐν τῷ νόμῳ δὲ τῷ ὑμετέρῳ γέγραπται ὅτι δύο ἀνθρώπων
ἡ μαρτυρία ἀληθής ἐστιν. 18. ἐγώ εἰμι ὁ μαρτυρῶν περὶ ἐμαυτοῦ,

For the conception of Jesus as "sent" by the Father, see
on 3¹⁷ 4³⁴. After ὁ πέμψας με ℵ°BLTΘW add πατήρ, but πατήρ
is omitted by ℵ*D, and it probably comes from v. 18.

17. γέγραπται. Jn. generally has γεγραμμένον ἐστίν where
the Synoptists would have γέγραπται (see on 2¹⁷). But γεγραμμένον ἐστίν here is attested by ℵ only; all other authorities
give γέγραπται, which must therefore be regarded as the true
reading. Abbott (*Diat.* 2588a) suggests that γέγραπται ὅτι is
used here to introduce a quotation not given exactly.

ἐν τῷ νόμῳ κτλ. This is a free reference to the maxim of
evidence in Deut. 19¹⁵ (cf. Num. 35³⁰, Deut. 17⁶; and see
2 Cor. 13¹, 1 Tim. 5¹⁹). For another reference by Jesus to this
legal maxim, cf. Mt. 18¹⁶.

The phrase "your law" challenges scrutiny. Jesus
accepted the "law," *i.e.* the Old Testament scriptures, very
explicitly (see Introd., pp. cxlvii, clv); and it is unlike the way
in which He was accustomed to speak of it, that he should
say "*your* law," thus dissociating Himself, as it were, from
any recognition of its authority. He is represented in 10³⁴ as
again using this expression, and in 15²⁵ as speaking to His
disciples of Scripture as "their law," *i.e.* the law of the Jews.
It is true that in 8¹⁷ and 10³⁴ the phrase appears in controversy
with the Jews, and it might be thought that it supplied an
argumentum ad hominem. Those who disputed with Jesus
were shown to be in the wrong, on their own principles. But in
the equally argumentative passage 7¹⁹· ²³, He speaks of "the
law" and "the law of Moses"; and no such explanation can
be given of the phrase "their law" in 15²⁵, which would
definitely dissociate Him from the people of Israel, by suggesting that their Scriptures were not His Scriptures. In every
place where ὁ νόμος is mentioned by Him in the Synoptists,
whether it refers to the law which He came "not to destroy,
but to fulfil," or in a wider sense to the O.T. books, He always
says "*the* Law" (cf. Mt. 5¹⁷· ¹⁸ 7¹² 11¹³ 12⁵ 22⁴⁰ 23²³, Lk.
2²²· ²⁴· ²⁷· ³⁹ 10²⁶ 16¹⁶; the word νόμος does not occur in Mk.).

It is difficult to think that in these Johannine texts (8¹⁷
10³⁴ 15²⁵) the words of Jesus have been exactly reproduced.[1]

18. The use of ἐγώ εἰμι in solemn affirmation has been
discussed in Introd., p. cxviii; and the present passage provides
an instructive example of this usage.

ἐγώ εἰμι ὁ μαρτυρῶν περὶ ἐμαυτοῦ. This is the style of Deity.
As the Pharisees had urged, a man's witness about himself

[1] See also McNeile in *Cambridge Biblical Essays*, p. 242.

καὶ μαρτυρεῖ περὶ ἐμοῦ ὁ πέμψας με Πατήρ.   19. ἔλεγον οὖν αὐτῷ
Ποῦ ἐστιν ὁ Πατήρ σου; ἀπεκρίθη Ἰησοῦς Οὔτε ἐμὲ οἴδατε οὔτε τὸν
Πατέρα μου· εἰ ἐμὲ ᾔδειτε, καὶ τὸν Πατέρα μου ἂν ᾔδειτε.   20. Ταῦτα

is not trustworthy (v. 13); but Jesus replies to this by
expressing Himself in terms which suggest His Divinity.
This, however, is not said explicitly; and the point of His
answer which the Pharisees understand is that He says that
there is a second Witness, sc. His Father who sent Him
(cf. 5³²). There is a prophetic passage, Isa. 43¹⁰, which has
close verbal relations with this and v. 28: γένεσθέ μοι μάρτυρες,
καὶ ἐγὼ μάρτυς, λέγει κύριος ὁ θεός, καὶ ὁ παῖς μου ὃν ἐξελεξάμην,
ἵνα γνῶτε καὶ πιστεύσητε, καὶ συνῆτε ὅτι ἐγώ εἰμι.   The thought
in Isa. 43¹⁰, however, is of witness being borne to Yahweh
(1) by the people, (2) by His Servant, and, according to the
LXX interpolation, (3) by Himself.

For the witness of the Father to the Son, see on 5³⁷.

19. ποῦ ἐστιν ὁ πατήρ σου; This is the rejoinder of the
Jewish objectors. They understand that by ὁ πατήρ (v. 16)
Jesus means God the Father, and they do not ask " *Who* is
He ? " But they say " *Where* is He ? " This second Witness,
of whom Jesus had spoken, is not visible, and therefore (according to the Rabbinical doctrine of evidence) no appeal can be
made to Him.

The answer of Jesus is, in effect, that their ignorance
is invincible. God cannot, of course, be perceived by the
senses. He is appealing to the witness of One whom no man
can see.

οὔτε ἐμὲ οἴδατε οὔτε τὸν πατέρα μου. There is no inconsistency with 7²⁸ κἀμὲ οἴδατε, for there Jesus speaks only of
the Jews' knowledge of Him as man, and of the family at
Nazareth; here He speaks of their ignorance of His true
Personality, which is Divine (cf. v. 14). Being ignorant of this,
and therefore of His relation to the Father, they betray ignorance also of the Father Himself.   Cf. οὐκ ἐγνώκατε αὐτόν (v. 55),
and οὐκ ἔγνωσαν τὸν πατέρα οὐδὲ ἐμέ (16³).   See Mt. 11²⁷,
Lk. 10²².

εἰ ἐμὲ ᾔδειτε, καὶ τὸν πατέρα μου ἂν ᾔδειτε. This principle is
repeated 14⁷, εἰ ἐγνώκειτέ με, καὶ τὸν πατέρα μου ἂν ᾔδειτε (cf. 12⁴⁵
and 14⁹), and it is deep rooted in the Fourth Gospel. Jesus
came to *reveal* the Father, not only by His words but by
His life.

Note that εἰ ἐμὲ ᾔδειτε of this verse is replaced by εἰ
ἐγνώκειτέ με at 14⁷, showing what precarious ground we are
on when an attempt is made to distinguish οἶδα from γιγνώσκω
(see on 1²⁶).

τὰ ῥήματα ἐλάλησεν ἐν τῷ γαζοφυλακίῳ διδάσκων ἐν τῷ ἱερῷ· καὶ οὐδεὶς ἐπίασεν αὐτόν, ὅτι οὔπω ἐληλύθει ἡ ὥρα αὐτοῦ.

21. Εἶπεν οὖν πάλιν αὐτοῖς Ἐγὼ ὑπάγω καὶ ζητήσετέ με, καὶ ἐν

20. ταῦτα τὰ ῥήματα. Emphatic, and therefore placed at the beginning of the sentence.

ἐλάλησεν ἐν τῷ γαζοφυλακίῳ. The γαζοφυλάκιον was the name for the treasure-chamber of the Temple (cf. Mk. 12⁴¹, Lk. 21¹, and 2 Macc. 3⁶ 4⁴²). It abutted on the Court of the Women, and against its walls were placed chests, trumpet-like in form, as receptacles for the offerings of the worshippers. It is not probable that Jesus was teaching *within* a treasure-chamber, and so it seems that ἐν should be taken as denoting proximity only, "*near* the treasury" (cf. ἐν δεξιᾷ τοῦ θεοῦ, Rom. 8³⁴). Hence ἐν τῷ γαζοφυλακίῳ διδάσκων ἐν τῷ ἱερῷ means " teaching in the Temple precincts (see on 2¹⁴) near the treasury chamber," *i.e.* in the colonnade between it and the open court (cf. Mk 12⁴¹). The hall where the Sanhedrim met was hard by, and probably within earshot of the place where Jesus was teaching.

καὶ οὐδεὶς ἐπίασεν αὐτόν κτλ., " and yet " (καί being used for καίτοι, as often in Jn.; see on 1¹⁰) " no man took Him, because His hour was not yet come." This is almost verbally repeated from 7³⁰, where see note. For οὔπω ἐληλύθει ἡ ὥρα αὐτοῦ, see also on 2⁴.

Jesus develops His lofty claims : some of the Jews who hear believe (vv. 21–30)

21. The occasion of the discourse which follows is not mentioned. It may be a continuation of what precedes (see on v. 26), and if so οὖν may be causative, having reference to the fact that Jesus had not been arrested (v. 20; cf. 7³³). But perhaps οὖν is used as a mere conjunction (see on 1²²), and πάλιν only marks (as in v. 12) the beginning of a new discourse. It is not possible to assign every discourse in Jn. to its original occasion; and one of the many rearrangements of the Gospel (that of F. W. Lewis) would place 8²¹⁻⁵⁹ after 7⁵². Ver. 21 reproduces, though not verbally, the warning of 7³³˙ ³⁴, and its last clause is addressed in identical terms to the disciples at 13³³ (where see note). But πάλιν is not to be taken as an allusion to the repetition of 7³⁴; as has been said, it may only mark the opening of a new discourse or paragraph (v. 12, 10⁷; and see on 1³⁵).

εἶπεν οὖν πάλιν αὐτοῖς. ΝΓΔΘ add ὁ Ἰησοῦς (from 7³³), but om. ℵBDLTW.

τῇ ἁμαρτίᾳ ὑμῶν ἀποθανεῖσθε· ὅπου ἐγὼ ὑπάγω ὑμεῖς οὐ δύνασθε ἐλθεῖν. 22. ἔλεγον οὖν οἱ Ἰουδαῖοι Μήτι ἀποκτενεῖ ἑαυτόν, ὅτι λέγει Ὅπου ἐγὼ ὑπάγω ὑμεῖς οὐ δύνασθε ἐλθεῖν; 23. καὶ ἔλεγεν αὐτοῖς Ὑμεῖς ἐκ τῶν κάτω ἐστέ, ἐγὼ ἐκ τῶν ἄνω εἰμί· ὑμεῖς ἐκ τούτου τοῦ

ἐγὼ ὑπάγω. For this verb and its usage in Jn., see on 7³³. " I go away," *sc.* to God.

καὶ ζητήσετέ με. As in 7³⁴, this is the search of despair; they will seek Jesus as their Messiah, when it is too late. καὶ οὐκ εὑρήσετέ με is added by a few manuscripts from 7³⁴, where it is part of the text; but it is implied in any case.

καὶ ἐν τῇ ἁμαρτίᾳ ὑμῶν ἀποθανεῖσθε, " and ye shall die in your sin," an O.T. phrase (cf. Ezek. 3¹⁸ 18¹⁸, and especially Prov. 24⁹ ἀποθνήσκει δὲ ἄφρων ἐν ἁμαρτίαις, of which LXX rendering the phrase in the text may be a reminiscence). It is repeated v. 24, where see note. Those who too late seek Jesus as the Messiah, shall die in a state of sin, unredeemed by Him.

ὅπου ἐγὼ ὑπάγω ὑμεῖς οὐ δύνασθε ἐλθεῖν, " whither I go ye cannot come ": this is repeated verbally at 13³³, where it is addressed to the disciples. Cf. 7³⁴, where the same thing (in substance) was said to the Jews, and see the note there.

22. ἔλεγον οὖν οἱ Ἰουδαῖοι, *sc.* the Jewish objectors.

μήτι ἀποκτενεῖ ἑαυτόν κτλ., " Is He going to kill Himself, that He says, ' Whither I am going you cannot come ' ? " This is a quite different rejoinder from that of 7³⁵, made in reply to the same warning, the occasion and the interlocutors both being different. It has often been suggested that the rejoinder carries a scornful allusion to the belief that the depths of hell were reserved for suicides (cf. Josephus, *B.J.* III. viii. 5, ᾅδης σκοτιώτερος); but this is not certain. In any case, the Jews speak ironically: " If we cannot follow you, it must be because you will be no longer alive." The saying of mystery, " Whither I go you cannot come," which was uttered more than once (7³⁴ 13³³), naturally provoked different comments from different persons.

23. καὶ ἔλεγεν. The rec. has εἶπεν, but ℵBDLNTWΘ have the imperfect ἔλεγεν, which suggests that what follows was a habitual saying of Jesus. He leaves their taunt unanswered, but adds that His origin and natural home were different from the origin and home of " the Jews." It was not surprising that they did not understand Him when He said that He was moving to a region where they could not follow. Cf. Mt. 6²¹.

ὑμεῖς ἐκ τῶν κάτω ἐστέ, " You are from beneath," *i.e.* " of the earth." Cf. ἐπὶ τῆς γῆς κάτω (Acts 2¹⁹). κάτω does not occur again in Jn. (but cf. 8⁸).

κόσμου ἐστέ, ἐγὼ οὐκ εἰμὶ ἐκ τοῦ κόσμου τούτου.   24. εἶπον οὖν
ὑμῖν ὅτι ἀποθανεῖσθε ἐν ταῖς ἁμαρτίαις ὑμῶν· ἐὰν γὰρ μὴ πιστεύσητε
ὅτι ἐγώ εἰμι, ἀποθανεῖσθε ἐν ταῖς ἁμαρτίαις ὑμῶν.   25. ἔλεγον οὖν

ἐγὼ ἐκ τῶν ἄνω εἰμί. The contrast is the same as that
of 3³¹. The implied argument, *sc.* that the Jews' failure of
understanding has its root in moral causes, has met us before
(5³⁸ᶠ· 7¹⁷ᶜ·), and is repeated 8⁴².

ὑμεῖς ἐκ τούτου τοῦ κόσμου ἐστέ. BT give the emphatic
τούτου τοῦ κόσμου here, but the more usual τοῦ κόσμου τούτου
in the second clause of the verse (so W in both clauses).
אDLΓΔ give τοῦ κόσμου τούτου in both clauses, and ὁ
κόσμος οὗτος is the order in every other N.T. passage where
the expression occurs. So, too, we always find ὁ αἰὼν οὗτος
(except Mt. 12³²).

The idea of imperfection which the word κόσμος, the
totality of created being, suggests in Jn. has been noted on 1⁹.
This idea is specially brought out in the phrase ὁ κόσμος οὗτος.
When thus limited, the word does not embrace any plane of
creation other than that of earth (11⁹), and "this world"
is contrasted with the spiritual or heavenly world, as being in a
special degree affected by evil powers (16¹¹), and as awaiting
the Judgment (9³⁹ 12³¹). The kingdom of Jesus is not of
"this world" (18³⁶), from which He passed after His Passion
(13¹). It is the place of our earthly discipline (1 Jn. 4¹⁷), in
which he who hates his life shall keep it to life eternal (12²⁵).
The phrase occurs with a like hint of evil, 1 Cor. 3¹⁹ 5¹⁰ 7³¹.[1]

So here it is said of the Jews ὑμεῖς ἐκ τοῦ κόσμου τούτου
ἐστέ. Cf. for the same construction εἶναι ἐκ, 1 Jn. 4⁵ αὐτοὶ ἐκ
τοῦ κόσμου εἰσί.

ἐγὼ (emphatic) οὐκ εἰμὶ ἐκ τοῦ κόσμου τούτου. Cf. 17¹⁴· ¹⁶.
It is the perpetual theme of the Fourth Gospel that He who
was not "of the world" came "into the world" for its rescue.

24. εἶπον οὖν ὑμῖν, *sc.* at v. 21, where see note.

ἀποθανεῖσθε ἐν ταῖς ἁμαρτίαις ὑμῶν, the singular τῇ ἁμαρτίᾳ
being changed to the plural. To this no significance is to
be attached, as when phrases are repeated in Jn., there are
generally slight verbal alterations (see on 3¹⁶).

ἐὰν γὰρ μὴ πιστεύσητε ὅτι ἐγώ εἰμι, ἀποθανεῖσθε κτλ. Jesus
repeats with an awful solemnity that if His hearers do not
accept Him for what He is, they will die in their sins. ὅτι ἐγώ
εἰμι may mean "that I am from above," as He had just
asserted of Himself, ἐγὼ ἐκ τῶν ἄνω εἰμί. But if this be
the construction, it is very elliptical. It is more probable
that we should take ἐγώ εἰμι absolutely, "I am He," *i.e.*

[1] Cf. Hobhouse, *The Church and the World*, p. 352, Note D.

αὐτῷ Σὺ τίς εἶ; εἶπεν αὐτοῖς ὁ Ἰησοῦς Τὴν ἀρχὴν ὅ τι καὶ λαλῶ
ὑμῖν. 26. πολλὰ ἔχω περὶ ὑμῶν λαλεῖν καὶ κρίνειν· ἀλλ᾽ ὁ πέμψας

" I am the Divine Deliverer," as at vv. 28, 58, and 13[19]. For
this use of ἐγώ εἰμι as the equivalent of the Hebrew אֲנִי־הוּא,
see Introd., p. cxx, where the expression is more fully discussed. We may here particularly compare Isa. 43[10] ἵνα
πιστεύσητε . . . ὅτι ἐγώ εἰμι (see on v. 18). Jesus had uttered
His message; henceforth they had no excuse for their
sin (15[22]).

25. ἔλεγον οὖν αὐτῷ Σὺ τίς εἶ; The Jews are puzzled
by the last words of Jesus. They sounded like the Divine
proclamations in the prophetical books. Who is this, that
says I AM? And they ask Him, "Who art Thou?" (cf. 1[19]).
But He gives no direct or simple answer (cf. 19[9]). Cf. 10[24]
for a similar question, and a similar indirectness of reply.

τὴν ἀρχὴν ὅ τι καὶ λαλῶ ὑμῖν, " Primarily (in essence),
what I am telling you," *i.e.* " I am what my words reveal."
We have already noted (see on 3[11]; and cf. 10[6] 12[49] 14[10] 16[18])
that λαλεῖν cannot always be sharply distinguished from
λέγειν; and the constr. ὅ τι λαλῶ is similar to ὁ λόγος ὃν
ἐλάλησα of 12[48], or ταῦτα λαλῶ of v. 28.

τὴν ἀρχήν is never used in Jn. for " from the beginning,"
which is expressed by ἐξ ἀρχῆς (16[4]), or more frequently by
ἀπ᾽ ἀρχῆς (15[27], 1 Jn. 1[1] and *passim*). In the LXX τὴν ἀρχήν
often stands for " at the beginning," " at the first "—*e.g.*
Gen. 43[20], Dan. 9[21] (LXX), and Dan. 8[1] (Theod.)—which is a
sound classical construction. (Cf. Herod. viii. 132 ἐόντες ἀρχὴν
ἑπτά, " being originally seven in number.") But in the present
passage the rendering " I have spoken at the beginning " is
inadmissible, inasmuch as the verb is in the present (λαλῶ)
and not in the aorist (ἐλάλησα). These considerations seem
to rule out the R.V. " Even that which I have also spoken
unto you from the beginning."

The R.V. margin treats the sentence as a question, and
for the relative ὅ τι substitutes ὅτι. Thus τὴν ἀρχὴν ὅτι καὶ
λαλῶ ὑμῖν; is translated " How is it that I even speak to you
at all ? " This rendering has the support of Chrysostom, and
there is no doubt that τὴν ἀρχήν may stand for ὅλως, *omnino*,
especially in negative sentences. An apposite parallel to such
a use is found in *Clem. Hom.* vi. 11, εἰ μὴ παρακολουθεῖς οἷς
λέγω, τί καὶ τὴν ἀρχὴν διαλέγομαι; (a sentence in which some
have found an echo of v. 25). The answer of Jesus, according
to this view, is a severe rebuke, which has a note of impatience,
comparable to Mk. 9[19], " O faithless generation, how long
shall I be with you ! " But it is difficult to connect a rebuke

με ἀληθής ἐστιν, κἀγὼ ἃ ἤκουσα παρ' αὐτοῦ, ταῦτα λαλῶ εἰς τὸν

of this kind with the words which immediately follow in v. 26,
πολλὰ ἔχω περὶ ὑμῶν λαλεῖν.

The Latin and Syriac vss. take the sentence as affirmative,
not as interrogative; and herein they are probably right. But
neither can be followed in detail. Syr. sin. gives " The chief
is that I should speak myself with you, seeing that I have much
that I should speak concerning you and judge"; but this
provides no answer to the question "Who art thou ?" Some
O.L. texts give " initium quod et loquor uobis," *i.e.* " I am
the Beginning (cf. Rev. 21⁶), that which I am saying to you ";
but τὴν ἀρχήν could not be attracted to ὅ τι in this way. The
Vulgate has " principium quia et loquor uobis," which is still
farther from the Greek.

We come back to the rendering, "Primarily, I am what I
am telling you," as the least open to objection of the many
renderings that have been offered of this difficult passage.
τὴν ἀρχήν means fundamentally or originally, or, in colloquial
English, " at bottom." In reply to the question "Who art
thou ?" Jesus declares to the Jews that He is essentially
what His words reveal, in particular such words as ἐγὼ ἐκ τῶν
ἄνω εἰμί (v. 23), and (above all) ἐγώ εἰμι (v. 24).

26. πολλὰ ἔχω περὶ ὑμῶν λαλεῖν καὶ κρίνειν. This seems
to take up the teaching of v. 16 above. Jesus does not dwell
upon His answer to the question " Who art thou ?" He goes
on with His discourse, as there was much still to say. With
πολλὰ ἔχω λαλεῖν cf. πολλὰ ἔχω λέγειν of 16¹², a comparison
which confirms the conclusion (reached in the note on 3¹¹)
that λαλεῖν and λέγειν are not sharply distinguished by Jn.,
and that they are sometimes interchangeable.

καὶ κρίνειν. His discourse was of judgment. He had
already said twice to the Jews that they would die in their sins
(vv. 21, 24), a κρίσις to which the words of v. 16 lead up.

ἀλλ' ὁ πέμψας με ἀληθής ἐστιν κτλ. This is again resumptive of v. 16, where Jesus had said that His judgment was
true, because it was not His own, but reflected the judgment of
the Father who had sent Him. The adversative ἀλλά points
back to the objection which He continually rebuts, *sc.* that
He has no authority behind Him. " Whatever objection you
raise to my claim to judge, you must remember that He who
sent me is true." See on v. 16 above; and cf. 3³³ 7²⁸.

κἀγὼ ἃ ἤκουσα παρ' αὐτοῦ, ταῦτα λαλῶ εἰς τὸν κόσμον. Cf.
15¹⁵ πάντα ἃ ἤκουσα παρὰ τοῦ πατρός μου ἐγνώρισα ὑμῖν, and
see vv. 38, 40. Here the sayings " heard from the Father "
were sayings of judgment, as at 5³⁰, καθὼς ἀκούω κρίνω. And,

κόσμον. 27. οὐκ ἔγνωσαν ὅτι τὸν Πατέρα αὐτοῖς ἔλεγεν. 28. εἶπεν οὖν ὁ Ἰησοῦς Ὅταν ὑψώσητε τὸν Υἱὸν τοῦ ἀνθρώπου, τότε γνώσεσθε ὅτι ἐγώ εἰμι, καὶ ἀπ᾽ ἐμαυτοῦ ποιῶ οὐδέν, ἀλλὰ καθὼς ἐδίδαξέν με ὁ

unlike those of 15[15], they were spoken " to the world" (cf. 18[20]).

To speak εἰς τὸν κόσμον is a constr. that is not found again in Jn.; but cf. 1 Cor. 14[9] εἰς ἀέρα λαλοῦντες, Mk. 13[10] εἰς πάντα τὰ ἔθνη δεῖ κηρυχθῆναι τὸ εὐαγγέλιον.

ταῦτα λαλῶ. So אBDLNTWΔΘ, but minor uncials substitute λέγω for λαλῶ.

27. οὐκ ἔγνωσαν ὅτι τὸν πατέρα αὐτοῖς ἔλεγεν. This is one of the evangelist's comments on his narrative (see Introd., p. xxxiv), and it seems to confirm what has been said on v. 25 about the Jews' misunderstanding of the words of mystery which Jesus had uttered.

28. εἶπεν οὖν ὁ Ἰησοῦς, " Jesus therefore said," *sc.* because of their misunderstanding. אDNΓΔΘ add αὐτοῖς, but om. BLTW; אD further add πάλιν.

ὅταν ὑψώσητε τὸν υἱὸν τοῦ ἀνθρώπου, " When you shall have lifted up," *sc.* on the Cross, " the Son of Man." See on 3[14] for ὑψοῦν in Jn., and cf. 12[32]. In the present passage ὑψοῦν must relate to the lifting up on the Cross, and not to the " lifting up " of the Ascension, for the latter was not in any sense the act of the Jews, as the Crucifixion was (cf. Acts 3[14]).

For the title " the Son of Man," see Introd., p. cxxxi.

τότε γνώσεσθε ὅτι ἐγώ εἰμι, " then ye shall know that I am (the Son of Man)," the predicate of ἐγώ εἰμι being understood from the preceding clause of the sentence. Otherwise, we must take ἐγώ εἰμι as used absolutely, as in v. 24 (cf. 8[58] 13[19]), the phrase being then identical with the self-designation of Yahweh in the prophets, אֲנִי־הוּא " I (am) He " (see Introd., p. cxx). On either interpretation, the *style* of the sentence is that of Divine proclamations: cf. Ezek. 11[10] ἐπιγνώσεσθε ὅτι ἐγὼ κύριος.

Too late, the pressure of facts, the fall of Jerusalem and the like, would convince them of the truth of His words: " cognoscetis ex re, quod nunc ex uerbo non creditis " (Bengel). This, rather than the conviction of sin wrought by the Holy Spirit (16[8f.]), seems to be the force of τότε γνώσεσθε.

ὅτι governs not only ἐγώ εἰμι, but also the next clause ἀπ᾽ ἐμαυτοῦ ποιῶ οὐδέν κτλ. This had been said before, 5[30] (cf. 12[49]). For its significance, see note on 5[19]. Ignatius (*Magn.* 7) has ὁ κύριος ἄνευ τοῦ πατρὸς οὐδὲν ἐποίησεν, a reminiscence of these Johannine phrases.

ἀλλὰ καθὼς ἐδίδαξέν με ὁ πατήρ. Cf. v. 26, and see

Πατήρ, ταῦτα λαλῶ. 29. καὶ ὁ πέμψας με μετ᾽ ἐμοῦ ἐστιν· οὐκ ἀφῆκέν με μόνον, ὅτι ἐγὼ τὰ ἀρεστὰ αὐτῷ ποιῶ πάντοτε. 30. Ταῦτα αὐτοῦ λαλοῦντος πολλοὶ ἐπίστευσαν εἰς αὐτόν.

7¹⁶. ¹⁷. After πατήρ, ΒΓΔ add μου, but om. אDLNTΘ. W om. ὁ πατήρ.

ταῦτα λαλῶ : ταῦτα referring to the specific teachings of this section. Cf. 12³⁶ ταῦτα ἐλάλησεν ὁ Ἰησοῦς, and v. 30 ταῦτα λαλοῦντος. With the sentence καθὼς ἐδίδαξέν . . . λαλῶ, cf. the parallels 12⁵⁰ and 14³¹.

29. καὶ ὁ πέμψας με (see on 3¹⁷ for the mission of the Son) μετ᾽ ἐμοῦ ἐστιν κτλ. This has already been said at v. 16, ὅτι μόνος οὐκ εἰμί, ἀλλ᾽ ἐγὼ καὶ ὁ πέμψας με, and is repeated 16³² in a different context. Much more is implied here than in the saying of Peter that "God was with Him" (Acts 10³⁸), for all through Jn. the ineffable union of the Son with the Father is behind the narrative (cf. 10³⁸).

οὐκ ἀφῆκέν με μόνον. ΓΔΝ add ὁ πατήρ unnecessarily; om. BDLTWΘ. The union of the preincarnate Son with the Father (17⁵) was continued after the Incarnation.

ὅτι is causal, "because I do the things pleasing to Him." Thus at 15¹⁰ Jesus tells His disciples that by keeping His commandments they will abide in His love, even as He by keeping His Father's commandments abides in the Father's love. The adj. ἀρεστός occurs again in Jn. only at 1 Jn. 3²², and there, as here, of doing the things that are pleasing to God, i.e. of keeping His commandments. See, for a similar use of ἀρεστός, Ex. 15²⁶, Wisd. 9¹⁸, Isa. 38³.

For the thought that the continual aim of Jesus was to do the will of the Father, cf. 4³⁴ 5³⁰ 6³⁸. Here He claims always (πάντοτε) to do that which is pleasing to the Father, a claim which implies a consciousness of sinlessness (cf. v. 46 below).

The language of Ignatius (Magn. 8), ὃς κατὰ πάντα εὐηρέστησεν τῷ πέμψαντι αὐτόν, seems to rest on this verse.

30. ταῦτα αὐτοῦ λαλοῦντος, "As He was saying these things." The gen. absolute is infrequent in Jn., partly because of his fondness for parataxis; he never uses it in his report of the words of Jesus.

πολλοὶ ἐπίστευσαν εἰς αὐτόν. For this favourite phrase of Jn., see on 4³⁹, where (as here) belief in Christ is due to what He said rather than to the "signs" which He wrought. Those who "believed in Him" were fewer in number than those who "believed Him"—a larger body who are addressed in the next verse, and of whom some, as the sequel shows, soon began to cavil at His teaching.

31. Ἔλεγεν οὖν ὁ Ἰησοῦς πρὸς τοὺς πεπιστευκότας αὐτῷ Ἰουδαίους Ἐὰν ὑμεῖς μείνητε ἐν τῷ λόγῳ τῷ ἐμῷ, ἀληθῶς μαθηταί μού ἐστε, 32. καὶ γνώσεσθε τὴν ἀλήθειαν, καὶ ἡ ἀλήθεια ἐλευθερώσει

Jesus tells the Jews who are inclined to believe Him, that truth would emancipate them from the slavery of sin (vv. 31–34)

31. ἔλεγεν οὖν . . . πρὸς τοὺς πεπιστευκότας αὐτῷ Ἰουδαίους, " So He began to say to the Jews that believed Him," *i.e.* those who had been impressed by His recent utterances (but cf. vv. 33 and 40). πιστεύειν followed by a dative does not represent so high a degree of faith as πιστεύειν εἰς τινα; but it indicates a stage on the way to discipleship. You must believe what a man says before you can believe in him. For the constr. πιστεύειν εἴς τινα, see on 1¹²; and cf. the note at 6³⁰ on πιστεύειν τινί. For the constr. ἔλεγεν πρός τινα, see on 2³.

ἐὰν ὑμεῖς μείνητε ἐν τῷ λόγῳ τῷ ἐμῷ κτλ. Cf. 2 Jn.⁹, where we have μὴ μένων ἐν τῇ διδαχῇ τοῦ Χριστοῦ θεὸν οὐκ ἔχει. In v. 37 and at 5³⁸ a different metaphor is employed, *sc.* that of the λόγος of God abiding in the believer. But (see on 5³⁸) the two expressions " abiding in His word " and " His word abiding in us " come to the same thing. See also on 6⁵⁶, 15⁷.

ἀληθῶς μαθηταί μού ἐστε. This is the highest rank among Christians, *sc.* those who have reached the stage of discipleship. See on 15⁸, where this is repeated.

32. καὶ γνώσεσθε τὴν ἀλήθειαν. For the conception of ἀλήθεια in Jn., see on 1¹⁴; and cf. vv. 40, 44, 45.

καὶ ἡ ἀλήθεια ἐλευθερώσει ὑμᾶς. The words express a great principle, which is applicable in many directions, and which has been enunciated by Jewish and heathen teachers as well as by Christian. It was a Stoic paradox ὅτι μόνος ὁ σοφὸς ἐλεύθερος καὶ πᾶς ἄφρων δοῦλος (Cicero, *Parad.* 5). This was repeated in another form by Seneca, " unum studium uere liberale est quod liberum facit, hoc est sapientiae " (*Ep.* lxxxviii. 2). Philo, in the same spirit, wrote a book to prove that the σπουδαῖος is free (*quod omnis probus liber sit*). In another book (*de confus. ling.* 20) he asks τίς οὖν ἐλευθερία βεβαιοτάτη; to which he gives the answer ἡ τοῦ μόνου θεραπεία σοφοῦ. But there is no trace of generalisations of this kind either in O.T. or N.T.

The freedom which truth brings (in the view of Jn.) is emancipation from the slavery of sin. This appears from v. 34, where see note. In v. 36 the Son is said to be the Agent of this emancipation (ἐὰν ὁ υἱὸς ὑμᾶς ἐλευθερώσῃ); and the

ὑμᾶς. 33. ἀπεκρίθησαν πρὸς αὐτὸν Σπέρμα Ἀβραάμ ἐσμεν, καὶ
οὐδενὶ δεδουλεύκαμεν πώποτε· πῶς σὺ λέγεις ὅτι Ἐλεύθεροι γενήσεσθε; 34. ἀπεκρίθη αὐτοῖς ὁ Ἰησοῦς Ἀμὴν ἀμὴν λέγω ὑμῖν ὅτι
πᾶς ὁ ποιῶν τὴν ἁμαρτίαν δοῦλός ἐστιν τῆς ἁμαρτίας.

juxtaposition of vv. 32, 36 is instructive, when the great utterance ἐγώ εἰμι ἡ ἀλήθεια (14⁶) is recalled. The purpose of the
self-consecration of Jesus is declared (17¹⁹) to be that His
disciples may be ἡγιασμένοι ἐν ἀληθείᾳ.

There is, perhaps, a hint of the emancipating influence of
truth at 1¹⁷: "The *law* came by Moses, but grace and *truth*
by Jesus Christ." See note *in loc.*

33. ἀπεκρίθησαν πρὸς αὐτόν. So אBDLWΘ 33 (see for
the constr. on 2³); but NΓΔ have ἀπεκρ. αὐτῷ. Those who
made the answer which follows were not the Jews who "believed Him" (v. 31), but the Jewish objectors, with whom
throughout the rest of this chapter Jesus is engaged in controversy. He could not have charged "the Jews who believed
Him" with seeking His life (vv. 37, 39).

Σπέρμα Ἀβραάμ ἐσμεν (cf. Ps. 105⁶, Isa. 41⁸). This was
the proudest boast of the Jews, that they were the heirs of the
covenant with Abraham, because of their direct descent from
him. Cf. Gen. 22¹⁷, Lk. 1⁵⁵.

καὶ οὐδενὶ δεδουλεύκαμεν πώποτε. This was, of course,
not true. The captivity in Babylon was only one instance of
the contrary; and they were under the yoke of Rome even
while they were speaking. But they would not admit, even to
themselves, that they were not a free people. They were not
bondslaves (δεδουλεύκαμεν), indeed, but Jesus had not used
the word δοῦλος yet. Their petulant retort really marked the
uneasy consciousness that they were not as free as they
would like to be: "How sayest thou, Ye shall become free
men?"

34. ἀπεκρ. αὐτοῖς ὁ Ἰησοῦς. B omits the art. before Ἰησοῦς
here (see on 1²⁹·⁵⁰). αὐτοῖς refers to the hostile Jews who are
in view throughout the rest of the chapter.

ἀμὴν ἀμὴν λέγω ὑμῖν, calling attention to a solemn pronouncement summing up what He has just said. Cf. vv. 51, 58;
and see on 1⁵¹.

πᾶς . . . δοῦλός ἐστιν τῆς ἁμαρτίας. D *b* and Syr. sin.,
with Clem. Alex. (*Strom.* ii. 5), omit τῆς ἁμαρτίας. The
omission would not, however, alter the sense, which must in
any case be that the sinner is the slave of sin (or of the devil).

πᾶς ὁ ποιῶν τὴν ἁμαρτίαν means (as it does 1 Jn. 3⁴·⁸)
"every one who lives in the practice of sin," just as ὁ ποιῶν τὴν
ἀλήθειαν (3²¹) means "he who lives in the practice of truth."

35. Ὁ δὲ δοῦλος οὐ μένει ἐν τῇ οἰκίᾳ εἰς τὸν αἰῶνα· ὁ υἱὸς μένει

It is habitual, rather than occasional, sin that is here in view when it is said that a man mastered by it is a slave.

The Hebrews regarded sin in the light of violation of God's law, rather than as a state of slavery. This latter doctrine is Greek rather than Hebrew; it is not often expressed by Greek writers so clearly as by Xenophon: ὅστις οὖν ἄρχεται ὑπὸ τῶν διὰ τοῦ σώματος ἡδονῶν, καὶ διὰ ταύτας μὴ δύναται πράττειν τὰ βέλτιστα, νομίζεις τοῦτον ἐλεύθερον εἶναι; Ἥκιστα, ἔφη (*Memorab.* iv. 5. 3). Cf. *Œconom.* i. § 22. Paul has the same idea when he speaks of sinners as δοῦλοι τῆς ἁμαρτίας (Rom. 6¹⁷· ²⁰), but it does not appear elsewhere in his epistles. He dwells often on the freedom of the Christian from the yoke of the Jewish law (Gal. 5¹· ¹³), but that is a different conception. In 2 Pet. 2¹⁹ we have the phrase δοῦλοι τῆς φθορᾶς, which is parallel to δοῦλοι τῆς ἁμαρτίας. But it is remarkable that the idea of sin as a master which makes slaves of men is found in the N.T. only here, and at Rom. 6¹⁷· ²⁰, 2 Pet. 2¹⁹. It is not quite apposite to cite Jas. 1²⁵ 2¹², 2 Cor. 3¹⁷, which express the principle that the Christian law is a law of liberty.

Jesus tells the Jews that they are only slaves without tenure in the household of God : they are not true sons of Abraham, for they try to kill Him : their father is the devil. It is just because they have not God for their Father that they will not believe Jesus, who offers them eternal life (vv. 35–51)

35. In the report of this discourse, there is at this point a sudden change of metaphor. In v. 34 the δοῦλος is the slave of sin (or of the devil); but in v. 35 a contrast is drawn between the positions of the δοῦλος and the υἱός in a household presided over by its rightful master. A slave may be cast out at any moment; he has no covenant with his master. But if the heir emancipates him from his state of serfdom, *sc.* to his lawful master, he becomes a free man and obtains a footing in the house comparable to that of a son. This seems to be the trend of the argument, but it involves a transition from a particular conception of the δοῦλος to a quite different conception.

ὁ δὲ δοῦλος οὐ μένει ἐν τῇ οἰκίᾳ εἰς τὸν αἰῶνα. The slave has no tenure. The story of Hagar and Ishmael (Gen. 21¹⁰) suggests itself, but it is not clear that Jn. intends any allusion to it, or to Paul's use of it (Gal. 4³⁰). If a slave offends his master, he is liable to expulsion from the household. This

εἰς τὸν αἰῶνα. 36. ἐὰν οὖν ὁ Υἱὸς ὑμᾶς ἐλευθερώσῃ, ὄντως ἐλεύθεροι ἔσεσθε. 37. οἶδα ὅτι σπέρμα Ἀβραάμ ἐστε· ἀλλὰ ζητεῖτέ με ἀποκτεῖναι, ὅτι ὁ λόγος ὁ ἐμὸς οὐ χωρεῖ ἐν ὑμῖν. 38. ἐγὼ ἃ ἑώρακα

seems to be meant as a warning to the Jews, who are really slaves because of their sins, that they have no fixed tenure in the household of God (cf. 4⁵³ for οἰκία as equivalent to " a household ").

ὁ υἱὸς μένει εἰς τὸν αἰῶνα. A similar contrast between the slave and the son appears Heb. 3⁵, where (quoting Num. 12⁷) Moses is described as a faithful servant (θεράπων) in the house (οἶκος) of God, but Christ as the Son of that house. For the οἰκία of the Father, cf. 14²; and for the permanence of a son's tenure in his father's house, cf. Lk. 15³¹: τέκνον, σὺ πάντοτε μετ' ἐμοῦ εἶ. For the phrase εἰς τὸν αἰῶνα in Jn., see on 4¹⁴.

The last clause, ὁ υἱὸς μένει εἰς τὸν αἰῶνα, is omitted by אWΓ 33 124 and in the quotation of the passage by Clem. Alex. (see on v. 34). But the omissions here and in the preceding verse only serve to show that the difficulties of the argument were felt by scribes and exegetes alike. It is possible that the whole of v. 35 is an early gloss, brought in from familiarity with such passages as Gal. 4³⁰, Heb. 3⁵.

36. ἐὰν οὖν ὁ υἱὸς ὑμᾶς ἐλευθερώσῃ κτλ. If v. 35 is part of the original text, then this sentence has in view the fact that the son and heir had a special privilege in the emancipation of his father's slaves. Cf. Gal. 5¹. But if v. 35 may be treated as a gloss, then v. 36 relates itself naturally to v. 34 : " You are the slaves of sin ; but if the Son (ὁ υἱός used absolutely, as at 3³⁵) make you free (cf. v. 32), you will be free indeed." What the Son does will be ratified by the Father.

ἐλεύθερος, ἐλευθεροῦν, do not occur elsewhere in Jn., and in the Synoptists only at Mt. 17²⁶ do we find ἐλεύθερος. ὄντως is not used elsewhere by Jn.

37. οἶδα ὅτι σπέρμα Ἀβραάμ ἐστε κτλ., "I know that you are of the stock of Abraham, but, despite that, you are the slaves of sin, for you seek to kill me, my word not being operative in you." This seems to be the sequence of the argument. The metaphor that they are the slaves of sin and need emancipation is now dropped; and Jesus tells them in the verses which follow that, sinners as they are, it is the devil who is their spiritual father.

ἀλλὰ ζητεῖτέ με ἀποκτεῖναι. Cf. 7¹· ²⁵.

ὅτι ὁ λόγος ὁ ἐμὸς οὐ χωρεῖ ἐν ὑμῖν. Cf. v. 31 above; and see note on 5³⁸, where we have τὸν λόγον αὐτοῦ οὐκ ἔχετε ἐν ὑμῖν μένοντα, which means almost the same. The real cause

παρὰ τῷ Πατρὶ μου λαλῶ· καὶ ὑμεῖς οὖν ἃ ἠκούσατε παρὰ τοῦ πατρὸς

of the Jews' enmity to Jesus was a moral cause; His revelation did not *abide* or *work* in their hearts.

χωρεῖν is used transitively 2⁶, and this use, "to hold," is common. But in the present passage it is used intransitively, and its precise meaning is hard to define. In 2 Macc. 3⁴⁰ it is used of the spreading of a report τὰ μὲν καθ᾽ Ἡλιόδωρον . . . οὕτως ἐχώρησεν; and the R.V. renders here "my word hath not free course in you," or, as Moffatt puts it, "makes no headway among you." This is, perhaps, to introduce the idea of *movement* a little more than is justifiable. Of the Latin versions, *a* has *requiescit*, *c* has *est*, and Jerome's Vulgate has *capit*. Accordingly, the R.V. margin gives as a possible rendering "hath no place in you,"[1] which would almost identify χωρεῖν here with μένειν at 5³⁸. We may compare Xenophon, *Œconom.* c. 20 § 21, τὸ γὰρ τὰς μὲν δαπάνας χωρεῖν ἐντελεῖς . . . of expenses *continuing undiminished*.[2] This we take to be the true meaning of χωρεῖ ἐν ὑμῖν, "continues in you," with a suggestion of operative activity. Jerome's literal rendering *non capit in uobis*, "does not hold in you," means the same thing.

38. The true text of this verse is doubtful, there being variants for nearly every word.

Westcott-Hort read: ἃ ἐγὼ ἑώρακα παρὰ τῷ πατρὶ λαλῶ· καὶ ὑμεῖς οὖν ἃ ἠκούσατε παρὰ τοῦ πατρὸς ποιεῖτε, giving as the "Western" reading ἐγὼ ἃ ἑώρακα παρὰ τῷ πατρί μου [ταῦτα] λαλῶ· καὶ ὑμεῖς οὖν ἃ ἑωράκατε παρὰ τῷ πατρὶ ὑμῶν ποιεῖτε.

אDNΓΔΘ and Syr. sin. support the insertion of μου (om. BCLTW) after πατρί in the first clause, and of ὑμῶν (also found in C) after πατρός in the second clause.

ἠκούσατε in the second clause is read by אᶜBCLWΘ, but א*DΓΔN and Syr. sin. have ἑωράκατε, probably by assimilation with the first clause: the rec. τῷ πατρί in the second clause (for τοῦ πατρός) is due to the same cause.

The Vulgate has: "ego quod uidi apud patrem loquor, et uos quae uidistis apud patrem uestrum facitis," and with this the evidence of Tatian agrees.

If the pronouns μου and ὑμῶν are omitted, ὁ πατήρ must stand for the same person in both clauses, and the second clause would have to be imperative: "do ye therefore the things

---

[1] In the passage from Alciphron (*Ep.* iii. 7) quoted by Field in support of this rendering, χωρεῖν is used transitively, and so the passage does not provide a parallel.

[2] Dr. L. C. Purser has pointed out this passage to me.

ὑμῶν ποιεῖτε. 39. ἀπεκρίθησαν καὶ εἶπαν αὐτῷ Ὁ πατὴρ ἡμῶν
Ἀβραάμ ἐστιν. λέγει αὐτοῖς ὁ Ἰησοῦς Εἰ τέκνα τοῦ Ἀβραάμ ἐστε,
τὰ ἔργα τοῦ Ἀβραὰμ ποιεῖτε· 40. νῦν δὲ ζητεῖτέ με ἀποκτεῖναι,

which ye heard from the Father." But this does not agree
well with the context.

We translate : " I speak of what I have seen with my
Father; but (καί being used for ἀλλά; see on 1¹⁰) you do
what you heard from your father," sc. the devil (v. 41). ἐγώ
and ὑμεῖς are placed for emphasis of distinction at the beginning of the two clauses respectively.

ἐγὼ ἃ ἑώρακα παρὰ τῷ πατρί μου λαλῶ. Cf. v. 28 above,
and see especially on 5¹⁹. παρὰ τῷ πατρί μου, apud patrem,
is not to be referred to the pre-incarnate life of the Son
(cf. 17⁵ παρὰ σεαυτῷ), or interpreted with Abbott (Diat. 2355)
as "in the home of my Father," i.e. heaven. The reference
is to the perpetual vision which the Incarnate Son had of
His Father's will (see 5¹⁹). For ἑώρακα as occasionally
used of spiritual vision, see on 3³². For λαλεῖν in Jn., see
on 3¹¹.

καὶ ὑμεῖς οὖν (cf. 16²²) κτλ. The contrast between λαλῶ
and ποιεῖτε is marked. Jesus speaks of the truths which
the Father has given Him, but the Jews do the sinful things
which the devil suggests, the pres. tense ποιεῖτε indicating
a continual doing. τοῦ πατρὸς ὑμῶν is identified with τοῦ διαβόλου
at v. 44 ; but this has not yet been made explicit by Jesus, and,
in fact, the Jews' reply shows that they do not yet understand
the tremendous severity of His words.

39. ὁ πατὴρ ἡμῶν Ἀβραάμ ἐστιν, " Our father is Abraham."
They repeat what they have said before (v. 33). It was true,
in so far as their physical pedigree was concerned; but Jesus
tells them that they are not true sons of Abraham if their
conduct is unlike his. His reply is almost in the words used
by Paul οὐδ᾽ ὅτι εἰσὶν σπέρμα Ἀβραάμ, πάντες τέκνα (Rom. 9⁷).
He had admitted (v. 37) that they were σπέρμα Ἀβραάμ, but
this natural descent did not, by itself, guarantee all the privileges which belong to the τέκνα who are Abraham's true heirs
(cf. Gal. 3⁷·⁹).

εἰ τέκνα τοῦ Ἀβραάμ ἐστε, τὰ ἔργα τοῦ Ἀβραὰμ ποιεῖτε. " If
you are Abraham's children, do Abraham's works," ποιεῖτε
being imperative.

ποιεῖτε, although only read by B, is probably the true
reading,[1] and should be rendered in the imperative mood, with
Syr. sin. ἐποιεῖτε ἄν (W omits ἄν) is read by א°CLNW; but

---

[1] Origen has it frequently (Comm. in Joann. 308, 313, 316, 317, etc. ;
but he has ἦτε . . . ἐποιειτε, 104).

ἄνθρωπον ὃς τὴν ἀλήθειαν ὑμῖν λελάληκα, ἣν ἤκουσα παρὰ τοῦ Θεοῦ. τοῦτο Ἀβραὰμ οὐκ ἐποίησεν. 41. ὑμεῖς ποιεῖτε τὰ ἔργα τοῦ πατρὸς ὑμῶν. εἶπαν αὐτῷ Ἡμεῖς ἐκ πορνείας οὐκ ἐγεννήθημεν, ἕνα Πατέρα

this requires the rec. ἦτε instead of ἐστέ in the first clause, while ἐστέ is read by אBDLT.

40. νῦν δέ, "but as things are," ζητεῖτέ με ἀποκτεῖναι: cf. v. 37 and 7[1. 25].

ἄνθρωπον. A difficulty has been found in the use of this word as applied (here only) to Himself by Jesus. Nowhere else in the N.T. is He described as " a man," for Rom. 5[15] and 1 Tim. 2[5] both imply that He was ἄνθρωπος in a unique sense. Cf. Acts 2[22] 17[31], where He is spoken of as ἀνήρ. But it is hypercritical to find offence in this manner of expression. It would be out of place in the writings of a second-century theologian, who had reached the point of seeing the difficulties in the formulation of the doctrine of the Incarnation; but for a first-century writer, who was combating with special care the idea that Christ had not come " in the flesh," it is quite natural.[1] The expression is used *sine preiudicio deitatis*, and that Jesus should have described Himself as " a person who has spoken the truth to you " in discussion with Jews who did not accept Him as divine is not surprising.

ἣν ἤκουσα παρὰ τοῦ θεοῦ. This is the perpetual teaching of Jesus in the Fourth Gospel, *sc.* that His words reveal the mind of the Father, who taught them to Him; cf. v. 26 and the references given in the note at that place.

τοῦτο Ἀβραὰμ οὐκ ἐποίησεν. Abraham welcomed the heavenly messengers (Gen. 18[3]); he did not seek to kill them.

41. *Paulatim procedit castigatio* is the comment of Grotius on the severe denunciation which follows.

ὑμεῖς ποιεῖτε τὰ ἔργα τοῦ πατρὸς ὑμῶν. " You," with emphasis, " do the works of your father," *sc.* the devil, although that is not yet said explicitly.

The Jews still misapprehend what is meant. They say, first, that if it is being suggested that they are not the legitimate descendants of Abraham and Sarah, it is not true; and secondly, that if it is spiritual and not physical descent that is in question, then their Father is God. The sentence is very much compressed.

ἡμεῖς ἐκ πορνείας οὐκ ἐγεννήθημεν (so BD*; οὐ γεγεννήμεθα is the rec. reading with א[c]CD[2]NWΓΔΘ). It has been held by some expositors, both ancient and modern, that the Jewish disputants mean to affirm by these words the legitimacy of the spiritual relation of Israel to Yahweh. See on 1[12]

[1] See on 1[14].

ἔχομεν τὸν Θεόν. 42. εἶπεν αὐτοῖς ὁ Ἰησοῦς Εἰ ὁ Θεὸς Πατὴρ ὑμῶν ἦν, ἠγαπᾶτε ἂν ἐμέ· ἐγὼ γὰρ ἐκ τοῦ Θεοῦ ἐξῆλθον καὶ ἥκω· οὐδὲ γὰρ

for the conception of Israel as Yahweh's wife, and Israelites as His children, in contradistinction to the heathen or Samaritans. Idolatry was fornication, and those who went after other gods were τέκνα πορνείας (Hos. 2⁴). This is a possible interpretation of ἐκ πορνείας οὐκ ἐγεννήθημεν, and accords well with what follows; but it is simpler to take the words literally and to regard them as a reaffirmation of σπέρμα Ἀβραάμ ἐσμεν . . . ὁ πατὴρ ἡμῶν Ἀβραάμ ἐστιν (vv. 33, 39), " we were not begotten of fornication " (see on 1¹³).

ἕνα πατέρα ἔχομεν τὸν θεόν. As for spiritual parentage, it was a fundamental and often expressed principle of the Israelites that Yahweh was their Father; cf. Ex. 4²², Deut. 32⁶, Isa. 63¹⁶ 64⁸. This is a wholly different figure from that of Israel as Yahweh's wife, and it is difficult to believe that there is a sudden transition from the one figure to the other, as we must suppose if ἡμεῖς ἐκ πορνείας οὐκ ἐγεννήθημεν is to be interpreted of spiritual fornication, i.e. idolatry.

The sentence " We have one Father, even God," is, then, not to be taken in strict connexion with what immediately precedes. It is a new plea, put forward for the Jewish disputants, who are beginning to understand that Jesus has been speaking of spiritual, not natural, parentage.

42. The rec. adds οὖν after εἶπεν, with אDΔ; om. BCLNTWΓΘ.

εἰ ὁ θεός κτλ., " If God were your Father, you would love me." This is the same argument as that in 1 Jn. 5¹· ², sc. " If you were the children of God, you would love God, and, as whoever loves a father loves his son, therefore you would love Jesus, His Son." The Jews have turned the argument, so that now *spiritual* fatherhood is in question, and Jesus shows them what the consequences of this spiritual fatherhood must be.

ἐγὼ γὰρ ἐκ τοῦ θεοῦ ἐξῆλθον, sc. " for *I*, even I who speak to you (ἐγώ being emphatic), came forth from God," i.e. in the Incarnation. ἐκ θεοῦ is a phrase that has found a place in the Nicene Creed; while as early as 196 B.C. Ptolemy Epiphanes was described as ὑπάρχων θεὸς ἐκ θεοῦ καὶ θεᾶς.[1]

Attempts have been made to distinguish ἐκ τοῦ θεοῦ (cf. 16²⁸) and ἀπὸ τοῦ θεοῦ (cf. 13³ 16³⁰), but they will not bear scrutiny. See on 1⁴⁴; and cf. 16²⁷ and the note there.

For ἐξῆλθον ἐκ, see on 4³⁰.

[1] i.e. on the Rosetta Stone ; see Moulton-Milligan, *Vocab. of N.T.*, s.v. ἐκ.

ἀπ᾽ ἐμαυτοῦ ἐλήλυθα, ἀλλ᾽ ἐκεῖνός με ἀπέστειλεν. 43. διὰ τί τὴν λαλιὰν τὴν ἐμὴν οὐ γινώσκετε; ὅτι οὐ δύνασθε ἀκούειν τὸν λόγον τὸν ἐμόν. 44. ὑμεῖς ἐκ τοῦ πατρὸς τοῦ διαβόλου ἐστὲ καὶ τὰς ἐπιθυμίας

καὶ ἥκω (cf. 1 Jn. 5²⁰). The present tense is emphatic, "and I am here."

οὐδὲ γὰρ ἀπ᾽ ἐμαυτοῦ ἐλήλυθα. This is repeated from 7²⁸, and with the same significance, "I have not come of myself," *i.e.* without a Divine mission, "but God sent me." For this "sending" of Christ by the Father, see on 3¹⁷; and cf. 17⁸.

For ἐκεῖνος in Jn., see on 1⁸, 19³⁵.

43. διὰ τί τὴν λαλιὰν τὴν ἐμὴν οὐ γινώσκετε; For λαλιά, see on 4⁴²: it does not mean "talk" in any disparaging sense (as it sometimes does in classical writers), but "manner of speech." The Jewish disputants did not appreciate the spiritual idiom of Jesus' words, in which they did not recognise the Divine accent.

ὅτι οὐ δύνασθε ἀκούειν τὸν λόγον τὸν ἐμόν. ἀκούειν with the accusative always means in Jn., to perceive by hearing, as distinct from hearing with appreciation and intelligence, when ἀκούειν takes the genitive (see on 3⁸; and cf. 5³⁷). Here, then, the incapacity of the Jews for "hearing" the message of Jesus is an even graver disability than that of their failure to understand it. As He said at v. 37, His λόγος or message had no place in them. It did not appeal to them at all. Their incapacity was, as it were, a spiritual deafness, and not merely an intellectual stupidity. See on 12⁴⁰; and cf. v. 47 below.

The contrast in the two clauses of the verse is between γινώσκειν and ἀκούειν rather than between λαλιά and λόγος. There is a difference between the usage of these words, but it cannot be sharply pressed in Jn.: see on 3¹¹.

44. ὑμεῖς (an emphatic beginning) ἐκ τοῦ πατρὸς τοῦ διαβόλου ἐστέ κτλ., "You are of your father, the devil." Similar language is ascribed to Jesus Mt. 13³⁸ 23¹⁵.

The sentence would admit of the translation, "You are of the father of the devil"; and Hilgenfeld, with some other critics, have found here a trace of Gnostic doctrine. According to the Ophites, Ialdabaoth, the God of the Jews, was the father of the serpent (Iren. *Hær.* I. xxx. 6, 10). But such a notion is not relevant to this context, the evangelist representing Jesus as telling the Jews plainly for the first time that they are the devil's children, a climax of denunciation to which the preceding verses have led up. Closely parallel in language and in thought is 1 Jn. 3⁸ ὁ ποιῶν τὴν ἁμαρτίαν ἐκ τοῦ διαβόλου ἐστίν, ὅτι ἀπ᾽ ἀρχῆς ὁ διάβολος ἁμαρτάνει.

For the constr. εἶναι ἐκ, see on v. 23 above.

τοῦ πατρὸς ὑμῶν θέλετε ποιεῖν. ἐκεῖνος ἀνθρωποκτόνος ἦν ἀπ᾽ ἀρχῆς, καὶ ἐν τῇ ἀληθείᾳ οὐκ ἔστηκεν, ὅτι οὐκ ἔστιν ἀλήθεια ἐν αὐτῷ. ὅταν λαλῇ τὸ ψεῦδος, ἐκ τῶν ἰδίων λαλεῖ, ὅτι ψεύστης ἐστὶν καὶ ὁ πατὴρ

καὶ τὰς ἐπιθυμίας τοῦ πατρὸς ὑμῶν θέλετε ποιεῖν, "And your will is to do the lusts of your father," θέλετε indicating a settled purpose of will.

ἀνθρωποκτόνος occurs elsewhere in the Greek Bible only at 1 Jn. 3¹⁵. In the *Apostolic Constitutions* (VIII. vii. 5) the devil is alluded to as ὁ ἀνθρωποκτόνος ὄφις.

That he was " a murderer from the beginning " is probably a reference to the Jewish doctrine that death was a consequence of the Fall, which was due to the devil's prompting; cf. Wisd. 2²⁴ φθόνῳ δὲ διαβόλου θάνατος εἰσῆλθεν εἰς τὸν κόσμον, and see Rom. 5¹². ἀπ᾽ ἀρχῆς is used thus in 1 Jn. 3⁸ (quoted above); cf. Eccles. 3¹¹, Mt. 19⁴. See on 15²⁷.

The allusion, however, may be to the murder of Abel by Cain. At 1 Jn. 3¹² we have Κάϊν ἐκ τοῦ πονηροῦ ἦν καὶ ἔσφαξε τὸν ἀδελφὸν αὐτοῦ, and three verses after we find ὁ μισῶν τὸν ἀδελφὸν αὐτοῦ ἀνθρωποκτόνος.

Whatever be the precise reference of the words ἐκεῖνος ἀνθρωποκτόνος ἦν ἀπ᾽ ἀρχῆς, their appositeness to the argument is derived from the fact that the Jews were seeking to kill Jesus (see vv. 37, 40), who now explains to them that their murderous intent is due to their spiritual parentage. They are doing the works of their father (v. 41).

καὶ ἐν τῇ ἀληθείᾳ οὐκ ἔστηκεν. οὐκ is read by אB*DLNWΘ, and must be preferred to the rec. οὐχ. Hence we have ἔστηκεν, and not ἔστηκεν, which would be the perfect of ἵστημι, used like a present, " has no footing in the truth." But ἔστηκεν, the impft. of στήκω, follows naturally after the impft. ἦν, *non stetit*, as the Vulgate renders it.

ὅτι οὐκ ἔστιν ἀλήθεια ἐν αὐτῷ. For ἀλήθεια in Jn. see on 1¹⁴. Mention of the *falseness* of the devil may have primary reference here to his deceitful words of temptation (Gen. 3⁴), which led to sin and death.

For the phrase " the truth is not in him (us)," cf. 1 Jn. 1⁸ 2⁴ and 1 Macc. 7¹⁸.

ὅταν λαλῇ τὸ ψεῦδος, ἐκ τῶν ἰδίων λαλεῖ. It is the devil's nature to be false; " when he tells a lie, he speaks out of his own inmost being ": cf. Mt. 12³⁴ ἐκ τοῦ περισσεύματος τῆς καρδίας τὸ στόμα λαλεῖ. Much stress is laid in Jn. on the repeated assurance of Jesus, ἐγὼ ἐξ ἐμαυτοῦ οὐκ ἐλάλησα (12⁴⁹; and see on 7¹⁷). His words always express the mind of God; while the devil's words only express his own false nature. In contradistinction to this, it is said (16¹³) that the Holy Spirit

αὐτοῦ. 45. ἐγὼ δὲ ὅτι τὴν ἀλήθειαν λέγω, οὐ πιστεύετέ μοι. 46. τίς
ἐξ ὑμῶν ἐλέγχει με περὶ ἁμαρτίας; εἰ ἀλήθειαν λέγω, διὰ τί ὑμεῖς οὐ
πιστεύετέ μοι; 47. ὁ ὢν ἐκ τοῦ Θεοῦ τὰ ῥήματα τοῦ Θεοῦ ἀκούει·

will lead into all truth, because " *He will not speak of Himself* (ἀφ' ἑαυτοῦ), but will speak of that which He shall hear."
This contrast is noted by Origen (Comm. *in Joann.* 346).

ὅτι ψεύστης ἐστὶν καὶ ὁ πατὴρ αὐτοῦ. Jn. uses the word
ψεύστης frequently (8⁵⁵, 1 Jn. 1¹⁰ 2⁴. ²² 4²⁰ 5¹⁰), just because
he dwells on the significance of ἀλήθεια (see on 1¹⁴). ὁ πατὴρ
αὐτοῦ may mean (*a*) the father of a *liar*, or (*b*) the father of a
lie, according as αὐτοῦ is masculine or neuter. Probably the
latter rendering is right, ὡς καὶ ὁ πατὴρ τοῦ ψεύδους ψεύστης
ἐστίν (Origen, Comm. *in Joann.* 347).

Westcott would render the sentence differently, *sc.* " Whenever a man speaketh a lie, he speaketh of his own, for his
father also is a liar." But it is difficult to supply a new subject
to the verb, between ὅταν and λαλῇ.[1] The point is not that the
Jews have been lying, for they have not been charged with
lying up to this point (cf. v. 55), but that they are following the
promptings of their father the devil, who is both a murderer
and a liar, in seeking to kill Jesus. And this leads up naturally
to the next verse. They are trusting to the promptings of a
liar, but they will not trust Jesus who tells them the truth.
Indeed, it is *because* He speaks the truth that His words
are unwelcome, for His hearers are spiritual sons of one in
whom the truth is not.

45. ἐγὼ δὲ ὅτι τὴν ἀλήθειαν λέγω, οὐ πιστεύετέ μοι, " But as
for me (ἐγώ being placed first for emphasis), because I speak
the truth, you do not believe me." Truth is uncongenial to
them. Cf. 3¹⁹; and see on 16⁷ for τὴν ἀλήθειαν λέγω.

πιστεύειν τινι is not to be confused with that deeper faith
which is expressed by πιστεύειν εἰς τινα (see on v. 31).

46. τίς ἐξ ὑμῶν ἐλέγχει με περὶ ἁμαρτίας; No answer
to this challenge is recorded. Probably no answer was
attempted. His hearers did not understand, of course, that
Jesus was literally χωρὶς ἁμαρτίας (Heb. 4¹⁵); but they could
prove nothing to the contrary, and they knew it. The phrase
ἐλέγχειν περὶ ἁμαρτίας occurs again 16⁸, where see note.

After a pause, as we may suppose, Jesus then resumes the
argument, " If I tell the truth (and none of you has accused
me of being a liar), why do you not believe me ? "

---

[1] Westcott s rendering was suggested by Middleton (*On the Greek
Article,* ed. 1808, p. 362), who mentions an emendation τις for τό
before ψεῦδος, which would remove the difficulty about the subject of
the verb.

διὰ τοῦτο ὑμεῖς οὐκ ἀκούετε, ὅτι ἐκ τοῦ Θεοῦ οὐκ ἐστέ. 48. Ἀπεκρίθησαν οἱ Ἰουδαῖοι καὶ εἶπαν αὐτῷ Οὐ καλῶς λέγομεν ἡμεῖς ὅτι
Σαμαρείτης εἶ σὺ καὶ δαιμόνιον ἔχεις; 49. ἀπεκρίθη Ἰησοῦς Ἐγὼ

47. ὁ ὢν ἐκ τοῦ θεοῦ, *i.e.* the true child of God: cf. 1 Jn.
3¹⁰ 4⁶ 5¹⁹, 3 Jn.¹¹, and see on ἐκ θεοῦ ἐγεννήθησαν (1¹³).

τὰ ῥήματα τοῦ θεοῦ. For this phrase, see on 3³⁴.

The principle that it is only the true child of God who
can hear God's words is frequently stated in Jn.; see on 7¹⁷ and
on 8⁴³ above. The man who is not " of God " is not in spiritual
affinity with Divine things, and does not catch the sound of the
Divine voice. As has been pointed out already (see on 3⁸ 5³⁷),
ἀκούειν with a following accusative signifies in Jn. a *mere*
hearing, while ἀκούειν with a genitive implies a hearing with
intelligence, the appreciation of the meaning of what has been
said. Thus at 1 Jn. 4⁶ the distinction between the man who is,
and the man who is not, ἐκ τοῦ θεοῦ is that the former understands the apostolic teaching (ἀκούει ἡμῶν), while the latter
does not understand it. This is not exactly the distinction
drawn out here, where the contrast is between the man who is
spiritually deaf and the man who hears God's voice, although
he may not be able perfectly to interpret it.

For the constr. διὰ τοῦτο, relating to what follows, see
on 5¹⁶.

ὅτι ἐκ τοῦ θεοῦ οὐκ ἐστέ. We should expect οὐκ ἐστέ to
precede ἐκ τοῦ θεοῦ (as at 10²⁶), but emphasis is gained by
altering the order of the words from that in the first clause of
the verse.

48. οὐ καλῶς λέγομεν ἡμεῖς κτλ., the emphasis resting on
ἡμεῖς : " *We* are right, after all." For καλῶς λέγειν, cf.
4¹⁷ 13¹³.

Σαμαρείτης εἶ σύ. For Σαμαρείτης, cf. 4⁹⁻ ³⁹. Jesus
had been combating their claim to be the true children of
Abraham (vv. 39, 40), and had thus challenged their boasted
spiritual privileges. This was a principal point with the
Samaritans, who would never allow that the Jews had any
exclusive right to the promises made to Abraham and his seed.
And so, observing, as they thought, that Jesus agreed with their
despised Samaritan neighbours, they said contemptuously,
" You, after all, are only a Samaritan." The position of σύ
at the end of the sentence is emphatic.

καὶ δαιμόνιον ἔχεις. This had been said before (7²⁰,
where see note) by the people, and it was said again (10²⁰).
The Jewish disputants say it here, with a touch of contempt:
" You must be mad, or you would not talk in this way."
There may be an allusion to the charge recorded by the

δαιμόνιον οὐκ ἔχω, ἀλλὰ τιμῶ τὸν Πατέρα μου, καὶ ὑμεῖς ἀτιμάζετέ
με. 50. ἐγὼ δὲ οὐ ζητῶ τὴν δόξαν μου· ἔστιν ὁ ζητῶν καὶ κρίνων.
51. ἀμὴν ἀμὴν λέγω ὑμῖν, ἐάν τις τὸν ἐμὸν λόγον τηρήσῃ, θάνατον
οὐ μὴ θεωρήσῃ εἰς τὸν αἰῶνα.

Synoptists (Mk. 3[22]) as having been made against Jesus by
scribes from Jerusalem, that "He casts out demons by the
prince of demons"; but the emphasis laid in Jn. on demoniac
possession is always in connexion with the *dementia* which
was supposed to be its consequence (see Introd., p. clxxvii).
It is not put forward in Jn. (either at 7[20] or 10[20]) as a sign
of wickedness, which is implied in Mk. 3[22].

49. Jesus does not take any notice of the imputation, "You
are a Samaritan." That was not so offensive to Him as it
was intended to be, for He looked to the day when the rivalries
between Jews and Samaritans would disappear (4[21]). His reply
is mild and calm: "I am not mad." His claim to be God's
messenger and to speak with a delegated authority (v. 42)
did not arise out of a disordered brain, but from His fixed
purpose of "honouring His Father," τιμῶ τὸν πατέρα μου.
Cf. 7[18] ὁ ζητῶν τὴν δόξαν τοῦ πέμψαντος αὐτόν. For ὁ πατήρ μου,
see on 2[16].

His Jewish adversaries, on the other hand, had been insulting, ὑμεῖς ἀτιμάζετέ με. Cf. 5[23], where it has been said
ὁ μὴ τιμῶν τὸν υἱὸν οὐ τιμᾷ τὸν πατέρα.

50. However, He goes on to explain that their insulting
words did not affect Him. ἐγὼ δὲ οὐ ζητῶ τὴν δόξαν μου: if
He did so, it would be nothing (cf. 5[41] 7[18] 8[54]).

ἔστιν ὁ ζητῶν καὶ κρίνων, "there is One who seeks (my
honour), and (in doing so) pronounces judgment (as between
us)." It is only the δόξα that comes from God that is worth
having (5[44] 8[54]). To win the approval of God for any act or
thought is to be "judged"; and this Jesus applied to Himself,
strange as the thought may be to us of the Father "judging"
the Son. But we cannot separate ζητῶν from κρίνων, and
ὁ ζητῶν refers to the Father as seeking to honour the Son
(see on v. 54).

There is no incongruity, even of expression, with 5[22], where
the office of the judgment of mankind is reserved to the Son
Himself.

51. ἀμὴν ἀμὴν λέγω ὑμῖν introduces a summary (see on 1[51])
of what Jesus has been leading up to (cf. vv. 34, 58). If they
keep His teaching, they will have eternal life.

ἐάν τις τὸν ἐμὸν λόγον κτλ. So אBCDLW; the rec., with
NO, has τὸν λόγον τὸν ἐμόν (from v. 43). "To keep the
word" of Christ or of God (τὸν λογὸν τηρεῖν) is a characteristic

52. Εἶπαν αὐτῷ οἱ Ἰουδαῖοι Νῦν ἐγνώκαμεν ὅτι δαιμόνιον ἔχεις.
Ἀβραὰμ ἀπέθανεν καὶ οἱ προφῆται, καὶ σὺ λέγεις Ἐάν τις τὸν λόγον

phrase in Jn.; cf. vv. 52, 55, 14²³· ²⁴ 15²⁰ 17⁶, 1 Jn. 2⁵. It
is practically identical in meaning with τηρεῖν τὰς ἐντολὰς τὰς
ἐμάς (see on 14²¹; and cf. Introd., p. lxvii). Cf. 5²⁴, where he
who "hears" and "believes" is promised eternal life; and
see 11²⁶ 12⁴⁷.

The phrase "shall never see death" is a Hebraism for
"shall never die." See on 3³ for ἰδεῖν, used as θεωρεῖν (see
on 2²³) is used here, in the sense of "participate in" or "have
experience of." "To see death," meaning "to die," is found
Ps. 89⁴⁸, Lk. 2²⁶, Heb. 11⁵. The promise given here is not, of
course, one of exemption from the death of the body, which
is not in question. But the man who "keeps the word" of
Christ has eternal life already. See 14²³.

*To the Jews' suggestion that Jesus is not as great as Abraham
was, despite His claims, He replies that He was in
existence before Abraham (vv. 52–58)*

52. אBCWΘ omit the rec. οὖν (so N) after εἶπαν.

For οἱ Ἰουδαῖοι (cf. vv. 22, 31, 48, 57), see on 1¹⁹. They
misunderstood the meaning of Christ's saying, interpreting
it of exemption from physical death. They thought He was
mad: νῦν ἐγνώκαμεν, "now we are sure," ὅτι δαιμόνιον ἔχεις.
Cf. v. 48.

Abraham and the prophets had "kept the word" of
Yahweh, and yet they had died (cf. Zech. 1⁵). Was Jesus
really claiming to be greater than Yahweh? Was His word
more powerful? He ventured to say ἐάν τις τὸν λόγον μου
τηρήσῃ, οὐ μὴ γεύσηται (the rec. has γεύσεται, but with insufficient support) θανάτου εἰς τὸν αἰῶνα.

γενεῖν θανάτου, "to taste of death," means "to die," and
is used of the death of Jesus Himself at Heb. 2⁹. Cf. for the
same usage Mt. 16²⁸, Mk. 9¹, Lk. 9²⁷, 2 Esd. 6²⁶. The phrase
is a Hebrew one, although not found in the O.T., and Wetstein
(on Mt. 16²⁸) has collected some instances of its use in the
Talmud. By pressing the distinction between θεωρεῖν θάνατον
in v. 51 and γενεῖν θανάτου in v. 52, it has been inferred that
Jn.'s report makes the Jews deliberately *misquote* what Jesus
had said; but this is not probable. That they *misunderstood*
it is certain.

In a saying of Jesus among the Oxyrhynchus Papyri¹

¹ *New Sayings of Jesus*, ed. B. P. Grenfell and A. S. Hunt (1904),
p. 12.

μου τηρήσῃ, οὐ μὴ γεύσηται θανάτου εἰς τὸν αἰῶνα.   53. μὴ σὺ
μείζων εἶ τοῦ πατρὸς ἡμῶν Ἀβραάμ, ὅστις ἀπέθανεν; καὶ οἱ προφῆται
ἀπέθανον· τίνα σεαυτὸν ποιεῖς;   54. ἀπεκρίθη Ἰησοῦς Ἐὰν ἐγὼ
δοξάσω ἐμαυτόν, ἡ δόξα μου οὐδέν ἐστιν· ἔστιν ὁ Πατήρ μου ὁ δοξάζων
με, ὃν ὑμεῖς λέγετε ὅτι Θεὸς ὑμῶν ἐστιν, 55. καὶ οὐκ ἐγνώκατε αὐτόν,

(about 280 A.D.) there is found, as restored by the editors:
[πᾶς ὅστις] ἂν τῶν λόγων τούτ[ων ἀκούσῃ, θανάτου] οὐ μὴ
γεύσηται. If the conjectural restoration is accurate, this
closely resembles Jn. 8⁵², and in any case οὐ μὴ γεύσηται provides a parallel.

53. μὴ σὺ μείζων εἶ τοῦ πατρὸς ἡμῶν Ἀβραάμ; Cf. the similar
question at 4¹².

ὅστις ἀπέθανεν. The relative ὅστις does not occur again in
Jn., although we have ἥτις (1 Jn. 1²) and ὅ τι. How could Jesus
claim exemption from death for those who kept His word,
when the saints of old, Abraham and the prophets, had died
like every one else ?

τίνα σεαυτὸν ποιεῖς; They are beginning to suspect that
His claims are blasphemous, an accusation which has not yet
been made in this discourse. Cf. 5¹⁸ 10³³ 19⁷. Who does He
really claim to be ? As usual, Jesus gives no explicit answer to
this question; but, having first defended Himself again in reply
to the charge of undue self-assertion (vv. 54, 55), He makes a
statement which implies that He *is* greater than Abraham (v. 56).

54. ἐὰν ἐγὼ δοξάσω (so אBC*DW, as against δοξάζω of LN
and the rec. text) **ἐμαυτόν, ἡ δόξα μου οὐδέν ἐστιν.** Cf. v. 50
and 5³¹· ⁴¹ 7¹⁸. In all these passages δόξα signifies *honour*
(see on 1¹⁴), and the contrast is between the δόξα that men
can bestow and that which comes from God.

ἔστιν ὁ πατήρ μου ὁ δοξάζων με, " it really is (ἔστιν being
placed first for emphasis) my Father who honours me "; *i.e.*
primarily by the honour given to Him in the power to do divine
acts, which is a form of the Father's " witness " (5³¹· ³⁶), but
more generally the reference is to the honour and glory of His
mission (3¹⁶· ¹⁷) throughout His Incarnate Life, although this
the Jews could not recognise. See on 17²²; and cf. 2 Pet. 1¹⁷,
λαβὼν παρὰ θεοῦ πατρὸς τιμὴν καὶ δόξαν, referring to the
Voice at the Transfiguration. See also on 1¹⁴.

ὃν ὑμεῖς λέγετε (cf. 10³⁶ for constr.) **ὅτι θεὸς ὑμῶν ἐστιν.**
So they had said (v. 41). This is, for the first time, an explicit
identification by Jesus of ὁ πατήρ μου with the God of Israel.

For ὑμῶν (אB*D, with the rec. text), AB²CLNWΔΘ have
ἡμῶν, ὅτι then being *recitantis*. The Coptic Q omits any
possessive pronoun before " God."

55. καὶ οὐκ ἐγνώκατε αὐτόν. So at 16³; and cf. 1¹⁰ 17²³· ²⁵,

ἐγὼ δὲ οἶδα αὐτόν. κἂν εἴπω ὅτι οὐκ οἶδα αὐτόν, ἔσομαι ὅμοιος ὑμῖν
ψεύστης· ἀλλὰ οἶδα αὐτὸν καὶ τὸν λόγον αὐτοῦ τηρῶ.   56. Ἀβραὰμ
ὁ πατὴρ ὑμῶν ἠγαλλιάσατο ἵνα εἴδῃ τὴν ἡμέραν τὴν ἐμήν, καὶ εἴδεν

1 Jn. 3[1, 6]. The verb οἶδα is used in similar contexts 7[28] (where
see note) 8[19] 15[21]. Although the Jews claimed God as their
Father (v. 41), they did not know Him.

ἐγὼ δὲ οἶδα αὐτόν. Cf. 7[29] ἐγὼ οἶδα αὐτὸν ὅτι παρ' αὐτοῦ
εἰμι, and for the same claim, the verb γινώσκω being used,
cf. 10[15] 17[25]. See note on 1[26].

This unique knowledge of the Father, Jesus could not
disclaim without denying the validity of His mission: ἔσομαι
ὅμοιος ὑμῖν ψεύστης. He had not yet directly accused the
Jewish objectors of lying, but He had told them that they were
the children of the devil, who is the father of lies (v. 44).

ὅμοιος ὑμῖν. So ABDW⊖. ὑμῶν is read by אCLNΓΔ
(cf. Job 35[8]), which would be doubtful Greek.

τὸν λόγον αὐτοῦ τηρῶ. See on v. 51 above.

56. Jesus now explains that He is truly " greater " than
Abraham (cf. v. 53).

Ἀβραὰμ ὁ πατὴρ ὑμῶν ἠγαλλιάσατο (exultauit, cf. 5[35]) ἵνα
εἴδῃ (this is the reading of אAB*) τὴν ἡμέραν τὴν ἐμήν, i.e.
probably the day of Christ's birth or appearance in the flesh
(cf. Job 3[1]). " The days of the Son of Man " (Lk. 17[22, 26])
was the Rabbinical description of the Messianic age generally.

The moment in Abraham's life to which reference is made
is not certain. Many expositors have referred to Gen. 17[17],
where Abraham " laughed " at the idea of Sarah becoming
" a mother of nations," but this was the laughter of incredulity.
That Abraham " received the promises " is noted at Heb. 11[17],
and it is probable that the Rabbinical idea was that Abraham
had welcomed the implicit promise that Messiah should be
born of his seed, in which all nations were to be blessed (Gen.
12[3], quoted Gal. 3[8] as Messianic). Westcott quotes a Jewish
tradition (Bereshith, R 44) that Abraham saw the whole
history of his descendants in the vision of Gen. 15[6f.], when he
" rejoiced with the joy of the law." With this agrees 2 Esd.
3[14], " Abraham . . . thou lovedst, and unto him only thou
shewedst the end of the times secretly by night." [1]

The constr. ἠγαλλιάσατο [2] ἵνα εἴδῃ seems to mean " exulted
in the anticipation of seeing," which is not far removed
from " desired to see "; and this rendering is adopted several

[1] Cf. a fanciful version of a similar idea in the Testament of Abraham,
§ ix. (A).
[2] F. H. Chase (J.T.S., July 1925, p. 381) suggested that ἠγαλλιάσατο
may be a primitive error for ἠγωνίσατο (cf. 18[36]).

καὶ ἐχάρη. 57. εἶπαν οὖν οἱ Ἰουδαῖοι πρὸς αὐτόν Πεντήκοντα ἔτη
οὔπω ἔχεις καὶ Ἀβραὰμ ἑώρακέ σε; 58. εἶπεν αὐτοῖς Ἰησοῦς Ἀμὴν
ἀμὴν λέγω ὑμῖν, πρὶν Ἀβραὰμ γενέσθαι ἐγὼ εἰμί.

times in the Latin version of Origen (*Lommatzsch*, vi. 38,
ix. 145, xiv. 425; cited by Abbott, *Diat.* 2688), and also appears
in the Syriac commentary of Isho'dad, which embodies much
early material. We should expect an infinitive instead of ἵνα
εἴδῃ, but ἵνα cannot be judged incorrect. Milligan [1] cites
from a third-century papyrus ἐχάρην ἵνα σὲ ἀσπάζομαι, " I
was glad to have an opportunity of greeting you."

καὶ εἶδεν καὶ ἐχάρη. This seems to say that Abraham in
the other world was joyfully conscious of Christ's appearance
in the flesh, a strange and mysterious saying, which is taken up
in one of the legends of the *Descensus ad inferos*. There it is
said that when the news of Christ came to Hades there was joy
among the O.T. saints, καὶ εὐθὺς ὁ πατὴρ ἡμῶν Ἀβραὰμ μετὰ τῶν
πατριαρχῶν καὶ τῶν προφητῶν ἐνωθείς, καὶ χαρᾶς ὁμοῦ πλησθέντες
εἶπον πρὸς ἀλλήλους.[2]

57. καὶ Ἀβραὰμ ἑώρακέ σε; The Jewish objectors are
represented as interpreting the reply of Jesus to mean that
Abraham, while alive on earth, had seen Him. The rec. καὶ
Ἀβραὰμ ἑώρακας; is strongly supported, being read by
ℵᶜACDN; but the true reading seems to be καὶ Ἀβραὰμ
ἑώρακέ σε; " And did Abraham see thee ? " This is
read by ℵ* and supported by Syr. sin. and the Coptic vss.
(including Q). BWΘ have ἑώρακες. The reading ἑώρακέ σε·
εἶπεν would be in uncials εωρακεϲεειπεν, which by dropping
one ε would become εωρακεϲειπεν or ἑώρακες· εἶπεν, and
then ἑώρακες was corrected into ἑώρακας, the rec. reading.
In v. 56 Jesus had not said that He had seen Abraham, but
that Abraham has seen Him, or His day; and there is no
reason to suppose that the Jews are represented as misquoting
His words, as we must assume if the received text be followed.

πεντήκοντα ἔτη οὔπω ἔχεις. Chrysostom reads τεσσαράκοντα,
but this is plainly due to an attempt to reconcile the
statement with such passages as Lk. 3²³. At fifty years of age,
the Levites were superannuated from further service (Num. 4³),
and all that the sentence means is, " You are not yet an old
man." Irenæus, however, resting his argument on this passage,
concludes that Jesus was not far short of fifty years of age at
the conclusion of His earthly ministry (*Hær.* ii. xxii. 6), and
that therefore its duration exceeded the single year which the
Synoptists suggest.

58. ἀμὴν ἀμὴν λέγω ὑμῖν. We have had this solemn

---

[1] *Vocab.*, s.v. ἵνα.   [2] *Evang. Nicodemi*, ii. ii. (18).

59. Ἦραν οὖν λίθους ἵνα βάλωσιν ἐπ' αὐτόν· Ἰησοῦς δὲ ἐκρύβη καὶ ἐξῆλθεν ἐκ τοῦ ἱεροῦ.

form of affirmation (see on 1⁵¹) twice before in this discourse, at vv. 34, 51; and in each case, as here, it sums up what has gone before.

πρὶν 'Αβραὰμ γενέσθαι ἐγὼ εἰμί, i.e. "before Abraham came into being, I AM." The contrast betweeen the verbs γίγνεσθαι and εἶναι is as unmistakable as it is in Ps. 90², πρὸ τοῦ ὄρη γενηθῆναι . . . ἀπὸ τοῦ αἰῶνος ἕως τοῦ αἰῶνος σὺ εἶ, "before the mountains came into being . . . from age to age THOU ART." ¹ Of God it could not be said that He "came into being" or "became," for He IS. Cf. 1¹⁸ and Col. 1¹⁷ for this absolute use of εἶναι; see also on 1¹. It has been pointed out already (see Introd., p. cxxi) that ἐγὼ εἰμί used absolutely, where no predicate is expressed or implied, is the equivalent of the solemn אֲנִי־הוּא, I (am) He, which is the self-designation of Yahweh in the prophets. A similar use of the phrase is found at 13¹⁹. It is clear that Jn. means to represent Jesus as thus claiming for Himself the timeless being of Deity, as distinct from the temporal existence of man. This is the teaching of the Prologue to the Gospel about Jesus (1¹· ¹⁸); but here (and at 13¹⁹) Jesus Himself is reported as having said I (am) He, which is a definite assertion of His Godhead, and was so understood by the Jews. They had listened to His argument up to this point; but they could bear with it no longer. These words of mystery were rank blasphemy (see 10³³), and they proceeded to stone Him.

For other occurrences in Jn. of ἐγὼ εἰμί without a predicate following, see 6²⁰ 9⁹ 18⁶, as well as vv. 24, 28 of the present chapter.

The angry people would stone Jesus, but He escapes from them into hiding (v. 59)

59. ἦραν οὖν λίθους κτλ. So again at 10³¹⁻³³, when He said "I and the Father are One," the Jews attempted to stone Him for blasphemy. The Temple was not finished, and stones

---

¹ Dr. L. C. Purser has pointed out to me a striking passage in Plutarch (De Ei apud Delphos, c. 20, p. 393) where εἶναι is similarly used for the timeless existence of Deity, being contrasted with γίγνεσθαι: Ἀλλ' ἔστιν ὁ θεὸς . . . καὶ ἔστι κατ' οὐδένα χρόνον ἀλλὰ κατὰ τὸν αἰῶνα τὸν ἀκίνητον καὶ ἄχρονον . . . καὶ μόνον ἐστὶ τὸ κατὰ τοῦτον ὄντως ὄν, οὐ γεγονὸς οὐδ' ἐσόμενον οὐδ' ἀρξάμενον οὐδὲ παυσόμενον. Plutarch uses the remarkable expression ἀλλ' εἰς ὢν ἑνὶ τῷ νῦν τὸ ἀεὶ πεπλήρωκε, "But He, being One with the One Now has filled up the Ever"; and adds that we should address God as εἶ ἕν, "Thou art One Being."

IX. 1. Καὶ παράγων εἶδεν ἄνθρωπον τυφλὸν ἐκ γενετῆς.   2. καὶ

were lying about its courts (cf. Mk. 13¹); Josephus (*Antt.* XVII. ix. 3) gives an account of the stoning of soldiers in the Temple precincts.

'Ιησοῦς δὲ ἐκρύβη, "But He hid Himseif," as again at 12³⁶.

After ἱεροῦ the rec. text (so N⊛ᶜᵒʳʳ) adds διελθὼν διὰ μέσου αὐτῶν (from Lk. 4³⁰) καὶ παρῆγεν οὕτως, probably suggesting that the escape of Jesus from the angry Jews was miraculous. But of this there is no trace in the true text, ending with ἱεροῦ, which is supported by ℵBDW⊛* latt sah arm. The words παρῆγεν οὕτω are added in the rec. text to the interpolation from Lk. 4³⁰, in order to introduce c. 9.

See 10³⁹, where Jesus again escapes from the hostile Jews.

IX. 1 ff. The narrative of c. 9 may be intended to follow immediately the disputes of 8²¹⁻⁵⁹, but there can be no certainty as to this. The day on which the blind man's sight was restored was a Sabbath (v. 14), as was also the day of the impotent man's cure at Bethesda (5¹⁰), but there may have been a considerable interval between the two healings. The next note of time that we have is the mention of the Feast of Dedication (10²²), and there is no doubt that cc. 9 and 10 must be taken together. The tone of the questioning and of the words of Jesus in c. 9 is different from that of c. 8, where the Jews become fiercely indignant with the claims which Jesus puts forward. It is probable that 9¹ marks the beginning of a fresh section of the narrative, which has no special relation with that of c. 8. The story in 9¹⁻³⁴ is told very vividly and with much lively detail.

Cure of a man blind from his birth (IX. 1-13)

1. καὶ παράγων εἶδεν κτλ. This is an abrupt beginning, but the introductory καί is thoroughly Johannine. παράγειν does not occur again in the Fourth Gospel; but cf. 1 Jn. 2⁸·¹⁷.

τυφλὸν ἐκ γενετῆς. Probably the man was a well-known figure, as he begged for alms (v. 8) near the Temple or at some other much-frequented place. γενετή does not appear again in the N.T., but the phrase τυφλὸς ἐκ γενετῆς is common in secular writers (see Wetstein).

It is not reported of any other case of healing in the Gospels that the person cured had been sick, blind, or lame *from his birth* (cf. Acts 3² 14⁸), and some critics have found here an

ἠρώτησαν αὐτὸν οἱ μαθηταὶ αὐτοῦ λέγοντες ʽΡαββεί, τίς ἥμαρτεν, οὗτος ἢ οἱ γονεῖς αὐτοῦ, ἵνα τυφλὸς γεννηθῇ; 3. ἀπεκρίθη Ἰησοῦς

instance of Jn.'s alleged habit of magnifying the miraculous element in the ministry of Jesus (see Introd., p. clxxx). This healing goes beyond any of the healings of blind men recorded by the Synoptists, Jn., after his wont, selecting one typical and notable case for record (see below on v. 6).

Diseases of the eye are common in the East, and it is not surprising that blind folk should have been brought for cure to Jesus. There is no mention in the O.T. of a blind person being cured (unless the case of Tob. 11[11] be reckoned as such); but to the prophet the blessings of the Messianic age included the opening of the eyes of the blind (Isa. 35[5]), and the Baptist was reminded of this in connexion with the cures wrought by Jesus (cf. Mt. 11[5]). Mk. records two special cases, *sc.* at Mk. 8[23] (to which further reference must be made) and Mk. 10[46] (cf. Mt. 20[29], Lk. 18[35]). See also Mt. 9[27] 12[22] (cf. Lk. 11[14]) 15[30] 21[14]. But the singularity of the case recorded by Jn. is that the blindness is said to have been congenital.

There is a passage in Justin (*Tryph.* 69) which seems to pre-suppose a knowledge of this verse. Justin has quoted Isa. 35[1-7], and he proceeds: πηγὴ ὕδατος ζῶντος παρὰ θεοῦ ἐν τῇ ἐρήμῳ γνώσεως θεοῦ . . . ἀνέβλυσεν, *sc.* Christ, τοὺς ἐκ γενετῆς καὶ κατὰ τὴν σάρκα πηροὺς καὶ κωφοὺς καὶ χωλοὺς ἰάσατο (cf. *Apol.* i. 22). πηρός is used of blindness, as well as of other bodily disabilities; but, apart from that, the phrase ἐκ γενετῆς indicates a knowledge of Jn. 9[1], for it occurs nowhere else in the Gospels, nor is the circumstance that Jesus healed men of *congenital* infirmities mentioned elsewhere in the N.T.

2. ἠρώτησαν αὐτὸν οἱ μαθηταὶ αὐτοῦ. These disciples may have been His Jewish adherents, as distinct from the Twelve, or the Twelve or some of them may be indicated (see on 2[2]). But the nature of the question which they put betrays an intimate relation of discipleship (note the word *Rabbi*, and see on 1[38]); and the close connexion of c. 9 with c. 10, in which the discourse about the Good Shepherd seems speci-ally appropriate to the inner circle of His followers, suggests that οἱ μαθηταὶ αὐτοῦ here at any rate includes the Twelve.

τίς ἥμαρτεν κτλ. The question is as old as humanity. The first of the alternative answers suggested is that the man himself had sinned and that his blindness was a punishment divinely sent. As to this, it may be true in an individual case, but the whole drift of the Book of Job is to show that suffering is *not* always due to sin, and with this may be compared the words of Jesus at Lk. 13[2, 4] (see on 5[14] above). In this particular

Οὔτε οὗτος ἥμαρτεν οὔτε οἱ γονεῖς αὐτοῦ, ἀλλ' ἵνα φανερωθῇ τὰ ἔργα τοῦ Θεοῦ ἐν αὐτῷ.   4. ἐμὲ δεῖ ἐργάζεσθαι τὰ ἔργα τοῦ πέμψαντός με

instance which drew forth the disciples' question. as the man had been blind from birth, if his blindness was a punishment for his own sin, it must have been prenatal sin. This was a possibility, according to some Rabbinical casuists (see *Bereshith*, R xxxiv, cited by Wetstein). Cf. v. 34. It is hardly likely that the questioners had in view sins committed in a former body, although the doctrine of the pre-existence of souls was not unknown to later Judaism; cf. Wisd. 8[19. 20].

The other alternative answer, as it seemed to the disciples, was that the man's blindness was divinely sent as a punishment for the sins of his parents, a doctrine which is frequently stated in the O.T. (Ex. 20[5] 34[7], Num. 14[18], Ps. 79[8], 109[14], Isa. 65[6. 7]). This was the doctrine of punishment which Ezekiel repudiated, declaring that justice is only to be found in the operation of the principle, " The soul that sinneth, *it* shall die " (Ezek. 18[20]).

The question of the relation between sin and suffering was discussed by the Gnostic Basilides in a passage quoted by Clem. Alex. (*Strom.* iv. 12), but although the problem raised is similar to that in the text, the discussion does not contain any allusion to the story before us.

3. ἀπεκρίθη 'Ιησοῦς. See for the omission of ὁ before 'Ιησ. on 1[50].

The answer of Jesus to the questioners approved neither of the alternatives which they put before Him. His answer, as set forth by Jn., is that the man's blindness was foreordained so that it might be the occasion of the exhibition of Divine power in his cure, ἵνα φανερωθῇ τὰ ἔργα τοῦ θεοῦ ἐν αὐτῷ.[1] Cf. 5[36] for the witness borne to the Divine mission of Jesus by His ἔργα; and 11[4] (where see note), where the sickness of Lazarus is said to have been "for the glory of God, that the Son of God may be glorified thereby."

The doctrine of predestination is apparent at every point in the Fourth Gospel, every incident being viewed *sub specie æternitatis*, as predetermined in the mind of God. See on 2[4] and 3[14].

4. ἐμὲ δεῖ ἐργάζεσθαι τὰ ἔργα τοῦ πέμψαντός με. So א[a]ACNΓΔΘ, the Lat. and Syr. vss. (including Syr. sin.). But א*BDLW read ἡμᾶς δεῖ, and for τοῦ πέμψαντός με, אLW read τοῦ πέμψαντος ἡμᾶς. The latter variant may be rejected, both on the MS. evidence and because the phrase " He that sent me " is characteristically Johannine (see on 4[34]), while " He that sent us " would be foreign to the phraseology of the

---

[1] For the ellipse in ἀλλ' ἵνα, cf. 13[18] 15[25], 1 Jn. 2[19].

ἕως ἡμέρα ἐστίν· ἔρχεται νὺξ ὅτε οὐδεὶς δύναται ἐργάζεσθαι. 5. ὅταν
ἐν τῷ κόσμῳ ὦ, φῶς εἰμὶ τοῦ κόσμου. 6. ταῦτα εἰπὼν ἔπτυσεν χαμαὶ

Gospels. But ἡμᾶς δεῖ ἐργάζεσθαι, etc., would give a tolerable
sense (see on 3¹¹). It is adopted by Westcott-Hort, and by the
R.V., as having the weight of uncial authority, the combination
of ℵ*BD (and also apparently the evidence of Origen) being
strong. Yet although it is true of all of us that " we must
work while it is day " (cf. Ecclus. 51³⁰), "the works of Him that
sent me " in this passage has special reference to the ἔργα
τοῦ θεοῦ, such as were made manifest in the cure of the blind
man, which could not be wrought by the disciples, but were
the " signs " of Jesus alone. In the doing of such ἔργα Jesus
never associated others with Himself.

Nor, again, is it in the manner of Jn. to report a mere
maxim of experience, such as " We must all work while it is
day " would be. The force of δεῖ goes deeper, for the words
of Jesus here (vv. 3, 4) express that Divine predestination of
events which is so prominently brought out in Jn. (see Introd.,
p. clii, and on 2⁴). The man's blindness had been foreordained in the Divine purpose ἵνα φανερωθῇ τὰ ἔργα τοῦ θεοῦ ἐν
αὐτῷ (v. 3); and in like manner there was a Divine necessity
that Jesus should do the works of " Him that sent Him " (see
on 4³⁴ for this phrase). The only reading that brings out the
force of the passage and gives consistency to the sentence is the
rec. reading ἐμὲ δεῖ ἐργάζεσθαι τὰ ἔργα τοῦ πέμψαντός με.

Some expositors find in these words an allusion to 5¹⁷
ὁ πατήρ μου ἕως ἄρτι ἐργάζεται, κἀγὼ ἐργάζομαι (see note
in loc.); this healing at Siloam, like the healing at Bethesda,
having been wrought on a Sabbath (v. 14). But the allusion
to 5¹⁷ is doubtful.

ἕως ἡμέρα ἐστίν. The day is the time for labour, while
the night is for rest (Ps. 104²³); and the day is none too long for
its appointed task. Jesus had already spoken of the shortness
of His time (see on 7³³). The " night " was coming for Him
in this sense only, that when His public ministry on earth was
ended, the " works " which it exhibited would no longer be
possible.

ἕως with the pres. indic. occurs in Jn. only here and at
21²². ²³ (but cf. 12³⁵), and is in these passages to be rendered
" while " (cf. 13³⁸, where, followed by οὗ, it is " until ").

ἔρχεται νύξ κτλ.: cf. 11⁹ 12³⁵.

5. ὅταν ἐν τῷ κόσμῳ ὦ, φῶς εἰμὶ τοῦ κόσμου. We had in
8¹² the majestic claim ἐγώ εἰμι τὸ φῶς τοῦ κόσμου (see note
in loc.). Here it reappears, but not in so universal or exclusive
a form: ἐγώ is omitted; so is the article before φῶς, and it is

introduced by a clause which seems to limit its application
to the time of the ministry of Jesus upon earth. "While I
am in the world, I am a light of the world," He says ; and He
proceeds to impress His meaning upon His hearers by restoring
his sight to the blind man. When Jn. says that Christ was
" in the world " (1^{10}) he refers quite definitely to the period of
His historical manifestation in the flesh (cf. also 17^{11}); and
the context in the present passage shows that the same meaning
must be given here to ἐν τῷ κόσμῳ. Christ is always, and
always has been, and will be, τὸ φῶς τοῦ κόσμου; but that
thought is not fully expressed by ὅταν ἐν τῷ κόσμῳ ὦ, φῶς εἰμὶ
τοῦ κόσμου. The thought here is that it had been eternally
ordered in the Divine purpose that He should "work the works of
God " during His earthly ministry ; and another way of expressing this is to say that while He is in the world He is, inevitably,
a light of the world, whose brightness cannot be hidden.

6. Jesus is represented here (as also at 5^{6}) as curing the
sufferer without waiting to be asked. This is unlike the Synoptic narratives of healing, e.g. Mk. 8^{23}, the cure of the blind
man at Bethsaida, who was brought to Jesus by his friends.
In that case, however, as in this, Jesus is said to have resorted
to the use of physical means for the recovery of the patient,
sc. the eyes were treated with spittle (cf. also Mk. 7^{33}).

The curative effects of saliva (especially of fasting saliva)
have been, and still are, accepted in many countries. " Magyars
believe that styes on the eye can be cured by some one spitting
on them." [1] A blind man who sought a cure from Vespasian
asked " ut . . . oculorum orbes dignaretur respergere oris
excremento " (Tacitus, Hist. iv. 81). Lightfoot (Hor. Hebr.
in loc.) quotes a Rabbinical story which embodies the same
idea. It was, apparently, a current belief in Judæa that spittle
was good for diseased eyes, and that Jesus accommodated
Himself to that belief is reported both by Mk. and Jn., although
in neither case is it stated that He Himself accepted it as well
founded. This tradition of Jesus curing blindness by means of
His spittle is not found in Mt. or Lk. It is evidently the oldest
tradition.

Severus Sammonicus, a second-century physician, quoted
by Wetstein, prescribes the use of clay for smearing bad eyes,
" turgentes oculos uili circumline cæno." [2]

These strange remedies may be compared with those
mentioned in a second-century inscription: [3] Οὐαλερίῳ Ἄπρῳ
στρατιώτῃ τυφλῷ ἐχρημάτισεν ὁ θεὸς ἐλθεῖν καὶ λαβεῖν αἷμα ἐξ

---

[1] See E.R.E. xi. 102, s.v. " Saliva."
[2] See, for other illustrations, Trench, Miracles, p. 294.
[3] See Moulton-Milligan, s.v. ἐπιχρίω.

καὶ ἐποίησεν πηλὸν ἐκ τοῦ πτύσματος, καὶ ἐπέχρισεν αὐτοῦ τὸν πηλὸν ἐπὶ τοὺς ὀφθαλμούς, 7. κἀὶ εἶπεν αὐτῷ Ὕπαγε νίψαι εἰς τὴν κολυμ-

ἀλεκτρυῶνος λευκοῦ μετὰ μέλιτος καὶ κολλυρίου συντρῖψαι (cf. the mixture of clay and spittle) καὶ ἐπὶ τρεῖς ἡμέρας ἐπιχρεῖσαι ἐπὶ τοὺς ὀφθαλμοὺς (cf. ἐπέχρισεν . . . ἐπὶ τοὺς ὀφθαλμούς, v. 6) καὶ ἀνέβλεψεν καὶ ἐλήλυθεν καὶ ηὐχαρίστησεν δημοσίᾳ τῷ θεῷ.[1]

ἔπτυσεν χαμαί. πτύειν occurs again only Mk. 7³³ 8²³; it should be noted that at Mk. 8²³ Jesus spat into the eyes of the blind man, πτύσας εἰς τὰ ὄμματα αὐτοῦ. χαμαί only occurs again 18⁶.

ἐπέχρισεν. So אADNWΘ; BC* give ἐπέθηκεν. In the N.T. ἐπιχρίω occurs again only at v. 11.

The true text (אBLNΘ) proceeds: αὐτοῦ τὸν πηλὸν ἐπὶ τοὺς ὀφθαλμούς, i.e. "and smeared its clay" (sc. the clay which He had mixed with His spittle) "on the eyes." The rec. text after ὀφθαλμούς adds τοῦ τυφλοῦ, "He smeared the clay on the eyes of the blind man."

Irenæus has a curious comment on the use of clay. He says (Hær. v. xv. 2) that the true work of God (cf. v. 3) is the creation of man, "plasmatio hominis," and he quotes Gen. 2⁷ of God making man out of the dust of the earth. He concludes that the use of clay for the cure of the blind man was similar to this; being blind from his birth, he had virtually no eyes, and Jesus created them out of the clay.

7. ὕπαγε. See on 7³³ for ὑπάγειν, a favourite verb with Jn.

νίψαι. For the aor. imperative, see on 2⁵.

εἰς τὴν κολυμβήθραν. The man interpreted this command (v. 11) as meaning, "Go to the Pool, and wash." νίψαι εἰς τήν κτλ., however, may be translated as "wash in the Pool," εἰς being often used where the verb of motion is not expressed but only implied, e.g. ἐλθὼν κατῴκησεν εἰς πόλιν κτλ. (Mt. 2²³; cf. Mt. 4¹³), and cf. ἐντετυλιγμένον εἰς ἕνα τόπον (20⁷). See, further, on 19¹³.

The man, apparently, was not directed to bathe in the Pool, but only to go there to wash off the clay with which his eyes had been smeared. The Egyptian vss. render νίψαι as meaning "wash thy face" (cf. v. 10).

The Pool of Siloam (there are two pools) is situated to the south of the Temple area, at the mouth of the Tyropœon Valley. It is mentioned Isa. 8⁶, where "the waters of Shiloah that go softly" are contrasted with "the waters of the Euphrates, strong and many," which typify the Assyrian power;

---

[1] The paratactic style of this inscription, καί . . . καί, is very like that of vv. 5-8, and shows that a redundance of καί conjunctions does not always point to a Semitic original (cf. Introd., p. lxvii).

βήθραν τοῦ Σιλωάμ (ὃ ἑρμηνεύεται Ἀπεσταλμένος). ἀπῆλθεν οὖν
καὶ ἐνίψατο, καὶ ἦλθεν βλέπων.   8. Οἱ οὖν γείτονες καὶ οἱ θεωροῦντες

cf. also Neh. 3¹⁵, Lk. 13⁴. The waters which gather in the
Pool are connected by a subterranean tunnel or conduit with
the Virgin's Well (see on 5²). שָׁלַח, *misit*, is the root of the
name Shiloah, or Siloam, which thus means, etymologically,
" sent," this name having been given to the Pool because the
water is " sent " or " conducted " thither by the artificial
aqueduct which goes back to the time of Hezekiah, or even
earlier.¹

In the note ὃ ἑρμηνεύεται Ἀπεσταλμένος we observe the
tendency to interpret Hebrew proper names for his Greek
readers, of which we have many instances in Jn. (see on 1³⁸).
Σιλωὰμ ὃ ἑρμηνεύεται Ἀπεσταλμένος is exactly parallel to Κηφᾶς
ὃ ἑρμηνεύεται Πέτρος (1⁴²). Hence it is unnecessary, and even
perverse, to seek esoteric symbolism in the note ὃ ἑρμ.
Ἀπεσταλμένος, such as is suggested by commentators who
call attention here to the fact that Jesus was " sent " by God
(6²⁹ etc.). The evangelist knew that the name Siloam was
given to the Pool because the water was conducted or " sent "
there artificially; and he naturally passes on the information
to his readers.² The word " Siloam " is not strictly a proper
name, and this Jn. indicates by prefixing the article, τοῦ Σιλωάμ,
as in Isa. 8⁶, Lk. 13⁴.

ἀπῆλθεν οὖν καὶ ἐνίψατο, καὶ ἦλθεν βλέπων. B omits οὖν
. . . ἦλθεν, an omission due to *homoioteleuton* (ἀπῆλθεν
. . . ἦλθεν). The man did as he was bidden. He was able
to find his way to the Pool of Siloam, for he was no doubt
familiar with the streets near the place where he was accustomed
to solicit alms. Apparently, he had some confidence in the
power of Jesus to heal him, for he did not hesitate, as Naaman
did when bidden to bathe in the Jordan.

ἦλθεν βλέπων. The mention of his neighbours in the next
verse suggests that ἦλθεν means that he went home after he
had visited the Pool. At any rate, it is not clearly said that
the cure was instantaneous (but cf. v. 11). The restoration or
improvement of sight may not have been observed for a day
or more; and some days may have elapsed between v. 7 and
v. 8. See v. 13 τόν ποτε τυφλόν.

8. The lively account which follows, of the experiences of
the blind man who had recovered his sight, may go back to
the evidence of the man himself.

---

¹ See G. A. Smith, *Jerusalem*, i. 102 ff.
² Grotius tried to identify *Siloam* with *Shiloh*, and noted that the
Vulgate of Gen. 49¹⁰ renders Shiloh by " qui mittendus est."

αὐτὸν τὸ πρότερον, ὅτι προσαίτης ἦν, ἔλεγον Οὐχ οὗτός ἐστιν ὁ καθήμενος καὶ προσαιτῶν; 9. ἄλλοι ἔλεγον ὅτι Οὗτός ἐστιν· ἄλλοι
ἔλεγον Οὐχί, ἀλλὰ ὅμοιος αὐτῷ ἐστιν. ἐκεῖνος ἔλεγεν ὅτι Ἐγώ εἰμι.
10. ἔλεγον οὖν αὐτῷ Πῶς οὖν ἠνεῴχθησάν σου οἱ ὀφθαλμοί;
11. ἀπεκρίθη ἐκεῖνος Ὁ ἄνθρωπος ὁ λεγόμενος Ἰησοῦς πηλὸν
ἐποίησεν καὶ ἐπέχρισέν μου τοὺς ὀφθαλμοὺς καὶ εἶπέν μοι ὅτι Ὑπαγε
εἰς τὸν Σιλωάμ καὶ νίψαι· ἀπελθὼν οὖν καὶ νιψάμενος ἀνέβλεψα.
12. καὶ εἶπαν αὐτῷ Ποῦ ἐστιν ἐκεῖνος; λέγει Οὐκ οἶδα.

οἱ θεωροῦντες αὐτὸν ὅτι κτλ. θεωρεῖν is used here (see on
2²³) of " taking notice," as at 10¹² 20⁶ etc. They noticed
the man *because* he was a familiar figure, as a blind beggar.
Burney urges that ὅτι must mean "when," and that it is a
misrendering of the Aramaic particle ־ֽ, which might be
translated either " that " or " when." But this is unnecessary.
They had noticed the man formerly *because* he used to beg
from them; cf. 12⁴¹.

For προσαίτης (אABC*DNW⊛) the rec. has τυφλός.

With ὁ καθήμενος καὶ προσαιτῶν cf. Mk. 10⁴⁶ τυφλὸς
προσαίτης ἐκάθητο παρὰ τὴν ὁδόν. A blind man begging by the
wayside is a common figure in the East.

9. His neighbours and those who had formerly noticed the
poor man, were not sure of his identity, now that his sight had
been restored. His appearance would naturally be changed.
Some said he was the man, others thought not. But he himself
(ἐκεῖνος, cf. vv. 11, 12, 25, 36) set them right. ἐγώ εἰμι, " I am
the man." This is a simple affirmation of identity, not to be
confused with the mystical use of ἐγώ εἰμι in Jn. (see Introd.,
p. cxx).

10. πῶς οὖν ἠνεῴχθησάν σου οἱ ὀφθαλμοί; The fact that
the man's sight had been restored is not challenged; it is
only the *manner* of the cure that is in question. See vv. 15,
19, 26.

11. Ὁ ἄνθρ. ὁ λεγόμενος Ἰησοῦς κτλ., " the man who is
called Jesus," etc. He does not yet acknowledge Jesus as the
Christ (cf. v. 36).

ὕπαγε εἰς τὸν Σιλωάμ καὶ νίψαι. Some Latin and Syriac
renderings give " wash thy eyes "; the Egyptian versions
have " wash thy face." (See on v. 7 above.)

νιψάμενος ἀνέβλεψα. For ἀναβλέπειν of recovering sight,
see Tob. 14², Mt. 11⁵, Mk. 10⁵¹, Lk. 18⁴¹; and cf. Lk. 4¹⁸. The
aor. ἀνέβλεψα would suggest that the man was cured immediately after the washing at the Pool of Siloam; but cf. v. 7
above. Strictly speaking, the verb is inappropriate to the
case of *congenital* blindness; but a parallel is cited from
Pausanias (*Messen.* iv. 12. 10), in which a man, who is described

13. Ἄγουσιν αὐτὸν πρὸς τοὺς Φαρισαίους, τόν ποτε τυφλόν. 14. ἦν δὲ σάββατον ἐν ᾗ ἡμέρᾳ τὸν πηλὸν ἐποίησεν ὁ Ἰησοῦς καὶ ἀνέῳξεν αὐτοῦ τοὺς ὀφθαλμούς. 15. πάλιν οὖν ἠρώτων αὐτὸν καὶ οἱ Φαρισαῖοι πῶς ἀνέβλεψεν. ὁ δὲ εἶπεν αὐτοῖς Πηλὸν ἐπέθηκέν μου ἐπὶ τοὺς ὀφθαλμούς, καὶ ἐνιψάμην, καὶ βλέπω. 16. ἔλεγον οὖν ἐκ τῶν Φαρισαίων τινές Οὐκ ἔστιν οὗτος παρὰ Θεοῦ ὁ ἄνθρωπος, ὅτι τὸ σάββατον οὐ τηρεῖ. ἄλλοι ἔλεγον Πῶς δύναται ἄνθρωπος ἁμαρτωλὸς

as τὸν ἐκ γενετῆς τυφλόν, after an attack of headache recovers his sight (ἀνέβλεψεν ἀπ᾽ αὐτοῦ), although only temporarily.

12. Ποῦ ἐστιν ἐκεῖνος;   See on 7¹¹ for the same question.

The Pharisees investigate the cure of the blind man on the Sabbath (vv. 13–34)

13. The cure was so striking, and the technical breach of the Sabbath so obvious, that some of those who had been interesting themselves in the case brought the man that had been cured before the Pharisees, as the most orthodox and austere of the religious leaders (see on 7³²). This was not on the day of the cure, but on a later day. Note τόν ποτε τυφλόν.

14. ἦν δὲ σάββατον (cf. 5⁹) ἐν ᾗ ἡμέρᾳ (so אBLW, but the rec. has simply ὅτε, with ADNΓΔΘ) τὸν πηλὸν ἐποίησεν. It was the kneading of the clay that primarily called for notice, as it was obviously a work of labour and so was a breach of the Sabbath.

15. πάλιν οὖν ἠρώτων κτλ. The questioning (see v. 10) had to begin all over again, for this was an official inquiry, and the brevity and sharpness of the man's answers now show that he is tired of replying to queries as to the manner and circumstances of his cure.

16. There was a division of opinion among the Pharisees who heard the story of the man whose sight had been restored. The strict legalists among them fastened on one point only, viz. that the Sabbath had been broken. οὐκ ἔστιν οὗτος παρὰ θεοῦ ὁ ἄνθρωπος, "this person is not from God," i.e. has not been sent by God, has no Divine mission. For παρά cf. 1⁶, also 1 Macc. 2¹⁵· ¹⁷; and see on 6⁴⁶ for the deeper meaning which παρὰ θεοῦ has elsewhere.

ὅτι τὸ σάββατον οὐ τηρεῖ. This was the charge that had been made against Jesus on a former occasion, when He healed the impotent man at Bethesda and told him to carry his mat away (5¹⁰). There was a twofold violation of the Sabbath laws apparent in this case, for not only had the clay been kneaded (v. 14), but it was specially forbidden to use spittle to cure bad

τοιαῦτα σημεῖα ποιεῖν; καὶ σχίσμα ἦν ἐν αὐτοῖς. 17. λέγουσιν οὖν
τῷ τυφλῷ πάλιν Τί σὺ λέγεις περὶ αὐτοῦ, ὅτι ἠνέῳξέν σου τοὺς ὀφθαλμούς; ὁ δὲ εἶπεν ὅτι Προφήτης ἐστίν. 18. οὐκ ἐπίστευσαν οὖν οἱ
Ἰουδαῖοι περὶ αὐτοῦ ὅτι ἦν τυφλὸς καὶ ἀνέβλεψεν, ἕως ὅτου ἐφώνησαν

eyes on the Sabbath: " As to fasting spittle; it is not lawful
to put it so much as upon the eyelids." [1]

It is curious that the phrase τὸ σάββατον τηρεῖν does not
occur again in the Greek Bible; but τηρεῖν is a favourite verb
with Jn. (see on 8[51]).

Others among the Pharisees took a larger view of the
situation, probably such men as Nicodemus or Joseph of
Arimathæa. They called attention to the σημεῖα of Jesus as
wonderful, no matter what the day was on which they were
wrought. πῶς δύναται ἄνθρωπος ἁμαρτωλὸς (this word " sinner "
is only found in Jn. in this chapter) τοιαῦτα σημεῖα (see on 2[11])
ποιεῖν; How could a sinner do such things?

καὶ σχίσμα ἦν ἐν αὐτοῖς. Cf. for similar divisions of
opinion, 7[43] 10[19]; and see also 6[52] 7[12].

17. λέγουσιν οὖν τῷ τυφλῷ πάλιν, "they," sc. the Pharisees
collectively who were present, " say again to the blind man,"
i.e. they resume their inquiry, to get more details.

τί σὺ λέγεις περὶ αὐτοῦ; "What do you say about
Him?"

ὅτι ἠνέῳξέν implies that as Jesus had opened his eyes, the
man's opinion was worth having. " What do you say, inasmuch as it was your eyes that He opened?" conveys the sense.
For the constr., cf. 2[18]. Burney suggested that ὅτι is here a
mistranslation of the Aramaic relative ד, and points to the
Vulgate qui aperuit. But it is not necessary to appeal to an
Aramaic original here. See Abbott, Diat. 2183.

The man's answer was προφήτης ἐστίν. He did not say
that Jesus was " the prophet," as the multitude said after the
miracle of the loaves (6[14]), but only that He was " a prophet,"
a simple answer like that of the Samaritan woman (4[19]), i.e.
that He was an extraordinary person who could do extraordinary things.

18. Up to this point the Pharisees have not directly
challenged the statement that the man's sight had been restored,
having confined themselves to the question about the breach
of the Sabbath which was involved. But the answer of the
man, προφήτης ἐστίν, leads the more hostile of them (οἱ Ἰουδαῖοι,
see on 5[10]) to suspect collusion between Jesus and the patient,
and so they summon the parents for further inquiry as to their
son's blindness and its cure.

[1] Shabb. c. 21, cited by Lightfoot, Hor. Hebr. on 9[6].

τοὺς γονεῖς αὐτοῦ τοῦ ἀναβλέψαντος, 19. καὶ ἠρώτησαν αὐτοὺς
λέγοντες Οὗτός ἐστιν ὁ υἱὸς ὑμῶν, ὃν ὑμεῖς λέγετε ὅτι τυφλὸς
ἐγεννήθη; πῶς οὖν βλέπει ἄρτι; 20. ἀπεκρίθησαν οὖν οἱ γονεῖς
αὐτοῦ καὶ εἶπαν Οἴδαμεν ὅτι οὗτός ἐστιν ὁ υἱὸς ἡμῶν καὶ ὅτι τυφλὸς
ἐγεννήθη· 21. πῶς δὲ νῦν βλέπει οὐκ οἴδαμεν, ἢ τίς ἤνοιξεν αὐτοῦ
τοὺς ὀφθαλμοὺς ἡμεῖς οὐκ οἴδαμεν· αὐτὸν ἐρωτήσατε, ἡλικίαν ἔχει,
αὐτὸς περὶ ἑαυτοῦ λαλήσει. 22. ταῦτα εἶπαν οἱ γονεῖς αὐτοῦ ὅτι
ἐφοβοῦντο τοὺς Ἰουδαίους· ἤδη γὰρ συνετέθειντο οἱ Ἰουδαῖοι ἵνα ἐάν

γονεῖς occurs in Jn. only in this chapter: the word in the
N.T. is always used in the plural.

19. The Pharisees now cross-examine the parents, in strict
fashion. " Is this your son ? the son whom you say was born
blind ? How is it that he now sees ? "

ἄρτι is a favourite word with Jn., and signifies " at this
moment," as distinct from the vaguer νῦν, " at the present
time." Cf. v. 25, 13[7. 33. 37] 16[12. 31].

20. ἀπεκρίθησαν οὖν οἱ γονεῖς κτλ. אB support οὖν, which
is omitted in the rec. text, αὐτοῖς being put in its place
(om. אBLW).

The parents were anxious to avoid responsibility in the
matter of the cure, being afraid of the Jewish leaders (v. 22).
They admit, of course, that the man was their son, and that he
had been born blind, but they disclaim all knowledge of the
manner of his cure. Perhaps they had not been present when
Jesus smeared the man's eyes. At any rate, they repudiate
with special emphasis any knowledge of who it was that healed
him : τίς ἤνοιξεν αὐτοῦ τοὺς ὀφθαλμοὺς ἡ μ ε ῖ ς οὐκ οἴδαμεν.

21. αὐτὸν ἐρωτήσατε, ἡλικίαν ἔχει, " ask him, he is of
age," and therefore a legal witness. ἡλικία in the Synoptists
always means " stature," but in this passage and at Heb. 11[11]
it means " age." ἡλικίαν ἔχει is a good classical phrase, and
is found in Plato. αὐτὸς περὶ ἑαυτοῦ λαλήσει, " he will tell
you about himself." The parents were much alarmed.

αὐτὸν ἐρωτήσατε is omitted by א*W b and the Sahidic vss.
(including Q), a remarkable combination.

22. ταῦτα εἶπαν . . . ὅτι ἐφοβοῦντο τοὺς Ἰουδαίους. The fear
of "the Jews" (see 1[19] 5[10]), the Jewish opponents of Jesus,
whose leaders were the Pharisees, was very definite (cf. 7[13]).
They were determined to check His success, and to put down
His popularity. Cf. 7[44f.].

ἤδη συνετέθειντο, they had formed a compact (cf. 7[32. 47-49]),
and decided that strong measures must be taken against any
one confessing (see on 1[20]) Jesus as Christ. He had not yet
declared Himself openly in Jerusalem (10[24]), but it had been
debated whether He were not indeed the Christ (7[26f.]).

τις αὐτὸν ὁμολογήσῃ Χριστόν, ἀποσυνάγωγος γένηται. 23. διὰ
τοῦτο οἱ γονεῖς αὐτοῦ εἶπαν ὅτι Ἡλικίαν ἔχει, αὐτὸν ἐπερωτήσατε.
24. Ἐφώνησαν οὖν τὸν ἄνθρωπον ἐκ δευτέρου ὃς ἦν τυφλός, καὶ
εἶπαν αὐτῷ Δὸς δόξαν τῷ Θεῷ· ἡμεῖς οἴδαμεν ὅτι οὗτος ὁ ἄνθρωπος
ἁμαρτωλός ἐστιν. 25. ἀπεκρίθη οὖν ἐκεῖνος Εἰ ἁμαρτωλός ἐστιν

Except when Jn. is interpreting Μεσσίας (1⁴¹ 4²⁵), this is
the only place in the Gospel where we find Χριστός without
the def. article: " if any one should confess Him as Christ."
Cf. Rom. 10⁹ for a similar constr.: ἐὰν ὁμολογήσῃς Κύριον
Ἰησοῦν, " if thou shalt confess Jesus as Lord."

ἀποσυνάγωγος, " excommunicate." The word is found in
the Greek Bible only here and at 12⁴² 16². Full excommunication involved a cutting off from the whole " congregation of
Israel " (cf. Mt. 18¹⁷); but it is probable that the lesser penalty
of exclusion from the synagogue for a month (the usual
period) is all that is indicated here. That he who acknowledged Jesus as the Messiah was to be treated as ἀποσυνάγωγος
is mentioned again 12⁴².[1]

23. διὰ τοῦτο, " wherefore," referring (as generally in
Greek) to what precedes; cf. 13¹¹ 15¹⁹ 16¹⁵ 19¹¹, 1 Jn. 4⁵. For
διὰ τοῦτο as referring to what follows, see on 5¹⁶.

ὅτι Ἡλικίαν ἔχει, αὐτὸν ἐπερωτήσατε (so אBW). ὅτι is
recitantis, purporting to introduce the actual words spoken.
Note that the order of the words has been changed, for in
v. 21 we have αὐτὸν ἐρωτήσατε, ἡλίκιαν ἔχει. Jn. is not
punctilious in his narrative about reproducing the exact words
or the order of words (see on 3¹⁶).

24. The Jewish leaders summon the man himself for
re-examination (ἐκ δευτέρου, cf. v. 17). They now press him
on the point of his former evidence, which they suggest was
not true.

δὸς δόξαν τῷ θεῷ. This does not mean here " Thank
God " (cf. Lk. 17¹⁸), but it is a form of adjuration meaning
" Speak the truth," as at Josh. 7¹⁹ (cf. 1 Esd. 9⁸).

ἡμεῖς οἴδαμεν ὅτι οὗτος ὁ ἄνθρωπος ἁμαρτωλός ἐστιν, " *we*
know," speaking with ecclesiastical authority, " that this man
is a sinner," although the blind man had said (v. 17) that He
was a prophet. They suggest that the man was lying, and was
in collusion with Jesus.

25. The shrewdness and obstinacy of the man reveal
themselves in his answer. He refuses to discuss their assertion
that Jesus was a sinner. " One thing I know, that being a
blind man, now I see." That is all he will say.

[1] See, for Jewish excommunications, Schürer, *History of Jewish
People*, II. ii. 61.

οὐκ οἶδα· ἓν οἶδα, ὅτι τυφλὸς ὢν ἄρτι βλέπω. 26. εἶπαν οὖν αὐτῷ
Τί ἐποίησέν σοι; πῶς ἤνοιξέν σου τοὺς ὀφθαλμούς; 27. ἀπεκρίθη
αὐτοῖς Εἶπον ὑμῖν ἤδη καὶ οὐκ ἠκούσατε· τί πάλιν θέλετε ἀκούειν;
μὴ καὶ ὑμεῖς θέλετε αὐτοῦ μαθηταὶ γενέσθαι; 28. καὶ ἐλοιδόρησαν
αὐτὸν καὶ εἶπαν Σὺ μαθητὴς εἶ ἐκείνου, ἡμεῖς δὲ τοῦ Μωϋσέως ἐσμὲν
μαθηταί· 29. ἡμεῖς οἴδαμεν ὅτι Μωϋσεῖ λελάληκεν ὁ Θεός, τοῦτον
δὲ οὐκ οἴδαμεν πόθεν ἐστίν. 30. ἀπεκρίθη ὁ ἄνθρωπος καὶ εἶπεν

26. Accordingly his questioners attempt a further cross-
examination, hoping to elicit some damaging admission.

After αὐτῷ, the rec. text has πάλιν (אᶜΑΝΓΔΘ), but om.
א*BDW.

27. The man who has recovered his sight now becomes
irritable, and turns on his questioners: εἶπον ὑμῖν ἤδη καὶ οὐκ
ἠκούσατε, "I told you already (v. 15), and you did not
hear," *i.e.* you did not heed. *Fam.* 13 have ἐπιστεύσατε for
ἠκούσατε, and the O.L. *r* has *creditis*, an attempt to interpret
ἠκούσατε.

μὴ καὶ ὑμεῖς θέλετε αὐτοῦ μαθηταὶ γενέσθαι; "Surely you do
not wish to become disciples of His?" He could not refrain
from this ironical gibe, which he must have known would
irritate the Pharisees. καί before ὑμεῖς, "you *also*," suggests
that it was known that Jesus had made *some* disciples already,
and that the Pharisees were aware of it.

28. καὶ ἐλοιδόρησαν αὐτόν, "and they reviled him." Having
failed to get anything out of the man which might be
damaging to Jesus, they angrily accuse him of being on the
side of Jesus.

Σὺ μαθητὴς εἶ ἐκείνου, "you yourself are a disciple of that
fellow." ἐκεῖνος conveys a suggestion of contempt; and, as
Bengel says, "hoc vocabulo remouent Iesum a sese."

ἡμεῖς δέ κτλ., "we, on the contrary, are disciples of
Moses," as all orthodox Rabbis claimed to be.

29. ἡμεῖς οἴδαμεν (cf. v. 24) ὅτι Μωϋσεῖ λελάληκεν ὁ θεός
(cf. Heb. 1¹): that was why they were proud to be disciples of
Moses.

τοῦτον δὲ οὐκ οἴδαμεν πόθεν ἐστίν. They profess complete
ignorance of the antecedents of Jesus. Some of the people of
Jerusalem knew, indeed, whence He came, τοῦτον οἴδαμεν πόθεν
ἐστίν (7²⁷, where see note), although there was a deeper sense in
which none of the Jews knew it (8¹⁴). But the Pharisees would
not admit that they either knew or cared what was His origin
or who were His kindred.

30. The man whose sight had been restored is now
thoroughly angry, and he goes on to argue in his turn, shrewdly
enough, beginning with a mocking retort.

αὐτοῖς Ἐν τούτῳ γὰρ τὸ θαυμαστόν ἐστιν, ὅτι ὑμεῖς οὐκ οἴδατε πόθεν
ἐστίν, καὶ ἤνοιξέν μου τοὺς ὀφθαλμούς. 31. οἴδαμεν ὅτι ἁμαρτωλῶν
ὁ Θεὸς οὐκ ἀκούει, ἀλλ᾽ ἐάν τις θεοσεβὴς ᾖ καὶ τὸ θέλημα αὐτοῦ ποιῇ,
τούτου ἀκούει. 32. ἐκ τοῦ αἰῶνος οὐκ ἠκούσθη ὅτι ἠνέῳξέν τις

ἐν τούτῳ γὰρ (this is the order of words in אBLΘ) τὸ
θαυμαστόν ἐστιν κτλ., "Why, then, here is an astonishing thing,
that you (ὑμεῖς, whose business it is to know about miracle-
workers) do not know whence He is, and yet (καί) He opened
my eyes!" Syr. sin., with a b c ff², om. γάρ, D and e replacing
it by οὖν; but γάρ must be retained. Blass says that we should
treat the sentence as an interrogative, "Is not this, then, an
astonishing thing?" (see Abbott, *Diat.* 2683). But it is
simpler to take γάρ as referring back to what had just been
said, "Why, if *that be so*, etc."

On καί for καιτοί, see on 1¹⁰.

31. The argument is clear. God does not hear the prayers
of sinners. Miracles are granted in answer to the prayers of
a good man. Jesus has worked a miracle. Therefore Jesus
is a good man.

οἴδαμεν, "we all know," introducing a maxim which
no one will dispute; cf. 3², 1 Jn. 5¹⁸.

ἁμαρτωλῶν ὁ Θεὸς οὐκ ἀκούει, "sinners are not heard by
God," ἁμαρτωλῶν being put in the first place (with אALNWΓΔ,
but BDΘ have ὁ θε. ἁμ.) for emphasis. ἀκούειν here takes the
genitive, because it implies a hearing with attention; see on 3⁸.

The principle that God does not hearken to the prayers
of sinners appears frequently in the O.T.; cf. Job 27⁹, Ps.
66¹⁸, Isa. 1¹⁵ 59², Ezek. 8¹⁸, Mic. 3⁴, Zech. 7¹³. For the converse principle, that God hears the prayer of a godly man, cf.
Ps. 34¹⁵ 145¹⁹, Prov. 15²⁹, Jas. 5¹⁶.

θεοσεβής is not found again in the N.T. (it occurs in the
LXX, *e.g.* Job 1¹); but cf. 1 Tim. 2¹⁰ for θεοσέβεια.

ἐάν τις . . . τὸ θέλημα αὐτοῦ ποιῇ, τούτου ἀκούει. That Jesus
"did the will of God" is a frequent thought in Jn.; see on
4³⁴. For the answer always given to His prayers, cf. 11²². ⁴¹.

32. ἐκ τοῦ αἰῶνος. The phrase ἀπὸ τοῦ αἰῶνος or ἀπ᾽ αἰῶνος
occurs Lk. 1⁷⁰, Acts 3²¹ 15¹⁸, and is common in the LXX
(1 Chron. 16³⁶, Ps. 25⁶ 90², Ecclus. 14¹⁷, Jer. 2²⁰, etc.), as it is
in the papyri. But ἐκ τοῦ αἰῶνος does not occur again in the
Greek Bible, the nearest phrase being ἐξ αἰῶνος, Prov. 8²¹.
(Wetstein illustrates it freely from non-Biblical authors.) We
have here an instance of the interchangeability of ἐκ and ἀπό
which we have already observed in Jn. (see on 1⁴⁴ 6³⁸).

ἐκ τοῦ αἰῶνος κτλ., "Since the world began it was unheard
of that any one opened the eyes of one who was born blind."

ὀφθαλμοὺς τυφλοῦ γεγεννημένου· 33. εἰ μὴ ἦν οὗτος παρὰ Θεοῦ, οὐκ ἠδύνατο ποιεῖν οὐδέν. 34. ἀπεκρίθησαν καὶ εἶπαν αὐτῷ Ἐν ἁμαρτίαις σὺ ἐγεννήθης ὅλος, καὶ σὺ διδάσκεις ἡμᾶς; καὶ ἐξέβαλον αὐτὸν ἔξω.

35. Ἤκουσεν Ἰησοῦς ὅτι ἐξέβαλον αὐτὸν ἔξω, καὶ εὑρὼν αὐτὸν εἶπεν Σὺ πιστεύεις εἰς τὸν Υἱὸν τοῦ ἀνθρώπου; 36. ἀπεκρίθη

It is this point, viz. that the blindness was congenital, that is insisted on throughout; whereas in the case of the cure of the man at Bethesda, the circumstance that he had been infirm for thirty-eight years (5⁵) passes out of view at once, and attention is concentrated on the fact that he was cured on a Sabbath day.

33. εἰ μὴ ἦν . . . ποιεῖν οὐδέν. This was a principle recognised by Nicodemus (3²), to which reference is made again at 10²¹. "If this man were not sent from God (cf. v. 16 for παρὰ θεοῦ), He could do nothing," sc. of this wonderful nature.

34. The Pharisees will not stoop to refute a low person who ventures to argue with them; but the retort ascribed to them is weak, for it admits what they had previously questioned (v. 19), viz. that the blindness was congenital, and assigns as a reason for it the man's prenatal sin (cf. v. 2).

ἐν ἁμαρτίαις (the emphatic words beginning the sentence) σὺ ἐγεννήθης ὅλος. Cf. Ps. 51⁵; and for ὅλος cf. 13¹⁰.

σὺ διδάσκεις ἡμᾶς; Every word is scornfully emphatic.

καὶ ἐξέβαλον αὐτὸν ἔξω. This does not signify "they excommunicated him " (v. 22), a formal act which could only be done at a formal sitting of the Sanhedrim. It only means "they put him out," sc. of their presence; cf. note on 6³⁷, where ἐκβάλλειν ἐκ is shown to be a Johannine phrase.

The man who was cured accepts Jesus as the Son of Man
(*vv. 35–38*)

35. ἤκουσεν Ἰησοῦς. א*B omit ὁ before Ἰησοῦς, perhaps rightly; see on 1²⁹·⁵⁰.

When Jesus heard of the repulse of the man by the Pharisees, after his courageous utterances, He sought him out. With εὑρὼν αὐτόν cf. 1⁴³ 5¹⁴.

σὺ πιστεύεις εἰς τὸν υἱὸν τοῦ ἀνθρώπου; The form of the question presupposes an affirmative reply, "Thou, at least, believest in the Son of Man?" The man's simplicity and constancy, in the presence of those whom he had good reason to fear, show Jesus that he is already on the way to become a disciple. Not only did he assert before the Pharisees that his Healer must have a Divine mission (παρὰ θεοῦ, v. 33), but his

ἐκεῖνος καὶ εἶπεν Καὶ τίς ἐστιν, Κύριε, ἵνα πιστεύσω εἰς αὐτόν;
37. εἶπεν αὐτῷ ὁ Ἰησοῦς Καὶ ἑώρακας αὐτὸν καὶ ὁ λαλῶν μετὰ

faith was beginning to go deeper. He was on the point of
believing in (see on 1¹² for the force of πιστεύειν εἰς . . . and
cf. 4³⁹) the Son of Man (see Introd., p. cxxxi). This is the
criterion of Christian discipleship which was placed before him.
We follow אBDW and Syr. sin. in reading τὸν υἱὸν τοῦ
ἀνθρώπου. But ALΘ and most vss. read τὸν υἱὸν τοῦ θεοῦ,
which is the usual title in Jn. when confession of faith is in
question. See, e.g., 1³⁴· ⁴⁹ 11²⁷; and cf. Mt. 16¹⁶. According
to 20³¹, the purpose of the Fourth Gospel is that readers may
believe that " Jesus is the Christ, *the Son of God*." But if
" the Son of God " were the original reading here, it is surprising that scribes should have altered it to " the Son of
Man," which does not appear in any of the other confessions
of faith; while the change from the unusual " Son of Man "
to " Son of God," the usual title in similar contexts, is
easily explicable (see 6⁶⁹ for a similar alteration by scribes).
Further, v. 36 shows that the would-be disciple did not understand who was meant by " the Son of Man " or that Jesus
was claiming such a title for Himself. As we have seen (1⁴⁹),
the Messiah was popularly designated " the Son of God," but
" the Son of Man " was not a recognised Messianic title (see
Introd., p. cxxx). The man to whom Jesus spoke was evidently
puzzled (cf. 12³⁴).

36. ἀπεκρίθη ἐκεῖνος καὶ εἶπεν καὶ τίς ἐστιν, κύριε; For this
BW have the shorter form καὶ τίς ἐστιν, ἔφη, κύριε;

The man had accepted Jesus as a prophet (v. 17), and so
he was ready to act on whatever Jesus bade him. He will put
his trust in the " Son of Man " if he is told who He is, and
where he may find Him.

καὶ τίς ἐστιν; " Who then is He ? " For the initial καί,
cf. καὶ τίς δύναται σωθῆναι; (Mk. 10²⁶, Lk. 18²⁶) and καὶ τίς ἐστίν
μου πλησίον; (Lk. 10²⁹). Cf. also 14²².

He addresses Jesus with respect : κύριε, " sir " (see on
12²¹). κύριε generally comes at the beginning of the sentence,
but here and at v. 38 it comes at the end.

ἵνα πιστεύσω εἰς αὐτόν, taking up the words of Jesus in
the preceding verse. There is an ellipsis before ἵνα, which has
full telic force. " Who is He ? *for I want to know* in order
that I may put my trust in Him." Cf., for a similar constr., 1²².

37. The reply of Jesus, beginning καὶ ἑώρακας αὐτόν, has
a special force as addressed to a man who had been blind from
his birth. " You have *seen* Him." This was one of the first
blessings which came to him through " the opening of his

σοῦ ἐκεῖνός ἐστιν.   38. ὁ δὲ ἔφη Πιστεύω, Κύριε· καὶ προσεκύνησεν
αὐτῷ.

39. Καὶ εἶπεν ὁ Ἰησοῦς Εἰς κρίμα ἐγὼ εἰς τὸν κόσμον τοῦτον

eyes." In his case, faith followed immediately on the "seeing " of Jesus, in marked contrast with the case of those to
whom it was said ἑωράκατέ [με] καὶ οὐ πιστεύετε (6³⁶, where
see note).

καὶ ὁ λαλῶν μετὰ σοῦ ἐκεῖνός ἐστιν, " He who is talking
with you is He." Cf. 4²⁶ for a similar discovery of Himself to
the Samaritan woman. For ἐκεῖνος, used by the speaker or
narrator of himself, see on 19³⁵.

38. The man's response is unhesitating : πιστεύω, κύριε,
" I believe, Lord " ; κύριε being now used with a respect
which has passed into reverence (see on 1³⁸ 4¹), for the narrator
adds καὶ προσεκύνησεν αὐτῷ, " and he worshipped Him."
προσκυνεῖν (see on 4²⁰) is always used in Jn. to express *divine*
worship.

The man who has been cured of his blindness now passes
out of the story.

The whole of v. 38 and the words καὶ εἶπεν ὁ Ἰησοῦς in
v. 39 are omitted in ℵ*W, the O.L. *b*, and the fourth-century
Coptic MS. described as Q. The O.L. *l* also omits the clause,
with the exception of καὶ προσεκύνησεν αὐτῷ. Such a con-
sensus of Greek, Coptic, and Latin authorities for this omission
is remarkable, as a textual phenomenon; but the omission
cannot be original.

*The inner meaning of the healing, and the condemnation
of the Pharisees (vv. 39–41)*

39. Here is given, in brief, the interpretation of the
story, for this miracle was a σημεῖον (v. 16). The cure of the
man's blindness was symbolic of the giving of spiritual vision
to those conscious of their spiritual blindness, who are therefore
willing to be healed. But some do not feel the need of a
Healer. This is the dividing line between man and man. And
the mission of Jesus leads up to judgment, according as men do
or do not recognise their Deliverer in Him.

εἰς κρίμα ἐγὼ εἰς τὸν κόσμον τοῦτον ἦλθον. Cf. 16²⁸ 18³⁷
for the saying " I am come into the world " ; and cf. also 6¹⁴.
For the phrase " *this* world," see on 8²³. It means the earthly
world, the home of fallen man, which is therefore imperfect.
κρίμα (a word not found again in Jn.) is the result of a κρίσις or
act of distinguishing between good and bad, and so of judging.
So the sentence means, " It was with a view to that ultimate

ἦλθον, ἵνα οἱ μὴ βλέποντες βλέπωσιν καὶ οἱ βλέποντες τυφλοὶ
γένωνται. 40. ἤκουσαν ἐκ τῶν Φαρισαίων ταῦτα οἱ μετ᾽ αὐτοῦ ὄντες
καὶ εἶπαν αὐτῷ Μὴ καὶ ἡμεῖς τυφλοί ἐσμεν; 41. εἶπεν αὐτοῖς ὁ

decision which shall distinguish man from man that I came
into this world," special emphasis being laid on ἐγώ.

There is no mention of the Agent of this Judgment,
i.e. of the Personality of the Judge, and so there is no inconsistency with 3¹⁷ (cf. 8¹⁵). Jesus does not say here that He
came to execute judgment (cf. 5²²), but in order that by His
coming men might be tested and so judgment reached at last.
The supreme test, as always (cf. v. 35, and see on 3¹⁵), is faith in
Himself. Those who recognise Him for what He is are in one
category; those who fail to do so, in another.

He came, not only to give recovery of sight to the physically
blind (Isa. 61², quoted by Himself Lk. 4¹⁸), but to open the
eyes of the spiritually blind. It was the challenge of a prophet,
" Look, ye blind, that ye may see " (Isa. 42¹⁸); and Jesus came
to bring this illumination to those conscious of their blindness,
ἵνα οἱ μὴ βλέποντες βλέπωσιν.

There is also a severer purpose in the coming of Jesus.
It was ἵνα . . . οἱ βλέποντες τυφλοὶ γένωνται, " that those
who see should become blind " (cf. Mk. 4¹²). There is a
darkening of moral vision which is caused by complacent
satisfaction with the light that is already enjoyed (cf. Rev.
3¹⁷·¹⁸). Those who see only dimly, and do not desire to see
more clearly, lose the power of sight wholly; they become
blind. This was the end of the Pharisees (the " blind guides "
of Mt. 23¹⁶), who did not see anything exceptional in Jesus.
They could not see at first, because they would not; and so the
judgment of blindness fell upon them. See further on 12⁴⁰.

40. Some Pharisees who were near overheard what Jesus
said, and interjected the scornful question, " Are we also
blind ? "

ἐκ τῶν Φαρισαίων . . . οἱ μετ᾽ αὐτοῦ ὄντες. The Sinai Syriac
renders " who were *near* Him," μετά indicating proximity
in place, but not necessarily any attachment of discipleship.
See τοὺς πτωχοὺς γὰρ πάντοτε ἔχετε μεθ᾽ ἑαυτῶν (12⁸); and
cf. Mt. 9¹⁵. The crushing reply of Jesus (v. 41) to their question
forbids the hypothesis that these Pharisees are to be reckoned
among the half-believing Jews mentioned at 8³¹.

μὴ καὶ ἡμεῖς τυφλοί ἐσμεν; " Are we also spiritually
blind," we who are the recognised religious teachers of the
nation ? The form of the question, μὴ καὶ ἡμεῖς . . ., suggests
that a negative answer is believed by the questioners to be
the obviously true answer See on 6⁶⁷.

Ἰησοῦς Εἰ τυφλοὶ ἦτε, οὐκ ἂν εἴχετε ἁμαρτίαν· νῦν δὲ λέγετε ὅτι Βλέπομεν· ἡ ἁμαρτία ὑμῶν μένει.

X. 19. Σχίσμα πάλιν ἐγένετο ἐν τοῖς Ἰουδαίοις διὰ τοὺς λόγους τούτους. 20. ἔλεγον δὲ πολλοὶ ἐξ αὐτῶν Δαιμόνιον ἔχει καὶ μαίνεται·

41. The answer of Jesus is as overwhelming as it was unforeseen. The Pharisees had expected that He would say, " Yes, you are blind, despite your authoritative position as religious guides " (cf. Mt. 23¹⁶). But instead of that, He said, " No, you are not wholly blind; that is the worst feature of your case."

εἰ τυφλοὶ ἦτε, οὐκ ἂν εἴχετε ἁμαρτίαν. If they were wholly and involuntarily blind to the presentation of the Divine which Jesus embodied, they would not be blameworthy for refusing to acknowledge it. Cf. εἰ μὴ ἦλθον καὶ ἐλάλησα αὐτοῖς ἁμαρτίαν οὐκ εἴχοσαν (15²²). But this was not their situation. The perpetual reproach with which Jesus challenged them (cf., e.g., 8⁴⁷) was that their failure to accept Him was a moral failure. Their self-satisfaction prevented them from seeing what they *ought* to have seen in Him (see on v. 39 above). Their claim to " see," βλέπομεν, was arrogant, and shut them out from the larger vision which had offered itself (cf. Prov. 26¹²). So " your sin abides," *i.e.* is not removed.

For the Johannine constr. ἔχειν ἁμαρτίαν, cf. 15²² 19¹¹ and 1 Jn. 1⁸.

ἡ ἁμαρτία ὑμῶν μένει. There is a sin against light which is eternal in its consequences. Cf. Mk. 3²⁹ for the Synoptic form of this tremendous judgment.

X. 19. The sequence of ideas brings vv. 19–29 into direct connexion with c. 9 rather than with 10¹⁻¹⁸, and they are printed accordingly at this point. See Introd., p. xxiv, for some considerations which favour the order 9⁴¹ 10¹⁹⁻²⁹ 10¹⁻¹⁸ 10³⁰ᶠᶠ.

Diversity of opinion about Jesus (vv. 19–22)

σχίσμα. A division of opinion had appeared before among the crowd (7⁴³), but this was among the Jewish critics of Jesus, the Pharisees, who were not all of one mind about Him. πάλιν refers back to the σχίσμα of 9¹⁶, which had originated in the cure of the blind man, and which is still apparent.

20. δαιμόνιον ἔχει. This was an easy way of accounting for the strangeness of the teaching of Jesus, and we have had it before 7²⁰ 8⁴⁸; cf. Wisd. 5⁴, and see Introd., p. clxxvii.

μαίνεται. This verb occurs only here in Jn.

τί αὐτοῦ ἀκούετε; 21. ἄλλοι ἔλεγον Ταῦτα τὰ ῥήματα οὐκ ἔστιν δαιμονιζομένου· μὴ δαιμόνιον δύναται τυφλῶν ὀφθαλμοὺς ἀνοῖξαι;
22. Ἐγένετο τότε τὰ ἐνκαίνια ἐν τοῖς Ἱεροσολύμοις· χειμὼν ἦν·

τί αὐτοῦ ἀκούετε; "Why do you heed Him?" ἀκούειν with the gen. always indicating in Jn. a hearing with attention and appreciation (see on 3⁸). The question betrays a certain uneasiness on the part of the questioners.

21. Others were less swayed by prejudice. "These are not the words of one possessed with a devil." δαιμονίζεσθαι is a familiar verb in Mk. and Mt., but it occurs only here in Jn., who prefers δαιμόνιον ἔχειν.

"Can a devil open the eyes of blind people?" Mt. represents the Pharisees as admitting the possibility of miracles wrought by demoniac agency (Mt. 12²⁴), but this idea does not appear in Jn. To open the eyes of the blind is a Divine prerogative (Ps. 146⁸).

ἀνοῖξαι, אBLWΘ fam. 13; the rec. has ἀνοίγειν.

The Feast of the Dedication: Jesus admits that He is Messiah, of which His words should have been sufficient proof (vv. 22-25)

22. ἐγένετο τότε τὰ ἐνκαίνια ἐν τοῖς Ἱεροσολύμοις. τότε is read by BLW, but it has been replaced by δέ in אADΘ and the rec. text. τότε is not common in Jn., and indicates here that some time had elapsed since the last date mentioned, viz. the Feast of Tabernacles (7³⁷). Chapters 8 and 9 describe a period of continual controversy with the Pharisees, which was brought to a head by the healing of the blind man and the claims subsequently made by Jesus. The Feast of Tabernacles was celebrated about the month of October, and it was now December. Jn. is forward to give dates when he can (see Introd., p. cii).

The Feast of the Dedication (חֲנֻכָּה, "Renewal") was instituted by Judas Maccabæus to commemorate the purification of the Temple from the pollutions of Antiochus Epiphanes by the dedication of a new altar (1 Macc. 4³⁶· ⁵⁹, 2 Macc. 10⁵· ⁶), and was kept at the winter solstice (Chislev, 25); and during the following week Josephus notes that it was customary to light the lamps on the "candlestick" as a mark of rejoicing, and that the Feast was sometimes called τὰ φῶτα (Antt. XII. vii. 6). The ceremonial was similar to that of Tabernacles (2 Macc. 10⁶), the idea of light being conspicuous in both festivals. Hence the words "I am the Light of the World" (8¹² 9⁵) would have been equally illustrated by the ritual of Tabernacles or of Dedication.

23. καὶ περιεπάτει ὁ Ἰησοῦς ἐν τῷ ἱερῷ ἐν τῇ στοᾷ τοῦ Σολομῶνος.
24. ἐκύκλωσαν οὖν αὐτὸν οἱ Ἰουδαῖοι καὶ ἔλεγον αὐτῷ Ἕως πότε
τὴν ψυχὴν ἡμῶν αἴρεις; εἰ σὺ εἶ ὁ Χριστός, εἰπὸν ἡμῖν παρρησίᾳ.

It was not a matter of obligation to attend at Jerusalem for
the Feast of τὰ ἐνκαίνια, which might be observed elsewhere;
and Jesus is not represented by Jn. as " going up " to Jerusalem
for it. It happened that the season of the Dedication came
on while He was there, and, as Jn. notes, it was winter.

Ἱεροσολύμοις. ABLWΘ prefix τοῖς, which אDΓΔ omit.
Jn. usually omits the article before Ἱεροσόλυμα (see on 2²³ ;
and cf. 1¹⁹).

χειμὼν ἦν. The rec. prefixes καί, but om. אBDLWΘ.

23. " It was winter, and Jesus was walking in the Temple,
in Solomon's porch." That is, He was giving His teaching
under shelter, because of the severity of the season, in the
eastern cloister of the Temple precincts (for τὸ ἱερόν, the Temple
enclosure, see on 2¹⁴). This vivid touch suggests that the
writer is thoroughly familiar with the place and the conditions
under which instruction was given there. At the time when
the Fourth Gospel was written, the Temple had been for some
years in ruins; but the note of time and circumstance is easily
explicable, if we have here the reminiscence of an eye-witness
of the scene.

ἡ στοὰ τοῦ Σολομῶνος is mentioned again, Acts 3¹¹ 5¹².

24. ἐκύκλωσαν οὖν αὐτὸν οἱ Ἰουδαῖοι. " The Jews (see on
1¹⁹) surrounded Him," sc. that they might settle the question
as to His claims.

ἕως πότε τὴν ψυχὴν ἡμῶν αἴρεις; " How long dost thou
hold us in suspense ? "   This rendering of the R.V. is probably
accurate, although no exact parallel for ψυχὴν αἴρειν in this
sense has been produced. We have the phrase at Ps. 25¹ 86⁴,
meaning " lift up my soul," and so Josephus uses it (Antt. iii.
ii. 3). Here it is, "How long do you excite our spirits," i.e.
arouse our expectations?—in other words, keep us in suspense.
The expression is idiomatic Greek, and has survived in modern
Greek : ὡς πότε θὰ μᾶς βγάζεις τὴν ψυχήν, " How long will you
plague us ? " [1]

εἰ σὺ εἶ ὁ Χριστός κτλ. " If thou be the Christ, etc.,"
σύ being emphatic, " If you are really the Christ."

εἰπὸν ἡμῖν παρρησίᾳ. Cf. Mt. 26⁶³, Lk. 22⁶⁷; and for παρρησίᾳ,
see on 7⁴.

25. " Art thou the Christ ? " is one of those questions
which cannot be answered by a direct " Yes " or " No," if
misunderstanding is to be avoided. If He had said " Yes,"

[1] See A. Pallis, Notes on St. Mark and St. Matthew (1903), p. v.

25. ἀπεκρίθη αὐτοῖς ὁ Ἰησοῦς Εἶπον ὑμῖν, καί οὐ πιστεύετε· τὰ ἔργα
ἃ ἐγὼ ποιῶ ἐν τῷ ὀνόματι τοῦ Πατρός μου, ταῦτα μαρτυρεῖ περὶ ἐμοῦ·

they would have assumed that He claimed to be the Messiah
of Jewish patriotic expectation; and this He was not. But
He could not say " No " without disavowing His mission.
So He answers by saying (1) that He had told them already,
and (2) that His works sufficiently exhibit Him as the Anointed
of God.

א*D omit αὐτοῖς, but ins. אᶜABLWΘ. B omits ὁ before
Ἰησοῦς, as it frequently does.

εἶπον ὑμῖν (see on 6³⁶ 11⁴⁰). The only open avowal by Jesus
of His Messiahship recorded by Jn. before this point in the
narrative is at 4²⁶, and this was addressed, not to the Jews but
to the Samaritan woman. But He had told them *indirectly*,
and more than once (*e.g.* 5³⁹ 8²⁴· ⁵⁶ 9³⁷; cf. 2¹⁶); if their thoughts
had been in tune with His, they would have understood.

καὶ οὐ πιστεύετε, " and yet (note καί for καίτοι or ἀλλά;
see on 1¹⁰) you do not believe," πιστεύειν being used absolutely;
see on 1⁷. The reason for their unbelief is explained in v. 26.

τὰ ἔργα. For ἔργα used of the " works " of Christ, see on 5²⁰.
The place of " signs " as generating faith in Christ has
already been discussed (see on 2¹¹); here He speaks, as at 5³⁶,
of the value of His " works " as " witnessing " to His claims,
which is the same thing put into different words. His works
bear witness as to the kind of Messiah which He is. For the
idea of " witness " in Jn., see Introd., p. xcii.

τὰ ἔργα ἃ ἐγὼ (emphatic) ποιῶ ἐν τῷ ὀνόματι τοῦ πατρός μου.
For the phrase " the Name of my Father," see on 5⁴³.
The works of Jesus were done, not only as the ambassador of
the Father and sent by Him (see on 3¹⁷), but as by one to whom
the " Name," that is the providential power of the Father,
had been given (see on 17¹¹, and cf. 14²⁶). There is no special
reference to the invocation of the Name of God comparable
with the invocation of names of power common in Gnostic
magic. In the Fourth Gospel the ἔργα of Christ *are* the ἔργα
of the Father (cf. v. 37).

ταῦτα, the subject of the sentence, repeated for the sake of
emphasis; see on 6⁴⁶.

*The Jews do not believe in Jesus, because they are not of His
flock.   He is their true Shepherd, would they but recognise it ; other shepherds are false guides (vv. 26–29, 1–6)*

26 ff. In our arrangement of the text we have at v. 26 the
first appearance in Jn. of the image of Jesus as the Shepherd,

and of His followers as His sheep. The image is introduced
without any explanation, but it is apparent from the Synoptic
Gospels that it was one which Jesus often used, and which
must have been familiar to His disciples. He called them His
" little flock " (Lk. 12[32]); and He declared His mission to be
primarily addressed to " the lost sheep of the house of Israel "
(Mt. 10[6] 15[24]). One of the most touching of His parables is
that in which He compared Himself with a shepherd seeking a
lost and strayed sheep, while the rest of his flock are left temporarily by themselves (Mt. 18[12], Lk. 15[4]). The wandering
crowds move His pity, because they are as " sheep without a
shepherd " (Mk. 6[34], Mt. 9[36]). He told His disciples, in words
from Zechariah, that when their Shepherd was smitten, they
would be like sheep scattered abroad (Mk. 14[27], Mt. 26[31]).
This was one of the illustrations by which Jesus was accustomed to describe His own ministry; and the apostolic writers
speak of Him in the next generation as the " Shepherd of
souls " (1 Pet. 2[25]), " the great Shepherd of the sheep " (Heb.
13[20]), without adding any comment or explanation.

This imagery, natural to a pastoral people, was already
familiar to the Jews. In the Psalms, Yahweh is the Shepherd
of His people (Ps. 23[1] 77[20] 79[13] 80[1] 95[7] 100[3]; cf. Ezek. 34[12-16]).
And it is particularly to be observed that Messiah is spoken of
in the O.T. as a Shepherd. Micah (5[4]) and Isaiah (40[11]) both
speak of the future Deliverer as one who will feed His flock;
and in the *Psalms of Solomon* (xvii. 45) the same picture is
found of the Messianic king tending the flock of Yahweh. Cf.
2 Esd. 2[34]. This idea of the Messiah as Shepherd is developed
in the verses which follow here.

The sequence of thought in vv. 26–29, 1–18, must now be
set out. In v. 24, the Jews ask Jesus for a plain answer to the
question, " Art thou the Messiah ? " In the note on v. 25
it has been pointed out that an answer " Yes " or " No "
might have been misleading. Jesus first replies that He has,
in effect, told them already, and then that His " works "
should be a sufficient witness. He now goes on to give a fuller
answer. The reason why the Jews did not realise at once
that He was the Messiah was that they were not His true
" sheep." Were they His sheep, they would recognise His
voice as that of their Shepherd, and would follow Him un-
hesitatingly (v. 27). He it is indeed who gives His sheep
eternal safety, and no one can snatch them out of His hand, or
out of the hand of God who gave them to Him (v. 28). They
are " the sheep of His hand," as the Psalmist has it (Ps. 95[7]).

It ought to be possible always to recognise a true shepherd.
He comes into the fold through the door, and does not climb

26. Ἀλλὰ ὑμεῖς οὐ πιστεύετε, ὅτι οὐκ ἐστὲ ἐκ ⲧῶν προβάτων τῶν

over the wall, as a thief would do (v. 1). The porter opens
the door to him, and the sheep recognise his voice: he calls
them by name, and leads them forth (v. 3). He leads and they
follow, recognising his voice (v. 4), while they would run from
that of a stranger (v. 5). But the Jews did not understand
what bearing this allegory had on the question they had asked,
sc. "Art thou the Messiah?" In particular, they cannot
perceive what or where is the door into the fold by which the
true shepherd enters. So Jesus explains this.

"I am the Door," He says (v. 7). Accordingly all claiming
to be your Messianic shepherds who did not pass through this
Door are thieves and robbers (v. 8), as is further established
by the fact that the sheep of Israel did not attend to them (v. 8).
"I am the Door," and not only for the shepherds, but for the
sheep. I am the Door for the shepherds *because* I am the
Door for the sheep. It is only through me that you can enter
the fold of safety, and be led out into good pastures (v. 9). The
thieves and robbers come only to destroy and kill. I am come
to give life abundantly (v. 10).

And then the main theme is resumed, the metaphor of
the Door having been explained. I am *the Good Shepherd*,
who gives His life for the sheep, unlike the hireling who runs
away when there is danger (vv. 11-13). I know my sheep,
and they know me (just as the Father knows me and I know
Him), vv. 14, 15. I have other sheep besides those of the Flock
of Israel: them also I must lead, and they too shall hear my
voice. So shall there be One Flock and One Shepherd (v. 16).

The Father loves me, because I am thus laying down my
life, to take it up again (v. 17). My death is voluntary. But
the Father knows and approves. Indeed this is *His* commandment (v. 18). The fact is, that I and my Father are One
(v. 30).

26. ἀλλὰ ὑμεῖς οὐ πιστεύετε, ὅτι οὐκ ἐστέ κτλ. So אBDLWΘ,
but the rec. has οὐ γὰρ ἐστέ. The thought is the same as that
at 8⁴⁷, where see the note. Those who are not of the flock of
Christ have no faith. This is natural, for faith, in the Fourth
Gospel, is born of a certain spiritual affinity.

The rec. adds at the end of the verse καθὼς εἶπον ὑμῖν, with
AD; but these words are not found in אBLWΘ, and cannot
be regarded as part of the true text. If genuine, they must
refer to something that has preceded, and cannot be associated
with what follows (Tatian links them with v. 27). It is not
easy to find any previous saying of Jesus in Jn., to which
καθὼς εἶπον ὑμῖν could be referred at this point, if the words

ἐμῶν. 27. τὰ πρόβατα τὰ ἐμὰ τῆς φωνῆς μου ἀκούουσιν, κἀγὼ
γινώσκω αὐτά, καὶ ἀκολουθοῦσίν μοι, 28. κἀγὼ δίδωμι αὐτοῖς ζωὴν
αἰώνιον, καὶ οὐ μὴ ἀπόλωνται εἰς τὸν αἰῶνα, καὶ οὐχ ἁρπάσει τις
αὐτὰ ἐκ τῆς χειρός μου. 29. ὁ Πατήρ μου ὃς δέδωκέν μοι πάντων

were genuine, other than such passages as 8⁴⁷ mentioned above
(cf. 6³⁶ 11⁴⁰ 14²). Even if the traditional arrangement of the
text be followed, there is nothing in vv. 1–18 which says
expressly that those who are not of Christ's flock have no faith.
Probably καθὼς εἶπον ὑμῖν is the interpolation of a scribe
working on the displaced text, who wished to connect τὰ
πρόβατα τὰ ἐμά of vv. 26, 27, with those of whom (as he supposed) vv. 1–18 had already told.

27. τὰ πρόβατα τὰ ἐμὰ τῆς φωνῆς μου ἀκούουσιν, *sc.* hear
with obedient attention.   Cf. vv. 3, 16; and see on 3⁸.

The rec. has ἀκούει (from v. 3), but אBLWΘ give
ἀκούουσιν (cf. v. 16).   So we have here the plural ἀκολουθοῦσιν,
while at v. 4 we have ἀκολουθεῖ.

The sheep, in Eastern lands, follow the shepherd, who
always goes before and leads.   Cf. Ignatius, *Philad.* 2, ὅπου
δὲ ὁ ποιμήν ἐστιν, ἐκεῖ ὡς πρόβατα ἀκολουθεῖτε.

κἀγὼ γινώσκω αὐτά.   Cf. v. 14.

28. κἀγὼ δίδωμι αὐτοῖς ζωὴν αἰώνιον.   (This is the order of
the words in אBL.)   This was the gift of Jesus to His sheep,
i.e. to His faithful disciples, as promised 6²⁷· ⁴⁰.   Cf. 1 Jn.
2²⁵ 5¹¹.

For ζωὴ αἰώνιος, see on 3¹⁵ 4¹⁴ above.

καὶ οὐ μὴ ἀπόλωνται εἰς τὸν αἰῶνα.   These sheep of His will
not be lost finally.   See on 3¹⁶; and cf. 6³⁹, 17¹² 18⁹.   The
words recall the Synoptic parable of the lost sheep rescued
by the Shepherd.

καὶ οὐχ ἁρπάσει (so ABWΓΔΘ, while אDL have ἁρπάσῃ) τις
αὐτὰ ἐκ τῆς χειρός μου.   This had already been promised by
Jesus (6³⁷· ³⁹).   For ἁρπάζειν in a similar sense, cf. v. 12; the
verb has occurred before at 6¹⁵.

29. ὁ πατήρ μου ὃς δέδωκέν μοι πάντων μείζων ἐστίν.   The
textual variants are puzzling.   For ὅς (AB²ΓΔΘ syrr. sah.),
אB*LW latt. have ὅ; and for μείζων (אDLΓΔW Syr. sin.
sah.), ABΘ latt. have μεῖζον.

Thus the weight of MS. authority favours the reading
ὅ . . . μεῖζον. The Vulgate, following the O.L., clearly
supports this: " pater meus, quod dedit mihi maius omnibus
est."   But the meaning then must be: " As for my Father, that
which He has given me (*i.e.* my flock of sheep) is greater than
all."   This is quite unsuited to the context, as not only here,
but in vv. 1–18, the main thought is of the weakness of the

μείζων ἐστίν, καὶ οὐδεὶς δύναται ἁρπάζειν ἐκ τῆς χειρὸς τοῦ Πατρός.
1. ἀμὴν ἀμὴν λέγω ὑμῖν, ὁ μὴ εἰσερχόμενος διὰ τῆς θύρας εἰς

sheep and their dependence on the Shepherd's strength. To
introduce at this point the idea of the Church as a mighty
organisation would be wholly irrelevant, and the reading ὁ
. . . μεῖζον is to be rejected.

ὁ πατήρ μου must be the subject of ἐστίν, and ὅς must be
preferred to ὅ. The neuter singular is used several times in Jn.
to denote the sum-total of those who have been given by the
Father to the Son ; and probably through reminiscence of such
phrases as πᾶν ὃ δέδωκέν μοι (6³⁹, and see note on 6³⁷) and πᾶν
ὃ δέδωκας αὐτῷ (17²), ὅ has got into the text at this point.
μείζων has then been changed to μεῖζον, so as to agree with ὅ.

Burney [1] found in the aberrant ὁ . . . μεῖζον an illustration
of his theory that in the Fourth Gospel we have to do with
a translation from an Aramaic source, רַבָּא . . . דִּ being
rendered ὁ . . . μεῖζον, instead of ὅς . . . μείζων. This
ingenious argument is, however, not necessary, as the variants
can be explained otherwise.

The rendering, then, of the text which we adopt is simple:
" My Father, who gave (them) to me, is greater than all
things," i.e. is all-powerful. For the " giving " by the Father
to the Son, see on 3³⁵; and cf. 17¹¹.

καὶ οὐδεὶς δύναται ἁρπάζειν ἐκ τῆς χειρὸς τοῦ πατρός. Jesus
has already given the assurance that " no one will snatch
His sheep away from Him." They are the sheep which His
all-powerful Father has given to Him, and He adds (as self-
evident) that " no one *can* snatch them away from the Father."
See Deut. 32³⁹ οὐκ ἔστιν ὃς ἐξελεῖται ἐκ τῶν χειρῶν μου; and cf.
Isa. 49² 51¹⁶. This is at the heart of the comfortable saying
of Wisd. 3¹ δικαίων δὲ ψυχαὶ ἐν χειρὶ θεοῦ.

The allegory of the Sheep and the Shepherd follows at this
point. No one can snatch the sheep of Jesus from His safe-
keeping, and He proceeds to explain with emphasis that it is
only with Him that safety is assured (see Introd., p. xxiv).

X. 1. ἀμὴν ἀμὴν λέγω ὑμῖν. For this solemn prelude to
sayings or discourses of special significance, see on 1⁵¹. It is
never used abruptly to introduce a fresh topic, out of connexion
with what has gone before, nor does it begin a new discourse.
It always has reference to something that has been said already,
which is expanded or set in a new light (cf. 8³⁴· ⁵¹· ⁵⁸). Thus
it introduces here the allegory of the sheep in the fold who recognise their shepherd, which arises out of the pronouncements

[1] *Aramaic Origin, etc.*, p. 102. Torrey agrees with this (*Harvard
Theol. Review*, Oct. 1923, p. 328).

τὴν αὐλὴν τῶν προβάτων ἀλλὰ ἀναβαίνων ἀλλαχόθεν, ἐκεῖνος κλέπτης ἐστὶν καὶ λῃστής· 2. ὁ δὲ εἰσερχόμενος διὰ τῆς θύρας ποιμήν
ἐστιν τῶν προβάτων. 3. τούτῳ ὁ θυρωρὸς ἀνοίγει, καὶ τὰ πρόβατα
τῆς φωνῆς αὐτοῦ ἀκούει, καὶ τὰ ἴδια πρόβατα φωνεῖ κατ' ὄνομα καὶ

in vv. 26–29. To begin this allegory by " Verily, verily," is
exactly in the Johannine manner.

Verses 1–5 are a παροιμία of general application, of which
Jesus explains the reference to Himself and His flock in
vv. 7–16.

The αὐλὴν τῶν προβάτων is the open courtyard in front of
the house, where the sheep were folded for the night. The
word is used thus in Homer, where the Trojans are compared
to ὄϊες πολυπάμονος ἀνδρὸς ἐν αὐλῇ (*Iliad*, iv. 433). So
Josephus represents Abraham as sitting παρὰ τῇ θύρᾳ τῆς αὐτοῦ
αὐλῆς, where the LXX has σκηνῆς (Gen. 18¹; cf. *Antt.* I.
xi. 2). A shepherd, who had access to the courtyard, would
naturally come in and go out by the θύρα. See on v. 16; and cf.
18¹⁵· ¹⁶ for these terms.

ἀλλὰ ἀναβαίνων ἀλλαχόθεν, " but one climbing up another
way," *sc.* a man who gets over the wall into the courtyard.
ἀλλαχόθεν (4 Macc. 1⁷) is a legitimate form for ἄλλοθεν, and
is found in the papyri (see Moulton-Milligan, *s.v.*). It does not
occur elsewhere in the N.T.

ἐκεῖνος, inserted for explicitness, as Jn. so frequently uses
it (see on 1⁸).

κλέπτης ἐστὶν καὶ λῃστής, " is a thief and a robber "; he
has, presumably, come to steal the sheep and to carry them
off with violence. See further on v. 8. κλέπτης is used again
of Judas (12⁶) and λῃστής of Barabbas (18⁴⁰). Cf. Obad.⁵ for
κλέπται and λῃσταί coming by night.

2. ὁ δὲ εἰσερχόμενος κτλ. On the other hand, a man coming
into the court or fold by the door presumably is entitled to do
so. He is a shepherd, whose business it is to look after the
sheep. He is ποιμὴν προβάτων (Gen. 4²). The application of
this to Jesus comes later. So far the picture is true of all
sheepfolds and shepherds.

3. τούτῳ ὁ θυρωρὸς ἀνοίγει, " to him the doorkeeper opens "
the door when he comes. This, again, is part of the general
picture. It does not appear that in the allegory the θυρωρός
is significant. In every parable there are details in which a
spiritual meaning is not necessarily to be sought.

καὶ τὰ πρόβατα τῆς φωνῆς αὐτοῦ ἀκούει κτλ. The sheep hear
his voice with obedient attention (see v. 27 and the note on
ἀκούειν with the gen. at 3⁸). That is, they recognise his voice
as that of a shepherd.

ἐξάγει αὐτά. 4. ὅταν τὰ ἴδια πάντα ἐκβάλῃ, ἔμπροσθεν αὐτῶν
πορεύεται, καὶ τὰ πρόβατα αὐτῷ ἀκολουθεῖ, ὅτι οἴδασιν τὴν φωνὴν
αὐτοῦ· 5. ἀλλοτρίῳ δὲ οὐ μὴ ἀκολουθήσουσιν, ἀλλὰ φεύξονται ἀπ'
αὐτοῦ, ὅτι οὐκ οἴδασιν τῶν ἀλλοτρίων τὴν φωνήν. 6. Ταύτην τὴν

τὰ ἴδια πρόβατα φωνεῖ κατ' ὄνομα. Several flocks under
different shepherds might be brought into the same fold for a
night. All the sheep might discern the note of authority in the
voice of any lawful shepherd. But it is only the sheep of his
own flock that a shepherd will call by name. This he does, as
he leads them out to pasture; and it is only " his own sheep "
that follow.

φωνεῖ. So אABDLW, as against the rec. καλεῖ (ΓΔΘ). Jn.
prefers φωνεῖν to καλεῖν; but cf. Isa. 40²⁶ 43¹ 45³ for the use of
καλεῖν with ὄνομα. See on 1⁴⁸.

It is still common for Eastern shepherds to give particular
names to their sheep, "descriptive of some trait or characteristic of the animal, as Long-ears, White-nose, etc." [1]

4. ὅταν τὰ ἴδια πάντα ἐκβάλῃ. So א^caBDLΘ, but ΑΓΔ
read πρόβατα for πάντα. The rec. has καὶ ὅταν (with ADΓΔ),
but אBLWΘ omit καί. It probably came in from καὶ τὰ ἴδια
in the preceding verse. "When he has put out (of the fold)
all his own ": he is careful to forget none, as he leads his
flock to pasture. ἐκβάλλειν suggests a certain measure of
constraint, the shepherd thrusting out a sheep that delays
unduly in coming forth at his call.

The shepherd, having collected his own flock from the fold,
goes before them (ἔμπροσθεν αὐτῶν). At 3²⁸ ἔμπροσθεν is used
of priority in time; here it refers to space, as at 12³⁷. His
own sheep follow him (cf. v. 27), because they know his voice
(cf. vv. 26, 3).

5. They will not follow an ἀλλότριος, that is, any one who
is not their own shepherd, whether he be the legitimate shepherd
of another flock, or an impostor and a thief (v. 1) Rather will
they run away from him, for they do not know or recognise
his voice. This, as we shall see (v. 8), is a specially significant
feature of the allegory. Cf. v. 26 above and v. 8 below.

ἀκολουθήσουσιν. So ABDΔ, but אLWΘ have ἀκολουθήσωσιν

6. ταύτην τὴν παροιμίαν εἶπ. κτλ. παροιμία occurs again
in N.T. only in Jn. 16²⁵· ²⁹ (as well as in 2 Pet. 2²²), where it
introduces a quotation from Prov. 26¹¹). On the other hand,
παραβολή does not occur outside the Synoptists, except at
Heb. 9⁹ 11¹⁹. In the LXX both words are used to translate

[1] C. T. Wilson, *Peasant Life in the Holy Land*, p. 165. The author's
observations illustrative of the relation of the shepherd to his sheep are
very apposite in connexion with c. 10.

παροιμίαν εἶπεν αὐτοῖς ὁ Ἰησοῦς· ἐκεῖνοι δὲ οὐκ ἔγνωσαν τίνα ἦν ἃ ἐλάλει αὐτοῖς.

7. Εἶπεν οὖν πάλιν αὐτοῖς ὁ Ἰησοῦς Ἀμὴν ἀμὴν λέγω ὑμῖν ὅτι

מָשָׁל : in Ezek. 12²³ 18²·³, the LXX having παραβολή and Symmachus παροιμία. In Ecclus. 47¹⁷ we find Solomon's ᾠδαί and παροιμίαι and παραβολαί all mentioned together.

Etymologically παραβολή suggests the placing of one thing beside another (παραβάλλειν) or a comparison, while παροιμία is derived from παρ' οἶμον, something said "by the way." But the distinction sometimes put forward, that παραβολή always stands for a fictitious narrative, intended to instruct the hearer, as in the "parables" of Christ, while παροιμία is a "proverb," a terse saying of wisdom, cannot be sustained. Thus in the passage now under consideration, παροιμία is the description of the allegory of the Shepherd and the Sheep, while at Lk. 4²³ the proverbial taunt, "Physician, heal thyself," is called a παραβολή (cf. Lk. 5³⁶). And in Ezekiel παραβολή is sometimes descriptive of an allegory (17²ᶠ·), and sometimes signifies a "proverb" (16⁴⁴ 18²). Cf. Ecclus. 8⁸, 39³, for the παροιμίαι of the wise and their hidden meaning.

All that can be said about these two Greek words here is that Jn. uses παροιμία, while the Synoptists prefer παραβολή, both doubtless going back to the Hebrew מָשָׁל, a saying or discourse which, either from its terseness or its veiled significance, may need explanation before it can be fully understood.

This παροιμία of the Shepherd and the Sheep was addressed to the Jews (see v. 25): εἶπεν αὐτοῖς ὁ Ἰησοῦς. They, however (ἐκεῖνοι, for clearness as to the persons indicated; see on 1⁸), did not understand its application; and accordingly Jesus proceeds to explain how it bears on what he had told them (v. 26). The idea of a shepherd as a spiritual leader was, of course, quite familiar to them (see on v. 26), as were also the ordinary habits of shepherds and sheep. But what they did not realise was the appositeness of the allegory in vv. 1–5, in relation to their question, "Art thou the Messiah?" (v. 24). In particular, what was the Door through which Jesus said the true shepherd must come?

Jesus is not only the Shepherd, He is the Door (vv. 7–10).

7. εἶπεν οὖν πάλιν ὁ Ἰησοῦς. οὖν is here more than a mere conjunction; it was because they did not understand that the explanation which follows was given. "Accordingly, Jesus said to them again"; πάλιν also being emphatic (cf. 8¹²·²¹).

ἐγώ εἰμι ἡ θύρα τῶν προβάτων.   8. πάντες ὅσοι ἦλθον πρὸ ἐμοῦ κλέπται εἰσὶν καὶ λησταί· ἀλλ' οὐκ ἤκουσαν αὐτῶν τὰ πρόβατα.

The rec. adds αὐτοῖς after πάλιν, but om. ℵ*B.

ἀμὴν ἀμὴν λέγω ὑμῖν.   Cf. v. 1; and see on 1⁵¹.

ὅτι (recitantis) is omitted by BL, but is found in ℵADW⊙.

ἐγώ εἰμι ἡ θύρα τῶν προβάτων.   For the use in Jn. of the dignified prelude ἐγώ εἰμι, which marks the style of deity, see Introd., p. cxviii.

ἡ θύρα τῶν προβάτων must mean primarily the gate by which the sheep enter and leave the αὐλή, and this would also be the gate used by the shepherd. The phrase cannot be translated, however, " the gate *to* the sheep," although that is involved. Cf. ἡ πύλη τῶν ἱππέων, " the horse gate " (2 Chron. 23¹⁵), meaning the gate by which the horses enter. " The sheep gate " (cf. 5²) in Neh. 3¹ is ἡ πύλη ἡ προβατική. Jn. never uses πύλη, while θύρα occurs again 18¹⁶ 20¹⁹. ²⁶.

When Jesus announces here that He is ἡ θύρα τῶν προβάτων, the primary meaning is that He is the legitimate door of access to the spiritual αὐλή, the Fold of the House of Israel, the door by which a true *shepherd* must enter. In v. 9 the thought is rather that He is the door which must be used by the *sheep*.

For ἡ θύρα, the Sahidic supports ὁ ποιμήν, which is adopted by Moffatt as the true reading here. But, apart from the fact that ἡ θύρα τῶν προβάτων has the weight of MS. authority overwhelmingly in its favour, ὁ ποιμήν would not fit the argument at this point. The Jewish inquirers could not have failed to understand that Jesus claimed to be the Shepherd (see v. 26); their difficulty was as to the interpretation of the *Door* which was so important in the allegory of vv. 1–5. Verses 7–10 are taken up with the explanation of this: " I am the Door," a figure verbally inconsistent indeed with the image of the Shepherd entering *by* the door, but being quite intelligible when taken by itself. See further on v. 9.[1]

8. πάντες ὅσοι ἦλθον πρὸ ἐμοῦ κλέπται εἰσὶν καὶ λησταί. So ℵᶜABDLW; but ℵ* om. πρὸ ἐμοῦ, with most vss., including the Latin, Sahidic, and Syriac; and Westcott-Hort treat the words as a " Western and perhaps Syrian " gloss. On the other hand, they may have been omitted by scribes to lessen the risk of the passage being interpreted as if it applied to the O.T. prophets.[2] πρὸ ἐμοῦ must relate to priority in time

---

[1] For a critical analysis of the parable of the Shepherd and the Sheep, see Holtzmann, *Life of Jesus*, Eng. Tr., p. 37 f.

[2] So Valentinus applied them (Hippol. *Ref.* vi. 35). Jülicher thinks (*Introd.*, p. 401) that the words have a Gnostic ring.

(cf., *e.g.*, Neh. 5¹⁵). But even if the words be omitted, ἦλθον involves a " coming " in the past; and we must translate " all that came before me are thieves and robbers."

The reference is, undoubtedly, to v. 1. He who enters the fold by any other way than the " door " is " a thief and a robber." Now Jesus claims to be the Door of the Fold of the Flock of Israel, and hence it follows that all who sought a way of access to the sheep before He was manifested as the " Door " may be described as " thieves and robbers." This, nakedly stated, is a harsh saying. But, if the sequence of the argument be followed from v. 23 onward (see on v. 26), it is not so intolerant as it sounds (see also on 14⁶). The distinction that is being drawn out is not that between the ministrations of older prophets and teachers, and the perfect ministration of Jesus, but rather (as Chrysostom points out) between those who falsely claimed to be heaven-sent deliverers and the true Messiah Himself.

The methods, *e.g.*, of Judas of Galilee, who instigated the people to revolt against Roman taxation about the year A.D. 6, were violent, and led to murder and robbery (so Josephus, *Antt.* XVIII. i. 6; cf. *B.J.* II. viii. 1 and Acts 5³⁷). According to Acts 5³⁶, Theudas was an earlier impostor of the same type, although Josephus (*Antt.* XX. v. 1) seems to put him later, if indeed he is describing the same person. And, apart from Judas and Theudas, we have the testimony of Josephus (*Antt.* XVII. x. 4, 18) that at the beginning of the first century Judæa was the scene of innumerable risings and disorders, which were caused, in part at any rate, by current misinterpretations of the Messianic idea, associated by the Zealots with militant activities. It is true that we have no knowledge of any Jew before Barcochba (A.D. 135) who claimed explicitly to be the Messiah. But there were many pretenders to the office of leadership of the nation, and to such the words of Jesus, " thieves and robbers," were fitly applied. And the present tense εἰσίν confirms the view that His allusion was to leaders of revolt who belonged to the first century, some of whom were probably living at the time.

The convincing proof that none of these was the divinely appointed Shepherd of Israel was: οὐκ ἤκουσαν αὐτῶν τὰ πρόβατα, " the sheep," *sc.* the true sheep of Israel, who are alone in view throughout this chapter, " did not listen to them " (cf. vv. 4, 5, where it was pointed out that sheep recognise their true shepherd's voice, while they will not listen to one who is only an impostor). It was just because the Jews who were arguing were *not* the true sheep of Israel that they did not accept Jesus as their Shepherd (v. 26).

9. ἐγώ εἰμι ἡ θύρα· δι' ἐμοῦ ἐάν τις εἰσέλθῃ, σωθήσεται, καὶ

9. ἐγώ εἰμι ἡ θύρα. This is repeated from v. 7, a repetition
in the Johannine manner (see on 3[16]), a slight change being
made in the form of the saying. In v. 7 the stress is laid on
Jesus being the Door through which a lawful *shepherd* would
enter. But here the thought is simpler. He is the Door
through which the *sheep* must enter the fold, a saying which
is not relevant to the allegory of this chapter, but is consonant
with the teaching of Jesus as presented by Jn. elsewhere. He
is the Door into the spiritual fold, as He is the Way (and the
only Way) of access to the Father (14[6]; cf. Eph. 2[18], Heb. 10[20]).
The αὐλή (see v. 1) to which He is the Door is the fold of the
house of Israel, the Jewish fold; nor has anything been said
up to this point which suggests any wider fold (cf. v. 16, where
the Gentile fold is indicated for the first time). But the saying
I am the Door has always been quoted, from the first century
onward, as having as wide an application as the parallel saying
I am the Way.

Clement of Rome, commenting on Ps. 118[19. 20], speaks
of " that gate (πύλη) which is in righteousness, even in
Christ " (§ 48). Ignatius (*Philad.* 9) speaks of Christ as
being θύρα τοῦ πατρός, " through whom Abraham and Isaac
and Jacob enter in, and the prophets and the apostles, and the
Church." Both these passages seem to carry an allusion to
ἐγώ εἰμι ἡ θύρα. So also Hermas (*Sim.* ix. 12) has: ἡ πέτρα
αὕτη καὶ ἡ πύλη ὁ υἱὸς τοῦ θεοῦ, the explanation being
added that the Rock is ancient, but the Gate recent (καινή),
because " He was made manifest in the last days of the
consumption," . . . ἵνα οἱ μέλλοντες σώζεσθαι δι' αὐτῆς
εἰς τὴν βασιλείαν εἰσέλθωσι τοῦ θεοῦ, words which recall
the teaching of v. 9. According to Hegesippus (Eus.
H.E. ii. xxiii. 8), James, the Lord's brother, was asked
by inquirers τίς ἡ θύρα τοῦ Ἰησοῦ; which carries an allusion
either to this passage or to a Synoptic precept such as Lk.
13[24] ἀγωνίζεσθε εἰσελθεῖν διὰ τῆς στενῆς θύρας (Mt. 7[13] has
πύλης).

Two reminiscences of the Johannine " I am the Door "
may be quoted from Gnostic sources. In the hymn in the
second-century *Acts of John* (§ 95), we find the phrases θύρα
εἰμί σοι [τῷ] κρούοντί με, ὁδός εἰμί σοι παροδίτῃ. The image of
one *knocking at* a door is not identical with that of one *entering
by* it; but it probably goes back to Jn. 10[9]. Again, Hippolytus
cites Jn. 10[9] from a Naassene writer in the form ἐγώ εἰμι ἡ πύλη
ἡ ἀληθινή, and he represents the Naassene as adding οὐ δύναται
σωθῆναι ὁ τέλειος ἄνθρωπος, ἐὰν μὴ ἀναγεννηθῇ διὰ ταύτης εἰσελθών

εἰσελεύσεται καὶ ἐξελεύσεται καὶ νομὴν εὑρήσει. 10. ὁ κλέπτης οὐκ ἔρχεται εἰ μὴ ἵνα κλέψῃ καὶ θύσῃ καὶ ἀπολέσῃ· ἐγὼ ἦλθον ἵνα ζωὴν ἔχωσιν καὶ περισσὸν ἔχωσιν.

τῆς πύλης (*Ref.* v. viii. 21), a passage which recalls Jn. 3⁵ as well as 10⁹.¹

Probably the proclamation " I am the Door " should be taken in connexion with the Synoptic saying about the Narrow Door (Mt. 7¹³, Lk. 13²⁴). Jn., however, is careful not to suggest that the Door is narrow, while he implies that there is only *one* Door. The comparison with the Synoptists suggests that the αὐλή or fold of the spiritual Israel represents the kingdom of God.

δι' ἐμοῦ ἐάν τις εἰσέλθῃ, σωθήσεται κτλ. δι' ἐμοῦ comes first for emphasis. The form ἐάν τις expresses the catholicity of the implied appeal (cf. 7¹⁷); *any one* may enter by this Door. And the sheep which enters the fold thus shall, first of all, be *safe* (σωθήσεται; see on 3¹⁷). As Jesus had said already, none can snatch His sheep from the Shepherd's hand (v. 28).

καί εἰσελεύσεται καὶ ἐξελεύσεται. The " going out and coming in " suggests being *at home* (Deut. 28⁶, Ps. 121⁸), the daily routine of the sheltered flock (cf. Acts 1²¹). Num. 27¹⁷, which speaks of the shepherd leading the sheep out and bringing them in again, is hardly apposite, for at this point the thought is of the *sheep* rather than of the shepherd. We must take the words in connexion with καὶ νομὴν εὑρήσει. The sheep which has entered the fold by the door is then safe, and he shall find pasture for his needs. Cf. 1 Chron. 4⁴⁰, where the same phrase εὑρίσκειν νομήν is found. The shepherd leads the sheep to pasture (v. 3 above; and cf. Ps. 23¹ 74¹ 95⁷ 100³, Ezek. 34¹⁴); but here the thought is of the happiness of the sheep rather than of the duty of the shepherd.

10. ὁ κλέπτης οὐκ ἔρχεται κτλ. The thief (cf. Ex. 22¹) comes only to steal and kill (κλέπτειν and θύειν do not occur again in Jn.) and destroy (see Jer. 23¹; and cf. v. 28, οὐ μὴ ἀπόλωνται εἰς τὸν αἰῶνα).

ἐγὼ ἦλθον κτλ., " I have come (on the contrary) that they may have life." Cf. v. 28 and 14⁶. The Fourth Gospel was written that believers might thus " have life " in the Name of Jesus (20³¹).

καὶ περισσὸν ἔχωσιν, "and may have it to the full." This is the περισσεία of Christ's grace (Rom. 5²⁰). So Xenophon (*Anab.* VII. vi. 31), περισσὸν ἔχειν, " to have a surplus."

¹ For an account of the nineteenth-century Persian reformer who called himself *Bāb*, or " the Gate," see *E.R.E.* ii. 299, *s.v.* " Bāb."

11. Ἐγώ εἰμι ὁ ποιμὴν ὁ καλός.   ὁ ποιμὴν ὁ καλὸς τὴν ψυχὴν

Jesus the Good Shepherd (vv. 11–30)

11. We have had the allegory of the Shepherd and the Sheep (vv. 1–5); then the explanation of what is meant by the Door (vv. 7–10); now we come to the great proclamation of Jesus as the Good Shepherd, as contrasted with the hireling.

Philo (de Agric. §§ 6, 9, 10) draws out a similar contrast between the ἀγαθὸς ποιμήν, who does not allow his sheep to scatter, and the mere herd (κτηνοτρόφος), who permits the flock to do as it likes.   But the similarity does not go beyond what may naturally be observed between the words of two writers who are expounding the same image; there is no *literary* connexion to be traced between Jn. 10 and Philo.

On ἐγώ εἰμι, and the special appropriateness of this phraseology in passages such as this, something has already been said in the Introduction (p. cxviii). Dods quotes, however, a striking parallel from Xenophon (*Mem.* II. vii. 14), where ἐγώ εἰμι is used only to mark a contrast, the sheep-dog being represented as saying to the sheep, ἐγὼ γάρ εἰμι ὁ καὶ ὑμᾶς αὐτὰς σώζων, ὥστε μήτε ὑπ᾿ ἀνθρώπων κλέπτεσθαι, μήτε ὑπὸ λύκων ἁρπάζεσθαι.   If this had been found in Philo, it would probably have been claimed by somebody as the source from which Jn. derived the language of these verses.   But literary parallels do not always imply literary obligation.

ὁ ποιμὴν ὁ καλός, "the Good Shepherd," *Pastor bonus*. We have already noticed that Philo calls his good shepherd ἀγαθός; and it is not possible to draw any clear distinction in such passages as the present between the two adjectives.   No doubt, goodness and beauty were closely associated in Greek minds; and, if we please, we can find the thought of the beauty of holiness suggested by the application of καλός to the Good Shepherd (cf. καλὰ ἔργα in v. 32).   But ὁ καλὸς οἶνος in 2¹⁰ is simply *good* wine, the adjective carrying no allusion either to moral or æsthetic beauty.   In Tob. 7⁷ and 2 Macc. 15¹² an "honest and good man" is καλὸς καὶ ἀγαθός, a frequent Greek combination.   And when καλός is combined, as here, with the description of a man pursuing a particular business, it simply conveys the idea that he discharges his office or fulfils his calling well, just as we would speak of "a good doctor." Thus we have καλοὶ οἰκονόμοι, "good stewards" (1 Pet. 4¹⁰); ὁ τοῦ μισθοῦ καλὸς ἀνταποδότης, "the good paymaster of the reward," *i.e.* he who will make no default (Barnabas, xix. 11); and "good priests," καλοὶ καὶ οἱ ἱερεῖς (Ignatius, *Philad.* 9),

αὐτοῦ τίθησιν ὑπὲρ τῶν προβάτων· 12. ὁ μισθωτὸς καὶ οὐκ ὢν

in comparison with the High Priest, who is κρείσσων. Barnabas in another place (vii. 1) speaks of "the good Lord," ὁ καλὸς κύριος. Here, then, ὁ ποιμὴν ὁ καλός is simply the Good Shepherd, One who tends His flock perfectly, without any failure of foresight or tenderness, of courage or unselfishness.[1]

τὴν ψυχὴν αὐτοῦ τίθησιν κτλ. He lays down His life for the sheep. All good shepherds are ready to risk their lives in defence of their flock (1 Sam. 17³⁵, Isa. 31⁴); He who is uniquely *the* Good Shepherd lays down His life.

For τίθησιν, א*D substitute the more usual δίδωσιν, but τὴν ψυχὴν αὐτοῦ τιθέναι is a characteristic Johannine expression for the " laying down " of His life by Jesus, occurring again vv. 15, 17, 13³⁷·³⁸, 1 Jn. 3¹⁶, and (of a disciple acting as Jesus did) 15¹³. It stands in contrast with the Synoptic δοῦναι τὴν ψυχὴν αὐτοῦ (Mk. 10⁴⁵, Mt. 20²⁸).

The expression τὴν ψυχὴν τιθέναι, "to lay down one's life," *ponere animam*, is not found in the Greek Bible outside Jn. (cf. 15¹³, 1 Jn. 3¹⁶). Nor is it a classical phrase, but from Hippocrates, ψυχὴν κατέθετο, "he died," is quoted by Dods, following Kypke. We have, indeed, in Judg. 12³ (cf. 1 Sam. 19⁵ 28²¹), ἔθηκα τὴν ψυχήν μου ἐν χειρί μου, " I took my life in my hand," *i.e.* I *risked* my life; but in Jn. τὴν ψυχὴν τιθέναι means rather " to divest oneself of life," as at Jn. 13⁴ τίθησι τὰ ἱμάτια means "He divests Himself of His garments."

ὑπὲρ τῶν προβάτων, "on behalf of the sheep." The Synoptists in similar contexts have ἀντί (Mt. 20²⁸, Mk. 10⁴⁵), but ἀντί occurs only once in Jn. (1¹⁶), and there it does not mean "instead of." In this passage the Death of Jesus is said to be "on behalf of the *sheep*": it is not explicitly declared that it was on behalf of *all men*, "to take away the sin of the world," as at 1²⁹, 1 Jn. 2². But there is no inconsistency with the catholicity of these great pronouncements; and, lest the allegory might be too narrowly interpreted, mention is made in v. 16 of "other sheep" who must learn to follow the Shepherd.

12. ὁ μισθωτὸς καὶ οὐκ ὢν ποιμήν. The rec. with ΑΓ has δέ after, אΔΘ have it before, μισθωτός: om. BLW. Syr. cur. has " the hireling, *the false one*," but this explanatory gloss is not in Syr. sin.

Blass (*Gram.* 255) suggests that οὐκ is a Hebraism, " since in the case of a participle with the article, the LXX render א֑ל by οὐ " (cf. στεῖρα ἡ οὐ τίκτουσα, Isa. 54¹). But although in

---

[1] καλός " denotes that kind of goodness which is at once seen to be good " (Hort, on 1 Pet. 2¹²).

ποιμήν, οὗ οὐκ ἔστιν τὰ πρόβατα ἴδια, θεωρεῖ τὸν λύκον ἐρχόμενον

v. 1 we have ὁ μὴ εἰσερχόμενος, "any one not coming through the door," at v. 12 οὐκ is preferable to μή before ὤν, because the hireling is *certainly* not the shepherd.

ὁ μισθωτός. The term occurs again in the N.T. only at Mk. 1[20], where it is used of the "hired servants" in Zebedee's boat. It occurs often in the LXX, and is not necessarily a term of reproach. In Job 7[2] it is used, as here, of a servant who thinks primarily of his wages. The μισθωτός may be an honest man; but the care of a herdsman who comes for wages to look after a flock of sheep can never be equal to that of their own shepherd, who knows each one and is ready to give his life for theirs. In vv. 1–5 the *shepherd* was contrasted with the *thief*, nothing being said about the excellence of the shepherd's service, the thought being only of his right to enter the fold. Here, in vv. 11–15, we have the contrast exhibited between a *good shepherd* and a *hired man* whose only interest in his flock comes from his wages. In vv. 12, 13, the conduct which may be expected from the μισθωτός in the hour of danger is described in terms contrasting strongly with the conduct of the really good shepherd. We must not confuse the "hireling" with the "thief" of v. 1, any more than with the "wolf" of v. 12. He is only blameworthy because his service is perfunctory, as compared with ὁ ποιμὴν ὁ καλός, who is the perfect shepherd.

The centre of the picture is the figure of "the Good Shepherd," that is, of Jesus Himself. His example of self-sacrifice and watchfulness has always been held up to the "pastors" of His Church (vv. 1–16 form the Gospel for the Ordering of Priests); but to these lesser pastors there is no direct reference in this passage, while the figure of the "hired man" supplies a warning to them all. Cf. 1 Pet. 5[2], where those who tend the flock of God are warned that they must not do their work "for filthy lucre, but of a ready mind."

οὗ οὐκ ἔστιν τὰ πρόβατα ἴδια, "whose own the sheep are not." There is no thought here of the *owner* of the sheep; that does not come into the allegory. But every true shepherd counts the sheep entrusted to his care as his own in a peculiar sense; this the μισθωτός does not feel.

θεωρεῖ τὸν λύκον ἐρχόμενον, "notices the wolf coming." For θεωρεῖν as signifying intelligent perception, see on 2[23], and cf. 9[8].

The wolf is the great danger to sheep in a country like Palestine (cf. Mt. 10[16]); and that "grievous wolves would enter in, not sparing the flock" (Acts 20[29]), was a warning to

καὶ ἀφίησιν τὰ πρόβατα καὶ φεύγει,—καὶ ὁ λύκος ἁρπάζει αὐτὰ καὶ σκορπίζει·—13. ὅτι μισθωτός ἐστιν καὶ οὐ μέλει αὐτῷ περὶ τῶν προβάτων. 14. ἐγώ εἰμι ὁ ποιμὴν ὁ καλός, καὶ γινώσκω τὰ ἐμὰ καὶ γινώσκουσί με τὰ ἐμά, 15. καθὼς γινώσκει με ὁ Πατὴρ κἀγὼ

the Church at Ephesus of which its leaders could not mistake the meaning. The μισθωτός is likely to leave the sheep and run away when the wolf appears. Cf. "ut non derelinquas nos, sicut pastor gregem suum in manibus luporum malignorum" (2 Esd. 5[18]). See Zech. 11[17].

ὁ λύκος ἁρπάζει αὐτά, "the wolf snatches them," as no enemy could snatch His sheep from the care of Jesus (v. 29). That is because He is "the Good Shepherd."

καὶ σκορπίζει. The rec. adds τὰ πρόβατα, but this explanatory addition is not necessary, and is not found in ℵBDW. A consequence of the carelessness of the man in charge of the sheep is described similarly in Jer. 10[21] καὶ διεσκορπίσθησαν (cf. Jer. 23[1]). And in the vision of Ezek. 34[5], when the shepherds neglected their duty "the sheep became meat to all the beasts of the field, and were scattered."

For σκορπίζομαι, διασκορπίζομαι, as applied to the "scattering" of the spiritual flock, cf. 11[52] 16[32]. One of the marks of the unworthy shepherd of Zech. 11[16] is τὸ ἐσκορπισμένον οὐ μὴ ζητήσῃ. Cf. also Zech. 13[7], "smite the shepherd, and the sheep shall be scattered."

The rec. repeats after σκορπίζει, ὁ δὲ μισθωτὸς φεύγει, but this unnecessary gloss is omitted by ℵBDLΘ. W om. this, and also the following ὅτι μισθωτός ἐστιν.

13. οὐ μέλει αὐτῷ περὶ τ. π. We have the same construction, descriptive of God's providence, at 1 Pet. 5[7] αὐτῷ μέλει περὶ ὑμῶν. Cf. Tob. 10[5], οὐ μέλει μοι.

14. ἐγώ εἰμι ὁ ποιμὴν ὁ καλός, repeated after the Johannine manner. Cf. v. 9 for the repetition of "I am the Door"; and see on 3[16].

καὶ γινώσκω τὰ ἐμά. This has been said already, v. 27, κἀγὼ γινώσκω αὐτά. It is one of the marks of a good shepherd; cf. v. 3, where it is noted as a habit of the shepherd to have individual names for his sheep. "The Lord knoweth them who are His" is a sentence of judgment (Num. 16[5]); but it may also be taken as a benediction (2 Tim. 2[19]). Cf. Nah. 1[7].

The rec. proceeds καὶ γινώσκομαι ὑπὸ τῶν ἐμῶν (see on 14[21]), following ΑΓΔΘ, but ℵBDLW read καὶ γινώσκουσί με τὰ ἐμά. This, too, has been said or implied before; cf. vv. 27, 3, 4. The sheep know their shepherd's voice.

15. καθὼς γιν. . . . κἀγὼ γινώσκω . . . We have seen on

6⁵⁷ that the constr. καθώς . . . κἀγώ may be taken in two different ways. In the present passage we may either (1) place a full stop after ἐμά, and then we have a new sentence, sc. " As the Father knoweth me, so I know the Father," the constr. being the same as that at 15⁹ 20²¹; or (2) we may treat καθώς γινώσκει . . . τὸν πατέρα as explanatory of the preceding words, sc. " I know mine, and mine know me, even as the Father knoweth me, and I know the Father," the constr. then being similar to that at 6⁵⁷ 17²¹. The A.V. follows (1), the R.V. adopts (2); and both are legitimate renderings of the Greek, and consistent with Johannine usage. The difficulty of (1) is that the words " As the Father knoweth me, so I know the Father," would seem to be irrelevant to the context, unless we are to connect them with what is said in v. 17, and understand by v. 15, " As the Father knoweth me, so I know the Father, and, *because I know Him and His will*, I lay down my life for the sheep." [1]   But this is to interpolate a thought which is not expressly stated.   On the other hand, it may be objected to the rendering (2), that it suggests that the knowledge of Christ by His true disciples is comparable in degree and in kind to the knowledge that He has of the Father.   No other statement in the Fourth Gospel or elsewhere claims for His disciples so intimate a knowledge of Christ as this would seem to do (the promise of 14²⁰ is for the future, not the present).   But we have seen (on 6⁵⁷) that καθώς . . . καί does not, in fact, imply a perfect or complete parallelism with what has gone before. All that is said here, if rendering (2) be adopted, as we believe it must be, is that the mutual knowledge by Christ's sheep of their Good Shepherd, and His knowledge of them, may be *compared* with the mutual knowledge of the Son and the Father; it is not the perfection or intimacy of the knowledge that is in view, it is its reciprocal character.   Cf. 1 Cor. 11³; and see further on 17¹⁸.

Adopting rendering (2), the sequence of thought in vv. 14, 15, is plain: " I am the Good Shepherd, as is shown *first* by my knowledge of my sheep and theirs of me, and *secondly* by my readiness to lay down my life on their behalf." These are the two principal marks of the Good Shepherd which have been noted in the preceding verses.

The mutual knowledge of the Father and the Son which is brought in here parenthetically is explicitly stated in the great declaration Mt. 11²⁷, Lk. 10²², and is implied at 17²¹ and at many other points in the Gospel.   That Jesus knew God in a unique manner and in pre-eminent degree was His constant claim (see on 7²⁹; and cf. also 8⁵⁵ 17²⁵).

[1] Cf. Abbott, *Diat.* 2125, 2126.

γινώσκω τὸν Πατερα, καὶ τὴν ψυχήν μου τίθημι ὑπὲρ τῶν προβάτων.
16. καὶ ἄλλα πρόβατα ἔχω ἃ οὐκ ἔστιν ἐκ τῆς αὐλῆς ταύτης· κἀκεῖνα

καὶ τὴν ψυχήν μου τίθημι κτλ. This is repeated, like a
refrain, from v. 11, in the Johannine manner. See note on
3¹⁶ for such repetitions.

For τίθημι, א*DW have δίδωμι. See the similar variant
in v. 11, and the note there.

16. ἄλλα πρόβατα ἔχω κτλ. These " other sheep " were the
Gentiles, who " were not of this fold," *i.e.* not of the Jewish
Church.[1] They were not, indeed, in any fold as yet, being
" scattered abroad " (11⁵²). Jesus claims them as already His:
" Other sheep I *have*," for such is the Divine purpose, which,
being certain of fulfilment, may be spoken of as already fulfilled.

κἀκεῖνα δεῖ με ἀγαγεῖν, " them also I *must* lead," δεῖ
expressing that inevitableness which belongs to what is foreordained by God (see on 3¹⁴). Not only had it been prophesied
of Messiah that He was to be a " Light to the Gentiles " (Isa.
42⁶ 49⁶), but there was the explicit promise, " The Lord God
which gathereth the outcasts of Israel saith, Yet will I gather
others to Him, beside His own that are gathered " (Isa. 56⁸).

All this is intelligible from the standpoint of a Christian
living at the end of the first century, when it had long been
conceded that the gospel was for the Gentile as well as for the
Jew. But it is not so easy to be sure how far Jesus taught
this explicitly. Had His teaching been clear on so important
a point, it is difficult to believe that the apostles could have
misunderstood it. Yet Acts and the Pauline Epistles show
that acute controversy arose in the apostolic circle about the
position of the Gentiles. All were ready to admit that, as
Jewish proselytes, they might pass into the Christian Church;
but could they be admitted to Christian baptism without passing
through the portal of Judaism? For this Paul contended
successfully, but his struggle was severe. Had he been able
to quote specific words of Christ determining the matter, his
task would have been easier; but this, seemingly, he was
unable to do. Did Jesus, then, teach plainly that Gentile and
Jew were equally heirs of the Gospel promises?

In Mk. (excluding the Appendix), the mission of Jesus to
those who professed the Jewish religion is the exclusive topic
of the narrative, and there is no saying of Jesus recorded which
would suggest that He had a mission also to the Gentiles.
Indeed, when He crossed the border into the country " of

---

[1] Clem. Alex. (*Strom.* vi. 14, p. 794 P) comments on the " other
sheep, deemed worthy of another fold and mansion, according to their
faith."

Tyre and Sidon," He did not wish His presence to be known
(Mk. 7²⁴); and when the Syrophœnician woman asked Him
to cure her daughter He is reported to have said to her, " Let
the children first be filled," adding that children's bread should
not be given to " dogs." This may have been a proverbial
saying (which would mitigate its seeming harshness); but
at any rate Mk. gives no hint that Jesus regarded non-Jews
as having any *claim* on His ministry. In Mt. (15²⁴) Jesus
actually says to the woman, " I was not sent but unto the
lost sheep of the house of Israel "; as He had said to the apostles
in an earlier passage (10⁵· ⁶), " Go not into any way of the
Gentiles, and enter not into any city of the Samaritans; but
go rather to the lost sheep of the house of Israel."

But these are only *seemingly* instances of Jewish particu-
larism. They do not explicitly convey more than that Jesus
regarded His mission as directed *in the first instance* to the
Jews; and, in fact, there are many indications that both Mt.
and Lk. believed the Gentiles to be included within the re-
deeming purpose of Christ. The prophecies about Messiah
being a light to the Gentiles are quoted (Mt. 4¹⁶ 12²¹; cf.
Lk. 2³²). The Roman centurion was commended for his
faith (Mt. 8¹⁰); so was the Samaritan leper (Lk. 17¹⁹); and
the example of the Good Samaritan is held up for imitation
(Lk. 10³⁷). The saying, " Many shall come from the east and
the west, and shall sit down with Abraham and Isaac and
Jacob," is in Mt. (8¹¹), and, in a different context, also in Lk.
(13²⁸). The command to preach to all nations is in the Marcan
Appendix (Mk. 16¹⁵) as well as in Mt. 28¹⁹; and, even if it be
supposed that we have not in the latter passage the *ipsissima
verba* of Christ, there can be no doubt that it represents one
aspect of His teaching (cf. Mt. 24¹⁴, Lk. 24⁴⁷).

In Jn.'s narrative the Gentiles come without argument or
apology within the scope of the Gospel. Jesus stays two days
with the Samaritan villagers, to teach them (4⁴⁰); He does not
admit that descent from Abraham is a sufficient ground for
spiritual self-satisfaction (8³⁹); He is approached by a party of
Greeks (12²⁰ᶠ·); He declares that He is the Light of the world
(8¹²), which implies that the Gentiles as well as the Jews are
the objects of His enlightening grace. And in the present
passage (10¹⁶) Jesus, in like manner, declares that He has
" other sheep " besides the Jews, while it is not to be overlooked that He puts them in the second place : " Them *also*
I must lead." They are not His first charge: that was to
shepherd " the lost sheep of the house of Israel." He " came
to His own " (1¹¹) in the first instance.

Jn., then, is in agreement with Mt. and Lk. in his repre-

δεῖ με ἀγαγεῖν, καὶ τῆς φωνῆς μου ἀκούσουσιν, καὶ γενήσεται μία

sentation of the teaching of Jesus about the Gentiles; and this teaching is accurately represented in the saying of Paul that the gospel was "to the Jew first, and also to the Greek" (Rom. 1¹⁶). Mk. is the only evangelist who says nothing about the inclusion of the Gentiles. The significance of what Jesus had said about this was perhaps not appreciated by Mk., any more than it was by those with whom Paul had his great controversy. See further on 11⁵² 12²¹.

καὶ τῆς φωνῆς μου ἀκούσουσιν. So He says again, v. 27 (cf. 18³⁷). So Paul said of the Gentiles, when the Jews at Rome had declined to accept his message: τοῖς ἔθνεσιν ἀπεστάλη τοῦτο τὸ σωτήριον τοῦ θεοῦ· αὐτοὶ καὶ ἀκούσονται, "*they* will hear it" (Acts 28²⁸). Note that ἀκούειν here takes the gen., as it does when it connotes hearing with understanding and obedience. See on 3⁸.

μία ποίμνη, εἷς ποιμήν, "one flock, one shepherd": the alliteration cannot be reproduced in another language.

A rendering of the Latin Vulgate in this verse has led to so much controversy, that the textual facts must be briefly stated. All Greek MSS. have ἐκ τῆς αὐλῆς ταύτης . . . μία ποίμνη, εἷς ποιμήν. The O.L. vss.[1] correctly preserve the distinction between αὐλή and ποίμνη, by rendering them respectively *ouile* (fold) and *grex* (flock). But Jerome's Vulgate has *ouile* in both places. This might be taken for a mere slip, were it not that in his *Comm. on Ezekiel* (46) he distinctly implies that the Greek word αὐλή is repeated, saying that he is dissatisfied with the old rendering *ouile* for αὐλή and suggesting *atrium*. Wordsworth and White (*in loc.*) regard this as establishing Jerome's reliance here on some Greek authority which had αὐλή in the last clause instead of ποίμνη. Into this question we need not enter, further than to note that no such Greek authority is now extant. However Jerome's eccentric rendering *unum ouile et unus pastor* arose, the weight of authority is overwhelmingly against it, although it has caused misunderstanding and perplexity for many centuries.

Jesus did not say there would be *one fold* (αὐλή): He said *one flock*, which is different. In one flock there may be many folds, all useful and each with advantages of its own, but the Flock is One, for there is only One Shepherd. The unity of the Hebrew people is indicated similarly in Ezekiel by the assurance that one shepherd will be set over them, as ruling over an undivided kingdom, Judah and Israel having come together

---

[1] Except Cod. Sangallensis (saec. ix.), which has *ouile vel pastorale* for ποίμνη.

ποίμνη, εἰς ποιμήν. 17. διὰ τοῦτό με ὁ Πατὴρ ἀγαπᾷ ὅτι ἐγὼ τίθημι τὴν ψυχήν μου, ἵνα πάλιν λάβω αὐτήν. 18. οὐδεὶς ἦρεν αὐτὴν ἀπ'

again: " I will set up one shepherd over them, even my servant David: he shall feed them " (Ezek. 34²³; cf. 37²⁴). The phrase " one shepherd " is also found in Eccles. 12¹¹, where it refers to God as the one source of wisdom.

Jn., in the next chapter, expresses the thought that the Death of Jesus had for its purpose the gathering into one of the scattered children of God: ἵνα τὰ τέκνα τοῦ θεοῦ τὰ διεσκορπισμένα συναγάγῃ εἰς ἕν (11⁵²). In 10¹⁶ Jesus is to " lead " (ἀγαγεῖν) the Gentile members of His flock: in 11⁵² He is to bring them together (συναγαγεῖν).

17. διὰ τοῦτο . . . ὅτι. See on 5¹⁶ for this favourite Johannine construction, διὰ τοῦτο referring to what follows. The meaning here is that God's love for Jesus is drawn out by His voluntary sacrifice of His life in order that He may resume it after the Passion for the benefit of man. The same idea is found in Paul: " *Wherefore* God also highly exalted Him " (Phil. 2⁹). See also Heb. 2⁹; and cf. Isa. 53¹².

με ὁ πατήρ. So אBDLΘ; the rec. has ὁ πατήρ με.

με ὁ πατὴρ ἀγαπᾷ. Jn. generally uses ἀγαπᾶν of the mutual love of the Father and the Son (see on 3¹⁶), but at 5²⁰ we find ὁ πατὴρ φιλεῖ τὸν υἱόν. See also on 3³⁵ 21¹⁷, as to the alleged distinction in usage between ἀγαπᾶν and φιλεῖν, a distinction which is not observed in the Fourth Gospel.

ὅτι ἐγὼ τίθημι τὴν ψυχήν μου, *sc.* as a good shepherd does for his sheep (see on v. 11 for the phrase). The self-sacrificing love of Jesus for man draws out the love of the Father to Him. Love evokes love.

ἵνα πάλιν λάβω αὐτήν. ἵνα must be given its full telic force. It was *in order that* He might resume His Life, glorified through suffering, that Jesus submitted Himself to death. Death was the inevitable prelude to the power of His Resurrection Life. It was only after He had been " lifted up " on the cross that He could draw all men to Himself (12³²). The Spirit could not come until after the Passion (7³⁹, where see note). The purpose of the Passion was not only to exhibit His unselfish love; it was *in order that* He might resume His life, now enriched with quickening power as never before.

18. οὐδεὶς ἦρεν αὐτὴν ἀπ' ἐμοῦ. א*B read ἦρεν, while the easier reading of the rec. text (אᶜADWΘ latt.) is αἴρει If the aorist ἦρεν is adopted, " no one *took it* from me," Jn. is representing Jesus as speaking *sub specie æternitatis.* The issue is so certain that He speaks of His death, which is still in the future, as if it were already past. Whether ἦρεν or αἴρει

ἐμοῦ, ἀλλ' ἐγὼ τίθημι αὐτὴν ἀπ' ἐμαυτοῦ. ἐξουσίαν ἔχω θεῖναι αὐτήν, καὶ ἐξουσίαν ἔχω πάλιν λαβεῖν αὐτήν· ταύτην τὴν ἐντολὴν ἔλαβον παρὰ τοῦ Πατρός μου.   30. ἐγὼ καὶ ὁ Πατὴρ ἕν ἐσμεν.

be read, it is the voluntariness of the Death of Jesus which is emphasised; cf. 18⁶, Mt. 26⁵³.

ἀλλ' ἐγὼ τίθημι αὐτὴν ἀπ' ἐμαυτοῦ. This clause is omitted by D, probably because of its apparent verbal inconsistency with 5¹⁹ (cf. 5³⁰ 7²⁸ 8²⁸) οὐ δύναται ὁ υἱὸς ποιεῖν ἀφ' ἑαυτοῦ οὐδέν. But there is no real inconsistency. ἀπ' ἐμαυτοῦ here does not mean *without authority from the Father*, for that authority is asserted in the next sentence. It only implies spontaneity, voluntariness, in the use of the authority which Jesus has received from the Father, and in the obeying of the Father's commandment. See on 5¹⁹.

ἐξουσίαν ἔχω θεῖναι αὐτήν. For ἐξουσία, "authority" as distinct from "power," in Jn., see on 1¹². The authority which Jesus claimed from the Father was, first, the authority to lay down His life spontaneously (which no one has unless he is assured that his death will directly serve the Divine purposes); and, secondly, the authority to resume it again. That He had been given this latter ἐξουσία is in accordance with the consistent teaching of the N.T. writers that it is God the Father who was the Agent of the Resurrection of Jesus. Jesus is not represented as raising Himself from the dead. See on 2¹⁹.

ταύτην τὴν ἐντολήν κτλ. This was the Father's commandment, viz. that He should die and rise again. See further on 12⁴⁹ for the Father's ἐντολή addressed to Christ. This Johannine expression is recalled in Hermas (*Sim.* v. vi. 3), δοὺς αὐτοῖς τὸν νόμον ὃν ἔλαβε παρὰ τοῦ πατρὸς αὐτοῦ.

He says "*my* Father" here and vv. 25, 29, 37. His relation to God was unique; see on 2¹⁶.

30. ἐγὼ καὶ ὁ πατὴρ ἕν ἐσμεν. As has been shown (Introd., p. xxv), this great utterance seems to have been made in explanation of v. 18, upon which it immediately follows in our arrangement of the text. None the less, it would not be out of place if it followed on v. 29, in the traditional order.

It has been customary, following the habit of the patristic commentators, to interpret these significant words in the light of the controversies of the fourth century. Bengel, *e.g.* (following Augustine), says: "Per *sumus* refutatur Sabellius, per *unum* Arius"; the words thus being taken to prove identity of *essence* between the Father and the Son, while the difference of *persons* is indicated by the plural ἐσμέν. But it is an anachronism to transfer the controversies of the fourth century to the theological statements of the first. We have a parallel

31. Ἐβάστασαν πάλιν λίθους οἱ Ἰουδαῖοι ἵνα λιθάσωσιν αὐτόν.
32. ἀπεκρίθη αὐτοῖς ὁ Ἰησοῦς Πολλὰ ἔργα ἔδειξα ὑμῖν καλὰ ἐκ τοῦ
Πατρός· διὰ ποῖον αὐτῶν ἔργον ἐμὲ λιθάζετε; 33. ἀπεκρίθησαν αὐτῷ

to ἕν ἐσμεν in 1 Cor. 3⁸, where Paul says ὁ φυτεύων καὶ ὁ ποτίζων
ἕν εἰσιν, meaning that both the " planter " and the " waterer "
of the seed are in the same category, as compared with God
who gives the increase. A unity of fellowship, of will, and of
purpose between the Father and the Son is a frequent theme
in the Fourth Gospel (cf. 5¹⁸· ¹⁹ 14⁹· ²³ and 17¹¹· ²²), and it is
tersely and powerfully expressed here; but to press the words
so as to make them indicate identity of οὐσία, is to introduce
thoughts which were not present to the theologians of the first
century.

Ignatius expresses the same thought as that conveyed in
this verse, when he writes ὁ κύριος ἄνευ τοῦ πατρὸς οὐδὲν
ἐποίησεν, ἡνωμένος ὤν (Magn. 7). Cf. 8²⁸ above.

The Jews accuse Jesus of blasphemy : He defends His claim to be Son of God (vv. 31-39)

31. The Jewish opponents of Jesus, with a true instinct,
perceived that He was claiming to be more than human.

ἐβάστασαν πάλιν (cf. 8⁵⁹) λίθους οἱ Ἰουδ. κτλ. For βαστάζειν,
see on 12⁶ below. Here it means " to lift up and carry
off," and expresses more than αἴρειν in the similar context
in 8⁵⁹. They fetched stones from a distance, that they might
stone Him. The verb λιθάζειν does not occur in the Synoptists, but cf. 11⁸.

32. ἀπεκρ. αὐτοῖς ὁ Ἰη. He did not withdraw Himself
immediately, as at 8⁵⁹, but proceeded to answer the thoughts
which urged them to kill Him. Cf. 5¹⁷ and Mk. 11¹⁴ for
ἀπεκρίνεσθαι used of an answer to acts, rather than to words.

πολλὰ ἔργα καλά, "many noble works," καλός expressing
goodness as well as beauty (see on v. 11; and cf. 1 Tim. 6¹⁸); His
works of healing were not only good works (as we use the phrase),
but were works significant of the beauty of holiness. See on
2²³ for " signs " which He showed at Jerusalem on an earlier
visit. These ἔργα were ἐκ τοῦ πατρός. This He had repeatedly
urged (5¹⁹· ³⁶ 9⁴ 10²⁵).

The rec. has μου after πατρός, but om. א*BDΘ. For
ἔδειξα, Θ has ἐδίδαξα.

διὰ ποῖον αὐτῶν ἔργον ἐμὲ λιθάζετε; He knew, indeed, that
it was not merely because He had cured the impotent and the
blind that they sought to kill Him, but because of the claims
which He consistently made as to the source of His power and

οἱ Ἰουδαῖοι Περὶ καλοῦ ἔργου οὐ λιθάζομέν σε ἀλλὰ περὶ βλασφημίας,
καὶ ὅτι σὺ ἄνθρωπος ὢν ποιεῖς σεαυτὸν Θεόν. 34. ἀπεκρίθη αὐτοῖς
ὁ Ἰησοῦς Οὐκ ἔστιν γεγραμμένον ἐν τῷ νόμῳ ὑμῶν ὅτι Ἐγὼ εἶπα

authority. He desired to bring this out, by putting to them
such a question, " For what kind of work among these do you
stone me ? " ποῖον directs their attention to the quality and
character of His works.

33. ἀπεκρίθησαν αὐτῷ οἱ Ἰουδαῖοι. The rec. adds λέγοντες,
but this is rightly omitted by אABLWΘ. ἀπεκρίθη followed
by the pres. part. λέγων is very rare in Jn. (see on 1²⁶), who
prefers to use two co-ordinate verbs, ἀπεκρ. καὶ εἶπεν (see on 1⁵⁰).

The Jewish opponents of Jesus give Him the answer that
He anticipated. They had set about stoning Him, because
death by stoning was the appointed penalty for blasphemy
(Lev. 24¹⁶; cf. 1 Kings 21¹⁰·¹³), and His language was, in
their ears, blasphemous, "making Himself God," as they said.
Cf. 5¹⁸, and 19⁷ below, where the charge against Him was more
accurately formulated, ἑαυτὸν υἱὸν θεοῦ ἐποίησεν.

περὶ βλασφημίας, " because of blasphemy "; cf. Acts 26⁷
περὶ ἧς ἐλπίδος ἐγκαλοῦμαι, where περί is used in the same way.
The word βλασφημία occurs in Jn. only in this passage.

34. For the formula of citation ἔστιν γεγραμμένον, see on 2¹⁷.

The quotation is from Ps. 82⁶, the "Law" embracing the
O.T. generally; cf. 12³⁴ 15²⁵, Rom. 3¹⁹, 1 Cor. 14²¹. Thus in
Philo, de Iona (§ 44, extant only in an Armenian version), we
find, " Hast thou not read in the Law . . . ?" quoting Ps. 102²⁶.
So also in Sanhedrin, f. 91. 2, cited by Wetstein: " Quomodo
probatur resurrectio mortuorum ex lege ? quia dicitur (in Ps.
84⁵) non *laudauerunt* sed *laudabunt* te."

ἐν τῷ νόμῳ ὑμῶν. So אᵃABL latt. and some syrr.; but
om. ὑμῶν א*DΘ and Syr. sin. For the phrase " your law "
on the lips of Jesus, see on 8¹⁷.

The argument is thoroughly Jewish : " In your Scriptures,
judges are addressed as אֱלֹהִים by the Divine voice, being
commissioned by God for their work and thus being His dele-
gates and representatives; where, then, is the blasphemy in my
description of myself as υἱὸς τοῦ θεοῦ, being (as I am) the Ambassador of God and sent by Him into the world ? " In Ps. 82,
which represents God as the Judge of judges, He is represented as reminding unjust judges that it is by His appointment
they hold their office, which is therefore divine: " I have said
(*sc.* when you were made judges), Ye are gods." Cf. Ex. 21⁶
22⁹·²⁸ for אֱלֹהִים used of judges in the same way. The argument is one which would never have occurred to a Greek
Christian, and its presence here reveals behind the narrative

Θεοί ἐστε; 35. εἰ ἐκείνους εἶπεν θεοὺς πρὸς οὓς ὁ λόγος τοῦ Θεοῦ
ἐγένετο, καὶ οὐ δύναται λυθῆναι ἡ γραφή, 36. ὃν ὁ Πατὴρ ἡγίασεν

a genuine reminiscence of one who remembered how Jesus
argued with the Rabbis on their own principles.

The natural retort (obvious to a modern mind) would be that
the argument is insecure, because it seems to pass from " gods "
in the lower sense to " God " in the highest sense of all.   But
(1) *ad hominem* the argument is complete.   On Jewish principles of exegesis it was quite sound.   Jesus never called Himself " son of Yahweh ";   such a phrase would be impossible
to a Jew.   But " sons of Elohim " occurs often in the O.T.
(Gen. 6², Job 1⁶, Ps. 29¹ 89⁶, etc.).   That Jesus should call
Himself υἱὸς τοῦ θεοῦ could not be *blasphemous*, having regard
to O.T. precedents, however unwarranted His opponents might
think the claim to be.   And (2) there is a deeper sense
in which the argument as presented in Jn. conveys truth.
The strict Hebrew doctrine of God left no place for the Incarnation.   God and man were set over against each other, as
wholly separate and distinct.   But even in the Jewish Scriptures
there are hints and foreshadowings of potential divinity in
man (cf. Ps. 82⁶, Zech. 12⁸); and it is to this feature of Hebrew
theology that attention is drawn in v. 34.   The doctrine of the
Incarnation has its roots, not in bare Deism, but in that view
of God which regards Him as entering into human life and
consecrating human activities to His own purposes.

35. εἰ ἐκείνους εἶπεν θεούς, " if then the Law (*i.e.* the Scripture) called them gods," πρὸς οὓς ὁ λόγος τοῦ θεοῦ ἐγένετο, " to
whom the message of God came," *sc.* at the moment of their
appointment to high office, which was a Divine call.   So it
was said of Jeremiah ὃς ἐγενήθη λόγος τοῦ θεοῦ πρὸς αὐτόν
(Jer. 1²), and of John the Baptist ἐγένετο ῥῆμα θεοῦ ἐπὶ Ἰωάνην
(Lk. 3²); and it is implied here that the same words are
applicable to the judge who is invested with authority to
execute justice in God's name.   The call of circumstance may
often be truly a " word of God " to the man to whom it comes.

καὶ οὐ δύναται λυθῆναι ἡ γραφή.   For λύειν used of " breaking " a law, see on 5¹⁸.   Here we should render " the Scripture
cannot be set at naught."   The opposite of setting the Scripture
at naught or " destroying " it is the " fulfilling " of it.   See
Mt. 5¹⁷.   The meaning of this parenthesis is that the words of
Ps. 82⁶ are full of permanent significance and must not be
ignored.   See Introd., p. clii.

ἡ γραφή, as always in Jn., signifies the actual passage of
the O.T. which is cited or indicated, and not the whole body of
the Hebrew Scriptures.   See on 2²².

καὶ ἀπέστειλεν εἰς τὸν κόσμον ὑμεῖς λέγετε ὅτι Βλασφημεῖς, ὅτι εἶπον, Υἱὸς τοῦ Θεοῦ εἰμί; 37. εἰ οὐ ποιῶ τὰ ἔργα τοῦ Πατρός μου, μὴ πιστεύετέ μοι· 38. εἰ δὲ ποιῶ, κἂν ἐμοὶ μὴ πιστεύητε, τοῖς ἔργοις πιστεύετε, ἵνα γνῶτε καὶ γινώσκητε ὅτι ἐν ἐμοὶ ὁ Πατὴρ κἀγὼ ἐν τῷ

36. ὃν ὁ πατὴρ ἡγίασεν. ἁγιάζειν is a Biblical word, connoting primarily the idea of setting apart for a holy purpose. Thus it is used of Yahweh hallowing the Sabbath (Ex. 20¹¹), and of the consecration of an altar (Lev. 16¹⁹). It is applied to men who are set apart for important work or high office, e.g. to Jeremiah as prophet (Jer. 1⁵), to the priests (2 Chron. 26¹⁸), to Moses (Ecclus. 45⁴), to the fathers of Israel (2 Macc. 1²⁵). In the N.T. οἱ ἡγιασμένοι are the Christian believers (Acts 20³² 26¹⁸, 1 Cor. 1², Heb. 2¹¹ 10¹⁰, 2 Tim. 2²¹), a form of expression which we have in Jn. 17¹⁹, where Jesus prays that the apostles may be ἡγιασμένοι ἐν ἀληθείᾳ. In that passage (where see note) He declares ἐγὼ ἁγιάζω ἐμαυτόν, but here the Agent of His consecration is the Father. In virtue of this hallowing, Jesus is ὁ ἅγιος τοῦ θεοῦ (6⁶⁹, where see note). That He was set apart for His mission by the Father, who sent Him into the world, is the constant doctrine of the Fourth Gospel.

καὶ ἀπέστειλεν εἰς τὸν κόσμον. Cf. 17¹⁸ ; and see on 3¹⁷.

ὑμεῖς λέγετε ὅτι κτλ., " Do *you* say . . ."; ὑμεῖς being emphatic.

ὅτι εἶπον, υἱὸς τοῦ θεοῦ εἰμί. This He had repeatedly said, by implication, if not explicitly (cf. especially v. 30 ; and see 5¹⁸ 19⁷). It was involved in the claim that He made when He spoke of God as " *my* Father ": see on 2¹⁶.

37. εἰ οὐ ποιῶ τὰ ἔργα τοῦ πατρός μου, μὴ πιστεύετέ μοι. He returns to the argument which He has put forward all through. They had seen His works of healing; He had declared consistently that they were really the ἔργα of God Himself, whose Ambassador He was (v. 25); if they did not recognise these as works of God and accept their witness. He did not expect them to believe His words (μὴ πιστεύετέ μοι : for πιστεύειν followed by a dative, see on 8³¹). Cf. 5³⁶.

38. εἰ δὲ ποιῶ κτλ. But, on the other hand, if they recognised the divine character of these ἔργα of Jesus, they should accept their witness as to His authority. This would not produce the highest kind of faith, but it would be a beginning. See 5³⁶⁻³⁸. The witness of the works will convince them of His trustworthiness, and so they will come to believe what He says. This, in turn, will lead on to belief " in Him " (see on 1¹²), to faith in the majesty of His Person.

ἵνα γνῶτε καὶ γινώσκητε, " that you may perceive, and so reach the fixed conviction of knowledge," ὅτι ἐν ἐμοὶ ὁ πατὴρ

Πατρί.   39. Ἐζήτουν οὖν αὐτὸν πάλιν πιάσαι· καὶ ἐξῆλθεν ἐκ τῆς χειρὸς αὐτῶν.

40. Καὶ ἀπῆλθεν πάλιν πέραν τοῦ Ἰορδάνου εἰς τὸν τόπον ὅπου

κἀγὼ ἐν τῷ πατρί, "that the Father is in me, and I in the Father" (cf. 17²¹). This faith would appreciate the saying at which they had stumbled, ἐγὼ καὶ ὁ πατὴρ ἕν ἐσμεν (v. 30).

γινώσκητε. So BLWΘ, but אΑΓΔ substitute πιστεύσητε. But there is nothing pleonastic in γνῶτε followed by γινώσκητε, the pres. subjunctive referring to a continuous appreciation and understanding, the aorist to the initial apprehension of the truth. Cf. ἵνα γινώσκουσιν (17³) and ἵνα γινώσκῃ (17²³).

The argument is repeated 14¹¹, πιστεύετέ μοι (i.e. believe my word) ὅτι ἐγὼ ἐν τῷ πατρὶ καὶ ὁ πατὴρ ἐν ἐμοί· εἰ δὲ μὴ (but, if you will not, then accept the lower form of witness) διὰ τὰ ἔργα αὐτὰ πιστεύετε. The reciprocal communion of the Father and the Son—"I in Him, and He in me"—is expressed again in the same mystical words at 17²¹; cf. 1 Jn. 3²⁴ 4¹⁵.

39. ἐζήτουν οὖν. So אALWΔ, but οὖν may have come in from 7³⁰ or may be an itacism; om. BΘ.

The project of stoning Him (v. 31) was abandoned, perhaps because v. 38 did not seem to express His equality with the Father so uncompromisingly as v. 30, but more probably because οἱ Ἰουδαῖοι (v. 33) found that, as before, the crowd were not in entire agreement with their policy of violence.

πάλιν. His Jewish opponents had sought His arrest more than once before (cf. 7¹· ³⁰· ⁴⁴ 8²⁰). א*D omit πάλιν.

For πιάζειν, see on 7³⁰.

καὶ ἐξῆλθεν ἐκ τῆς χειρὸς αὐτῶν. There is no suggestion of His escape being miraculous, any more than at 8⁵⁹ (q.v.).

For the redundant ἐξῆλθεν ἐκ, see on 4³⁰.

Jesus retires beyond the Jordan, and many believe on Him there (vv. 40–42)

40. It had become apparent that the Jews were not to be persuaded of the claims of Jesus, to whom their hostility was increasing. So he retired beyond the Jordan to the scene of His earliest ministry, where He had called His first disciples; and there He found what must have been a welcome response to His teaching.

καὶ ἀπῆλθεν πάλιν κτλ. πάλιν is omitted by Syr. sin. and by e; but it is a favourite word with Jn. when he wishes to indicate that one is going back to a place that has been visited

ἦν Ἰωάνης τὸ πρῶτον βαπτίζων, καὶ ἔμενεν ἐκεῖ. 41. καὶ πολλοὶ
ἦλθον πρὸς αὐτὸν καὶ ἔλεγον ὅτι Ἰωάνης μὲν σημεῖον ἐποίησεν οὐδέν,
πάντα δὲ ὅσα εἶπεν Ἰωάνης περὶ τούτου ἀληθῆ ἦν. 42. καὶ πολλοὶ
ἐπίστευσαν εἰς αὐτὸν ἐκεῖ.

before (see on 4³). The use of πάλιν does not suggest that
the former visit was a recent one, as Lange and others have
supposed. Jesus returned to Bethany (or Bethabara) beyond
Jordan (see on 1²⁸ for different views as to the exact place),
which was in the district called Peræa; and it is probable that
this visit is to be identified with that mentioned Mk. 10¹,
Mt. 19¹.

For the constr. ὅπου ἦν Ἰω. βαπτίζων, see on 1²⁸. Jn. is
careful to note that he means the place where John was baptizing
first, not " Ænon near Salim," where we find him exercising
his ministry at 3²².

For τὸ πρῶτον, אDΘ give τὸ πρότερον; but the constr. τὸ
πρῶτον appears again 12¹⁶ 19³⁹.

καὶ ἔμενεν ἐκεῖ. Jesus seems to have remained in Peræa,
until He went to Bethany for the raising of Lazarus (11⁷),
i.e. perhaps about three months.

41. That the people flocked to hear His teaching in Peræa
is confirmed by the Marcan tradition (Mk. 10¹, Mt. 19¹). They
remembered what John the Baptist had said about Him, and
remembered too that his witness had been found trustworthy.
This was the reason why they came now in such numbers to
see and hear Jesus.

Of John the Baptist, too, they remembered that he did no
" sign," such as might be expected of a prophet; but nevertheless, although it was not confirmed by signs (see on 2¹¹), his
witness was true. For the witness of the Baptist, cf. 1⁷. ²⁹⁻³⁴
3²⁷⁻³⁰ 5³³. It made a profound impression.

אD omit ὅτι after ἔλεγον, apparently not realising that
ὅτι here is *recitantis*. The words which follow are set down as
the actual words which the people used.

42. πολλοὶ ἐπίστευσαν εἰς αὐτόν, a favourite phrase of Jn.
See on 4³⁹.

For the constr. πιστεύειν εἴς τινα, see on 1¹².

ἐκεῖ comes before εἰς αὐτόν in the rec. text ; but
אABDLWΘ place it at the end of the sentence, as at v. 40,
perhaps for emphasis. It often comes last in Jn., *e.g.* 2¹
11⁸. ¹⁵. ³¹ 12².

XI. 1. Ἦν δέ τις ἀσθενῶν, Λάζαρος ἀπὸ Βηθανίας, ἐκ τῆς κώμης Μαρίας καὶ Μάρθας τῆς ἀδελφῆς αὐτῆς. 2. ἦν δὲ Μαρία ἡ ἀλείψασα τὸν Κύριον μύρῳ καὶ ἐκμάξασα τοὺς πόδας αὐτοῦ ταῖς θριξὶν αὐτῆς,

The sickness of Lazarus, and the discussion of it by Jesus and His disciples (XI. 1-16)

XI. 1. ἦν δέ τις ἀσθενῶν. For the constr. of ἦν with a participle, cf. 3[23] 18[25], and see note on 1[28].

The name *Lazarus*, לְעָזָר, is a shortened form of *Eleazar*, אֶלְעָזָר, and is found again in the N.T. only in the parable of Lk. 16. Bethany, which is about 2 miles from Jerusalem, is now called *El 'Azariyeh*, from the tradition of the miracle narrated here.

Lazarus is described as ἀπὸ Βηθανίας, ἐκ τῆς κώμης Μαρίας (אD have τῆς Μαρίας) καὶ Μάρθας. So Philip is described as ἀπὸ Βηθσαϊδά, ἐκ τῆς πόλεως Ἀνδρέου καὶ Πέτρου (1[44], where see note). It has been suggested that we ought to distinguish "Bethany" from "the village of Mary and Martha," and place the latter (see Lk. 10[38]) in Galilee. But Lk. does not always arrange the incidents he narrates in such strict order that we can be sure either of the locality or the time at which a given incident is to be placed. It can hardly be doubted (cf. 12[1]) that Lazarus, Mary, and Martha lived at Bethany together. The attempt to distinguish between ἀπό and ἐκ, so as to regard ἀπὸ Βηθανίας as indicating *domicile*, while ἐκ τῆς κώμης κτλ. would indicate *place of origin* (see Abbott, *Diat.* 2289 f.), is not only without corroborative evidence as to such a use of the two prepositions, but would make the opening sentence of this chapter very clumsy. See on 1[44].

Mary is mentioned before Martha, while elsewhere (Jn. 11[19], Lk. 10[38]) Martha, as the mistress of their house, is named before Mary. At the time the Fourth Gospel was written, Mary was the more prominent of the two in Christian tradition, as is recorded in Mk. (14[9]): "Wheresoever the gospel shall be preached throughout the whole world, that also which this woman hath done shall be spoken of for a memorial of her."

2. This verse seems to be an explanatory gloss added by an editor. There are two non-Johannine touches of style. The phrase τὸν κύριον (see on 4[1]) appears instead of Jn.'s usual τὸν Ἰησοῦν. And, secondly, the characteristically Johannine ἦν ἀσθενῶν (v. 1) is altered to the more classical ἠσθένει.

The story by which Mary is identified is that of her anointing Jesus, and wiping His feet with her hair, which Jn. tells

ἧς ὁ ἀδελφὸς Λάζαρος ἠσθένει. 3. ἀπέστειλαν οὖν αἱ ἀδελφαὶ πρὸς
αὐτὸν λέγουσαι Κύριε, ἴδε ὃν φιλεῖς ἀσθενεῖ. 4. ἀκούσας δὲ ὁ
Ἰησοῦς εἶπεν Αὕτη ἡ ἀσθένεια οὐκ ἔστιν πρὸς θάνατον ἀλλ' ὑπὲρ τῆς

in the next chapter. But this story is also told of the sinful
woman of Lk. 7[38]. Christian readers of the next generation
would not be helped by an explanatory note which might
equally be applied to two distinct women; and the conclusion
is inevitable that Jn. (or his editor) regarded Mary of Bethany
as the same person who is described by Lk. as ἁμαρτωλός.[1]
The easiest way to identify her for the reader is to recall the
singular gesture by which she was best known, and which she
had enacted not once only, but twice. She was the best-known
member of her family, and the note recalls that it was *her*
brother, Lazarus, who was sick.

It is worth observing, in view of the discrepancy between
Mk. 14[3] and Jn. 12[3], as to whether it was the *head* or the *feet*
of Jesus that Mary anointed, that this note evades the difficulty
by saying simply "anointed the Lord." ἀλείφειν, μύρον,
ἐκμάσσειν, θρίξ, are words common to this passage with both
Lk. 7[38] and Jn. 12[3]; and the reference is probably to both
incidents. ἐκμάσσειν is only found again in N.T. at 13[5], and
there, as in Lk. 7, Jn. 12, of wiping *feet*.

Μαριάμ, rather than Μαρία, seems to be the best-attested
spelling of Mary's name throughout Jn., although *here*
אADLWΘ have Μαρία, B 33 alone supporting Μαριάμ.[2] This
provides another reason for suspecting v. 2 to be non-
Johannine. Cf., however, v. 20, 12[3]; and see 19[25].

3. ἀπέστειλαν οὖν αἱ ἀδελφαὶ πρὸς αὐτόν. "So the sisters
sent to Him," *i.e.* to Jesus ; D *b c e* support πρὸς τὸν Ἰησοῦν.

κύριε. It is thus that the sisters address Jesus throughout
(vv. 21, 27, 32, 34, 39), although Martha speaks to Mary of
Jesus as ὁ διδάσκαλος (v. 28), and the disciples address Him as
Rabbi (v. 8). See the note on 1[38]; and cf. 4[1] 13[13].

ἴδε : a favourite word with Jn. (see on 1[29]).

ὃν φιλεῖς ἀσθενεῖ, "he whom thou lovest is sick." They
feel it unnecessary to send any explicit invitation to Jesus to
come and heal their brother: "Sufficit ut noueris. Non enim
amas et deseris " (Augustine).

ὃν φιλεῖς. So v. 36 ἴδε, πῶς ἐφίλει αὐτόν (cf. 20[2]). But at
v. 5 we have ἠγάπα ὁ Ἰησοῦς . . . τὸν Λάζαρον. There is no
real distinction in meaning between the two verbs. Cf. 3[35]
5[20], and note on 21[17]. See Introd., p. xxxvii n.

4. αὕτη ἡ ἀσθένεια οὐκ ἔστιν πρὸς θάνατον. This was the

---

[1] Cf. Introductory Note on the Anointing at Bethany (12[1-8]).

[2] See Westcott-Hort, Appendix, 156, for details as to the spelling.

δόξης τοῦ Θεοῦ, ἵνα δοξασθῇ ὁ Υἱὸς τοῦ Θεοῦ δι᾽ αὐτῆς.   5. ἠγάπα

comment of Jesus when the tidings of Lazarus' illness reached Him. It was not a direct reply to the sisters' message, and we do not know if it was reported to them (v. 40).

The constr. πρὸς θάνατον is unusual, occurring again in the N.T. only at 1 Jn. 5¹⁶ ἁμαρτία πρὸς θάνατον, and in the LXX at 4 Macc. 14⁴ 17¹, while εἰς θάνατον is common (cf. 2 Kings 20¹, where it is said of Hezekiah that he was sick εἰς θάνατον). If a distinction is to be drawn between the two constructions, perhaps " this sickness is not πρὸς θάνατον " is more reassuring than " this sickness is not εἰς θάνατον." The latter would mean that the sickness would not have death as its final issue; the former ought to mean that the sick person is not in danger at all, that his sickness is not " dangerous," as we would put it. Consequently the meaning that the disciples inevitably took from the words of Jesus was that Lazarus was not dead at the time of speaking, and further that Jesus was convinced he would recover. No doubt, the evangelist means his readers to understand that this was not the real meaning of Jesus' words (see v. 11). But it is strange that he should translate them by using πρός instead of εἰς ; for, in fact, Lazarus' sickness was πρὸς θάνατον, although it might plausibly be argued that it was not εἰς θάνατον, as death was not the final issue.

Jesus adds that this illness had come upon Lazarus ὑπὲρ τῆς δόξης τοῦ θεοῦ, " on behalf of God's glory," i.e. in order that the glory and power of God might be revealed. The attempt to give ὑπέρ a semi-sacrificial sense here, as if the sickness were a voluntary offering by Lazarus, is fanciful ὑπέρ is used exactly as in 1³⁰ 10¹¹, " on behalf of." The issue of the sickness and death of Lazarus was the revelation of the glory of God, as exhibited in his miraculous resuscitation. The miracle was more than a "wonder "; it was a "sign " of ἡ δόξα τοῦ θεοῦ. And so Martha was reminded, when it was over, that she had been told that she would see this glory (v. 40).

The glory of God was exhibited through the person and works of Jesus; this sickness, with its issue, had for its purpose ἵνα δοξασθῇ ὁ υἱὸς τοῦ θεοῦ, that He might be honoured by this revelation of His Father (cf. 8⁵⁴ ἔστιν ὁ πατήρ μου ὁ δοξάζων με). We have seen (on 7³⁹) that the supreme " glorification " of Jesus is identified by Jn. with the Passion and its sequel, and it has been thought by some that this too is the reference in the present passage. If so, ἵνα δοξασθῇ ὁ υἱὸς τοῦ θεοῦ would mean here that the final cause of Lazarus' sickness was that it might lead up to the Passion by making

δὲ ὁ Ἰησοῦς τὴν Μάρθαν καὶ τὴν ἀδελφὴν αὐτῆς καὶ τὸν Λάζαρον.

public the power of Jesus and thereby bringing the hostility of his enemies to a crisis (Westcott). But this is over subtle. The true parallel to 11[4b] is 8[54]. This revelation of "the glory of God" was that the Son might be honoured or "glorified" by so signal a mark of His Father's favour as the power to raise a dead man would exhibit. As in the O.T., "the glory of God" is the visible manifestation of His presence. See also on 9[3] 10[25] 14[13]; and cf. 17[1].

For the title "the Son of God," see on 1[34] and 5[25]. Only here and at 5[25] 10[36] is Jesus said to have used this title as descriptive of Himself.

5. Moffatt transposes this verse, placing it after the parenthetical v. 2; and this is the most natural position for it, as it then explains in proper sequence why it was that the sisters sent to Jesus the news that Lazarus was ill. Jesus was their friend, and they hoped that He would come and heal their sick brother. In the traditional position of v. 5, it seems to suggest as the reason why Jesus did not immediately leave Peræa and start for the sick man's house, that *because* He loved the household at Bethany, He stayed for two days longer where He was. That is, no doubt, a possible explanation of His action or delay, *sc.* that because He loved them, He wished to exhibit in their case the greatness of His power and the reach of His compassion. But, if that were so, He was content to leave the sisters in the agony of grief for three or four days, in order that the "glory of God" might be more signally vindicated in the end.

There is no textual authority for Moffatt's transposition of the text, and I have left v. 5 in its traditional position. It is possible, however, that v. 5 is an explanatory gloss added by an editor which has got into the wrong place (see 4[44] for a like case of displacement). Two small points suggest that v. 5 is not from the pen of the author of vv. 1, 3. In v. 1 we have *Mary and her sister Martha*, while in v. 5 we have the more usual order, *Martha and her sister*,[1] a sudden change (but cf. v. 19). Again, the verb twice used in this chapter for the affection which Jesus had for Lazarus is φιλεῖν (vv. 3, 36), while in v. 5 it is ἀγαπᾶν. We must not, indeed, sharply distinguish these verbs (see on 21[17]); but we should expect the same verb to be used in v. 3 and v. 5. It is possible that v. 5 is a non-Johannine gloss, which ought to be placed where Moffatt places it, after v. 2.

---

[1] This is the true reading, but Θ *fam.* 13 give in v. 5 τὴν Μαριὰμ καὶ τὴν ἀδελφὴν αὐτῆς Μάρθαν, being influenced by v. 1.

6. ὡς οὖν ἤκουσεν ὅτι ἀσθενεῖ, τότε μὲν ἔμεινεν ἐν ᾧ ἦν τόπῳ δύο ἡμέρας· 7. ἔπειτα μετὰ τοῦτο λέγει τοῖς μαθηταῖς Ἄγωμεν εἰς τὴν Ἰουδαίαν πάλιν. 8. λέγουσιν αὐτῷ οἱ μαθηταί Ῥαββεί, νῦν ἐζήτουν σε λιθάσαι οἱ Ἰουδαῖοι, καὶ πάλιν ὑπάγεις ἐκεῖ; 9. ἀπεκρίθη Ἰησοῦς

6. ὡς οὖν ἤκουσεν κτλ. οὖν is resumptive, and looks back to v. 4, " And so, when He heard, etc." It was because of His confidence that the sickness was not πρὸς θάνατον, and that the issue of it would be for the glory of God, that He did not hasten to the bedside of His friend. For ὡς οὖν, see on 4⁴⁰.

ὅτι is *recitantis*: what the messenger from Bethany had said was ἀσθενεῖ.

τότε μὲν ἔμεινεν κτλ. He remained where He was for two days. Jn. consistently represents Jesus as never being in haste. He always knew when the time to move had come (cf. 2⁴ 7⁶· ⁸).

Jn.'s tendency to indicate the time between one event and another has been already mentioned (see Introd., p. cii). He notes here that Jesus remained in His Peræan retreat for two days (cf. 4⁴⁰) after the condition of Lazarus had been reported. From Bethany or Bethabara beyond Jordan (see on 1²⁸), whatever its exact situation, it would be a long and rough day's walk to Bethany near Jerusalem, and the journey may well have occupied part of a second day. When Jesus reached the tomb, Lazarus had been dead more than three days (v. 39). Jn. may intend to convey that the patient was dead at the time that the message reached Jesus; but, on the other hand, Martha's words in v. 21 suggest that she thought that if Jesus had started at once, He would have arrived while Lazarus was yet alive.

7. ἔπειτα (only here in Jn.) μετὰ τοῦτο, i.e. *deinde postea.* μετὰ τοῦτο implies a short interval: cf. v. 11 and 2¹² 19²⁸. See Introd., p. cviii.

After μαθηταῖς, ΑΔΓΔ add αὐτοῦ, but אBLWΘ omit. For οἱ μαθηταί used absolutely, see on 2² ; and cf. vv. 8, 12, 54.

ἄγωμεν. This intransitive form occurs again 11¹⁵· ¹⁶ and 14³¹ (so Mk. 14⁴², Mt. 26⁴⁶): " let us go." So in Homer we have ἄγε used intransitively " go."

εἰς τὴν Ἰουδαίαν πάλιν, "back to Judæa," whence they had come to avoid the danger caused by the hostility of the Jews (10³⁹· ⁴⁰).

8. Ῥαββεί. So the disciples called Him. See on 1³⁸ for the use of this title in Jn.

νῦν κτλ., sc. " quite recently (10³¹· ³⁹), the Jews (see on 1¹⁹) were seeking to stone Thee " : cf. 7¹ 8⁵⁹.

καὶ πάλιν ὑπάγεις ἐκεῖ; "and are you going back there?"

Οὐχὶ δώδεκα ὧραί εἰσιν τῆς ἡμέρας; ἐάν τις περιπατῇ ἐν τῇ ἡμέρᾳ, οὐ προσκόπτει, ὅτι τὸ φῶς τοῦ κόσμου τούτου βλέπει· 10. ἐὰν δέ τις περιπατῇ ἐν τῇ νυκτί, προσκόπτει, ὅτι τὸ φῶς οὐκ ἔστιν ἐν αὐτῷ.

For the Johannine use of ὑπάγειν, see on 7³³. Probably their apprehension of danger was on their own account, as well as on that of their Master.

9. ἀπεκρίθη Ἰησοῦς. See on 1²⁹ for the omission of the article before Ἰησοῦς in this phrase.

οὐχὶ δώδεκα ὧραί εἰσιν τῆς ἡμέρας; " Are there not twelve hours in the day ? " That is, Jesus tells them that their anxiety is premature. The hour of danger had not yet come. Jesus never acted before the appropriate time (see on v. 6).

This saying is the counterpart of 9⁴. There Jesus had said that work must be done during the day, and that it could not be postponed until night without failure, and that this law applied to Him as well as to mankind at large. He implied that but a short time remained to Him. But in this passage the thought is different. The hour of His Passion was near, but it had not yet arrived. There was no need for undue haste. The " twelve hours " of His day were not yet exhausted.

For the twelve hours of the Jewish day, see on 1³⁹.

ἐάν τις περιπατῇ ἐν τῇ ἡμέρᾳ κτλ. We have already had the contrast between walking in the light and walking in darkness (see note on 8¹² for its significance). Here this solemn aphorism is put in connexion with what goes before. The disciples were apprehensive. But Jesus assured them that the night had not yet come. So long as men walk in the light of day they are safe, but it is the night that is the time of hazard.

Here, however, a mystical meaning lurks behind the literal meaning of the words employed. It is literally true that a man walking in the daytime does not stumble, because he sees **τὸ φῶς τοῦ κόσμου τούτου,** that is, the sun (see for the expression ὁ κόσμος οὗτος on 9³⁹). But Jesus had already spoken of Himself as the Light of the World (see on 8¹²), and the suggestion is the same as in the former passage, sc. that he who walks by the light that Jesus gives does not walk in darkness.

The answer of Jesus to the disciples, then, in these verses implies first that there is no danger yet, for the day—His day— is not yet over; and suggests also that danger need not be dreaded by those who follow Him on His appointed way.

10. ἐὰν δέ τις περιπατῇ ἐν τῇ νυκτί κτλ. In this second clause it is the mystical and not the literal sense which is most clearly expressed. For we should expect v. 10 to run, " If any one walk in the night, he stumbles because he has no

11. ταῦτα εἶπεν, καὶ μετὰ τοῦτο λέγει αὐτοῖς Λάζαρος ὁ φίλος ἡμῶν κεκοίμηται· ἀλλὰ πορεύομαι ἵνα ἐξυπνίσω αὐτόν.   12. εἶπαν οὖν οἱ

light," or, as it is expressed at 12³⁵ (a parallel passage), "He that walketh in the darkness knoweth not whither he goeth " (cf. 1 Jn. 2¹¹). But instead we have ὅτι τὸ φῶς οὐκ ἔστιν ἐν αὐτῷ (not ἐν αὐτῇ, which D reads in an attempt to simplify the passage). This departs from the literal application of the illustration of a guiding light, and directs the thought of the reader to the idea of spiritual enlightenment. Cf. 8¹² and Mt. 6²³. With the picture of one stumbling in the darkness, cf. Jer. 13¹⁶.

11. ταῦτα εἶπεν, i.e. vv. 9, 10, which but for this explicit statement might be treated as a comment of the evangelist (see on 3¹⁶) rather than as words spoken by Jesus on this occasion.

καὶ μετὰ τοῦτο. Some interval between vv. 8–10 and v. 11 is implied; see on v. 7 above.

Λάζαρος ὁ φίλος ἡμῶν. Lazarus was the friend of the disciples, as well as of the Master; and it is implied that if Jesus ventured into Judæa to visit him, they also ought to be ready to do so. Lazarus was within the circle of those whom Jesus called His "friends" (see 15¹⁴, Lk. 12⁴; and cf. v. 3 above).

κεκοίμηται, "has fallen asleep." The natural interpretation of this verb would be that put upon it by the disciples, sc. that the sick man had fallen into a refreshing slumber. In ordinary Greek, as throughout the LXX, κοιμᾶσθαι is generally used in this, its primary, meaning. But in poetry it is sometimes used of the sleep of death, e.g. in Homer, Il. xi. 241; in Job 3¹³ 14¹² 21¹³. ²⁶, Ezek. 32¹⁹. ²⁰. ²⁷, as well as in the oft-repeated phrase, "he slept with his fathers." Cf. also 2 Macc. 12⁴⁵. In the N.T. this euphemistic use is found 13 times, as against 3 occurrences of the verb in the sense of ordinary sleep (Mt. 28¹³, Lk. 22⁴⁵, Acts 12⁶). Although this use was not original to Christianity, or even to Judaism, κοιμᾶσθαι (and κοιμητήριον; see Moulton-Milligan, s.v.) came to be more frequently applied to the sleep of death after the Christian era than before.

The verb does not occur again in Jn.; but its interpretation by the disciples here as indicating physical sleep was no stupid misunderstanding but natural, and almost inevitable, having regard to the circumstances.

ἀλλὰ πορεύομαι ἵνα ἐξυπνίσω αὐτόν, "but I am going to wake him up." ἐξυπνίζω is a Hellenistic word, not occurring again in the N.T. We find it in the LXX (1 Kings 3¹⁵), and may especially note Job 14¹², where, as here, it is associated with

μαθηταὶ αὐτῷ Κύριε, εἰ κεκοίμηται, σωθήσεται. 13. εἰρήκει δὲ ὁ
Ἰησοῦς περὶ τοῦ θανάτου αὐτοῦ· ἐκεῖνοι δὲ ἔδοξαν ὅτι περὶ τῆς
κοιμήσεως τοῦ ὕπνου λέγει. 14. τότε οὖν εἶπεν αὐτοῖς ὁ Ἰησοῦς
παρρησίᾳ Λάζαρος ἀπέθανεν, 15. καὶ χαίρω δι᾽ ὑμᾶς, ἵνα πιστεύσητε,
ὅτι οὐκ ἤμην ἐκεῖ· ἀλλὰ ἄγωμεν πρὸς αὐτόν. 16. εἶπεν οὖν Θωμᾶς

κοιμᾶσθαι, used of the sleep of death: ἄνθρωπος δὲ κοιμηθεὶς
. . . οὐκ ἐξυπνισθήσονται ἐξ ὕπνου αὐτῶν.

12. εἶπαν οὖν οἱ μαθηταὶ αὐτῷ. So BC*Θ against the rec.
οἱ μαθηταὶ αὐτοῦ : אDW have αὐτῷ οἱ μαθηταί.

κύριε. For this mode of address, see on 1²⁸ and 13¹³.

εἰ κεκοίμηται, σωθήσεται, " if he has fallen asleep, he will
recover." They understood Jesus to mean that the sick man
had fallen into a natural sleep—not the sleep of death. This
was a favourable symptom, and suggested that Lazarus would
get well. It puzzled them to think that Jesus would wish to
wake him from health-giving sleep. No doubt, they were glad
of another argument by which they might dissuade their Master
from facing the dangers of Judæa. The journey would be to
no good purpose.

σωθήσεται, " he will get well." For this use of σώζειν, see
on 3¹⁷.

13. εἰρήκει δὲ ὁ Ἰησοῦς κτλ., " But Jesus had been speaking about his death." This is one of those parenthetical
comments which are so frequent in the Fourth Gospel (see
Introd., p. xxxiv), the writer calling attention to a misunderstanding by the disciples of the words of Jesus. They thought
that Jesus was using the word κοιμᾶσθαι of natural sleep,
whereas he was really using it of death.

ἐκεῖνοι δὲ ἔδοξαν κτλ., " but *they* thought, etc.," ἐκεῖνος
being employed to mark distinctly the subject of the verb.
It is often used by Jn. to make his point, just as an English
writer may resort to italics for the sake of clearness (see on 1⁸).

κοίμησις does not occur again in the N.T. It is used
euphemistically at Ecclus. 46¹⁹ 48¹³ of the sleep of death, but
not elsewhere in the LXX in any sense.

14. τότε οὖν κτλ. " At this point, Jesus said plainly,
Lazarus died "; He no longer spoke enigmatically to the
disciples. For παρρησίᾳ, see on 7⁴.

15. καὶ χαίρω δι᾽ ὑμᾶς, ἵνα πιστεύσητε, ὅτι οὐκ ἤμην ἐκεῖ,
" And I rejoice for your sakes that I was not there, so that
you may believe." The implication is that the recovery of
Lazarus from death would be a more remarkable " sign "
than his recovery from a sick-bed would have been. The
disciples were already " believers," or they would not have been
" disciples " ; but faith is always growing, if it be alive, and

ὁ λεγόμενος Δίδυμος τοῖς συνμαθηταῖς Ἄγωμεν καὶ ἡμεῖς ἵνα ἀποθάνωμεν μετ' αὐτοῦ.

the Twelve knew that theirs was susceptible of increase (cf. Lk. 17[5]). Although His friend has died and the sisters are in grief, Jesus rejoices because of His confidence not only that Lazarus will be called back to life, but because this sign of power will increase the faith of His disciples, and promote the glory of God (v. 4).

Abbott (*Diat.* 2099) translates, " I am glad on account of you, that ye may believe, *because* I was not there," which is, indeed, a possible rendering, but unnecessarily subtle.

ἵνα πιστεύσητε is, as it were, in parenthesis, explaining why Jesus was glad that He was not present when Lazarus was still alive. For πιστεύειν used absolutely, as here, the object of belief being left unexpressed, see on 1[7].

Bengel notes that no one is said to have died in the *presence* of Jesus, and suggests that perhaps death was impossible where He was: " Cum decoro divino pulchre congruit, quod praesente uitae duce nemo unquam legitur mortuus." But we cannot infer from the narrative that Jn. means to hint at this.

χαίρω is not elsewhere placed in the lips of Jesus, but He speaks of His joy (ἡ χαρὰ ἡ ἐμή) at 15[11] 17[13]; and at 4[36] we have ἵνα ὁ σπείρων ὁμοῦ χαίρῃ καὶ ὁ θερίζων, where He refers to Himself as the Sower. In all these passages, it will be noticed that His rejoicing is connected with the fulfilment of His mission. So also at Lk. 10[21] it is said of Him ἠγαλλιάσατο τῷ Πνεύματι τῷ Ἁγίῳ, because of the acceptance of His message by the Seventy, and of their success. And the rejoicing of the shepherd, when the lost sheep is found (Mt. 18[13], Lk. 15[6]), is, in like manner, drawn out by the happy issue of his labours.

ἀλλὰ ἄγωμεν πρὸς αὐτόν, "but, anyway, let us go to him," as He had said before ἄγωμεν εἰς τὴν Ἰουδαίαν (v. 7, where see note on ἄγωμεν). The repetition of this invitation, even though Lazarus was now dead and a visit to his bedside for the purpose of healing him was now impossible, seems to have convinced the hesitating disciples that Jesus had some great purpose in view when He proposed to return to a place where He and they would be in danger. At all events, no further objection is raised, and the loyal outburst of Thomas, " Let us also go, that we may die with Him," is acted on by all.

16. Θωμᾶς ὁ λεγόμενος Δίδυμος. םאֹת is a "twin" (found only in Gen. 25[24] 38[27], Cant. 4[5] 7[3], always in the plural, and always rendered by δίδυμα or δίδυμοι), and of this Θωμᾶς is a

transliteration. Three times in Jn. (cf. 20²⁴ 21²) to this name
the note is added ὁ λεγόμενος Δίδυμος, an appellation which is
not found in the Synoptists. This suggests (see on 4²⁵) that
the apostle was called " Didymus " in Greek circles; if Jn.
only meant to interpret *Thomas*, he would probably have
written ὃ ἑρμηνεύεται Δίδυμος (as at 1⁴²).[1]

The personal name of the apostle is given as *Judas* in
the *Acta Thomæ* and elsewhere; and the attribution of this
name to him led afterwards to the attempted identification of
Thomas with " Judas of James " and " Judas the Lord's
brother."

The character of Thomas comes out as clearly in the Fourth
Gospel as does that of Nicodemus (see on 3¹). The notices of
him here, at 14⁵ and 20²⁴ᶠ·, are remarkably consistent, one with
the other, and reveal a man whose temper of mind we can
thoroughly understand. Thomas always looks at the dark
side of things, and is a pessimist by disposition, while entirely
loyal to his convictions and ready to act on them at all cost.
He is a man of independent mind who says what he thinks, and
does not wait for the promptings of others. Here Thomas
foresaw only too clearly that Jesus was going to His death,
and he realised that to enter Judæa as His disciple was to risk
the same fate. But Jesus was his Master, and he would not
draw back when he found that Jesus was resolved to go back
to Judæa. εἶπεν οὖν Θωμᾶς κτλ., " Thomas *thereupon* said, Let
us also go (for ἄγωμεν, see on v. 7) that we may die with
Him."

This challenge was addressed to his " fellow-disciples."
συνμαθηταί does not occur again in the N.T., but as used here
it suggests the Twelve, of whom Thomas was one, rather than
any outer circle of μαθηταί (see on 2²). It is not implied that
all of the Twelve were present during the retreat to Peræa
or at Bethany when Lazarus was recovered from the tomb;
but συνμαθηταῖς suggests that the disciples who were with Jesus
on this occasion were of the inner circle.

It is probable that Peter was not among them. He is not
mentioned once in Part II. of the Gospel, and there is no indication in Mk. (which is thought to depend on Peter's information) that Peter knew anything about this Jerusalem ministry.
Probably the Galilæan disciples were often at their homes
when Jesus was in Judæa or in Peræa. If Peter had been
present, we might have expected that he would take the lead [2]

---

[1] The extraordinary statement in the Greek *Acta Thomæ* (§ 31)
that he was the twin brother of Jesus seems to be due to a misunderstanding of the original Syriac.

[2] Cf. Introd., p. clxxxiii.

17. Ἐλθὼν οὖν ὁ Ἰησοῦς εὗρεν αὐτὸν τέσσαρας ἤδη ἡμέρας ἔχοντα ἐν τῷ μνημείῳ. 18. ἦν δὲ Βηθανία ἐγγὺς τῶν Ἱεροσολύμων ὡς ἀπὸ σταδίων δεκαπέντε. 19. πολλοὶ δὲ ἐκ τῶν Ἰουδαίων

in assuring Jesus that His disciples would not abandon Him, just as he was foremost when the danger was even nearer (13³⁷). From the Synoptists we should not have gathered that Thomas was one of the leaders of the apostolic company; but the notices of him in Jn. (see above; and also 21², where he is named immediately after Peter) indicate that he was prominent among them, so that the statement that he acted as spokesman for the rest on this occasion is not surprising.

Jesus goes to Bethany : His conversation with Martha
(vv. 17–27)

17. ἐλθὼν οὖν κτλ., " Jesus, then, having come, etc." οὖν is resumptive, not causal.

εὗρεν αὐτὸν τέσσαρας ἤδη ἡμέρας ἔχοντα κτλ. He found Lazarus had been already four days in the tomb. For the constr. ἡμέρας ἔχειν, see on 5⁵. ἤδη is om. by A*D, and its position varies in other MSS., but the weight of authority is in favour of its retention.

For the " four days," see on v. 6 above; and cf. v. 39. The burial would have taken place as soon as possible after death (cf. Acts 5⁶).

Augustine (in loc.) finds allegory in the "four days ": one day of death for original sin, one for violation of natural law, one for breaking the law of Moses, and one for transgressing the Gospel. This is no more, and no less, fantastic than the efforts of modern expositors to find allegory in Jn.'s narrative.

18. Moffatt places vv. 18, 19, between v. 30 and v. 31, where they would fit very well. But there is no insuperable difficulty in their traditional position, and I do not venture to alter it.

ἦν δὲ Βηθανία κτλ. Jn. alone of the evangelists uses ἦν in this way (cf. 18¹ 19⁴¹, and perhaps 6¹⁰); Meyer suggested that it is employed by him thus instead of the present ἐστί because he is writing after the devastation of Jerusalem and its suburbs. But if (as we hold) his narrative reproduces the reminiscences of the aged apostle John, looking back on many years, ἦν is more natural than ἐστί, without assuming any allusion to the fall of Jerusalem. See on 5².

The rec. inserts ἡ before Βηθανία, with א°ACDLWΘ; but א*B om. ἡ, as in v. 1.

For the form τῶν Ἱεροσολύμων, see on 1¹⁹.

ὡς ἀπὸ σταδίων δεκαπέντε, "about fifteen furlongs." Bethany

ἐληλύθεισαν πρὸς τὴν Μάρθαν καὶ Μαριάμ, ἵνα παραμυθήσωνται

is a little less than 2 miles from the city. The constr. of ἀπό with the genitive to indicate distance is not necessarily a Latinism, as, e.g., *a millibus passuum duobus* (Cæsar, *Bell. Gall.* ii. 7). It occurs again at 21⁸; cf. Rev. 14²⁰, and see Hermas, *Vis.* iv. 1, οὕτω γὰρ ἦν ἀπ᾽ ἐμοῦ ὡς ἀπὸ σταδίου.

19. πολλοὶ δέ. So אBCDLWΘ, as against the rec. καὶ πολλοί (ΑΓΔ).

ἐκ τῶν Ἰουδαίων, *i.e.* of the citizens of Jerusalem. οἱ Ἰουδαῖοι often represents in Jn. the Jews who were hostile to Jesus (see on 1¹⁹ 5¹⁰); but here that suggestion is not present.

Jerusalem being so near (v. 18), it was natural that many friends from the city should come to condole with Martha and Mary on the death of their brother. Lightfoot gives (*Hor. Hebr.*, in loc.) curious details about the ceremonial which was customary at these mournful gatherings. The first three days after death were kept with severity, the next four days with less strictness, the period of observance lasting for thirty days altogether. Cf. for the " seven days of mourning for the dead " (Ecclus. 22¹²), 1 Sam. 31¹³, Job 2¹³, Judith 16²⁴; and for the visits of neighbours to console, 2 Esd. 10².

παραμυθεῖσθαι, " to comfort," is found in the Greek Bible only here, v. 31, 1 Thess. 2¹¹ 5¹⁴, and 2 Macc. 15⁹.

πρὸς τὴν Μάρθαν καὶ Μαριάμ is the best-attested reading (אBC*L), but the article should be prefixed to both or to neither of the names. D has πρὸς Μάρθαν καὶ Μαριάμ. Syr. sin. seems, on the other hand, to presuppose the article in both places, and reads " went forth *to Bethany* that they might comfort Martha and Mary," omitting " concerning their brother." See on v. 24 for Jn.'s consistent use of ἡ Μάρθα, ἡ Μαριάμ.

The rec. text, with ΑC³ΓΔΘ, has ἐληλύθεισαν πρὸς τὰς περὶ Μάρθαν καὶ Μαριάμ, which ought to mean " came to the women of the household of Martha and Mary"; but it can hardly be genuine. Perhaps τὰς περί came in from [αὐ]τὰς περί in the next line. After ἀδελφοῦ ΑCΓΔ add αὐτῶν, but om. אBDLWΘ.

20. The congruity of the characters of Martha and Mary, as suggested by what we read of them in Lk. 10³⁸ᶠ·, with what Jn. tells in this chapter about their demeanour is remarkable.[1] Martha is the busy housewife who, as the mistress of the house, is the first to be told of the approach of Jesus (v. 20). She goes to meet Him, and expresses at once her own conviction and that of Mary (vv. 21, 32), that if He had been present, Lazarus would not have died. She is puzzled by the enigmatical words

[1] See Lightfoot, *Biblical Essays*, p. 38.

αὐτὰς περὶ τοῦ ἀδελφοῦ. 20. ἡ οὖν Μάρθα ὡς ἤκουσεν ὅτι Ἰησοῦς
ἔρχεται, ὑπήντησεν αὐτῷ· Μαριὰμ δὲ ἐν τῷ οἴκῳ ἐκαθέζετο. 21. εἶπεν
οὖν ἡ Μάρθα πρὸς Ἰησοῦν Κύριε, εἰ ἦς ὧδε, οὐκ ἂν ἀπέθανεν ὁ

of hope which Jesus addresses to her (v. 23), and supposes
that He is giving the usual orthodox consolation (v. 24). She
does not understand what He then says (vv. 25, 26); but her
faith in Him as the Messiah is strong, and of this she assures
Him (v. 27), although she does not expect that He can do
anything *now* to restore her brother. Then she goes to tell
her sister that Jesus has arrived and is asking for her.

Before Martha told her, Mary had not heard of the arrival
of Jesus (v. 29): she was seated inside the house (v. 20) as a
mourner, and it had been to her that the condolences of the
friends who had come from Jerusalem were specially addressed
(v. 45). But as soon as she learnt that Jesus had come, she
got up hastily and left the house without acquainting the
mourners of her purpose in going out (v. 29). Her friends
thought that she was going to wail at the tomb (v. 30). When
she met Jesus, she fell at His feet (unlike her more staid sister),
greeting him with the same assurance that Martha had given
(v. 32), but wailing unrestrainedly (v. 33). Her cries of grief
seem to have affected the human heart of Jesus as the grave
sorrow of Martha did not do (v. 33). But, as they proceed to
the tomb, Martha is with them, and, practical woman as she is,
demurs to its being opened (v. 39). Throughout, her figure
is in sharp contrast with that of her more emotional sister.
See further, Introd., p. clxxxv.

ἡ οὖν Μάρθα ὡς ἤκουσεν ὅτι κτλ. She is the first to be told,
as the mistress of the house. ὅτι is *recitantis*: what was said
to her was Ἰησοῦς ἔρχεται.

The rec. has ὁ Ἰησ., but om. ὁ אABCDW. See on 1[29].

ὑπήντησεν αὐτῷ, "met Him," but without any display of
emotion such as Mary exhibited. She met Jesus before He
entered the village (see v. 30).

ἐν τῷ οἴκῳ ἐκαθέζετο, "she was seated in the house"; see
on 4[6] for ἐκαθέζετο. It was customary for mourners to be
seated when receiving the condolences of their friends; see
Job 2[8, 13], and cf. Ezek. 8[14]. Sitting down was also a common
posture for mourners among the Romans. It was adopted,
e.g., by Cato after Pharsalia, and Varro after Cannæ (Plutarch,
Cato, 56).

Μαρία is attested by most authorities, but Θ 33 give Μαριάμ
(see also 12[3]), in accordance with the general usage of Jn.
(see on v. 2).

21. εἶπεν οὖν (οὖν being resumptive) ἡ Μάρθα πρὸς Ἰησοῦν.

ἀδελφός μου.   **22.** καὶ νῦν οἶδα ὅτι ὅσα ἂν αἰτήσῃ τὸν Θεὸν δώσει

Cf. 2³ for the constr. λέγειν πρός τινα. The rec., with AC²DLWΘ, inserts τόν before Ἰησοῦν, but om. ℵBC*. See on 1²⁹.

κύριε. See on v. 3.

εἰ ἦς ὧδε κτλ., " if thou hadst been here, my brother had not died." Mary greets Jesus with the same words (v. 32). No doubt, Martha and Mary had said this to each other many times during the last four days. The greeting may imply a reproach, suggesting that if Jesus had started immediately after He heard of Lazarus' illness, He would have kept him from death (see on v. 6). On the other hand, the sisters do not say " if thou hadst *come* here," but " if thou hadst *been* here," which may only imply wistful regret.

ἀπέθανεν. So ℵBC*DLW, but AC³ΓΔ have ἐτεθνήκει. Θ has τεθνήκει.

22. The rec. inserts ἀλλά before καὶ νῦν: om. ℵ*BC*. Jn. often uses καί adversatively (see on 1¹⁰), and ἀλλά is not needed here.[1] " Even now (although my brother is dead) I know that whatsoever thou shalt ask of God, God will give it thee." This is a deeper confidence than that which recognises the efficacy of the prayers of any good man (see 9³¹). Martha wistfully expresses faith in Jesus not only as her friend, but as the Son of God (v. 27). She understands, though dimly, that He stands in a special relation to God; and the repetition of ὁ θεός at the end of the sentence is emphatic. Perhaps His remark in v. 4 had been reported to her.

ὅσα ἂν αἰτήσῃ τὸν θεόν. Martha used, however, a verb to describe the prayers of Jesus which (according to Jn.) Jesus never used of them. αἰτεῖν is often used in the Gospels of *men's* prayers to God, and Jesus uses it thus at Jn. 14¹³ 15¹⁶ 16²³, but the word that He uses of His own prayers is ἐρωτᾶν. In Jn. (and in Jn. only) ἐρωτᾶν is used of prayer to God; and in the Gospel it is not generally used of the prayers of men, but of the prayers of Jesus (14¹⁶ 16²⁶ 17⁹·¹⁵·²⁰). Too much, however, must not be made of this usage, for the distinction between αἰτεῖν and ἐρωτᾶν had almost disappeared in later Greek (cf. Acts 3²·³), and at 1 Jn. 5¹⁶ ἐρωτᾶν is used of the prayer of Christians. See further on 16²³. It is remarkable that the words προσεύχεσθαι, παρακαλεῖν, and δεῖσθαι, which are all used elsewhere of prayer, do not occur in Jn.

But Martha, although she uses a word about the prayers of Jesus which He never applies to them, is right in substance;

---

[1] Abbott (*Diat.* 1915) prefers to take καὶ νῦν as at 14²⁹ 17⁵, indicating as it were a last word on the subject ; cf. Deut. 10¹², Ps. 39⁷.

σοι ὁ Θεός. 23. λέγει αὐτῇ ὁ Ἰησοῦς Ἀναστήσεται ὁ ἀδελφός σου.
24. λέγει αὐτῷ ἡ Μάρθα Οἶδα ὅτι ἀναστήσεται ἐν τῇ ἀναστάσει ἐν τῇ
ἐσχάτῃ ἡμέρᾳ. 25. εἶπεν αὐτῇ ὁ Ἰησοῦς Ἐγώ εἰμι ἡ ἀνάστασις καὶ

and her confession is a true, if imperfect, statement of what
Jesus says Himself at v. 41.

23. ἀναστήσεται ὁ ἀδελφός σου. This must often have
been said both to Martha and Mary during the past four
days ; it was (and is) a commonplace of consolation in bereavement offered by friends. By the first century, belief in
the resurrection, at any rate of good men, was widely spread
among the Jews (see on 5²⁸). The doctrine is plainly expressed
in the *Psalms of Solomon* (about 80 B.C.): οἱ δὲ φοβούμενοι
κύριον ἀναστήσονται εἰς ζωὴν αἰώνιον (iii. 16). And Jesus com-
mends this assurance to Martha as a truth which should
assuage her grief. A doctrine which is trite may, nevertheless,
be both true and important.

24. Martha's reply is not sceptical or querulous. She
does not deny the tremendous doctrine of resurrection at the
Last Day. She replies, wistfully enough, that she knows it
and accepts it. But, like many another mourner, she fails to
derive much immediate consolation from it. The Last Day
seems very far off. Meanwhile, where is her brother ? And
what are the conditions of this Resurrection ? What *is* the
Resurrection ?

The answer of Jesus is unexpected indeed. " *I* am the
Resurrection ": the soul that has touched me has touched
life; and the life of God is eternal. That is the whole answer.
And Martha, not fully understanding it, recognises that He
who spoke to her, spoke with an awful prescience, as befitted
Him in whom she saw the Messiah.

λέγει αὐτῷ ἡ Μάρθα. The article, which is omitted by
אAC³ΓΔW, must be retained with BC*DLΘ. Throughout the
chapter (except at vv. 1, 39, which are not true exceptions),
Jn. writes ἡ Μάρθα. See on vv. 2, 20.

For the doctrine of the Last Things in Jn., see Introd.,
p. clviii; and for the phrase ἡ ἐσχάτη ἡμέρα, which is peculiar
to Jn., see on 6³⁹. For the word ἀνάστασις, used of a resurrection from death, see on 5²⁸.

25. ἐγώ εἰμι ἡ ἀνάστασις καὶ ἡ ζωή. For the form of
this solemn pronouncement, ἐγώ εἰμι . . ., and for the claim
to an equality with God which is involved in such a way of
speaking, see Introd., p. cxix.

For the Divine prerogative of Jesus as a " quickener " of
the dead, see 5²¹ and the note there. It is asserted again in
the proclamation, four times repeated, ἀναστήσω αὐτὸ [ἐν] τῇ

ἐσχάτῃ ἡμέρᾳ (see note on 6³⁹).   Here, what is said goes beyond
even that great assurance.

All the great similitudes by which Jesus describes Himself
in the Fourth Gospel are introduced by the opening phrase
ἐγώ εἰμι, which marks the style of Deity (see Introd., p. cxviii).
But ἐγώ εἰμι ἡ ἀνάστασις differs from the other pronouncements in this respect, that it is *not* a similitude.   When Jesus
is represented as saying that He is the Bread of Life, or the
Light of the World, or the Door, or the Way, or the True Vine,
or the Good Shepherd, every one understands that these are
only figures of speech, used to illustrate and explain that He
strengthens and guides mankind.   Here, however, in reply to
Martha's allusion to the Resurrection at the Last Day, Jesus
uses no explanatory figure of speech.   "I am the Resurrection"
is not a similitude; it is the reference to Himself of what
Martha had said about the final resurrection.   The sentence is
comparable to ἐγώ εἰμι ὁ μαρτυρῶν περὶ ἐμαυτοῦ (8¹⁸), rather
than to any of the so-called similitudes; but it is more difficult
to interpret.   For how can a person represent an event in the
future?   Yet this is what is asserted.   ἡ ἀνάστασις in v. 25
must refer back to ἡ ἀνάστασις in v. 24.   Jesus does not say ἐγώ
εἰμι ἀνάστασις (without the article), or identify Himself with the
act or process of "rising again"; but He diverts the thought
of Martha, as it were, from the Resurrection at the Last Day,
which she feels is very far distant, to the Resurrection of which
He is potentially the Source as well as the Agent.

"I will raise him up at the Last Day."   That is a frequent
theme of the Fourth Gospel (see on 6³⁹).   But, if Jesus had
said no more on the subject, it would have postponed the possibility of resurrection to the new and heavenly life until the day
of the Final Assize.   And it is equally, and more particularly, a
doctrine of the Fourth Gospel, that as men are judged *now*, so
the entrance on the ζωὴ αἰώνιος is a present possibility (see
Introd., p. clx).   Jesus is the Door to the Kingdom, *i.e.* to the
enjoyment of "eternal life"; and it is through Him that man
enters into its possession here and now.

Thus, in vv. 24, 25, the old Jewish and the new Christian
eschatology are explicitly confronted with each other.   Jn.
never represents Jesus as denying the Jewish doctrine of a Last
Judgment; but he perpetually represents Him as insisting
upon the judgment of the present hour, not pronounced by a
fiat of external authority, but determined by the man's own self
and his relation to God in Christ (see on 3¹⁸).

So ἐγώ εἰμι ἡ ἀνάστασις is meant to convey to Martha,
not indeed a rebuke for her belief in the General Resurrection
at last, but an assurance that the "rising again" of believers

ἡ ζωή· ὁ πιστεύων εἰς ἐμὲ κἂν ἀποθάνῃ ζήσεται, 26. καὶ πᾶς ὁ ζῶν

in Him is not to be postponed until then.   If a man believe
in Him, although his body dies yet his true self shall live (v. 25).
Or, as it may be put in other words, no believer in Jesus shall
ever die, so far as his spirit is concerned (v. 26).   The consolation which Jesus offers to those mourning the death of a Christian believer is *not* that their friend will rise again at some
distant day when the dead shall be raised by a catastrophic
act of God (however true that may be), but that the Christian
believer *never* dies, his true life is never extinguished.   " Youɪ
friend is alive now; for in me he touched the life of God
which is eternal; in me he had already risen, before his body
perished."   This is the Johannine doctrine of life (see Introd.,
p. clxi); it is also the doctrine of Paul (cf. Col. 3¹).

Neither Jn. nor Paul discuss or contemplate the future life
of those who are not " in Christ."   The assurance of life, here
and hereafter, in the Fourth Gospel, is for all "believers ";
and in this passage no others are in view.

καὶ ἡ ζωή.   This second clause in the great pronouncement
of Jesus is omitted by Syr. sin., and also by Cyprian (*de Mortal.*
21), who quotes these verses in the form: " Ego sum Resurrectio.   Qui credit in me, licet moriatur, uiuet; et omnis qui
uiuit et credit in me non morietur in aeternum."   Cyprian
appears to have missed the distinction between the two clauses
25*b* and 26, and he may have omitted *et uita*, not perceiving
that the words are essential, if what follows is to be understood.
But this does not explain the omission in Syr. sin.   All other
authorities have the words καὶ ἡ ζωή, which are indispens-
able for the argument.

Jesus is not only the Resurrection, and thus the pledge and
the source of the believer's revival after death; but He is the
Life, for this revival is unending.   In the two sentences which
follow, the twofold presentation of Jesus as the Resurrection
and as the Life is expanded and explained.   He is the Resurrection, and therefore the believer in Him, though he die, yet
shall live again.   He is the Life, and therefore the believer in
Him, who has been " raised from the dead " and is spiritually
alive, shall never die.   See further on v. 26.

That Jesus is the Life is, in one sense, the main theme
of the Fourth Gospel.   Cf. 1⁴ 6⁵⁷ 14⁶ 20³¹; and see Introd.,
p. clxi.

ὁ πιστεύων εἰς ἐμέ κτλ., " he who believes in me " (see on
1¹² for the constr. πιστεύειν εἰς, and cf. 9³⁵) " even if he die
(*sc.* physically), yet shall he live " (*sc.* spiritually, in the spiritual
body, as Paul has it).   So it has been said already (3³⁶).

καὶ πιστεύων εἰς ἐμὲ οὐ μὴ ἀποθάνῃ εἰς τὸν αἰῶνα· πιστεύεις τοῦτο;

Westcott compares Philo's saying that " the wise man who appears to have died in respect of this corruptible life, lives in respect of the incorruptible life " (*quod det. pot.* 15). But the distinctive feature of the Johannine teaching is that the privilege of the immortal, spiritual life is for him who " believes in Christ," and so has touched the life of God.

26. καὶ πᾶς ὁ ζῶν κτλ. The verse is susceptible of two meanings. (1) If πᾶς ὁ ζῶν is understood as meaning " every living man," *sc.* living in this earthly life (cf. ἐνώπιον παντὸς ζῶντος, Tob. 13⁴), then v. 26 is but the repetition in other words of what has already been said in v. 25, " no living man who believes in me shall ever die." Such repetition is quite in the Johannine style (see 3³·⁵), and it gives a good sense here. (2) But inasmuch as ζήσεται in v. 25 refers to spiritual life, the life of the believer after the death of the body, it is preferable to take ζῶν in v. 26 as having the same reference, and to treat v. 26 as continuing the topic of v. 25, but not repeating it. " Every one who is living (*sc.* in the heavenly life) and a believer in me shall never die." Verse 25 gives only the promise of life after physical death ; v. 26 gives the assurance of that future life being immortal. For this use of ζῶν as indicating one who is living, not on earth, but in the spiritual world, cf. the saying of Jesus to the Sadducees, that God is not the God of the dead, but of the living (ζώντων, Mk. 12²⁷ and parallels).

For this use of εἰς τὸν αἰῶνα, " shall never die," cf. 4¹⁴, and esp. 8⁵¹.

It should be observed that vv. 25, 26, do not suggest to Martha that Lazarus will live again *on earth.* They are general pronouncements applying to every believer in Jesus, and the emphasis is laid on the words ὁ πιστεύων εἰς ἐμέ. It is this essential condition of life in its deepest sense that is proclaimed to Martha. She is asked if she believes it, and she says " Yes "; but her answer does not indicate that she understood what was involved.

27. Martha's reply is a confession of Jesus as the Messiah. It hardly goes farther; although, in terms, it embraces all that Jn. hopes his readers will reach, *sc.* that full faith which leads to life (20³¹). She hastens to summon Mary, who may be expected to understand the mysterious sayings of Jesus better than she (cf. Lk. 10³⁹).

Ναί. Cf. 21¹⁵·¹⁶ and Mk. 7²⁸. She acquiesces in the truth of what Jesus had said, because she believed Him to be the Christ.

κύριε. See on v. 3.

27. λέγει αὐτῷ Ναί, Κύριε· ἐγὼ πεπίστευκα ὅτι σὺ εἶ ὁ Χριστὸς ὁ Υἱὸς τοῦ Θεοῦ ὁ εἰς τὸν κόσμον ἐρχόμενος.

28. Καὶ τοῦτο εἰποῦσα ἀπῆλθεν καὶ ἐφώνησεν Μαριὰμ τὴν ἀδελφὴν αὐτῆς λάθρα εἰποῦσα Ὁ Διδάσκαλος πάρεστιν καὶ φωνεῖ σε.

29. ἐκείνη δὲ ὡς ἤκουσεν, ἠγέρθη ταχὺ καὶ ἤρχετο πρὸς αὐτόν.

ἐγὼ πεπίστευκα. With the perfect tense cf. 6⁶⁹ and 1 Jn. 4¹⁶; ἐγώ is emphatic. Certainly Martha accepts the word of Jesus as true, for she has believed for some time past in His Messiahship. ὅτι σὺ εἶ ὁ Χριστός. For the form of the confession σὺ εἶ, cf. 1⁴⁹ 6⁶⁹, Mk. 8²⁹, Mt. 16¹⁶.

ὁ υἱὸς τοῦ θεοῦ—a recognised title of Messiah. See on 1³⁴ for its usage and significance. Cf. the note on 6⁶⁹ for the confession of Jesus as the Christ by Peter; and see further on v. 40. Note that the exact terms, ὁ χριστός, ὁ υἱὸς τοῦ θεοῦ, appear together again at 20³¹, where Jn. defines the faith which he aims to inspire in his readers.

ὁ εἰς τὸν κόσμον ἐρχόμενος. This is the way in which the coming Prophet was described in popular discourse (see 6¹⁴, Mt. 11³). Jesus used the expression of Himself more than once (9³⁹ 16²⁸ 18³⁷).

Mary, being informed of Jesus' presence, hastens to speak to Him (vv. 28-32)

28. τοῦτο εἰποῦσα. This is the true reading, with אBCLW, rather than ταῦτα of ΑΔΓΔΘ. Martha said one thing only in response to Jesus' words of mystery; she did not make a speech.

She called (ἐφώνησεν) "Mary." Μαριάμ does not take the article here, suggesting that the actual name was called out by Martha.

λάθρα, "secretly," presumably because she wished Mary to see Jesus privately, without the crowd of mourning friends being present. However, this did not succeed, for they followed Mary out of the house (v. 31). λάθρα occurs elsewhere in N.T. at Mt. 1¹⁹ 2⁷, Acts 16³⁷. D reads σιωπῇ, which gives the same sense.

ὁ διδάσκαλος. So they called Jesus among themselves, although they addressed Him as κύριε. See on 1³⁸ 13¹³ ; and cf. 20¹⁶.

καὶ φωνεῖ σε. No mention has been made hitherto of the desire of Jesus to see Mary.

29. ἐκείνη δέ. δέ should be retained with אBC*LW. ἐκείνη designates the person who has just been mentioned (see on 1⁸).

ἠγέρθη ταχὺ καὶ ἤρχετο πρὸς αὐτόν. With her natural impul-

30. οὔπω δὲ ἐληλύθει ὁ Ἰησοῦς εἰς τὴν κώμην, ἀλλ᾽ ἦν ἔτι ἐν τῷ τόπῳ ὅπου ὑπήντησεν αὐτῷ ἡ Μάρθα. 31. οἱ οὖν Ἰουδαῖοι οἱ ὄντες μετ᾽ αὐτῆς ἐν τῇ οἰκίᾳ καὶ παραμυθούμενοι αὐτήν, ἰδόντες τὴν Μαριὰμ ὅτι ταχέως ἀνέστη καὶ ἐξῆλθεν, ἠκολούθησαν αὐτῇ, δόξαντες ὅτι ὑπάγει εἰς τὸ μνημεῖον ἵνα κλαύσῃ ἐκεῖ. 32. ἡ οὖν Μαριὰμ ὡς ἦλθεν ὅπου ἦν Ἰησοῦς, ἰδοῦσα αὐτὸν ἔπεσεν αὐτοῦ πρὸς τοὺς πόδας, λέγουσα αὐτῷ Κύριε, εἰ ἦς ὧδε, οὐκ ἄν μου ἀπέθανεν ὁ ἀδελφός.

siveness (see Introductory Note on 12$^{1-8}$), Mary rose up quickly from the seat of mourning (see on v. 20), and went to meet Jesus, as she had been bidden to do. The rec. (with AΘ) has ἐγείρεται . . . ἔρχεται, but the aorist and imperfect tenses are significant.

30. οὔπω δέ κτλ. It is useless to make guesses as to why Jesus had not yet come into the village. He may have been resting at the spot where Martha met Him first.

ἔτι is om. by ADLΓΔ, but ins. אBCW. Θ has ἐπὶ τῷ τόπῳ.

At this point Moffatt places vv. 18, 19. See on v. 18 above.

31. The friends who had come out from Jerusalem to mourn with the sisters (see v. 19), when they saw Mary rise up (see on v. 20) and leave the house suddenly without giving any explanation, supposed that she had gone to wail at the tomb, a common habit of mourners.

κλαίειν does not indicate *silent* weeping (cf. v. 35), but the unrestrained wailing of Orientals. It is used elsewhere, as here, of wailing for the dead; cf. Mk. 5^{38} (of the wailing for Jairus' daughter), Lk. 7^{13} (for the widow of Nain's son), Acts 9^{39} (for Dorcas), Mt. 2^{18} (Rachel wailing for her children). See on 16^{20}.

It is noteworthy, in view of the identity of Mary the sister of Martha with Mary Magdalene,[1] that Mary Magdalene is represented (20$^{11.\ 13.\ 15}$) as *wailing* (κλαίουσα) at the tomb of Jesus.

δόξαντες. So אBC*DLW; the rec., with AC^{2}ΓΔΘ, has λέγοντες.

32. When Mary met Jesus, she fell at His feet, impulsive and demonstrative creature as she was, and said, as Martha had said, " Lord, if thou hadst been here, my brother had not died " (see on v. 21). She is described by Lk. (10^{39}) as sitting at His feet for instruction, and later she anointed His feet (12^3), probably for the second time (see Introductory Note on 12$^{1-8}$).

πρὸς τοὺς πόδας. So אBC*DLW, but AC^{3}ΓΔΘ give εἰς τοὺς πόδας. πρός is the preposition used by Mk. (5^{22} 7^{25}) when telling of Jairus and the Syrophœnician woman falling at the feet of Jesus. So, too, is it used in Rev. 1^{17} and (in the

[1] Cf. Introductory Note on 12$^{1-8}$.

33. Ἰησοῦς οὖν ὡς εἶδεν αὐτὴν κλαίουσαν καὶ τοὺς συνελθόντας αὐτῇ Ἰουδαίους κλαίοντας, ἐνεβριμήσατο τῷ πνεύματι καὶ ἐτάραξεν

LXX) at Esth. 8³. But εἰς τοὺς πόδας in a context like this would be curious Greek. Lk. prefers to use παρά (8⁴¹ 17¹⁶; but cf. Acts 5¹⁰)

Jesus weeps, and, being directed by the mourners, goes to the tomb (vv. 33-38)

33. Ἰησοῦς οὖν ὡς εἶδεν αὐτὴν κλαίουσαν κτλ., " Jesus, then, when He saw her wailing and the Jews which came with her also wailing."

ἐνεβριμήσατο τῷ πνεύματι. Cf. v. 38 ἐμβριμώμενος ἐν ἑαυτῷ, this being the only other occurrence of the verb in Jn. In its primary sense, ἐμβριμᾶσθαι is " to snort " like a horse (cf. Æsch. *Septem c. Theb.* 461); while in the LXX it means " to show indignation " (Dan. 11³⁰), ἐμβρίμημα being used of the anger of Yahweh at Lam. 2⁶. A similar use of the cognate words occurs Ps. 7¹² (Aq.), Isa. 17¹³ (Symm.), and Ezek. 21³¹. In Mk. 14⁵ ἐνεβριμῶντο αὐτῇ carries the idea of indignation: " they roared against her," *sc.* in their indignation at the waste of the ointment. But in Mk. 1⁴³, Mt. 9³⁰, ἐμβριμησάμενος αὐτῷ and ἐνεβριμήσατο αὐτοῖς can hardly mean that Jesus was angry with the leper or the blind men whom He had cured: " strictly charged them " is the rendering of the R.V., but it is doubtful if this adequately represents ἐμβριμᾶσθαι, or if any Greek parallel can be cited for such a meaning.

All three occasions on which this rare word is applied to Jesus (Mk. 1⁴³, Mt. 9³⁰, Jn. 11³³˙ ³⁸) were occasions, as we must suppose, of intense emotion. The cure of a leper, the restoring of sight to the blind, the preparation of Himself for so stupendous a task as the raising of Lazarus from the tomb, must have involved the output of spiritual energy in a degree which we cannot measure. The narrative of vv. 33-43 reveals, as no other passage in the N.T. does, that the working of " miracles " (however we try to explain them) was not achieved without spiritual effort or without the agitation of the human spirit of Jesus. " He shuddered " (ἐτάραξεν ἑαυτόν): " He shed tears " (ἐδάκρυσεν). And the verb ἐμβριμᾶσθαι may well express the physical effect of powerful emotion upon His voice. It represents the inarticulate sounds which escape men when they are physically overwhelmed by a great wave of emotion. And Jesus, the Perfect Man, experienced this as He experienced all else that is human and not sinful. As He charged the leper and the blind whom He had relieved to tell

ἑαυτόν, 34. καὶ εἶπεν Ποῦ τεθείκατε αὐτόν; λέγουσιν αὐτῷ Κύριε,

nothing of what had been done for them, He stumbled over the words, the loud and harsh tone of His voice indicating His agitation. "He roared at them" would not exactly convey the sense, for that would suggest violence of speech or of command. But it is nearer the primary meaning of ἐνεβριμήσατο than "strictly charged them." So in the present passage "He groaned in spirit" is probably the best rendering; but, if not explained, it might suggest the groaning of one in sorrow, and this ἐνεβριμήσατο cannot mean. But the groaning, like the tears and the shuddering, were the outward and bodily indications of a tremendous spiritual agitation and effort.[1] ἐμβριμώμενος ἐν ἑαυτῷ, He arrived at the tomb, not "indignant" at anything nor "groaning" with loud outbursts of sorrow, but making those inarticulate sounds which are the expression of mental agitation and strain.

D has the variant ἐταράχθη τῷ πνεύματι ὡς ἐνβρειμούμενος, which *d* renders "conturbatus est spiritu sicut *ira plenus.*" But, as has been said, *anger* is not primarily suggested by the verb ἐμβριμᾶσθαι, nor does the idea of Jesus being angry enter into the story of the Raising of Lazarus.[2]

ἐνεβριμήσατο τῷ πνεύματι καὶ ἐτάραξεν ἑαυτόν. Cf. 12²⁷ ἡ ψυχή μου τετάρακται and 13²¹ ὁ Ἰησοῦς ἐταράχθη τῷ πνεύματι. Putting these passages side by side, it is not easy to make a distinction between the use of ψυχή and πνεῦμα. In each case the "soul" of Jesus, as we would say, was troubled. So again Jn. tells of His death in the words παρέδωκεν τὸ πνεῦμα (19³⁰; see note *in loc.*); but he makes Jesus speak of His death in 10¹⁷ in the words ἐγὼ τίθημι τὴν ψυχήν μου. We have not now to do with the psychological doctrine of Paul; we are only concerned with the Johannine use of the two words πνεῦμα and ψυχή; and while recognising that πνεῦμα *suggests* what is Divine (4²⁴), and that ψυχή *suggests* the bodily life (12²⁵) in Jn. as in other writers, it is not legitimate to differentiate them sharply in a verse like that before us. The Lucan parallelism (Lk. 1⁴⁷):

μεγαλύνει ἡ ψυχή μου τὸν κύριον,
καὶ ἠγαλλίασεν τὸ πνεῦμά μου ἐπὶ τῷ θεῷ . . .

shows that the words may be used synonymously; and the Johannine usage agrees with this. See on 12²⁵.

34. καὶ εἶπεν Ποῦ τεθείκατε αὐτόν; "Where have you

---

[1] See on 1¹⁴ for Jn.'s emphasis on the true humanity of Jesus.

[2] See also, for ἐμβριμάομαι, Abbott, *Diat.* x. iii. 254 f. I am indebted to Dr. Purser for valuable help in connexion with this word.

ἔρχου καὶ ἴδε.   35. ἐδάκρυσεν ὁ Ἰησοῦς.   36. ἔλεγον οὖν οἱ Ἰουδαῖο
Ἴδε πῶς ἐφίλει αὐτόν.   37. τινὲς δὲ ἐξ αὐτῶν εἶπαν Οὐκ ἐδύνατο
οὗτος ὁ ἀνοίξας τοὺς ὀφθαλμοὺς τοῦ τυφλοῦ ποιῆσαι ἵνα καὶ οὗτος μὴ

laid him ? " This is a simple request for information. See on
6⁶ for other examples of questions asked by Jesus.

λέγουσιν αὐτῷ, sc. (apparently) Martha and Mary, who
preface their reply with the κύριε of respect (see on v. 3).

ἔρχου καὶ ἴδε. Cf. 1³⁹.

35. ἐδάκρυσεν ὁ Ἰησοῦς. אDΘ prefix καί to ἐδάκρυσεν, but
it is quite in the style of Jn. to begin the sentence without
any conjunction. δακρύειν does not occur again in the N.T.
It means " to shed tears," but not to " wail." The word in
Lk. 19⁴¹, where Jesus " wept " over Jerusalem, is ἔκλαυσεν: cf.
Heb. 5⁷, of Gethsemane, μετὰ κραυγῆς ἰσχυρᾶς καὶ δακρύων.

It is not said in the Gospels that Jesus " laughed," while
it is told here, and suggested elsewhere, that He " wept." But
to draw the inference that He never laughed would be misleading. To be incapable of laughter would be to fall short
of the perfection of manhood. This was perceived by the
compilers of the apocryphal gospels: cf. *Gospel of Thomas*, A 8,
ἐγέλασε τὸ παιδίον μέγα, and *Pseudo-Matth.* 31, " Jesus
laeto vultu subridens."

The ethics of Jesus were not those of the Stoics, and Jn.
brings out, perhaps more clearly than the Synoptists, that He
did not aim at the Stoic ἀπάθεια. Juvenal finely says of
human tears, " haec nostri pars optima sensus " (*Sat.* xv. 133).

36. The visitors from Jerusalem were impressed by the
sight of Jesus weeping, and said to each other, " See, how He
loved him," how great a friend of Lazarus He was! Cf. vv.
3, 5, for ἐφίλει.

37. Some of them, however (δέ), expressed surprise that
He who had cured the blind man at Jerusalem (9⁶· ⁷) could
not have kept His friend from death. Like Martha (v. 21)
and Mary (v. 32), they seem to think that if Jesus had been
present, Lazarus would not have died, although they are not
so sure of it. They are not contemplating any raising of
Lazarus from the dead; such a thing does not occur to them.
They refer merely to a healing miracle at Jerusalem, of which
they had recently heard, and which they may have witnessed.

A reference here to the Galilæan miracles of raising from
the dead (Mk. 5³⁵ᶠ·, Lk. 7¹¹ᶠ·) could hardly have been resisted
by a writer who was *inventing* the story of the raising of Lazarus.
But these citizens of Jerusalem may not have heard of any
Galilæan miracles.

38. That the article ὁ is omitted before Ἰησοῦς in all the

ἀποθάνῃ; 38. Ἰησοῦς οὖν πάλιν ἐμβριμώμενος ἐν ἑαυτῷ ἔρχεται εἰς τὸ μνημεῖον· ἦν δὲ σπήλαιον, καὶ λίθος ἐπέκειτο ἐπ᾽ αὐτῷ.

39. Λέγει ὁ Ἰησοῦς Ἄρατε τὸν λίθον. λέγει αὐτῷ ἡ ἀδελφὴ τοῦ τετελευτηκότος Μάρθα Κύριε, ἤδη ὄζει· τεταρταῖος γάρ ἐστιν.

MSS. except Θ and 33 (which, however, preserves some good readings in this chapter; cf. v. 20) is contrary to the general usage of Jn. (see on 1²⁹).

Again (πάλιν) the agitation of Jesus was noticeable (ἐμβριμώμενος ἐν ἑαυτῷ, see on v. 33), as He was approaching the tomb of Lazarus. It was a cave, such as was often used as a burial-place (cf. Gen. 23¹⁹, Isa. 22¹⁶, 2 Chron. 16¹⁴), the cavern being sometimes natural, sometimes artificial. The body was either let down through a horizontal opening, as is the European practice, or placed in a tomb cut in the face of the rock. In either case the opening was closed by a stone, which had to be a heavy one to keep wild animals out. Cf. 20¹, Mk. 15⁴⁶, Mt. 27⁶⁰, Lk. 24². If the cave were a subterranean one, then λίθος ἐπέκειτο ἐπ᾽ αὐτῷ must be rendered "a stone lay *upon* it"; if it were cut in the face of the rock, then the stone lay *against* the opening.

The raising of Lazarus (vv. 39–44)

39. ἄρατε. The aorist imperative is the command of authority; see on 2⁵. The same verb is used of the removal of the stone at the tomb of Jesus (cf. 20¹).

ἡ ἀδελφὴ τοῦ τετελευτηκότος, "the sister of the deceased." τελευτάω occurs only here in Jn., and is infrequent in the N.T. (cf. Mk. 9⁴⁸). The rec. substitutes the more usual τεθνηκότος.

Martha, although she had joined the party which was visiting the tomb, had no thought of the resuscitation of her brother, and, with her strong sense of decorum (Lk. 10⁴⁰), was horrified to think of the exposure of the corpse, it being now the fourth day after death. She was sure that putrefaction had begun, which shows that the body had not been embalmed, but had only been bound with swathes (v. 44), spices being probably used, after the Jewish custom (cf. 19⁴⁰). It is not alleged by Jn. that Martha was stating a fact when she said ὄζει, "he stinketh." That was merely what she thought must be the case.

ὄζειν is only used again in the Greek Bible at Ex. 8¹⁴, where it is used of the dead frogs.

τεταρταῖος does not occur again in the Greek Bible (except by mistake for τέταρτος in the A text of 2 Sam. 3⁴); but in Herod. ii. 89 τεταρταῖος γενέσθαι is "to be four days dead,"

40. λέγει αὐτῇ ὁ Ἰησοῦς Οὐκ εἶπόν σοι ὅτι ἐὰν πιστεύσῃς ὄψῃ τὴν

as here.   Lightfoot (*Hor. Hebr.* in loc.) cites a Jewish tradition to the effect that " for three days (after death) the spirit wanders about the sepulchre, expecting if it may return into the body. But when it sees that the form or aspect of the face is changed, then it hovers no more, but leaves the body to itself " (*Beresh. Rabba*, fol. 114. 3).   The same tradition is found in *The Rest of the Words of Baruch*, § 9 (ed. Harris, p. 62).

For the three days of weeping, followed by four days of lamentation, see on v. 19; and cf. v. 17 for τεταρταῖος.

40. Jesus rebukes Martha, although gently, for her lack of understanding: " Said I not to thee, that if thou believedst, thou shouldest see the glory of God ? "   Some commentators suppose the allusion to be to what Jesus had said about the sickness of Lazarus being for " the glory of God " (v. 4, where see note).   But this was said to the disciples in Peræa, not to Martha, and there is no hint that it was reported to her.   Nor is there anything in v. 4 about *belief* being a condition precedent to the *vision* of the Divine glory.   It is more probable that the reference is to Martha's previous conversation with Jesus (vv. 25-27), where she declared her belief in Him as the Christ. Such confessions of faith are elsewhere (see on 1[51]) answered by a benediction from Jesus, in which He promises to the faithful as a reward a vision of the Advent of the Son of Man in glory; and it may be that some such promise, although not recorded, was given by Jesus to Martha [1] (see on 6[36] 10[25]).

ἐὰν πιστεύσῃς ὄψῃ τὴν δόξαν τοῦ θεοῦ.   Whatever this promised vision was to be, it was a *spiritual* vision that is meant, for ὄπτομαι is always used in Jn. of seeing spiritual or heavenly realities, as at 1[51] (where see note).   Bearing this in mind, it is difficult to suppose that " thou shalt see the glory of God " means " thou shalt see Lazarus restored from the grave," nor is there any suggestion that Martha understood this to be the meaning.   Paul's phrase that Christ was " raised from the dead, through the glory of the Father " (Rom. 6[4]), may, however, be thought to supply a parallel; and the " glory of God " which Martha was to " see " with the eye of faith would then be the Divine power which was put forth in the raising of Lazarus.   Thus the larger promise of vision, which it may be supposed was given in response to Martha's confession of faith, was about to receive a special exemplification in the revival of her brother.   Even this, however, is not free from difficulty; for it would suggest that the sight of the raising of Lazarus could have been perceived only by those who

[1] Cf. Abbott, *Diat.* 2545.

δόξαν τοῦ Θεοῦ; 41. ἦραν οὖν τὸν λίθον. ὁ δὲ Ἰησοῦς ἦρεν τοὺς ὀφθαλμοὺς ἄνω καὶ εἶπεν Πάτερ, εὐχαριστῶ σοι ὅτι ἤκουσάς μου. 42. ἐγὼ δὲ ἤδειν ὅτι πάντοτέ μου ἀκούεις· ἀλλὰ διὰ τὸν ὄχλον

had faith (ἐὰν πιστεύσῃς), whereas the whole tenor of the story is that all the bystanders, Jews and disciples alike, were witnesses of it. But perhaps what is meant is that only those who had faith could see the inner meaning of this " sign," and discern in it the exhibition of the Divine glory.

41. ἦραν οὖν τὸν λίθον, as Jesus had bidden them (v. 39). The rec. text adds after λίθον the explanatory gloss οὗ ἦν ὁ τεθνηκὼς κείμενος: om. אBC*LD.

ἦρεν τοὺς ὀφθαλμοὺς ἄνω. This is a natural prelude to prayer or thanksgiving: cf. Ps. 121[1] ἦρα τοὺς ὀφθαλμούς μου εἰς τὰ ὄρη, and Lk. 18[13]. So, again, did Jesus " lift up His eyes " before His great high-priestly prayer (17[1]); and, as the Synoptists tell (Mk. 6[41]), before the blessing of the loaves, although Jn. omits this detail (see note on 6[11]). " To lift the eyes " is used more generally of any careful or deliberate gaze (see on 4[35] 6[5]).

καὶ εἶπεν πάτερ. It was thus that Jesus began His own prayers or thanksgivings, even as He taught men to begin with " Our Father." Other instances in Jn. are 12[27] 17[1]; and in the Synoptists, Mk. 14[36], Lk. 22[42] (cf. Mt. 26[39]), Lk. 10[21] (Mt. 11[25]), and Lk. 23[34, 46]. He does not say " Our Father," but " My Father " (see on 5[17]), or " Father," simply, as here; for His relation to the Eternal Godhead is different from that of men in general. Bengel's comment on the simple invocation πάτερ (at 17[1]) is suggestive : " nomina dei non sunt cumulanda in oratione."

εὐχαριστῶ σοι. For εὐχαριστεῖν in Jn., see on 6[11].

ὅτι ἤκουσάς μου, "because Thou didst hear me," the aor. indicating some definite act of prayer, whether spoken or only mental, perhaps before v. 4. He gives thanks before the visible answer to His prayer, because He is in no doubt as to the issue. His prayers were always directed to the realisation of the Father's will (5[30]), and this cannot be frustrated (see on 12[28]).

For ἀκούειν with a gen. case as connoting *sympathetic* or *appreciative* hearing, see on 3[8].

42. ἐγὼ δὲ ἤδειν κτλ., " But I knew that thou hearest me always." This is a phase of Jesus' consciousness of Himself as in unique relation with the Father, which appears all through the Fourth Gospel, and which is most explicitly stated in the words ἐγὼ καὶ ὁ πατὴρ ἕν ἐσμεν (10[30]).

We examine, first, the rec. reading ἀλλὰ διὰ τὸν ὄχλον τὸν

τὸν παρεστῶτά μοι ποιῶ, ἵνα πιστεύσωσιν ὅτι σύ με ἀπέστειλας.

περιεστῶτα εἶπον, " but for the sake of the crowd standing round,
I said it "; *i.e.* He said aloud εὐχαριστῶ σοι ὅτι ἤκουσάς μου,
not merely because of thankfulness to His Father for an answer
to His prayer (for of this He had been sure), but because
He wished the bystanders to appreciate the true secret of His
power. The prayer of Elijah, " Hear me, O Lord, that this
people may know that thou art God " (1 Kings 18³⁷), is not
a true parallel, for Elijah had not the *certainty* of his prayer
being answered as he wished, that Jesus had. See, however,
12³⁰, where Jesus is represented as saying that the voice from
heaven was not for His sake, but for the sake of the wondering
crowd; and cf. 17¹³. ἵνα πιστεύσωσιν ὅτι σύ με ἀπέστειλας,
" that they might believe (cf. 17⁸· ²¹) that thou hast sent me."
This, according to the rec. text, was the purpose with which
Jesus had uttered aloud His thanksgiving and His assurance
that the Father always heard Him, *sc.* that He might fix the
attention of the bystanders upon His claim, that He was
" sent " by the Father (see on 3¹⁷; and cf. 6²⁹). For the
reiterated claim, σύ με ἀπέστειλας, cf. 17⁸· ¹⁸· ²¹· ²³· ²⁵. It is
difficult to accept the rec. text as exactly representing the
motive behind the words εὐχαριστῶ σοι ὅτι ἤκουσάς μου. Without the addition of v. 42, these words commend themselves to
every reader as a sublime expression of thankfulness. But v. 42
represents them as having been uttered in order to impress the
crowd. Perhaps we might take v. 42 as a comment or interpretative gloss of the evangelist rather than as a saying of
Jesus.[1]

Probably, however, the rec. text is corrupt. In one uncial
(Θ) there is a variant reading which we take to represent the
original, viz.: διὰ τὸν ὄχλον τὸν παρεστῶτά μοι ποιῶ, ἵνα κτλ.

First, παρεστῶτα is read not only by Θ and the allied cursive
28, but also by 235 and the ninth-century uncial Λ. Further,
the Vulgate G has *adstantem,* not *circumstantem* (which
is the usual rendering of the rec. περιεστῶτα). Again,
περιΐστάναι is never used by Jn. elsewhere, and in N.T. only
at Acts 25⁷ " to surround him " (used transitively), and at
2 Tim. 2¹⁶, Tit. 3⁹ " to shun "; while Jn. has παρεστηκώς at
18²² and παρεστῶτα at 19²⁶. For παρίστημι followed by a
dative (as in παρεστῶτά μοι), cf. Acts 1¹⁰ 9³⁹ 27²³. On all
grounds, παρεστῶτά μοι, " standing by me," is preferable to
περιεστῶτα, " standing round," which would be a unique
instance in the N.T. of this intransitive sense.

[1] See Garvie, *The Beloved Disciple,* pp. 19, 198, for a similar explanation.

Secondly, the reading of Θ, ΜΟΙΠΟΙω, might readily be corrupted into the rec. ΕΙΠΟΝ; and the verb ποιῶ gives us a meaning as unexceptionable as εἶπον is difficult. At 5³⁶ Jesus says τὰ ἔργα ἃ ποιῶ μαρτυρεῖ περὶ ἐμοῦ ὅτι ὁ πατήρ με ἀπέσταλκεν (cf. also 10²⁵· ³⁸). And so here, reading ποιῶ, we translate " because of the multitude standing by *I do it*, that they may believe that thou didst send me." There is thus no intimation that the thanksgiving of Jesus in v. 41 was uttered only to impress the bystanders. The words of v. 41 were the inmost expression of His personal life. Rather in v. 42 does He speak of the purpose with which He is about to perform the sign that will convince the onlookers of His Divine mission.

The only authority, as it seems, corroborating ποιῶ, the reading of Θ, is the Armenian version, which, for the widely attested " I said it," gives " I do it." This appears also in two Armenian MSS. of Ephraem's Commentary on Tatian's *Diatessaron*,¹ as well as in a homily on the Raising of Lazarus ascribed to Hippolytus, part of which is extant only in Armenian.² The text of Θ (whose home is in the neighbourhood of Armenia) has been thought to show special affinities to the Armenian version;³ and it is possible that " I do it " in Jn. 11⁴² has been taken over by an Armenian (or Georgian⁴) scribe from the version with which he was most familiar, not only in Θ, but in Ephraem's *Commentary* and in the Hippolytus homily. If this be so, the reading ποιῶ has its roots in the Armenian version, the sources of which are imperfectly known.

It has been shown⁵ that the Armenian version of the Gospels rests in part on the Old Syriac. In this instance, however, the Syriac gives no support to ποιῶ, the Armenian deserting the Syriac here as in other instances;⁶ and it is probable that here some Greek authority is behind the Armenian vulgate.

The attestation of παρεστῶτά μοι ποιῶ is undoubtedly weak, but the phrase could so readily be corrupted into περιεστῶτα εἶπον (which has the non-Johannine περιεστῶτα as well as the disconcerting εἶπον), that παρεστῶτά μοι ποιῶ has been adopted in this edition as probably the original Greek.

¹ See Dr. J. A. Robinson's *Appendix* to Hamlyn Hill's *Earliest Life of Christ*, etc., p. 367, to which he has kindly directed me.
² See Pitra, *Analecta Sacra*, ii. pp. 226–230, or Achelis's edition of Hippolytus, *Kleinere Schriften*, p. 224.
³ See Streeter, *The Four Gospels*, p. 86 f.
⁴ See Blake, *Harvard Theological Review* for July 1923.
⁵ By J. A. Robinson, *Euthaliana*, p. 73 f.
⁶ Streeter, *loc. cit.* p. 89.

43. καὶ ταῦτα εἰπὼν φωνῇ μεγάλῃ ἐκραύγασεν Λάζαρε, δεῦρο ἔξω.

43. φωνῇ μεγάλῃ ἐκραύγασεν κτλ. As in the Synoptic accounts of the raising of Jairus' daughter (Mk. 5[41]) and of the widow of Nain's son (Lk. 7[14]), the dead person was recalled to life by an authoritative command from Jesus Himself. This is repeated with emphasis at 12[17]. It is His voice which, being heard by the dead as addressing them personally, is spoken of as the effective instrument of their resurrection (cf. 5[28, 29]).

The verb κραυγάζειν occurs only once in the LXX, and there, as here, is associated with "a loud voice"; ὁ λαὸς ἐκραύγασε φωνῇ μεγάλῃ (Ezra 3[13]) describes the joyful shouts of the people. The verb is found in the N.T. (in the best texts) only in Jn., who has it six times (cf. 12[13] 18[40] 19[6, 12, 15]), and at Mt. 12[19], where the words of Isa. 42[1] are rendered "He shall not cry aloud" (οὐδὲ κραυγάσει).[1] It is only here that the verb is used of an utterance of Jesus.

Two of the Words from the Cross are said to have been uttered φωνῇ μεγάλῃ (Mk. 15[34, 37]); and in Rev. 1[10] the voice of the glorified Son of Man is described as φωνὴ μεγάλη, as is also (Mt. 24[31]) the voice of the Trumpet at the coming in glory of the Son of Man. Cf. Rev. 21[3]. Jn. represents the voice of Jesus when He summoned Lazarus from the grave as in like manner "a great voice."

Λάζαρε (note the *personal* call), δεῦρο ἔξω, *huc foras*, "Come out." δεῦρο occurs only here in Jn.

44. The rec. text, with אAC³WΓΔΘ, prefixes καί to ἐξῆλθεν, but om. BC*L. The absence of a conjunction is quite in Jn.'s manner.

The dead body had been bound as to feet and hands with swathes (cf. 19[40]), and the face had been bound with a napkin (cf. 20[7]), after the Jewish custom. It is idle to speculate as to how the evangelist means us to understand the emergence from the tomb. The bandages would, seemingly, forbid the free use of the limbs; and they had to be loosened (λύσατε αὐτόν) as soon as Lazarus appeared.

The word κειρία appears elsewhere in the Greek Bible only at Prov. 7[16], where it stands for part of the covering of a bed. Moulton-Milligan (*s.v.*) note its occurrence in the form κηρία in a medical papyrus. However, there is no doubt as to its meaning here, *sc*. "bandage" or "swathe."

For ὄψις, see on 7[24].

σουδάριον is a Latin word, "a napkin"; it occurs again in N.T. at 20[7], Lk. 19[20], Acts 19[12].

[1] Cf. Abbott, *Diat.* 1752b.

44. ἐξῆλθεν ὁ τεθνηκὼς δεδεμένος τοὺς πόδας καὶ τὰς χεῖρας κειρίαις, καὶ ἡ ὄψις αὐτοῦ σουδαρίῳ περιεδέδετο. λέγει αὐτοῖς ὁ Ἰησοῦς Λύσατε αὐτὸν καὶ ἄφετε αὐτὸν ὑπάγειν.

45. Πολλοὶ οὖν ἐκ τῶν Ἰουδαίων, οἱ ἐλθόντες πρὸς τὴν Μαριὰμ

BC*L have ἄφετε αὐτόν. אADΓΔ om. αὐτόν. Θ has ἐάσατε αὐτόν.

For ὑπάγειν, see on 7³³: ἄφετε αὐτὸν ὑπάγειν is equivalent to "let him go home." This simple and kindly counsel is comparable with that of Mk. 5⁴³ ; cf. also Lk. 7¹⁵.

It is noteworthy how few are the apocryphal legends about Lazarus. *A priori*, it might have been expected that pious fancy would have delighted in depicting his experiences in the unseen world, and his sayings when he was restored to earth. But there is little of the kind. Epiphanius says that among the traditions with which he was familiar, there was one which gave the age of Lazarus at thirty, and alleged that he lived for thirty years longer after his resuscitation (*Hær.* lxvi. 34). There is nothing impossible in that. The grim legend (cited by Trench, without giving his authority) that after Lazarus returned from the tomb, he was never known to smile, is probably a mediæval fancy. The *Anaphora of Pilate* (B 5) says that Lazarus was raised from the dead on a Sabbath day, an idea which is probably due to imperfect recollection of the healings in cc. 5 and 9. A Sahidic sermon in F. Robinson's *Coptic Apocryphal Gospels*, p. 170 f., represents the miracle as having been wrought by Jesus in order to convince Thomas, who expressed a desire to see a man raised from the grave; and that Jesus told him that His action in calling Lazarus forth was a figure of what would happen at the Resurrection on the Last Day.

The impression made on the bystanders (vv. 45, 46)

45. Many of the spectators became believers in Jesus because of the raising of Lazarus (cf. 12¹¹), just as many had become believers after former healings (7³¹). Some of them reported the story to the Pharisees.

πολλοὶ οὖν ἐκ τῶν Ἰουδαίων, οἱ ἐλθόντες κτλ. must be rendered "many, therefore, of the Jews, *sc.* those who had come to Mary (vv. 19, 31), and had seen what He did, believed on Him." The "many" are defined as those who had come to visit Mary.

D for οἱ ἐλθόντες reads τῶν ἐλθόντων, altering the sense, which then would be that many of the Jews who had come to visit the sisters believed on Jesus in consequence of the

καὶ θεασάμενοι ὃ ἐποίησεν, ἐπίστευσαν εἰς αὐτόν· 46. τινὲς δὲ ἐξ
αὐτῶν ἀπῆλθον πρὸς τοὺς Φαρισαίους καὶ εἶπαν αὐτοῖς ἃ ἐποίησεν
Ἰησοῦς.

47. Συνήγαγον οὖν οἱ ἀρχιερεῖς καὶ οἱ Φαρισαῖοι συνέδριον, καὶ

miracle, but not all of them. Some (v. 46) went off to report
it to the Pharisees, the implication being that they were *not*
among those who believed in Him, and that their action was
prompted by hostility or malevolence. But ἐλθόντες is undoubtedly the true reading, and it conveys the meaning that
the many Jews (the phrase is repeated from v. 19) who had
come to condole with the sisters were all convinced by the
miracle of the claims of Jesus.

Syr. sin. has a reading unsupported by the uncials, *sc.*
" Many Jews that came unto Jesus, because of Mary, from
that hour believed in Jesus."

θεασάμενοι. θεᾶσθαι is always used in Jn. of physical vision,
of seeing with the eyes of the body (see on 1¹⁴). For the effect
of the miracle, cf. 2²³.

ὃ ἐποίησεν. So A²BC*D; but אALWΓΔΘ have ἃ (perhaps
from v. 46). Before ἐποίησεν the rec. adds ὁ Ἰησοῦς (from
v. 46); but om. ABC*W.

ἐπίστευσαν εἰς αὐτόν. For this phrase, see on 4³⁹.

46. τινὲς δὲ ἐξ αὐτῶν κτλ. There is nothing to prove that this
action of some of the citizens who had come to Bethany and had
been convinced of the claims of Jesus by the raising of Lazarus
was malevolent. δέ means no more here than "however."

ἀπῆλθον πρὸς τοὺς Φαρισαίους, " went off to the Pharisees,"
i.e. to the religious leaders who formed the most zealous
and orthodox party in the Sanhedrim (see on 7³²). An event
of such religious significance as the miracle at Bethany seemed
to be would naturally be brought before them, and those who
reported it probably did so without meaning to injure Jesus.
See on 5¹⁵ for a similar case.

If the plural ἃ before ἐποίησεν is to be pressed, it means
that not only the raising of Lazarus, but other actions of Jesus
which they had observed or of which they had heard, were
included in their report (cf. πολλὰ σημεῖα, v. 47).

Counsel of Caiaphas to the Sanhedrim, and their resolve
(*vv.* 47–53)

47. οἱ ἀρχιερεῖς καὶ οἱ Φαρισαῖοι, *sc.* the principal members
of the Sanhedrim (see on 7³²). From this time onwards,
the chief priests take the lead in the arraignment of Jesus.
These leaders summoned an informal council.

ἔλεγον Τί ποιοῦμεν, ὅτι οὗτος ὁ ἄνθρωπος πολλὰ ποιεῖ σημεῖα; 48. ἐὰν ἀφῶμεν αὐτὸν οὕτως, πάντες πιστεύσουσιν εἰς αὐτόν, καὶ ἐλεύσονται οἱ Ῥωμαῖοι καὶ ἀροῦσιν ἡμῶν καὶ τὸν τόπον καὶ τὸ ἔθνος.

συνήγαγον . . . συνέδριον, the Ferrar cursives adding the explanatory gloss κατὰ τοῦ Ἰησοῦ. This is the only occurrence of the word συνέδριον in Jn.

καὶ ἔλεγον Τί ποιοῦμεν; "They were saying (to each other), What are we doing ? " sc. Why are we doing nothing ? The parallel Acts 4[16] τί ποιήσωμεν; "What are we to do ? " has a slightly different tinge of meaning. ποιοῦμεν in the present tense cannot be rendered "What *shall* we do ? "[1]

ὅτι οὗτος ὁ ἄνθρωπος κτλ., "for this person is doing many signs "; the turn of phrase expressing contempt. For "many signs " in Jerusalem, cf. 2[23]; but the reference here is to the report brought by those who had been present at the raising of Lazarus (v. 46).

48. The Jewish leaders were anxious lest the growing fame of Jesus should suggest to those who were being convinced of His claims, that He was the national Deliverer of their expectation (cf. 6[15]); and that thus a rebellion should break out, which would call down stern punishment from their Roman rulers. It was, indeed, the charge preferred against Him before Pilate that He claimed to be the "King of the Jews " (cf. 18[33f.]).

ἐὰν ἀφῶμεν αὐτὸν οὕτως κτλ., "if we let Him go thus," *i.e.* without intervening and curbing His activities, "every one will believe in Him " (cf. v. 45).

καὶ ἐλεύσονται οἱ Ῥωμαῖοι. This has a verbal resemblance to the LXX of Dan. 11[30] καὶ ἥξουσι Ῥωμαῖοι, but there is no allusion here to that passage. "Romans " are not mentioned by the Synoptists (cf. 19[20]).

καὶ ἀροῦσιν ἡμῶν καὶ τὸν τόπον καὶ τὸ ἔθνος. The position of ἡμῶν is emphatic. "They will suppress our place and our nation." ὁ τόπος seems to mean the Holy Place, *i.e.* the Temple, with which the chief priests were specially concerned. Cf. 4[20] and Mt. 24[15], Acts 6[13, 14] 21[28]. At 2 Macc. 5[19] the τόπος is the Temple, and the fortunes of the τόπος and the ἔθνος are associated, as they are here.

The apprehension attributed in this verse to the Jewish leaders, of the destruction of the Temple and the nation, might, no doubt, be regarded as a prophecy after the event, for Jerusalem had fallen twenty years or more before the Fourth Gospel was written. But, on the other hand, there is an antecedent probability that such anxieties must always have been present.

[1] Cf. Abbott, *Diat.* 2493, 2766.

49. εἷς δέ τις ἐξ αὐτῶν Καϊάφας, ἀρχιερεὺς ὢν τοῦ ἐνιαυτοῦ ἐκείνου, εἶπεν αὐτοῖς Ὑμεῖς οὐκ οἴδατε οὐδέν, 50. οὐδὲ λογίζεσθε ὅτι συμφέρει

during the first century, to the minds of the chief priests, who were well aware that any Messianic rebellion would be sternly repressed by their Roman masters.

49. εἷς δέ τις ἐξ αὐτῶν. For ἐκ before a gen. pl. in sentences of this kind, see on 1⁴⁰.

Καϊάφας, ἀρχιερεὺς ὤν. The office of high priest, under the ancient Hebrew laws, was for life; but in Roman times the high priest only held his position at the pleasure of the imperial authority. He might be high priest for one year only, or for a term of years, according as he pleased his Roman masters. Annas was high priest from 6 A.D. to 15 A.D., when he was deposed by the procurator Valerius Gratus. But he retained his influence throughout his life, and several of his sons held the office after him. In the year 18 A.D., Joseph Caiaphas (as Josephus calls him), the son-in-law of Annas, succeeded to this great position, which he held until 36 A.D., thus being high priest throughout the whole period of Pontius Pilate's procuratorship. His name is not mentioned by Mk., but he appears as the principal person at the trial of Jesus in Mt. 26⁵⁷; see further on 18¹⁹ᶠ.

The phrase ἀρχιερεὺς ὢν τοῦ ἐνιαυτοῦ ἐκείνου is applied to him thrice (v. 51, 18¹³) by Jn. This does not imply that Jn. supposed mistakenly that the high priest was appointed annually, like the Asiarchs. But the phrase is repeated with emphasis, " high priest in that *fateful* year " (for such a use of ἐκεῖνος, cf. 1⁴⁰ 20¹⁹), because Jn. thinks it so remarkable that the high priest, whose duty it was to enter the holy of holies and offer the atonement for *that* year, should unconsciously utter a prophecy of the efficacy of the Atonement which was presently to be offered on the Cross. This was the acceptable year of the Lord.[1]

ὑμεῖς οὐκ οἴδατε οὐδέν κτλ. The council was an informal one, and Caiaphas was not presiding. But he speaks very sharply to the other members, for their irresolution. " You people " (ὑμεῖς is contemptuous) " know nothing at all "; you do not understand that it is in your interests that the man should die. Why hesitate about it ? This is the obvious policy. Caiaphas was evidently a strong man, who knew his own mind; and the sharpness of his speech provides an illustration of what Josephus says about Sadducee manners : " The behaviour of the Sadducees to one another is rather rude, and their intercourse with their equals is rough, as with strangers "

[1] Cf. Lightfoot, *Biblical Essays*, p. 29.

ὑμῖν ἵνα εἰς ἄνθρωπος ἀποθάνῃ ὑπὲρ τοῦ λαοῦ καὶ μὴ ὅλον τὸ ἔθνος

(*Bell. Jud.* ii. viii. 14). For the relation of the Sadducee or priestly party to the Pharisees, see on 7³².

50. οὐδὲ λογίζεσθε. So אABDLW, as against the rec. δια-λογίζεσθε. Neither verb occurs again in Jn.; the simple verb being customary in Paul, and the compound in the Synoptists.

ὅτι συμφέρει ὑμῖν (cf. 16⁷ for the constr.; and cf. 18¹⁴ for ἵνα . . . ἀποθάνῃ), " that it is expedient for you," perhaps spoken contemptuously.

BDLΓ, with some Latin and Coptic vss., have ὑμῖν. ἡμῖν is read by AΔΘW, with Latin, Syriac (including Syr. sin. and Syr. cur.), and Coptic support (including Q).

ἵνα εἰς ἄνθρωπος ἀποθάνῃ ὑπὲρ τοῦ λαοῦ κτλ.: a fine sentiment in its proper setting, and one which could be copiously illustrated from history. Caiaphas, from his point of view, was giving politic if cynical advice. Better that one man die than that the nation perish.

λαός is used by Jn. only in this saying of Caiaphas (repeated 18¹⁴) ; ἔθνος is used by him only in this passage and at 18³⁵. ἔθνος has reference to the Jews as a political unit, organised for civic and social life; λαός is used when their relation to God, as His peculiar people, is in view. But it is as impossible to provide exact and exclusive definitions of these two Greek words as of the English words " nation " and " people." It is doubtful if in this verse any stress should be laid on the difference between ἔθνος and λαός. ἔθνος is used of the Jewish nation at Lk. 7⁵ 23² and elsewhere; while ἔθνη in the plural is always in sharp contrast to λαός.

51. This is one of those editorial comments of which Jn. gives his readers many (cf. Introd., p. xxxiv). The words of Caiaphas, he notes, were an unconscious prophecy, for it was true in a deeper sense than Caiaphas understood that the Death of Jesus would be expedient for the Jews, as well as for the wider circle of all God's children.

The Jews ascribed a measure of prophetic faculty to the high priest, when, after being duly vested, he " inquired of Yahweh " (Ex. 28³⁰, Lev. 8⁸, Num. 27²¹). Josephus has left on record that he, as a priest, claimed to have power to read the future (*B.J.* iii. viii. 3). And Philo says that the true priest is always potentially a prophet (*de const. principum*, 8). The word ἐπροφήτευσεν is applied to Zacharias the priest (Lk. 1⁶⁷), just as it is here (its only occurrence in Jn.) to Caiaphas: " He, being high priest that year (see on v. 49), *prophesied.*"

Caiaphas spoke not " of himself," but being, as it were, inspired by the Spirit of God, ἐπροφήτευσεν. See on 19²¹.

ἀπόληται. 51. τοῦτο δὲ ἀφ' ἑαυτοῦ οὐκ εἶπεν, ἀλλὰ ἀρχιερεὺς ὢν τοῦ ἐνιαυτοῦ ἐκείνου ἐπροφήτευσεν ὅτι ἤμελλεν Ἰησοῦς ἀποθνήσκειν ὑπὲρ τοῦ ἔθνους, 52. καὶ οὐχ ὑπὲρ τοῦ ἔθνους μόνον, ἀλλ' ἵνα καὶ τὰ

Note that ἐπροφήτευσεν (אBDLΘ) is the true form of the aorist, not προεφήτευσεν, with the rec. text. The augment precedes the preposition, there being no simple verb φητεύω.

ὅτι ἤμελλεν Ἰησοῦς ἀποθνήσκειν κτλ. For ἤμελλεν (ABDLWΘ) א has ἔμελλεν. The def. art. before Ἰησοῦς is omitted by אABDLW (see on 1[29]).

For ἤμελλεν, used of the Death of Jesus, cf. 12[33] 18[32]. It conveys in these passages the sense of predestined inevitableness, which is always present to the mind of Jn. (see on 2[4] 3[14]; and cf. Introd., p. cii). See also for μέλλειν on 4[47] 6[71].

ὑπὲρ τοῦ ἔθνους. See for ὑπέρ on 1[30]; and cf. 6[51] 10[11]. Jn. alters the phrase of Caiaphas ὑπὲρ τοῦ λαοῦ (v. 50) to ὑπὲρ τοῦ ἔθνους, perhaps because he wishes to suggest that by their rejection of Jesus the Jews had forfeited their privilege as the λαός of God. But he is prone, when he repeats a phrase, to alter it slightly (see on 3[16]); and in any case, as we have seen, we cannot distinguish very sharply between ἔθνος and λαός.

52. The Death of Jesus was not only on behalf of Jews. This is the teaching of Jn. Cf. 3[16] 10[16] 12[32], 1 Jn. 2[2], as a few of the passages which make this plain. It is natural that in a Gospel written amid Greek surroundings and primarily for Greek readers, the scope of the Christian message of salvation as extending beyond the borders of Judaism should be explained with special emphasis.

Its larger purpose was "to gather into one the scattered children of God," ἵνα καὶ τὰ τέκνα τοῦ θεοῦ τὰ διεσκορπισμένα συναγάγῃ εἰς ἕν. The phrase looks onward to the future, when those who are potentially God's children shall have become τέκνα θεοῦ, begotten of God, through faith in Jesus (see on 1[12. 13] for τέκνα θεοῦ in Jn.); and it looks onward also to the more distant future, when all these children of God shall be gathered into one. It should be observed again at this point (see on 1[12]) that the ideas of the universal Fatherhood of God, and of the whole human family as His children, are not explicit in Jn. All who will "believe" may become His children; but this faith is presupposed.

τὰ διεσκορπισμένα. These potential children of God are "scattered," as Jn. writes. They are, to his mind, in every part of the world. The verb διασκορπίζω does not occur again in Jn., but is frequently used in the LXX of the scattering of Israel among the nations, which is a thought foreign to the

τέκνα τοῦ Θεοῦ τὰ διεσκορπισμένα συναγάγῃ εἰς ἕν.   53. ἀπ᾽ ἐκείνης
οὖν τῆς ἡμέρας ἐβουλεύσαντο ἵνα ἀποκτείνωσιν αὐτόν.

54. Ὁ οὖν Ἰησοῦς οὐκέτι παρρησίᾳ περιεπάτει ἐν τοῖς Ἰουδαίοις,
ἀλλὰ ἀπῆλθεν ἐκεῖθεν εἰς τὴν χώραν ἐγγὺς τῆς ἐρήμου, εἰς Ἐφραὶμ

context here; for the "children of God who are scattered
abroad" are not all of Israel. Jn. has σκορπίζω at 10¹², but
there the allusion is to the wolf scattering the flock, of which
there is no suggestion in the present passage.

There seems to be a reminiscence of this verse in the
Didache (ix. 4), where mention is made of the Eucharistic
loaf: ὥσπερ ἦν τοῦτο τὸ κλάσμα διεσκορπισμένον ἐπάνω τῶν ὀρέων
καὶ συναχθὲν ἐγένετο ἕν, οὕτω συναχθήτω σου ἡ ἐκκλησία ἀπὸ τῶν
περάτων τῆς γῆς εἰς τὴν σὴν βασιλείαν.   See on 6¹².

συναγάγῃ εἰς ἕν.   Cf. 10¹⁶, δεῖ με ἀγαγεῖν κτλ., where see note.
For the nature of this unity, see on 17²¹; and cf. Eph. 2¹⁴.

53. ἀπ᾽ ἐκείνης οὖν τῆς ἡμέρας κτλ.   "From that day,
therefore (*sc.* because they were impressed by the advice of
Caiaphas), their plan was to kill Him." The hostility of the
ecclesiastical authorities had been gradually intensified; it
began with the cures on Sabbath days, and the claim of Jesus
to Divine authority (5¹⁸ 7³² 9²²); but after the raising of Lazarus,
and Caiaphas' warning, they came to the decision (ἐβουλεύσαντο
ἵνα) that He must die (cf. 12¹⁰ for a similar phrase).

For ἡμέρας, L reads ὥρας : there is a similar variant at
19²⁷, where see note. Jn. is prone to note the *time* at which
things happened: see Introd., p. cii.

Jesus withdraws to the north-east of Jerusalem (*vv.* 54-57)

54. ὁ οὖν (because of the machinations of His enemies)
Ἰησοῦς οὐκέτι παρρησίᾳ (see for this word on 7⁴) περιεπάτει
(see on 7¹) ἐν τοῖς Ἰουδαίοις (the hostile Jews; see on 1¹⁹
5¹⁰).

He withdrew "to the country near the desert," *i.e.* the hill
country to the north-east of Jerusalem, which was thinly
populated. The town or village of Ephraim is not mentioned
elsewhere in the N.T. "But it is mentioned by Josephus
(*Bell. Jud.* IV. ix. 9), in connexion with the mountain district
(ἡ ὀρεινή) north of Jerusalem, as a small fort (πολίχνιον). . . .
Josephus couples it with Bethel, and it is a coincidence that
where it occurs in 2 Chron. 13¹⁹ (τὴν Ἐφρών) Bethel is named
with it. The two places were probably not far apart." [1]   It is
generally identified with El-Tayibeh, 4 miles north-east of

[1] Lightfoot, *Biblical Essays*, p. 177 ; cf. G. A. Smith, *Hist. Geogr.*,
p. 352.

λεγομένην πόλιν, κἀκεῖ ἔμεινεν μετὰ τῶν μαθητῶν. 55. ἦν δὲ ἐγγὺς τὸ πάσχα τῶν Ἰουδαίων, καὶ ἀνέβησαν πολλοὶ εἰς Ἱεροσόλυμα ἐκ τῆς χώρας πρὸ τοῦ πάσχα, ἵνα ἁγνίσωσιν ἑαυτούς. 56. ἐζήτουν οὖν τὸν Ἰησοῦν καὶ ἔλεγον μετ᾽ ἀλλήλων ἐν τῷ ἱερῷ ἑστηκότες Τί δοκεῖ ὑμῖν;

Bethel, on the road from Samaria to Jericho, from which it is distant about 15 miles.

Cod. Bezæ after χώραν inserts CAMΦOYPEIM (*Sapfurim*). Harris [1] ingeniously suggests that Σαμφουρείμ " is a mere corruption from the Syriac words answering to *whose name is Ephraim*," which were inserted as a gloss, σαμ standing for the Hebrew םשׁ. Sepphoris in Galilee has been supposed by some to be indicated by Σαμφουρείμ, but this place is too far away to suit the conditions of the narrative.

κἀκεῖ ἔμεινεν. This is the reading of אBLW (cf. 10⁴⁰). ΑΔΓΔΘ read διέτριβεν, which occurs at 3²² ἐκεῖ διέτριβεν μετ᾽ αὐτῶν. μένειν is a favourite word with Jn. (cf. *e.g.* 2¹² 4⁴⁰), and is used with μέτα, as here, at 1 Jn. 2¹⁹.

The rec. text adds αὐτοῦ after μαθητῶν : om. אBDLW. See on 2².

55. ἦν δὲ ἐγγὺς τὸ πάσχα τῶν Ἰουδαίων. For this phrase, see on 2¹³, as also for the phrase καὶ ἀνέβησαν εἰς Ἱεροσόλυμα (cf. 1¹⁹).

ἐκ τῆς χώρας. Many went up " from the country parts," ἡ χώρα not referring here to the Ephraim district (v. 54).

ἵνα ἁγνίσωσιν ἑαυτούς. Ceremonial purity was requisite if a man was to keep the Passover duly (cf. Num. 9¹⁰, 2 Chron. 30¹⁷. ¹⁸); and the necessary ritual of purification might last a whole week, or a much shorter time if the pilgrim had not been gravely polluted (see Lightfoot, *Hor. Hebr.* in loc.). Accordingly many pilgrims had to arrive in Jerusalem some days before the Passover, πρὸ τοῦ πάσχα. See 18²⁸ for the emphasis that was laid on ritual purity; and cf. Acts 21²⁴.

ἁγνίζειν is not found in the Synoptists, and is used by Jn. again only at 1 Jn. 3³ (of *spiritual* purification).

56. Just as at an earlier Passover (7¹¹), the pilgrims were curious to see and hear Jesus: ἐζήτουν οὖν τὸν Ἰησοῦν. And the knots of people in the Temple precincts, where they naturally gathered, as well as because it was here that Jesus had been accustomed to teach, were full of eager speculation. " What do you think ? " " Surely He isn't coming to the Feast ? " This, they thought, was unlikely, because of the order for His arrest which had been made by the authorities.

D reads τί δοκεῖτε; instead of τί δοκεῖ ὑμῖν; and Syr. sin.

[1] Rendel Harris, *Codex Bezæ*, p. 184.

ὅτι οὐ μὴ ἔλθῃ εἰς τὴν ἑορτήν; 57. δεδώκεισαν δὲ οἱ ἀρχιερεῖς καὶ οἱ Φαρισαῖοι ἐντολὰς ἵνα ἐάν τις γνῷ ποῦ ἐστιν μηνύσῃ, ὅπως πιάσωσιν αὐτόν.

puts the two questions into one, " Do ye suppose that *per-chance* He cometh not to the Feast ? " The A.V. takes the Greek similarly: " What think ye, that He will not come to the Feast ? " But the better reading, and the better rendering of the Greek, give two short ejaculatory questions instead of one (see Abbott, *Diat.* 2184).

57. δεδώκεισαν δέ. The rec. text, with D, adds καί, the effect of which is to disconnect v. 57 from v. 56. But καί must be omitted with אABLWΔΘ. It spoils the sense, which clearly is that the people thought it improbable that Jesus would come up to Jerusalem, for the Sanhedrim had given orders (δεδώκεισαν δέ) for His arrest.

For οἱ ἀρχιερεῖς καὶ οἱ Φαρισαῖοι, cf. v. 47 ; and see on 7³².

ἐντολάς (אBW) seems to be preferable to ἐντολήν of the rec. text (ADLΓΔΘ): they gave " directions," that if any one knew where Jesus was, he should give information (μηνύσῃ, only here in Jn., but cf. Acts 23³⁰), in order that they might arrest Him.

ὅπως πιάσωσιν αὐτόν. This is the only place where Jn. has ὅπως, it being used here (as Blass suggests, *Gram.*, p. 211) for variety, as ἵνα has occurred immediately before.

INTRODUCTORY NOTE ON THE ANOINTING AT BETHANY
(c. 12¹⁻⁸)

There are three evangelical traditions of the anointing of Jesus at an entertainment in a private house : that of Mk. 14³⁻⁹ (followed by Mt. 26⁶⁻¹³), that of Jn. 12¹⁻⁸, and that of Lk. 7³⁶⁻⁵⁰. From the second century to our own time the comparison of these narratives has been attempted by critical readers, and various answers have been given to the questions which arise. Were there three anointings or only two ? Or did one incident furnish the material for all three stories ?

Few modern expositors hesitate to identify the incident described in Mk. 14 with that of Jn. 12. The place is the same, viz. the κώμη or village of Bethany near Jerusalem; and in both traditions the scene is laid in the week before the Cruci-fixion, Jn. putting it on the Sabbath before the Passover, while Mk. suggests (although he does not say it explicitly) that it is to be dated two days only before that feast (cf. Mk. 14¹· ³). Mk. does not name the woman who anointed Jesus, but Jn. says that it was Mary, the sister of Martha and Lazarus. In

Mk. the host is " Simon the Leper," [1] but Jn. says that Martha
waited on the company, which might mean that she was the
mistress of the house; Lazarus, in any case, is included among
those at table.   In the Marcan story the woman anoints the
head of Jesus (a frequent mark of honour to a distinguished
guest; cf. Lk. 7[46]), no mention being made of His *feet*, or of
the use of her hair as a towel.   Jn., however, says nothing
either of anointing the head of Jesus or of washing His feet;
but he relates that Mary *anointed His feet*, and then wiped
them with her hair.   This is, *prima facie*, a strange statement.
Anointing the feet of a guest might follow the washing of them,
but why should the ointment be wiped off ?   And it is improbable that a suitable towel (see 13[4]) would not be at Mary's
disposal in a house where the acting hostess was her sister.
That she should have used her hair for the purpose of wiping
the feet of Jesus on this occasion, either after washing or
anointing them, is an extraordinary circumstance, to which we
shall return presently.

It is not doubtful, however, despite the superficial differences
between the Marcan and Johannine stories, that they refer to
the same incident, and that Jn. is conscious of the fact and
familiar with the earlier narrative.   Like Mk., Jn. mentions
the criticism made about the waste of the precious ointment
(a criticism which he ascribes to Judas); and like Mk., he
recalls the Lord's rebuke, " The poor ye have always with you,
but me ye have not always."   Again, Mk.'s προέλαβεν μυρίσαι
τὸ σῶμά μου εἰς τὸν ἐνταφιασμόν is reflected in Jn.'s ἵνα εἰς τὴν
ἡμέραν τοῦ ἐνταφιασμοῦ μου τηρήσῃ αὐτό.   And Jn.'s νάρδου
πιστικῆς πολυτίμου is a reproduction of Mk.'s νάρδου πιστικῆς
πολυτελοῦς.   We may say with confidence that the Marcan
and Johannine narratives are versions of the same story,
Jn. having corrected Mk. where he thought it necessary
to do so.[2]

The narrative of Lk. 7[36f.] is markedly different from both
Jn. and Mk.   The place where the incident happened is not
named, but the context suggests that it was somewhere in
Galilee, and that it occurred during the period of John the
Baptist's imprisonment.   But Lk. does not always observe
strict chronological sequence, and the story may have been
inserted at this point in connexion with the accusation that
Jesus was " a friend of publicans and sinners " (v. 34).   The
host, on this occasion, was a Pharisee named Simon, and the
woman who is the central figure was " a sinner " (ἁμαρτωλός).

---

[1] Attempts have been made to treat this Simon as the *father*, or as
the *husband*, of Martha ; but there is no early evidence.
[2] See Introd., p. xcvi, for the parallels in full.

The story tells of her coming into the house—uninvited, as was possible in a country where meals were often semi-public—and standing behind Jesus, as He reclined at table. As she wept, her tears dropped on His feet, and she wiped them off with her long flowing hair. Then she kissed them, and anointed them with ointment which she had brought with her, probably with the hope of being allowed to anoint His *head*. This would have been an ordinary act of courtesy, but anointing of the *feet* is not mentioned again (except Jn. 12³) in Scripture, and was evidently unusual.[1] Simon the Pharisee was shocked that a guest who had been entertained as a possible prophet should submit to the ministrations of a sinful woman; but Jesus rebuked him with the parable of the Two Debtors, and the story ends with the benediction given to her who had been forgiven much and who had therefore loved much.

The moral of this narrative is wholly unlike anything in the narratives of Mk. 14 and Jn. 12; nor does there seem to be any connexion with the narrative of Mk. 14. The name of the host, indeed, both in Lk. and Mk. was Simon, but Simon the Pharisee is not necessarily to be identified with Simon the Leper, for Simon was the commonest of Jewish names. Nor can we suppose that a leading Pharisee would have entertained Jesus at his house during the week before His Passion, when He was already the subject of orthodox suspicion. The unnamed woman may be the same in both narratives, nevertheless, although Mk. does not note that she was or had been a sinner; but that Mk. and Lk. deal with quite different incidents is plain.

The resemblances, however, of the Lucan story to that in Jn. 12 are striking. In both, it is the *feet* (not the *head*, as in Mk.) which are anointed, and the language used is similar in both cases. Thus Lk. 7³⁸ has τοῖς δάκρυσιν ἤρξατο βρέχειν τοὺς πόδας αὐτοῦ καὶ ταῖς θριξὶν τῆς κεφαλῆς αὐτῆς ἐξέμασσεν . . . καὶ ἤλειφεν τῷ μύρῳ, while Jn. 12³ has ἤλειψεν τοὺς πόδας τοῦ Ἰησοῦ καὶ ἐξέμαξεν ταῖς θριξὶν αὐτῆς τοὺς πόδας αὐτοῦ.

It will be observed that there is no formal *washing* of Jesus' feet in either story, and that the falling of the woman's tears upon them, which is so touching a feature of Lk.'s account, has no place in Jn. But the linguistic similarities between the two verses just cited show conclusively that Jn. intended to tell a story similar to that told by Lk.; while, on the other hand, his version is as puzzling as Lk.'s is lucid. Why should Mary of Bethany appear with dishevelled hair, and use this instead of a towel ? Why should she anoint the *feet* of Jesus

---

[1] J. B. Mayor (*D.B.*, iii. 280) cites Aristoph. *Vespæ* 608, where a daughter is represented as anointing and kissing her father's feet.

at all ? The woman of Lk. 7 did so from penitent humility,
but does this apply to Mary of Bethany ? And why should
Mary wipe off the unguent once it was applied ? The
ἁμαρτωλός only wiped off her falling tears.

We shall approach these difficulties presently, but at this
point we seem called to recognise the fact that Jn. is writing
in terms of the Lucan story. He is not necessarily describing
the same incident as Lk., but he is describing an incident so
similar in some exceptional features, that we must believe him
to be writing of the same woman that Lk. has depicted. This
involves the conclusion that Jn. regarded Mary of Bethany as
the sinful woman of whom Lk. tells. Lk. does not make this
identification. He mentions Mary afterwards as being at the
house of Martha her sister, the situation of which is not indicated (10³⁸), and records how Mary was praised by Jesus
as having " chosen the good part," in comparison with the
housewifely activities of her sister. This is not inconsistent
with the conclusion that Mary had formerly been of loose
behaviour, but it does not suggest it directly.

The relations between the various evangelical narratives
of the anointing of Jesus have been discussed at length, both
in ancient and modern times, and we cannot stay here to
examine the opinions of individual Fathers or critics.[1] Clement
of Alexandria (*Pæd.* ii. 61) identifies the anointings of Lk. 7
and of Jn. 12, Mk. 14; so does Tertullian (*de pudic.* xi.).
Origen is not consistent with himself, at one time speaking of
three (Comm. *in Mt.* 77) or two anointings (Hom. *in Cant.* 1¹²),
at another time of only one (Fragm. *in Joann.* 11², ed. Brooke,
ii. 287). Ephraim Syrus (Hom. i. " On our Lord ") has a
lengthy commentary on the sinful woman, whom he explicitly
distinguishes from Mary of Bethany. Tatian treats the story
of Lk. 7 in like manner as distinct from the story of Jn. 12,
Mk. 14. But, since the time of Gregory the Great, the Roman
Church has been accustomed to identify Mary of Bethany,
Mary Magdalene, and the ἁμαρτωλός of Lk. 7. The Breviary
office for the Feast of St. Mary Magdalen (July 22) draws out
this identification, and treats the story of Mary as that of one
who, once a great sinner, became a great saint.

This identification has been accepted in the present
commentary. Of Mary Magdalene, *i.e.* Mary of Magdala
(a village some 3 miles from Capernaum, now called *Mejdel*),
Lk. tells that " seven devils had gone out of her " (Lk. 8²), a
statement that is made immediately after the story of the
ἁμαρτωλός. She is named along with other women who had

[1] A good and convenient summary will be found in J. B. Mayor's
article, " Mary," in *D.B.*, vol. iii.

been "healed of evil spirits and infirmities"; and Lk.'s
statement about her is repeated in the Marcan Appendix: "He
appeared first to Mary Magdalene, from whom He had cast
out seven devils" (Mk. 16⁹). This description would not
necessarily point to special vice, for it might only refer to
madness; but it remains, for all that, a very apt description
of a woman who had been rescued as the ἁμαρτωλός was, and
would be a convenient euphemism. Further, the identification of Mary Magdalene with Mary of Bethany enables us to
interpret the otherwise difficult words of Jn. 12⁷, "Suffer her
to keep it against the day of my burying" (cf. Mk. 14⁸, Mt.
26¹²). No evangelist speaks expressly of Mary of Bethany as
going to the tomb to anoint the Lord's body on the day of the
Resurrection; but all four name Mary Magdalene as taking
part. The equation of Mary Magdalene to Mary of Bethany
explains quite simply the Lord's words about the latter at the
Supper at Bethany (Jn. 12⁷, where see note)—words which are
otherwise left without fulfilment.

We hold, then, that a comparison of Jn. 12 with Lk. 7
makes it necessary to identify the woman that was a sinner
with Mary Magdalene and also with Mary of Bethany, or
at any rate to recognise that Jn. identified them.

There is another significant bit of evidence for the latter
conclusion. At Jn. 11² is a parenthetical explanation (whether
by Jn. or by a later editor need not now be discussed; see note
in loc.), that Mary of Bethany is ἡ ἀλείψασα τὸν κύριον μύρῳ
καὶ ἐκμάξασα τοὺς πόδας αὐτοῦ ταῖς θριξὶν αὐτῆς. Now this
would not identify Mary of Bethany for the reader, if
another woman had also "anointed the Lord with ointment and
wiped His feet with her hair." If we distinguish the woman
of Lk. 7 from the woman of Jn. 12, this singular gesture may be
attributed to *two* women, and thus the note of 11² would be
useless for its purpose of identification. It is plain that the
Fourth Gospel regards the ἁμαρτωλός of Lk. 7 as the sister of
Lazarus and Martha.

It is to be observed, however, that while Jn. uses the same
words of Mary's action that Lk. does of the action of the
ἁμαρτωλός, he does not necessarily imply that the narratives
of Jn. 12³ and Lk. 7³⁸ refer to the same incident. Mary may
have, in the days of His public ministry, anointed the feet of
Jesus in penitence (Lk. 7³⁸); and then, having repented and
returned to her family, when Jesus came to her home the day
before His entry to Jerusalem, have repeated an act so full of
memories for her (Jn. 12³). No emphasis is laid in Lk. on the
costliness of the ἀλάβαστρον μύρου; the woman had brought
with her an ordinary supply of unguent. But in Jn. and Mk.

XII. 1. Ὁ οὖν Ἰησοῦς πρὸ ἓξ ἡμερῶν τοῦ πάσχα ἦλθεν εἰς

the special quality of the ointment is a principal feature of
the story. It was "very precious," so exceptionally costly
that the use of it called forth criticism. If Mary desired to
repeat the act which had in the first instance called forth the
benediction of Jesus, it would be quite natural that she should
provide herself with unguent of specially fine quality. And the
circumstance that she used her hair for a towel would also be
explained by her purpose of reproducing the former scene.
It could not be *exactly* reproduced; there were no tears of
penitence on the second occasion. But, just on that account,
a true narrative of what happened would be at once like and
unlike the story of Lk. 7; and this is what we find in Jn. 12
Thus, while we do not identify the incident recorded in Lk. 7
with that recorded in Jn. 12 and Mk. 14, we may regard Lk. 7
as telling of the first occasion on which Mary anointed Jesus,
the second being that narrated in Jn. 12 [1] and (with less
exactness) in Mk. 14, Mk. missing the point that it was the
feet (not the head) of Jesus that were anointed at the house in
Bethany shortly before His Passion.

The Supper at Bethany (XII. 1–8)

XII. 1. ὁ οὖν Ἰησοῦς. οὖν is not causal: it does not carry
us back to 11[57], where it is said that the priests were planning
to arrest Him. His motive in going to Bethany was not to
seek a place of safety, but it was on His way to Jerusalem,
whither He was proceeding for the feast. οὖν is only copula-
tive, "and so" (see on 1[22]). He knew, indeed, of the enmity
of the priestly party; but that did not move Him from His
purpose. Indeed, Jn. lays special emphasis on the continual
consciousness on the part of Jesus of what was impending
(cf. 18[4]).

According to the Synoptists (Mk. 11[11], Mt. 21[17], Lk. 21[37]),
He lodged at Bethany during the nights that remained before
the end.

πρὸ ἓξ ἡμερῶν τοῦ πάσχα, a transposition of πρό, the phrase
meaning "six days before the Passover." Meyer cites Amos
1[1] πρὸ δυὸ ἐτῶν τοῦ σεισμοῦ for the same construction. Jn. is
prone to record dates (see Introd., p. cii); and he notes that the
day of the arrival of Jesus at Bethany was the Sabbath before
the Passover, *i.e.*, in our reckoning, the Saturday preceding

---

[1] Salmon held Jn. to believe that Mary had anointed the Lord's
feet twice, but he did not discuss the matter fully (*Human Element in
the Gospels*, p. 484).

Βηθανίαν, ὅπου ἦν Λάζαρος, ὃν ἤγειρεν ἐκ νεκρῶν Ἰησοῦς. **2.** ἐποίησαν οὖν αὐτῷ δεῖπνον ἐκεῖ, καὶ ἡ Μάρθα διηκόνει, ὁ δὲ Λάζαρος εἰς

Palm Sunday. He may have arrived just as the Sabbath was
beginning, *i.e.* on the Friday evening; or He may have only
come from a short distance, and so have refrained from exceeding the limit of a Sabbath day's journey.

From Mk. 14^1, Mt. 26^1, we might infer that the supper at
Bethany was held later in the week, "*two* days before the
Passover," but neither statement is quite definite as to the
date. What Jn. tells here is more probably accurate.

ὅπου ἦν Λάζαρος. On this account, Bethany was a place
of special danger. It was no place to come for one who feared
the vindictiveness of the priests which had been excited by
the raising of Lazarus.

For the constr. ὅπου ἦν, see on 1^{28}.

ὁ τεθνηκώς is added after Λάζαρος by ΑΔΓΔΘ, with support
from the vss., including the Coptic Q, but om. אBLW.

ὃν ἤγειρεν ἐκ νεκρῶν Ἰησοῦς. The rec. text omits Ἰησοῦς,
which indeed is unnecessary to the sentence, but א *BW
insert it. Perhaps all the words after Λάζαρος, *sc.* [ὁ τεθνηκώς]
ὃν ἤγειρεν ἐκ νεκρῶν Ἰησοῦς, are a gloss that has crept in from
v. 9, where ὃν ἤγειρεν ἐκ νεκρῶν is quite in place and apposite;
here it is superfluous. Cf. v. 17.

Syr. sin. gives here: " came Jesus to the village Beth
Ania unto Lazar, him that was dead and lived. And he made
for Him a supper there, and Lazar was one of the guests that
sat down to meat with Him, but Martha was occupied in
serving."

2. ἐποίησαν οὖν αὐτῷ δεῖπνον ἐκεῖ. The subject of ἐποίησαν
is undefined. Probably we should understand that the
villagers of Bethany prepared a supper for Jesus, having
still in vivid recollection the fame of His recent miracle. Mk.
says that the entertainment was in "the house of Simon the
Leper," and this may be an accurate report, although of Simon
we know nothing (see p. 410). From the way in which the
presence of Lazarus as one of the company is mentioned by
Jn., it would seem probable that at any rate the supper was not
in *his* house. On the other hand, ἐποίησαν οὖν αὐτῷ δεῖπνον
might mean that it was the well-known household of Bethany,
Martha and Mary and Lazarus, who gave the feast, and the
Sinai Syriac (quoted on v. 1) understands the text thus.
Lazarus would in any case be a figure to attract attention and
curiosity, which may account for the words ὁ δὲ Λάζαρος εἰς
ἦν ἐκ τῶν ἀνακειμένων σὺν αὐτῷ. That Martha was serving
(διηκόνει) would be more natural if she were in her own house,

ἦν ἐκ τῶν ἀνακειμένων σὺν αὐτῷ· 3. ἡ οὖν Μαριὰμ λαβοῦσα λίτραν μύρου νάρδου πιστικῆς πολυτίμου ἤλειψεν τοὺς πόδας τοῦ Ἰησοῦ καὶ

as at Lk. 10⁴⁰, where it is said of her περιεσπᾶτο περὶ πολλὴν διακονίαν.

The rec. text omits ἐκ before τῶν ἀνακειμ., with ADWΓΔΘ; but ἐκ is inserted by אBL, and this is consonant with Jn.'s style (see on 1⁴⁰).

For ἀνακειμένων σὺν αὐτῷ (אABDLΘ), the rec. (W) reads συνανακειμένων αὐτῷ. The better-attested reading is interesting because of the preposition σύν, which is used again by Jn. only at 18¹ 21³ (it does not occur in Rev.). Abbott (*Diat.* 2799, ii.) remarks that Jn. agrees with Demosthenes and Epictetus in hardly ever using σύν, the reason being that σύν belongs to literary, as distinct from spoken, Greek. Thus Lk. (Gospel and Acts) employs σύν more frequently than all the other N.T. writers put together.

3. ἡ οὖν Μαριάμ. This is the reading of B 33, and is probably right, despite the authority of אADLWΘ for Μαρία. See on 11²⁰.

λαβοῦσα λίτραν μύρου. λίτρα (*libra*) occurs again in N.T. only at 19³⁹. Mk. says of the woman (whom he does not name) ἔχουσα ἀλάβαστρον μύρου, "having an alabaster cruse or flask of ointment," and then goes on to tell that she broke the flask and poured the contents on the head of Jesus. To anoint the head of a guest (cf. Ps. 23⁵) was an act of Eastern courtesy and respect, but Jn. treats the incident differently, and tells that Mary anointed Jesus' *feet*. The Lat. *fuldensis* tries to combine the two, and its text here gives "habens alabastrum . . . et fracto effudit super caput ihesu recumbentis et unxit pedes." Syr. sin. has a similar conflate text.

This marked difference between the narratives of Mk. and Jn., which clearly refer to the same incident, is considered above (p. 410).

νάρδου πιστικῆς πολυτίμου. This is almost identical with Mk.'s νάρδου πιστικῆς πολυτελοῦς. A special point is made in both narratives (not in the earlier story, Lk. 7³⁸) of the costliness of the ointment provided (cf. "the chief ointments" of Amos 6⁶). The adj. πιστικός (only here and at Mk. 14³ in the Greek Bible) is of uncertain meaning. It may be derived from πίστις, and it is applied, as Abbott (*Diat.* 1736*d*) has pointed out, to a "faithful" wife. Thus it might mean here *genuine*, as indicating the quality of the spikenard. The vg., however, at Mk. 14³ (but not here), renders it *spicati*, and Wetstein called attention to the word σπίκατον, which means a

ἐξέμαξεν ταῖς θριξὶν αὐτῆς τοὺς πόδας αὐτοῦ· ἡ δὲ οἰκία ἐπληρώθη ἐκ

luxurious unguent. It is possible that, as Abbott suggests, some form of σπίκατον originally stood in the Gospel texts, and that it was altered to πιστικός by an attempt at allegorical interpretation. Swete quotes Jerome as playing on the word thus: "ideo uos uocati estis *pistici*." Another, less likely, derivation of πιστικός is from πίνω, so that it would mean "potable," as some perfumes were; but this would be quite out of place in the present context. Yet another explanation is quoted by Dods (*in loc.*) from the *Classical Review* (July 1890), *sc.* that we should read not πιστικῆς, but πιστακῆς, the latter word referring to the *Pistacia terebinthus*, which grows in Palestine "and yields a turpentine in such inconsiderable quantities as to be very costly." Whatever the precise derivation of the word may be, the combination νάρδου πιστικῆς (νάρδου, like πιστικῆς, occurring again in the N.T. only at Mk. 14³) is so unusual, that we must suppose Jn. to have followed here either the actual text of Mk., or a familiar tradition embodying these words.

With this costly unguent, Jn. tells that Mary anointed the feet of Jesus. He insists upon the word *feet*, repeating τοὺς πόδας twice, that there may be no misunderstanding, and to show that he is deliberately correcting Mk.'s account. He adds, in words that reproduce Lk.'s story of the sinful woman (Lk. 7³⁸), that Mary wiped the Lord's feet with her hair (καὶ ἐξέμαξεν ταῖς θριξὶν αὐτῆς τοὺς πόδας αὐτοῦ). Attention has already (p. 411) been directed to the fact that a perfumed anointing of *feet* (as distinct from the washing of them, of which there is no mention here) is a custom not mentioned in Scripture elsewhere than here and Lk. 7³⁸. It is further to be observed that for a woman to have her hair unbound was counted immodest by the Jews,[1] and that Mary should unloose her hair at an entertainment where men were present requires some special explanation. A towel would be readily accessible (cf. 13⁵) whether this supper was in the house of Martha and Mary, or not; and it would be more seemly and convenient to use it. But for what purpose were the Lord's feet wiped *after* the unguent had been applied? In the story of Lk. 7³⁸ the woman wiped His feet with her unbound hair, because her tears had fallen on them by inadvertence, but she did not wipe off the *ointment*. These considerations seem to prove that when Jn. reproduces as nearly as possible the words of the earlier narrative (Lk. 7³⁸) he does so, not by any inadvertence or mistaken recollection, but because the act of Mary recorded

[1] See Lightfoot, *Hor. Hebr.* in Jn. 12³.

τῆς ὀσμῆς τοῦ μύρου. 4. λέγει δὲ Ἰούδας ὁ Ἰσκαριώτης εἷς τῶν

here did actually reproduce her former gesture, then dictated
by a sudden impulse of penitence, now inspired by adoring
homage of her Master. The moment of her " conversion,"
to use the modern word, was the moment to which she looked
back as the most memorable in her life; and when she learnt
that Jesus was to honour a supper in Bethany by His presence,
she decided that she would once again anoint His feet, and
present herself in the guise of a penitent and grateful disciple,
the significance of whose strange gesture would be well understood by all her friends, as well as by Jesus.

This, at least, is what Jn. seems to indicate. If he did not
regard Mary as identical with the unnamed sinner of the
earlier incident, he has told the story of the anointing at Bethany
in a way which is unintelligible.

ἡ δὲ οἰκία ἐπληρώθη ἐκ τῆς ὀσμῆς τοῦ μύρου. For this
use of ἐκ as indicating " with," cf. Rev. 8⁵, Mt. 23²⁵.

This detail is peculiar to Jn., and suggests that the narrative
is due to the recollection of some one who was present on the
occasion. It seems to have been known to Ignatius, who
interprets the savour of the ointment pervading the whole
house as typifying the fragrance of incorruptibility diffused
throughout the Church from the Person of Christ (*Eph.* 17).
Cf. also Clem. Alex. *Pæd.* ii. 8 (P 205) for a similar spiritual-
ising of the incident.

Wetstein quotes from *Midr. Koheleth*, vii. 1: " A good
unguent spreads from the bedroom to the dining-hall ; so
does a good name from one end of the world to the other."
The latter clause recalls Mk. 14⁹, " Wherever the gospel is
preached in the whole world, what she hath done shall be told
for a memorial of her," a saying which Jn. does not record. It
is possible, but improbable, that the circumstance told by Jn.,
that the house was filled with the odour of the ointment, gave
rise, by an allegorical interpretation, to the saying of Mk. 14⁹.
But the idea that Jn. *meant* it to be taken allegorically is devoid
of evidence and may be confidently rejected.

4. The description of Judas is almost identical with that
given in 6⁷¹ (where see note).

We must read δέ (אBW) for the rec. οὖν.

Apparently we should omit ἐκ before τῶν μαθητῶν (with
BLW 33 249), although it is inserted, in accordance with Jn.'s
general habit (see on 1⁴⁰), by אADΘ. ἐκ is also omitted in
similar sentences at 18²² 19³⁴.

אBLW, *fam.* 1, and most vss. read here Ἰούδας ὁ
Ἰσκαριώτης (cf. 14²² for ὁ Ἰσκ.); but ΑΓΔΘ have Ἰούδας

μαθητῶν αὐτοῦ, ὁ μέλλων αὐτὸν παραδιδόναι, 5. Διὰ τί τοῦτο τὸ
μύρον οὐκ ἐπράθη τριακοσίων δηναρίων καὶ ἐδόθη πτωχοῖς; 6. εἶπεν
δὲ τοῦτο οὐχ ὅτι περὶ τῶν πτωχῶν ἔμελεν αὐτῷ, ἀλλ' ὅτι κλέπτης ἦν

Σίμωνος Ἰσκαριώτης, introducing the name of his father
(as at 6⁷¹ 13²).

The rec. text, following ADΘ, places the sentence εἰς [ἐκ]
τῶν μαθητῶν αὐτοῦ before Ἰούδας ; but אBLW place it after
Ἰσκαριώτης.

For ὁ μέλλων, D has ὃς ἤμελλεν (perhaps a reminiscence
of 6⁷¹). μέλλων may convey the idea that Judas was *predestined* to betray Jesus (see on 3¹⁴ and 6⁷¹).

According to the Synoptists (Mk. 14⁴, Mt. 26⁸), the uneasy
feeling that the ointment was wasted was shared by several of
the onlookers, but Jn. specifically mentions Judas as the one
who remonstrated. Perhaps he first suggested to the others
the extravagance of what had been done by Mary in purchasing
exceptionally rare and costly ointment.

5. This verse reproduces Mk. 14⁵ ἠδύνατο γὰρ τοῦτο τὸ
μύρον πραθῆναι ἐπάνω δηναρίων τριακοσίων καὶ δοθῆναι τοῖς
πτωχοῖς. 300 *denarii* would be about ten guineas, a large
sum. To suppose, as Schmiedel does (*E.B.* 1797), that 300 is
a symbolical number indicating "the symmetrical body of
humanity," is fantastic. The Gospel of St. Mark, at any rate,
does not deal in allegories of this cryptic kind.

Jn. here follows Mk.,[1] just as he does at 6⁷ when he recalls
200 *denarii* as the estimated cost of bread for the multitude.

6. εἶπεν δὲ τοῦτο κτλ. This is the evangelist's comment
(cf. 7²²; and see Introd., p. xxxiv). It has been thought by
some that he is unfair to Judas, and that he is so possessed with
the conviction of the baseness of his treachery, that he imputes
the lowest of motives to him (see on 6⁷⁰ 18⁵). The criticism
that the money spent on the costly ointment might have been
better spent is very natural on the lips of the disciple who, as
keeper of the common purse, was responsible for the moneys
spent by the Twelve, amounting in all, we may be sure, to no
large sum. But Jn. roundly says that he was a thief. Judas
was not above a bribe, for he took the thirty pieces of silver;
but he was not therefore dishonest, although the value which
he attached to money may have made ill-gotten gains a strong
temptation. "Temptation commonly comes through that
for which we are naturally fitted " (Westcott), *i.e.* in this case
the handling of money. And it may have been found out,
after the secession of Judas, that, as Jn. says, he had been guilty
of small peculations, for which he had full opportunity. How-

[1] See Introd., p. xcvi.

καὶ τὸ γλωσσόκομον ἔχων τὰ βαλλόμενα ἐβάσταζεν. 7. εἶπεν οὖν

ever that may be, the bitterness of the words about Judas in this verse is easily explained if they go back to one who was a former comrade in the inner circle of the Twelve, who had had no suspicions even at the end (see on 13²⁸· ²⁹), and whose indignation, when disillusioned, was all the more severe.

τὸ γλωσσόκομον: cf. 13²⁹. A γλωσσοκομεῖον originally meant a case to hold the reeds or *tongues* (γλῶσσαι) of musical instruments, and hence any kind of *box*, e.g. it is used for a *coffin* (by Aquila, Gen. 50²⁶). The word became accepted by Aramaic speakers, and appears as נלפוסמא in the Talmud. It stands for a coffer into which money is cast, at 2 Chron. 24⁸· ¹⁰ ἐνέβαλλον εἰς τὸ γλωσσόκομον, and this is the sense in which the word is used here. The γλωσσόκομον or money-box of the disciples was kept by Judas (it was not necessarily carried about with him habitually: τὸ γλωσσόκομον ἔχων is the phrase), and into it well-wishers (cf. Lk. 8³) were wont to throw (βάλλειν) small coins to provide for the needs of Jesus and His followers. In this it was like the begging-bowl of an Eastern holy man. To translate it " purse " is misleading; and the Latin vss. rightly render it by *loculi*, *i.e.* a box or coffer with several compartments. See Field, *in loc.*, on γλωσσόκομον and βαστάζειν.

For ἔχων (אBDLWΘ) the rec. has εἶχεν καί (ΑΓΔ).

τὰ βαλλόμενα, *sc.* the moneys cast into the box by well-wishers and friends; cf. 2 Chron. 24¹⁰ quoted above.

ἐβάσταζεν. The verb βαστάζειν is used (10³¹ 16¹² 19¹⁷) of carrying or bearing something heavy; but here and at 20¹⁵ it is equivalent to the vulgar English " to lift," *i.e.* to carry off furtively or unscrupulously, and so " to steal." Field gives a convincing illustration of this usage from Diog. Laert. iv. 59 μαθόντα δὲ ταῦτα τὰ θεραπόντια . . . ὅσα ἐβούλετο ἐβάσταζεν, " When therefore the servants found this out, they used to *steal* whatever they pleased." Deissmann (*Bible Studies*, Eng. Tr., p. 257) cites some further instances from the papyri of this use of βαστάζειν.[1]

Hence we must translate, " he was a thief, and having the money-box used to steal what was cast into it." To render ἐβάσταζεν here as if it only meant that Judas, as the treasurer, used to " carry about " what was put into it, would give a tame and superfluous ending to the sentence.

7. With vv. 7, 8, cf. Mk. 14⁶⁻⁹.

The rec. text, with ΑΓΔ, omits ἵνα and reads τετήρηκεν, while אBDLWΘ support ἵνα . . . τηρήσῃ.

[1] See also Moulton-Milligan, *Vocab.* 106.

ὁ Ἰησοῦς Ἄφες αὐτήν, ἵνα εἰς τὴν ἡμέραν τοῦ ἐνταφιασμοῦ μοι τηρήσῃ αὐτό· 8. τοὺς πτωχοὺς γὰρ πάντοτε ἔχετε μεθ᾽ ἑαυτῶν, ἐμὲ δὲ οὐ πάντοτε ἔχετε.

We must render " let her alone, in order that she may keep it (sc. the remainder of the spikenard) against the day of my burying." In Mk.'s narrative (here being corrected silently by Jn.[1]) the flask of ointment was broken and its entire contents poured upon the head of Jesus; but Jn. says nothing of the flask being broken, and it is not to be supposed that all the ointment was used for His feet. ἐνταφιασμός (cf. 19⁴⁰) is " preparation for burial," and might or might not include the anointing of the whole body. The words of Jesus tell of His impending death and burial to any of the company who had sufficient insight; the rest of the spikenard will soon be needed, and will not be wasted.

We have above (p. 412) identified Mary of Bethany with Mary Magdalene ; and thus she who began His ἐνταφιασμός by anointing the Lord's feet in Bethany, was among the women who finished the anointing of His body eight days later (cf. 20¹, Mk. 16¹).

For ἄφες αὐτήν, cf. Mk. 14⁶, Mt. 15¹⁴, 2 Sam. 16¹¹, 2 Kings 4²⁷. We might translate (with R.V.ᵐᵍ) " Let her alone; (it was) that she might keep it," or (with R.V.ᵗˣᵗ) " Suffer her to keep it," but we prefer to render " Let her alone, in order that, etc."

8. This verse is identical with Mt. 26¹¹, and both Jn. and Mt. reproduce exactly the words of Mk. 14⁷, both of them omitting Mk.'s καὶ ὅταν θέλητε, δύνασθε αὐτοὺς εὖ ποιῆσαι. But that Jn. is using Mk. rather than Mt. all through the story is not doubtful.[2]

D and Syr. sin. omit the whole verse here for some unknown reason, perhaps because ἐμὲ δὲ οὐ πάντοτε ἔχετε was (mistakenly) deemed to be at variance with Mt. 28²⁰. But cf 17¹¹ οὐκέτι εἰμὶ ἐν τῷ κόσμῳ.

With πτωχοὺς πάντοτε ἔχετε μεθ᾽ ἑαυτῶν, cf. Deut. 15¹¹.

The people's curiosity about Lazarus, and the hostility of the priests (vv. 9-11)

9. ὁ ὄχλος πολύς is read by אB*L, and at v. 12 by BLΘ, but in both places many authorities omit ὁ. If we omit ὁ and read ὄχλος πολύς, " a great multitude," then no difficulty presents itself. We had ὄχλος πολύς before at 6², and πολὺς ὄχλος at 6⁵: cf. Mk. 5²¹· ²⁴ 6³⁴ 9¹⁴, Acts 6⁷, Rev. 7⁹.

But ὁ πολὺς ὄχλος is undoubtedly the right reading at Mk.

¹ See Introd., p. xcvii.   ² *Ibid.*, p. xcvi.

9. Ἔγνω οὖν ὄχλος πολὺς ἐκ τῶν Ἰουδαίων ὅτι ἐκεῖ ἐστιν, καὶ ἦλθον οὐ διὰ τὸν Ἰησοῦν μόνον, ἀλλ᾽ ἵνα καὶ τὸν Λάζαρον ἴδωσιν ὃν ἤγειρεν ἐκ νεκρῶν. 10. ἐβουλεύσαντο δὲ οἱ ἀρχιερεῖς ἵνα καὶ τὸν

12³⁷, and it means there the mob, the mass of the people, or, as the E.V. has it, " _the common people_ heard Him gladly "; and of this use of ὁ πολὺς ὄχλος Field (in Mk. 12³⁷) gives some classical instances. This, too, would suit the context well in the present passage, for crowds are generally composed of "the common people" and include "riff-raff." But, as Abbott points out (_Diat._ 1739-1740), the variant of Jn. gives here and at v. 12, _not_ ὁ πολὺς ὄχλος (as at Mk. 12³⁷), but ὁ ὄχλος πολύς, which is bad Greek. Westcott suggests that ὄχλος πολύς here must be treated as " a compound noun," but why Jn. should adopt such a usage is not explained.

Having regard to the grammatical difficulty presented by ὁ ὄχλος πολύς, and to the fact that both Latin and Syriac versions give " a great crowd " as the rendering, the balance of evidence seems to be against ὁ, and we therefore read ὄχλος πολύς both here and at v. 12.

ἔγνω οὖν. The rumour of the supper at Bethany spread quickly, and the people generally were much excited by the expectation of seeing not only Jesus, but Lazarus whom He raised from the dead (for ὃν ἤγειρεν ἐκ νεκρῶν, cf. vv. 1, 17).

ὄχλος πολὺς ἐκ τῶν Ἰουδαίων, " a great crowd of the Jews," _sc._ of the people of Judæa, who were _generally_ hostile to Jesus. But "the Jews" does not specially indicate here, as at 5¹⁰ 6⁴¹, etc., the party of opposition to Him; it includes those who favoured (v. 11) as well as those who did not favour His claims (see on 1¹⁹). A "great crowd" of them came to Bethany, apparently on the evening of the Sabbath, to see the man who had come back from the dead, as well as to see Jesus who raised him. To see one returned from the dead would indeed be a great experience (cf. Lk. 16³¹).

10. ἐβουλεύσαντο δὲ οἱ ἀρχιερεῖς κτλ. The Sanhedrim (see on 7³²) had given directions that the movements of Jesus should be reported to them (11⁵⁷); and having heard of the excitement caused by the presence of Lazarus as well as of Jesus at Bethany, they made up their minds that both Lazarus and Jesus should die: ἵνα καὶ τὸν Λάζ. ἀποκτείνωσιν, "that they would kill Lazarus _also_." The priests, being of the Sadducean party, who rejected the idea of resurrection, were naturally disconcerted by the report that Lazarus had been raised from the dead ; and they were unscrupulous as to the means which they employed to put an end to what they regarded as mischievous talk.

Λάζαρον ἀποκτείνωσιν, 11. ὅτι πολλοὶ δι' αὐτὸν ὑπῆγον τῶν
Ἰουδαίων καὶ ἐπίστευον εἰς τὸν Ἰησοῦν.

12. Τῇ ἐπαύριον ὄχλος πολὺς ὁ ἐλθὼν εἰς τὴν ἑορτήν, ἀκούσαντες
ὅτι ἔρχεται Ἰησοῦς εἰς Ἱεροσόλυμα, 13. ἔλαβον τὰ βαΐα τῶν

11. The priests were specially urgent about the putting
away of Lazarus, because, on his account (δι' αὐτόν), many of
the Jews (cf. 11⁴⁵) " began to go away " (ὑπῆγον), perhaps to
Bethany, which was the centre of attraction, " and began to
believe in Jesus " (ἐπίστευον εἰς τὸν Ἰησοῦν ; cf. note on
1¹²). The force of the imperfect tenses must be observed.
The verb ὑπάγειν, " to withdraw," is a favourite word with
Jn. (see on 7³³), and ὑπῆγον here may mean simply "they began
to withdraw," *i.e.* from their allegiance to the chief priests,
as at 6⁶⁷, where Jesus asks His disciples, " Would you also go
away ? "

The triumphal entry to Jerusalem (vv. 12–19)

12. The Synoptic accounts of the entry to Jerusalem are
found at Mk. 11⁷⁻¹⁰, Mt. 21⁴⁻⁹, Lk. 19³⁵⁻³⁸. As has been pointed
out above (on v. 1), Mk. (followed by Mt.) places the supper
at Bethany later in the week of the Passion, but Jn., putting
it on Saturday, Nisan 9, halts Jesus and the disciples at Bethany
for that night, the entry taking place on Sunday, Nisan 10.
Christian tradition has followed Jn. in putting the triumphal
entry on Palm Sunday.

τῇ ἐπαύριον, *sc.* on the Sunday. Jn is fond of these notes
of time (see Introd., p. cii).

ὄχλος πολύς (see on v. 9) κτλ., " a great crowd that had come
up to the feast," *sc.* those that came from the country parts to
the metropolis, including doubtless many Galilæans (see 4⁴⁵).

ἀκούσαντες, " having heard," *sc.* from those who had come
by way of Bethany. ὅτι is *recitantis*. The words they heard
were: ἔρχεται Ἰησοῦς εἰς Ἱεροσόλυμα. B⊖ prefix ὁ to Ἰησοῦς,
while אADLW omit; it is usually B that omits the def. art.
(see on 1²⁹).

The entry of Jesus would naturally provoke curiosity and
enthusiasm, coming (as Jn. represents it to have done) not
long after the raising of Lazarus (11⁵⁵· ⁵⁶). The most conspicuous discrepancy between Mk. and Jn. is at this point,
Mk. not mentioning Lazarus at all, but describing none the
less the triumphal entry, while the enthusiasm with which
Jesus was received is expressly connected by Jn. with the
miracle at Bethany (see Introd., p. clxxxiii).

13. ἔλαβον τὰ βαΐα τῶν φοινίκων. βαΐον, a " palm branch,"

φοινίκων καὶ ἐξῆλθον εἰς ὑπάντησιν αὐτῷ, καὶ ἐκραύγαζον
Ὡσαννά
εὐλογημένος ὁ ἐρχόμενος ἐν ὀνόματι Κυρίου,
καὶ ὁ Βασιλεὺς τοῦ Ἰσραήλ.

occurs again in the Greek Bible only at 1 Macc. 13⁵¹, in the
account of Simon's triumphal entry into Jerusalem, μετὰ
αἰνέσεως καὶ βαΐων κτλ. (cf. 2 Macc. 10⁷). To carry palms
was a mark of triumphant homage to a victor or a king
(cf. Rev. 7⁹). Either βαΐα or φοίνικες, separately, would
mean "palms," so that Jn.'s τὰ βαΐα τῶν φοινίκων is super-
fluously precise (see Abbott, *Diat.* 2047), "the palm branches
of the palm trees," perhaps trees which grew on the slopes of
Olivet. The Synoptists do not mention the bearing of palms:
Mk. has στιβάδας, *i.e.* "litter" of leaves, etc., which were
strewn in the road; Mt. says ἔκοπτον κλάδους ἀπὸ τῶν δένδρων
καὶ ἐστρώννυον ἐν τῇ ὁδῷ. There seem to have been two
crowds, one accompanying Jesus, the other going out from the
city to meet Him (ἐξῆλθον εἰς ὑπάντησιν αὐτῷ); see Swete on
Mk. 11⁹, and cf. v. 18 below.

καὶ ἐκραύγαζον κτλ., "they kept crying out Hosanna."
ἐκραύγαζον is read by אB³DLW, as against ἔκραζον of the
rec. text (ΑΓΔΘ). For κραυγάζειν applied to the shouting
of crowds, cf. Ezra 3¹³ ; and see note on 11⁴³ above.

Before Ὡσαννά, the rec., with אADW, ins. λέγοντες: om.
BLΓΔΘ.

The words from the Psalter with which (according to the
Synoptists as well as Jn.) the acclaiming crowds greeted Jesus
as He rode into the city, were the words with which in the
original use of the Psalm the priests blessed the procession entering the Temple. "Hosanna : Blessed in the Name of Yahweh
is he that cometh" (Ps. 118²⁵·²⁶). The sense is missed if ἐν
ὀνόματι κυρίου is connected with ὁ ἐρχόμενος. The Hebrew
priests were chosen "to bless in the name of Yahweh" (Deut.
21⁵); and so also it is written of David εὐλόγησεν τὸν λαὸν
ἐν ὀνόματι κυρίου (2 Sam. 6¹⁸). Cf. also 1 Kings 22¹⁶, 2 Kings
2²⁴ ; and see note on 16²³.

The quotation of Ps. 118²⁵·²⁶ by the crowds who hailed
Jesus on His entry to Jerusalem was something more than a
mere blessing of welcome, as of One who had done wonderful
things (cf. Ps. 129⁸). It recognised in Him ὁ ἐρχόμενος, "the
Coming One," even as Martha had said to Him σὺ εἶ . . . ὁ
εἰς τὸν κόσμον ἐρχόμενος (11²⁷ ; cf. Mt. 11³).

The cry of *Hosanna* (in Aramaic אנעשׁוה, rendered
σῶσον δή in the LXX of Ps. 118²⁵) was the refrain sung by the
people in the processional recitation of Ps. 118 at the Feast of

14. εὑρὼν δὲ ὁ Ἰησοῦς ὀνάριον ἐκάθισεν ἐπ᾽ αὐτό, καθώς ἐστιν γεγραμμένον

Tabernacles. When v. 25 was reached, the palm branches which were carried by the worshippers were waved; and hence these sprigs of palm with myrtle and willow (*lulab* was the technical name) came themselves to be called *hosannas*.

The practice, however, of bearing palm sprigs and crying *Hosanna* was not confined to the Feast of Tabernacles, although it originated in the Temple services at that festival; and we have already cited from 1 Macc. 13⁵¹ an instance of palm branches being borne on the occasion of a popular welcome to a hero at another time of the year. There is thus no historical improbability in Jn.'s statement that palms and hosannas were accompaniments of the entry of Jesus to the city.[1]

καὶ ὁ βασιλεὺς τοῦ Ἰσραήλ. Mk. has instead of this εὐλογημένη ἡ ἐρχομένη βασιλεία τοῦ πατρὸς ἡμῶν Δαυείδ, which conveys the same idea, *sc.* that the crowds were acclaiming Jesus as the Messianic king. Lk. has ὁ ἐρχόμενος ὁ βασιλεύς, but Mt. puts it differently, reporting the cry as Ὡσαννὰ τῷ υἱῷ Δαυείδ (a different use of *hosanna*, perhaps derived from some liturgical refrain). Jn. has already (1⁴⁹) attributed the confession σὺ βασιλεὺς εἶ τοῦ Ἰσραήλ to Nathanael. It was this public acclamation of Jesus as King of Israel or King of the Jews which was the foundation of the charge made against Him before Pilate (18³³). He had refused earlier in His ministry to allow the eager people to "make Him king" (6¹⁵); but now He did not disclaim the title (cf. Lk. 19³⁸⁻⁴⁰). Pseudo-Peter represents the inscription on the cross as being in the form οὗτος ἐστιν ὁ βασιλεὺς τοῦ Ἰσραήλ (see on 19¹⁹).

14. εὑρὼν δὲ ὁ Ἰησοῦς ὀνάριον κτλ. This is not verbally consistent with the Synoptists, who tell that it was the *disciples* who had found the ass, in accordance with the directions given them by Jesus (Mk. 11²⁻⁶). Chrysostom is at unnecessary pains to reconcile the various statements; see v. 16 below.

ἐκάθισεν ἐπ᾽ αὐτό. So Mk. 11⁷; Lk. 19³⁵ says ἐπεβίβασαν τὸν Ἰησοῦν.

καθώς ἐστιν γεγραμμένον. See on 2¹⁷ for this formula of citation.

15. The quotation is from Zech. 9⁹, in an abbreviated form. The LXX has πῶλον νέον, whereas Jn. has πῶλον ὄνου, a more literal rendering of the Hebrew; for the opening words, "Exult greatly," he gives μὴ φοβοῦ. Mk. and Lk., while

[1] See Dalman, *Words of Jesus*, p. 220 f. ; Cooper, in *D.C.G.* i. 749 ; and Cheyne, in *E.B.* 2117, for the word *hosanna*.

15.   Μὴ φοβοῦ, θυγάτηρ Σιών·
      ἰδοὺ ὁ Βασιλεύς σου ἔρχεται,
      καθήμενος ἐπὶ πῶλον ὄνου.

narrating the entry into Jerusalem, do not quote the prophecy.
Mt. (21⁵) gives it in the form Εἴπατε τῇ θυγατρὶ Σιών, Ἰδού,
ὁ βασιλεύς σου ἔρχεταί σοι πραῢς καὶ ἐπιβεβηκὼς ἐπὶ ὄνον καὶ ἐπὶ
πῶλον υἱὸν ὑποζυγίου. Jn. notes (v. 16) that the application
of this prophecy of Zechariah to the entry of Jesus was not
thought of until a later time; but Mt. introduces his account
with the formula ἵνα πληρωθῇ τὸ ῥηθὲν διὰ τοῦ προφήτου λέγοντος
. . . (see Introd., p. cliv).

The full quotation, as given by Mt., is misleading. The
story, as told by the other evangelists, is simply that an ass's
colt was found and that Jesus rode on it. But Mt., misunderstanding the Hebrew repetition in Zech. 9⁹,

          ". . . upon an ass,
    and upon a colt, the foal of a she-ass,"

where only one animal is indicated, tells us that *two* animals
were fetched,[1] and garments put on them that they might be
ridden. Jn., on the contrary, gives only that part of the
prophecy which is relevant, *sc.* " sitting on an ass's colt."

It is not to be thought that there is any suggestion of
humility in riding upon an ass. On the contrary, the ass and
the mule were the animals used in peace by great persons for
their progresses, as the horse was used in war. The sons of
the judges rode upon asses (Judg. 10⁴ 12¹⁴); so did Ahithophel
(2 Sam. 17²³); so did Mephibosheth, Saul's son, when he went
to Jerusalem to meet David (2 Sam. 19²⁶); cf. Judg. 5¹⁰. Indeed
Zech. 9¹⁰ shows plainly that the prophecy was specially of
One coming *in peace*.

The LXX translators did not understand this. They have
πώλους only in Judg. 10⁴ 12¹⁴, probably because they thought
of an ass as a beast of burden exclusively; thus in Zech. 9⁹
they have not noticed that אָתוֹן is the regular word for *she-ass*
(Gen. 32¹⁵), which may be either used for riding or for carrying
loads.

The king, then, in the vision of Zechariah, rode upon an
ass to signify that he came in peace, not to destroy but to
save; and the entry of Jesus to Jerusalem on an ass was understood by the populace, in like manner, as the entry of the
Prince of Peace.

16. A similar reminiscence of the evangelist is set down at
2²², where see note. The saying of Jesus about restoration,

[1] Justin (*Dial.* 53) follows Mt. in this, and specially dwells upon
the choice of *two* animals.

16. Ταῦτα οὐκ ἔγνωσαν αὐτοῦ οἱ μαθηταὶ τὸ πρῶτον, ἀλλ' ὅτε ἐδοξάσθη Ἰησοῦς, τότε ἐμνήσθησαν ὅτι ταῦτα ἦν ἐπ' αὐτῷ γεγραμμένα καὶ ταῦτα ἐποίησαν αὐτῷ. 17. Ἐμαρτύρει οὖν ὁ ὄχλος ὁ ὢν μετ' αὐτοῦ ὅτε τὸν Λάζαρον ἐφώνησεν ἐκ τοῦ μνημείου καὶ ἤγειρεν αὐτὸν

after the Cleansing of the Temple, was not understood by the disciples until after His Resurrection. So, too, they did not perceive the significance in connexion with prophecy of His entry into Jerusalem, riding upon an ass, until He was " glorified," and they began to reflect upon the events of His ministry.

For ἐδοξάσθη, see on 7³⁹ 12²³. Cf. also 13³¹.

אBLW⊙ omit δέ after the first ταῦτα, which the rec. inserts. αὐτοῦ οἱ μαθηταί (אB⊙) is the true order of words.

The rec. (with DW⊙) inserts ὁ before Ἰησοῦς, which is omitted in אABL. This omission of the article is not in accordance with Jn.'s general usage (see on 1²⁹), and it is possible that the whole verse is an explanatory gloss added by an editor other than the evangelist himself. The threefold repetition of ταῦτα is somewhat clumsy, and can hardly be intentional. Again, the phrase ἐπ' αὐτῷ γεγραμμένα is unlike Jn. (cf. Rev. 10¹¹ 22¹⁶): it must mean that the Scriptures quoted were, as it were, " based on Him." D substitutes περὶ αὐτοῦ for ἐπ' αὐτῷ, recognising the difficulty. And, finally, the last clause of the verse, which says that the disciples afterwards remembered " that they had done these things to Him," invites the question, " What things? " Evidently, the answer is that the reference is to the search for the ass, in accordance with the instructions of Jesus, of which the Synoptists tell. But, as we have seen, Jn. tells nothing of this incident. He says only (v. 14) that " Jesus having found the ass, sat thereon," but he does not mention the co-operation of the disciples in this, or that they took any part in the entry to the city. It seems likely that the comment preserved in the last clause of this verse is due to some one who was thinking of the Synoptic narrative.

17. The interpretation of this verse depends mainly upon whether ὅτε (rec. with אABWΓΔ⊙) or ὅτι (DL) is adopted as the true reading before τὸν Λάζαρον. If ὅτι be approved (with Tischendorf), we translate, " So the crowd that was with Him was testifying that *He called Lazarus from the tomb, and raised him from the dead*," ὅτι introducing the actual words used by the crowd when acclaiming the entry of Jesus. Cf. Lk. 19³⁷: " the whole multitude of the disciples began to rejoice and praise God with a loud voice for all the mighty works which they had seen." According to this rendering, the shouts of the crowd made special reference to the raising of

ἐκ νεκρῶν.   18. διὰ τοῦτο καὶ ὑπήντησεν αὐτῷ ὁ ὄχλος, ὅτι ἤκουσαν
τοῦτο αὐτὸν πεποιηκέναι τὸ σημεῖον.   19. οἱ οὖν Φαρισαῖοι εἶπαν
πρὸς ἑαυτούς Θεωρεῖτε ὅτι οὐκ ὠφελεῖτε οὐδέν· ἴδε ὁ κόσμος ὀπίσω
αὐτοῦ ἀπῆλθεν.

Lazarus. This is entirely consistent with the view which Jn.
gives his readers of the extraordinary effect which that miracle
had on the public mind (vv. 9, 18). But, attractive as this
rendering is, ὅτε must be preferred to ὅτι on the MS. evidence;
and we translate: " So the crowd that was with Him when He
called Lazarus from the tomb, and raised him from the dead,"
i.e. the onlookers at the scene described 11³³⁻⁴⁴, " bore their
testimony." The true authors of the ovation were the people
who had been spectators of the miracle, who no doubt inspired
all their acquaintances with their wondering enthusiasm.
They " bore their witness." See for the idea of μαρτυρία in
Jn., the note on 1⁷ ; and cf. Introd., p. xc.

18. διὰ τοῦτο (see on 5¹⁶ for this opening) καὶ ὑπήντησεν αὐτῷ
ὁ ὄχλος, "for this reason the crowd also met Him," *sc.*
the multitude mentioned v. 13, as distinct from the crowd
accompanying Him from Bethany, where they had seen the
raising of Lazarus. There were two streams of people : one
escorting Jesus, the other meeting Him (see on v. 13), " because
they heard (ἤκουσαν is preferable to the rec. ἤκουσε) that He
had done this sign."

For the σημεῖα of Jesus, see on 2¹¹.

19. οἱ οὖν Φαρισαῖοι. The Pharisees formed the party
who were most deeply opposed to the teaching of Jesus (see
on 1²⁴), and who initiated the movement for His arrest, which
was ultimately carried out by the authority of the ἀρχιερεῖς
(v. 10), who were the most influential members of the Sanhedrim
(see on 7³²). They were in despair at the reception given to
Jesus at His entry into the city, and said to each other, " Do
you notice (θεωρεῖτε is probably indicative, rather than imperative) that you don't do any good ? " θεωρεῖν is used here
of mental perception and understanding of the situation (see
on 2²³).

With οὐκ ὠφελεῖτε οὐδέν; cf. 6⁶³ ἡ σὰρξ οὐκ ὠφελεῖ
οὐδέν.

For ἴδε in Jn., see on 1²⁹.

ὁ κόσμος. DL add ὅλος to bring out the sense, " the
whole world," everybody, *tout le monde.* Wetstein quotes a
Rabbinical story of a priest of whom it was said, in like manner,
" all the world was going after him." For κόσμος in Jn.,
see on 1⁹.

ὀπίσω αὐτοῦ ἀπῆλθεν. The aor. ἀπῆλθεν is here equivalent to " has gone," or, as the Sinai Syriac renders, " is going." The movement which the Pharisees regretted was in progress.

For the use of ὀπίσω, cf. 2 Sam. 15¹³ ἐγενήθη ἡ καρδία ἀνδρῶν Ἰσραὴλ ὀπίσω Ἀβεσσαλώμ.

The Greek inquirers (vv. 20-22)

20. The episode of the Greek inquirers is introduced immediately after the complaint made by the Pharisees, " the world is gone after Him." Among those who were excited and moved by the reports about Jesus and Lazarus were some Greek pilgrims; it was not only Jews and Galilæans who were attracted by what they had heard of the wonderful things that had happened at Bethany, but Greeks as well. And Jn., alone among the evangelists, notes that some of them told Philip of their desire to see Jesus, and that Jesus was informed of it. This incident is naturally recalled in a Gospel written primarily for Greek readers. It is, however, not explicitly said that the request of the Greeks for an interview with Jesus was granted, or that they were present while the sayings of vv. 23-28 were being pronounced.

But, although there is no positive statement to this effect in the text, it has been generally held since the days of Tatian that v. 20 begins a new section of the Gospel, and that vv. 20-22 are to be read in connexion with what follows. On this supposition, it is natural to seek in the words of Jesus here some message which may be taken as specially appropriate to Greeks. It has been suggested, *e.g.* by Lange, that the tremendous paradox of v. 25, " he that loveth his life loseth it, and he that hateth his life shall keep it," has a peculiar applicability, if regarded as the judgment of Christ on Greek ideals of life. For the Greek, the ideal of manhood was to reach the fulness of personal life; a man should develop his own personality; the larger and richer his life, the more nearly he approached his highest. There is something of this in Christianity as well as in Greek paganism, for Christianity holds up the Perfect Man as exemplar. But the Christian ideal involves *sacrifice*, and this was foreign to the philosophy of Greece. Jn *may* mean us to understand v. 25 as implying the condemnation by Jesus of Greek ideals of life. Again, v. 32, " I will draw all men to myself," is a universal promise, including not only Jews but Gentiles like the Greek inquirers. And some have found in the exhortation, " Believe in the light, that ye may become sons of light " (v. 36), an allusion to the prophecy, " The glory of the Lord is risen upon thee. . . . Nations

20. Ἦσαν δὲ Ἕλληνές τινες ἐκ τῶν ἀναβαινόντων ἵνα προσκυνήσωσιν ἐν τῇ ἑορτῇ· 21. οὗτοι οὖν προσῆλθον Φιλίππῳ τῷ ἀπὸ
Βηθσαϊδὰ τῆς Γαλιλαίας, καὶ ἠρώτων αὐτὸν λέγοντες Κύριε, θέλομεν

(ἔθνη) shall come to thy light, and kings to thy brightness"
(Isa. 60¹· ³).

Yet it must be owned that if vv. 23-28 are to be interpreted
as addressed in particular to the Greeks whom Jesus now saw
for the first time, the use of the Jewish title "Son of Man"
(see Introd., p. cxxxii) is puzzling (v. 23); and it is even more
difficult to suppose that Jesus revealed to these strangers the
anguish of His soul in words like those of v. 27. It is possible
that vv. 20-22 should be treated as linked closely with v. 19, but
as having no special relation with vv. 23 ff., a new paragraph
beginning at v. 23 (where see note).

ἦσαν δὲ Ἕλληνές τινες (this is the reading of אBDLW, as
against τινες Ἕλληνες of the rec. text) ἐκ τῶν ἀναβαινόντων
(for ἀναβαίνειν of "going up" to Jerusalem, cf. 2¹³) ἵνα
προσκυνήσωσιν (see on 4²⁰ for the absolute constr. of προσκυνεῖν)
ἐν τῇ ἑορτῇ. Among (ἐκ) those who went up to the feast
were many strangers (cf. 1 Kings 8⁴¹). These men were not
Ἑλληνισταί, i.e. Greek-speaking Jews (see on 7³⁵), but
Ἕλληνες, Greeks who had become proselytes of the gate, and
accordingly attended the Jewish festivals (see Acts 17⁴ for
"devout Greeks" at Thessalonica ; and cf. Acts 8²⁷ for the
Ethiopian eunuch who came up to Jerusalem to worship). To
such proselytes the Court of the Gentiles in the Temple precincts
was appropriated. It was from this court (see on 2¹⁴) that the
moneychangers and the cattle were expelled by Jesus on the
occasion when He cleansed the Temple; and if this episode is
rightly placed by the Synoptists in the last week of Jesus'
ministry (but see on 2¹³ᶠ·), the Greek inquirers may have been
moved to seek speech with Him by the impression which His
strong action had made on them, as well as by the reports of
the raising of Lazarus.

21. οὗτοι οὖν προσῆλθον Φιλίππῳ τῷ ἀπὸ Βηθσαϊδὰ τῆς
Γαλιλαίας. For the notices of Philip in Jn., see on 1⁴³· ⁴⁴. He
had a Greek name, and this may have encouraged the Greek
proselytes to speak to him. They may have come from the
Greek cities of Decapolis.

Objection has been taken to the phrase "Bethsaida of
Galilee," i.e. Bethsaida Julias, for no other Bethsaida is known
(see on 6¹), on the ground that the next appearance of this
descriptive title is in Claudius Ptolemæus (c. 140 A.D.), and
that such language suggests a second-century writer. But
there is abundance of evidence that the north-eastern side of

τὸν Ἰησοῦν ἰδεῖν. 22. ἔρχεται ὁ Φίλιππος καὶ λέγει τῷ Ἀνδρέᾳ
ἔρχεται Ἀνδρέας καὶ Φίλιππος καὶ λέγουσιν τῷ Ἰησοῦ.

the lake, where Bethsaida is situated, was reckoned as in the
province of Galilee by the year A.D. 80.[1]

The Greeks address Philip with respect, as κύριε, "Sir."
He was not a Rabbi or teacher, but κύριε was an appropriate
mode of address from those who saw in Philip the disciple
and friend of One on whom they looked with reverential
admiration (see on 1[38]).

θέλομεν τὸν Ἰησοῦν ἰδεῖν. There is no suggestion that they
understood or imagined that Jesus was the Christ. They
say τὸν Ἰησοῦν (using His personal name ; cf. 18[5]), not τὸν
Χριστόν. And they mean by "seeing" Him, having a private
conversation; any one could see Him in the Temple courts,
but they wished for something more intimate.

The request may well have embarrassed Philip. The
Twelve had been forbidden to preach to Gentiles (Mt. 10[5, 6]);
and although the Jews at Jerusalem had wondered whether one
of the mysterious sayings of Jesus could mean that He proposed
"to teach the Greeks" (7[35]), it is a question how far Jesus had
explained to the apostles the full scope of His mission. This
has been considered above (see on 10[16]); but we must mark
here that although in the Fourth Gospel the Gentiles are more
explicitly than in the Synoptists brought within the range of
Jesus' mission, it is in that Gospel that we can most clearly
trace a hesitation on the part of one of the Twelve to admit
that Jesus has a message for Greeks as well as for Jews. As
has been said above (on v. 20), we are not told whether Jesus
gave an interview to these inquirers or whether He refused it.

22. ἔρχεται ὁ Φίλιππος καὶ λέγει τῷ Ἀνδρέᾳ. For the close
association between Philip and Andrew, and for the vivid
characterisation of each which is apparent in Jn., see on 6[8].
Philip is cautious, perhaps a little dull; Andrew is the practical
man to whom others appeal in a difficulty. Andrew is one of
the inner circle of the Twelve (Mk. 13[3]), and perhaps might
venture to proffer an unusual request to Jesus, where Philip
would hesitate.

For the second ἔρχεται the rec. text has καὶ πάλιν, omitting
καί before λέγουσι. But the best-attested reading is ἔρχεται
Ἀνδρέας καὶ Φίλιππος καὶ λέγουσιν τῷ Ἰησοῦ. The singular
ἔρχεται followed by the plur. λέγουσιν is quite a classical usage
in a sentence like this.

[1] See Sanday, *Sacred Sites*, p. 95 ; G. A. Smith, *Hist. Geogr. of Holy
Land*, p. 458 ; Rix, *Tent and Testament*, pp. 265 ff. ; the last-named
work giving a full discussion of the situation of Bethsaida.

23. Ὁ δὲ Ἰησοῦς ἀποκρίνεται αὐτοῖς λέγων Ἐλήλυθεν ἡ ὥρα ἵνα

*Jesus announces His impending Passion (v. 23); here is the
supreme exemplification of the Law of Life through
Death (vv. 24–26)*

23. ἀποκρίνεται. So ℵBLW, as against ἀπεκρίνατο (see on
5[17]) of the rec. text, with ADΓΔ. Θ *fam.* 13 have ἀπεκρίθη.
The pres. tense does not occur in the Synoptists, and in Jn.
only twice again, 13[26. 38].

ἀποκρίνεται αὐτοῖς, *sc.* He answers Andrew and Philip.
The Greeks may have heard what He said, but there is no
hint of it in what follows.

For the unusual constr. ἀποκρίνεται λέγων, see on 1[26] ; and
cf. 1[50].

ἐλήλυθεν ἡ ὥρα. The time of the Passion had come. Cf.
13[1] ἦλθεν αὐτοῦ ἡ ὥρα and 17[1] ἐλήλυθεν ἡ ὥρα. The phrase
occurs in the Synoptists only in the account of the words of
Jesus at Gethsemane immediately before the Betrayal, ἦλθεν
ἡ ὥρα, Mk. 14[41], Mt. 26[45] (cf. ὁ καιρός μου ἐγγύς ἐστιν, Mt. 26[18],
which was said at an earlier stage, before the preparation of
the Last Supper).

The Fourth Gospel is written throughout, as Jesus Himself
spoke, *sub specie æternitatis.* He is represented as knowing
from the beginning the time and manner and sequel of the
end of His public ministry in the flesh. Twice in this Gospel
He is made to say " my time (καιρός) is not yet come " (7[6. 8]);
and twice Jn. comments " His hour (ὥρα) was not yet come"
(7[30] 8[20]; see on 2[4]).

It will be noticed that, with the possible exception of this
passage (12[23]), the phrase " the hour has come " is always
(13[1] 17[1], Mk. 14[41]) applied to the hour immediately before the
Betrayal. It is not used loosely, as if it only meant " the time
is near," and in every case the verb ἐλήλυθεν (ἦλθεν) comes
first, the phrase ἐλήλυθεν ἡ ὥρα being strikingly and austerely
impressive and final. Its presence suggests that what is about
to be narrated relates to the last scenes, and we shall see (on
v. 27) that there are some indications that in what follows Jn.
is giving us his version of the prayers of Jesus at Gethsemane.

ἐλήλυθεν ἡ ὥρα ἵνα δοξασθῇ ὁ υἱὸς τοῦ ἀνθρώπου, " the
hour is come that the Son of Man should be glorified." For
δοξασθῇ, " glorified," *sc.* in His Death, see on 7[39]; and cf.
12[16] 13[31]. This is quite a different use of δοξάζεσθαι from that
at 11[4], where ἵνα δοξασθῇ ὁ υἱὸς τοῦ θεοῦ means " that the
Son of God might be glorified " by the manifestation of the
Father's power in the recovery of Lazarus. Here, with the

δοξασθῇ ὁ Υἱὸς τοῦ ἀνθρώπου. 24. ἀμὴν ἀμὴν λέγω ὑμῖν, ἐὰν μὴ
ὁ κόκκος τοῦ σίτου πεσὼν εἰς τὴν γῆν ἀποθάνῃ, αὐτὸς μόνος μένει·
ἐὰν δὲ ἀποθάνῃ, πολὺν καρπὸν φέρει. 25. ὁ φιλῶν τὴν ψυχὴν αὐτοῦ

Passion in view, Jesus does not speak of Himself as "Son of
God," but as "Son of Man"; cf. 3¹⁴ 6⁵³ 8²⁸, and see Introd.,
p. cxxxii.

The glorification of Jesus as Son of Man would be in His
Passion, as He now Himself declares. This is the paradox of
the Cross. But it is a paradox only to those who have not
considered its threefold illustration in nature and in human
life : (1) the seed must die that it may be fruitful, v. 24 ; (2)
the true life of man is achieved only through sacrifice, v. 25 ;
(3) the life of service, of ministry, is the life of honour, of the
true glory, v. 26.

ἐλήλυθεν ἡ ὥρα ἵνα δοξασθῇ κτλ. ἵνα seems *prima facie* to
be used as equivalent to "when"; and Burney finds an explanation of this in his suggestion that ἵνα is often a translation
or mistranslation of the Aramaic ח, which may bear this meaning. But if we compare 13¹ 16². ³², we see that in each case
where ἵνα is used as here, it always follows "the hour has
come " or "the hour cometh." When God's predestined
hour has come, the purpose which He has in view must follow.
It has come *in order that* this purpose may be fulfilled. The
use of ἵνα in such passages is an illustration of that view of the
sequence of events, which is constantly present to the mind of
Jn., and which he does not hesitate to ascribe to Jesus Himself
(see on 2⁴).

24. ἀμὴν ἀμήν κτλ. See on 1⁵¹ for this formula introducing
a saying of special solemnity. Here it is prefixed to the *first*
illustration of the paradox that Life comes through Death,
viz. the law that the grain of wheat (ὁ κόκκος. *any* grain)
must die before it can bear fruit. To this law Paul appeals
in his statement of the resurrection of man (1 Cor. 15³⁶). It
has, perhaps, a special applicability here, in reference to what
precedes ; for Christ, who is about to be glorified in Death,
claimed to be, Himself, the *Bread* of Life.

Hippolytus (*Ref.* vi. 16) quotes from the *Apophasis* of
Simon Magus (a work written about A.D. 100) a passage that
Schmiedel[1] thinks is behind this verse. Simon says that a
tree abiding alone and bearing no fruit is destroyed (ἐὰν δὲ
μείνῃ δένδρον μόνον, καρπὸν μὴ ποιοῦν, <μὴ> ἐξεικονισμένον
ἀφανίζεται), but he goes on to cite Mt. 3¹⁰. There is a verbal
similarity with Jn., but the thought is quite different.

25. We now come to the *second* illustration of the great

[1] *E.B.*, 1829, *s.v.* "Gospels."

ἀπολλύει αὐτήν, καὶ ὁ μισῶν τὴν ψυχὴν αὐτοῦ ἐν τῷ κόσμῳ τούτῳ εἰς ζωὴν αἰώνιον φυλάξει αὐτήν. 26. ἐὰν ἐμοί τις διακονῇ, ἐμοὶ ἀκο-

paradox of the Cross: "He that loveth his life (ψυχή) loseth it (ἀπολλύει, with אBLW, is to be preferred to the rec. ἀπολέσει), and he that hateth his life in this world (ἐν τῷ κόσμῳ τούτῳ, cf. 8²³) shall keep it unto life eternal (for ζωὴ αἰώνιος, see on 4¹⁴)."

ψυχή is the conscious organ of feeling and desire, not so near the Divine as πνεῦμα, sometimes (as here) to be distinguished from πνεῦμα, but often used as its equivalent, just as in English we do not always sharply differentiate "soul" from "spirit" (see on 11³³).

This great saying may have been repeated by Jesus more than once, representing as it does the central lesson of His teaching and His life. In the Marcan tradition it is placed after the Confession of Peter (Mk. 8³⁵, Mt. 16²⁵, Lk. 9²⁴), when Jesus began to tell the Twelve that His Mission would issue in death. It is found also in other settings in the Mt.–Lk. tradition (Mt. 10³⁹, Lk. 17³³), where it comes from the source Q. In its most literal meaning it was applicable to the choice between martyrdom and apostasy, which Christians of the first century (as well as later) were sometimes called to make. But selfishness is always the death of the true life of man.

The strong expression "*hateth* his life" (ὁ μισῶν τὴν ψυχὴν αὐτοῦ) is softened down in the Synoptic parallels, but it is found in another context, Lk. 14²⁶.

26. In this verse is the *third* illustration of the paradox of v. 23, that the Passion of Jesus is His glorification. The life of ministry is a life of honour.

ἐὰν ἐμοί τις διακονῇ κτλ. The doctrine of διακονία, *i.e.* of the dignity of ministry, occupies a large place in all the Gospels. It is, naturally, an instinct of discipleship to minister to a master ; and the ministry of women disciples to Jesus (Mk. 1³¹ 15⁴¹, Lk. 10⁴⁰, Jn. 12²) needs no special comment. A servant is not thankworthy because he thus ministers (Lk. 17⁹). But the repeated teaching of Jesus goes much beyond this. He taught that the path to pre-eminence in His Kingdom is the path of service, of ministry (Mk. 10⁴³), and that true greatness cannot be otherwise attained (Mk. 9³⁵). Actually, the test by which His professed disciples shall be judged at the Last Judgment is the test of ministry; have they ministered to man, and therefore to Christ ? (Mt. 25⁴⁴). This is the *essentia* of discipleship, for ministry was the essential characteristic of the life of Christ, who came not διακονηθῆναι ἀλλὰ

λουθείτω, καὶ ὅπου εἰμὶ ἐγώ, ἐκεῖ καὶ ὁ διάκονος ὁ ἐμὸς ἔσται· ἐάν τις ἐμοὶ διακονῇ, τιμήσει αὐτὸν ὁ Πατήρ.

διακονῆσαι (Mk. 10⁴⁵); and the issue of His ministry was death, δοῦναι τὴν ψυχὴν αὐτοῦ λύτρον ἀντὶ πολλῶν.

In the present passage, He suggests that this, too, may be the portion of His faithful disciples. He has laid down the universal law of sacrifice, " he that hateth his life in this world shall keep it to life eternal " (v. 25). And He warns those to whom He has just foretold His death (v. 23), that His disciple-ship means following Him, and this may mean a following in the way of death.

ἐὰν ἐμοί τις διακονῇ. This is the true order of words (אABLW), although the rec. has διακονῇ τις. ἐμοί here is emphatic. It is the service of Christ that involves a perilous following.

ἐμοὶ ἀκολουθείτω, "me let him follow." See on 21¹⁹.

καὶ ὅπου εἰμὶ ἐγώ κτλ., "and where I am, there shall my minister be," in spiritual companionship, both here and (as is promised later) hereafter (14³ 17²⁴). εἰμί is the *essential* present, not necessarily conveying the idea of the visible presence of Christ (cf. 8⁵⁸). He does not say ἐγώ εἰμι—that would suggest different thoughts (see Introd., p. cxx)—but εἰμὶ ἐγώ. On the other hand, He had said to the Jews ὅπου εἰμὶ ἐγώ, ὑμεῖς οὐ δύνασθε ἐλθεῖν (7³⁴, where see note).

The rec. inserts καί after ἔσται, but om. אBDLWΘ.

ἐάν τις ἐμοὶ διακονῇ. Here τις is the emphatic word ; the promise that follows is for all true disciples.

τιμήσει αὐτὸν ὁ πατήρ, " him shall the Father honour " ; but the honour may be the kind of honour with which Christ was honoured (v. 23). For τιμᾶν, see on 5²³.

Jesus' agony of spirit (v. 27) ; a Voice from heaven (vv. 28–30) ; the world's condemnation (v. 31) ; the universal appeal of the Cross (v. 32)

27. Jn. does not give any account of the Agony in Geth-semane (see on 18¹); but the prayer recorded here corresponds very closely to the prayer in the garden recorded by the Synop-tists (Mk. 14³⁵·³⁶, Mt. 26³⁹, Lk. 22⁴²); and it may be that he intends vv. 27–29 to be his version of that tremendous spiritual crisis (see on v. 23). Thus ἡ ψυχή μου τετάρακται corre-sponds with Mk. 14³⁴ περιλυπός ἐστιν ἡ ψυχή μου ἕως θανάτου: σῶσόν με ἐκ τῆς ὥρας ταύτης corresponds to Mk. 14³⁵ προσηύχετο ἵνα εἰ δυνατόν ἐστι παρέλθῃ ἀπ' αὐτοῦ ἡ ὥρα: and the repeated πάτερ . . . πάτερ may reflect ἄββα ὁ πατήρ of Mk. 14³⁶ (cf.

27. Νῦν ἡ ψυχή μου τετάρακται, καὶ τί εἴπω; Πάτερ, σῶσόν με

Lk. 22⁴²). Indeed, no passage in Jn. illustrates so powerfully as this the words of Mk. 14³⁸ τὸ μὲν πνεῦμα πρόθυμον, ἡ δὲ σὰρξ ἀσθενής. And, finally, in Lk.'s narrative the sequel of the Agony is ὤφθη δὲ αὐτῷ ἄγγελος ἀπ᾽ οὐρανοῦ ἐνισχύων αὐτόν (Lk. 22⁴³). Is this another version of Jn. 12²⁹ ἄλλοι ἔλεγον, ἄγγελος αὐτῷ λελάληκεν?

It is noteworthy that while Mk., followed by Mt., asserts that John the son of Zebedee was present with Peter and James when the Agony of spirit began (Mk. 14³³), Lk. does not mention the names of any disciples as specially witnesses of the scene in the garden. The tradition of Mk. is different from the tradition of Lk.; and it would seem that the tradition of Jn. as to the Agony is different from both of his predecessors. Such a crisis of spiritual decision may, indeed, have recurred, Jn. mentioning the earlier occasion, while the Synoptists tell only of the later. But even this does not give a complete solution of the questions raised by the divergences of the evangelists in regard to the Agony; for Jn. at 18¹¹ puts the saying, "The cup which the Father hath given me, shall I not drink it?" (cf. Mk. 14³⁶, Lk. 22⁴²), into the mouth of Jesus *at Gethsemane* (although after His arrest) and not in connexion with the narrative of c. 12.

Nor, again, is it a sufficient explanation to say that Jn. does not narrate the Agony in the garden because he wishes to bring out the Divine self-surrender exhibited in the last scenes; for Jn. all through his Gospel lays special stress on the human emotions which Jesus felt. Jn. knew of the Agony in the garden, but we cannot tell why he chooses to reproduce some of the words then spoken by Jesus at the point in the narrative which we have now reached, rather than in what is (apparently) the proper place, viz. c. 18.

νῦν, "now, *at last*": the hour had come; cf. v. 23.

ἡ ψυχή μου τετάρακται. Cf. 13²¹ and 11³³, where see the note. As is there shown, we cannot in such phrases distinguish ψυχή from πνεῦμα. His "soul" was troubled. See the note on 4⁶ for the emphasis laid by Jn. on the complete humanity of Jesus; and cf. Ps. 42⁷ πρὸς ἐμαυτὸν ἡ ψυχή μου ἐταράχθη (cf. also Ps. 6⁴). This troubling of spirit was truly human (Heb. 5⁷).

καὶ τί εἴπω; "and what shall I say?" εἴπω, the *deliberative* subjunctive (see Abbott, *Diat.* 2512), being used to express a genuine, if momentary, indecision.

πάτερ, σῶσόν με ἐκ τῆς ὥρας ταύτης. This is the natural, human prayer of One face to face with a cruel death.

ἐκ τῆς ὥρας ταύτης. ἀλλὰ διὰ τοῦτο ἦλθον εἰς τὴν ὥραν ταύτην.
28. Πάτερ, δόξασόν σου τὸ ὄνομα. ἦλθεν οὖν φωνὴ ἐκ τοῦ οὐρανοῦ

For σώζειν see on 3¹⁷.

πάτερ. So Jesus was accustomed to begin His prayers;
see on 11⁴¹. For the aor. imper. σῶσον, see on 2⁵.

ἐκ τῆς ὥρας ταύτης : the hour had come (v. 23), and He
wished to be saved from its horrors. No distinction can be
drawn between ἐκ and ἀπό in a constr. like this (see on 1⁴⁴ 6³⁸).

ἀλλὰ διὰ τοῦτο κτλ., "and yet for this very purpose,"
sc. that His ministry should be consummated in the Passion,
"did I come to this hour"; cf. 18³⁷. He cannot now draw
back from the accomplishment of what He had come to do, in
fulfilment of the mission He had received. "Concurrebat
horror mortis et ardor obedientiae " (Bengel).

28. πάτερ, δόξασόν σου τὸ ὄνομα, "Father (see on preceding verse), make Thy Name glorious," sc. in the fulfilment
of the mission of Redemption, which was the Passion of Christ.
As "save me from this hour " is the prayer of the σάρξ, so
this is the prayer of the πνεῦμα, willing to suffer all, if thereby
the Name of God may be glorified. For "the Name " of
God, as expressing His character revealed in and by the Son,
see on 1¹² 5⁴³ 17¹¹. The "glory " of His Name is His glory as
exhibited in the world (cf. Isa. 63¹⁴ 66⁵); and that the Father
was "glorified " in the Death of Jesus is said again at 13³¹.
where see note.

In Ps. 79⁹ we have βοήθησον ἡμῖν, ὁ θεὸς ὁ σωτὴρ ἡμῶν,
ἕνεκα τῆς δόξης τοῦ ὀνόματός σου, but the Psalmist's prayer
was that the people might be delivered, and that in this deliverance the glory of the Name might be exhibited. Here
the prayer is not for deliverance; it is a prayer of submission
to what was impending, because through the Passion God's
Name would be glorified. This is the most complete and
perfect example of the prayer enjoined upon every disciple,
ἁγιασθήτω τὸ ὄνομά σου (Mt. 6⁹). In the Lord's Prayer this
comes first, before any petition; it is the condition to be accepted
before the petition "deliver us from evil " can be offered.
But in the case of Jesus it involved the surrender of all thought
of such deliverance. "Glorify Thy Name " carries with it
the "Thy will be done " of resignation.

There is a variant reading (L 1, 13, 33), δόξασόν σου τὸν
υἱόν, which may (as Abbott suggests, Diat. 2769) have arisen
by the misreading of a scribe, τοονομα being written τογνομα,
and then τογν at the end of a line being read as τ̄ο̄γ̄ν̄, "the
Son." But it is more likely that δόξασόν σου τὸν υἱόν has
been imported here from 17¹; and the fact that D adds ἐν τῇ

δόξῃ ᾗ εἶχον παρὰ σοὶ πρὸ τοῦ τὸν κόσμον γένεσθαι from 17[5] makes this probable. In any case, " glorify Thy Son " has a wholly different meaning (see note on 17[1]) from " glorify Thy Name," which is undoubtedly the true reading in the present passage.

It must be observed that πάτερ, δόξασόν σου τὸ ὄνομα is not a prayer that God's Name may be glorified by Jesus or by the world (for which idea, cf. Ps. 86[12], Isa. 42[10], Mal. 1[11]), but that God may *Himself* make it glorious. This is to be, indeed, through the voluntary Death of Jesus ; but the ministry of Jesus is treated throughout the Gospel as fulfilled in the Name of the Father, His words and works being, as it were, words and works of the Father (see on 5[43] 10[25] 17[11]).

ἦλθεν οὖν φωνὴ ἐκ τοῦ οὐρανοῦ, " there came then," *sc.* in answer to the prayer, " a Voice from heaven." This expression first appears Dan. 4[31], where a voice from heaven warns Nebuchadnezzar. The phrase became common in later Judaism. In the O.T. there are many indications of the belief that God may speak to men with audible and articulate voice (*e.g.* 1 Sam. 3[4], 1 Kings 19[13], Job 4[16]). The Rabbis, however, hesitated to use so anthropomorphic a form of speech as " God said," and they preferred to speak of a " voice from heaven." For examples, see *Enoch* lxv. 4, *Jubilees* xvii. 15, 2 Esd. 6[13. 17], and the first-century *Apocalypse of Baruch* xxii. 1, which has " The heavens were opened, and . . . a voice was heard from on high, and it said, Baruch, why art thou troubled ? " Cf. also a remarkable parallel to the passage before us in *Test. of XII. Patr.* (Levi, xviii. 6): " The heavens shall be opened, and from the temple of glory shall come upon him sanctification, with the Father's voice as from Abraham to Isaac, and the glory of the Most High shall be uttered over him."

In Rabbinical literature the heavenly voice is often mentioned under the name of *bath-qôl*, בת קול, *i.e.* " the daughter of a voice." The days of the prophets being over, the *bath-qôl* was regarded as the only medium of Divine revelation, and was generally counted as miraculous.[1] Two points only can be noted here: (1) the revelations of the *bath-qôl* were often expressed in Scripture phrases,[2] and (2) there are instances of the *bath-qôl* taking the form of an echo of words spoken on earth.[3]

In the N.T. voices from heaven are spoken of in Acts 11[7], Rev. 10[4], and besides in three passages of the Gospels, *sc.* the Synoptic narratives of the Baptism (Mk. 1[11]) and the Trans-

---

[1] For a full and learned account of the doctrine of *bath-qôl*, see Abbott, *Diat.* 726 f.; and cf. Dalman, *Words of Jesus*, p. 204 f.

[2] See Box, *D.C.G.* ii. 810.   [3] Abbott, *Diat.* 783.

figuration (Mk. 9⁷) of Jesus, and the present verse. In both the Synoptic passages, *sc.* of the Baptism and Transfiguration, the *bath-qôl* or heavenly Voice speaks in almost the same words. It combines Ps. 2⁷ and Isa. 42¹: "Thou art My Son . . . My chosen in whom My soul delighteth"; that is, it was expressed in Scripture phrases. Jn. does not tell of the Transfiguration, and he says nothing about the voice from heaven at the Baptism (cf. 1³². ³³). But he mentions here a *bath-qôl* of which, on the other hand, the Synoptists say nothing. Even if we are right in regarding vv. 28–30 as the Johannine version of the agonised prayer at Gethsemane, there is nothing in any of the Synoptic accounts of Gethsemane which corresponds with this comforting voice, although Lk. (22⁴³) tells of angelic ministration.

That is, according to the Gospel narratives, heavenly voices were heard by Jesus at three great moments of crisis and consecration in His ministry : after His Baptism, at His Transfiguration, and just before His Passion. In no case is it said that others understood or interpreted these " voices "; and if we put this into our modern ways of speech, we should say that their messages were *subjective* in the sense that they conveyed a meaning to none but Him to whom they were addressed, while *objective* in the sense that He was not deluded or deceived, for they were truly messages from God.

In v. 28 the Voice is an answer to the prayer δόξασον τὸ ὄνομα, and according to Jn. it said to Jesus καὶ ἐδόξασα καὶ πάλιν δοξάσω, *i.e.* " I did glorify My Name, and will glorify it again." This is not a quotation from the O.T., as the *bath-qôl* often was, although there are O.T. passages verbally like it. The pregnant saying of 1 Sam. 2³⁰ τοὺς δοξάζοντάς με δοξάσω, and the promise of Divine deliverance in Ps. 91¹⁵, which ends ἐξελοῦμαι καὶ δοξάσω αὐτόν, both speak of God " glorifying " His pious servants ; but the thought here is of God glorifying *His own Name*, which is quite different. The *bath-qôl*, if it may be so called, in this passage is of the nature of an *echo*, the word " glorify " in the prayer being twice repeated in answer. It is just possible, as Abbott suggests (*Diat.* 782 f.), that we should illustrate this by the one or two instances of an echoing *bath-qôl* that appear in the Talmud. But, whether this be so or not, it is plain that Jn. means us to understand that a sound was heard after Jesus had prayed, which conveyed an assurance to Him that His prayer was answered, while at the same time it impressed the bystanders with the sense that, at all events, something unusual was taking place.

ἐδόξασα, as, *e.g.*, at the raising of Lazarus, where the spectators saw τὴν δόξαν τοῦ θεοῦ (11⁴⁰). All the ἔργα of Jesus during His earthly ministry were *ad maiorem Dei gloriam*.

Καὶ ἐδόξασα καὶ πάλιν δοξάσω. 29. ὁ οὖν ὄχλος ὁ ἑστὼς καὶ ἀκούσας ἔλεγεν βροντὴν γεγονέναι· ἄλλοι ἔλεγον Ἄγγελος αὐτῷ λελάληκεν. 30. ἀπεκρίθη Ἰησοῦς καὶ εἶπεν Οὐ δι' ἐμὲ ἡ φωνὴ αὕτη

πάλιν δοξάσω, *sc.* in the approaching Passion of Jesus, when ὁ θεὸς ἐδοξάσθη ἐν αὐτῷ (13[31]). Nor need the promise πάλιν δοξάσω be thus restricted, for in every fresh triumph of the Christian spirit may be seen its fulfilment.

Aphrahat (*Sel. Dem.* xxi. 17) attributes the words "I have glorified and will glorify" to Jesus Himself—a curious slip of memory, unless it is a deliberate attempt to evade the difficulty of the passage.

29. ὁ οὖν ὄχλος ὁ ἑστὼς (ADWΘ have ἑστήκως ; cf. 3[29]) **καὶ ἀκούσας κτλ.,** " the crowd (that is, most of the bystanders) that stood by and heard said that it had thundered." That thunder is the Voice of God is a commonplace in the O.T. (cf. Ex. 9[28], 2 Sam. 22[14], Ps. 29[3], Job 37[5], Jer. 10[13]); and when the crowd said that it had thundered, they meant that the thunder was a Divine response to what Jesus had said, although they did not catch any articulate words. This is the only place in the N.T. where mention is made of a thunderclap.

ἄλλοι ἔλεγον, ἄγγελος αὐτῷ λελάληκεν, " others," that is, a few of the crowd, discerned that Jesus had received a definite message of comfort, and that something more than a clap of thunder had been heard. But none of the bystanders heard any articulate words; and this Jn. is careful to make clear. In this particular, the narrative is like that of the Voice from heaven at the conversion of Paul, where his companions heard a sound (ἀκούοντες τῆς φωνῆς, Acts 9[7]) but did not distinguish the words (τὴν φωνὴν οὐκ ἤκουσαν τοῦ λαλοῦντός μοι, Acts 22[9]; see note above on 3[8]).

Wetstein illustrates the passage by the prayer of Anchises, which has some verbal similarities (Virg. *Æn.* ii. 692):

> " Da deinde augurium, pater, atque haec omina firma
> Vix ea fatus erat senior, subitoque fragore
> Intonuit laeuum."

30. ἀπεκρίθη Ἰησοῦς καὶ εἶπεν. See on 1[49. 50].

οὐ δι' ἐμὲ ἡ φωνὴ αὕτη (this is the order of אABDLWΘ) **γέγονεν ἀλλὰ δι' ὑμᾶς,** " this voice has not happened for my sake but for yours." (For γέγονεν D has ἦλθεν, and Θ has ἐλήλυθεν.)

This statement presents difficulties similar to those which the traditional text offers at 11[42]; for it represents the Voice from heaven as without any significance for Jesus Himself, and as

γέγονεν ἀλλὰ δι' ὑμᾶς. 31. νῦν κρίσις ἐστὶν τοῦ κόσμου τούτου·
νῦν ὁ ἄρχων τοῦ κόσμου τούτου ἐκβληθήσεται ἔξω· 32. κἀγὼ ἐὰν

intended only to impress the crowd. No doubt, it might be said
that the sound, whatever it was, suggested to the crowd that
they would do well to mark what was happening, for it seemed
to be a heavenly signal in answer to the prayer of Jesus. It
was the signal for the judgment of the world (v. 31), now beginning. But we cannot attach any meaning to the words καὶ
ἐδόξασα καὶ πάλιν δοξάσω (v. 28), which the crowd were not
able to catch (v. 29), if they had no significance for Jesus. It
was to Him that the heavenly Voice seemed to come, and in
coming to give assurance to His spirit, that His impending
Death was to the greater glory of God. It is not impossible
that v. 30 has been added by the evangelist, in order to emphasise the *voluntariness* of Christ's surrender of Himself, as
a superhuman Person who needed no support for His soul
even in this dark hour. But v. 31, for all that, follows v. 30
in a true sequence: "The Voice was on *your* account. For
now is the world of men like you being judged."

31. νῦν. The Passion is conceived of as already begun
(see on v. 23 and 13³¹). It is a judging (κρίσις), a testing of
men (see 3¹⁷ 8¹⁵ 9³⁹).

For τοῦ κόσμου τούτου, see on 8²³, and v. 25 above.

The phrase ὁ ἄρχων τοῦ κόσμου τούτου appears again
14³⁰ 16¹¹, but nowhere else in the N.T. (cf., however, ὁ θεὸς τοῦ
αἰῶνος τούτου 2 Cor. 4⁴ and Eph. 2² 6¹²). The title " the
ruler of this world " is applied to Beliar in the earlier part of the
Ascension of Isaiah (i. 3, ii. 4, x. 29), which is probably contemporary with the Fourth Gospel; and Ignatius has ὁ ἄρχων
τοῦ αἰῶνος τούτου several times, *e.g. Eph.* xvii. xix. According to Lightfoot (*Hor. Hebr.* in loc.) שַׂר הָעוֹלָם was a well-
known Jewish title for Satan [1] (or for Sammael, the Angel of
Death), and it may be that the Johannine ὁ ἄρχων τοῦ κόσμου
τούτου goes back to this.

" The prince of this world has been already judged "
(16¹¹); but here is in view the issue of the judgment, when
he shall be finally cast out (ἐκβληθήσεται ἔξω) of the world
over which he claims dominion (cf. 1 Jn. 4⁴). For ἐκβάλλειν ἐκ,
see on 6³⁷.

32. ἐὰν ὑψωθῶ ἐκ τῆς γῆς, *sc.* on the Cross. See the note
on 3¹⁴ ; and cf. 8²⁸. ἐκ τῆς γῆς is "*from* the earth " and not
"*out* of the earth " as R.V. marg. has it, and as Westcott
interprets because he finds the Ascension indicated here by
ὑψωθῶ.

[1] Cf. also Schlatter, *Die Sprache, etc.*, p. 121.

ὑψωθῶ ἐκ τῆς γῆς, πάντας ἑλκύσω πρὸς ἐμαυτόν. 33. τοῦτο δὲ
ἔλεγεν σημαίνων ποίῳ θανάτῳ ἤμελλεν ἀποθνήσκειν.

πάντας ἑλκύσω πρὸς ἐμαυτόν. For the verb ἑλκύειν, see on
6⁴⁴. For ἐμαυτός in Jn., see on 5³⁰.

It has often been suggested (the criticism goes back to
Celsus; see Origen, c. Cels. ii. 13) that the predictions of His
Passion which the evangelists place in the mouth of Jesus are
vaticinia ex eventu, and that in particular these predictions, as
recorded by Jn., are so precise that they cannot be regarded as
historical. It is not, indeed, impossible that in some instances
the evangelists, and especially Jn. and Mt., ascribed language
to Jesus which was coloured by their knowledge of the sequel
of His ministry. But that He foresaw the end is certain.
He knew, and apparently was conscious from a very early stage
in His ministry, what its issue would be. And wonderful
as a prophecy like δεῖ ὑψωθῆναι τὸν υἱὸν τοῦ ἀνθρώπου (v. 34)
seems to be, and is, it is not more wonderful than that we should
find in a document of the first century the prophecy ἐὰν ὑψωθῶ
ἐκ τῆς γῆς, πάντας ἑλκύσω πρὸς ἐμαυτόν, " I will draw all
men to myself " (cf. 10¹⁶). The continuous fulfilment of this
prophecy throughout many centuries and among all races of
men is a fact of history. It is not any easier to believe that
the prophecy is an invention of the evangelist, than that he
recorded it because he had heard that his Master uttered it.
Whether we have in Jn. 12³² a genuine saying of Christ or
a saying which Jn. thought would be appropriate to Him,
it is a saying of remarkable prescience. The Word of
the Cross (1 Cor. 1¹⁸) has always been a word of power;
and the Appeal of the Cross has been the most effective that
the world has known. It draws " all men," πάντας, to the
Crucified.

There is a variant reading πάντα (א*D) which, if genuine,
would embrace the whole creation within the circle of the
attraction of Christ. But πάντας is better authenticated.

33. τοῦτο δὲ ἔλεγεν, introducing a comment of the evangelist,
as at 2²¹ 6⁶, " this He was saying, etc." (For the impft.
ἔλεγεν, cf. 5¹⁸ 6⁷¹ 8³¹.) This explanatory comment is repeated
18³², and it shows the interpretation which Jn. gives to ὑψωθῶ.
In the Fourth Gospel ὑψοῦν always has reference to the lifting
up of the Son of Man on the Cross. See note on 3¹⁴.

σημαίνων ποίῳ θανάτῳ κτλ. Cf. 21¹⁹.

ἤμελλεν. So ABDW. א has ἔμελλεν. Perhaps ἤμελλεν
ἀποθνήσκειν, as also at 11⁵¹ 18³², carries the idea of the
inevitableness of the Death of Jesus, as foreordained by God.
See on 6⁷¹.

34. Ἀπεκρίθη οὖν αὐτῷ ὁ ὄχλος Ἡμεῖς ἠκούσαμεν ἐκ τοῦ νόμου
ὅτι ὁ Χριστὸς μένει εἰς τὸν αἰῶνα, καὶ πῶς λέγεις σὺ ὅτι δεῖ ὑψωθῆναι
τὸν Υἱὸν τοῦ ἀνθρώπου; τίς ἐστιν οὗτος ὁ Υἱὸς τοῦ ἀνθρώπου;

*The people ask who the "Son of Man" is (v. 34), and Jesus
warns them to use the light while they can (vv. 35, 36)*

34. ἀπεκρ. οὖν αὐτῷ κτλ. אBLW support οὖν, which Θ and
the rec. text omit.

**ἡμεῖς ἠκούσαμεν ἐκ τοῦ νόμου ὅτι ὁ Χριστὸς μένει εἰς τὸν
αἰῶνα.** "The Law" (see on 10³⁴) often includes more
than the Pentateuch, and the reference is somewhat vague.
Ezek. 37²⁵ has "David my servant shall be their prince for
ever"; Ps. 89⁴ 110⁴ are apposite, as also Isa. 9⁷. Cf. *Orac.
Sibyll.* iii. 767, and *Psalms of Solomon*, xvii. 4.

**πῶς λέγεις σὺ ὅτι δεῖ ὑψωθῆναι τὸν υἱὸν τοῦ ἄνθρώπου; τίς
ἐστιν οὗτος ὁ υἱὸς τοῦ ἀνθρώπου;** We have seen (Introd.,
p. cxxiii) that Jesus habitually spoke of Himself in the third
person as "the Son of Man," and Jn. implies here that Jesus
had used this way of speech when He said that He would be
"lifted up," *i.e.* crucified. But His present hearers did not
understand what He meant; they were not accustomed to His
habits of speech, and the title "the Son of Man" was unfamiliar to them (cf. 9³⁵). "Who is this 'Son of Man'?"
they asked. The form of the question is exactly the same as
τίς ἐστιν οὗτος ὁ λόγος ὃν εἶπεν; (7³⁶). There is no emphasis
on οὗτος in either passage. We must not translate "Who is
this Son of Man," as if there were another "Son of Man," of
whom they had often heard; for Jn. does not express emphasis
by such a use of οὗτος, and "the Son of Man" was not a
recognised title of the Christ.[1]

On the other hand, if we could suppose that in popular
speech the Christ was sometimes called "the Son of Man,"
the meaning of the passage would be somewhat different. It
would represent the crowd as puzzled that any one should
seem to tell them that the Christ was to suffer a dishonourable
death. "The Son of Man must be crucified, you say . . .
Who can *this* Son of Man be ? . . . He cannot be the Christ
or the Son of Man of Daniel's vision (Dan. 7¹³), whose dominion
is to be everlasting." Cf. *Enoch*, lxii. 14, "With that Son of
Man will they eat and lie down and rise up for ever." But if
this was what the objectors meant, we should have expected
them to say, "*the Son of Man* abides for ever," rather than
"the Christ abides for ever," as more apposite to the objection
which they are putting forward. We prefer the view that the

[1] Cf. Introd., p. cxxiii.

35. εἶπεν οὖν αὐτοῖς ὁ Ἰησοῦς Ἔτι μικρὸν χρόνον τὸ φῶς ἐν ὑμῖν ἐστιν. περιπατεῖτε ὡς τὸ φῶς ἔχετε, ἵνα μὴ σκοτία ὑμᾶς καταλάβῃ· καὶ ὁ περιπατῶν ἐν τῇ σκοτίᾳ οὐκ οἶδεν ποῦ ὑπάγει. 36. ὡς τὸ φῶς ἔχετε, πιστεύετε εἰς τὸ φῶς, ἵνα υἱοὶ φωτὸς γένησθε.

title " Son of Man " as applied to Messiah was unfamiliar to them.[1]

There is a passage in Justin (*Tryph.* 32) which recalls their argument on any interpretation. Justin has quoted Dan. 7, and Trypho the Jew objects, " These scriptures indeed compel us to expect that Great and Glorious One who as a son of man receives the eternal kingdom from the Ancient of Days; but this your so-called Christ became dishonoured and inglorious so that he fell under the last curse in the law of God (Deut. 21[23]), for he was crucified." The Jews, with whom Trypho was in accord, did not expect a Suffering Messiah.

35. " Who is this *Son of Man* ? " Jesus does not answer the question, or explain Himself further. But He repeats the austere warning which He gave before (9[4] and 7[33], where see note), that He would not be much longer among them: it would only be μικρὸν χρόνον, " for a little while." Even this He expresses in mystic words which not all could have understood in their fulness; or, at least, the evangelist represents Him as speaking only indirectly of Himself and His approaching departure, when He said ἔτι μικρὸν χρόνον τὸ φῶς ἐν ὑμῖν ἐστιν. He had claimed to be the Light of the World (8[12]), but not many had believed that the Light was really among them, or had grasped what was meant.

ἐν ὑμῖν is the true reading (אBDWΘ and the Latin vss.) rather than the rec. μεθ᾽ ὑμῶν (A). Cf. for ἐν as equivalent to " among," Acts 4[34]; and note ἐσκήνωσεν ἐν ἡμῖν (1[14]).

He goes on with an exhortation: " Walk while ye have the light " [2] (ὡς τὸ φῶς ἔχετε, not ἕως of the rec. text, is the best attested reading). For περιπατεῖν as used of conduct, cf. 8[12]; and see especially 9[4] 11[9, 10].

ἵνα μὴ σκοτία ὑμᾶς καταλάβῃ, " lest darkness *overtake* you," and so get the better of you. See on 1[5], the only other place where καταλαμβάνειν is found in Jn. (but cf. [8[4]] and note on 6[17]); and cf. 1 Thess. 5[4], where the " day " is said to " overtake " one engaged in dark pursuits.

The second half of the verse is almost verbally identical with 1 Jn. 2[11] ἐν τῇ σκοτίᾳ περιπατεῖ καὶ οὐκ οἶδεν ποῦ ὑπάγει. See 11[10].

[1] Cf. Abbott, *Diat.* 2998 (xxi. *b*).
[2] So R.V. It is possible that we should translate ὡς by " according as."

44. Ἰησοῦς δὲ ἔκραξεν καὶ εἶπεν Ὁ πιστεύων εἰς ἐμὲ οὐ πιστεύει εἰς ἐμὲ ἀλλὰ εἰς τὸν πέμψαντά με, 45. καὶ ὁ θεωρῶν ἐμὲ θεωρεῖ τὸν

36. ὡς τὸ φῶς ἔχετε, *sc.* while Jesus was among them; but the exhortation has a wider application, and is for all time.

πιστεύετε εἰς τὸ φῶς. For the Johannine phrase πιστεύειν εἰς . . . see on 1¹²; τὸ φῶς indicates here the Person who *is* the Light (1⁴). To trust the Light, and walk in confidence that it will not mislead, is necessary for those who would become " sons of light."

υἱοὶ φωτός. The Oriental " looked upon any very intimate relationship—whether of connexion, origin, or dependence—as a relation of sonship, even in the spiritual sphere ";[1] but there is nothing necessarily Hebraic in such a phrase as υἱὸς φωτός, which is not alien to the genius of the Greek language (cf. 17¹²). It is equivalent to " an enlightened man," and first appears in a saying of Jesus recorded in Lk. 16⁸, that the υἱοὶ τοῦ αἰῶνος τούτου are sometimes more prudent than the υἱοὶ τοῦ φωτός. The contrast between those who are in darkness and those who are υἱοὶ φωτός, as Paul called his converts, appears in 1 Thess. 5⁵; and there is a similar exhortation in Eph. 5⁸ ὡς τέκνα φωτὸς περιπατεῖτε. φωτισμός became soon the regular word for the grace of baptism (cf. Heb. 6⁴, 10³²); but there is no trace of this usage in Jn.

Jesus reiterates His august claims (*vv.* 44–50)

44–50. We place these verses after v. 36ᵃ (see Introd., p. xxv). There is now a sequence of thought, the ideas of *light* and *truth* in v. 36ᵃ being the subjects of vv. 44–46.

The section vv. 44–50 can represent only a summary of the teaching of Jesus on the occasion. See below on vv. 36ᵇ–43. His final warning recalls the lament over Jerusalem's unbelief and its rejection of His claims preserved in Mt. 23³⁷⁻³⁹, Lk. 13³⁴, ³⁵.

44. Ἰησοῦς δὲ ἔκραξεν καὶ εἶπεν. The def. art. is omitted here before Ἰησοῦς, contrary to the general usage of Jn. (see on 1²⁹). But he often omits it in the phrase ἀπεκρίθη Ἰη. καὶ εἶπεν (see on 1⁵⁰), which is like the phrase here. For ἔκραξεν, see on 7²⁸.

ὁ πιστεύων εἰς ἐμέ κτλ., " he that believeth on me, believeth not on me (only), but on Him that sent me." The affirmative sentence, followed by a negative clause to bring out the sense, is thoroughly Johannine. See on 1²⁰; and cf. 3³².

[1] Cf. Deissmann, *Bible Studies*, pp. 161 ff., for a full discussion of υἱός with a genitive following.

πέμψαντά με. 46. ἐγὼ φῶς εἰς τὸν κόσμον ἐλήλιθα, ἵνα πᾶς ὁ πιστεύων εἰς ἐμὲ ἐν τῇ σκοτίᾳ μὴ μείνῃ. 47. καὶ ἐάν τίς μου ἀκούσῃ

For πιστεύειν εἰς. . . , a characteristically Johannine constr., see on 1[12] ; and for the idea of the Father " sending " the Son, which is so frequent in Jn., see on 3[17]. Cf. v. 49.

That he who believes on (or accepts) the Son accepts the Father, is a saying found in the Synoptists: ὁ ἐμὲ δεχόμενος δέχεται τὸν ἀποστείλαντά με (Mt. 10[40]; cf. Lk. 9[48]). Jn. here substitutes his favourite word πιστεύειν for δέχεσθαι, and also uses πέμπειν for ἀποστέλλειν (see on 3[17]); but in 13[20] (where see note) he has λαμβάνειν instead of πιστεύειν in a second citation of this saying of Jesus.

Cf. 5[24] πιστεύων τῷ πέμψαντί με, and (for the general sense of the verse) 8[19. 42]. In 14[1] the argument is turned round: " Ye believe in God; believe also in me."

45. ὁ θεωρῶν ἐμέ κτλ. θεωρεῖν is used here (as at 6[40] 14[19]) of spiritual vision. Not all those who saw Jesus with bodily eyes " saw the Father." For θεωρεῖν, see on 2[23] ; and cf. the saying ὁ ἑωρακὼς ἐμὲ ἑώρακεν τὸν πατέρα (14[9], where see note). So at v. 41 Jn. identifies the δόξα of Christ with the δόξα of God. Cf. 8[19].

τὸν πέμψαντά με. *Fam.* 13 read ἀποστείλαντα (see on 3[17] for πέμπω and ἀποστέλλω).

46. ἐγὼ φῶς εἰς τὸν κόσμον ἐλήλυθα. Cf. 3[19] τὸ φῶς ἐλήλυθεν εἰς τὸν κόσμον, and 9[5] ὅταν ἐν τῷ κόσμῳ ὦ, φῶς εἰμὶ τοῦ κόσμου. That Christ is the Light of the world is a principal topic with Jn.; cf. also 1[4. 5. 9] 8[12].

ἵνα πᾶς (B om. πᾶς *per incuriam*) ὁ πιστεύων εἰς ἐμέ κτλ., " in order that every one that believeth in me may not remain in darkness " (going back to v. 35), *sc.* in the darkness which is the normal state of man before the revelation of Christ (cf. 1 Jn. 2[9. 11]). The form of the sentence is that of 3[16] ἵνα πᾶς ὁ πιστεύων εἰς αὐτὸν μὴ ἀπόληται, and the meaning is the same, although a different metaphor is employed. *Christus Illuminator* is *Christus Saluator.*

47. ἐάν τίς μου ἀκούσῃ τῶν ῥημάτων, *sc.* with appreciation and understanding of what they signify: if it were only the mere physical hearing that was meant, ἀκούειν would take the acc., and we should have τὰ ῥήματα. See on 3[8]. It is only the man who is neglectful of Christ's words, while understanding them all the time, that is here contemplated.

μὴ φυλάξῃ. So אABDLW, but rec. has πιστεύσῃ. DΘ omit μή before φυλάξῃ, the motive apparently being to place vv. 47 and 48 in sharp contrast. But v. 48 is, in fact, a reaffirmation of v. 47; the distinction suggested by Westcott,

τῶν ῥημάτων καὶ μὴ φυλάξῃ, ἐγὼ οὐ κρίνω αὐτόν· οὐ γὰρ ἦλθον ἵνα
κρίνω τὸν κόσμον, ἀλλ᾽ ἵνα σώσω τὸν κόσμον. 48. ὁ ἀθετῶν ἐμὲ καὶ
μὴ λαμβάνων τὰ ῥήματά μου ἔχει τὸν κρίνοντα αὐτόν· ὁ λόγος ὃν
ἐλάλησα, ἐκεῖνος κρινεῖ αὐτὸν ἐν τῇ ἐσχάτῃ ἡμέρᾳ. 49. ὅτι ἐγὼ ἐξ

that v. 47 contemplates the listener who does not put into
practice what he has heard, while v. 48 contemplates the man
who defiantly does not listen at all, is over subtle.

φυλάττειν is used in Mk. 10²⁰ of "keeping" the Ten
Commandments; cf. Lk. 11²⁸. In the Sermon on the Mount,
the man "who hears these words and does them not" (Mt.
7²⁶) is compared to one who builds on the sand. Of him Jesus
says here ἐγὼ οὐ κρίνω αὐτόν (see note on 8¹⁵); He came not
to judge the world, but to save the world (see on 3¹⁷). There is
a sense in which "judgment" is inevitably the issue of His
Advent (cf. 9³⁹), but it was not the main purpose of that Advent.
See on 1³³.

The clause, "I came not to judge the world, but to save
the world," recalls an addition to the text at Lk. 9⁵⁵. In that
passage Jesus rebuked James and John, the true text, according to אABCL, being στραφεὶς δὲ ἐπετίμησεν αὐτοῖς. But a
"Western and Syrian" addition (to use the nomenclature of
Westcott-Hort) gives: "and said, Ye know not what spirit
ye are of, for the Son of man came not to destroy men's lives,
but to save them." If this Western text represents a true
tradition (whether it be Lucan or not) of words addressed by
Jesus to John the son of Zebedee, it is significant that similar
words should be ascribed to Jesus in the "Gospel according to
St. John." If, however, the words ὁ γὰρ υἱὸς τοῦ ἀνθρώπου οὐκ
ἦλθεν ψυχὰς ἀνθρώπων ἀπολέσαι, ἀλλὰ σῶσαι may be taken as
Lucan, then we have here another point of contact between
Lk. and Jn., where Jn. is seemingly correcting Lk. (see Introd.,
p. xcix). Cf. 20⁵ for a similar instance.

48. ἀθετεῖν is not found again in Jn.; but cf. Lk. 10¹⁶.
For the phrase λαμβάνων τὰ ῥήματά μου, cf. 17⁸ ; and see Mt.
13²⁰.

He who receives not the word of Christ "has one who
judges him," sc. the "word" itself, which shall rise up in
judgment against him at the Last Day (cf. Deut. 18¹⁹). The
λόγος is the "saying," or the sum of the ῥήματα, the words
spoken. With this passage cf. Mt. 10³², Lk. 12⁸· ⁹ ; and see
Introd., p. clix.

For the Johannine use of ἐκεῖνος, see on 1⁸ ; and for the
phrase "the Last Day," peculiar to Jn., see on 6³⁹.

49. The reason why His word is final and absolute, is that
it is not His own merely, but that it is the word of God who

ἐμαυτοῦ οὐκ ἐλάλησα, ἀλλ' ὁ πέμψας με Πατὴρ αὐτός μοι ἐντολὴν
δέδωκεν τί εἴπω καὶ τί λαλήσω.   50. καὶ οἶδα ὅτι ἡ ἐντολὴ αὐτοῦ
ζωὴ αἰώνιός ἐστιν.   ἃ οὖν ἐγὼ λαλῶ, καθὼς εἴρηκέν μοι ὁ Πατήρ,
οὕτως λαλῶ.

sent Him, and thus provides the ultimate test by which men
are judged.

ἐγὼ ἐξ ἐμαυτοῦ οὐκ ἐλάλησα. He had said this before
(7¹⁷). We cannot distinguish ἀπ' ἐμαυτοῦ from ἐξ ἐμαυτοῦ;
see on 1⁴⁴. As He had said that He could *do* nothing of Himself (5³⁰), so now He declares of His words that they, too, are
words of the Father. For His " mission " from the Father,
see on 3¹⁷ and the references given there.

αὐτός μοι ἐντολὴν δέδωκεν, " Himself hath given me
commandment . . .," the pft. tense expressing continuing
action (cf. 14³¹). The rec. ἔδωκε has only secondary uncial
support. See 17⁸ τὰ ῥήματα ἃ ἔδωκάς μοι δέδωκα αὐτοῖς; and
cf. 10¹⁸ 14³¹ 15¹⁰ for the ἐντολή of the Father to Christ. Of the
Prophet to come (Deut. 18¹⁸), Yahweh had said, " I will put
my words in His mouth, and He shall speak unto them all
that I shall command Him." Indeed, the formula of all the
prophets was, " Thus saith Yahweh."

τί εἴπω καὶ τί λαλήσω. Perhaps both the *substance* and
the *form* of His words are suggested by the two verbs; but it
seems simpler to treat them as identical in meaning here (see
λαλῶ, v. 50), the repetition being in the style of dignity.

Justin (*Tryph.* 56) recalls this Johannine doctrine of the
relation of the Son to the Father: " He never did anything
except what God willed Him to do or to speak " (βεβούληται
καὶ πρᾶξαι καὶ ὁμιλῆσαι).

50. καὶ οἶδα ὅτι κτλ. Cf. 5³² 8⁵⁵, this form of solemn
assurance being used in each case by Jesus, when speaking
of His knowledge of the " witness " or " commandment " of
God, or of God Himself.

ἡ ἐντολὴ αὐτοῦ ζωὴ αἰώνιός ἐστιν. See for ζωὴ αἰώνιος
on 3¹⁵; and cf. 6⁶⁸, where Peter confesses to Jesus ῥήματα ζωῆς
αἰωνίου ἔχεις. It is instructive to recall the Synoptic story
that the answer to the young man who asked τί ποιήσω ἵνα
ζωὴν αἰώνιον κληρονομήσω; was to refer him to the Ten Commandments (Mk. 10¹⁸). It is not only for Jn., but for the
Synoptists too, that the Divine Commandment, when fully
realised, *is* Eternal Life, although in the Synoptists the idea
of eternal life as already present is only latent and is not made
explicit.

καθὼς εἴρηκέν μοι ὁ πατήρ, οὕτως λαλῶ. This is the secret
of the absolute value of the words of Jesus; cf. 8²⁸ and 14³¹.

36ᵇ. Ταῦτα ἐλάλησεν Ἰησοῦς, καὶ ἀπελθὼν ἐκρύβη ἀπ' αὐτῶν. 37. Τοσαῦτα δὲ αὐτοῦ σημεῖα πεποιηκότος ἔμπροσθεν αὐτῶν οὐκ ἐπίστευον εἰς αὐτόν, 38. ἵνα ὁ λόγος Ἡσαΐου τοῦ προφήτου πληρωθῇ

The final rejection by the Jews : the evangelist's comment on their unbelief as foreordained in prophecy (vv. 36ᵇ-43)

36ᵇ. It is explained above (on v. 44) that the section vv. 44–50 has been transposed, so as to place v. 44 immediately after v. 36ᵃ. Thus the connexion of ideas is unbroken, and we now come to v. 36ᵇ.

" These things spake Jesus, and He departed and hid Himself from them." This is the conclusion of Part II. of the Gospel,[1] the climax of the Jerusalem ministry, the rejection of Jesus by the Jews. He had hidden Himself before (8⁵⁹), when the Jews sought to stone Him ; but He went into seclusion now because He had given His last warning. The time for teaching was over.

In Mk. (13³⁵, ³⁶) the final word to the Jews is, " Watch, . . . lest the Master coming suddenly find you sleeping." But the final word in Jn. is more sombre, and is suggestive in its phrases of the judgment that afterwards came on the Jews : " Walk while ye have the Light, lest darkness overtake you. . . . While ye have the Light, believe in the Light " (vv. 35, 36). He had reiterated His august claims (vv. 44–50), and then He withdrew. Jn. does not say *where* He withdrew, but according to Lk. 21³⁷ it seems to have been in Bethany that He passed the last nights.

37. Verses 37–43 contain an explanatory commentary by the evangelist upon the Rejection of Jesus by the Jews, its causes and its extent.[2]

τοσαῦτα, " so many " (cf. 6⁹ 21¹¹), not " so great." For the term σημεῖα, see on 2¹¹, ²³. Many had believed in consequence of the " signs " that had been wrought ; cf. 2²³ 4⁴⁵ 7³¹ 11⁴⁷, ⁴⁸, it being clear that Jn. knew of many " signs " other than those which he describes (cf. 20³⁰). But the nation as a whole did not accept Him (cf. 1¹¹ 3¹¹, ³² 5⁴³ 15²⁴), although some in high station were among those that believed, while they were afraid to confess it (v. 42). For the constr. ἐπίστευον εἰς αὐτόν, see on 1¹².

38. Jn. does not hesitate to say that the unbelief of the Jews was " in order that " the prophecies of Isaiah should be fulfilled. ἵνα πληρωθῇ must be given its full telic force ; see Introd., p. cliv. Paul (Rom. 10¹⁶) quotes Isa. 53¹ to illustrate this unbelief and as a prophecy of it, but he does not say ἵνα πληρ. as Jn. does (cf. 1²⁹ 19³⁰).

[1] Cf. Introd., p. xxx.   [2] Cf. Introd., p. xxxiv.

ὃν εἶπεν Κύριε, τίς ἐπίστευσεν τῇ ἀκοῇ ἡμῶν; καὶ ὁ βραχίων Κυρίου τίνι ἀπεκαλύφθη; 39. διὰ τοῦτο οὐκ ἠδύναντο πιστεύειν, ὅτι πάλιν εἶπεν Ἡσαίας 40. Τετύφλωκεν αὐτῶν τοὺς ὀφθαλμοὺς καὶ ἐπώρωσεν αὐτῶν τὴν καρδίαν, ἵνα μὴ ἴδωσιν τοῖς ὀφθαλμοῖς καὶ νοήσωσιν τῇ

The quotation is from Isa. 53[1. 2], introduced by the opening word κύριε, which is also added in the LXX. Here, probably, Jn. is influenced by the LXX version.

There was a twofold fulfilment: (1) the people did not believe the words of Jesus, and (2) they did not recognise the " arm of the Lord " in His signs. In the O.T. the " arm of God " is often figurative of His power (Deut. 5[15], cf. Lk. 1[51]), especially in Deutero-Isaiah (40[10] 51[9] 52[10] 63[5]). One of the theses of Cyprian's *Testimonia* (ii. 4) is " Quod Christus idem manus et *brachium Dei*," and he quotes Isa. 53[1. 2] as here; but it would be to go beyond the evidence to conclude that this idea is in the thought of Jn.

39. διὰ τοῦτο, *i.e.* because of the prophetic words of Isaiah which follow: they *had* to be fulfilled, for they were the expression of Divine foreknowledge.[1]

διὰ τοῦτο refers to what *follows*, not to what *precedes*; see note on 5[16], and cf. 1 Jn. 3[1].

ὅτι πάλιν κτλ., " because again Isaiah said, etc."

40. This second quotation, from Isa. 6[10], differs markedly from the LXX. (1) The LXX has altered the Hebrew, which ascribes the hardening of Israel's heart to God's agency, and throws the sentence into a passive form: ἐπαχύνθη γὰρ ἡ καρδία τοῦ λαοῦ τούτου κτλ. Jn., however, reproduces the sense (although not the exact phrases) of the Hebrew " He hath hardened their heart." (2) The LXX has μήποτε ἴδωσιν τοῖς ὀφθαλμοῖς. Now Jn. (and it is one of the notable features of his style) never uses μήποτε. Instead, he has ἵνα μὴ here and elsewhere (see on 3[20]), which may represent the Aramaic דִּלְאָ. Indeed דִּלְאָ is actually reproduced in the Pesh. rendering of Isa. 6[10]. Burney infers[2] that Jn. is here translating direct from the Aramaic.

The passage Isa. 6[10] is quoted also by Mt. (13[15]), who takes it verbally from the LXX. He places it in the mouth of Jesus Himself; it is not in Mt., as in Jn., an illustrative passage quoted by the evangelist. It is quoted also in Acts 28[26] from the LXX, where Paul is represented as applying its words to the Jews at Rome. Probably Isa. 6[10] was regarded by Christians from the beginning as predictive of the Rejection of Jesus by the Jews (cf. Mk. 4[12], Lk. 8[10]).

The prophets often speak of people who " have eyes and

---

[1] Cf. Introd., p. cliv.　　　　[2] *Aramaic Origin*, p. 100.

καρδίᾳ καὶ στραφῶσιν, καὶ ἰάσομαι αὐτούς. 41. ταῦτα εἶπεν Ἡσαίας

see not, and ears and hear not " (Jer. 5²¹, Ezek. 12²; cf. Isa. 42²⁰), and the same thing may be observed in every age and country. The child's story of "Eyes and no Eyes" has a universal application. But Isa. 6¹⁰ speaks of a *penal* blindness, an insensibility which was, as it were, a Divine punishment for sin. So at Isa. 44¹⁸ we have, "He hath shut their eyes, that they cannot see; and their hearts, that they cannot understand." And in Deut. 29⁴ the comment of Moses when the Israelites did not recognise the meaning of the "signs" in Egypt is, "The Lord hath not given you an heart to know and eyes to see and ears to hear unto this day." Paul makes this doctrine his own: "God gave them eyes that they should not see, and ears that they should not hear " (Rom. 11⁸). That sin causes a blindness of the soul, a moral insensibility to spiritual truths, is a law of the natural, that is of the Divine, order.

Jesus rebukes the multitude (Mk. 8¹⁸) who did not rightly interpret the miracle of the loaves, by saying, "Having eyes, see ye not? and having ears, hear ye not?" In explaining the Parable of the Sower to His disciples, while He did not explain it to the multitudes, He gave the reason, "Unto them that are without all things are done in parables, that seeing they may see and not perceive, and hearing they may hear and not understand, lest haply they should turn again and it should be forgiven them " (Mk. 4¹¹· ¹², Lk. 8¹⁰). Mt. 13¹³ gives the same saying, and represents Jesus as quoting Isa. 6⁹· ¹⁰ in full from the LXX, which does not ascribe the moral blindness of the people to the agency of God.

Jn., however, never shrinks from a direct statement of events as predestined; if things happened, it was because God intended them to happen. He does not attempt here to soften down the tremendous judgment of Isa. 6⁹· ¹⁰.

The verb ἐπώρωσεν has been generally translated "hardened." But this is a misleading rendering.[1] πώρωσις is *numbness*, rather than *hardness*; and the prophet's ἐπώρωσεν αὐτῶν τὴν καρδίαν is strictly parallel to the first half of the verse, τετύφλωκεν αὐτῶν τοὺς ὀφθαλμούς. We should translate:

"He hath blinded their eyes,
and darkened their hearts,"

for πώρωσις τῆς καρδίας is precisely "blindness of heart." See 9³⁹ above; and cf. 8⁴³.

ἐπώρωσεν. So AB*LWΘ; the rec. has πεπώρωκεν (ΓΔ).

στραφῶσιν is read by אBD*, and is therefore to be preferred

[1] See, for a full note on πώρωσις, J. A. Robinson, *Ephesians,* pp. 264 ff.

ὅτι εἶδεν τὴν δόξαν αὐτοῦ, καὶ ἐλάλησεν περὶ αὐτοῦ. 42. ὅμως
μέντοι καὶ ἐκ τῶν ἀρχόντων πολλοὶ ἐπίστευσαν εἰς αὐτόν, ἀλλὰ διὰ

to the rec. ἐπιστραφῶσιν. LWΘ have ἐπιστρέψωσιν. Field
points out that στραφῶσιν is to be taken in a *middle* sense,
" turn themselves "; cf. a similar usage at 20¹⁴. ¹⁶.

41. The true reading is ὅτι (אABLΘ), not ὅτε of the rec.
text or ἔπει with W. It was not *when* Isaiah saw his vision of
Yahweh and the seraphim that he announced the blindness of
men's eyes (Isa. 6¹. ². ¹⁰), but it was *because* the vision was so
dazzling that he realised how far men were from being equal
to it.

The vision was not with the eye of sense; it was spiritually
that Isaiah " saw the Lord," a statement that the Targum
characteristically softens by saying he saw *the glory of the Lord*.
But Jn. goes farther. He declares that in this vision Isaiah
saw the glory of *Christ*, and spake of Him (εἶδεν τὴν δόξαν
αὐτοῦ, καὶ ἐλάλησεν περὶ αὐτοῦ, αὐτοῦ necessarily referring
to the same person in both limbs of the sentence). This
illustrates well the freedom, so to speak, with which Jn. treats
the O.T. In the vision of Isa. 6, the prophet contemplates the
awful glory of the invisible God; but the evangelist, in affirm-
ing that he spoke of the glory of *Christ*, identifies Christ with
the Yahweh of Israel. It was a later Christian thought that
the Logos was the agent of the O.T. theophanies, and it may
be that Jn. means to suggest this. In any case, he seems to
be aware of the Targum which says that Isaiah saw *the glory*
of Yahweh (see on 1¹⁴).

42. ὅμως μέντοι. The Coptic Q omits both words.
Neither of them is used by the Synoptists, ὅμως occurring again
in N.T. only 1 Cor. 14⁷, Gal. 3¹⁵. For μέντοι, cf. 4²⁷ 7¹³ 20⁵ 21⁴.

τῶν ἀρχόντων, sc. the principal men in the Sanhedrim ;
cf. 7²⁶. ⁴⁸, and see on 7³² for the composition of the Sanhedrim.

καὶ ἐκ τῶν ἀρχ. κτλ., " *even* of the rulers," who were most
difficult to convince, " many believed on Him " (for the constr.
see on 1¹²), *e.g.* men like Nicodemus (3¹) and Joseph of
Arimathæa. See note on 8³⁰ for the phrase πολλοὶ ἐπίστευσαν
εἰς αὐτόν. The Pharisees had put it to the common folk,
many of whom were attracted by Jesus (vv. 11, 37), as a test
question, " Hath any of the rulers believed on Him ? " (7⁴⁸).
This had now actually come to pass, but fear of the fanaticism
of the Pharisees (cf. v. 19) prevented their belief from showing
itself in open confession of the claims of Jesus. It has been
suggested that the young ruler who made the Great Refusal [1]
may have been among these secret disciples.

---

[1] Lk. 18¹⁸ᶠ. Cf. Garvie, *The Beloved Disciple*, p. 231.

τοὺς Φαρισαίους οὐχ ὡμολόγουν, ἵνα μὴ ἀποσυνάγωγοι γένωνται·
43. ἠγάπησαν γὰρ τὴν δόξαν τῶν ἀνθρώπων μᾶλλον ἤπερ τὴν δόξαν
τοῦ Θεοῦ.

οὐχ ὡμολόγουν, "they were not confessing Him." For
ὁμολογεῖν used of "confessing" Christ, see 1²⁰ 9²², 1 Jn. 2²³
4². ³. ¹⁵, Rom. 10⁹.

ἵνα μή . . . For this favourite constr. of Jn., see on 3²⁰.

For ἀποσυνάγωγοι, see on 9²². To be forbidden to enter a
synagogue, even for a short period, would be a serious matter
for a member of the Sanhedrim. To be shut off from the
common worship of one's friends and colleagues is a grave
penalty, especially for an ecclesiastical personage.

43. ἠγάπησαν γὰρ τὴν δόξαν τῶν ἀνθρώπων κτλ., "for they
loved the honour that men bestow rather than the honour that
God bestows" (see 5⁴⁴ and the note there). The genitives
ἀνθρώπων . . . θεοῦ are both genitives of origin, the thought
being similar to that in 5⁴⁴, where the same contrast is drawn.
δόξα is used in the sense of "honour" (see on 1¹⁴); it would
be quite unfitting to speak of any one *loving* the *glory* of God,
in the sense in which δόξα has been used above at v. 41.

The form of the sentence is like 3¹⁹, ἠγάπησαν οἱ ἄνθρωποι
μᾶλλον τὸ σκότος ἢ τὸ φῶς, except that here Jn. has ἤπερ for ἤ.
ἤπερ occurs only here in the N.T. (cf. 2 Macc. 14⁴²), and is
perhaps more emphatic than ἤ, μᾶλλον ἤπερ signifying "*much*
more than." אLW 1, 33, 69 have ὑπέρ, but ABDΓΔΘ give
ἤπερ, which was altered to ὑπέρ as the more ordinary word.

This comment, in which Jn. attributes low motives to those
of whom he writes, may be compared with what he says about
Judas (12⁶). A grave and austere judgment on the discipleship that prefers to be in secret (see on v. 42) is the last comment
of the evangelist on the rejection of Jesus by the Jews, as
described in Part II.

PART III.—THE PASSION AND RESURRECTION
(XIII.–XX.)

HITHERTO the exoteric or public teaching of Jesus has been
expounded: in Part I. as addressed to would-be disciples,
and in Part II. to Jews, for the most part incredulous. In Part
III. we have only the esoteric and private teaching reserved by
Jesus for His chosen friends and future ambassadors.

XIII. 1. Πρὸ δὲ τῆς ἑορτῆς τοῦ πάσχα εἰδὼς ὁ Ἰησοῦς ὅτι ἦλθεν
αὐτοῦ ἡ ὥρα ἵνα μεταβῇ ἐκ τοῦ κόσμου τούτου πρὸς τὸν Πατέρα,
ἀγαπήσας τοὺς ἰδίους τοὺς ἐν τῷ κόσμῳ, εἰς τέλος ἠγάπησεν αὐτούς.

Part III. begins with a carefully constructed editorial
introduction (13¹). It is noteworthy that, while vv. 1–3 are
full of Johannine phrases, a greater use is made of subordinate
and dependent clauses than is customary with Jn., who prefers
parataxis in narration.

The Feet-washing at the Last Supper (vv. 1–11)

XIII. 1. πρὸ δὲ τῆς ἑορτῆς τοῦ πάσχα. δέ is resumptive, the
Passover being that mentioned 12¹. What is now to be narrated
took place on the eve of the Passover, *i.e.* on the evening of
Nisan 13.

εἰδώς. Attention is specially called in this narrative
(vv. 3, 11, 18) to the perfect insight and foresight which Jesus
exhibited as to the time and circumstances of the Passion; cf.
18⁴, 19²⁸. He knew that "His hour had come" (cf. 12²³);
see on 2⁴ for this feature of the Fourth Gospel, that it represents
the predestined end as foreseen from the beginning.

For ἦλθεν (אABLWΘ) the rec. has ἐλήλυθεν. D has παρῆν.
For ἵνα in the sense of "when," see on 12²³.

ἵνα μεταβῇ κτλ. Harris has suggested that this is Passover
language ; and in one of Bede's *Homilies* we find "Pascha
transitus interpretatur."[1] But μεταβαίνειν is never used elsewhere in the Greek Bible with this suggestion. Its use here
of a departure from this life to the unseen world is, indeed, also
without Biblical parallels; but cf. 5²⁴, 1 Jn. 3¹⁴.

ἐκ τοῦ κόσμου τούτου. See for this phrase the note on 8²³.
For κόσμος generally, see on 1⁹.

πρὸς τὸν πατέρα. Christ's departure or ascension is
spoken of again as a "going to the Father," 14¹². ²⁸ 16¹⁰. ²⁸.

τοὺς ἰδίους. "His own intimate friends and disciples,"
not, as at 1¹¹, "His own people, the Jews." Cf. Mk. 4³⁴.

τοὺς ἐν τῷ κόσμῳ. They were "in the world," as He said
17¹¹, although in another sense they are distinguished from
"the world," out of which they had been given to Him (17⁶. ⁹).
These men He had loved.

εἰς τέλος ἠγάπησεν αὐτούς. To translate these words
"He loved them unto the end," although linguistically defensible, reduces the sentence to a platitude. This verse introduces an incident to which Jn. gives a good deal of space, and
which he regards as of high consequence. "Jesus, knowing

[1] See *Expository Times*, Nov. 1926, p. 88, and Feb. 1927, p. 233.

2. καὶ δείπνου γινομένου, τοῦ διαβόλου ἤδη βεβληκότος εἰς τὴν καρδίαν ἵνα παραδοῖ αὐτὸν Ἰούδας Σίμωνος Ἰσκαριώτης, 3. εἰδὼς ὅτι

that His hour was come that He should depart out of this world unto the Father, . . ." The reader expects that this solemn prelude is to be followed by a statement that Jesus did or said something of special significance. The statement is εἰς τέλος ἠγάπησεν αὐτούς, and it seems to mean, " He *exhibited His love* for them *to the uttermost*," *i.e.* in a remarkable manner.

First, as to ἠγάπησεν. If " He continued to love them " were the meaning, we should expect the impf. rather than the aor. tense. The aor. indicates a definite act, rather than a continuing emotion; so ἠγάπησεν in 3¹⁶ is used of the love of God *as exhibited* in the gift of His Son. Abbott (*Diat.* 1744) quotes a similar Pauline use in Rom. 8³⁷, Gal. 2²⁰, Eph. 5², and also Ignatius, *Magn.* 6. Thus ἠγάπησεν may mean here " He showed His love," *sc.* by His action, unprecedented for a master, in washing the feet of His disciples. And so the words καθὼς ἠγάπησα ὑμᾶς of v. 34 bear a definite reference to ἠγάπησεν in v. 1 and to the feet-washing which followed.

Secondly, εἰς τέλος is often used as equivalent to " wholly " or " utterly," as at Josh. 3¹⁶, 1 Chron. 28⁹, 2 Macc. 8²⁹, 1 Thess. 2¹⁶. Abbott (*Diat.* 2322c) cites Hermas, *Vis.* III. x. 5, where ἱλαρὰ εἰς τέλος means " joyful exceedingly," or " joyful *to the uttermost*." It can equally well mean " to the end," *e.g.* Mt. 10²², where it is said that " he that endures εἰς τέλος shall be saved "; but this rendering does not suit the context here.

Accordingly, we translate v. 1, " Jesus, knowing that His hour was come that He should depart out of this world unto the Father, having loved His own which were in the world, exhibited His love for them to the uttermost," *i.e.* gave that remarkable manifestation of His love for His disciples which is told in the narrative of the feet-washing that follows.

2. For γινομένου (א*BLW) the rec. text, with אᶜADΓΔΘ, has γενομένου, which wrongly suggests that the supper was ended.

δείπνου γινομένου, " while a supper was going on," " during supper," there being no def. art. and no suggestion that this was *the* supper of the Passover feast, as the Synoptists state.

τοῦ διαβόλου ἤδη βεβληκότος κτλ., " the devil having *already* put it into the heart of Judas, etc." So the Synoptists (Mk. 14¹⁰, Mt. 26¹⁴, Lk. 22³) represent the matter, Judas having made his bargain with the chief priests on a previous day of the same week; Lk. alone (as Jn. does here) ascribing

πάντα ἔδωκεν αὐτῷ ὁ Πατὴρ εἰς τὰς χεῖρας, καὶ ὅτι ἀπὸ Θεοῦ ἐξῆλθεν

his treachery to the instigation of the devil, εἰσῆλθεν Σατανᾶς εἰς Ἰούδαν. This is repeated by Jn. at v. 27, when Judas decided on the final and fatal step. Cf. Acts 5³.

The rec. text, with ΑΔΓΔΘ, has a smoother order of words, εἰς τὴν καρδίαν Ἰούδα Σίμωνος Ἰσκαριώτου, ἵνα αὐτὸν παραδῷ, which does not differ in meaning from the better supported εἰς τὴν καρδίαν ἵνα παραδοῖ αὐτὸν Ἰούδας Σίμωνος Ἰσκαριώτης (so אBL).

For παραδίδωμι, see on 6⁶⁴. For Ἰσκαριώτης, see on 6⁷¹. It is applied here to Judas, as there to his father Simon.

3. After εἰδώς, ΑΘ add ὁ Ἰησοῦς for the sake of clearness; om. אBDLW. For ἔδωκεν (אBLW) the rec. has δέδωκεν with ΑΔΓΔΘ.

εἰδώς, as in v. 1; but here it signifies that Jesus set Himself to the humble office of washing His disciples' feet, with full consciousness of the majesty of His Person, and even because of it. He knew that the Father had given all things into His hands, and that therefore He could evade the Passion which was impending, if He wished. Cf. 3³⁵ ὁ πατὴρ ἀγαπᾷ τὸν υἱὸν καὶ πάντα δέδωκεν ἐν τῇ χειρὶ αὐτοῦ. We cannot distinguish ἐν τῇ χειρὶ αὐτοῦ in that passage from αὐτῷ εἰς τὰς χεῖρας in this. So at Dan. 1² the LXX has παρέδωκεν . . . εἰς χεῖρας αὐτοῦ, where Theodotion has ἔδωκεν ἐν χειρὶ αὐτοῦ. ἐν and εἰς are not always to be distinguished.

Jn. says of Jesus that He knew ὅτι ἀπὸ θεοῦ ἐξῆλθεν. So Nicodemus was ready to admit, ἀπὸ θεοῦ ἐλήλυθας διδάσκαλος (3²); and on the night before the Passion the apostles made the same confession, ἀπὸ θεοῦ ἐξῆλθες (16³⁰). Jn. never makes Jesus speak thus of Himself. He does not say ἀπὸ τοῦ πατρὸς ἐξῆλθον, but always uses either παρὰ or ἐκ in such contexts. Yet, again, the distinction of prepositions cannot be pressed (see on 1¹⁴, ⁴⁴ 16²⁸).

καὶ πρὸς τὸν θεὸν ὑπάγει, "and is going to God," the historic present which vividly reproduces the situation. For ὑπάγειν, see on 7³³ 16⁷, ¹⁰.

There seems to be a reminiscence of this teaching (see also 16²⁸) in Ignatius, *Magn.* 7, Ἰησοῦν Χριστὸν τὸν ἀφ᾽ ἑνὸς πατρὸς προελθόντα καὶ εἰς ἕνα ὄντα καὶ χωρήσαντα. See on 1¹⁸.

INTRODUCTORY NOTE ON THE LAST SUPPER

Before we examine Jn.'s narrative of the Last Supper, we set down what we conceive to have been the actual order of events. Although the Synoptists treat the Last Supper as

the Paschal Feast, which Jn. pointedly does not do, there can
be no doubt that Jn. 13 is intended to describe the same supper
as that of Mk. 14, Mt. 26, Lk. 22. We cannot harmonise the
various narratives precisely, but they have much in common.
We place the incidents in order as follows:

1. The supper begins.
2. The disciples dispute about precedence (Lk. 22$^{24f.}$;
   not in Mk., Mt., Jn.).
3. Jesus washes the feet of the disciples, by His example
   rebuking their self-seeking, and bidding them
   remember that their Master was content to act
   as their slave (Jn. 13$^{4-10}$; cf. Jn. 13$^{15.\ 16}$ and
   Lk. 22$^{26.\ 27}$).
4. Jesus announces that a traitor is in their midst (Jn.
   13$^{10.\ 11.\ 18.\ 21}$, Mk. 14^{18}, Mt. 26^{21}, Lk. 22^{21}).
5. The disciples begin to ask which of them was thus
   designated (Jn. 13$^{22f.}$, Mk. 14^{19}, Mt. 26^{22},
   Lk. 22^{23}).
6. Jesus tells John the beloved disciple that the traitor
   is the one to whom He will give the sop from the
   dish (Jn. 13$^{25.\ 26}$; cf. Mk. 14^{20}, Mt. 26^{23}; not in Lk.).
7. Jesus gives the sop to Judas (Jn. 13^{26}), and thus or
   otherwise conveys to Judas that He knows of his
   intentions (Mt. 26^{25}). This is not in Mk. or
   Lk., neither of whom at this point names Judas
   as the traitor.
8. Judas goes out at once (Jn. 13^{30}; not in Mk., Mt., Lk.).
9. The Eucharist is instituted (Mk. 14$^{22f.}$, Mt. 26$^{26f.}$,
   Lk. 22$^{19f.}$; not in Jn., but cf. Jn. 6^{51b-58}).
10. Jesus predicts His impending Passion in the words,
    " I will no more drink of the fruit of the vine,
    until I drink it new in the kingdom of God "
    (Mk. 14^{25}, Mt. 26^{29}, Lk. 22^{18}; not given thus
    by Jn., but cf. Jn. 13$^{31-35}$ and 15$^{1-13}$).
11. Jesus warns Peter that he will deny Him (Jn.
    13$^{36-38}$, Mk. 14$^{29f.}$, Mt. 26$^{33f.}$, Lk. 22$^{31f.}$).

On examination of this table, it will be noticed, first that
Jn. and Mk. (whom Mt. follows) never disagree as to the
order of the various incidents; the important differences being
that Jn. describes the Feet-washing, which Mk. does not
mention, and that he omits the Institution of the Eucharist.
Jn. also tells that it was to the beloved disciple that Jesus conveyed the hint which might have enabled the company to
have identified the traitor (see on 13^{26}); and he alone mentions
expressly that Judas left the room.

καὶ πρὸς τὸν Θεὸν ὑπάγει, 4. ἐγείρεται ἐκ τοῦ δείπνου καὶ τίθησιν τὰ

The order, however, in which Lk. mentions the several incidents is different.   His order is 1, 10, 9, 4, 5, 2, 11, omitting 3, 6, 7, 8; the most remarkable feature in his narrative being that he puts the announcement that a traitor was present after the Institution of the Eucharist, thus implying that Judas received the Bread and the Cup along with the rest.   The position, also, which he gives to the mysterious saying numbered 10 above, differs from that assigned to it by Mk. and Mt.   Lk., in short, follows a different tradition from that of Mk. and Mt. in his narrative of the Eucharist.   The longer recension of the words of Institution as given by him (see Introd., p. clxxii) seems to have been derived from Paul; but that cannot be said of the Western version, which may be the original.   From whatever source Lk. has derived his narrative of the Last Supper, it has marks of confusion.   We are justified, then, in preferring to his order of incidents here that which is given in the two Gospels Mk. and Jn., which probably rest respectively on the reminiscences of Peter and of John the son of Zebedee, both of whom were present at the Supper.

At what point in the narrative of Jn. are we to suppose that the Institution of the Eucharist took place ?   The foregoing comparison with Mk. suggests that we should put it after Judas had left (v. 30), and before the prediction of the Passion as near (vv. 31, 32).   That Jn. knew of the Institution of the Eucharist is certain; [1] and we have found reason for holding that the words of Institution are reproduced in 6[51b], where see note.   We hold that there has been a dislocation of the text after 13[30], and that the original order was c. 15, c. 16, c. 13[31-38], c. 14, c. 17.[2]   It may be that a paragraph has been lost after 13[30], and it is tempting to conjecture that this paragraph told of the first Eucharist.[3]   But, if this were not so (and there is no external evidence for it), we must fall back on the conclusion that Jn. has designedly omitted to tell of the Institution of the Eucharist (although he betrays his knowledge of it in c. 6), while his reasons for this omission cannot now be discovered.   See on v. 31.

XIII. 4. ἐγείρεται ἐκ τοῦ δείπνου, " He rises from the supper," that is, from the couch on which He had been reclining.   This shows that the Feet-washing which follows was not *before* supper, and so is not to be regarded as the cleansing

---

[1] Cf. Introd., p. clxvi f.   [2] See Introd., p. xx f.
[3] This idea was put forward first by Spitta (*Zur Gesch. u. Litt. d. Urchristentums*, i. 186 f.).

ἱμάτια, καὶ λαβὼν λέντιον διέζωσεν ἑαυτόν· 5. εἶτα βάλλει ὕδωρ εἰς

of the feet which was preparatory to a meal. Where sandals
are worn, the feet get dusty and tired, and it was a courtesy
of hospitality to arrange that water was available for washing
them (Lk. 7⁴⁴; cf. Gen. 18⁴ 19² 24³² 43²⁴, Judg. 19²¹, 1 Sam.
25⁴¹, 1 Tim. 5¹⁰). But in this case, the supper had not only
begun, but was probably ending. In the talk that followed,
the disciples began to dispute about their precedence (Lk. 22²⁴),
perhaps in reference to the order in which they were placed at
the meal; and Jesus, rising from His place, proceeds to give
them an object-lesson. " Whether is greater, he that sitteth
at meat, or he that serveth ? Is not he that sitteth at meat ?
But I am in the midst of you as he that serveth " (Lk. 22²⁷).
So, stripping off His outer robe or *tallith* (ἱμάτιον) and appearing
in His tunic only, He girded Himself with a towel, as a slave
would do, that He might pour water upon their feet. Wetstein
recalls the story of Caligula, who was wont to insult members of
the Senate by making them wait at table *succinctos linteo*
(Suetonius, *Cal.* 26). This story indicates how great an act of
condescension the Feet-washing by Christ must have seemed
to His disciples to be.

After ἱμάτια D adds αὐτοῦ.

With διέζωσεν, cf. 21⁷: Lk. 12³⁷ 17⁸ illustrate the " girding " himself for his work which was appropriate to a slave.
The towel (*linteum*) was fastened to the shoulder, so as to
leave both hands free.

5. The word νιπτήρ does not occur again in Greek literature,[1] Biblical or secular, except in quotations of this passage.
It must mean some washing utensil, but " bason " may easily
convey a wrong impression. Orientals do not wash, as we do,
in a bason which visibly retains the water that has been used;
that they would regard as an unclean practice. The Eastern
habit is to pour water from a ewer over hands or feet (cf.
2 Kings 3¹¹, where Elisha performs this duty for his master
Elijah), the water being caught below in a bason with a strainer,
and then passing through the strainer out of sight. The
assistance of a servant is necessary, as both the ewer and the
bason have to be held. At the Last Supper, the disciples were
reclining on the usual divans or couches, their feet being
stretched out behind (see Lk. 7³⁸, where the sinful woman was
" standing behind " at the feet of Jesus, when she let her tears
fall upon them). Jesus first poured (βάλλει, cf. Mt. 9¹⁷) water
into the νιπτήρ, which was ready in the room for such a purpose (τὸν νιπτῆρα, " *the* ewer "), and then He poured the

---

[1] The Coptic Q has λακάνη, the later form of λεκάνη, a dish or pot.

τὸν νιπτῆρα, καὶ ἤρξατο νίπτειν τοὺς πόδας τῶν μαθητῶν καὶ ἐκμάσ-
σειν τῷ λεντίῳ ᾧ ἦν διεζωσμένος.   6. ἔρχεται οὖν πρὸς Σίμωνα
Πέτρον· λέγει αὐτῷ Κύριε, σύ μου νίπτεις τοὺς πόδας; 7. ἀπεκρίθη
Ἰησοῦς καὶ εἶπεν αὐτῷ Ὃ ἐγὼ ποιῶ σὺ οὐκ οἶδας ἄρτι, γνώσῃ

water over the disciples' feet, drying them with the towel with
which He had girded Himself.   He did all that was the duty
of a slave for his master who was having his feet washed.[1]

καὶ ἤρξατο κτλ.   The verb ἄρχεσθαι does not occur again
in Jn. (but cf. [8⁹]).   He *began* to wash the disciples' feet,[2] but it
is not said in what order, nor is this now possible to determine.   Some have thought that the order was that in which
they sat at table, and that Judas came first (see on v. 23 below).
Or it may have been Peter, for οὖν in the phrase ἔρχεται οὖν
πρὸς Σίμωνα Πέτρον (v. 6) is not causative (see on 1²²).   οὖν is a
favourite conjunction with Jn., and vv. 5, 6 may be rendered in
accordance with his usage, " He began to wash the disciples'
feet . . . and *so* He comes to Simon Peter."   We do not know.

After μαθητῶν, D, for clearness, adds αὐτοῦ.   οἱ μαθηταί
here are the Twelve, the inner circle (cf. v. 1), not the general
body of the disciples (see on 2²).

ἐκμάσσειν is always used in Lk. and Jn. for " wiping " the
feet after washing (Lk. 7³⁸⋅ ⁴⁴, Jn. 11² 12³).

ᾧ ἦν διεζωσμένος.   ᾧ is, by attraction, for ὅ.

6. After Σίμωνα Πέτρον, the rec. adds καί, with אAWΓΔΘ;
but the conjunction is omitted by BDL, and this suits the
abrupt style of the narrative.   After λέγει αὐτῷ, in like manner,
ἐκεῖνος is added by rec. text, with אᶜADLWΓΔΘ, to make the
sense clear; om. א*B.

κύριε.   Peter does not say " Rabbi," as in the early days;
see on 1³⁸, and cf. vv. 9, 36.

σύ μου νίπτεις τοὺς πόδας; " Dost *Thou* wash *my* feet ? "
both pronouns being emphatic, and special stress lying on μου,
as following another pronoun directly.   Peter, we may suppose,
drew his feet up, as he spoke, in his impulsive humility.
There is a pseudo-reverence which is near akin to irreverence.[3]

7. ὃ ἐγὼ (emphatic) ποιῶ σὺ (emphatic) οὐκ οἶδας κτλ.,
" What *I* do *thou* knowest not at this moment (ἄρτι; see on

---

[1] See, for details, art. " Bason " in *D.C.G.*

[2] For the pleonastic use of ἄρχεσθαι in the Synoptists, see Hunkin
in *J.T.S.*, July 1924, p. 390.   Here, however, ἤρξατο is not pleonastic,
the aorist marking the definite time when the feet-washing began.

[3] A curious turn is given to this incident in the eccentric Latin
paraphrase of the Gospels known as the Huntington Palimpsest, of
which E. S. Buchanan has printed the text (New York, 1917).   It
represents Jesus as " washing the feet of Simon *Iscariot*," and Simon
Peter protesting, " Thou wilt not wash *his* feet ! "

δὲ μετὰ ταῦτα. 8. λέγει αὐτῷ Πέτρος Οὐ μὴ νίψῃς μου τοὺς πόδας εἰς τὸν αἰῶνα. ἀπεκρίθη Ἰησοῦς αὐτῷ Ἐὰν μὴ νίψω σε, οὐκ ἔχεις μέρος μετ᾽ ἐμοῦ. 9. λέγει αὐτῷ Σίμων Πέτρος Κύριε, μὴ τοὺς πόδας

9¹⁹), but thou shalt know presently." μετὰ ταῦτα (see Introd., p. cviii) is equivalent to " afterwards," and is quite vague as to the length of time that is to elapse.

For the distinction between εἰδέναι and γινώσκειν, see on 1²⁶; cf. v. 12.

The Feet-washing is explained vv. 12 f. as being a lesson in humility. The disciples had been disputing about precedence (see on v. 4 above), and Jesus reminds them, as He had done before, of the dignity of service and ministry. See on 12²⁶, where the high place which διακονία occupies in the teaching of Christ is discussed. Here He illustrates, by His action (cf. Lk. 22²⁷), this essential feature of His mission, and He bids His disciples to follow His example (v. 16). As to the possibility of a deeper symbolism, see on v. 10 below.

8. οὐ μὴ νίψῃς μου τοὺς πόδας, " Thou shalt assuredly never (εἰς τὸν αἰῶνα; see on 4¹⁴) wash *my* feet," μου being emphatic because of its position in the sentence (acc. to BCL; but the rec. text, with אΑΓΘ, puts it after πόδας).

The answer of Jesus, " If I wash thee not, thou hast no part with me," is very severe. " To have part with another," or to be his partner, is to share in his work, and ultimately in his reward. Thus the unfaithful slave is condemned to have his part (τὸ μέρος αὐτοῦ) with the hypocrites (Mt. 24⁵¹; cf. Ps. 50¹⁸). The Levites had no part in the inheritance of Israel, their work being different from that of the other tribes (Deut. 10⁹ 12¹²) ; Simon Magus had no part in the apostolic endowments of the Spirit, being animated by ideals wholly different from those of the apostles (Acts 8²¹); a Christian has no part with an unbelieving heathen (2 Cor. 6¹⁵). So to decline the call of ministry, to which every disciple is called, is to have no part with Christ, to be no partner of His, for His work was pre-eminently a work of ministry (see on 12²⁶). Peter's refusal to allow his Master to minister to him was really to reject that principle of the dignity of ministry and service which was behind the work of Jesus.

It was not said affirmatively that he whom Jesus washed was thereby recognised as His partner; for the feet of Judas were washed by Him, and He knew Judas for a traitor.

9. For Σίμων Πέτρος, B has Πέτρος Σίμων, by inadvertence: D omits Σίμων.

Peter does not yet understand what is meant by the strange act of his Master. He now thinks that the " washing "

μου μόνον ἀλλὰ καὶ τὰς χεῖρας καὶ τὴν κεφαλήν. 10. λέγει αὐτῷ
ὁ Ἰησοῦς Ὁ λελουμένος οὐκ ἔχει χρείαν εἰ μὴ τοὺς πόδας νίψασθαι,

of which Jesus has spoken is for bodily cleansing, or (perhaps)
is a symbol of spiritual cleansing; and he cries with his
accustomed impulsiveness, "Lord (א* om. κύριε), not my
feet only, but also my hands and my head," thus missing the
point of the action of Jesus. It was not a symbol of cleansing,
but an illustration of the dignity of service, even menial service ; and therefore the washing was of the *feet*, rather than
of the hands or the head.

10. B om. ὁ before Ἰησ., ins. אACDWΘ. For the rec. order
οὐ χρείαν ἔχει, אABC*W have οὐκ ἔχει χρείαν.

א omits the words εἰ μὴ τοὺς πόδας, possibly, as Abbott
(*Diat.* 2659e) suggests, by *homoioteleuton*. א sometimes
writes ει as ι, and Abbott thinks the archetype may have been

OYKEXIXPEIANI
MHTOYCΠOΔACNI
ΨACΘAI

However that may be, BC*L retain εἰ μὴ τοὺς πόδας, AC³
having ἢ τοὺς πόδας, while E² has τοὺς πόδας only; D expands
and gives οὐ χρείαν ἔχει τὴν κεφαλὴν νίψασθαι εἰ μὴ τοὺς πόδας
μόνον.

If the words εἰ μὴ τοὺς πόδας are omitted (א, with Origen
and some O.L. authorities), the answer of Jesus is clear, " He
that has been bathed needs not to wash," thus indicating that
His words and actions have had nothing to do with *cleansing*,
as Peter supposed; the *pedilauium* was an illustration only
of the dignity of ministry. But the variants show that τοὺς
πόδας was probably in the original text, and that the omission
of the words is due either to *homoioteleuton* or to the difficulty
of reconciling εἰ μὴ τοὺς πόδας with the words ἀλλ' ἔστιν
καθαρὸς ὅλος which follow.

ὁ λελουμένος κτλ. λούειν is frequently used of bathing
the whole body (*e.g.* Lev. 14⁹ 16⁴ 17¹⁶, Num. 19⁷, Deut. 23¹¹,
Acts 9³⁷). Guests were accustomed to bathe before they went
to a feast (Wetstein gives many illustrations of this); when they
arrived at the house where they were to have dinner or supper,
it was only necessary that their feet should be washed (see on
v. 4). There was no need for the head or the hands to be
washed. And so Jesus reminds Peter, who has been wrong
in thinking that the washing of his feet by his Master was for
the purpose of bodily cleansing. The man who has bathed
before the meal is καθαρὸς ὅλος, and Jesus adds, of the disciples
who were present, ὑμεῖς καθαροί ἐστε.

ἀλλ' ἔστιν καθαρὸς ὅλος· καὶ ὑμεῖς καθαροί ἐστε, ἀλλ' οὐχὶ πάντες.

καθαρός is often used of external cleanliness, as at Mt.
23²⁶ 27⁵⁹, and cf. Heb. 10²² λελουσμένοι τὸ σῶμα ὕδατι καθαρῷ,
where καθαρός refers to the purity of the water to be used in
baptism; but in the only other place where it occurs in Jn.
(15³) the word is used of *spiritual* purity. To this other meaning of καθαρός Jesus reverts here ; then to the words " ye are
clean " He adds, " but not all," Judas being the exception.
As far as bodily cleanliness was concerned, no doubt Judas
was on a par with the rest; but not in a spiritual sense.

ἀλλ' οὐχὶ πάντες. This, according to Jn., is the first hint
given by Jesus that one of the Twelve would be a traitor;
although Jn. has stated (6⁶⁴) that He had known this ἐξ ἀρχῆς,
and repeats the statement here (v. 11).

In this verse a new idea emerges, *sc.* that of spiritual
purity, being suggested by the double meaning of καθαρός ;
and we have to inquire if (as some have thought) Jn. sees a
deeper symbolism in the feet-washing than the lessons of
humility and of the dignity of service. In v. 8 we had, " If I
wash thee not, thou hast no part with me." This, apart from
its context, would naturally refer to the spiritual cleansing
which is needful before the disciple can be Christ's partner,
and perhaps (see on v. 9) Peter understood it thus. But in
the narrative this is not the interpretation of His action
furnished by Jesus Himself (vv. 13–16); although it has been
thought that Jn. tells the story in terms which imply it.

Yet (1) if the cleansing be the spiritual purification which
is the issue of Christ's atonement, then we have an idea introduced which is foreign to the context and which does not
appear again in c. 13. It is worth adding that the conception
of Christ washing away sin *in* His blood is not explicit anywhere in the N.T. (In Rev. 1⁵ the true reading is λύσαντι,
not λούσαντι, and Rev. 7¹⁴ refers to *man's* part in redemption,
" *they* washed their robes in the blood of the Lamb.")

(2) More plausible is the interpretation which finds in the
pedilauium the symbol of baptism. This goes back to Tertullian (*de bapt.* xii.), but Tertullian is inclined to find a foreshadowing of baptism in any N.T. phrase which alludes to
water. The *washing* of Christian disciples in the water of
baptism is, however, a familiar image in the N.T.; cf. 1 Cor. 6¹¹,
Eph. 5²⁶, Tit. 3⁵, and Heb. 10²² λελουσμένοι τὸ σῶμα ὕδατι καθαρῷ.

Holtzmann suggested [1] that Jn. in this passage is giving
an account of the institution of Baptism as a Christian rite,
and that he gives it here instead of narrating, as the Synoptists

[1] *Life of Jesus*, Eng. Tr., p. 42.

11. ᾔδει γὰρ τὸν παραδιδόντα αὐτόν· διὰ τοῦτο εἶπεν ὅτι Οὐχὶ πάντες καθαροί ἐστε.

do, the institution of the Eucharist, because he wishes to call attention to the high dignity of baptism. "In doing so, he at the same time very plainly offers the suggestion that washing the feet should be allowed to take the place of complete immersion." The last sentence is not only an anachronism, for baptism by affusion rather than by immersion is, so far as we know, a concession much later than the latest date that can be assigned to the Fourth Gospel; [1] but no baptismal rite has ever been known which substituted the pouring water on the feet for pouring it on the head or the body. The *pedilauium*, indeed, is prescribed in some early Gallican "Ordines Baptismi" and also in the baptismal offices of the Celtic Church. But it was no part of the actual baptism; it was a supplementary ceremony, intended to illustrate for the new Christian what manner of life his should be—humble and ministerial, as was his Master's.

If there be any allusion to baptism here, it must lurk in the word λελουμένος, "bathed," and this is specially contrasted with the "washing" (νίπτειν) of the feet. The esoteric meaning of v. 10 would then be that, as baptism cannot be repeated, the baptized person needs but to have regard to the removal of the occasional defilements of sin with which he is troubled. Even this seems over subtle.

The simplest explanation is that provided in vv. 13–16; the sudden turn of the argument in v. 11 being due to the ambiguity of the word καθαρός, which suggests the introduction of the saving clause "but not all."

11. The saying "but not all" was not understood by the disciples, who did not suspect Judas. After the Passion, it would have needed no explanation; but Jn., in explaining what it meant, is reproducing the situation as it presented itself to an eye-witness.

ᾔδει γὰρ τὸν παραδιδόντα αὐτόν, "for He knew the man that was delivering Him up," the pres. part. indicating that the movement of treachery had already begun (see on v. 2). Jn. is always careful to bring out the insight of Jesus in regard to men's characters and motives (see on 2²⁵). This explanatory comment is characteristic of his manner of writing (see on 2²¹).

διὰ τοῦτο εἶπεν ὅτι κτλ.. "wherefore He said, etc." ὅτι (om. אΑΓΔΘ, but ins. BCLW) is *recitantis*, introducing the words actually spoken.

[1] See Abrahams, in *J.T.S.*, July 1911, in reply to C. F. Rogers in the same journal for April 1911, on the Jewish method of baptism.

12. *Ὅτε οὖν ἔνιψεν τοὺς πόδας αὐτῶν καὶ ἔλαβεν τὰ ἱμάτια αὐτοῦ καὶ ἀνέπεσεν πάλιν, εἶπεν αὐτοῖς Γινώσκετε τί πεποίηκα ὑμῖν, 13. ὑμεῖς φωνεῖτέ με Ὁ Διδάσκαλος καὶ ὁ Κύριος, καὶ καλῶς λέγετε· εἰμὶ γάρ. 14. εἰ οὖν ἐγὼ ἔνιψα ὑμῶν τοὺς πόδας ὁ Κύριος καὶ ὁ Διδάσκαλος, καὶ ὑμεῖς ὀφείλετε ἀλλήλων νίπτειν τοὺς πόδας·

οὐχὶ πάντες . . . Cf. v. 18 οὐ περὶ πάντων ὑμῶν (and Mt. 7²¹) for this Greek order of words.

The spiritual meaning of the Feet-washing (vv. 12-20)

12. ὅτε . . . αὐτῶν, " When then He had washed their feet," αὐτῶν indicating that He ministered to them all.

καὶ ἔλαβεν τὰ ἱμάτια αὐτοῦ, " and had taken His garments," *i.e.* had resumed the *tallith* which He had taken off (v. 4).

καὶ ἀνέπεσεν πάλιν, " and had reclined (or, as we should say, *sat down*) again." He resumed His place at the table, which He had left when ἐγείρεται ἐκ τοῦ δείπνου (v. 4).

For καὶ ἀνέπεσεν, C³DΘ have ἀναπεσών.

εἶπεν αὐτοῖς Γινώσκετε τί πεποίηκα ὑμῖν; γινώσκετε may be either *imperative* (as at Josh. 23¹³, Dan. 3¹⁵, Jn. 15¹⁸) or *interrogative*, as it has usually been understood. Abbott (*Diat.* 2243) prefers to take γινώσκετε as imperative here, the Lord bidding the disciples to recognise, and mark the meaning of, His ministry to them. The words go back to γνώσῃ μετὰ ταῦτα of v. 7, in any case. They introduce the interpretation of the strange action of Jesus in washing the disciples' feet.

For γινώσκειν, see on 1⁴⁸.

13. ὑμεῖς φωνεῖτέ με κτλ., " You address me as Teacher and Lord." φωνεῖν (see on 1⁴⁸) is the word regularly used by Jn. for calling a person by his name or title.

For the titles *Rabbi* (διδάσκαλε) and *Mari* (κύριε), by which the disciples were accustomed to address Jesus, see on 1³⁸ above. ὁ διδάοκαλος, ὁ κύριος, are called by the grammarians titular nominatives.

καὶ καλῶς λέγετε, εἰμὶ γάρ, " and you say well, for so I am." Cf. with εἰμὶ γάρ the καί ἐσμεν of 1 Jn. 3¹. Christ affirms His own dignity, even while stooping to what the disciples counted a menial office. He will not permit them to be in any doubt about this.

14. εἰ οὖν ἐγώ κτλ., " If then, *I*, your Lord and Teacher, have washed *your* feet, *a fortiori*, you ought to wash the feet of one another." By this example were the dignity and the duty of mutual διακονία recommended (see on 12²⁶) to Christian disciples.

The precept was not taken by the Church to be the initiation

15. ὑπόδειγμα γὰρ ἔδωκα ὑμῖν ἵνα καθὼς ἐγὼ ἐποίησα ὑμῖν καὶ ὑμεῖς ποιῆτε. 16. ἀμὴν ἀμὴν λέγω ὑμῖν, οὐκ ἔστιν δοῦλος μείζων τοῦ κυρίου αὐτοῦ, οὐδὲ ἀπόστολος μείζων τοῦ πέμψαντος αὐτόν. 17. εἰ

of a sacramental rite; the *pedilauium* was never counted as a sacrament, although the custom grew up by the fourth century, in certain parts of the Western Church, of washing the feet of the poor on the Thursday before Easter. In England, the sovereign, or in his stead the Lord High Almoner, used to do this with ceremony until 1731; and in Rome the Pope still presides at the *pedilauium*. The pious widows described in 1 Tim. 5¹⁰ " washed the saints' feet," but only as an incident of their hospitable ministrations.

ὀφείλετε. The verb occurs again in Jn. at 19⁷, 1 Jn. 2⁶ 3¹⁶ 4¹¹.

15. ὑπόδειγμα is not found again in Jn., and is applied nowhere else in the N.T. to the example of Christ. It is used of the noble example of Eleazar's death at 2 Macc. 6²⁸. Cf. Heb. 4¹¹ 8⁵ 9²³, Jas. 5¹⁰, 2 Pet. 2⁶.

The rec. ἔδωκα (BCDW⊛) is perhaps to be preferred to δέδωκα of ℵA *fam*. 13.

ἵνα καθὼς ἐγώ κτλ., " that as I have done to you, so you should do ": a practical illustration having been provided of the meaning of the precept, " Learn of me, for I am meek and lowly in heart " (Mt. 11²⁹). For the constr. καθὼς . . . καί, cf. vv. 33, 34.

16. ἀμὴν ἀμήν κτλ., as usual, introduces an aphorism of special significance. See on 1⁵¹.

οὐκ ἔστιν δοῦλος μείζων τοῦ κυρίου αὐτοῦ. Lk. 6⁴⁰ has οὐκ ἔστιν μαθητὴς ὑπὲρ τὸν διδάσκαλον; and Mt. 10²⁴ combines the Johannine and Lucan forms of the saying. It is, of course, beyond question that the servant is not greater than his master (cf. Lk. 22²⁷) ; but it is stated here to reinforce the lesson of the true dignity of service, which Jesus has been teaching by His example. If He may stoop to minister, without losing dignity, *a fortiori* may His disciples do so. The saying is repeated 15²⁰, where a different lesson is drawn from it.

οὐδὲ ἀπόστολος κτλ., " nor is he that is sent greater than Him that sent him." ἀπόστολος is not found again in Jn., and is here used in its etymological sense of a " messenger," as at 1 Kings 14⁶, 2 Cor. 8²³, Phil. 2²⁵. The Synoptists tell that Jesus gave the title ἀπόστολοι to the Twelve (Lk. 6¹³), and they occasionally apply it to them. But Jn. always uses the older descriptions " the Twelve," or " the Disciples." It is possible that Jn. discovers a special allusion to the Twelve in the words " he that is sent is not greater than Him that sent

ταῦτα οἴδατε, μακάριοί ἐστε ἐὰν ποιῆτε αὐτά.   18. οὐ περὶ πάντων
ὑμῶν λέγω· ἐγὼ οἶδα τίνας ἐξελεξάμην· ἀλλ' ἵνα ἡ γραφὴ πληρωθῇ
ʽΟ τρώγων μου τὸν ἄρτον ἐπῆρεν ἐπ' ἐμὲ τὴν πτέρναν αὐτοῦ.   19. ἀπ'

him," and that the word ἀπόστολος is specially significant here
of their mission; but this is not certain. See on 2².

17. εἰ ταῦτα οἴδατε κτλ., "If ye know these things," *sc.* if
you thoroughly understand and appreciate what I have been
saying to you (for the force of οἴδατε, see on 1²⁶). Judas had
not reached to this point.

μακάριοί ἐστε κτλ., "blessed are ye, if ye do them." The
dignity of διακονία is an easy lesson to understand, but is
hard to put into practice (cf. Lk. 11²⁸). Yet it is he who does
this, who humbles himself like a child, who is great in the
kingdom of heaven (Mt. 18⁴). μακάριος is used only once
again by Jn., at 20²⁹, where he quotes other words of Jesus,
μακάριοι οἱ μὴ ἰδόντες καὶ πιστεύσαντες. This latter saying is
the Benediction of Faith ; that in 13¹⁷ is the Benediction of
Ministry. Both are *blessed*, not only εὐλογητός that is, lauded
by men, but μακάριος, as God is μακάριος (1 Tim. 1¹¹ 6¹⁵).

18. οὐ περὶ πάντων ὑμῶν λέγω. So He had said before
(v. 10). The treachery of Judas (who had no share in the
benediction of v. 17) did not come upon Jesus unawares (see
on 6⁶⁴).

τίνας (אBCL) is to be preferred to the rec. οὕς (ADW⊖)
before ἐξελεξάμην: "I know *the kind of men* whom I chose,"
sc. when selecting the Twelve out of a larger company of
disciples. See 6⁷⁰, where the same word ἐξελεξάμην is used ;
and cf. 15¹⁶· ¹⁹.

ἀλλ' ἵνα ἡ γραφὴ πληρωθῇ κτλ., may be a note added by
the evangelist after his manner,[1] but possibly he intends to
place the phrase and the quotation in the mouth of Jesus
Himself (cf. 17¹²). If this be so, the sentence is elliptical,
and we must understand the meaning to be: "I know whom I
chose, but *none the less this treachery will come*, that the
Scripture might be fulfilled " (cf. 9³ 15²⁵ for a like ellipse).
The treachery of Judas was foreordained in the eternal counsels
of God; he was destined to deliver up Jesus to the Jews (see
6⁷¹ 12⁴).

The quotation is from the Hebrew (not the LXX) of Ps. 41⁹ :
"he that eateth my bread lifted up his heel against me." To
eat bread at the table of a superior was to offer a pledge of
loyalty (2 Sam. 9⁷· ¹⁴, 1 Kings 18¹⁹, 2 Kings 25²⁹); and to
betray one with whom bread had been eaten, one's "mess-
mate," was a gross breach of the traditions of hospitality

[1] Cf. Introd., p. clv.

ἄρτι λέγω ὑμῖν πρὸ τοῦ γενέσθαι, ἵνα πιστεύσητε ὅταν γένηται ὅτι ἐγώ

"To lift up the heel" against any one is to offer him brutal violence. The Synoptists do not quote this Psalm in connexion with the treachery of Judas; but Jn. is especially prone to find fulfilment of prophecy in the incidents of the Passion.[1]

The LXX of this passage is: ὁ ἐσθίων ἄρτους μου ἐμεγάλυνει ἐπ᾽ ἐμὲ πτερνισμόν. It is noteworthy that Jn. does not say ὁ ἐσθίων, but ὁ τρώγων, a less usual word which he employs four times (6[54. 56. 57. 58]) for the "feeding" on Christ in the Eucharist (see note on 6[54]). Here he almost goes out of his way to use it of the "eating" at the Last Supper.

For μου after τρώγων, אADWΓΔΘ give μετ᾽ ἐμοῦ, but μου is nearer the Hebrew and is better supported (BCL). The Coptic Q has the conflate rendering, "eats my bread with me."

19. ἀπ᾽ ἄρτι λέγω ὑμῖν κτλ., "From now I tell you," etc. For ἀπ᾽ ἄρτι, cf. 14[7], Rev. 14[13], Mt. 23[29] 26[29. 64]; the phrase does not occur elsewhere in the N.T.

The startling announcement that one of the Twelve would betray Him was not made explicitly by Jesus before, but it is now distinctly stated, so that when the Betrayal took place they might not be scandalised and perplexed (cf. 16[1]).

ἵνα πιστεύσητε ὅταν γένηται κτλ., "in order that ye may believe, when it comes to pass, that *I am He.*" ἐγώ εἰμι in this sentence is used absolutely, no predicate being expressed or suggested by the context. It is an instance (see Introd., p. cxx.; and cf. 8[58]) of the employment of the phrase as the equivalent of אֲנִי־הוּא, *I (am) He,* which is the prophetic self-designation of Yahweh in the O.T. And the whole passage λέγω ὑμῖν πρὸ τοῦ γενέσθαι, ἵνα πιστεύσητε ὅταν γένηται ὅτι ἐγώ εἰμι, recalls prophetic words which speak of the foretelling of the future as the prerogative of Yahweh. "Before it came to pass I showed it to thee" (Isa. 48[5]) may be compared with Isa. 41[26], where the implied answer to the question, "Who hath declared it from the beginning that we may know?" is evidently "None but God." Cf. also Ezek. 24[24], . . . ὅταν ἔλθῃ ταῦτα, καὶ ἐπιγνώσεσθε διότι ἐγὼ κύριος.

Jesus assumes to Himself this prerogative 3 times in Jn.: here, where He announces that He will be betrayed by one of His disciples; in 16[4], where, having forewarned His disciples of future persecution, he says ταῦτα λελάληκα ὑμῖν ἵνα ὅταν ἔλθῃ ἡ ὥρα αὐτῶν μνημονεύητε αὐτῶν, ὅτι ἐγὼ εἶπον ὑμῖν, and again in 14[29], where, having spoken of the Coming of the Paraclete, He adds νῦν εἴρηκα ὑμῖν πρὶν γενέσθαι, ἵνα ὅταν

[1] Cf. Introd., p. cliv.

εἰμί. 20. ἀμὴν ἀμὴν λέγω ὑμῖν, ὁ λαμβάνων ἄν τινα πέμψω ἐμὲ λαμβάνει, ὁ δὲ ἐμὲ λαμβάνων λαμβάνει τὸν πέμψαντά με.

21. Ταῦτα εἰπὼν Ἰησοῦς ἐταράχθη τῷ πνεύματι καὶ ἐμαρτύρησεν

γένηται πιστεύσητε. A similar phrase occurs in Mt. 24²⁵, where He has been speaking of the false Christs that would appear: ἰδού προείρηκα ὑμῖν. See on 2²².

πιστεύσητε (as at 14²⁹) is read by ℵADLWΓΔΘ; πιστεύητε (cf. 17²¹), by BC. Cf. Abbott, *Diat.* 2526 f.

Origen (*in loc.*) takes ἐγώ εἰμι as meaning "I am He, of whom it was written, He that eateth my bread, etc." (v. 18); but this would be a strange ellipse, although the meaning would be suitable to the context.

20. ἀμὴν ἀμήν κτλ. See on 1⁵¹.

Jesus has reminded the apostles that their dignity is not greater than His (v. 16); but lest they should make any mistake, He now reminds them that their dignity is, none the less, very great. The man who receives those whom He has sent, receives Him; and he who receives Jesus receives God who sent Him. The latter part of this aphorism has been stated already in other words (12⁴⁴, where see note). It is a Synoptic saying, and its form here is very like Mk. 9³⁷ and Mt. 10⁴⁰ ὁ δεχόμενος ὑμᾶς ἐμὲ δέχεται, καὶ ὁ ἐμὲ δεχόμενος δέχεται τὸν ἀποστείλαντά με (cf. Lk. 9⁴⁸). Jn. substituted for δέχεσθαι the verb λαμβάνειν (cf. 1¹²), and for ἀποστέλλειν the verb πέμπειν (see on 3¹⁷), after his manner.[1] It is a general principle that the reverence paid to an ambassador is reckoned as reverence to his sovereign; and so it was claimed by the Great Ambassador, both in respect of His own relation to the Father, and of the relation of His apostles to Himself.

Jesus foretells His betrayal, the others not recognising that Judas is designated by being handed a sop : Judas leaves the room (vv. 21-31)

21. ACDW read ὁ Ἰησοῦς, but om. ὁ ℵBL. See on 1²⁹.

ἐταράχθη τῷ πνεύματι. See note on 11³³, and cf. 12²⁷, ταράσσειν being used in both cases of the troubled spirit of Jesus (in 14¹· ²⁷ it is said of the disciples). Jn., who lays such stress on the consciousness which Jesus had of His oneness with God (cf. 5¹⁹), is no less emphatic about His true humanity (see on 1¹⁴). The emotion with which He announced explicitly to His chosen companions that a traitor was among them is very human.

[1] Cf. Ignatius, *Eph.* vi. οὕτως δεῖ ἡμᾶς αὐτὸν δέχεσθαι, ὡς αὐτὸν τὸν πέμψαντα.

καὶ εἶπεν Ἀμὴν ἀμὴν λέγω ὑμῖν ὅτι εἷς ἐξ ὑμῶν παραδώσει με.
22. ἔβλεπον εἰς ἀλλήλους οἱ μαθηταὶ ἀπορούμενοι περὶ τίνος λέγει.
23. ἦν ἀνακείμενος εἷς ἐκ τῶν μαθητῶν αὐτοῦ ἐν τῷ κόλπῳ τοῦ Ἰησοῦ,

καὶ ἐμαρτύρησεν, the verb being used here of an explicit and definite pronouncement of Jesus, as at 4⁴⁴ 18³⁷. For the idea of "witness" in Jn., see Introd., p. xc ; and for the μαρτυρία of Jesus, cf. 3¹¹· ³² 7⁷ 8¹⁴· ¹⁸.

ἀμὴν ἀμήν κτλ.   See on 1⁵¹.   ὅτι is *recitantis.*

εἷς ἐξ ὑμῶν.   For this constr., see on 1⁴⁰.

παραδώσει με, " shall deliver me up."   See on 6⁶⁴ for the exact meaning of παραδιδόναι.   All the evangelists (cf. Mk. 14¹⁸, followed by Mt. 26²¹, Lk. 22²¹) agree that this startling announcement was made for the first time at the Last Supper; even then, Jesus gave no clue as to who the traitor was (see on vv. 10, 26).   Indeed, if He had done so, Judas could hardly have escaped with his life.

22. The rec., with ℵ*ADLWΘ, ins. οὖν after ἔβλεπον, but om. ℵᶜBC.

The bewilderment (cf. Lk. 24⁴, Gal. 4²⁰, for ἀπορεῖν) and distress of the apostles at this announcement are noted by the Synoptists as well as by Jn.; possibly the dissension as to precedence which seems to have taken place that evening (see on v. 16) may have accentuated the perplexity which they felt.   Judas did not suggest by his demeanour that he was the guilty one, for they noticed nothing of the sort.

This is the moment chosen by Leonardo da Vinci for his wonderful picture of the scene.

23. After ἦν the rec., with ℵAC²DWΘ, ins. δέ, but om. BC*L.

For the constr. ἦν ἀνακείμενος, where we should expect the impf., see on 1²⁸.

εἷς ἐκ τῶν μαθ.   Θ om. ἐκ, but ins. ℵABCDW; see on 1⁴⁰.

ὃν ἠγάπα ὁ Ἰησοῦς.   Cf. 19²⁶ 20² 21⁷· ²⁰.   We have argued in the Introduction (p. xxxv f.) that this disciple was John the son of Zebedee.   The question has been raised, indeed, whether we may not suppose others, outside the circle of the Twelve, to have been present at the Last Supper, of whom " the beloved disciple " may have been one.   But the language of Mk. 14¹⁷, " He cometh with *the Twelve*," is explicit; so too Lk. 22¹⁴, " He sat down, and *the apostles* with Him."   There is no hint anywhere of the presence of any except the twelve chosen companions of the Lord (cf. v. 18), of whom therefore the beloved disciple must be one.   Sanday's suggestion [1] that the beloved

¹ *Criticism of Fourth Gospel,* p. 98.

disciple may have been present as a young and favoured follower, a " supernumerary apostle," lacks evidence. It is highly unlikely that Jesus would have bestowed special marks of His love and favour on one whom He did not include within the circle of the Twelve, and of whom, besides, the Synoptists know absolutely nothing.[1]

The posture at table of guests at a feast seems to have been that of reclining sideways on couches or divans, the left arm on a cushion which was on the table, the right hand being thus free for taking food; the feet were stretched out behind. The host or principal person was in the centre, and the place of honour was above him, that is, to his left; the next highest place being below him, or to his right.[2] Thus the person on the right of the host would be so placed that his head would be close to the host's breast, and that it would be easy therefore to say a word to him confidentially. The host would occupy a similar position in relation to the chief guest on his left, and would readily be able to address *him* privately.

It is plain that, at the Supper, the beloved disciple (*i.e.*, as we take it, John the son of Zebedee) lay on the *right* of Jesus, ἀνακείμενος ἐν τῷ κόλπῳ τοῦ Ἰησοῦ. There is no certain indication as to the disciple on His *left* (which was the place of honour). Some have thought it was Peter, but, if that were so, he would have addressed his question (v. 24) to Jesus directly, without the intervention of John. And the fact that he made signs to John would suggest that he was not very near him at table. It is more probable that the chief place (on the left of Jesus) was occupied by Judas, for Jesus was able to speak to him privately without the conversation being overheard (see v. 27 and cf. Mt. 26[25]). That Judas was the treasurer of the little company (see on 12[6]) may point to his enjoyment of some kind of precedence; and if this were so, he would naturally occupy the chief place at table, next to Jesus. See also on 6[71].

That John the son of Zebedee was given a place of honour at the supper is reminiscent of the request of Mk. 10[37] that he and his brother should be given the two highest seats in the Messianic kingdom; and it is possible that it was their custom to occupy the places of honour at the common meals of the Lord and His disciples. This would suggest that James was on the left of Jesus, as John was on His right, at the Last Supper; but more probably on this occasion Judas was next his Master.

[1] Cf. Jülicher (*Introd.*, p. 413), who holds, however, that the " beloved disciple " is only an ideal figure.
[2] See Lightfoot, *Hor. Hebr.* in loc., and in Mt. 26[22].

ὅν ἠγάπα ὁ Ἰησοῦς· 24. νεύει οὖν τούτῳ Σίμων Πέτρος πυθέσθαι τίς
ἂν εἴη. 25. ἀναπεσὼν ἐκεῖνος οὕτως ἐπὶ τὸ στῆθος τοῦ Ἰησοῦ λέγει

24. **νεύει οὖν τούτῳ Σίμων Πέτρος.** " Simon Peter," taking
the initiative as usual, beckons to him, *sc.* to John. The
text in the latter part of the verse is not quite certain.

(1) BCL and the Latin vss., followed by most modern
editors, after Πέτρος read καὶ λέγει αὐτῷ Εἰπὲ τίς ἐστιν περὶ οὗ
λέγει. But the verb νεύειν, " to make signs," is not usually
accompanied by an intimation that the person making signs
also *spoke*.[1] Again, εἰπέ is difficult to translate. The R.V.
renders "tell *us*"; but why should Peter have expected
John to answer out of his own knowledge? They were all
puzzled, and John knew no more than the others. Abbott
(*Diat.* 1359) takes εἰπέ as meaning " say," *sc.* to Jesus, that
is, " *ask* Him." But why, then, do we not find ἐρώτησον?
(*a c f q* add *interroga*).

(2) The other reading, νεύει οὖν τούτῳ Σίμων Πέτρος πυθέσθαι
τίς ἂν εἴη, has in its favour that νεύειν is followed by an
infinitive, as it is in the only other place where it occurs in
the N.T. (Acts 24[10]), and that it does not represent Peter as
making signs and speaking as well. It is supported by
ADWΓΔΘ and the Syriac vss. (including the Sinai Syriac).[2]
πυθέσθαι is a Johannine word, occurring at 4[52]. The only
objection to this reading is that the optative mood (εἴη) is very
rare in the N.T., as it was going out of use at this period, and
that it never occurs again in Jn.

In any case, according to the Fourth Gospel, John is
prompted by Peter to ask Jesus whom He had in mind. Mk.,
followed by Mt., represents all the disciples as asking " Is it
I ? " Lk. says that they questioned each other. Perhaps all
these things happened, but it may at least be claimed that
Jn.'s narrative is peculiarly vivid.

25. **ἀναπεσών.** So אᶜBC*L, as at 21[20]; the rec. ἐπιπεσών,
following א*AC³DWΓΔΘ, suggests too violent a change of
posture for the occasion. The rec. inserts δέ after ἐπιπεσών,
with AΘ, but it is om. by BC; אDLW have οὖν.

ἀναπεσὼν ἐκεῖνος οὕτως ἐπὶ τὸ στῆθος τοῦ Ἰη.,[3] " he (*i.e.*
John) leaning back just as he was (cf. 4[6] for οὕτως) on the
breast of Jesus," *i.e.* leaning back, keeping the same attitude

---

[1] See Field, *in loc.*

[2] א combines both readings in a confused fashion, thus showing that
both are earlier than the date of that manuscript.

[3] The phrase is quoted verbatim, as descriptive of John, by
Irenæus (III. i. 1) and Polycrates (Eus. *H.E.* v. 24). See Introd.,
p. l.

αὐτῷ Κύριε, τίς ἐστιν ; 26. ἀποκρίνεται οὖν ὁ Ἰησοῦς Ἐκεῖνός ἐστιν ᾧ ἐγὼ βάψω τὸ ψωμίον καὶ δώσω αὐτῷ. βάψας οὖν τὸ ψωμίον λαμβάνει

that has been described in **v. 23**. For the frequent use of ἐκεῖνος by Jn., see on 1[8].

οὕτως is omitted by the rec., with אADWΘ ; but BCLΔ have it, and it gives an intimate touch to the narrative here.

λέγει αὐτῷ, " saith to Him," viz. in a whisper so that the others could not hear, which his position on the right of Jesus would enable him to do.

τίς ἐστιν ; "Who is it ? " But Jesus does not give the name of the traitor in reply. He answers in a way that even John does not seem to have been able to interpret (see on vv. 21, 28).

26. ἀποκρίνεται οὖν, " So Jesus answers " (cf. for the pres. tense 12[23]) ; see for οὖν on 1[22]. οὖν is omitted (wrongly) by א*AC³DWΓΔΘ, but is read by אᶜBC*L. B omits, after its frequent habit (see on 1[26]), ὁ before Ἰησοῦς. אD and *fam.* 13 add καὶ λέγει after Ἰησοῦς, but om. ABCLWΘ.

ψωμίον, " a morsel," is not found in the N.T. outside this passage, but is a common word, and is the usual word for " bread " in modern Greek (cf. Judg. 19[5]). The best reading (BCL cop.) is ἐγὼ βάψω τὸ ψωμίον καὶ δώσω αὐτῷ, the constr. βάψω καὶ δώσω being thoroughly Johannine; but the rec. text has ἐγὼ βάψας τὸ ψωμίον ἐπιδώσω, following אAD. For βάψας in the second clause of the verse, the rec. has ἐμβάψας (ΑΓΔΘ). After the second ψωμίον the rec. omits λαμβάνει καί (with א*ADWΓΔΘ), but the words are found in אᶜᵃBCL and must be retained, as adding a new and vivid detail. For Ἰσκαριώτου (the true reading here ; see on 6[71]), which is found in אBCΘ, the rec. has Ἰσκαριώτῃ (ΑWΓΔ).

In Mk. (followed by Mt.), the same reply in substance is given to the disciples' eager inquiry as to which of them would be the traitor (ὁ ἐμβαπτόμενος μετ᾽ ἐμοῦ εἰς τὸ τρύβλιον, Mk. 14[20]); Lk. does not mention it. Jn. relates that Jesus gave to the beloved disciple a more precise clue, by saying that the traitor would be he to whom Jesus would Himself give the " sop," having first dipped it. This is, no doubt, a correct detail. But it does not appear that John identified the traitor even when this clue was provided (v. 28).

It was a token of intimacy, to allow a guest to dip his bread in the common dish or τρύβλιον: thus Boaz says to Ruth βάψεις τὸν ψωμόν σου τῷ ὄξει (Ruth 2[14]). And it is still a favour of Eastern hospitality for the host to dip a choice morsel in the central dish and hand it to a guest. This is what Jesus did for Judas, who was probably reclining at table next to

καὶ δίδωσιν Ἰούδᾳ Σίμωνος Ἰσκαριώτου. 27. καὶ μετὰ τὸ ψωμίον τότε εἰσῆλθεν εἰς ἐκεῖνον ὁ Σατανᾶς. λέγει οὖν αὐτῷ ὁ Ἰησοῦς "Ο

Him (see on v. 23); but it was so usual a courtesy that it escaped the notice of the others, and did not seem even to John to have any special significance, despite what he had been told. If John understood, we must suppose him to have kept silent, and to have refrained from telling the others, which is highly improbable.

βάψας οὖν τὸ ψωμίον κτλ., "having dipped the sop, He takes and gives it to Judas." According to Mt. 26²⁵, Judas asked, "Is it I?" to which the answer "Thou hast said" was given. This could have happened without attracting the attention of any one, as Judas was reclining next to Jesus. In any case, whether by word or act, Judas was made aware that Jesus knew what was in his heart. There was still time for him to abandon his purpose. But the quiet word and the courteous gesture of giving him the sop did but harden him. This was the last appeal to his better nature, and there was no response.

27. μετὰ τὸ ψωμίον, sc. after the whole incident of the giving of the sop, a classical use of μετά with a substantive following.

τότε, "then," a graphic word, calling attention to the moment of final decision.

εἰσῆλθεν εἰς ἐκ. κτλ., "Satan entered into that one," ἐκεῖνος being used as indicating the alien mind of Judas, and not merely for emphasis (see on 1⁸). Lk. (22³) has the same phrase εἰσῆλθεν ὁ Σατανᾶς εἰς Ἰούδαν, but he uses it of him at an earlier stage. See v. 2; and cf. 6⁷⁰. It was a natural way of explaining a course of treachery, so abhorrent to the evangelists, by whom the direct agency of Satan was firmly believed in. εἰσέρχομαι is the verb used by the Synoptists to describe the "entering in" of evil spirits (cf. Mk. 5¹², Lk. 8³⁰ 11²⁶). The evangelist can no otherwise explain to himself the devilish treachery that followed.

ὁ Ἰησοῦς. BL om. ὁ. (See on 1²⁹; and cf. v. 26.)

ποίησον is imperative. "What thou doest, do more quickly" (see on 2⁵).

τάχιον (or τάχειον) is the comparative, occurring again in the N.T. only at Jn. 20⁴, Heb. 13¹⁹· ²³; cf. Wisd. 13⁹. Possibly Judas had not intended to consummate his treachery so soon, and was waiting until the Passover was past. But, whether this be so or not, the stern word "Do it more quickly" is human, indeed, in its context. "How am I straitened until it be finished!" is an earlier saying which Lk. (12⁵⁰) ascribes to

ποιεῖς ποίησον τάχιον. 28. τοῦτο δὲ οὐδεὶς ἔγνω τῶν ἀνακειμένων
πρὸς τί εἶπεν αὐτῷ· 29. τινὲς γὰρ ἐδόκουν, ἐπεὶ τὸ γλωσσόκομον
εἶχεν Ἰούδας, ὅτι λέγει αὐτῷ Ἰησοῦς Ἀγόρασον ὧν χρείαν ἔχομεν εἰς
τὴν ἑορτήν, ἢ τοῖς πτωχοῖς ἵνα τι δῷ. 30. λαβὼν οὖν τὸ ψωμίον
ἐκεῖνος ἐξῆλθεν εὐθύς· ἦν δὲ νύξ.

Jesus. The looking forward to the inevitable Passion was
torture; that there should be no longer delay was the natural
wish of His heart. Attention has been called above (1^{14}) to
the emphasis laid by Jn. on the true humanity of Jesus, as
indicated by the human emotions of which Jn. tells.

28. τοῦτο δὲ οὐδείς κτλ. None of the disciples understood
what was the reference of this injunction " Do it more
quickly," which had been said aloud so that all could hear it.
This explicit statement must include the beloved disciple
as well as the rest (see on v. 26).[1]

For the constr. οὐδεὶς τῶν ἀνακειμένων, οὐδείς not being
followed by ἐκ, cf. 21^{12}, and see on 1^{40} 7^{19} ; and for the position
of οὐδείς in the sentence, see on 1^{18}.

29. τινὲς γάρ κτλ. Jn. is apt thus to introduce with γάρ
his own comments on the incidents or sayings which he records;
see on 3^{16}.

The disciples did not know what the order " Do it more
quickly " meant, and they held different views about it. Judas,
being the treasurer (for τὸ γλωσσόκομον, see on 12^6), was naturally
also the purveyor and the almoner of the little company. Some
thought that he was bidden to hasten the purchase of what was
needed for the Passover feast. This indicates again that the
Passover was still to come, and that the Last Supper, for Jn.,
was not the Paschal meal (see on v. 1); for, had it been Passover
night, nothing could have been bought. Another explanation
was that Judas was told to give some alms to the poor, as he
was accustomed to do (12^6), perhaps in order that aid might be
given to a poor household to provide the Paschal lamb for the
morrow.

In v. 29, ὁ is omitted before Ἰούδας and Ἰησοῦς by אB.
See vv. 26, 27, and note on 1^{29}.

30. λαβὼν οὖν τὸ ψωμίον κτλ., " So, having taken the sop,
that one went out immediately." Jn. lays stress on the acceptance of the sop by Judas, the suggestion being that Judas had
recognised the significance of the offer of it by Jesus, and
understanding now that Jesus knew his purpose he proceeds

---

[1] Newman's astounding comment on " What thou doest, do
quickly," as justifying or illustrating the rapid recitation of the words
in the Canon of the Mass, is one of the curiosities of literature (*Loss
and Gain*, ch. xx.).

31. Ὅτε οὖν ἐξῆλθεν, λέγει Ἰησοῦς XV. 1. Ἐγώ εἰμι ἡ ἄμπελος

to execute it at once, whatever he may have intended before as to the day or hour of the betrayal.

ἐξῆλθεν εὐθύς. This is the right order (אBCDLW), as against εὐθέως ἐξῆλθεν of AΘ and the rec. text: so also at 19³⁴. The emphasis is on εὐθύς ; Judas hurried away at once.

There is a variant εὐθέως (AΓΔΘ), but εὐθύς is read here by אBCDLW. Abbott (*Diat.* 1911 f.) seems to draw a distinction in use between these forms, but his argument is over subtle. For εὐθύς, see on 5⁹ ; and cf. 1²².

ἦν δὲ νύξ. This may be only a note of time, such as Jn. is apt to give (see on 1²⁹); but it is remarkably impressive here, and the dramatic horror of the moment is brought before the reader. Judas went out into the darkness. The symbolic meaning of this can hardly have been absent from the mind of the evangelist. Cf. Lk. 22⁵³, Rev. 21²⁵ 22⁵.

The departure of Judas from the room is not mentioned by the Synoptists, although it is assumed.

31ᵃ. ὅτε οὖν ἐξῆλθεν. The rec. omits οὖν, with A, but ins אBCDLWΘ. Some commentators, *e.g.* Bengel, omitting it, connect the preceding words ἦν δὲ νύξ with ὅτε ἐξῆλθεν, and this repetition of ἐξῆλθεν would be quite in the style of Jn. But the MS. evidence is conclusive for οὖν, and this disposes of such an arrangement of the words. The sentence ends dramatically with the monosyllable νύξ.

Here there seems to have been a dislocation of the original text,[1] and in this commentary we take the text in the order cc. 13³¹ᵃ 15 16 13³¹ᵇ⁻³⁸ 14 17. This is also the time (see Introductory Note to v. 4) at which we must suppose the Eucharist to have been instituted. Whether Jn.'s account of this has been lost, or whether he did not describe the institution at all, is not certain; but in any case it is at this point in the narrative that we suppose it to have taken place.

XIII. 31ᵃ, XV. 1. ὅτε οὖν ἐξῆλθεν, λέγει Ἰησοῦς Ἐγώ εἰμι ἡ ἄμπελος ἡ ἀληθινή. οὖν is emphatic. Such a discourse as this of the True Vine which follows was only for the faithful.

It has been suggested [2] that cc. 14–17 are more easily understood if we suppose them to represent discourses of Jesus which belong to His post-resurrection life on earth, rather than discourses spoken on the eve of His Passion. That their

---

[1] See Introd., p. xx.
[2] See R. T. Byrn in the *Irish Church Quarterly* for April and Oct. 1909 ; and G. Henslow in the *Interpreter*, 1917. Cf., *contra*, Garvie, *The Beloved Disciple*, p. 157.

teachings are specially apposite, when read in public worship between Easter and Pentecost, has been recognised by Christendom for many centuries, the Greek, Syrian, and Latin Churches (as well as the Anglican) making use of selections from these chapters as the Gospels for some of the Sundays after Easter. It is not impossible that Jn. has preserved in cc. 14–17 some of the Lord's post-resurrection counsels with other words spoken after the Last Supper. Thus 16⁷⁻¹¹ present an interesting resemblance to words ascribed to Jesus after His Resurrection in an addition to Mk. 16¹⁴, preserved in the Freer MS. (see on 16¹¹ below). But it can hardly be doubted that cc. 14–17 belong to the eve of the Passion, or that 16⁵ must precede 13³⁶.

The Vine and the branches (vv. 1–8)

XV. 1. The comparison of Jesus to a Tree, and of His disciples to the branches which derive their life from the life of the Tree, is similar in some respects to an illustration used by Paul to explain the relation of the individual Israelite to his forefathers, Abraham and the rest. " If the root is holy, so are the branches " (Rom. 11¹⁶). Israel is compared to an olive tree, the roots being the patriarchs and the branches their descendants. But the illustration of Jesus conveys a deeper lesson, as we shall see.

The question presents itself: Why is the *vine* selected as the tree best fitted to bring out the lesson which it was the purpose of Jesus to teach ? A vine has none of the dignity of the olive, with its fine trunk and spreading branches. Vines, indeed, in the East generally trail on the ground, although they are sometimes supported on stakes (cf. Ezek. 17⁶ᶠ·), or entwine themselves round a greater tree (as in the parable in Hermas, *Sim.* ii.). The olive was regarded in an older parable as fit to be the king of trees (Judg. 9⁸). It is the most important of the fruit trees of Palestine, and was a familiar object in Jerusalem, as the name " the Mount of Olives " indicates. Vines were also plentiful, especially in Judæa (cf. Gen. 49¹¹), but for strength and stateliness they are much inferior to the olive, as to many other trees.

The reason generally assigned by exegetes for the employment here of the figure of a *vine* is that it is frequently used in the O.T. as a type of Israel. But it is always thus used of *degenerate* Israel. " What is the vine tree more than any other tree ? " Ezekiel asks (15²), and he declares that as vine branches are only fit for burning, the vine of Jerusalem must be devoured by fire. So again (Ezek. 19¹⁰), Israel was once a fruitful vine, but she was plucked up and destroyed. The choicest vine was planted in the vineyard of Yahweh, but it only brought forth wild grapes (Isa. 5¹). Israel was planted as a noble vine, but it became degenerate (Jer. 2²¹). Israel is a luxuriant vine, but judgment comes on her (Hos. 10¹). The vine from Egypt of God's planting spread far and wide, but the fences of its vineyard were broken, and it was ravaged by wild beasts (Ps. 80⁸⁻¹³). God had chosen " of all the trees . . . one vine," as He had chosen one people, but it came to dishonour (2 Esd. 5²³). Always in the O.T., where Israel is compared to a vine, the comparison introduces a lament over her degeneracy, or a prophecy of her speedy destruction. See also Rev. 14¹⁹, where the vintage of the earth is cast into the winepress of the wrath of God. None the less, the vine was the national emblem, and on the coins of the Maccabees Israel is represented by a vine. And it has been thought that when Jesus said " I am the True Vine," the comparison in view was that between the degenerate vine of Israel and the Ideal Vine represented by Himself. That is to say, the True Vine is now brought before the disciples as the new ideal of the spiritual Israel.

This, however, involves a comparison of the *Church of Christ* with the True Vine (cf. Justin, *Tryph.* 110), rather than an identification of *Christ Himself* with it. No doubt, by describing His disciples as the branches, Jesus connected them as well as Himself with the mystic vine of His similitude; but the emphasis in the sentence ἐγώ εἰμι ἡ ἄμπελος ἡ ἀληθινή is on ἐγώ, as in all the other great similitudes of the Fourth Gospel. ἐγώ εἰμι marks the style of Deity, which cannot be shared (see Introd., p. cxviii). The main thought is not of the Vine as the Church, but of the Vine as representing Him who is the source of the Church's life. We take the view that the Vine of the allegory was directly suggested here by the wine of the first Eucharist, which had just been celebrated.¹

ἡ ἄμπελος ἡ ἀληθινή. Burkitt ² points out that an early Syriac rendering of this similitude was " I am the Vineyard of Truth," *i.e.* the True Vineyard. This does not appear in Syr. sin. or the Peshitta, but it may have been in the *Diatessaron*. The confusion between *Vineyard* and *Vine* may be due to ἄμπελος having been taken as equivalent to ἀμπελών, a usage which Moulton-Milligan (*s.v.*) illustrate from the papyri. ἄμπελος occurs again in the N.T. only in Jas. 3¹², Rev. 14¹⁸, ¹⁹, and Mk. 14²⁵ (and parls.), where Jesus said that He would not drink again of τὸ γένημα τῆς ἀμπέλου until He drank it new in the kingdom of God.

For ἀληθινός, see on 1⁹. Jesus is the *genuine* Vine.

¹ See Introd., p. xxi.   ² *Ev. da Mepharr.*, ii. 143, 151.

ἡ ἀληθινή, καὶ ὁ Πατήρ μου ὁ γεωργός ἐστιν.   2. πᾶν κλῆμα ἐν ἐμοὶ
μὴ φέρον καρπόν, αἴρει αὐτό, καὶ πᾶν τὸ καρπὸν φέρον, καθαίρει αὐτὸ

καὶ ὁ πατήρ μου (see on 2¹⁶) **ὁ γεωργός ἐστιν.** γεωργός occurs
again only at 2 Tim. 2⁶, Jas. 5⁷, and in the parable of the
wicked husbandmen (Mk. 12¹ and parallels).   Cf. 1 Cor. 3⁹
θεοῦ γεώργιον . . . ἐστέ.

2. πᾶν κλῆμα κτλ. Note the pendent nominative, as at 6³⁹ 17².
κλῆμα is a word which does not appear again in the N.T.;
but it is habitually used in the LXX for the " shoot " of a
vine (*e.g.* Num. 13²⁴, Ezek. 17⁶), as distinct from the " branch "
(κλάδος) of other trees.

ἐν ἐμοὶ μὴ φέρον καρπόν. Note that a κλῆμα or branch may
be truly *in* Christ, and yet may not bear fruit.   μή expresses
a hypothetical possibility.   This severe warning, coming so
soon after the beginning of the allegory, was probably an
allusion to the failure and doom of Judas, who had gone
forth to his treachery just before, in the arrangement of chapters
here adopted.

αἴρει αὐτό. " He takes it away." So, too, the κλάδοι of
the olive which represented Israel in Paul's illustration, were
of the true stock, but some of them were broken off by God
(Rom. 11¹⁶· ¹⁷).   The action of the Great Husbandman in this
is like that of every earthly γεωργός : *inutilesque falce ramos
amputans* (Horace, *Epod.* ii. 13).   Cf. Mt. 3¹⁰, Lk. 3⁹.

καὶ πᾶν τὸ καρπὸν φέρον, καθαίρει αὐτό. The play on
the words αἴρειν, καθαίρειν (*suavis rhythmus*, as Bengel
says), cannot be reproduced in English.

καθαίρειν, *to cleanse*, occurs in the N.T. again only at
Heb. 10² (of religious cleansing), and is rare in the LXX.   It
is used here in the sense of " to cleanse by pruning," as it is in
Philo (*de somn.* ii. 9, cited by Cremer): " As superfluous
shoots grow on plants, which are a great injury to the genuine
shoots (τῶν γνησίων), and which the husbandmen (γεωργοῦντες)
cleanse and prune (καθαίρουσι καὶ ἀποτέμνουσι), knowing
what is necessary ; so likewise the false and arrogant life grows
up beside the true and humble life, of which to this day no
husbandman (γεωργός) has been found to cut off by the roots
the superfluous and injurious growth."   In this passage
καθαίρειν, " to cleanse," can hardly be distinguished from
ἀποτέμνειν, " to prune."

In the verse before us, however, the Great Husbandman
does " cleanse " the fruitful branches by pruning off useless
shoots, so that they may bear fruit more abundantly.   It is not
as if the branches were foul; on the contrary, they are already
clean by virtue of their share in the life of the Vine (v. 3).

ἵνα καρπὸν πλείονα φέρῃ. 3. ἤδη ὑμεῖς καθαροί ἐστε διὰ τὸν λόγον
ὃν λελάληκα ὑμῖν· 4. μείνατε ἐν ἐμοί, κἀγὼ ἐν ὑμῖν. καθὼς τὸ
κλῆμα οὐ δύναται καρπὸν φέρειν ἀφ᾿ ἑαυτοῦ ἐὰν μὴ μένῃ ἐν τῇ

But pruning may be good for them, none the less. Such
pruning, according to Justin (*Tryph.* 110), illustrates God's
painful discipline for His true servants. The vine is a tree
which specially needs attention, and it is essential to its fruit-
fulness that the already fruitful branches should be pruned
regularly. Perhaps this is a warning anticipatory of the more
explicit warning of vv. 20, 21.

ἵνα καρπὸν πλείονα φέρῃ. Cf. Mt. 13[12]. The order καρπὸν
πλείονα is that of אBL latt.

3. ἤδη ὑμεῖς καθαροί ἐστε. So Jesus had said before
(13[10]), the primary reference then being to bodily cleanness,
although with an allusion to spiritual purity as well (see note
in loc.). Here, the thought is carried on from v. 2, which spoke
of the cleansing of the branches by the Great Husbandman
(καθαίρειν). The disciples were not useless branches, presently
to be cut off; they were in the way of bearing fruit, and already
they had been " cleansed " διὰ τὸν λόγον ὃν λελάληκα ὑμῖν,
" by the word which I have spoken to you."

We have seen (on 6[57]) that διά followed by an acc. is to be
distinguished from διά with a gen. The text here is not
διὰ τοῦ λόγου, which would suggest that the Word of Jesus is
the *instrument* of cleansing ; but διὰ τὸν λόγον signifies rather
that it is because of the Word abiding in them (v. 7) that they
are kept pure. The λόγος which had thus, in some measure,
been assimilated by them (cf. 5[38], 8[43]) was the whole message
that Jesus had delivered during His training of the Twelve. In
so far as this continued to " abide " in them (v. 7), in that
degree were they " clean." As it abides in them, so do they
abide in the True Vine (1 Jn. 2[24]).

The cleansing τοῦ ὕδατος ἐν ῥήματι of Eph. 5[26] does not
constitute a true parallel to the thought here.

4. μείνατε ἐν ἐμοί, κἀγὼ ἐν ὑμῖν. This is an imperative
sentence (for the aor. imper. see on 2[5]). No doubt, the practical
precept which was the issue of all the teaching of Jesus was just
this; but we must not join the words to the preceding διὰ τὸν
λόγον ὃν λελάληκα ὑμῖν, as if the precept itself were the λόγος.
The words ἐν ἐμοὶ μένει, κἀγὼ ἐν αὐτῷ had been used before
(6[56]), but the promise of that passage has not heretofore been
turned into an explicit precept (cf. 14[20]). For λόγος as signifying not a single sentence, but the whole purport of the Divine
revelation given by Christ, see on 5[38].

καθὼς τὸ κλῆμα κτλ. Even the fruitful branch does not

ἀμπέλῳ, οὕτως οὐδὲ ὑμεῖς ἐὰν μὴ ἐν ἐμοὶ μένητε. 5. ἐγώ εἰμι ἡ
ἄμπελος, ὑμεῖς τὰ κλήματα. ὁ μένων ἐν ἐμοὶ κἀγὼ ἐν αὐτῷ, οὗτος
φέρει καρπὸν πολύν, ὅτι χωρὶς ἐμοῦ οὐ δύνασθε ποιεῖν οὐδέν. 6. ἐὰν
μή τις μένῃ ἐν ἐμοί, ἐβλήθη ἔξω ὡς τὸ κλῆμα καὶ ἐξηράνθη, καὶ

bear fruit *of itself* (cf. for ἀφ᾽ ἑαυτοῦ, 5¹⁹ 7¹⁸ 11⁵¹ 16¹³), but only
in so far as it assimilates and is nourished by the sap of the
vine. So the disciple of Jesus cannot bear fruit, unless he
abide (ἐὰν μὴ μένῃ) in the Vine. Here is the difference between the natural and the spiritual order. The vine shoot
has not the power of choosing whether it will " abide " in the
vine, or cut itself loose. But in the spiritual sphere this
" abiding " is not maintained without the constant and conscious
endeavour of the disciple's own will. Hence the urgency of
the precept μείνατε ἐν ἐμοί.

5. ἐγώ εἰμι ἡ ἄμπελος κτλ., " I am the Vine, ye are the
branches," the main theme being repeated with slight verbal
alteration, as frequently in Jn. Cf. the repetitions of " I am
the Bread of Life " (6³⁵· ⁴¹· ⁴⁸· ⁵¹), " I am the Door " (10⁸· ⁹),
" I am the Good Shepherd " (10¹¹· ¹⁴); and see on 3¹⁶.

ὁ μένων ἐν ἐμοὶ κἀγὼ ἐν αὐτῷ. The two " abidings " go
together; see on 6⁵⁶.

οὗτος φέρει καρπὸν πολύν. This was the purpose for
which the disciples were chosen (v. 16). For the emphatic
οὗτος, " he it is that . . .," cf. 4⁴⁷.

ὅτι χωρὶς ἐμοῦ οὐ δύνασθε ποιεῖν οὐδέν. The branch is
wholly dependent on the tree, by whose sap it is quickened
and made fruitful.

6. ἐὰν μή τις μένῃ κτλ. μένῃ is the true reading (א*ABD)
as against the rec. μείνῃ. ἐὰν μή with the pres. subj. is rare
in the N.T., but we have it three times in vv. 4, 6.

ἐβλήθη ἔξω. The branch that does not bear grapes is cast
out (apparently, out of the *vineyard*). The aorists ἐβλήθη,
ἐξηράνθη, seem to look forward to the future Judgment of
mankind, and treat it as already past, so certain and inevitable
is it. Abbott (*Diat.* 2445) compares Isa. 40⁷· ⁸ ἐξηράνθη ὁ
χόρτος καὶ τὸ ἄνθος ἐξέπεσεν, τὸ δὲ ῥῆμα τοῦ θεοῦ ἡμῶν μένει,
where the aorists are used in the same way. But a Greek aorist
may be used without reference to any special moment of time.

ἐξηράνθη (it does not occur again in Jn.) is the word used,
Mk. 4⁶, of the withering of the seed that had no root, as here
of the vine shoot that is no longer " in " the vine.

καὶ συνάγουσιν αὐτό. So אDLΔ *fam.* 13; the rec. has
αὐτά with ABΓΘ. " They " (*sc.* the servants of the Lord of
the Vineyard, the subject being understood. but not expressed)
" collect " the useless branches.

συνάγουσιν αὐτὸ καὶ εἰς τὸ πῦρ βάλλουσιν, καὶ καίεται.   7. ἐὰν
μείνητε ἐν ἐμοὶ καὶ τὰ ῥήματά μου ἐν ὑμῖν μείνῃ, ὃ ἐὰν θέλητε
αἰτήσασθε, καὶ γενήσεται ὑμῖν.   8. ἐν τούτῳ ἐδοξάσθη ὁ Πατήρ μου,
ἵνα καρπὸν πολὺν φέρητε καὶ γενήσεσθε ἐμοὶ μαθηταί.

καὶ εἰς τὸ πῦρ βάλλουσιν κτλ., " and fling them into the
fire." Cf. Ezek. 15⁴, where the prophet says of the vine branch,
" it is cast into the fire for fuel." The vivid picture of the
labourers burning at the harvest all that is worthless, appears
also in Mt. 13⁴⁰ as an illustration of the Last Judgment.

7. The figure of the tree and its branches is left aside for the
moment; and the consequence of abiding in Christ is declared
to be not only the capacity for " bearing fruit," but the acquisi-
tion of the power of efficacious prayer. This is the secret of
the saints.

ἐὰν μείνητε ἐν ἐμοὶ (cf. v. 4 and 8³¹) καὶ τὰ ῥήματά μου
(sc. the " sayings " which make up the λόγος of v. 3) ἐν ὑμῖν
μείνῃ κτλ. The man of whom this is true is a master of prayer,
and his petitions will be answered. In the Synoptists faith is
the prerequisite for efficacious prayer: πάντα ὅσα προσεύχεσθε
καὶ αἰτεῖσθε, πιστεύετε ὅτι ἐλάβετε καὶ ἔσται ὑμῖν (Mk. 11²⁴);
" if you had faith you would say to this tree, Be uprooted and
planted in the sea, and it would obey you " (Lk. 17⁶; cf. Mt.
17²⁰). πάντα δυνατὰ τῷ πιστεύοντι (Mk. 9²³) is true of the
life of prayer. But in Jn. faith in Christ is more than belief
in His message, or fitful attraction to His Person; it is a continual abiding " in Him." See further on v. 16 below; and
cf. 6²⁹.

ὃ ἐὰν θέλητε αἰτήσασθε. For ὃ ἐάν (ADLΘ), B has ὃ ἄν,
and א has ὅσα ἐάν. ABDL support the imperative αἰτήσασθε,
while אΘ have αἰτήσεσθε.

ὃ ἐὰν θέλητε κτλ., " whatever you will, etc."; petitions
prompted by the indwelling words of Jesus cannot fail to be
in harmony with the Divine Will. A petitioner who " abides
in Christ " asks habitually " in His Name "; i.e. he asks as
Christ would ask, and so his satisfaction is sure. See 14¹³ and
the note there; cf. also v. 16 below, and 16²³.

γενήσεται ὑμῖν, " it shall come to pass for you," not as a
boon granted arbitrarily, but as the inevitable sequence of the
prayer.

8. ἐν τούτῳ, sc. in the fact that His followers abide in
Christ (v. 7), the reference being retrospective: " in this is
my Father glorified, that ye bear much fruit." The γεωργός
(v. 1) is always glorified if the trees of his planting are fruitful;
and so in Isa. 61³ the purpose of the mission of Yahweh's
servant was " that they might be called trees of righteousness,

9. Καθὼς ἠγάπησέν με ὁ Πατήρ, κἀγὼ ὑμᾶς ἠγάπησα· μείνατε

the planting of the Lord, that He might be glorified." The perfection of human character is the glory of God: all good works are *ad maiorem Dei gloriam* (cf. Mt. 5[16]). So Jesus spoke of His signs as exhibiting the glory of God (11[40]). The aor. ἐδοξάσθη is used proleptically. The issue is so sure that it is spoken of as already a fact. See, for a similar usage, v. 6 and 12[23] 13[1. 31].

For the phrase ὁ πατήρ μου, see on 2[16].

γενήσεσθε. So אA: γένησθε is read by BDL⊙. If γένησθε is read, the rendering is " that ye bear much fruit and become my disciples." But γενήσεσθε is better: " that ye bear much fruit: so shall you become my disciples," or literally " disciples to me," ἐμοί (cf. 13[35]) expressing the relationship more affectionately than μου (which is read by D*). Cf. 8[31], " if ye abide in my word, ye are truly my disciples."

It is to have gone a long way in the Christian course to be able to appropriate the promise of v. 7; but the final cause of such progress is that " fruit " may appear, not in service only but in the development of character, to the glory of God. And the highest aspiration of all is to become " a disciple." " True discipleship is hardly begun until the earthly life is near its end and the fruit hangs thick and ripe upon the branches of the Vine "[1] Cf. the saying of Ignatius, when on his way to martyrdom, νῦν ἄρχομαι μαθητὴς εἶναι (*Rom.* 5).

The love of Jesus for His disciples (vv. 9-11)

9. καθὼς ἠγάπησέν με ὁ πατήρ (cf. 5[20] 17[24]), κἀγὼ ὑμᾶς ἠγά-πησα (13[34]), " As the Father loved me, so also I loved you." The words are spoken in retrospect of His association with the apostles, now that the hour of parting has come; but they convey an assurance of the depth and intimacy of His love to all future disciples.

For the constr. καθὼς . . . κἀγώ in Jn., see on 6[57] 10[15]; and cf. also 17[18]. For the verb ἀγαπᾶν, see on 21[15].

μείνατε ἐν τῇ ἀγάπῃ τῇ ἐμῇ, " abide in my love," *i.e.* " continue in the shelter of my love for you." See on 5[42] for the Johannine use of the phrase ἡ ἀγάπη τοῦ Χριστοῦ. Judas had fallen away from the reach of this love of Christ, and so may any disciple. Hence the need of the precept μείνατε, ·' continue." (Cf. Jude[21] ἑαυτοὺς ἐν ἀγάπῃ θεοῦ τηρήσατε.) This " is perhaps the nearest approach to an authoritative command to obey a moral or spiritual precept " that occurs

[1] Swete, *The Last Discourse, etc.,* p. 81.

ἐν τῇ ἀγάπῃ τῇ ἐμῇ.   10. ἐὰν τὰς ἐντολάς μου τηρήσητε, μενεῖτε
ἐν τῇ ἀγάπῃ μου, καθὼς ἐγὼ τοῦ Πατρός μου τὰς ἐντολὰς τετήρηκα

in Jn. (Abbott, *Diat.* 2438).   For the aor. imperative μείνατε,
see on 2⁵.

10. The precept is "abide in my love," and the way to
obey it is to keep His commandments : ἐὰν τὰς ἐντολάς μου
τηρήσητε, μενεῖτε ἐν τῇ ἀγάπῃ μου.   The ἀγάπη is the love of
Jesus for His disciples, not their love for Him, as it is in 14¹⁵.
It is over subtle to attempt a distinction between ἐν τῇ ἀγάπῃ τῇ
ἐμῇ of v. 9 and ἐν τῇ ἀγάπῃ μου of v. 10.   Both phrases mean the
same thing, *sc.* the love of Jesus for His own.   Jn. is specially
fond of ἐμός, which occurs 37 times in the Gospel, and always
in words of Jesus.[1]

καθὼς ἐγὼ (אD have καθὼς κἀγώ) τοῦ πατρός μου (B. om. μοῦ)
τὰς ἐντολὰς τετήρηκα.   This is the high example set before
the Christian disciple.   Jesus had claimed (8²⁹) ἐγὼ τὰ ἀρεστὰ
αὐτῷ ποιῶ πάντοτε, and now, looking back, He can say τετήρηκα
(cf. 17⁴).   No man could say with such complete assurance, "I
have kept the commandments of my Father " ; while it is possible
at the end to say, with Paul, τὴν πίστιν τετήρηκα (2 Tim. 4⁷).

καὶ μένω αὐτοῦ ἐν τῇ ἀγάπῃ.   This is the eternal issue of the
ministry of Christ, the resumption of His place in the bosom of
Deity, who is Love (cf. 17²⁴).

Westcott [2] finds here an *advance* on the teaching of 14¹⁵· ²¹ ;
and if this could surely be traced, the traditional order of
chapters (c. 14 preceding c. 15) would be in some degree
corroborated.   But his reasoning is precarious.   The idea of
the ἐντολαί given by Jesus is only found in cc. 13, 14, 15;
and the relevant passages are quite consistent with the order of
chapters adopted here, viz.:

> 15¹⁰ "If ye keep my commandments, ye will abide
> in my love."   As we have seen, this is the funda-
> mental idea in the Allegory of the Vine.

> 15¹² Next, Jesus bids them love one another.

> 13³⁴ This commandment is repeated and described as
> "new."   See Introd., p. xxi.

> 14¹⁵ He tells His disciples that if they love Him, they
> must keep His commandments.

> 14²¹ And, finally, He gives them the great promise, that
> if they thus show their love for Him, the Father
> will love them, and He Himself will love them
> and will manifest Himself to them.   There is
> no "advance " on this teaching in c. 15, nor could
> there be.

[1] Cf. Introd., p. lxvi.   [2] *St. John*, i. p. cxxx.

καὶ μένω αὐτοῦ ἐν τῇ ἀγάπῃ. 11. Ταῦτα λελάληκα ὑμῖν ἵνα ἡ χαρὰ ἡ ἐμὴ ἐν ὑμῖν ᾖ καὶ ἡ χαρὰ ὑμῶν πληρωθῇ.

12. Αὕτη ἐστὶν ἡ ἐντολὴ ἡ ἐμή, ἵνα ἀγαπᾶτε ἀλλήλους καθὼς

The truth is, that we must not expect a continuous logical sequence in the discourses of the Fourth Gospel. The sacred words are set down as they are remembered by the aged disciple of Jesus,[1] but there is no attempt to present them in the manner which would be suitable to a theological treatise.

11. In these Last Discourses the phrase ταῦτα λελάληκα ὑμῖν recurs like a solemn refrain seven times (15¹¹ 16¹· ⁴· ⁶· ²⁵· ³³ 14²⁵), just as ἐγὼ κύριος λελάληκα recurs several times in Ezekiel (5¹³· ¹⁵· ¹⁷ 6¹⁰ 17²¹· ²⁴ etc.). The ἐγώ of dignity (see Introd., p. cxvii) is, however, not prefixed to λελάληκα in Jn. It is improbable that there is significance in there being *seven* repetitions of ταῦτα λελάληκα ὑμῖν and no more.[2] 16⁶ is a reference to 16⁵ "*because* I said these things"; and in 16²⁵ ἐν παροιμίαις comes between ταῦτα and λελάληκα, the emphasis being on the words "in proverbs" and not on "these things have I spoken." See, for similar refrains, on 6³³· ³⁹.

In each case ταῦτα refers to what has been said in the preceding sentences; and in three cases the purpose of the teaching is indicated, sc. that the disciples might have joy (15¹¹), that they might have peace (16³³), and that they might be warned of future persecution (16¹· ⁴).

To come back on a phrase in this way is thoroughly characteristic of the style of Jn.: cf. note on 3¹⁶.

ἵνα ἡ χαρὰ ἡ ἐμή κτλ. Paul afterwards expressed the hope that his joy might be the joy of his disciples (2 Cor. 2³; cf. Phil. 2²); but ἵνα ἡ χαρὰ ἡ ἐμὴ ἐν ὑμῖν ᾖ has a more mystical significance here. Jesus had spoken ταῦτα, *i.e.* ἐὰν τὰς ἐντολάς μου τηρήσητε, μενεῖτε ἐν τῇ ἀγάπῃ τῇ ἐμῇ, and He now says that the purpose of His speaking these words was ἵνα ἡ χαρὰ ἡ ἐμὴ ἐν ὑμῖν ᾖ. For the joy of Christ must be shared by those who abide in His love. So shall their "joy be fulfilled" (cf. 16²⁴, and especially 17¹³). This is a favourite expression of Jn.; cf. 1 Jn. 1⁴ and 2 Jn.¹², as also Jn. 3²⁹, where it is put into the mouth of John the Baptist.

The New Commandment to love the brethren (vv. 12-17)

12. αὕτη ἐστὶν ἡ ἐντολὴ ἡ ἐμή κτλ. Jesus had spoken of "commandments" to the disciples whom He was so soon to leave, and had promised that if they kept His commandments they would "abide in His love." But He gives no

¹ Cf. Introd., p. cxiv.　　　　² Cf. Introd., p. lxxxix.

ἠγάπησα ὑμᾶς. 13. μείζονα ταύτης ἀγάπην οὐδεὶς ἔχει, ἵνα τις τὴν ψυχὴν αὐτοῦ θῇ ὑπὲρ τῶν φίλων αὐτοῦ. 14. ὑμεῖς φίλοι μού ἐστε,

detailed instructions, no set of precepts for the conduct of their lives. He gives only *one* commandment, for it will be enough, if fully realised.

ἵνα ἀγαπᾶτε ἀλλήλους κτλ., "that you love one another." This was the commandment, repeated a little later in the evening, when it is described as a *new* commandment, as something that had never been enjoined before (13³⁴, where see note). That Christian disciple must "love" Christian disciple, because of their common discipleship, was a new idea, perhaps not yet universally understood.

καθὼς ἠγάπησα ὑμᾶς. This mutual love is to be no faint affection of goodwill; it must be a love which will pour itself out in sacrifice, if it is to be like the love of Jesus for all of them. This is the commandment which must be fulfilled by the disciple who will claim the promise "Ye shall abide in my love" (v. 10). You can live in the shelter of my love only if you love one another. Cf. Eph. 5².

Abbott (*Diat.* 2529) calls attention to the frequent use of the present subjunctive in these Last Discourses, "that you may be loving," etc., the precept extending to all future generations of Christian disciples.

13. μείζονα ταύτης ἀγάπην κτλ. He reminds the disciples what was the measure of His love for them, having just told them that their love for each other must be of the same type. He was about to lay down His life for them, and this is the supreme sacrifice of love. A man can show no greater proof of his love for his friends than to die on their behalf. The love of God, indeed, has a wider range, as Paul reminds us: "While we were yet sinners, Christ died for us," thus showing the all-embracing character of God's love (Rom. 5⁷· ⁸). But here something less is commended to the imitation of the Christian disciple, for the "new commandment" does not speak of universal brotherhood, but only of the obligations of Christian brethren to each other. The precept is reproduced, 1 Jn. 3¹⁶: ἐν τούτῳ ἐγνώκαμεν τὴν ἀγάπην, ὅτι ἐκεῖνος ὑπὲρ ἡμῶν τὴν ψυχὴν αὐτοῦ ἔθηκεν· καὶ ἡμεῖς ὀφείλομεν ὑπὲρ τῶν ἀδελφῶν τὰς ψυχὰς θεῖναι. For the expression τὴν ψυχὴν τιθέναι, see on 10¹¹; and for the position of οὐδείς, see on 1¹⁸.

ἵνα τις τὴν ψυχήν κτλ. This is in apposition to ταύτης: cf. 4³⁴ for a similar use of ἵνα. τις is omitted by א*D*Θ and some Latin vss., but אᶜABD²L have it.

14. ὑμεῖς φίλοι μού ἐστε κτλ. This is another way of expressing what has already been said in v. 10. Those who

ἐὰν ποιῆτε ἃ ἐγὼ ἐντέλλομαι ὑμῖν.   15. οὐκέτι λέγω ὑμᾶς δούλους,

abide in Christ's ἀγάπη are His φίλοι: see on 21¹⁵ for ἀγαπᾶν
and φιλεῖν.

ἃ ἐγὼ ἐντέλλομαι ὑμῖν.   According to Mt. 28²⁰, this was also
to be the burden of the apostles' preaching: διδάσκοντες αὐτοὺς
τηρεῖν πάντα ὅσα ἐνετειλάμην ὑμῖν.

ἃ. So אDL *fam.* 13. B has ὅ, and ΑΓΔΘ have ὅσα.

15. οὐκέτι λέγω ὑμᾶς δούλους κτλ. They were accustomed
to call Him *Mar* as well as *Rabbi* (see on 1³⁸, 13¹³), and δοῦλος,
"slave," is the correlative of *Mar*, "Lord." He had applied
the term δοῦλος to them, 13¹⁶; and He had implied that to be
His διάκονος was a dignity.

There is nothing derogatory in being described as δοῦλος
κυρίου, עֶבֶד יְהֹוָה ; on the contrary, it was a title of honour,
and as such is used of Joshua (Josh. 24²⁹), Moses (Deut. 34⁵),
David (Ps. 89²⁰ etc.); in the N.T. Simeon uses it of himself
(Lk. 2²⁹), the Epistle to Titus begins Παῦλος δοῦλος Θεοῦ, and
the Epistle of James has Ἰάκωβος Θεοῦ καὶ Κυρίου Ἰησοῦ Χριστοῦ
δοῦλος (Jas. 1¹). To this day, *Abd-allah* is a favourite
name in the East. Abraham was singularly honoured by
being called the *friend* of Yahweh (Ἀβραὰμ ὃν ἠγάπησα,
Isa. 41⁸; cf. 2 Chron. 20⁷, Jas. 2²³), and still is called by the
Arabs, *El-Khalil*.

This distinction between God's "slave" and His "friend"
appears in Philo. He says that while we speak of God as the
δεσπότης or κύριος of the external world, in reference to the
spiritual world (τὸ νοητὸν ἀγαθόν) He is called σωτὴρ καὶ
εὐεργέτης. "For wisdom is God's friend rather than His
slave" (φίλον γὰρ τὸ σοφὸν θεῷ μᾶλλον ἢ δοῦλον, *de sobrietate*,
11). Philo then cites Gen. 18¹⁷ in the form "Shall I hide it
from Abraham my friend?" According to the Book of
Wisdom (7²⁷), to be God's friend (φίλος) is a privilege of holy
men in every generation.

Thus the difference drawn out in the text between the
δοῦλοι and the φίλοι of Jesus corresponds to the difference,
familiar to the Jews, between the δοῦλοι and the φίλοι of
God, and conveys an additional suggestion of the Divinity of
Jesus, which is behind the teaching of the Fourth Gospel from
beginning to end.

The chief officials of an Eastern monarch were called his
"friends" (1 Macc. 2¹⁸ 3³⁸ 10⁶⁵ etc.), and Swete suggests that
there is here an allusion to this nomenclature. "He has lifted
them out of the condition of menial service, and raised them
gradually into that of the friends of the Messianic king." But
this does not seem to be in harmony with vv. 14, 15ᵇ, where the

ὅτι ὁ δοῦλος οὐκ οἶδεν τί ποιεῖ αὐτοῦ ὁ κύριος· ὑμᾶς δὲ εἴρηκα φίλους,
ὅτι πάντα ἃ ἤκουσα παρὰ τοῦ Πατρός μου ἐγνώρισα ὑμῖν.   16. οὐχ
ὑμεῖς με ἐξελέξασθε, ἀλλ᾽ ἐγὼ ἐξελεξάμην ὑμᾶς, καὶ ἔθηκα ὑμᾶς ἵνα

duties and privileges of "friends" as distinct from "slaves"
are explained.

To be a δοῦλος of Jesus was the first stage in the progress
of a Christian disciple; and the early Christian leaders, speaking
of themselves, claim to be His δοῦλοι (Acts 4²⁹, Rom. 1¹,
Gal. 1¹⁰, etc.), while they do not venture to claim the further
honour of His φιλία which was given to the Eleven on the
eve of the Lord's Passion. The difference appears in this,
that a slave obeys his lord, without claiming to know the
reason for his lord's actions, while a friend shares his knowledge and is admitted to his secrets. ὁ δοῦλος οὐκ οἶδεν κτλ.
Thus the apostles did not know the significance of the action
of Jesus in washing their feet (13⁷· ¹²).

ὑμᾶς δὲ εἴρηκα φίλους. So Luke records (Lk. 12⁴), at an
earlier stage of their training, that Jesus addressed His disciples
as "my friends." And He had *implied* many times that they
were His friends, because He had expounded to them more
freely than to others the mysteries of the kingdom of God
(Mk. 4¹¹).

ὅτι πάντα ἃ ἤκουσα παρὰ τοῦ π. κτλ. Always His message
was of the things which He had "heard" from His Father
(cf. 8²⁶· ⁴⁰); but He did not disclose everything to the multitudes. It was only to His chosen friends that He had made
known the ὄνομα of the Father (17²⁶); but from them He had
hidden nothing that they were able to bear (cf. 16¹²).

γνωρίζειν, "to make known," occurs in Jn. again only at
17²⁶.

16. The apostles were henceforth His chosen friends,
and herein was encouragement for them, who were so
soon to take up their mission, in the absence of their Master.
It would be a mission of difficulty, but their *Call* was their
Power.

οὐχ ὑμεῖς με ἐξελέξασθε, ἀλλ᾽ ἐγὼ ἐξελεξάμην ὑμᾶς, "You
did not choose me, but I chose you," the personal pronouns being repeated for emphasis. See on 6⁷⁰ 13¹⁸ and v. 19,
where the aor. ἐξελεξάμην is used as here to mark the
moment when the apostles were selected from the larger body
of disciples. Each of them was a σκεῦος ἐκλογῆς (Acts
9¹⁵), and had been chosen by Jesus after a night of prayer
(Lk. 6¹³). It is constantly taught in the Fourth Gospel that
God's love precedes the movement of man's soul to Him
(see on 3¹⁶).

ὑμεῖς ὑπάγητε καὶ καρπὸν φέρητε καὶ ὁ καρπὸς ὑμῶν μένῃ, ἵνα ὅ τι
ἂν αἰτήσητε τὸν Πατέρα ἐν τῷ ὀνόματί μου δῷ ὑμῖν. 17. ταῦτα

καὶ ἔθηκα ὑμᾶς,[1] "and appointed you," *sc.* to your special
work; cf. for τίθημι used thus, Acts 20²⁸, 1 Tim. 1¹².

ἵνα ὑμεῖς ὑπάγητε. ὑπάγειν is used at Lk. 10³ of the
" going forth " of the Seventy on their mission. For ὑπάγειν
in Jn., see on 7³³.

καὶ καρπὸν φέρητε, primarily the fruit of success in their
apostolic labours, but also indicating the perfecting of personal
character (cf. v. 4).

καὶ ὁ καρπὸς ὑμῶν μένῃ, "and your fruit may abide."
Jesus had said to a group of disciples on a former occasion,
ὁ θερίζων . . . συνάγει καρπὸν εἰς ζωὴν αἰώνιον (4³⁶), and the
thought is the same in this passage. Cf. Rev. 14¹³ and
1 Cor. 15⁵⁸.

ἵνα ὅ τι ἂν αἰτήσητε (so אADNΘ, but BL have αἰτῆτε)
τὸν πατέρα ἐν τῷ ὀνόματί μου δῷ ὑμῖν (cf. v. 7). This great
promise occurs six times (with slight variations) in the Last
Discourses (cf. 16²³· ²⁴· ²⁶ 14¹³· ¹⁴); and in these passages the
philosophy, so to speak, of Christian prayer is unfolded, as
nowhere else in the N.T.

In the Sermon on the Mount we have the simple words
αἰτεῖτε καὶ δοθήσεται ὑμῖν (Mt. 7⁷). But, when the Lord's
Prayer is prescribed for use, it is made plain that there are
conditions which must be fulfilled, if prayer is to be acceptably
offered, and one of these is *Thy Will be done.* Prayer that is
not submissive to that condition has no promise of answer.
Another condition is suggested Mt. 18¹⁹: "If two of you shall
agree as touching anything that they shall ask, it shall be
done for them by my Father." Prayer may be selfish, so that
the granting of one man's petition may be the refusal of
another's. But *if men agree,* that barrier is removed. If all
men agreed in asking the Eternal for the same thing, the
prayer could be offered with entire confidence. And Jn. tells
that Jesus expressed the supreme condition of Christian prayer
by saying that it must be offered ἐν τῷ ὀνόματί μου, "in my
Name." For Christ embraces all men. He is *the* Man.
A petition which is one that *He* could offer is one the fulfilment
of which could hurt none and would benefit all (cf. 11²²). So,
in Johannine language, the prayer which is of certain efficacy
must be ἐν τῷ ὀνόματι αὐτοῦ, and that is enough. Jn. does

---

[1] The words καὶ ἔθηκα ὑμᾶς are omitted (because of homoioteleuton,
ἐξελεξάμην ὑμᾶς immediately preceding) by Δ 13 250, suggesting
that the exemplars of these MSS. were written in lines of twelve letters
(cf. Introd., p. xxix).

ἐντέλλομαι ὑμῖν, ἵνα ἀγαπᾶτε ἀλλήλους.   18. Εἰ ὁ κόσμος ὑμᾶς

not speak of importunity in prayer, as Lk. does (Lk. 11⁸); but it is reiterated in the Fourth Gospel that the will of the man who prays must be in harmony with Christ's will (cf. 1 Jn. 5¹⁴). The man must be ἐν ἐμοί, a phrase used several times in these Last Discourses (14²⁰ 15⁴· ⁷ 16³³ ; cf. 6⁵⁶, 1 Jn. 5²⁰), with which Paul's ἐν Χριστῷ should be compared (Rom. 12⁵ 16⁷, 1 Cor. 15¹⁸, 2 Cor. 5¹⁷).[1] This condition has been already expressed in different words at v. 7 : "If ye abide in me, and my sayings abide in you, ask (αἰτήσασθε) what you will, and it shall be done to you." To pray " in the Name " of Christ is not any magical invocation of the Name, nor is it enough to add *per Jesum Christum Dominum nostrum*, but it is to pray as one who is " in Christ." Such are the prayers of the saints.

For the significance of "the Name," see on 1¹²; and for ἐν τῷ ὀνόματί μου in other contexts, cf. Lk. 10¹⁷, Jn. 14²⁶ 20³¹, Eph. 5²⁰.

The repeated ἵνα . . . ἵνα challenges attention. The final cause of the choice of the apostles was that they should " go forth and bear fruit," in their own lives as well as in their missionary labours, so that at last they should become masters of effectual prayer.

17. ταῦτα ἐντέλλομαι ὑμῖν (cf. v. 14), ἵνα ἀγαπᾶτε ἀλλήλους (v. 12). The purpose of these instructions was that they might appreciate the urgency of this novel precept (see on 13³⁴) which enjoined the love of Christian disciple for Christian disciple. This is not any vague recommendation of universal brotherhood; it is something much more definite. Indeed, as vv. 18, 19 show, the doctrine of mutual love cannot be extended so as to embrace all mankind. For the " world " hates Christians, as it hated Christ. There can be no reciprocity of ἀγάπη, in the special sense in which it is here enjoined, between the Church and the world.

See on 1⁹ for the Johannine use of the term κόσμος. It is solemnly repeated five times in vv. 18, 19.

The world hates Christian disciples because it hated Christ (vv. 18–25)

18. εἰ ὁ κόσμος ὑμᾶς μισεῖ κτλ. The disciples are not to expect that the *world* will love them (cf. 1 Jn. 3¹³), and of its future hostility they are now warned explicitly (see on 16⁴ below). Jesus had told His " brethren " that the world could

[1] Cf. Introd., p. cxxxvii.

μισεῖ, γινώσκετε ὅτι ἐμὲ πρῶτον ὑμῶν μεμίσηκεν. 19. εἰ ἐκ τοῦ κόσμου ἦτε, ὁ κόσμος ἂν τὸ ἴδιον ἐφίλει· ὅτι δὲ ἐκ τοῦ κόσμου οὐκ ἐστέ, ἀλλ' ἐγὼ ἐξελεξάμην ὑμᾶς ἐκ τοῦ κόσμου, διὰ τοῦτο μισεῖ ὑμᾶς

not hate *them* (7⁷), but that was because they were on the world's side, and not on His, as all His disciples must be.

γινώσκετε ὅτι ἐμὲ πρῶτον ὑμῶν μεμίσηκεν, "know (*scitote*) that it has hated me first." γινώσκετε is imperative, like μνημονεύετε in v. 20. Despite His words on a former occasion (7⁷), the disciples had not yet realised the measure of the " world's " hatred for Jesus, the world being here represented by the hostile Jews.

ὑμῶν is omitted by ℵ*D *a b c e ff²*, but is found in ℵᶜABLNΘ *f g l* vg. etc. and the Syriac vss. If it be omitted, the constr. is easy; but if it be retained, πρῶτον ὑμῶν presents the same difficulties as πρῶτός μου in 1¹⁵. Abbott (*Diat.* 1901) would translate here "that it hath hated me, *your Chief*," which might be defended by the vg. *priorem uobis*. But this seems unsatisfactory, and it is best to take πρῶτον ὑμῶν as if it were πρότερον ὑμῶν (see on 1¹⁵).

19. εἰ ἐκ τοῦ κόσμου ἦτε. Those who are " of the world " (cf. 1 Jn. 4⁵) are sharply contrasted by Jn. with the Christian disciples, whose " otherworldliness " he always speaks of with emphasis. See, particularly, 17¹⁴· ¹⁶. One of the characteristics of the writings of Jn. is that he always paints in black and white, without allowing for intermediate shades of colour. He will have no compromise with evil. For him the Church and the world are set over against each other, and he does not contemplate their reconcilement.[1]

ὁ κόσμος ἂν τὸ ἴδιον ἐφίλει, "the world would have loved its own," that which is in harmony with worldly ideals. The apostles, on the other hand, are not " of the world." Out of it they had been chosen (see v. 16, and cf. 13¹⁸), and so the world hated them. διὰ τοῦτο refers to what has gone before, as at 6⁶⁵. Thus vv. 16–20 taught the apostles that if to abide in Christ is the secret of fruitful lives and of effectiveness in prayer, it also provokes the world's hostility. But this hostility carries with it a promise and a benediction (cf. 1 Pet. 4¹⁴, Mt. 5¹¹).

With the Johannine teaching as to the hatred of the Church by the world (7⁷ 17¹⁴, 1 Jn. 3¹³), cf. the fine saying of Ignatius: " Christianity (χριστιανισμός) is not talk, but power, when it is hated by the world " (*Rom.* 3).

---

[1] See, for this contrast, Hobhouse, *The Church and the World*; cf. Westcott, *Epp. of St. John*, p. 250 f., and Gore, *Epp. of St. John*, p. 154 f.

ὁ κόσμος. 20. μνημονεύετε τοῦ λόγου οὗ ἐγὼ εἶπον ὑμῖν Οὐκ ἔστιν δοῦλος μείζων τοῦ κυρίου αὐτοῦ. εἰ ἐμὲ ἐδίωξαν, καὶ ὑμᾶς διώξουσιν· εἰ τὸν λόγον μου ἐτήρησαν, καὶ τὸν ὑμέτερον τηρήσουσιν. 21. ἀλλὰ

20. μνημονεύετε τοῦ λόγου οὗ ἐγὼ εἶπον ὑμῖν, "Be mindful of the saying which I said to you." μνημονεύειν occurs again in Jn. only at 16⁴· ²¹. א reads here τὸν λόγον ὃν ἐγὼ ἐλάλησα ὑμῖν.

We have already had the saying οὐκ ἔστιν δοῦλος μείζων τοῦ κυρίου αὐτοῦ at 13¹⁶ (where see note), but Jesus probably repeated it more than once, the reference here perhaps being to the occasion when He gave a charge to the newly chosen apostles (Mt. 10²⁴; cf. Lk. 6⁴⁰). They had been warned then that they would not be exempt from persecution (cf. Mt. 10¹⁷⁻²³); it was even more necessary that they should bear this in mind in the days that were coming. He had told them that He counted them as friends rather than servants (v. 15), but for all that the saying "The servant is not greater than his lord" would be applicable to their situation in a hostile world. The moral He had drawn from this saying at the Last Supper, earlier in the evening, was different (13¹⁶).

εἰ ἐμὲ ἐδίωξαν, "If they persecuted me," the subject being ὁ κόσμος, taken as a noun of multitude, from v. 19. Jn. has already spoken of the persecution (ἐδίωκον) of Jesus by the Jews, because of the freedom with which He treated the rules of the Sabbath (5¹⁶).

καὶ ὑμᾶς διώξουσιν, "they will persecute you also," a warning repeated in other language at 16³³. Lk. records a similar warning (Lk. 21¹²), and Mk. 10³⁰ notes that Jesus accompanied a promise of temporal blessings to the faithful with the significant addition of μετὰ διωγμῶν. There is no reason to doubt that Jesus did thus predict that persecution would be the lot of His disciples; and it is unnecessary to accumulate proofs that the prediction came true (cf. 1 Cor. 4¹², 2 Cor. 4⁹, Gal. 4²⁹, 2 Tim. 3¹²).

εἰ τὸν λόγον μου ἐτήρησαν, καὶ τὸν ὑμέτερον τηρήσουσιν, "if they kept my word, they will keep yours also." For the phrase τὸν λόγον τηρεῖν, a favourite phrase in Jn., see on 8⁵¹ 14¹⁵. In Ezek. 3⁷ Yahweh is represented as saying to the prophet, "They will not hearken unto thee, because they will not hearken unto me"; and this would apply to the apostles of Jesus. But the saying recorded here by Jn. goes farther. Those who observe the word of Jesus will also observe the word of His apostles, it being implied of course that the apostles will utter no "word" for which they have not the authority of their Master. A world which "observed" the teaching of

ταῦτα πάντα ποιήσουσιν εἰς ὑμᾶς διὰ τὸ ὄνομά μου, ὅτι οὐκ οἴδασιν

Jesus would inevitably " observe " the teaching of those who could rightly claim His commission. The difficulty of drawing inferences from this great assurance, once Christendom was divided, is illustrated by the whole course of Christian history. Jesus, however, goes on to insist that it is the other alternative which the apostles must prepare to face; not acquiescence, but opposition, will be the portion of those who proclaim His gospel.

21. ἀλλὰ ταῦτα πάντα ποιήσουσιν εἰς ὑμᾶς (the rec. has ὑμῖν, with AD²ΝΓ, but אᵃBD*LΘ support εἰς ὑμᾶς), " but all these things will they do to you." The " things " are not defined here. The whole verse is repeated in slightly different words at 16³ (see note), where it follows the mention of excommunication and death; and if we could treat it here as a gloss that has crept into the text from below, the sequence of thought in vv. 20–24 would be easier to follow. But this would be an arbitrary alteration of the text. The sequence in Jn. is not always determined by logical considerations, and his reports of the words of Jesus are not to be taken as complete or exhaustive. Much more, doubtless, was said on this last night; what is preserved represents the long-pondered reminiscences of an aged disciple.

διὰ τὸ ὄνομά μου, " for my Name's sake." Persecution will come, but it will be easier to bear if they remember *why* it comes, and whose cause it is that they are upholding. This, again, had been said to them before, when they received their apostolic commission: ἔσεσθε μισούμενοι ὑπὸ πάντων διὰ τὸ ὄνομά μου (Mt. 10²²; see above on v. 20). The same warning appears in the Marcan tradition in a different context (Mk. 13¹³, Mt. 24⁹, Lk. 21¹⁷), but in identical terms. A few verses before these passages in Mk. and Lk., the apostles had been told that they would be haled before rulers and kings, ἕνεκεν ἐμοῦ (Mk. 13⁹) or ἕνεκεν τοῦ ὀνόματός μου (Lk. 21¹²); and there is no substantial difference in meaning between these expressions and διὰ τὸ ὄνομά μου.

The Name of God is equivalent in the O.T. to His revealed character (see on 1¹²); and in 1 Sam. 12²², 2 Chron. 6³², Jer. 14²¹, we find διὰ τὸ ὄνομα [τὸ μέγα], " on account of His great Name," *sc.* because He is what He is. In the N.T. we have the phrase διὰ τὸ ὄνομα αὐτοῦ, used of the Name of Christ, not only in the passages cited above, but at 1 Jn. 2¹², Rev. 2³. His " Name " signified His revealed character, His Person; and those who suffered " on account of His Name " suffered because they proclaimed His Name as supreme.   Cf. Polycarp,

τὸν πέμψαντά με. 22. εἰ μὴ ἦλθον καὶ ἐλάλησα αὐτοῖς, ἁμαρτίαν οὐκ εἴχοσαν· νῦν δὲ πρόφασιν οὐκ ἔχουσιν περὶ τῆς ἁμαρτίας αὐτῶν. 23. ὁ ἐμὲ μισῶν καὶ τὸν Πατέρα μου μισεῖ. 24. εἰ τὰ ἔργα μὴ

Phil. 8: ἐὰν πάσχωμεν διὰ τὸ ὄνομα αὐτοῦ, δοξάζωμεν αὐτόν. In the persecutions of the early centuries, to confess "the Name" was to court death. Cf. 1 Pet. 4¹⁴, Acts 5⁴¹; Ignatius, *Eph.* 3.

ὅτι οὐκ οἴδασιν τὸν πέμψαντά με. Ignorance of the character of God is the cause of failure to recognise the claims of Christ, who came as the Ambassador of the Father. Cf. Lk. 23³⁴, Acts 3¹⁷, for ignorance as the cause of the Jews' rejection of Christ ; and see further on 16³.

Jesus said before (8¹⁹; cf. 14⁹) that to know Him is to know the Father; here He says that to know the Father is to know Him (cf. 8⁴²). For the conception of Jesus as " sent " by the Father, which so frequently appears in Jn., see on 3¹⁷.

22. That the Jews did not " know " God as revealed in Christ would be the cause of their hatred of Christ and of Christians (v. 21); and this ignorance is now shown to be inexcusable, (*a*) because the *words* of Jesus should have found an echo in their minds (v. 22), and (*b*) because His *works* should have convinced them of His Divine mission (v. 24).

The constr. εἰ μὴ . . . ἁμαρτίαν οὐκ εἴχοσαν· νῦν δὲ . . . is identical in vv. 22, 24; and it is noteworthy that ἄν is omitted, which perhaps makes the sentence more emphatic, " If I had not . . . *assuredly* they would have no sin." In both verses εἴχοσαν (אBLN) is to be preferred to the rec. εἶχον.

εἰ μὴ ἦλθον. This is the Messianic ἔρχεσθαι. He who was to come had come.

καὶ ἐλάλησα αὐτοῖς, " and discoursed to them " ; see on 3¹¹ for λαλεῖν. Cf. 12⁴⁸.

ἁμαρτίαν οὐκ εἴχοσαν. For ἁμαρτίαν ἔχειν, cf. 9⁴¹ 19¹¹, 1 Jn. 1⁸. But their failure to accept Jesus, when they had heard Him speak, was a moral failure, and therefore blameworthy. See on the parallel passage 9⁴¹. Involuntary ignorance, on the other hand, is excusable; cf. Acts 17³⁰.

νῦν δέ, " but now, as things are."

πρόφασιν οὐκ ἔχουσιν κτλ. πρόφασις does not occur again in Jn.; cf. Ps. 141⁴ (LXX).

23. Those who hate Christ, hate God, because in Christ's words and works God is revealed.

ὁ ἐμὲ μισῶν κτλ Cf. 5²³, 1 Jn. 2²³.

24. εἰ τὰ ἔργα μὴ ἐποίησα κτλ. The Jews were blameworthy because they did not recognise that the "works," as well as the "words" of Jesus revealed God.

ἐποίησα ἐν αὐτοῖς ἃ οὐδεὶς ἄλλος ἐποίησεν, ἁμαρτίαν οὐκ εἴχοσαν·
νῦν δὲ καὶ ἑωράκασιν καὶ μεμισήκασιν καὶ ἐμὲ καὶ τὸν Πατέρα μου.
25. ἀλλ' ἵνα πληρωθῇ ὁ λόγος ὁ ἐν τῷ νόμῳ αὐτῶν γεγραμμένος ὅτι
Ἐμίσησάν με δωρεάν.

In all the Gospels, the impression made by His works of
wonder is noted; *e.g.* Mk. 1²⁷, Lk. 4³⁶, Jn. 3² (where see note)
and 7³¹. It is not the highest kind of faith that is thus generated (14¹¹), but nevertheless such faith is, in its measure,
worthy and laudable (see on 2¹¹). And, more than once in the
Fourth Gospel, Jesus Himself appeals to the witness of His
ἔργα in confirmation of His Divine mission (5³⁶ 10³². ³⁷), as He
does here. As His words were greater than those of any other
(7⁴⁶), so were His works such as οὐδεὶς ἄλλος ἐποίησεν (cf. 9³²,
Mt. 9³³). If He had not wrought works of this wonderful
character among them (ἐν αὐτοῖς), the Jews would not have
been counted blameworthy; but as things were, they were left
without excuse (Mt. 11²¹, Lk. 10¹³).

ἐποίησεν. So ℵABDLΘ; the rec. has πεποίηκεν.

νῦν δὲ καὶ κτλ., " but now they have both seen and hated
both me and my Father," the perfects indicating the persistence
of their hostility (cf. Abbott, *Diat.* 2443). The construction
of the sentence, καί being four times repeated, shows that
ἑωράκασιν as well as μεμισήκασιν governs τὸν πατέρα μου no
less than ἐμέ. Jesus said later on ὁ ἑωρακὼς ἐμὲ ἑώρακεν τὸν
πατέρα (14⁹); but the original fault of the Jews was, as He had
said before (6³⁶), ἑωράκατέ με καὶ οὐ πιστεύετε (see on 14⁷).
Neither in His words nor in His works did they discern the
Divine mission of Jesus; and, not discerning who had sent
Him, they hated Him and therefore implicitly His Father
(v. 23).

25. For the ellipse ἀλλ' ἵνα, cf. 9³; and see on 13¹⁸.

ἵνα πληρωθῇ ὁ λόγος κτλ. The hatred of the Jews for Jesus
was part of the mysterious purpose of God, disclosed in the
O.T. scriptures. See Introd., p. clv.

The phrase "their law" has already been discussed in the
note on 8¹⁷. "The law" is used for the whole of Scripture
(see on 12³⁴); but although a Greek Christian might readily
say "*their* law," to suppose that Jesus thus separated Himself
from the Jewish race is hard of credence. Two of His Words
from the Cross are quotations from the Psalms, which, if the
phrase "their law" be His, He declines to recognise as having
any special value for Him.

The allusion is either to Ps. 35¹⁹ or Ps. 69⁴ (most probably from Ps. 69, as this was regarded as a Messianic Psalm;
see on 2¹⁷), in both of which οἱ μισοῦντές με δωρεάν faithfully

reproduces the Hebrew.   The hatred of the Jews for Jesus was gratuitous and without cause (δωρεάν; cf. πρόφασιν οὐκ ἔχουσιν of v. 22).

INTRODUCTORY NOTE ON Παράκλητος (v. 26).

The term παράκλητος does not occur in the Greek Bible outside the Johannine writings.   On the other hand, Jn does not use παρακαλεῖν or παράκλησις, the latter word being specially Lucan and Pauline, while the former is common to most of the N.T. writers.

Etymologically, παράκλητος is a passive form, and is equivalent to the Latin *aduocatus*, signifying one who is " called in " to give help or advice, and being especially used of the counsel for the defence.[1]   In classical writers this is always the meaning.   Demosthenes (*de falsa leg*. 341) has αἱ τῶν παρακλήτων δεήσεις καὶ σπουδαί, and in Diog. Laert. iv. 50, Bion is made to say, " I will do what is sufficient for you if you will send παράκλητοι (*sc.* representatives) and don't come yourself." The term is used in the same way in Philo.   Thus the city of Alexandria is called the παράκλητος by whom the emperor might be propitiated (*in Flaccum*, 4; cf. also *de Josepho*, 40).   In *de opif. mundi*, 6, Philo says that God employed no παράκλητος (*i.e.* helper) in the work of creation.   Again, in *Vit. Mos*. iii. 14, speaking of the high priest, " one consecrated to the Father of the world," Philo says that it was necessary that he should employ as his παράκλητος, " a son most perfect in virtue." [2]   In like manner, Barnabas (§ 20) has πλουσίων παράκλητοι, " advocates of the wealthy " ; and in *2 Clem*. 6 we have the question, " Who shall be our παράκλητος, *i.e.* our advocate, if we are not found doing what is right ? "   So in the Letter of the Churches of Lyons and Vienne (about 177 A.D., Eus. *H.E.* v. 1), it is said that Vettius Epagathus, confessing that he was a Christian, was taken into the order of martyrs (εἰς τὸν κλῆρον τῶν μαρτυρῶν), being called παράκλητος Χριστιανῶν, having the Paraclete within himself.

It may be added that the word was borrowed from the Greek by the Jews, and appears in Talmudic writings (see Wetstein on Jn. 14[16]) as פרקלט in the sense of *aduocatus*.

Although the verb παρακαλεῖν does not appear in Jn., an

---

[1] See Lightfoot, *Revision of N.T.*, p. 50 f.
[2] This " son " is not the Logos (as has been erroneously stated), but the Cosmos (cf. Drummond, *Philo Judæus*, ii. 238 ; Sanday, *Criticism of Fourth Gospel*, 197 ; and Bacon, *Fourth Gospel*, 298). Philo's use of παράκλητος does not relate the term to his Logos.

examination of its usage throws some additional light on the meaning of παράκλητος.

παρακαλεῖν is to call a person *to stand by one* (παρά), and hence *to help* in various ways, *e.g.*

(a) as a *witness*, to be present when a thing is done. Cf. Demosthenes, *c. Phorm.* § 29.

(b) as an *adviser*. Cf. Xenophon, *Anab.* I. vi. 5, Κλέαρχον δὲ καὶ εἴσω παρεκάλεσε σύμβουλον.

(c) as an *advocate*. Cf. Æschines, *Fals. Leg.*, § 184: παρακαλῶ δ᾽ Εὔβουλον μὲν ἐκ τῶν πολιτικῶν καὶ σωφρόνων ἄνδρα συνήγορον.

The verb is specially applied to the invoking of a *god*, and calling him in to help: *e.g.* Thucydides, i. 118 *fin.*, αὐτὸς ἔφη ξυλλήψεσθαι καὶ παρακαλούμενος καὶ ἄκλητος; Epictetus, *Diss.* III. xxi. 12, τοὺς θεοὺς παρακαλεῖν βοηθούς; Plutarch, *Alexander* 33, παρεκάλει τοὺς θεούς.

It appears from these passages that παράκλητος is naturally used for a Divine helper called in, either as a *witness* (15[26]), or as an *advocate* (16[8]), or as an *adviser* (16[13]). παρακαλεῖν is also used in the sense of *encourage*, *e.g.* Polybius, III. xix. 4, οἱ περὶ τὸν Δημήτριον συναθροίσαντες σφᾶς αὐτοὺς καὶ παρακαλέσαντες; but παράκλητος, being a passive form, cannot be equivalent to " one who encourages."

The familiar rendering " Comforter " was introduced into our English versions by Wyclif, who meant by it " confortator," *i.e.* strengthener, not *consoler* (see his rendering of Phil. 4[13]). But there is some patristic authority for the translation " consoler." Origen (*de princ.* II. vii. 4) says distinctly that while in I Jn. 2[1] παράκλητος means *intercessor*, in the Fourth Gospel it means *consoler*. So, too, Cyril of Jerusalem says (*Cat.* xvi. 20) that the Spirit is called παράκλητος from παρακαλεῖν, " to console," as well as because He " helps our infirmities " and " makes intercession " for us (Rom. 8[26]). Gregory of Nyssa (*c. Eunom.* ii. 14) also calls attention to the two meanings of the verb παρακαλεῖν. It is perhaps in consequence of an early interpretation of παράκλητος in Jn. 14 as " consoler," that Aquila and Theodotion render נָחַם in Job 16[2] by παράκλητος, where the LXX has παρακλήτωρ. But the weight of evidence is undoubtedly in favour of " advocate " rather than " comforter " as the rendering of παράκλητος in Jn.; and the notes on 14[16. 26] 16[7] will show also that this rendering is more in accordance with the contexts in which it occurs. At I Jn. 2[1] " advocate " is the only possible rendering.

The R.V. margin suggests " Helper " as an alternative, and this is adopted by Moffatt. This might include the idea

26. Ὅταν ἔλθῃ ὁ Παράκλητος ὃν ἐγὼ πέμψω ὑμῖν παρὰ τοῦ

of consoling as well as of pleading one's cause; but its vague-
ness veils the meaning here and at 16⁷.

Witness to Christ in the future will be borne by the Para-
clete as well as by Christian disciples (vv. 26, 27)

26. ὅταν ἔλθῃ ὁ παράκλ. After ὅταν the rec. inserts δέ,
with ADLΓΘ, but om. אBΔ; the omission of a connecting
particle is a familiar feature of Jn.'s style.

Verses 26, 27, follow at once upon the rebuke (vv. 21-25)
pronounced upon the enemies of Jesus. Their hostility was
blameworthy. And in the future they will be proved in the
wrong by the witness of the Spirit (v. 26) as well as by the
witness of the apostles (v. 27).

The rendering of ὁ παράκλητος by *advocate* is here demanded by the context, to which the rendering *comforter* would
be quite foreign. Jesus had explained that the hostility of the
Jews to Him was sinful, for they ought to have recognised
His Divine mission in His words and works (vv. 22-24). They
hated Him, not knowing Him, although they ought to have
known Him. But when the Paraclete came, *He* would bear
true testimony to Jesus, being indeed the Spirit of Truth
(v. 26). The Paraclete is the Divine *aduocatus* defending
the Righteous One, and pleading His cause against false
accusers. He is not, as at 1 Jn. 2¹, represented as pleading
the cause of man with God, but rather as pleading the cause
of Christ with the world. See further on 16⁸ ; and cf. Introd.,
p. xxi.

ὃν ἐγὼ πέμψω ὑμῖν κτλ. So also at 16⁷, the promise is that
Jesus will send the Paraclete; but at 14¹⁶ He is to be given by
the Father in response to the prayer of Jesus, and at 14²⁶ the
Father is to send Him in the Name of Jesus. The Lucan
doctrine is that Jesus sends the Spirit, "the promise of the
Father" (Lk. 24⁴⁹, Acts 2³³) ; see further on 14²⁶.

παρὰ τοῦ πατρός. Cf. 16²⁷ 17⁸ and see on 1¹⁴ for παρά as
expressing the relation of the Son to the Father. The Paraclete
is to be sent " from the Father's side."

τὸ πνεῦμα τῆς ἀληθείας. The full phrase occurs again
16¹³ 14¹⁷, 1 Jn. 4⁶. In the last passage it is contrasted with
τὸ πνεῦμα τῆς πλάνης, as in *Testaments of XII. Patriarchs*
(Judah, xx.), where the spirit of truth and the spirit of deceit
both wait upon man, and it is said that "the spirit of truth
testifieth all things and accuseth all." It is probable that this
sentence is a Christian interpolation introduced into the text

Πατρός, τὸ Πνεῦμα τῆς ἀληθείας ὃ παρὰ τοῦ Πατρὸς ἐκπορεύεται,

of the *Testaments*; but see on 1⁹, where there is another parallel to their language.

In these Last Discourses, however, τὸ πνεῦμα τῆς ἀληθείας is but another name for the Paraclete who is to be sent after Jesus has been withdrawn from the sight of men. The spirit of truth is the Spirit which brings truth and impresses it on the conscience of the world. In this passage the leading thought is of the witness of the Spirit to Jesus, infallibly true, however perverted the opinion of the world about Him may be.

The phrase τὸ πνεῦμα τῆς ἀληθείας has, like the phrase ὁ ἄρτος τῆς ζωῆς (see on 6³⁵), a double meaning. Primarily (*a*) it is the Spirit which brings truth and gives true testimony, but (*b*) this is the case because the Spirit has truth as the essential characteristic of His Being. So, also, the Logos is πλήρης ἀληθείας (1¹⁴), and Jesus says, later in this discourse, ἐγώ εἰμι . . . ἡ ἀλήθεια (14⁶).

ὃ παρὰ τοῦ πατρὸς ἐκπορεύεται. ἐκπορεύεσθαι occurs once elsewhere in Jn., *sc.* at 5²⁹, where it is used of the dead "coming forth" out of their graves. Here it is used in the same way of the Spirit "coming forth" from God in His mission of witness (cf. ἐν πνεύματι ἁγίῳ ἀποσταλέντι ἀπ' οὐρανοῦ, 1 Pet. 1¹²). To interpret the phrase of what is called "the Eternal Procession" of the Spirit has been a habit of theologians, which has been the cause of the endless disputes between East and West as to the "Procession" of the Spirit from the Son as well as from the Father. As far back as the fourth century, at all events,[1] the clause τὸ ἐκ (not παρά) τοῦ πατρὸς ἐκπορευόμενον has found a place in the Creed as descriptive of the Holy Spirit, and is taken from the verse before us. But to claim that this interpretation was present to the mind of Jn. would be to import into the Gospel the controversies and doctrines of the fourth century. ὃ παρὰ τοῦ πατρὸς ἐκπορεύεται does not refer to the mysterious relationships between the Persons of the Holy Trinity, but only to the fact that the Spirit who bears witness of Jesus Christ has come from God (cf. Rev. 22¹, where in like manner the river of the water of life is described as ἐκπορευόμενον ἐκ τοῦ θρόνου τοῦ θεοῦ).

ἐκεῖνος μαρτυρήσει περὶ ἐμοῦ. ἐκεῖνος calls special attention to the Spirit as the subject of the sentence, exactly as at 14²⁶. It is He, and none less than He, who shall bear august and true witness to the world about Christ. Cf. 1 Jn. 5⁶ τὸ πνεῦμά ἐστιν τὸ μαρτυροῦν, ὅτι τὸ πνεῦμά ἐστιν ἡ ἀλήθεια.

[1] See Hort, *Two Dissertations*, p. 86.

ἐκεῖνος μαρτυρήσει περὶ ἐμοῦ· 27. καὶ ὑμεῖς δὲ μαρτυρεῖτε, ὅτι ἀπ᾽ ἀρχῆς μετ᾽ ἐμοῦ ἐστέ.

XVI. 1. Ταῦτα λελάληκα ὑμῖν ἵνα μὴ σκανδαλισθῆτε. 2. ἀποσυναγώγους ποιήσουσιν ὑμᾶς· ἀλλ᾽ ἔρχεται ὥρα ἵνα πᾶς ὁ ἀποκτείνας

However little modern conceptions of *personality* and of what it implies were present to the mind of the first century, the repeated application of ἐκεῖνος to the Spirit in these chapters (16[8. 13. 14] 14[26]) shows that for Jn. τὸ πνεῦμα τῆς ἀληθείας meant more than a mere tendency or influence.

27. The Spirit was to be a Witness concerning Jesus in the future: the disciples' ministry of witness had already begun.

καὶ ὑμεῖς δὲ μαρτυρεῖτε, " ye also bear witness " (a state ment of fact, not an imperative) ; cf. Lk. 24[48]. The twofold witness of the Spirit and of the disciples is indicated Acts 5[32]; but Jn. specially dwells on this witness of the first disciples (cf. 3[11], 1 Jn. 1[2] 4[14], 3 Jn.[12]; and see Introd., p. xci).

The qualification for " witness " is personal intimacy, ὅτι ἀπ᾽ ἀρχῆς μετ᾽ ἐμοῦ ἐστέ : cf. Lk. 1[2], Acts 1[21].

ἀπ᾽ ἀρχῆς occurs again 8[44] only, but is frequent in the Johannine Epistles, sometimes (*e.g.* 1 Jn. 2[7. 24] 3[11], 2 Jn.[5. 6]) referring to the beginning of Jesus' ministry, as here, but some-times also to the beginning of all things (*e.g.* 1 Jn. 1[1] 2[13. 14] 3[8], as always in the Synoptists). See 8[44] 16[4].

ἐστέ, " ye *are* with me from the beginning." So Jesus said τοσοῦτον χρόνον μεθ᾽ ὑμῶν εἰμί (14[9]), using the present tense as here. The Twelve had been chosen ἵνα ὦσιν μετ᾽ αὐτοῦ (Mk. 3[14]), and they continued to be in close fellowship with Him.

Future persecution (XVI. 1–4)

XVI. 1. ταῦτα λελάληκα ὑμῖν: see on 15[11]. ταῦτα covers all that has been said about future persecution (15[20]), as well as about the promise of the Paraclete, who was to bear witness concerning Christ.

ἵνα μὴ σκανδαλισθῆτε. This image of the σκάνδαλα of faith, the stumbling-blocks which trip up a disciple, is very common in the Synoptists, but in Jn. only here and at 6[61] (cf. 1 Jn. 2[10]). These parting counsels were given in order that they might not be surprised or "offended" when troubles came.

2. ἀποσυναγώγους ποιήσουσιν ὑμᾶς, " they will put you out of synagogue," *i.e.* excommunicate you. For ἀποσυνάγωγος, see on 9[22] and 12[42].

ἀλλ᾽ ἔρχεται ὥρα, "indeed, furthermore, a time is coming."

56 739

ὑμᾶς δόξῃ λατρειαν προσφέρειν τῷ Θεῷ.   3. καὶ ταῦτα ποιήσουσιν
ὑμῖν ὅτι οὐκ ἔγνωσαν τὸν Πατέρα οὐδὲ ἐμέ.   4. ἀλλὰ ταῦτα λελάληκα

ἀλλά has no adversative sense here, nor must we press ὥρα to
mean "*the* predestined time," as if it were ἡ ὥρα (but cf. v. 4),
although, as we have seen (2⁴), the idea of the inevitableness
of what has been foreordained is a favourite one in Jn. See 4²¹.

ἵνα, *i.e.* "when"; see note on 12²³.

πᾶς ὁ ἀποκτείνας ὑμᾶς, "whosoever killeth you," whether
he be Jew or Gentile.

δόξῃ λατρείαν προσφέρειν τῷ θεῷ, "shall think (so blind
will he be) that he is offering service to God." (λατρεία does
not occur elsewhere in the Gospels.) Paul's persecution of the
early disciples was a notable instance of such mistaken zeal
(cf. Acts 22³⁻⁴ 26⁹, also 8¹ 9¹). A Midrash on Num. 25¹³
(cited by De Wette) has the maxim, "Quisquis effundit
sanguinem impii idem facit ac si sacrificium offerat." And
among Gentiles the same fanaticism has often displayed
itself. Tacitus (*Ann.* xv. 44) evidently thought that persecution of Christians to their death was morally justified.
Many persecutors are sincere, but their sincerity does not
excuse them, if they might have learnt the truth, and did not
do so.

3. ταῦτα ποιήσουσιν ὑμῖν. The rec., with ℵDL and some
vss., retains ὑμῖν, which ΑΒΓΔΘ omit. Probably it ought
to be retained (cf. 15²¹).

ὅτι οὐκ ἔγνωσαν κτλ., "because they did not recognise the
Father or me." This is virtually repeated from 15²¹ (where see
note). That the Jews did not "know" God, and thus did
not recognise Divinity in Jesus, has been said several times
before (7²⁸ 8¹⁹); and that "the world knew Him not" (1¹⁰)
when He came is the constant theme of the "Gospel of the
Rejection."

Ignorance, or want of appreciation of the true bearing of
facts, may often be at the root of wrong doing, and it is wholesome
to remember this. "When some one does you an injury or
speaks ill of you, remember that he either does it or speaks it,
believing that it is right and meet for him to do so. . . . So
you will bear a gentle mind towards him . . . saying each
time, *So it appeared to him*" (Epictetus, *Enchir.* 42). Cf.
Lk. 23³⁴, Acts 3¹⁷, 1 Cor. 2⁸.

But the ignorance of the Jews of the true character of
Jesus is always treated in Jn. as blameworthy and as deserving
of punishment, for they *ought* to have known.

4. For ταῦτα λελάληκα ὑμῖν, see on 15¹¹. It is preceded by
ἀλλά, not because what follows is in contrast with what goes

ὑμῖν ἵνα ὅταν ἔλθῃ ἡ ὥρα αὐτῶν μνημονεύητε αὐτῶν, ὅτι ἐγὼ εἶπον ὑμῖν.

Ταῦτα δὲ ὑμῖν ἐξ ἀρχῆς οὐκ εἶπον, ὅτι μεθ᾽ ὑμῶν ἤμην. 5. νῦν δὲ

before, but as a resumptive particle, v. 3 being in the nature of an explanatory parenthesis.

ἡ ὥρα αὐτῶν is the true reading (ABΘ syrr.), although αὐτῶν is omitted by אDΓΔ, to assimilate the sentence to the more usual ἔλθῃ ἡ ὥρα.

ταῦτα refers primarily (but cf. v. 1) to the persecutions which have been foreshadowed (15²⁰ 16¹⁻³), of which Jesus says that when their hour comes the disciples will remember that He had predicted them. See on 13¹⁹ ; and cf. 2²².

ἐγώ is emphatic, " that *I* told you." See Introd., p. cxvii.

ταῦτα δὲ ὑμῖν ἐξ ἀρχῆς οὐκ εἶπον. We cannot distinguish ἐξ ἀρχῆς from ἀπ᾽ ἀρχῆς of 15²⁷ (see on 6⁶⁴). The statement is precise: " These things I did not tell you from the beginning"; that is, He did not speak in the early stages of His teaching of the persecutions which would come upon His disciples after He had gone. That is what one would have expected; and the predictions of future persecutions in the Synoptists are mainly found at the close of His ministry, *e.g.* Mt. 23³⁴, Mk. 13⁹ᶠ·=Lk. 21¹²ᶠ·. It is true that Mt. puts his parallel passage to Mk. 13⁹ᶠ· as early as the tenth chapter (Mt. 10¹⁷ᶠ·); and it is also noteworthy that persecution is foreshadowed in the Sermon on the Mount (Mt. 5¹⁰· ¹¹, Lk. 6²²). But Mt. has rearranged our Lord's sayings in such contexts as suit the frame of his narrative, and it is not surprising that he has placed the warning about persecution immediately after the charge to the Twelve. Nor is it to be thought that all the reported sayings in the Sermon on the Mount were delivered at one time: the Beatitude of the Persecuted would naturally be one of the last that would have been proclaimed, so austere a saying is it. There is, therefore, no good reason for doubting the statement which Jn. places in the mouth of Jesus, *sc.* that He did not speak at the beginning of His ministry of the *ardua* in store for His followers, although the perpetual burden of His exhortation was that they must be ready to " take up the cross." Cf. 15¹⁸.

The reason assigned for this reserve is ὅτι μεθ᾽ ὑμῶν ἤμην, " because I was with you." That is, seemingly, as long as He was there, the attacks of His enemies would be directed against *Him* rather than against *them*; persecution of a serious kind would come upon them only after His departure.

ὑπάγω πρὸς τὸν πέμψαντά με, καὶ οὐδεὶς ἐξ ὑμῶν ἐρωτᾷ με Ποῦ ὑπάγεις; 6. ἀλλ' ὅτι ταῦτα λελάληκα ὑμῖν, ἡ λύπη πεπλήρωκεν ὑμῶν τὴν καρδίαν. 7. ἀλλ' ἐγὼ τὴν ἀλήθειαν λέγω ὑμῖν, συμφέρει

The coming of the Paraclete consequent on the departure of Jesus (vv. 5–7)

5. ὑπάγω πρὸς τὸν πέμψαντά με, repeated verbally from 7³³, where see note on ὑπάγειν. Cf. vv. 10, 17, 28, and 14¹².

καὶ οὐδεὶς κτλ. καί is used for ἀλλά, as often in Jn.: see note on 1¹⁰. These words show that 13³⁶ 14⁵ came *after* the present chapter in their original setting (see Introd., p. xx); for ποῦ ὑπάγεις; is the question put by Peter directly, and indirectly by Thomas at 14⁵. At the point which the discourse has now reached, the disciples were thinking rather of themselves and of the dangers in front of them (15²¹ 16². ³), than of the issue of their Master's mission.

For the Johannine use of ἐρωτᾶν, primarily meaning " to ask a question," see on 11²².

The " going " of Jesus " to the Father " throughout this chapter refers directly to His Death, when He re-entered the world of spirit (cf. Lk. 23⁴⁶). This was the moment when His mission was completed: τετέλεσται (19³⁰). Jn. lays no stress on the Ascension as distinct from the Resurrection of Christ (although he makes allusion to the Ascension as a specific event, 6⁶²). See 20¹⁷. For him the hour of the " glorification " of Jesus was the hour of His Passion (cf. 13³¹ and 14⁷).

6. ὅτι ταῦτα λελάληκα ὑμῖν, *sc.* because He had told them of the persecutions which they would experience : see on 15¹¹.

λύπη is found in Jn. in this chapter only (vv. 20, 21, 22); λύπη, λυπεῖν, are never used of Jesus in the Gospels.

7. For the asseveration τὴν ἀλήθειαν λέγω, cf. Rom. 9¹, 1 Tim. 2⁷. Jesus had used it before, in disputation with the Jews (8⁴⁵. ⁴⁶). Here, however, it introduces with solemnity the enigmatical saying " it is expedient for you that I go away," and is used like the prelude ἀμὴν ἀμὴν λέγω ὑμῖν (vv. 20, 23), which is a feature of the Fourth Gospel (see on 1⁵¹).

συμφέρει (cf. 11⁵⁰ 18¹⁴) ὑμῖν ἵνα ἐγὼ ἀπέλθω. This was a hard and perplexing saying. The disciples, who had been accustomed to look to Jesus for counsel and guidance in every difficulty, were now told that it would be better for them that He should go away than that He should stay with them. (1) Hitherto, He had trained them for His service by precept and visible example, but this method of spiritual direction was only preliminary. His strange words told them now that there is a better education in discipleship than that which can be

ὑμῖν ἵνα ἐγὼ ἀπέλθω. ἐὰν γὰρ μὴ ἀπέλθω, ὁ Παράκλητος οὐκ

supplied by a visible master, whose will for his disciples can never be misunderstood. The braver and more perfect disciple is he who can walk by faith, and not by sight only (cf. 20²⁹). So much might be reasoned out after reflexion on the way in which Jesus dealt with some would-be disciples who wished to be always by His side (cf. Lk. 8³⁸ 9⁵⁷). (2) But the reason assigned by Jesus Himself for the profitableness to His disciples of His departure is quite different. He said that if He did not go away from them, the Paraclete would not come to them, and that the mission of the Spirit could not begin until He had gone. This is one of those profound spiritual sayings in the Fourth Gospel which cannot be fully explained ; but we have it hinted at before in the evangelist's words, " the Spirit was not yet, for Jesus was not yet glorified " (7³⁹). *Why* the Spirit's influence could not be released during the earthly ministry of Jesus, as it was after His Passion and Resurrection, is a question to which no complete answer can be given. Perhaps it provides the supreme illustration of the gospel law that life comes only through death: a principle which is applied by Paul as well as by Jn., when he speaks of the Risen Christ (who had passed through death) as a Quickening Spirit. See further on 7³⁹ above.[1] It has been well said that " the Coming of the Holy Ghost was not merely to supply the absence of the Son, but to complete His presence." [2]

ἀπέλθω. Three verbs are used in this passage (vv. 7–9) of Jesus " going " to God; and attempts have been made to distinguish their meaning. Thus, ἀπέρχεσθαι is " to depart," simply; πορεύεσθαι is " to journey," *sc.* with a definite purpose, the purpose here being the sending of the Paraclete; while ὑπάγειν, the word most commonly used in Jn. by Jesus of His " going to the Father " (see on 7³³), is " to withdraw," *sc.* from the visible presence of men. But such distinctions are over subtle ; *e.g.* in 11⁸ ὑπάγειν is not used of a withdrawal, but of going to Judæa with a definite purpose. Again, Mk. 14²¹ has ὑπάγει where the parallel Lk. 22²² has πορεύεται; in Tob. 8²¹ B has πορεύεσθαι, while א has ὑπάγειν. These verbs are discussed at length by Abbott (*Diat.* 1652–1664), who endeavours to distinguish the Johannine usage of each: see on 7³³, and cf. 6⁶⁷.

ἐὰν γὰρ μὴ ἀπέλθω. After ἐὰν γάρ ΑΓΔ ins. the emphatic ἐγώ, as in the preceding clause; but om. אBDLΘ.

---

[1] I have discussed this great topic more fully in *Studia Sacra*, pp. 117–120.

[2] Gore, *Bampton Lectures*, p. 132.

ἐλεύσεται πρὸς ὑμᾶς· ἐὰν δὲ πορευθῶ, πέμψω αὐτὸν πρὸς ὑμᾶς.

ὁ παράκλητος (see on 15²⁶) οὐκ ἐλεύσεται πρὸς ὑμᾶς. So ℵADΘ ; but BL have οὐ μὴ ἔλθῃ, an even stronger negative.

The language of this passage implies that the mission of the Paraclete, to help and to bear witness, will be of a different order from that influence of the Spirit of God which is a frequent topic of the O.T. writers. His mission will, henceforth, be primarily a mission of *witness*, bearing testimony to Jesus as the Revealer of God. The Spirit of God had always been at work in the world, inspiring, enlightening, strengthening mankind; but that He was to come as the παράκλητος of Jesus and His disciples was a new thing. Henceforth He will come ἐν ὀνόματι Χριστοῦ (see note on 14²⁶).

ἐὰν δὲ πορευθῶ, πέμψω αὐτὸν πρὸς ὑμᾶς. See 15²⁶, where we have ἐγὼ πέμψω ὑμῖν, ὑμῖν and πρὸς ὑμᾶς being identical in meaning. Jn. is apt (see on 3¹⁷) to repeat an important statement in slightly different words.

The work of the Paraclete (vv. 8–15)

8. In the following verses the work of the Paraclete is predicted in some detail. We have already had His office described as one of witness (15²⁶): He is to vindicate Jesus to the world. But He is also to vindicate the apostles in the testimony which they are to deliver (15²⁷). They will be exposed to persecution (16¹·²) ; but, notwithstanding this, they will have a powerful advocate by their side (16⁷). He will be *their* παράκλητος no less than the παράκλητος of Jesus; or, rather, He will be theirs because He is His.

In the Synoptists, this promise of support and Divine help in persecution is recorded more briefly, but quite explicitly. "When they lead you to judgment . . . be not anxious what you shall speak . . . ; for it is not you that speak, but the Holy Spirit " (Mk. 13¹¹, Mt. 10¹⁹, Lk. 12¹¹ 21¹⁵). Here is assured to the apostles the help of the παράκλητος, as the advocate for their defence, who speaks through their mouths. In the present passage Jn. presents this thought more fully. The παράκλητος will not only provide their defence, but He will assume the part of the prosecutor, who convicts their accusers and the accusers of Jesus of being in the wrong. All early Christian preaching was, of necessity, apologetic and polemical. The first heralds of the gospel had to defend their new message, and were constrained to attack the Jewish and heathen doctrines in which much of evil was present. Both in defence and attack, the Holy Spirit was their unseen παράκλητος.

8. καὶ ἐλθὼν ἐκεῖνος ἐλέγξει τὸν κόσμον περὶ ἁμαρτίας καὶ περὶ δικαιοσύνης καὶ περὶ κρίσεως· 9. περὶ ἁμαρτίας μέν, ὅτι οὐ πισ-

καὶ ἐλθὼν ἐκεῖνος ἐλέγξει κτλ. ἐλέγχειν τινα περί τινος (cf. 8⁴⁶) is a classical construction (Aristoph. *Plutus*, 574), "to convict one of anything." ἐλέγχειν is to cross-examine for the purpose of convincing or refuting an opponent (the word being specially used of legal proceedings), and the ἔλεγχος may be brought to a head by means of witness or testimony.¹ Philo speaks of the ἔλεγχος of a man's conscience, and in one place identifies it with the Logos (τὸν σωφρονιστὴν ἔλεγχον, τὸν ἑαυτοῦ λόγον, *quod det. pot*, c. 40; cf. also c. 8). In another passage (*de animal. sacr. idon.* 11), when speaking of a penitent going into the Temple, he calls the ἔλεγχος or conviction of his soul (ὁ κατὰ ψυχὴν ἔλεγχος) a "blameless advocate," παράκλητος οὐ μεμπτός. This brings together the ideas of παράκλητος and ἔλεγχος, as in the verse before us.

ἐλέγξει τὸν κόσμον (see on 1⁹ for the Johannine use of κόσμος) περὶ ἁμαρτίας. Jesus had confidently asked τίς . . . ἐλέγχει με περὶ ἁμαρτίας; (8⁴⁶; cf. Lk. 3¹⁹ for the constr.); but the Paraclete would definitely convict the world of sin, as Jesus Himself had begun to do while He was in the flesh (7⁷). This would not be until the Passion had been fulfilled (cf. 8²⁸; and see on v. 7 above). An early illustration of this "conviction" is given Acts 2³⁶, ³⁷, where the crowds who had heard Peter's inspired preaching were "pricked to the heart": cf. 1 Cor. 14²⁴, ²⁵. It will be observed that in vv. 7–11, as well as at 15²⁶, the Paraclete is spoken of, not as man's advocate with God (1 Jn. 2¹), but as Christ's advocate with the world. See Introd., p. xxi.

9. Abbott (*Diat.* 2077) notes that in Johannine words of Jesus, μέν occurs only twice (here and at v. 22), in both cases being followed by δέ.

περὶ ἁμαρτίας μέν, ὅτι οὐ πιστεύουσιν εἰς ἐμέ. This was the sin to which He had just referred (15²²), and which He had already said (15²⁶) that the witness of the Paraclete would expose. It is the touchstone of moral character to discern God in Christ, as is repeatedly insisted on by Jn.: cf. 3¹⁸, ³⁶ 9⁴¹, 1 Jn. 5¹⁰. This is "to believe on Him": cf. 1¹² 4³⁹, and see 8²⁴.

The primary thought is of the vindication of Jesus to the world, which shall be "convicted" by the Paraclete of the sin which is inherent in its rejection of Jesus. But, although it is not directly stated here, the fact that the Spirit "convicts" of sin has been the experience of every disciple, as well as of the antagonists, of Jesus.

¹ Cf. Lucian, *Pseudol.* 4 : παρακλητέος ἡμῖν . . . ὁ Ἔλεγχος.

τεύουσιν εἰς ἐμέ· 10. περὶ δικαιοσύνης δέ, ὅτι πρὸς τὸν Πατέρα ὑπάγω καὶ οὐκέτι θεωρεῖτέ με· 11. περὶ δὲ κρίσεως, ὅτι ὁ ἄρχων τοῦ κόσμου

10. περὶ δικαιοσύνης. Syr. sin. has (at v. 8) "He will reprove the world in its sins and about *His* righteousness." This brings out that the δικαιοσύνη of which the world will be "convinced" to its shame is the δικαιοσύνη of Christ. It will be "convicted of righteousness" by pointing to Christ the Righteous One (1 Jn. 2¹, 1 Pet. 3¹⁸, Acts 3¹⁴ 7⁵²). The Jews, as Paul says, were "ignorant of God's righteousness" (Rom. 10³); they had not perceived that a new type of righteousness had been exhibited in the Person of Jesus, in whom was "no unrighteousness" (7¹⁸ above). But the words used here go deeper.

"He shall convict the world of righteousness, *because* I go to the Father." Absolute Righteousness could be revealed only in the Risen Christ. With the Passion, His Revelation of the Father was completed (see on v. 5); and henceforth the Paraclete was to convince the world of the Perfect Righteousness which is in Christ revealed and made accessible to men.

It is apposite to cite here the testimony of one of the most impartial of modern historians. "It was reserved for Christianity," writes Lecky,[1] "to present to the world an ideal character, which through all the changes of eighteen centuries has inspired the hearts of men with an impassioned love; has shown itself capable of acting on all ages, nations, temperaments, and conditions; has been not only the highest pattern of virtue, but the strongest incentive to its practice; and has exercised so deep an influence that it may be truly said that the simple record of three short years of active life has done more to regenerate and soften mankind than all the disquisitions of philosophers and all the exhortations of moralists." If we put this tribute into Johannine language, we shall say that the Spirit has convinced the world of the Righteousness of Christ.

ὅτι πρὸς τὸν πατέρα ὑπάγω. Cf. vv. 5, 16, 17, 19, 28 ; and see 7³³ for ὑπάγω. After πατέρα, the rec. inserts μου, with ΑΓΔΘ, but om. אBDLW.

καὶ οὐκέτι θεωρεῖτέ με, "and ye behold me no longer," *sc.* with the bodily eyes, for Jesus will have entered into the region of spirit: cf. vv. 16, 17, 19. There is no contradiction between this and ὑμεῖς θεωρεῖτέ με of 14¹⁹ (*q.v.*), θεωρεῖν being there used of spiritual vision. See on 2²³ for the various usage of this verb in Jn.

11. περὶ δὲ κρίσεως. As the Spirit will convict the world of its sin, and reveal the true δικαιοσύνη, thereby the spiritual

[1] *History of European Morals*, ii. 8.

significance of judgment will be disclosed (cf. 5³⁰, Acts 17³¹).
There is nothing arbitrary in the Divine judgment; it is the
inevitable issue of moral laws.   Good is not the same as evil,
and the sharpness of the distinction is revealed by the Spirit in
His assurance of κρίσις, *i.e.* separation or judgment.   He will
convince the world at once of the *justice* and the *inevitableness*
of God's judgments.

The world (see 8²³) is not yet judged; but it will be judged
at last; and the assurance of this is part of the message of
Christ's Passion ; for in this, which was apparently defeat but
really victory, ὁ ἄρχων τοῦ κοσμοῦ τούτου (cf. 12³¹ 14³⁰ for
this title) κέκριται, "the prince of this world has been judged."
See on 12³¹, where this has been said before, in similar words;
and cf. 13³¹, where the Passion is regarded as already begun.
For this aspect of the Passion, that it is the defeat of the Evil
One, cf. Heb. 2¹⁴, "that through death He might bring to
nought him that had the power of death, that is, the devil."
In later times, pious imagination played round the idea of the
defeat and judgment of Satan, and the legend of the Harrowing
of Hell, first found in the Gospel of Nicodemus, was widespread.
All that is said in Jn. is κέκριται, "he has already been
judged " (cf. Lk. 10¹⁸), and this will issue in final expulsion
from the domain over which he claims rule (12³¹).

In the fifth century Freer MS. (W), which contains the
last twelve verses of Mark, there is interpolated after Mk.
16¹⁴, in which Jesus has rebuked the unbelief of the disciples,
a remarkable passage which recalls the order of ideas in Jn.
16⁸⁻¹¹, as follows: " And they excused themselves, saying that
this age of lawlessness and unbelief is under Satan, who,
through the agency of unclean spirits, does not allow the true
power of God to be apprehended.   Wherefore, they said to
Christ, reveal now Thy righteousness.   And Christ said to
them, The limit of the years of Satan's authority has been
fulfilled (πεπλήρωται ὁ ὅρος τῶν ἐτῶν τῆς ἐξουσίας τοῦ Σατανᾶ),
but other terrors (δεῖνα) draw near, and I was delivered up
to death on behalf of those that have sinned, that they may
be turned to the truth and sin no more, so that they may
inherit the spiritual and incorruptible glory of righteousness in heaven.   But go ye into all the world, etc."   Here we
have a complaint of unbelief caused by Satan, to be cured by
the revelation of Christ's righteousness, to which Christ replies
that Satan's power is ended, that is, "he has been judged "
(Jn. 16¹¹).   The impending "terrors" may be the persecutions foretold in Jn. 16². ³.   In this *apocryphon* there may
be preserved an independent tradition of words recorded in
Jn. 16²⁻¹¹.

τούτου κέκριται. 12. Ἔτι πολλὰ ἔχω ὑμῖν λέγειν, ἀλλ' οὐ δύνασθε βαστάζειν ἄρτι· 13. ὅταν δὲ ἔλθῃ ἐκεῖνος, τὸ Πνεῦμα τῆς ἀληθείας, ὁδηγήσει ὑμᾶς εἰς τὴν ἀλήθειαν πᾶσαν· οὐ γὰρ λαλήσει ἀφ' ἑαυτοῦ,

12. ἔτι πολλὰ ἔχω ὑμῖν λέγειν κτλ. So אBL, but the rec. has λέγειν ὑμῖν. The constr. is thoroughly classical; cf. Demosth. *Olynth.* ii. τὰ μὲν ἄλλα σιωπῶ, πολλ' ἂν ἔχων εἰπεῖν.

At 15¹⁵ Jesus had assured His disciples that He had withheld from them nothing of His Father's purpose, but this was necessarily subject to the reservation that there were some matters which they could not understand. All revelation is subject to the condition "Quicquid recipitur, recipitur ad modum recipientis." So He now tells them that there are many things which they cannot yet bear (cf. 1 Cor. 3²). βαστάζειν is used figuratively (as at Acts 15¹⁰) of "bearing" a mental burden; see on 12⁶. For ἄρτι, see on 9¹⁹: its position here at the end of the sentence gives it emphasis.

The words of this verse show that the full Christian message is not contained in such teaching as, *e.g.*, is found in the Synoptic Gospels. That marks a stage only in the revelation of God in Christ. If the challenge "Back to Jesus" means that we may safely neglect the interpretation of His gospel put forth by the Christians of the Apostolic age, then it is misleading. It is part of the teaching of Jesus Himself, if Jn. 16¹² truly expresses His mind, that much would be learnt of Divine things under the guidance of the Spirit, which could not have been taught with profit during His public ministry on earth.

13. We have here a new thought as to the office of the Paraclete. Hitherto He has been presented as the vindicator of Jesus to the world, by His witness (15²⁶), and His convincing and convicting power (16⁹⁻¹¹). But now He appears in a different capacity, *sc.* as a Guide and Teacher of the faithful (vv. 13–15). Cf. 14²⁶, where a short summary is given of what is said more fully here as to the office of the Spirit in relation to the Church.

ὅταν δὲ ἔλθῃ ἐκεῖνος, τὸ πνεῦμα τῆς ἀληθείας. This is repeated from 15²⁶, where see the note.

ὁδηγήσει ὑμᾶς εἰς τὴν ἀλήθειαν πᾶσαν. So AB, but the rec. has πᾶσαν τὴν ἀλήθειαν. ἐν τῇ ἀληθείᾳ πάσῃ is read by אDLW⊖, and supported by many O.L. texts: a reading perhaps due to the greater frequency of ἐν than εἰς after ὁδηγέω in the Psalms (*e.g.* 5⁸ 27¹¹ 67⁴ 106⁹ 119³⁵).

The Vulgate rendering *docebit uos omnem ueritatem* has been thought to represent διηγήσεται ὑμῖν τὴν ἀλ. πᾶσ., a reading which is found in Cyril Hier. (*Cat.* xvii. 11) and in Eusebius, but which is not supported by any extant Greek

MS. of the Gospel. Wordsworth and White (*in loc.*) suggest that we have here a trace of a Greek MS. used by Jerome which is now lost, but the inference is doubtful.[1] Neither διηγέομαι nor ὁδηγέω are used elsewhere by Jn., but the true Greek reading may be taken to be ὁδηγήσει ὑμᾶς εἰς κτλ. The Spirit is represented as the Guide or Leader who points the Way (ὁδός) to the Truth (ἀλήθεια), Christ being Himself both the Way and the Truth (14⁶).

In Rev. 7¹⁷ ὁδηγεῖν is used of the Lamb leading the saints to fountains of living water; but the thought and the language of the verse before us seem to go back to the O.T. conception of the Divine leadership of Israel as a whole and of individual Israelites, which is so often expressed in the Psalms. Cf. Ps. 143¹⁰ τὸ πνεῦμά σου τὸ ἅγιον (*v.l.* ἀγαθόν) ὁδηγήσει με ἐν τῇ εὐθείᾳ, Ps. 25⁵ ὁδήγησόν με ἐπὶ τὴν ἀλήθειάν σου. See also Ps. 107⁷.

We have a similar phrase in Philo (*de vit. Mos.* iii. 36), who says that sometimes a guess is akin to a prophecy, for the mind would not hit on the point so directly, were not a divine spirit leading it towards the truth, εἰ μὴ καὶ θεῖον ἦν πνεῦμα τὸ ποδηγετοῦν πρὸς αὐτὴν τὴν ἀλήθειαν.

In this verse, then, the work of the Paraclete as a guide is brought into close relation with what is said in the Psalms (especially Ps. 143¹⁰) as to the work of the Spirit of Yahweh. The Paraclete is not *explicitly* identified with the "Holy Spirit," a Name familiar to every Jew, until 14²⁶; but what is said at this point prepares us for the identification.

ὁδηγήσει ὑμᾶς κτλ., "He will guide *you*," *sc.* the apostles, to whom the words were addressed. It is natural, and in a sense legitimate, for modern readers to give the promise a wider reference, and to interpret it of a gradual revelation of the truth to the Church under the guidance of the Spirit.[2] But it is not clear that the author of the Fourth Gospel would have recognised such an interpretation of the words which he records. For him, the revelation to the apostles after the Descent of the Spirit was final and complete (cf. 20²² and Heb. 1¹). In any case, by "all the truth" is meant here "all the truth about Christ and His Gospel"; the thought of the gradual revelation of scientific truth, and the ever-increasing knowledge of the works of God in nature, is not present in the text. The promise to the apostles did not mean, *e.g.*, that they would be divinely guided into all truth as to economic law or as to the distribution of property (Acts 4³⁵). See further on 14²⁶.

[1] I have discussed this point in *Hermathena* (1895, p. 189, and 1901, p. 340).

[2] Cf. Justin (*Tryph.* 39), οἱ ἐκ πάσης τῆς ἀληθείας μεμαθητευομένοι.

ἀλλ' ὅσα ἀκούσει λαλήσει, καὶ τὰ ἐρχόμενα ἀναγγελεῖ ὑμῖν.

οὐ γὰρ λαλήσει ἀφ' ἑαυτοῦ. This is the reason why the guidance of the Paraclete is sure and trustworthy in the things of God and Christ. As the Son did not speak "of Himself" (12⁴⁹ 14¹⁰, and cf. 7¹⁷ 5¹⁹), so the Spirit will not speak "of Himself."

ἀλλ' ὅσα ἀκούσει λαλήσει. So BDW; the rec. has ὅσα ἂν ἀκούσῃ; ⊝ has ὅσα ἂν ἀκούσει; אL read ἀκούει. "Whatsoever He shall hear (sc. from God), that will He speak"; cf. 8²⁶, where Jesus says, "The things which I heard from Him, these I speak unto the world." Westcott calls attention to the difference of tense, ἤκουσα at 8²⁶, ἀκούσει here. In the former passage, the message which the Son had to deliver was complete and definite, but here the thought is of a message being enlarged from time to time. This is attractive, but it is not certain (see above) that this thought of the continuous education of the Church was really present to the mind of the evangelist.

καὶ τὰ ἐρχόμενα ἀναγγελεῖ ὑμῖν. It was popularly believed that Messiah when He came would reveal new truths: cf. ἀναγγελεῖ ἡμῖν πάντα (4²⁵, where see note; and cf. 16²⁵ for ἀναγγέλλειν, "to report"). Here it is thrice repeated (vv. 14, 15) that the Spirit's office will also include that of "declaring" or "reporting" Divine things.

To report τὰ ἐρχόμενα is to predict the future, so that prophecy in the sense of prediction is included here in the work of the Paraclete. This is the only place in Jn. where any of the Pauline χαρίσματα of the Spirit is mentioned (cf. 1 Cor. 12²⁹. ³⁰); and Wendt would treat the words τὰ ἐρχ. . . . . ὑμῖν as an editorial addition, regarding them as out of harmony with the context.[1] But we have already seen that the description of the Paraclete's office as "guiding into truth" recalls O.T. phrases as to the work of the Holy Spirit, a main part of which, to Jewish thought, was the inspiration of the prophets. That it should be said of the promised Paraclete τὰ ἐρχόμενα ἀναγγελεῖ ὑμῖν is entirely in harmony with the identification of Him with the Divine Spirit (cf. Rev. 1¹ 22⁶).

To Jewish thought the expected Christ was ὁ ἐρχόμενος, the Coming One (Lk. 7²⁰, Jn. 6¹⁴); and to Christian thought He is still ὁ ἐρχόμενος, for He is, in some sense, to come again. There is a hint of apocalyptic prevision of the Last Things in τὰ ἐρχόμενα ἀναγγελεῖ, such as Jn. keeps in the background for the most part, although we have it in the Synoptists (Mk. 13²⁶). See Introd., p. clix.

[1] *St. John's Gospel*, pp. 163, 203.

14. ἐκεῖνος ἐμὲ δοξάσει, ὅτι ἐκ τοῦ ἐμοῦ λήμψεται καὶ ἀναγγελεῖ ὑμῖν. 15. πάντα ὅσα ἔχει ὁ Πατὴρ ἐμά ἐστιν· διὰ τοῦτο εἶπον ὅτι ἐκ τοῦ ἐμοῦ λαμβάνει καὶ ἀναγγελεῖ ὑμῖν.

14. ἐκεῖνος ἐμὲ δοξάσει. The Spirit was not to come until Jesus had been " glorified," *i.e.* in His Passion (7³⁹); but thenceforth every fresh revelation of the Spirit, all new insight into the meaning of Christ's gospel, would be a fresh " glorification " of Christ, an enlargement of man's sense of His majesty. As the Son had " glorified " the Father while He was on earth (17⁴), so the Spirit will " glorify " the Son after He has departed from human vision.

ὅτι ἐκ τοῦ ἐμοῦ λήμψεται καὶ ἀναγγελεῖ ὑμῖν. This " glorification " will be brought about by the Spirit's revelation of Christian truth. The advanced Christology of the Pauline Epistles, and of the Fourth Gospel itself, as compared with that to which the apostles had attained before the Passion, is a signal illustration of this.

See 14²², where the question of Jude shows that very different thoughts as to the future " glorification " of Jesus filled the hearts of the apostles. They expected a visible manifestation in glory, which should convict the world and put it to shame.

15. πάντα ὅσα ἔχει ὁ πατὴρ ἐμά ἐστιν. This is the perpetual claim of the Johannine Christ, repeated once more at 17¹⁰. So Paul can speak of " the unsearchable wealth of the Christ " (Eph. 3⁸).

διὰ τοῦτο, referring to what precedes (see on 5¹⁶). " Wherefore I said that (ὅτι *recitantis*) He takes of mine and shall show it unto you," repeated from v. 14, with the slight verbal change of λαμβάνει (BDLNWΘ) for λήμψεται of v. 14 (which is retained by the rec. with ℵᶜA, the Latin vss., and Syr. sin.). This repetition of a striking phrase, a word or two being altered, is a feature of Johannine style (see on 3¹⁶).

ἀναγγελεῖ ὑμῖν, thrice repeated at the end of vv. 13, 14, 15, is like a solemn refrain, calling special attention to the *revealing* office of the Spirit.

The disciples' perplexity as to Jesus' return (vv. 16–19)

16. μικρόν, " a little while ": see on 7³³ 13³³ 14¹⁹.   Jesus dwells again and again on the nearness of His Passion.

οὐκέτι is the true reading at this point (ℵBDᵍʳWNΘ); but the rec. has οὐ (assimilated to v. 17), with AΓΔ.   καὶ οὐκέτι θεωρεῖτέ με is here repeated from v. 10.

" A little while, and ye no longer behold me," *sc.* with the

16. Μικρὸν καὶ οὐκέτι θεωρεῖτέ με, καὶ πάλιν μικρὸν καὶ ὄψεσθέ με. 17. Εἶπαν οὖν ἐκ τῶν μαθητῶν αὐτοῦ πρὸς ἀλλήλους Τί ἐστιν τοῦτο ὃ λέγει ἡμῖν Μικρὸν καὶ οὐ θεωρεῖτέ με, καὶ πάλιν μικρὸν καὶ ὄψεσθέ με; καί Ὅτι ὑπάγω πρὸς τὸν Πατέρα; 18. ἔλεγον οὖν Τί ἐστιν τοῦτο ὃ λέγει, τὸ μικρόν; οὐκ οἴδαμεν τί λαλεῖ. 19. ἔγνω

bodily eyes (see on 2²³ for θεωρεῖν). On the day after these words were spoken, He would meet death, after which they would no longer be able to look upon His face as heretofore. It is to be observed that οὐκέτι (see on 4⁴²) always means " no longer " in Jn., sc. that the action in question is discontinued; it does not necessarily mean " never again."

καὶ πάλιν μικρὸν καὶ ὄψεσθέ με, "And again, a little while," sc. the period between His Death and His Resurrection, "and ye shall see me." ὄπτομαι, a verb always used in Jn. of the vision of *spiritual* realities (see on 1⁵¹), now takes the place of θεωρεῖν. παλὶν δὲ ὄψομαι ὑμᾶς, Jesus says, in like manner, at v. 22. The " seeing " of the Risen Lord in His spiritual body, and His " seeing " of His disciples after His Resurrection, are more suitably expressed by ὄπτεσθαι than by θεωρεῖν (although cf. 20¹⁴).

The rec. adds (from v. 10 or v. 17), after ὄψεσθέ με, ὅτι ἐγὼ ὑπάγω πρὸς τὸν πατέρα, with ΑΝΔΘ; but the phrase is not found at this point in אBDLW or Pap. Oxy. 1781.

17. The disciples were puzzled. ὑπάγω πρὸς τὸν πατέρα (v. 10) seemed to indicate a final withdrawal of His visible presence, and yet He used the word μικρόν (v. 16), which suggested that it would be only temporary.

εἶπαν οὖν ἐκ τῶν μαθητῶν αὐτοῦ κτλ. We must supply τινές. For a similar elliptical construction, cf. 7⁴⁰; and for πρὸς ἀλλήλους, cf. 4³³.

They repeated the enigmatic words of Jesus to each other, being unable to catch their meaning.

Note that they quote Jesus as having said Μικρὸν καὶ οὐ (*not* οὐκέτι) θεωρεῖτέ με, and Jesus is represented in verse 19 as repeating οὐ θεωρεῖτε. This provides one more illustration of Jn.'s habit of altering slightly a striking phrase when it is reproduced for the second or third time (see on 3¹⁶). Such verbal alterations are not to be taken as indicating a subtle change of meaning; they exemplify merely the freedom of Jn.'s style.

18. τί ἐστιν τοῦτο. So אBD*LΘ and Pap. Oxy. 1781; but the rec. has τοῦτο τί ἐστιν, with AD²ΔN.

ὃ λέγει, τὸ μικρόν; "What is this that He says, this word μικρόν?" τό before μικρόν singles out the word as the point of difficulty.

Ἰησοῦς ὅτι ἤθελον αὐτὸν ἐρωτᾶν, καὶ εἶπεν αὐτοῖς Περὶ τούτου ζητεῖτε μετ' ἀλλήλων ὅτι εἶπον Μικρὸν καὶ οὐ θεωρεῖτέ με, καὶ πάλιν μικρὸν καὶ ὄψεσθέ με; 20. ἀμὴν ἀμὴν λέγω ὑμῖν ὅτι κλαύσετε καὶ θρηνήσετε ὑμεῖς, ὁ δὲ κόσμος χαρήσεται· ὑμεῖς λυπηθήσεσθε, ἀλλ' ἡ

οὐκ οἴδαμεν τί λαλεῖ. (See on 3¹¹ for the frequent interchangeability of λέγειν and λαλεῖν in Jn.) "That which is quite clear to us was to them all mystery. If Jesus were about to found an earthly kingdom, why should He depart? If not, why should He return?" (Godet).

19. ἔγνω Ἰησοῦς ὅτι κτλ. He recognised that the disciples wished to interrogate Him (see below on v. 23 for ἐρωτᾶν). Cf. 2²⁴.

The rec. adds οὖν after ἔγνω, with ΑΔΝ; but om. ℵBDLW. For οὖν, Θ has δέ. Also the rec. has ὁ before Ἰησοῦς, with ℵADNΘ; but om. BLW and Pap. Oxy. 1781. See on 1²⁹; and cf. 6¹⁵.

The repetition of phrases in vv. 16-19 is quite in the Oriental manner of narrative. The crucial word μικρόν is repeated 7 times; and "A little while, and ye behold me not, and again, a little while, and ye shall see me," is said 3 times over. Although the Fourth Gospel is thoroughly Greek, the Semitic undertone is often present.

Words of comfort and hope (vv. 20-24)

20. In the answer which Jesus gives to the bewildered disciples, He fixes on the word μικρόν, which was the centre of their difficulty, and says nothing about the meaning of "I go to the Father." Their short time of sorrow at His departure will be followed by a season of joy. That is enough for them to know at the moment.

ἀμὴν ἀμήν κτλ. See on 1⁵¹.

κλαύσετε καὶ θρηνήσετε. These are the verbs used of the loud wailings and lamentations customary in the East after a death. They both occur Jer. 22¹⁰; for κλαίειν see on 11³¹, and for θρηνεῖν cf. 2 Sam. 1¹⁷. That the women lamented for Jesus (ἐθρήνουν αὐτόν) on the way to the Cross is told Lk. 23²⁷; and that they were wailing (κλαίειν) on the morning of the Resurrection is mentioned Mk. 16¹⁰; cf. Jn. 20¹¹ Μαριάμ . . . κλαίουσα. Pseudo-Peter (§ 12) adds that the apostles also exhibited their sorrow by weeping, ἡμεῖς . . . ἐκλαίομεν καὶ ἐλυπούμεθα. It is plain that κλαύσετε καὶ θρηνήσετε in the present passage refers to the grief which the disciples will display when their Master is taken from them.

ὁ δὲ κόσμος χαρήσεται: but the hostile world, i.e. the Jewish

λύπη ὑμῶν εἰς χαρὰν γενήσεται. 21. ἡ γυνὴ ὅταν τίκτῃ λύπην ἔχει, ὅτι ἦλθεν ἡ ὥρα αὐτῆς· ὅταν δὲ γεννήσῃ τὸ παιδίον, οὐκέτι μνημονεύει τῆς θλίψεως διὰ τὴν χαρὰν ὅτι ἐγεννήθη ἄνθρωπος εἰς τὸν κόσμον. 22. καὶ ὑμεῖς οὖν νῦν μὲν λύπην ἔχετε· πάλιν δὲ ὄψομαι ὑμᾶς, καὶ χαρήσεται ὑμῶν ἡ καρδία, καὶ τὴν χαρὰν ὑμῶν οὐδεὶς αἴρει

adversaries of Jesus, will rejoice that the Prophet whom they hate (15¹⁸) has been removed.

ὑμεῖς λυπηθήσεσθε, referring to the *inward* grief which they will feel (cf. 21¹⁷, the only other place where the verb is found in Jn.). ὑμεῖς is emphatic.

ἀλλ' ἡ λύπη ὑμῶν εἰς χαρὰν γενήσεται. So it came to pass. ἐχάρησαν οἱ μαθηταὶ ἰδόντες τὸν κύριον (20²⁰). Cf. ἀπὸ πένθους εἰς χαράν (Esth. 9²² ; and see Jer. 31¹³). See also 2 Esd. 2²⁷.

21. ἡ γυνή, *sc. any* woman, what follows being universally true; cf. ὁ κόκκος (12²⁴) or ὁ δοῦλος (15¹⁵). Abbott (*Diat.* 1948) takes the article as indicating that it is *the* woman of a household, *i.e.* the wife, that is in question. But this is to miss the point.

The image of a woman in travail is frequent in the O.T., where the suddenness and inevitableness of travail pains are often mentioned (*e.g.* Isa. 26¹⁷, 2 Esd. 16³⁸); but the thought of the joy which follows the pain does not occur except here. Some expositors have thought that the Birth of the Church and the travail pains of the Passion are contemplated in this passage (cf. Isa. 66⁷, Hos. 13¹³, Mk. 13⁸); but it is over subtle and inconsistent with the context to bring in such an idea. The apostles were not in travail with the Church that was to be. The true (and only) exposition of this beautiful image is given in the verse which follows. The image provides a familiar and touching illustration of the truth that pain is often the necessary antecedent to the supreme joys of life.

22. καὶ ὑμεῖς οὖν. For the constr. see 8³⁸. *This* is the application of the image of the joy which follows the pain of childbirth. " You now, indeed (for μέν, see on v. 9), have grief," but presently you will rejoice. ἔχετε (א*BCΔ) is to be preferred to ἕξετε of א°ADLΘ.

πάλιν δὲ ὄψομαι ὑμᾶς. Here is even a greater promise than ὄψεσθέ με of v. 16: it is better to be seen of God than to see Him (cf. Gal. 4⁹). This was the promise of Jesus, that He would see His disciples after He was risen.

καὶ χαρήσεται ὑμῶν ἡ καρδία. The phrase is identical with that of Isa. 66¹⁴ (ὄψεσθε, καὶ χαρήσεται ἡ καρδία ὑμῶν: cf. also Ps. 33²¹) Cf 20¹⁴⁻¹⁶, when the promise was fulfilled in the first instance. Such joy is inalienable, οὐδεὶς αἴρει ἀφ' ὑμῶν, the future which is certain being represented by a present

ἀφ᾽ ὑμῶν. 23. καὶ ἐν ἐκείνῃ τῇ ἡμέρᾳ ἐμὲ οὐκ ἐρωτήσετε οὐδέν.

tense. Nevertheless BD*N Pap. Oxy. 1781 have ἀρεῖ, which Westcott adopts. But אACD²LΔΘ and Pap. Oxy. 1228 give αἴρει. W has ἀφέρει.

23. ἐν ἐκείνῃ τῇ ἡμέρᾳ. This phrase occurs again at v. 26, and at 14²⁰; and in each case it signifies the day when the Spirit has been released, Jesus having been " glorified " (see on 7³⁹). The teaching of the Fourth Gospel is that the moment of consummation of the work of Jesus is the moment of His Death: τετέλεσται (19³⁰). After His Resurrection, He gave the Spirit to the assembled disciples: λάβετε πνεῦμα ἅγιον (20²²). The Day of Pentecost is described in Acts 2 as a Day when a special gift of spiritual power was manifested, and there is nothing in Jn. which is inconsistent with such a manifestation. But for Jn. the Day of the Spirit's Advent is the Day of the Resurrection of Jesus; and to introduce the thoughts of what happened at Pentecost into the exegesis of these Last Discourses is to make confusion. ἐν ἐκείνῃ τῇ ἡμέρᾳ signifies the new Dispensation or Era of the Spirit, which began with the Resurrection, to the thought of Jn.

ἐμὲ οὐκ ἐρωτήσετε οὐδέν. ἐρωτᾶν may mean *either* " to ask a question," as often in Jn. (1¹⁹· ²¹· ²⁵ 5¹² 9²· ¹⁵· ¹⁹· ²¹· ²³ 16⁵· ¹⁹· ³⁰ 18¹⁹· ²¹), *or* " to entreat, to beseech, to ask a boon " (as at 4³¹· ⁴⁰· ⁴⁷ 12²¹ 19³¹· ³⁸). We have already noted (on 11²²) that it is the verb used of the *prayers* of Jesus by Himself (16²⁶ 14¹⁶ 17⁹· ¹⁵· ²⁰), but that it is not used elsewhere in the Gospel of the prayers of *men* (cf., however, 1 Jn. 5¹⁶).

Hence ἐμὲ οὐκ ἐρωτήσετε οὐδέν may be translated in two ways:

(1) " In that day ye shall ask me no questions," as they had desired to do, v. 19; cf. v. 30. When the Paraclete came, they would no longer need to ask Jesus questions, such as those addressed to Him at 13³⁶ 14⁵· ²²; for the Spirit would teach them all things (14²⁶ 16¹³). But this seems to break the sequence of thought, and there is no mention of the Spirit in the immediate context. Further, as Field points out, the emphatic position of ἐμέ before the negative and the verb, naturally suggests a comparison with τὸν πατέρα in the next clause.

(2) It is better to render, " In that day, ye shall ask nothing of *me*." The visible company of Jesus would be withdrawn, so that they would no longer be able to ask favours of Him or proffer requests to Him, face to face. But there is a great compensation, and its promise is introduced by the solemn prelude ἀμὴν ἀμὴν λέγω ὑμῖν (see on 1⁵¹). They can henceforth have direct access to the Father, and whatever they ask of

ἀμὴν ἀμὴν λέγω ὑμῖν, ἄν τι αἰτήσητε τὸν Πατέρα δώσει ὑμῖν ἐν τῷ

Him, the due conditions of Christian prayer being observed (see on 15¹⁶), shall be given.

The view that the contrast is between "asking *me*" and "asking the *Father*" has been rejected by some commentators because ἐρωτᾶν is used in the first case, and αἰτεῖν in the second. But (see on 11²²) these verbs are not sharply distinguished in later Greek (cf. Acts 3². ³ for an illustration of their being used interchangeably). The general purport of the teaching of these discourses is that it will be spiritually beneficial for the disciples that their Master should depart (16⁷). New sources of knowledge and spiritual power will henceforth be available for them. They will be empowered to achieve great things on earth (14¹²), and their prayers will have a potential efficacy, such as could not have been before it was possible to offer them in the Name of Jesus.

δώσει ὑμῖν ἐν τῷ ὀνόματί μου. This is the order of words in אBC*LΔ, and is supported by Origen and the paraphrase of Nonnus. The rec. has ἐν τῷ ὀνόματί μου δώσει ὑμῖν, with AC³DNWΓΘ, the Syriac and Latin vss. generally.

If we adopt the former reading, which *prima facie* has the weight of MS. authority, the natural rendering of the sentence is, "If you ask anything of the Father, He will give it to you in my Name." This is difficult of interpretation. It is true that Jesus speaks later of "the Holy Spirit whom the Father will send in my Name" (14²⁶, where see note), but that is a way of speaking which has parallels at 5⁴³ 10²⁵. To say that the Father gives in the Name of the Son a boon which has been sought in prayer is unlike anything elsewhere in the N.T. It is not adequate to interpret this as meaning only that the Son is the medium through which prayer is answered as well as offered. That is true in a sense (see on 14¹³), but to speak of the Father acting ἐν ὀνόματι τοῦ υἱοῦ is foreign alike to Johannine doctrine and to Johannine phraseology. The phrase ἐν τῷ ὀνόματί μου occurs 15¹⁶ 16²³. ²⁴. ²⁶ 14¹³. ¹⁴. ²⁶ (7 times in all) in these Last Discourses; and in every case (except the last, 14²⁶, to which reference has already been made) it has reference to the essential condition of Christian prayer, *sc.* that it should be offered "in the Name" of Christ.

The Greek, however, does not necessarily require us to connect ἐν τῷ ὀνόματί μου here with δώσει ὑμῖν, even if δώσει ὑμῖν precedes ἐν τῷ ὀνόματί μου. For we have seen above (on 12¹³) that εὐλογημένος ὁ ἐρχόμενος ἐν ὀνόματι κυρίου must be rendered "Blessed in the Name of the Lord is He that cometh," ἐν ὀνόματι κυρίου being taken with εὐλογημένος, although ὁ ἐρχό-

ὀνόματί μου.   24. ἕως ἄρτι οὐκ ᾐτήσατε οὐδὲν ἐν τῷ ὀνόματί μου·
αἰτεῖτε, καὶ λήμψεσθε, ἵνα ἡ χαρὰ ὑμῶν ᾖ πεπληρωμένη.

25. Ταῦτα ἐν παροιμίαις λελάληκα ὑμῖν· ἔρχεται ὥρα ὅτε οὐκέτι

μενος immediately precedes.   In the present passage, in like
manner, it is legitimate to take ἐν τῷ ὀνόματί μου with αἰτήσητε
τὸν πατέρα, although δώσει ὑμῖν immediately precedes.   The
meaning, then, is exactly similar to that of 15¹⁶ ἵνα ὅ τι ἂν
αἰτήσητε τὸν πατέρα ἐν τῷ ὀνόματί μου δῷ ὑμῖν.   See notes
on 14¹³ 15¹⁶.   And that this is here also the true sequence of
words is confirmed by the next verse, where Jesus goes on to
say that hitherto the apostles had asked nothing in His Name.
See on 20³¹.

24. For ἕως ἄρτι, cf. 2¹⁰ 5¹⁷.

Hitherto they had asked nothing in the Name of Jesus.
They could not have done so, nor had they before this been
taught to do so.   The dispensation of the Spirit had not yet
begun.   Not yet could a Christian disciple say δι' αὐτοῦ ἔχομεν
τὴν προσαγωγὴν . . . ἐν ἑνὶ πνεύματι πρὸς τὸν πατέρα (Eph. 2¹⁸).

αἰτεῖτε, " Be asking," the pres. indicating continuous
prayer; καὶ λήμψεσθε, "and ye shall receive."   The new
mode of prayer has a more certain promise of response than
anything that had gone before, although αἰτεῖτε καὶ δοθήσεται
ὑμῖν (Mt. 7⁷) had been a precept of the Sermon on the Mount
(see on 14¹³).

ἵνα ἡ χαρὰ ὑμῶν ᾖ πεπληρωμένη.   Christian prayer issues
in the fulness of Christian joy.   For this thought of " joy
being fulfilled," which is frequent in Jn., see on 15¹¹ above,
with the references there given.

*Jesus ceases to speak in parables, and promises the disciples direct
access to the Father who loves them and to whom He
returns (vv. 25–28)*

25. ταῦτα ἐν παροιμίαις λελάληκα ὑμῖν.   For παροιμία, see on
10⁶; cf. Ps. 78².

We have seen (on 15¹¹) that ταῦτα in the seven-times-
repeated ταῦτα λελάληκα ὑμῖν refers in each case to what has
immediately preceded.   So here ταῦτα points back to the
sayings in 16¹⁵ᶠᶠ· about the approaching departure of Jesus.
The apostles had not understood the meaning of ὑπάγω πρὸς
τὸν πατέρα (v. 18), or of what Jesus had said about their seeing
Him again.   He puts it more plainly in v. 28, whereupon they
reply at once that now they know what He means (v. 29).
Whatever allusion ταῦτα ἐν παροιμίαις λελάληκα ὑμῖν may
carry to the veiled teachings suggested by the images of the

ἐν παροιμίαις λαλήσω ὑμῖν, ἀλλὰ παρρησίᾳ περὶ τοῦ Πατρὸς ἀπαγγελῶ ὑμῖν. 26. ἐν ἐκείνῃ τῇ ἡμέρᾳ ἐν τῷ ὀνόματί μου αἰτήσεσθε, καὶ οὐ λέγω ὑμῖν ὅτι ἐγὼ ἐρωτήσω τὸν Πατέρα περὶ ὑμῶν· 27. αὐτὸς γὰρ

Vine (15[1]) and of the Woman in Travail (16[21]), or more generally by the parables of the Ministry (Mk. 4[33]), the primary reference here is to vv. 15–18.

For the phrase ἔρχεται ὥρα, see on v. 2 and 4[21]. Here it must be equated with ἐν ἐκείνῃ τῇ ἡμέρᾳ of v. 26 (see v. 23 above). When the visible presence of Jesus was withdrawn, and when His oral teaching was replaced by the fuller teaching of the Spirit (see on 14[26]), then His revelation of the Father (the central theme of His ministry), conveyed through the Spirit, would be plainer.

For παρρησία, " unreserved and open speech," see on 7[4].

ἀπαγγελῶ. So ABC*DLWΘ, but the rec. (with N) has ἀναγγελῶ (from vv. 13, 14, 15). On the other hand, ἀπαγγέλλειν occurs again in Jn. only twice (1 Jn. 1[2, 3]), while we have ἀναγγέλλειν at Jn. 4[25] 5[15] 16[13, 14₂ 15], 1 Jn. 1[5]. It is doubtful if any distinction in meaning can be traced. παρρησίᾳ περὶ τοῦ πατρὸς ἀπαγγελῶ ὑμῖν means " I will bring word to you plainly about the Father "; ἀπαγγέλλειν, " to report," being a quite appropriate word to employ of the revelations which the Spirit is to bring.

If it be urged that ἀπαγγελῶ must refer to some future oral teachings of Jesus Himself, then we must suppose that the post-Resurrection discourses contained such fuller and plainer doctrine (cf. 20[17]); but it is most likely that the future disclosures of the Spirit are in view.

26. ἐν ἐκείνῃ τῇ ἡμέρᾳ (see on v. 23) ἐν τῷ ὀνόματί μου αἰτήσεσθε (see on 15[16] for this phrase). With the coming of the Paraclete, the doctrine of the Fatherhood of God as revealed in Christ would be better understood. They would know more of God as Father, and so would be bolder and more ambitious in prayer (cf. 1 Jn. 5[14] αὕτη ἐστὶν ἡ παρρησία ἣν ἔχομεν πρὸς αὐτόν, ὅτι ἐάν τι αἰτώμεθα κατὰ τὸ θέλημα αὐτοῦ, ἀκούει ἡμῶν). *Cognitio parit orationem* (Bengel).

καὶ οὐ λέγω ὑμῖν ὅτι ἐγὼ ἐρωτήσω τὸν πατέρα περὶ ὑμῶν, " I do not say to you that I will entreat the Father for you " (see for ἐρωτᾷν on 11[22] 16[23]), because in the dispensation of the Spirit prayer in the Name of Jesus does not fail to reach the Father and to receive its answer. The prayers of those who are " in Christ," and offered " in His Name," are virtually *His* prayers. *Before* the Coming of the Spirit He did pray for His disciples (14[16] 17[9, 15, 20]), but here the thought is of the ideal disciple *after* the Spirit has descended. This does

ὁ Πατὴρ φιλεῖ ὑμᾶς, ὅτι ὑμεῖς ἐμὲ πεφιλήκατε καὶ πεπιστεύκατε ὅτι
ἐγὼ παρὰ τοῦ Θεοῦ ἐξῆλθον. 28. ἐξῆλθον ἐκ τοῦ Πατρὸς καὶ ἐλή-

not exclude the perpetual intercession of Jesus for sinful
disciples ; ἐάν τις ἁμάρτῃ, παράκλητον ἔχομεν πρὸς τὸν πατέρα,
Ἰησοῦν Χριστὸν δίκαιον (1 Jn. 2¹; cf. Rom. 8³⁴, Heb. 7²⁵).
But the true disciple is encouraged to be bold in prayer for
himself, and the reason why he may be bold is now stated.

27. αὐτὸς γὰρ ὁ πατὴρ φιλεῖ ὑμᾶς, "for the Father Himself
loveth you." There will be no reluctance in His answer to
the prayers of those who love Jesus and have faith that His
mission was from the Father.

Field calls attention to the " elegant Greek use " of αὐτός
in the sense of αὐτόματος, *proprio motu*, and compares Homer,
Iliad, viii. 293, τί με σπεύδοντα καὶ αὐτὸν ὀτρύνεις. This is
one of the many passages in which the Greek of the Fourth
Gospel does not resemble translation-Greek.

At 3¹⁶, the love of God for the κόσμος (all mankind) has
been mentioned; here and at 14²¹·²³ 17²³ it is rather the special
love of God for those who are disciples of Jesus that is in view
(as at 1 Jn. 4¹⁹). Here the verb φιλεῖν is used, the *only* instance in which Jn. employs it to express the love of God for
man; in the other passages he uses ἀγαπᾶν. It is clear (see
further on 21¹⁵) that the attempt to distinguish ἀγαπᾶν from
φιλεῖν in Jn. cannot be sustained.

ὅτι ὑμεῖς ἐμὲ πεφιλήκατε, " because you are they who have
loved me," ὑμεῖς and ἐμέ being both emphasised. Here,
again, φιλεῖν is used of the love of His disciples for Jesus
(21¹⁵⁻¹⁷ providing the only other examples of this phraseology
in Jn.; but cf. Mt. 10³⁷, 1 Cor. 16²²); while in 14¹⁵·²¹·²³·²⁴·²⁸,
ἀγαπᾶν is consistently used to express this affection (cf. 21¹⁵·¹⁶).

καὶ πεπιστεύκατε (the perfect tenses bring back the discourse from a prospect of the future to the facts of the present)
ὅτι ἐγὼ παρὰ τοῦ θεοῦ ἐξῆλθον. To have believed this is to have
accepted the central message of the Gospel.

παρὰ τοῦ θεοῦ ἐξῆλθον. So ℵ*AC³NWΓ and Syr. sin.
(see on 8⁴²). The rec. for θεοῦ has πατρός (from v. 28), with
ℵᶜᵃBC*DL. W om. the repeated ἐξῆλθον παρὰ τοῦ πατρός in the
next verse.

Cf. παρὰ σοῦ ἐξῆλθον (17⁸); and see on 1¹⁴ 7²⁹ for παρά as
expressing the relation of the Son to the Father. See on 13³
for ἀπὸ θεοῦ ἐξῆλθεν.

28. Here, in four short phrases, we have the Pre-existence
of Christ, His Incarnation, His Death, and His Ascension.

ἐκ τοῦ πατρός. For ἐκ (BCL) the rec. has (from v. 27) παρά,
with ℵAC²NΓΔΘ.

λυθα εἰς τὸν κόσμον· πάλιν ἀφίημι τὸν κόσμον καὶ πορεύομαι πρὸς τὸν Πατέρα.

29. Λέγουσιν οἱ μαθηταὶ αὐτοῦ Ἴδε νῦν ἐν παρρησίᾳ λαλεῖς, καὶ παροιμίαν οὐδεμίαν λέγεις. 30. νῦν οἴδαμεν ὅτι οἶδας πάντα καὶ οὐ

παρά in v. 27 and ἐκ in v. 28 cannot be differentiated in meaning without over subtlety. The classical distinction between these prepositions was being obliterated by the first century. To interpret ἐκ θεοῦ or ἐκ τοῦ πατρός in the Fourth Gospel as if we had to do with the formal theology of the Nicene Creed is not legitimate (see on 8⁴²). We cannot press the force of ἐκ so as to make it indicate the unique relation of the Son to the Father, in a fashion that παρά will not indicate it equally well. It must be remembered that ὁ ὢν ἐκ τοῦ θεοῦ at 8⁴⁷ does *not* mean Jesus, the Eternal Son, but any man who hears with understanding the Divine message.

παρά in v. 27, ἐκ in v. 28, and ἀπό in v. 30 carry the same meaning for Jn.

καὶ ἐλήλυθα (D has ἦλθον) εἰς τὸν κόσμον, *sc.* at the Incarnation. Cf. 11²⁷ 18³⁷ for this phrase; and for κόσμος, see on 1¹⁰.

πάλιν (next, marking the sequence; cf. 1 Jn. 2⁸) ἀφίημι τὸν κόσμον. Hitherto the apostles had not understood that He was going to leave the world.

καὶ πορεύομαι πρὸς τὸν πατέρα. We shall have this phrase again 14¹². ²⁸; it is not to be distinguished from ὑπάγω πρὸς τὸν πατέρα (16¹⁰. ¹⁷; cf. 7³³ 16⁵ and note on 16⁷).

The disciples now become confident of their faith, and are warned that it will fail them in the hour of trial (vv. 29-32)

29. The rec. adds αὐτῷ after λέγουσιν, but om. ℵ*BC*D*NWΘ.
Ἴδε, an interjection of astonished admiration; see on 1²⁹ for its frequency in Jn.

νῦν ἐν παρρησίᾳ λαλεῖς, "*now* you are speaking explicitly." But they did not really understand, as they thought they did. The promise of teaching ἐν παρρησίᾳ in v. 25 was for a future day.

The rec. omits ἐν before παρρησίᾳ, but ins. ℵBCD.

καὶ παροιμίαν οὐδεμίαν λέγεις. For παροιμία, cf. v. 25; and see note on 10⁶.

In the latter part of the *Epistle to Diognetus*, which Lightfoot places at the end of the second century, there is a reference to the manifestation of the Logos, παρρησίᾳ λαλῶν (§ 11), which may be a reminiscence of this verse. See on 17³.

χρείαν ἔχεις ἵνα τίς σε ἐρωτᾷ· ἐν τούτῳ πιστεύομεν ὅτι ἀπὸ Θεοῦ
ἐξῆλθες.   31. ἀπεκρίθη αὐτοῖς Ἰησοῦς Ἄρτι πιστεύετε, 32. ἰδοὺ

30. νῦν οἴδαμεν κτλ. They were so surprised that He had
discerned their thoughts, and so bewildered at His words
(see v. 19), that they assure Him of their absolute confidence
in Him as all-knowing. With οἶδας πάντα cf. 21[17]. Jn.
comes back again and again to the penetrating insight of
Jesus into men's thoughts; see on 2[25].

ἵνα τίς σε ἐρωτᾷ, " that any one shall question thee," ἐρωτᾶν
being here used in its most frequent sense of asking questions; see on v. 23 above.

ἐν τούτῳ, " by this," ἐν being used in a quasi-causal
sense, as at 13[35], where see note.

πιστεύομεν ὅτι ἀπὸ Θεοῦ ἐξῆλθες. Nicodemus had confessed
as much (3[2]); what Jesus had said of their faith was that they
had come to believe ὅτι ἐγὼ παρὰ τοῦ πατρὸς ἐξῆλθον. But they
were not yet strong in this faith, as He reminds them in His
reply.   See note on 13[3] and also on v. 28 above. Strictly,
ἀπό ought to signify *mission*, while παρά or (especially) ἐκ
ought to signify *origin*; but these prepositions are not sharply
distinguished in Jn.

31. The form of the reply of Jesus is comparable with that in
13[38], the disciples' expression of confidence being repeated, and
then a warning given.   Here, however, the reply does not begin
with an interrogative.   The stress is on ἄρτι, coming at the
beginning of the sentence (cf. Rev. 12[10]).

ἄρτι πιστεύετε, " at this moment you believe." He had
just before recognised their belief as genuine, so far as it
went (v. 27; cf. 17[8]), and He does not question it now. But
He goes on to warn them that this faith will not keep them
faithful in the time of danger which is imminent.

To translate " Do ye now believe ? " is inconsistent with
what has gone before, and also with the position of ἄρτι in the
sentence.

For ἄρτι as compared with νῦν, see on 9[19].

32. For ἰδού, see on 4[35]; it has an adversative force: " At
this moment you believe, it is true, *but* an hour is imminent
when you will all abandon me."

ἔρχεται ὥρα, " an hour is coming." See on 4[23] and on vv. 2,
25. It is not ἡ ὥρα, which would indicate the inevitableness of
the predestined hour, and this thought is not prominent yet.

καὶ ἐλήλυθεν. The time for His arrest was at hand ; cf.
ἐλήλυθεν ἡ ὥρα (12[23]), and cf. 4[23], 5[25].

After καὶ the rec. text has νῦν (with NΘ), but om.
אABC*D*L.

ἔρχεται ὥρα καὶ ἐλήλυθεν ἵνα σκορπισθῆτε ἕκαστος εἰς τὰ ἴδια κἀμὲ
μόνον ἀφῆτε· καὶ οὐκ εἰμὶ μόνος, ὅτι ὁ Πατὴρ μετ᾽ ἐμοῦ ἐστίν.

33. Ταῦτα λελάληκα ὑμῖν ἵνα ἐν ἐμοὶ εἰρήνην ἔχητε. ἐν τῷ

ἵνα σκορπισθῆτε. The ἵνα marks the predestined sequence
of events. σκορπίζειν occurs again at 10¹², and we find
διασκορπίζειν at 11⁵².

The prophecy Zech. 13⁷, which (in the A text) runs as
follows, πατάξον τὸν ποιμένα καὶ διασκορπισθήσονται τὰ πρόβατα.
is cited as a prediction of the arrest of Jesus by Mk. 14²⁷
(followed by Mt. 26³¹), as well as by Barnabas (v. 12) and
Justin (*Tryph.* 53). Jn. does not mention Zechariah, but he
places in the mouth of Jesus a prediction which reproduces
the significant word σκορπισθῆτε.

Cf. the verbal parallel ἐσκορπίσθησαν ἕκαστος εἰς τὸν τόπον
αὐτοῦ (1 Macc. 6⁵⁴).

For εἰς τὰ ἴδια, " to his own home," see note on 19²⁷ below.
Cf. Appian, vi. 23 (quoted by Field), ἀπέλυε τοὺς αἰχμαλώτους
εἰς τὰ ἴδια.

κἀμὲ μόνον ἀφῆτε, "and shall leave me alone." This is the
only word of reproach, and it is softened by the next words,
" yet not alone, because, etc."

καί, " and yet." Jn. never uses καίτοι : see on 1¹⁰.

οὐκ εἰμὶ μόνος, ὅτι ὁ πατὴρ μετ᾽ ἐμοῦ ἐστίν. So Jesus had said
before, and in almost identical terms. See 8¹⁶· ²⁹ and the notes
there.

Jn. does not tell of the disciples' abandonment of Jesus after
His arrest, as in Mk. 14⁵⁰, except by implication (see on 18¹⁵).

*Jesus bids His disciples to be courageous, for He has overcome
the world (v. 33), in the Passion, which is His glorification
(XIII. 31ᵇ, 32)*

33. ταῦτα λελάληκα ὑμῖν : see on 15¹¹. Here ταῦτα seems
to refer to what has been said in v. 32 about the dispersion of
His disciples after their Master's arrest (cf. 16¹· ⁴).

The purpose of these instructions was ἵνα ἐν ἐμοὶ εἰρήνην
ἔχητε (see for εἰρήνη on 14²⁷). Peace can be found only in
Christ (cf. 15⁵⁻⁷); ἐν ἐμοί is in antithesis to ἐν τῷ κόσμῳ which
follows. For κόσμος, see on 1⁹; here it is "the world" which
"hates" Christ's disciples (cf. 15¹⁸), and in which therefore
"tribulation" must be their portion.

θλίψις occurs in Jn. only here and at v. 21; but cf. Rev.
1⁹ 2²² and Acts 14²², where Paul exhorts the disciples of Antioch
ὅτι διὰ πολλῶν θλίψεων δεῖ ἡμᾶς εἰσελθεῖν εἰς τὴν βασιλείαν τοῦ
θεοῦ.

κόσμῳ θλίψιν ἔχετε· ἀλλὰ θαρσεῖτε, ἐγὼ νενίκηκα τὸν κόσμον.
XIII. 31ᵇ. Νῦν ἐδοξάσθη ὁ Υἱὸς τοῦ ἀνθρώπου, καὶ ὁ Θεὸς ἐδοξάσθη

The rec. text (cf. v. 22) has ἕξετε with D 69, but the true
reading is ἔχετε, " ye are having tribulation "; their trial has
begun.

θαρσεῖν occurs only here in Jn. (cf. Mk. 6⁵⁰, Mt. 9². ²²); but
the same counsel in different words is given again 14¹· ²⁷.

ἐγώ is the ἐγώ of dignity (see Introd., p. cxvii).

νικᾶν is rare in the LXX except in the later books, and
in the N.T. except in the Apocalypse. It does not occur again
in the Fourth Gospel, but is found 6 times in 1 Jn. Sometimes
it is transitive, as here and at Lk. 11²², Rom. 12²¹, Rev. 11⁷ 12¹¹
13⁷ 17¹⁴, and 1 Jn. 2¹³· ¹⁴ 4⁴ 5⁴· ⁵; sometimes it is used absolutely,
as in Rev. 2⁷· ¹¹· ¹⁷· ²⁶ 3⁵· ¹²· ²¹ 5⁵ 6² 15² 21⁷. The verb is only
once used in the LXX of God as the Conqueror, sc. Ps. 51⁴
(quoted Rom. 3⁴), νικήσῃς ἐν τῷ κρίνεσθαι ; and in the N.T. it is
applied to the conquests of Christ only here and at Rev. 3²¹ 5⁵ 6²
17¹⁴. (Cf. 1 Esd. 3¹² ὑπὲρ δὲ πάντα νικᾷ ἡ ἀλήθεια.) In all the
passages of 1 Jn. where it appears, it is used of the spiritual
conquests of Christian believers. νικᾶν, then, is a favourite
word both with the author of the Fourth Gospel and the author
of the Apocalypse, both of whom apply it—alone among N.T.
writers—to the victory of Christ.

The phrase νικᾶν τὸν κόσμον is found only here and at
1 Jn. 5⁴· ⁵. Here the majestic announcement ἐγὼ νενίκηκα
τὸν κόσμον is placed in the mouth of Jesus, when His public
ministry had, to all seeming, ended in failure. In 1 Jn., the
apostle claims for himself and his fellow-believers that their
faith is " the victory which overcomes the world." The words
of Jn. 14¹² that they should do " greater things " than their
Master did, are coming within the range of their spiritual
understanding. ἐγὼ νενίκηκα τὸν κόσμον is thus a prophetic
word for those who are " in Christ."

XIII. 31ᵇ. νῦν ἐδοξάσθη ὁ υἱὸς τοῦ ἀνθρώπου κτλ. We now go
on with 13³¹ᶠ·.¹ The note of triumph in the words ἐγὼ
νενίκηκα τὸν κόσμον (16³³) is continued. νῦν, Now " has the
Son of Man been glorified."

The aorist ἐδοξάσθη challenges attention, for we should
expect the future tense, " Now shall the Son of Man be glorified." But it is a Hebrew usage to employ an aorist with
prophetic anticipation of the future. Thus to Abraham it was
said (Gen. 15¹⁸), " Unto thy seed have I given this land,"
where the LXX marks the meaning by the rendering δώσω.
And this way of speaking is specially appropriate when the

---

¹ See Introd., p. xx f.

ἐν αὐτῷ· 32. εἰ ὁ Θεὸς ἐδοξάσθη ἐν αὐτῷ, καὶ ὁ Θεὸς δοξάσει αὐτὸν
ἐν αὐτῷ, καὶ εὐθὺς δοξάσει αὐτόν.   33. τεκνία, ἔτι μικρὸν μεθ᾽ ὑμῶν

Speaker is Divine (which Jn. never allows his readers to forget
when he is recording the words of Jesus), and is One to whom
the inevitable future is involved in the present, and is foreseen.
See also, for this use of the aorist, on 12²³ 15⁸.

ὁ Θεὸς ἐδοξάσθη ἐν αὐτῷ. This is a different thought from
that expressed in the first clause of the verse. Not only was
Christ " glorified " in His Passion (see on 7³⁹), but God was
glorified thereby (cf. 12²⁸). Martyrdom is always a glorifying
of God, in whose name the martyr lays down his life. See 21¹⁹,
and the note there.[1] In other passages of the Gospel we have
the idea of the Father being glorified in Christ (e.g. 14¹³ 15⁸ 17⁴,
and cf. 1 Pet. 4¹¹) because of Christ's ministry and works; but
here the idea is confined to that " glorification " of God by
Christ's Passion, of which lower illustrations may be found in
every martyrdom.

32. The reading εἰ ὁ Θεὸς ἐδοξάσθη ἐν αὐτῷ at the beginning of the verse is supported by אᶜAC²ΓΘΔ, with many
MSS., including the Vulgate, which has " Nunc clarificatus est
filius hominis et Deus clarificatus est in eo. Si Deus clarificatus est in eo, et Deus clarificabit eum in semet ipso, etc."
This redundant style is characteristic of Jn., and the words
may stand part of the text. But they do not appear in
א*BC*DLW and the majority of the Old Latin vss. with
Syr. sin. Yet they might easily have dropped out by homoioteleuton (ἐν αὐτῷ . . . ἐν αὐτῷ).

καὶ ὁ Θεὸς δοξάσει αὐτὸν ἐν αὐτῷ (some texts have ἑαυτῷ),
" and God shall glorify Him in Himself." This goes beyond
the " glorification " of Christ *in* His Passion (v. 31); it is the
" glorification " which succeeded it, God the Father glorifying
Him in Himself, by taking up the humanity of Christ into the
Godhead, after the Passion. This great concepton appears
again and is more fully expressed at 17⁵. It is of this consummation that Peter said ὁ Θεὸς Ἀβραὰμ καὶ Ἰσαὰκ καὶ Ἰακὼβ
ἐδόξασεν τὸν παῖδα αὐτοῦ Ἰησοῦν (Acts 3¹³).

καὶ εὐθὺς δοξάσει αὐτόν, " and straightway He will glorify
Him." The time was near; the Passion would be short, for
it is to this thought of His impending Death that the Speaker
returns. For εὐθύς, see on 5⁹.

[1] In the Collect for Innocents' Day it is said that the infants were
made to " glorify " God by their deaths.

εἰμί· ζητήσετέ με, καὶ καθὼς εἶπον τοῖς Ἰουδαίοις ὅτι Ὅπου ἐγὼ ὑπάγω ὑμεῖς οὐ δύνασθε ἐλθεῖν, καὶ ὑμῖν λέγω ἄρτι.   34. ἐντολὴν

Jesus gives the New Commandment of brotherly love to those whom He leaves behind (vv. 33–35)

33. τεκνία. From the thought of what the Passion means for Him, Jesus turns to the thought of how it will affect His disciples when He is gone and they are like fatherless orphans (14¹⁸). So He addresses them tenderly, as the Head of His little family (τεκνία, "children "). τεκνίον is a Johannine word (1 Jn. 2¹· ¹²· ²⁸ 3⁷· ¹⁸ 4⁴ 5²¹, only again in N.T. at Gal. 4¹⁹; cf. τέκνα, Mk. 10²⁴).

ἔτι μικρὸν μεθ᾽ ὑμῶν εἰμί. The rec., with אLWT, adds χρόνον after μικρόν, this being a reminiscence of 7³³ (where see note). The verse reproduces the words of 7³³· ³⁴ and of 8²¹, the warning, which in those passages was addressed to unbelieving Jews, being repeated for the disciples, but not now in rebuke; and being followed in v. 36 by the consolatory promise that, although the disciples could not go where He was going immediately, yet they should follow afterwards. See on 7³⁴.

ζητήσετέ με. This would not be like the remorseful search which was in store for the unbelieving Jews (see on 7³⁴ 8²¹); but it would be a search in perplexity and tears, when their Master was taken fom them (cf. 14¹· ²).

καθὼς εἶπον τοῖς Ἰουδαίοις κτλ. It is not certain whether the reference is to 7³³· ³⁴ or to 8²¹. Jn. represents the warning to the Jews as having been given twice, and it may have been so.

ὅπου ἐγὼ ὑπάγω ὑμεῖς οὐ δύνασθε ἐλθεῖν. This is verbally identified with 8²¹. See the note on 7³⁴ for the meaning.

καὶ ὑμῖν λέγω ἄρτι, "so I tell *you* at this moment." ἄρτι is a favourite word with Jn. (see on 9¹⁹).

34. ἐντολὴν καινήν. For ἐντολή as a commandment given by Jesus, cf. 15¹⁰· ¹² 14¹⁵· ²¹, 1 Jn. 2³· ⁴ 3²⁴. He claimed to " give commandments," and so claimed to be equal with God. See on 14¹⁵.

Mandatum nouum do vobis. So the Latin vulgate renders, and hence Thursday before Easter has been commonly called *Maundy* (Mandati) *Thursday*, from the words of the Antiphon appointed for that day in the Latin rite.

The disciples had been disputing that evening about precedence (see on v. 4), and the " New Commandment " bade them " love one another." This ἐντολὴ καινή had been already mentioned (15¹², although it is not there called "new "). It is often mentioned in 1 Jn. (*e.g.* 2⁷⁻¹⁰ 3¹¹· ²³; cf. 2 Jn.⁵): " Love one another, as I have loved you." The Old Command-

καινὴν δίδωμι ὑμῖν, ἵνα ἀγαπᾶτε ἀλλήλους, καθὼς ἠγάπησα ὑμᾶς

ment was, "Thou shalt love thy neighbour as thyself" (Lev. 19[18]), and Jesus had explained the wide range of the term "neighbour" (Lk. 10[29. 36]); this was never superseded, and Paul notes its importance (Rom. 13[8], Col. 3[14]). But the New Commandment is narrower in range, and is inspired by a new motive. φιλαδελφία, "love of the brethren," is not so wide in its reference as ἀγάπη, but to cultivate it is a *new* commandment. A new circle, an inner circle, has been formed, and in this a special obligation is due from each to each (cf. Gal. 6[10]). Here is the test of true discipleship: "We know that we have passed out of death into life, because we love *the brethren*" (1 Jn. 3[14]). A later writer makes it clear that this is not the highest of Christian graces; to φιλαδελφία must be superadded ἀγάπη (2 Pet. 1[7]), the love which is like the Love of God in the catholicity of its range (see on 3[16]). But the idea that φιλαδελφία, the love of Christian disciple for Christian disciple, is a virtue at all was a new idea; and this grace is inspired by a new motive: "Love one another, *as I have loved you.*" The common love which Jesus has for His own binds them to each other.

The story preserved by Jerome (*ad Galat.* vi. 10), that John the son of Zebedee, in his old age, never ceased to repeat "Little children, love one another," as his most important counsel, shows how deeply the precept had impressed itself upon the first generation of Christians.

καθὼς ἠγάπησα ὑμᾶς. The idea of the love of Jesus for His own hardly needs references, but cf. Rom. 8[37], Rev. 1[5]. Observe that their love for each other is to be like His love for them, *sc.* it is to be a love which is ready to pour itself out in sacrifice (cf. 1 Jn. 3[16]).

The words of this verse are repeated from 15[12]. There may be a distant allusion to 13[1], where the love of Jesus for His disciples is specially mentioned; and to the incident of the Feet-washing, which was a remarkable illustration of it. As His love for the Twelve was exhibited by His ministrations to them, so ought the love of Christian for Christian to be exhibited by mutual service. Some expositors have found in the "New Commandment" a reference to the institution of the Eucharist, which is the sacrament of unity (cf. 1 Cor. 10[16. 17]). But, whatever allusion it may carry to the duty of ministering to each other, or to the sacrament by which Christians are united in communion with each other as well as with Christ, there can be no doubt that the primary and essential obligation of the ἐντολὴ καινή is brotherly love, and was so understood by Jn.

ἵνα καὶ ὑμεῖς ἀγαπᾶτε ἀλλήλους.   35. ἐν τούτῳ γνώσονται πάντες ὅτι ἐμοὶ μαθηταί ἐστε, ἐὰν ἀγάπην ἔχητε ἐν ἀλλήλοις.

36. Λέγει αὐτῷ Σίμων Πέτρος Κύριε, ποῦ ὑπάγεις; ἀπεκρίθη

That the verb φιλεῖν is never used in Jn. of man's love for man, but always ἀγαπᾶν (cf. 15¹². ¹⁷, 1 Jn. 2¹⁰ 3¹⁰. ¹⁴. ³³ 4⁷. ²⁰), does not justify us in distinguishing sharply between the meaning of the two verbs (see on 21¹⁶).

For the constr. in this verse, ἵνα . . . καθὼς . . ἵνα, see on 17².

35. ἐν τούτῳ γνώσονται κτλ.   This use of ἐν τούτῳ, followed by γινώσκομεν, is thoroughly Johannine; cf. 1 Jn. 2³ 3¹⁶. ¹⁹. ²⁴ 4¹³ 5². We have ἐν τούτῳ πιστεύομεν at 16³⁰. " In this " in such passages is equivalent to " by this." The causal or instrumental use of ἐν is illustrated from the papyri by Moulton-Milligan, and is not necessarily a Semitism, although its frequent employment in the Apocalypse points that way.[1]

γνώσονται πάντες κτλ., " all men (cf. ὁ κόσμος, 14³¹ 17²¹) shall know that ye are my disciples " (cf. 1 Jn. 3¹⁴). μαθητής is the highest title of a Christian: the apostles can aspire to nothing higher than ἐμοὶ μαθηταί implies (see on 15⁸).

The badge of discipleship was to be mutual love, and so it proved. Cf. Tertullian, *Apol.* 39, " Vide, inquiunt, ut inuicem se diligant."

Peter breaks in with a wish to follow Jesus even to death: he is warned that he will soon deny his Master (vv. 36-38)

36. The story of the warning to Peter, and the prediction that he would deny Jesus, are common to all four Gospels (cf. Mk. 14²⁷ᶠ·, Mt. 26³¹ᶠ·, Lk. 22³¹ᶠ·).   Mk., followed by Mt., says the warning was given after they had left the house and were on the way to Gethsemane.   Jn. agrees with Lk. in placing the incident in the upper room; but the narrative of Jn. connects it more closely with what went before, *sc.* the announcement of the approaching departure of Jesus, than does that of Lk.

λέγει αὐτῷ Σίμων Π.   As usual, Peter is the first with his question, and he fastens on what Jesus had said about His " going away," not only in its relation to Him, but in its relation to the disciples.   What is to happen to them ?   They had already found difficulty in the saying ὑπάγω πρὸς τὸν πατέρα (16¹⁷, where see note).

κύριε, ποῦ ὑπάγεις; *Domine, quo uadis?* words which

[1] See Charles, *Revelation*, 1. cxxx; cf. Abbott, *Diat.* 2332.

Ἰησοῦς "Οπου ὑπάγω οὐ δύνασαί μοι νῦν ἀκολουθῆσαι, ἀκολουθήσεις
δὲ ὕστερον. 37. λέγει αὐτῷ Πέτρος Κύριε, διὰ τί οὐ δύναμαί σοι
ἀκολουθῆσαι ἄρτι; τὴν ψυχήν μου ὑπὲρ σοῦ θήσω. 38. ἀποκρίνεται Ἰησοῦς Τὴν ψυχήν σου ὑπὲρ ἐμοῦ θήσεις; ἀμὴν ἀμὴν λέγω
σοι, οὐ μὴ ἀλέκτωρ φωνήσῃ ἕως οὗ ἀρνήσῃ με τρίς.

became very familiar from their use in the beautiful legend of
the death of Peter, found in *Acta Petri et Pauli*, § 82. See
on 14⁵.

For ὑπάγειν, see on 7³³; and cf. 16⁵.

ἀπεκρίθη Ἰησοῦς. So BC*L; the rec. has ἀπεκρίθη αὐτῷ
ὁ Ἰησοῦς. See on 1²⁶ and on 1⁵⁰.

ὅπου ὑπάγω. אD and *fam.* 13 ins. ἐγώ after ὅπου (as in
v. 33); om. ABCW⊕.

οὐ δύνασαί μοι κτλ., "thou canst not follow me now,"
sc. into the heavenly places; see on v. 33.

ἀκολουθήσεις δὲ ὕστερον, "thou shalt follow afterwards."
There is no reference, as it seems, to Peter's death by martyrdom (cf. 21¹⁹, 2 Pet. 1¹⁴); the promise is not confined to martyrs
(cf. 14². ³.).

37. διὰ τί οὐ δύναμαι κτλ. "Why can I not follow thee
this minute?" (ἄρτι, see on 9¹⁹). Peter had not yet realised
that the death of Jesus was near, and that it was this which
was in His mind; but even if to follow Him was dangerous, he
was confident that he would take all risks. Thomas had
expressed similar feelings (11¹⁶).

τὴν ψυχήν μου ὑπὲρ σοῦ θήσω. This willingness is the mark
of the Good Shepherd (10¹¹); it is the mark also of a true
disciple.

38. ἀποκρίνεται Ἰησοῦς. This is the true reading
(אABC*LW⊕), as against the rec. ἀπεκρίθη αὐτῷ ὁ Ἰησοῦς,
which would be the usual Johannine form. For the pres.
ἀποκρίνεται, see on 12²³; and for Ἰησοῦς without ὁ, see on 1²⁹· ⁵⁰.

τὴν ψυχήν σου κτλ. This repetition of the words used by
Peter is thoroughly Johannine; cf. 16¹⁶ᶠ· and 16³¹.

ἀμὴν ἀμὴν λέγω σοι. The prophetic warning to Peter is introduced in Mk. 14³⁰ by the same solemn ἀμὴν λέγω σοι. See on 1⁵¹.

οὐ μὴ ἀλέκτωρ φωνήσῃ ἕως οὗ ἀρνήσῃ με τρίς. This is almost
verbally identical with Lk. 22³⁴, where the word σήμερον is
added. Mk. (followed by Mt.) has "this night."

Mk.'s version of this warning is peculiar in that it runs "the
cock shall not crow *twice* (δίς, etc.); and, accordingly, a
second cock-crowing is narrated Mk. 14⁷². No other Gospel
has this, but it is found also in a Fayyûm papyrus fragment.[1]

[1] See Zahn, *Canon*, ii. 785; there is an English version of the fragment in James's *Apocryphal N.T.*, p. 25.

It seems to be an eccentric variant, rather than a relic of genuine tradition. At all events, Jn., who knew Mk.,[1] and who betrays knowledge of Mk.'s version of this warning by prefacing it with ἀμήν, does not accept it. His report of Jesus' prediction is simply that He told Peter that he would deny Him thrice before the cock crew. The fulfilment of the prediction is recorded in 18²⁷, where see the note.

φωνήσῃ. So אABW; the rec. has φωνήσει.

ἀρνήσῃ. So BDL; but אACWΓΔΘ give ἀπαρνήσῃ, which is perhaps due to a reminiscence of Mk. 14³⁰.

It is not recorded that Peter gave any reply to this prediction, which, introduced as it was by the solemn "Verily, verily," must have been a grievous blow to him. He does not appear again until 18¹⁵.

XIV. 1 ff. The opening verses of c. 14 are among the most familiar and the most precious in our Authorised Version of the Bible. It is an ungrateful task to disturb their beautiful cadences, charged with many memories, by offering a different rendering of the Greek text. But it must be attempted here, as at other points in the Fourth Gospel, if we are to express as nearly as we can the meaning of the evangelist's words. In v. 1, as will be seen, Tyndale's translation of 1534 has been preferred to the A.V. of 1611.

The promise of a future life, where the disciples would be with Jesus (XIV. 1–4)

1. D prefixes καὶ εἶπεν τοῖς μαθηταῖς αὐτοῦ, probably to soften the apparent abruptness of the words which follow. But no introduction is necessary; for there is an intimate connexion between 13³⁸ and 14¹. The warning to Peter that he would presently deny his Master must have shocked him, as it silenced him. He is not among the disciples who ask questions as to the meaning of Jesus' sayings in c. 14, nor is he mentioned again until c. 18. But the other disciples, too, must have been startled and saddened by the thought that the foremost among them would fail in the hour of trial. If that were so, who among them could be confident of himself? Indeed, they had already been warned that their faith would not be strong enough to keep them at the side of Jesus when the dark hour of His arrest came (16³¹· ³²). But this renewed suggestion of the instability of their allegiance, superadded to the announcements that Jesus had made of His impending

[1] Cf. Introd., pp. xcvi ff.

XIV. 1. Μὴ ταρασσέσθω ὑμῶν ἡ καρδία· πιστεύετε εἰς τὸν Θεόν, καὶ εἰς ἐμὲ πιστεύετε. 2. ἐν τῇ οἰκίᾳ τοῦ Πατρός μου μοναὶ πολλαί εἰσιν·

departure from them ($16^{5\text{-}7}$ $13^{33.\ 36}$), and of the persecutions which were in store for them ($15^{18\text{-}21}$ 16^{33}), had filled them with deep sorrow. So He sought to reassure them with a new message of consolation, which taught them to look beyond this earthly life to the life after death.

μὴ ταρασσέσθω ὑμῶν ἡ καρδία. The human experience of a "troubled" spirit had been His, more than once, during the last weeks (cf. 11^{33} 12^{27} 13^{21}), and He knew how painful it was.

πιστεύετε εἰς τὸν θεόν, καὶ εἰς ἐμὲ πιστεύετε. These are probably both imperatives: "believe in God (cf. Mk. 11^{22}); in me also believe." Belief in God should, of itself, turn their thoughts to the security of the future life; and then, if they believed in Jesus, they would recall promises to them which He had made about this (see v. 3, with its two clauses).

Grammatically, πιστεύετε might be pres. indicative in either place or in both, and the familiar "Ye believe in God; believe also in me," gives a good sense. But it seems more natural to take πιστεύετε in the same way in the first clause as in the second.

The true source of consolation for a troubled spirit is faith in God (cf. Ps. 27^{13} 141^8 etc.), and in Jesus whom God sent (cf. Mk. 5^{36}). The disciples had already professed (16^{30}) their faith in Jesus, but He had warned them that it was not invincible (16^{31}).

For the constr. εἰς τινὰ πιστεύειν, never used by Jn. of faith in man, see on 1^{12}.

2. ἐν τῇ οἰκίᾳ τοῦ πατρός μου κτλ., i.e. heaven; cf. Philo, who speaks of the soul returning εἰς τὸν πατρῷον οἶκον (de somn. i. 43).

μοναὶ πολλαί. The idea that there are "many mansions" in heaven, corresponding to different degrees of human merit, may not have been entirely new in Jewish religion. In the Sclavonic *Book of the Secrets of Enoch* (lxi. 2) we find: "In the world to come . . . there are many mansions prepared for men : good for the good; evil for evil" (cf. *Ethiopic Enoch*, xxxix. 4 : "The mansions of the holy, and the resting-places of the righteous "). Charles dates the Sclavonic *Enoch* as between 1 and 50 A.D.; but we cannot be sure that it was known in Palestine during our Lord's ministry. Nor can we be sure that μοναί was the Greek behind the Sclavonic word which Charles translates "mansions." If it were, then μοναί meant "mansions" in the sense of "abodes," not of "stages," which are only halting-places.

μονή is found elsewhere in the Greek Bible only at v. 23 (where it must mean " permanent abode," not a mere passing stage) and 1 Macc. 7³⁸ (where again the idea of permanence is involved).   In Pausanias (x. 41) μονή is used in the sense of a *stopping-place*, a *station* on a journey; and this sense, if introduced into the present passage, suggests interesting speculations.

Thus Origen (*de Princip.* ii. xi. 6) says that departed saints first live in some place " on the earth, which Scripture calls Paradise," where they receive instruction.   If worthy, they quickly ascend to a place in the air and reach the kingdom, through *mansions*, " which the Greeks call *spheres*, but Scripture *heavens* "; following Jesus, who " passed through the heavens " (Heb. 4¹⁴).   Origen then quotes Jn. 14². ³, showing that he understood μοναί, as stations or halting-places on the journey to God.   His singular interpretation is not likely to be accepted, but his use of μονή is to be noted.

An earlier citation of Jn. 14² is to be found in a passage quoted by Irenæus (*adv. Hær.* v. xxxvi. 12) from the " Sayings of the Elders," which is probably an extract from Papias.[1] According to the Elders, some good men will be counted worthy of a διατρίβη in heaven; others will enjoy paradise; others " the city," the Saviour being seen of them all.   This, the Elders say, is what is meant by the distinction between the thirtyfold, sixtyfold, hundredfold harvests in the Parable of the Sower.   καὶ διὰ τοῦτο εἰρηκέναι τὸν κύριον, Ἐν τοῖς τοῦ πατρός μου μονὰς εἶναι πολλάς.   For all are of God, who gives to each his appropriate οἴκησις.   This is the *triclinium*, the couch for three, on which shall recline those who are called to the Marriage Feast.   This, the Elders said, is the *dispositio* of those who are saved, who advance by steps of this kind, through the Spirit to the Son, and through the Son to the Father.

The first part of this implies that the μοναί are the permanent abodes of the blessed, which vary in glory; but the last sentence suggests, on the contrary, that the μοναί are stages, and that a saint may pass from one to another.   The general patristic interpretation of μοναί is, however, " abiding-places "; not *mansiones*, which are like inns on a journey, but permanent habitations.

Clement of Alexandria often has the word μονή, and always with allusion to Jn. 14².   In *Strom.* vi. 14 he refers (as Papias does) to the thirtyfold, sixtyfold, hundredfold harvests, which he says hint at (αἰνίσσομαι) the three μοναί where the saints dwell according to their respective merits.   So, again, he says (*Strom.* iv. 6) that there are with the Lord καὶ μισθοὶ καὶ

[1] Cf. Lightfoot, *Supernatural Religion*, p. 194, and *Biblical Essays*, p. 68.

εἰ δὲ μή, εἶπον ἂν ὑμῖν ὅτι πορεύομαι ἑτοιμάσαι τόπον ὑμῖν; 3. καὶ

μοναὶ πλείονες κατὰ ἀναλογίαν βίων. Clement taught consistently that there were degrees of glory in the heavenly world. In *Strom.* vii. 14 he explains that the " other sheep not of this fold " (Jn. 10[16]) are deemed worthy of another fold and another μονή in proportion to their faith." Once more, in *Strom.* v. 1, he uses μονή for the dwelling-place of God, as distinct from τόπος, which is the locality where the μονή is situated.

These citations show that μοναί in v. 2 (as in v. 23 and 1 Macc. 7[38]) must mean "abodes" or permanent dwelling-places, not merely temporary stations on a journey. The idea conveyed by the saying "In my Father's house are many mansions " is that of a hospitable palace with many chambers, rather than of a journey with many stages.

οἰκία is hardly to be distinguished from οἶκος, except that οἰκία is the larger word, embracing the precincts of the house as well as the house itself. Cf. 8[35], 2 Cor. 5[1]; and see on 2[16]. For the significance of the full phrase " *My* Father," cf. 2[16] 5[17] and vv. 20–23.

In heaven there are "many mansions," *i.e.* there is room for all the faithful, although it is not said that they shall all be housed with equal dignity.

εἰ δὲ μή occurs again in Jn. at v. 23 only ; and then after an imperative. It seems here to mean " if it were not *so*," *i.e.* if the preceding statement were not true. Cf. Abbott, *Diat.* 2080.

ὅτι before πορεύομαι is omitted in the rec. text, with C[corr]ΝΓΔΘ *a e f q*. Accordingly the A.V. places a full stop after " told you," and proceeds with " I go to prepare a place for you," as a new sentence. But ὅτι must be retained with אABC*DLW, *b c ff*[2] syrr. and cop. vss. How to translate it is not obvious, for ὅτι may mean either *because* or *that*.

(*a*) The R.V. takes ὅτι as equivalent to *because*, with Meyer, Westcott, Godet, Swete, and others. " If it were not so, I would have told you, for (i.e. *because*) I go to prepare a place for you." It is difficult to accept the sequence of thought which this rendering involves, *sc.*: if there was *not* plenty of room, He would have told them this bad news, *because* He is going to prepare a place. But that He was going to prepare a place for them could not be a reason for telling them that there was not plenty of room. This translation, when analysed, is hardly intelligible.

(*b*) A second expedient is to treat εἰ δὲ μή, εἶπον ἂν ὑμῖν, as parenthetical, and to connect directly " In my Father's house are many mansions " with "because I go to prepare a place for you." But again the sequence fails, for we should rather

ἐὰν πορευθῶ καὶ ἑτοιμάσω τόπον ὑμῖν, πάλιν ἔρχομαι καὶ παραλήμ-

expect, " I go to prepare a place for you, *because* in my Father's house are many mansions."

(c) It is more natural to take ὅτι after εἶπον ἂν ὑμῖν as meaning *that*; *sc.*, it is what the grammarians call ὅτι *recitantis*, introducing the actual words that might have been spoken. Syr. sin takes it thus: " I should have said that I go." Then we render: " In my Father's house are many mansions. If it were not so, I would have told you that I am going to prepare a place for you." But the difficulty of this is that He *was* going to prepare a place for them, as v. 3 implies. Origen took the verse thus, assuming that ὅτι is *recitantis*, although he notices the contradiction with v. 3.[1]

(d) The remaining alternative is to take εἶπον ἂν ὑμῖν ὅτι κτλ. as *interrogative*: " If there were not many mansions, would I have said to you that I go to prepare a place for you ? " There is only one difficulty about this rendering, *sc.* that hitherto there has been no record of Jesus having told His disciples that He was going to prepare a place for them. At 13³⁶ He had told Peter that he would follow Him later, and no doubt the other disciples expected that this promise was to be fulfilled in their case also. But the explicit words " I go to prepare a place for you " do not appear before this verse. Jn., however, more than once records references made by Jesus to former sayings of His which cannot be traced with certainty (see 6³⁶ 10²⁵ 11⁴⁰), so that there is no insuperable difficulty, on this head, of taking the sentence interrogatively. This rendering is adopted by Moffatt, Strachan, and W. Bauer.[2]

πορεύομαι. See on 16⁷ for this verb.

ἑτοιμάσαι τόπον ὑμῖν. This was one of the purposes of His impending departure. He was the πρόδρομος of all the faithful (Heb. 6²⁰). Jn. does not use ἑτοιμάζειν elsewhere, but the verb is used Mk. 10⁴⁰, Mt. 20²³, of the highest seats in the Messianic kindgom which have been " prepared " by God for those whom He has chosen (cf. Heb. 11¹⁶). In the present passage, ἑτοιμάζειν does not carry the idea of predestination; it is only " to make ready," as at Mk. 14¹⁶, Lk. 9⁵².

τόπος is used of a " place " in heaven, Rev. 12⁸; also in Clem. Rom. 5, where it is said of Peter ἐπορεύθη εἰς τὸν ὀφειλόμενον τόπον τῆς δόξης. In the *Revelation of Peter*, τόπος is similarly used; and also in the *Acts of Thomas*, c. 22.

3. καὶ ἐὰν πορευθῶ, repeated in substance from 16⁷.

[1] Cf. Origen's Comm. *in Joh*. (ed. Brooke, ii. 308).
[2] Cf. also Lowther Clarke, *Theology*, July 1924, p. 41 ; and Abbott, *Diat.* 2186.

ψομαι ὑμᾶς πρὸς ἐμαυτόν, ἵνα ὅπου εἰμὶ ἐγὼ καὶ ὑμεῖς ἦτε. 4. καὶ ὅπου ἐγὼ ὑπάγω οἴδατε, καὶ τὴν ὁδὸν οἴδατε.

τόπον ὑμῖν is the order of words in אBDLN ; but the rec. has ὑμῖν τόπον, with WΘ.

πάλιν ἔρχομαι. The present tense expresses the certainty of the future return: " I am coming back." This is an explicit announcement of the Parousia, or Second Advent. Not as much is said about this in Jn. as in the Synoptists ; but it is nevertheless an integral element in Johannine doctrine, more emphatic in the First Epistle than in the Gospel (cf. 21²². ²³ and 1 Jn. 2²⁸).[1]

καὶ παραλήμψομαι κτλ. Perhaps παραλαμβάνειν has here, as at 1¹¹, the meaning of receiving with *welcome* (cf. Cant. 8²); but at 19¹⁷ it is equivalent to " seize." For this meeting of Master and disciples, cf. 1 Thess. 4¹⁷.

ἵνα ὅπου εἰμὶ ἐγὼ καὶ ὑμεῖς ἦτε. This is, in a sense, true of earthly discipleship (12²⁶), but it is to be fulfilled more perfectly hereafter (17²⁴).

4. ὅπου ἐγὼ ὑπάγω οἴδατε τὴν ὁδόν is the reading of אBC*LW. But, as Field has pointed out, this is an ungrammatical construction. τὴν ὁδὸν ὅπου ὑπάγω is not good Greek, if it means τὴν ὁδὸν ἣν ὑπάγω. Furthermore, the comment of Thomas in v. 5 distinguishes clearly between the *goal* and the *way*, so that we should expect to find the same distinction inherent in the words of Jesus which drew it forth The rec. text is ὅπου ἐγὼ ὑπάγω οἴδατε, καὶ τὴν ὁδὸν οἴδατε. This is supported by AC³DNΓΔΘ with most cursives, and by the Syriac, Coptic, and O.L. vss. generally. If this were the original reading, we can see how easily the words οἴδατε καί might have dropped out, the eye being caught by the second οἴδατε. To claim that the uncials אB must outweigh the evidence of practically all the ancient versions, especially when they present an ungrammatical reading, is to claim too much for them. Accordingly, we follow the *textus receptus* here.

ὅπου ἐγὼ ὑπάγω οἴδατε. Peter had already shown that he, at any rate, did not know this, for he asked ποῦ ὑπάγεις; (13³⁶). But the disciples *ought* to have known, for Jesus had told them several times. He was going, He had said, πρὸς τὸν πέμψαντά με (7³³ 16⁵), or πρὸς τὸν πατέρα (16¹⁰. ²⁸), or to His Father's house (v. 2). The phrase ὑπάγω πρὸς τὸν πατέρα had already been the subject of perplexed comment by the disciples (16¹⁷). They had not understood *how* Jesus was to " go to the Father," but that this was the goal of the journey, of which He had spoken to them so often on this last night, He had

[1] See Introd., p. clviii f.

5. Λέγει αὐτῷ Θωμᾶς Κύριε, οὐκ οἴδαμεν ποῦ ὑπάγεις· πῶς οἴδαμεν

repeated again and again. And so He said now, " You know *where* I am going."

καὶ τὴν ὁδὸν οἴδατε. This too they should have understood. They did not yet know that for Him the Way to the Father was the Way of Death (see on 16⁵), for even yet they had not realised that He was soon about to die. They may not have understood that they, too, must die before they could inhabit the heavenly mansions where He was to prepare a place for them (v. 2). It is not clear that they had abandoned hopes of a Messianic kingdom shortly to be established on earth, in which high stations of honour should be theirs. τὴν ὁδὸν οἴδατε did not mean that they knew, or ought to have known, that the way to the Father was through death. But they ought to have " known " that the way to the Father's house was in fellowship with Jesus. This, in some measure, they must have realised at the end of their training; and so He reminds them that they " know the way," *sc.* they know that only in that fellowship with Him which Jn. calls " believing on Him " could the way to life be trodden.

The question of Thomas, and the answer to it (vv. 5-7)

5. Thomas now intervenes. Peter was the first to interrupt the great discourse by asking, " Whither goest thou ? " (see 13³⁶). Thomas presses the question, and urges that they could not be expected to know the answer. The Eleven had been perplexed when this " going " of Jesus to the Father had been mentioned at an earlier point in the discourse (16¹⁷), and their perplexities had not yet been removed. We have already had Thomas appearing as spokesman for the rest (11¹⁶), Peter perhaps being absent on that occasion. But Peter is silent now, although present, probably because of the severity of the rebuke and warning which he had just received (13³⁸). He would hardly venture again to interrupt Jesus by questions.

For κύριε, see on 1³⁸. Thomas declares that they do not know where Jesus was going, and that therefore they cannot be expected to know the way. Yet one may know the way without knowing exactly the goal of one's journey; and this is specially true of the Christian pilgrimage.

There are unimportant variants. אAC²ΝΓΔΘ, with most vss., have καί after ὑπάγεις, and this may be right; but BC*LW and Syr. sin. omit καί, the omission being characteristic of Jn.'s paratactic style. Again, for πῶς οἴδαμεν τὴν ὁδόν; (BC*D *a b c*), the rec., with AC²LNWΓΔΘ, has πῶς

τὴν ὁδόν; 6. λέγει αὐτῷ Ἰησοῦς Ἐγώ εἰμι ἡ ὁδὸς καὶ ἡ ἀλήθεια καὶ

δυνάμεθα τὴν ὁδὸν εἰδέναι; which looks like an explanatory correction of the shorter reading.

6. ℵC*L om. ὁ before Ἰησοῦς, but ins. ABC³DNWΘ.
See on 1²⁹.

ἐγώ εἰμι. On this majestic construction, see Introd.,
pp. cxvii–cxxi.

ἐγώ εἰμι ἡ ὁδός. This is the central thought here, the
words following, *sc.* καὶ ἡ ἀλήθεια καὶ ἡ ζωή, being not directly
involved in the context, but added to complete the great
declaration.

To walk in God's way has been the aspiration of pious men
of every race; and Israel was especially warned not to turn
aside from the ὁδός which God had commanded (Deut. 5³². ³³
31²⁹; cf. Isa. 30²¹ 35⁸). " Teach me Thy way " is the Psalmist's
prayer (Ps. 27¹¹; cf. Ps. 25⁴ 86¹¹). Philo, after his manner,
describes the " royal way " (ὁδός) as philosophy, and he says
that Scripture calls it the ῥῆμα and λόγος of God (*de post.
Caini*, 30), quoting Deut. 17¹¹. More apposite here, however,
is the declaration of the Epistle to the Hebrews that the way
to the holy place was not made plain before Christ (Heb. 9⁸),
who dedicated " a new and living way " through the veil of
His flesh (Heb. 10²⁰). This is the doctrine which becomes
explicit (cf. Eph. 2¹⁸) in the words " I am the Way." In the
Acts (9² 19⁹) the Christian profession is called " the Way,"
but this does not provide a true parallel to the present verse.
Again, in the second-century *Acts of John* (§ 95) there is a
Gnostic hymn ascribed to Christ which ends with ὁδός εἰμί
σοι προοδίτη, " A Way am I to thee, a wayfarer." This,
however, does not go as far as the claim involved in ἐγώ εἰμι
ἡ ὁδός. The uniqueness of Christ's claim in Jn. is that He is
the Way, *i.e.* the *only* Way, to God. This is the heart of the
Johannine message, which admits of no compromise with non-
Christian religions, and in fact takes no account of such. See
on 10⁹.

For ἀλήθεια in Jn., see on 1⁴¹. Both the exclusiveness
and the inclusiveness (cf. Col. 2³) of the claim ἐγώ εἰμι . . .
ἡ ἀλήθεια are thoroughly Johannine. This is to say much more
than to admit, as the Pharisees did, that Jesus taught τὴν ὁδὸν
τοῦ θεοῦ ἐπ᾽ ἀληθείας (Mk. 12¹⁴, Mt. 22¹⁶, Lk. 20²¹).

The idea of Christ's teaching as *true* does not strictly come
into the argument or exposition here; and it would seem that
the juxtaposition of ἡ ὁδός and ἡ ἀλήθεια is due to a reminiscence of O.T. phraseology. Cf. " I have chosen the way of
truth " (Ps. 119³⁰); and see the same expression, ὁδὸς ἀληθείας,

ἡ ζωή· οὐδεὶς ἔρχεται πρὸς τὸν Πατέρα εἰ μὴ δι᾽ ἐμοῦ.   7. εἰ ἐγνώκειτέ

at Wisd. 5⁶, Tob. 1³ (cf. 2 Pet. 2²). More striking still is, "Teach me thy Way, O Lord; I will walk in thy Truth" (Ps. 86¹¹; cf. Ps. 26³), where the " Truth " is a synonym for the " Way." So, again, a Psalmist says that the ὁδοί of the Lord *are* mercy and *truth* (Ps. 25¹⁰). Perhaps the close association in O.T. phraseology between ἡ ὁδός and ἡ ἀλήθεια may account for the introduction of the word ἀλήθεια at this point.

καὶ ἡ ζωή. This is included in another of the great Similitudes, ἐγώ εἰμι ἡ ἀνάστασις καὶ ἡ ζωή (11²⁵). ζωή is one of the keywords of the Fourth Gospel : " in Him was life " is the explicit pronouncement of the Prologue (1⁴), and that men might have " life in His Name " was the purpose of the composition of the book (20³¹). Cf. Col. 3⁴. The declaration " I am the Life " could not be out of place at any point of the Gospel (cf. v. 19); but nevertheless it does not help the exposition at this point, where the thought is specially of Christ as the Way.

Here again we are reminded of the O.T. phrase " the way (or ' ways ') of life " (Prov. 6²³ 10¹⁷ 15²⁴): cf. ἐγνώρισάς μοι ὁδοὺς ζωῆς (Ps. 16¹¹). In Mt. 7¹⁴ the way that leads to life is described as straitened ; and in Heb. 10²⁰ we hear of the " living way " (ὁδὸς ζῶσα) which Jesus dedicated. The thought of Jesus as the Way would naturally be associated with the thought of Him as the Life. Cf. also Heb. 7²⁵.

Lightfoot (*Hor. Hebr.*) suggests that the idiom here is Hebrew, *the Way and the Truth and the Life* meaning *the True and Living Way.* (He compares Jer. 29¹¹, where the Hebrew " a latter end and hope " means " a hoped-for latter end.") This at any rate brings out the point, that the emphasis is on *the Way*, as the concluding words, " No one comes to the Father but *through me,*" show. To claim to be not only *a* way to God, but *the only Way*, is in effect to claim to be the Truth and the Life.

There is a curious Christian interpolation in the Vulgate text of Ecclus. 24²⁵, which is a paraphrase of this Similitude. Wisdom says of herself, " In me gratia omnis uiae et ueritatis, in me omnis spes uitae et uirtutis," where the triple alliteration, *Via, Veritas, Vita,* is reinforced by a fourth word, *Virtus.*

7. The verb contains a rebuke. The disciples ought to have known what was meant by going to " the Father." That they did not know the Father was due to the fact that they had not yet learnt to know the Son.

εἰ ἐγνώκειτέ με, καὶ τὸν πατέρα μου ἂν ᾔδειτε. Jesus had said the same thing to His Jewish critics (8¹⁹), in identical

με, καὶ τὸν Πατέρα μου ἂν ᾔδειτε. ἀπ' ἄρτι γινώσκετε αὐτὸν καὶ ἑωράκατε αὐτόν.

language, except that in the former passage we have εἰ ἐμὲ ᾔδειτε instead of εἰ ἐγνώκειτέ με. But we cannot distinguish οἶδα from γινώσκω in passages like this (see on 1²⁶ for the usage of these verbs).

For ἐγνώκειτε (ABCD²LNΘ) and ᾔδειτε (BC*L), אD* have ἐγνώκατε and γνώσεσθε, which would turn the rebuke into a promise. Syr. sin. gives, " If me ye have not known, my Father also will ye know ? " For ᾔδειτε the rec. substitutes ἐγνώκειτε (AC³D²NΓΔΘ), so that the same verb may appear in both clauses.

ἀπ' ἄρτι κτλ. So BC*L, omitting the prefatory καί : this would be consonant with Jn.'s paratactic style. But ins. אAC²DNΓΔΘ, a strong combination. If καί is retained, it stands for καίτοι, in accordance with a Johannine idiom (see on 3¹¹). In any case, there is a contrast between the rebuke in the first part of the verse and the assurance in the second part.

ἀπ' ἄρτι γινώσκετε αὐτὸν κτλ., " from now (see on 13¹⁹ for ἀπ' ἄρτι) you are beginning to know Him." This is the force of the present tense γινώσκετε, which א tries to emphasise by reading γνώσεσθε. The moment marked by ἀπ' ἄρτι is the moment of the Passion; cf. νῦν ἐδοξάσθη ὁ υἱὸς τοῦ ἀνθρώπου (13³¹), and see on 16⁵. The Revelation of the Father was not complete until Jesus had removed His visible presence. Only after that did His disciples begin to understand how much He had revealed of God's nature and purpose (cf. 17³). In the next generation, Jn. could say of his younger fellow-disciples ἐγνώκατε τὸν πατέρα (1 Jn. 2¹³). But during the earthly ministry of Jesus that claim could not have been made. (" No one knoweth (γινώσκει) who the Father is, save the Son, and he to whom the Son willeth to reveal Him " (Lk. 10²²; cf. Mt. 11²⁷, who substitutes ἐπιγινώσκει, signifying complete knowledge, for the simple γινώσκει).

καὶ ἑωράκατε αὐτόν. BC* omit αὐτόν (perhaps because of the difficulty of the phrase), but ins. אAC³DLNWΘ. The verb ὁρᾶν in the pres. and pft. tenses (see on 3³²; and cf. 1⁵¹) is generally, but not always, used in Jn. of seeing with the eyes of the body. θεὸν οὐδεὶς ἑώρακεν πώποτε (1¹⁸; cf. 5³⁷) is a general principle of Judaism: the only One of whom it could be said ἑώρακεν τὸν πατέρα is Jesus (6⁴⁶), and in that case the reference is to *spiritual* vision. But at v. 9 we have ὁ ἑωρακὼς ἐμὲ ἑώρακεν τὸν πατέρα, which is parallel to ὁ θεωρῶν ἐμὲ θεωρεῖ τὸν πέμψαντά με (12⁴⁵, where see note). In neither case can the verb for " seeing " be taken as representing physical vision,

8. Λέγει αὐτῷ Φίλιππος Κύριε, δεῖξον ἡμῖν τὸν Πατέρα, καὶ

for many of the opponents of Jesus who " saw " Him in the flesh did not thereby " see the Father." Accordingly θεωρῶν at 12⁴⁵ and ἑώρακεν in v. 9 must imply spiritual insight in some degree. Those who saw in the Works and Life of Christ something of His purpose and personality, thereby saw something of the nature of God who sent Him. Those who " saw and hated " Jesus, on the other hand, could be justly said to have " seen and hated " God the Father (15²⁴); the false impression which they acquired of Jesus, issuing in an equally false impression of God. Thus the strange statement, as it must have seemed, " You are beginning to know Him, and (indeed) *have seen* Him," must mean that while the disciples would begin henceforth consciously to appropriate the new revelation of God as He is, they had already (although unconsciously) " seen " the reflection of His mind and purpose in the life of Jesus, with whom they had long been in close intimacy.

Abbott (*Diat.* 2760–2764) suggests as possible another rendering (apparently favoured by Nonnus) of ἀπ' ἄρτι γινώσκετε αὐτὸν καὶ ἑωράκατε αὐτόν, which takes γινώσκετε as an imperative, " From henceforth begin to know Him, and (then) you have seen Him." But this makes ἑωράκατε αὐτόν even more difficult than it is when we take γινώσκετε as indicative, for with this rendering there can be no reference to " seeing " God in Jesus, visible in the flesh.

Philip asks to be shown the Father. The coinherence of the Father and the Son explained (vv. 8–14)

8. λέγει αὐτῷ Φίλιππος κτλ. For Philip, see on 1⁴³. This is the *third* interruption of the discourse by a disciple. Their intimacy with Jesus was such that they ventured, even at this solemn hour and while He was bidding them farewell, to ask questions at any point where they did not understand Him; always addressing Him with the Κύριε of respect (13³⁷ 14⁵· ²²). Philip goes beyond a mere question. His remark is rather an argumentative challenge: " Show us the Father, and it is enough for us."

ἀρκεῖν has occurred before at 6⁷; Moulton-Milligan illustrate (*s.v.*) the impersonal use of the verb, as here, from the papyri.

δεῖξον ἡμῖν τὸν πατέρα. Probably Philip wished for a theophany, such as that which Ex. 33¹⁸ᶠ· tells was granted to Moses when he prayed " Show me Thy glory." Judas the son of James had similar desires and perplexities (see v. 22).

ἀρκεῖ ἡμῖν. 9. λέγει αὐτῷ ὁ Ἰησοῦς Τοσοῦτον χρόνον μεθ' ὑμῶν εἰμὶ καὶ οὐκ ἔγνωκάς με, Φίλιππε; ὁ ἑωρακὼς ἐμὲ ἑώρακεν τὸν Πατέρα. πῶς σὺ λέγεις Δεῖξον ἡμῖν τὸν Πατέρα; 10. οὐ πιστεύεις ὅτι ἐγὼ ἐν τῷ Πατρὶ καὶ ὁ Πατὴρ ἐν ἐμοί ἐστιν; τὰ ῥήματα ἃ ἐγὼ λέγω ὑμῖν

9. τοσοῦτον χρόνον. So ΑΒΝΓΔΘ, but אDLW have the dative τοσούτῳ χρόνῳ.

There is something of pathos in the reproach, " Have I been so long with you all (μεθ' ὑμῶν), and hast thou not learnt to know me, Philip ? " the personal name (cf. 20¹⁶ 21¹⁵) suggesting affectionate regard. The sheep know (γινώσκουσιν) their shepherd (10¹⁴), and Philip ought to have " known " Jesus by this time. But to fail to see God in Jesus was to fail to know Jesus.

ὁ ἑωρακὼς ἐμὲ ἑώρακεν τὸν πατέρα. See on v. 7 above ; and cf. Col. 1¹⁵, Heb. 1³.

After πατέρα, the rec. ins. καί with ΑDLΝΓΔΘ, but om. אB.

πῶς σὺ λέγεις κτλ., " how is that *you* say, etc.," σύ being emphatic, "*you* who have followed me from the beginning " (1⁴³ᶠ·).

10. οὐ πιστεύεις κτλ. This was to expect a greater faith than He asked of the blind man (9³⁵), or even of Martha (11²⁷). Jesus expected of the Eleven, who had enjoyed a longer and more intimate association with Him than others, that they should appreciate in some measure the deeper secrets of His being. The " evolution " of faith is always towards a larger faith.

ὅτι ἐγὼ ἐν τῷ πατρί κτλ. Here is the mystery of that oneness with the Father which is always prominent in Jn. Jesus had held this Divine coinherence up to the Jews as a belief which they might ultimately recognise as true (10³⁸), but He did not reproach them for not having reached it yet. Philip was in a different position, and ought to have learnt something of it before now. The two lines of testimony to which Jesus appeals in support of His claim to reciprocal communion with the Father, here as elsewhere, are His *words* and His *works*. See on 10³⁸, where the argument is almost identical with that of vv. 10, 11, and expressed in the same terms.

τὰ ῥήματα. See on 3³⁴ for the " words " of Jesus as divine.

τὰ ῥήματα ἃ ἐγὼ λέγω ὑμῖν. The rec., with אΑΓΔΘ, has λαλῶ from the next clause, but B²LN have λέγω (which has been omitted in B* through misreading ἐγὼ λέγω). λέγω is often used in Jn. interchangeably with λαλῶ, as here. See on 3¹¹.

ἀπ᾽ ἐμαυτοῦ οὐ λαλῶ· ὁ δὲ Πατὴρ ὁ ἐν ἐμοὶ μένων ποιεῖ τὰ ἔργα αὐτοῦ.
11. πιστεύετέ μοι ὅτι ἐγὼ ἐν τῷ Πατρὶ καὶ ὁ Πατὴρ ἐν ἐμοί· εἰ δὲ
μή, διὰ τὰ ἔργα αὐτὰ πιστεύετέ μοι. 12. ἀμὴν ἀμὴν λέγω ὑμῖν,
ὁ πιστεύων εἰς ἐμὲ τὰ ἔργα ἃ ἐγὼ ποιῶ κἀκεῖνος ποιήσει, καὶ μείζονα

ἀπ᾽ ἐμαυτοῦ οὐ λαλῶ. This He had said several times. See
the references given in the note on 7¹⁷.

ὁ δὲ πατὴρ ὁ ἐν ἐμοὶ μένων. The second ὁ is omitted in BL,
but is preserved in ℵADNWΘ.

ποιεῖ τὰ ἔργα αὐτοῦ. So ℵBD; but the rec., with ΑΓΔΘ,
has αὐτὸς ποιεῖ τὰ ἔργα, a correction due to the tendency to
describe the miracles as Christ's rather than as the Father's.
But to distinguish thus is contrary to Johannine teaching.
See especially on 5¹⁹. The ἔργα of Jesus are also the ἔργα of
God the Father.

In this verse the *words* of Jesus are treated as among his
works. Both are, as it were, the λαλία of the Father. But
they may be considered separately, His words appealing more
directly to the conscience and spiritual insight of His hearers,
His works appealing rather to their intellect, as indicative of
His superhuman personality.

11. πιστεύετέ μοι. The plural shows that Jesus now
addresses Himself not to Philip individually, but to the disciples
collectively, whose spokesman for the moment Philip was.
" Believe me," *sc.* believe my words when I tell you that I am
in the Father and the Father in me (repeated in identical terms
from v. 10). He does not say " Believe *in* me " here. He
merely appeals (as at 5⁴⁷ 10³⁸) to the testimony of His own
sayings, as worthy of credit (cf. 4²¹).

εἰ δὲ μή, διὰ τὰ ἔργα αὐτὰ πιστεύετέ μοι. This is the
appeal to His miraculous *works* (cf. 3² 5³⁶ 10³⁷) in support of
His great claim of unity with the Father. The faith which is
generated by an appeal like this is not the highest type of faith,
but it is not despised by Jesus. Better to believe because of
miracles than not to believe at all. See on 6³⁶ 10³⁸; and cf.
2²³ 3² 4⁴⁸.

The concluding μοι is omitted after πιστεύετε by ℵDLW,
but ins. ΑΒΓΔΘ.

12. ἀμὴν ἀμὴν λέγω ὑμῖν, the customary prelude to a solemn
and unexpected saying. See on 1⁵¹.

He had appealed to His ἔργα. He now assures His hearers
that the Christian believer shall be endued with power to do
the like or even greater things, and in particular that he shall
have the secret of efficacious prayer (vv. 13, 14).

ὁ πιστεύων εἰς ἐμέ. This He had bidden them all to do
(v. 1), and He returns to the phrase, which involves more than

τούτων ποιήσει, ὅτι ἐγὼ πρὸς τὸν Πατέρα πορεύομαι· 13. καὶ ὅ τι ἂν

πιστεύετέ μοι of v. 11 (see on 1¹²). But, as Bengel says, " qui Christo de se loquenti credit, in Christum credit."

τὰ ἔργα ἃ ἐγὼ ποιῶ κἀκεῖνος ποιήσει. He had already given such power to the Twelve (Mk. 6⁷· ¹³), and in [Mk.] 16¹⁷ it is recorded that He renewed this assurance after His Resurrection.

καὶ μείζονα τούτων, " greater things," not necessarily more extraordinary " miracles," to the eye of the unspiritual observer. These works of wonder, healing the blind and the sick, etc., were not reckoned by Jesus among His own "greater " works (see on 5²⁰). The " greater things " which the apostles were to achieve, were the far-reaching spiritual effects which their preaching was to bring about. The teaching of the Incarnate Son was confined to one country, and while He was in the flesh His adherents were few. But His Church made conquest of the nations of the world.

ὅτι ἐγὼ πρὸς τὸν πατέρα πορεύομαι. His departure from their visible presence increased the apostles' spiritual power (see on 16⁷ above). As He goes on to explain (vv. 13, 14), their spiritual effectiveness in prayer will be increased beyond all limits hitherto presupposed, for their prayers will be offered " in His Name."

For πρὸς τὸν πατέρα πορεύομαι, cf. v. 28 ; and see on 16²⁸.

13. καὶ ὅ τι ἂν αἰτήσητε κτλ. " And " (further, in addition to the promise of v. 12, and following from it) "whatsoever ye shall ask in my Name, I will do it." See on 15¹⁶ for this great promise, here repeated for the fifth time.

It is not said here to whom the prayer is addressed, but we should probably understand τὸν πατέρα as at 15¹⁶ 16²³. Jesus is the Way (v. 6), and while prayers are naturally addressed to the Father, they are addressed through Jesus, " in the Name of " Jesus.

There is, however, an advance here on the teaching of 15¹⁶ 16²³. In the former passages it is the Father who answers prayer, who gives what the faithful petitioner asks; but here and at v. 14 it is the Son who is to grant the boon, ποιήσω being twice repeated. For, in the teaching of Jesus as presented in Jn., what the Father does, the Son does (cf. 10³⁰). Swete's paraphrase is thoroughly Johannine. " We pray to the Father in Christ's Name; we receive the answer from the Father. Yet we receive it through the Son and by the action of the Son." The difference between δώσει, " He will give," of 16²³, and ποιήσω, " I will do," of 14¹³ is the difference between the Jewish and the Christian doctrine of prayer.

αἰτήσητε ἐν τῷ ὀνόματί μου, τοῦτο ποιήσω, ἵνα δοξασθῇ ὁ Πατὴρ ἐν τῷ Υἱῷ. 14. ἐάν τι αἰτήσητε ἐν τῷ ὀνόματί μου, ἐγὼ ποιήσω.

ἵνα δοξασθῇ ὁ πατὴρ ἐν τῷ υἱῷ. This is only verbally similar to 13³¹, where see note. All that is done by Christ in His heavenly ministry is a " glorification " of the Father, a revelation to men of His power and compassion. This is the final cause of Christ's work.

For the absolute use of υἱός in Jn., see on 3³⁵.

14. This verse is wholly omitted in two minor uncials, as well as in 1, 22, *b*, *ful*, the Sinai Syriac, and Nonnus—a strong and unusual combination. The omission may be due to homoioteleuton, v. 14 being repeated from v. 13. ABL and *fam.* 13, indeed, repeat τοῦτο ποιήσω from v. 13, but אDWΘ in v. 14 replace τοῦτο by ἐγώ. So ADL follow v. 13 in reading αἰτήσητε ἐν κτλ, but אBWΓΔΘ have αἰτήσητέ με ἐν κτλ.

If the verse is to be retained, it must be taken as a repetition in slightly different terms of what has been said already: a construction which is quite in the style of Jn.[1] ἐγώ clearly lays special emphasis on Jesus being Himself the answerer of the prayer: "*I* will see that it is done."

But the insertion of με after αἰτήσητε, which the best MSS support, involves the harsh and unexampled phrase, " If ye shall ask *me* in *my* Name." No doubt, it may be urged that the man who is *in* Christ alone can offer petitions *to* Christ which are certain of acceptance. He whose will is in harmony with Christ's will, and who therefore can truly pray " in His Name," may be assured that Christ will perform what he asks. Yet the expression " ask me in my Name " is awkward, and does not occur elsewhere, the other passages in these discourses in which prayers in the Name of Christ are recommended explicitly mentioning the Father as Him to whom these prayers should be addressed (cf. 15¹⁶ 16²³·²⁴). The Johannine teaching would not indeed stumble at the addressing of prayer to Christ. He who prays to the Father, prays to the Son, so intimate is their ineffable union (cf. 10³⁰); but, nevertheless, no explicit mention of prayer to the Son is found elsewhere in Jn., unless 16²³ (where see note) is an exception.

We conclude that με must be rejected here,[2] despite its strong MS. support; and we read ἐάν τι αἰτήσητε ἐν τῷ ὀνόματί μου, ἐγὼ ποιήσω, the thought being carried on from the previous verse, a special emphasis being laid upon ἐγώ.

[1] See on 3¹⁴.   [2] Blass omits με.

15. Ἐὰν ἀγαπᾶτέ με, τὰς ἐντολὰς τὰς ἐμὰς τηρήσετε. 16. κἀγὼ
ἐρωτήσω τὸν Πατέρα καὶ ἄλλον Παράκλητον δώσει ὑμῖν ἵνα ᾖ μεθ'
ὑμῶν εἰς τὸν αἰῶνα, 17. τὸ Πνεῦμα τῆς ἀληθείας, ὃ ὁ κόσμος οὐ

*Love issuing in obedience will be followed by the gift of the
Paraclete, revealing the union of the Father and the Son
(vv. 15-20)*

15. ἐὰν ἀγαπᾶτέ με, τὰς ἐντολὰς τὰς ἐμὰς τηρήσετε (so אBL,
which is to be preferred to τηρήσατε of ADΘ and the rec.
text), "if you love me, you will keep my commandments,"
as it is said again (v. 23), ἐάν τις ἀγαπᾷ με, τὸν λόγον μου τηρήσει.
Love issues in obedience. The converse, "he who keeps my
commandments loves me," is found at v. 21 (the love then
fulfilling itself in knowledge, 1 Jn. 2³). For the verb ἀγαπᾶν,
as used in Jn. of the love of His disciples for Jesus, see
on 3¹⁶.

The phrase τηρεῖν τὰς ἐντολάς is thoroughly Johannine
(cf. 15¹⁰, 1 Jn. 2³·⁴ 3²²·²⁴ 5²·³). It is the phrase used for
"keeping" the Ten Commandments (cf. Mt. 19¹⁷, 1 Cor. 7¹⁹);
and that the precept "keep *my* commandments" should be
placed in the mouth of Jesus is significant of His claim to be
equal with God (cf. 13³⁴).

In Jn. τηρεῖν τὰς ἐντολάς μου is used interchangeably with
τηρεῖν τὸν λόγον μου (8⁵¹ 14²³·²⁴ 15²⁰, 1 Jn. 2⁵).

16. κἀγὼ ἐρωτήσω τὸν πατέρα. See on 11²² 16²³·²⁶ on
ἐρωτᾶν as the verb used of the prayers of Jesus Himself; cf. 17⁹.

καὶ ἄλλον παράκλητον δώσει ὑμῖν. The Sinai Syriac renders
"He will give you Another, the Paraclete"; but the more
natural rendering is "He will give you another Paraclete,"
sc. another besides myself. Jesus does not directly call
Himself a "Paraclete," nor is the term applied to Him anywhere in the Gospels (cf. 1 Jn. 2¹); but He has just spoken of
Himself (vv. 13, 14) as discharging in the future the functions of
a παράκλητος, or a Helper and Friend at the court of heaven,
in that it is He who will cause to be fulfilled the prayers which
are addressed to the Father. For παράκλητος see on 15²⁶.

ἵνα ᾖ μεθ' ὑμῶν. The rec. text (with ADΓΔΘ) has μένῃ for
ᾖ (perhaps from v. 17).

εἰς τὸν αἰῶνα. Jesus had been with them as Helper and
Friend on earth only for a short time, but the "other Paraclete"
would be in fellowship with them "for ever," *i.e.* until the
end of the present dispensation (cf. Mt. 28²⁰). See on 4¹⁴ for
εἰς τὸν αἰῶνα, which is generally used as including eternity.

17. For τὸ πν. τῆς ἀληθείας, see on 15²⁶.
With the sharp contrast between the "world" and

δύναται λαβεῖν, ὅτι οὐ θεωρεῖ αὐτὸ οὐδὲ γινώσκει· ὑμεῖς γινώσκετε αὐτό, ὅτι παρ' ὑμῖν μένει καὶ ἐν ὑμῖν ἐστίν. 18. οὐκ ἀφήσω ὑμᾶς ὀρφανούς, ἔρχομαι πρὸς ὑμᾶς. 19. ἔτι μικρὸν καὶ ὁ κόσμος

the "disciples" in regard to their faculty of spiritual perception, cf. 1 Cor. 2¹⁴.

ὃ ὁ κόσμος οὐ δύναται λαβεῖν. It could not have been said to the "world," λάβετε πνεῦμα ἅγιον (20²²). That gift could be received only by spiritually minded men.

ὅτι οὐ θεωρεῖ αὐτό. θεωρεῖν (see on 2²³) is generally used in Jn. of bodily vision, but sometimes (as at 6⁴⁰ 12⁴⁵) of mental and spiritual appreciation. The analogy of v. 19 would suggest that bodily vision is intended here, as there. The only kind of vision that the "world" has is physical, and with this the Spirit cannot be perceived. Observe that it is not said that the disciples could thus (θεωροῦσι) behold the Spirit.

οὐδὲ γινώσκει. So it is said in the Prologue (1¹⁰), ὁ κόσμος αὐτὸν οὐκ ἔγνω. The world did not recognise Jesus as the Word: nor does it recognise the Spirit.

ὑμεῖς γινώσκετε αὐτό. Disciples are not "of the world" (15¹⁹): they can, and will, recognise the workings of the Spirit, as they have in some measure recognised Christ for what He was (cf. v. 9).

ὅτι παρ' ὑμῖν μένει, "because He abides with you," καὶ ἐν ὑμῖν ἐστίν, "and is in you," the present tenses being used proleptically of the future. The rec. has ἔσται (with אAD²L⊖), which is a correction of the better reading ἐστίν (BD*W).

First it is said that the Spirit of Truth abides μετὰ ὑμῶν, then παρ' ὑμῖν, and finally ἐν ὑμῖν, the last phrase signifying the indwelling of the Spirit in the individual disciple (Rom. 8⁹, 1 Jn. 2²⁷, 2 Jn.²), while the other phrases (the former of which occurs also in 2 Jn.²) lay the emphasis on the fellowship of the Spirit with the disciples collectively, that is, with the Church (cf. ἡ κοινωνία τοῦ ἁγίου πνεύματος μετὰ πάντων ὑμῶν, 2 Cor. 13¹⁴).

18. οὐκ ἀφήσω ὑμᾶς ὀρφανούς. ὀρφανός occurs in the N.T. again only at Jas. 1²⁷, and there in its primary meaning of "fatherless." It has been thought that this is the idea here also; at 13³³ Jesus addressed his disciples as τεκνία, which suggests the relation of a father to his children. But, although ὀρφανός, both in the LXX and in classical literature, generally means "fatherless" in the most literal sense, it may be used of bereavement of any kind. ὀρφανῷ σὺ ἦσθα βοηθός (Ps. 10¹⁴) appears in Coverdale's Psalter as "Thou art the helper of the *friendless*," which brings out the sense well. Milligan (*Vocab.* s.v.) quotes a modern Greek song where *friendless* must be the meaning; and also Epictetus, III. xxiv. 14 for this more general

με οὐκέτι θεωρεῖ, ὑμεῖς δὲ θεωρεῖτέ με, ὅτι ἐγὼ ζῶ καὶ ὑμεῖς

sense. The rendering " comfortless " of the A.V. cannot be defended.

" I will not leave you friendless " means, then, " I will not leave you without a Helper and Friend (a παράκλητος), such as I have been."

ἔρχομαι πρὸς ὑμᾶς, " I am coming to you," *not*, as in v. 3, in the Parousia, but after His Resurrection, when the Spirit will be imparted (20²²). See on 16²³ for the Day of the Spirit's Advent.

19. ἔτι μικρὸν (see on 16¹⁶) καὶ ὁ κόσμος με οὐκέτι θεωρεῖ, " the world perceiveth me no longer," θεωρεῖν (see on 2²³) being used here of any kind of vision, for Jesus will have been removed from the world's sight after His Passion.

ὑμεῖς δὲ θεωρεῖτέ με, " but *you* perceive me," *sc.* with the spiritual perception which the disciples were to have of the Risen Lord. Jesus had indeed told them at an earlier point in this last discourse that, like the world, they would see Him no longer with the eyes of the body after His Passion: οὐκέτι θεωρεῖτέ με (16¹⁰). The assurance of the present verse is in verbal, although not real, contradiction with the former warning. He had led them on step by step, in the endeavour to make them understand that it was better for them that He should be removed from their bodily eyes (16⁷), and that He would be present with them spiritually. And, at last, He assures them—so intimate and vital will His presence be— " *you* shall perceive me " ὑμεῖς θεωρεῖτέ με, the present tense being used proleptically to mark the certainty of the future.

θεωρεῖν is the verb used of Mary's " seeing " the Risen Lord (20¹⁴), as it is used here of the disciples' " seeing " Him after His Passion, while such " seeing " would be impossible for the unbelieving world.

A comparison of 14¹⁹ with 16¹⁰ goes far to show that 16¹⁰ must be regarded as an earlier utterance than 14¹⁹. See Introd., p. xxi.

ὅτι ἐγὼ ζῶ καὶ ὑμεῖς ζήσετε. So BL, but ℵADΓΔΘ have ζήσεσθε. This had been said before (6⁵⁷, where see note), and the thought is present also in Paul (Rom. 5¹⁰, 1 Cor. 15²¹· ²², Gal. 2²⁰, Eph. 2⁵; cf. Rev. 20⁴). But the words " because I live, you also shall live," have here a direct connexion with the context. Jesus has just assured the disciples that they shall " see " Him in His Risen Life. But this would only be possible—for ordinary physical vision is not in question—for those who are in spiritual sympathy with Him, who are " in Him " and in whom He abides (v. 20), who share His Life.

ζήσετε. 20. ἐν ἐκείνῃ τῇ ἡμέρᾳ γνώσεσθε ὑμεῖς ὅτι ἐγὼ ἐν τῷ
Πατρί μου καὶ ὑμεῖς ἐν ἐμοὶ κἀγὼ ἐν ὑμῖν. 21. ὁ ἔχων τὰς ἐντολάς
μου καὶ τηρῶν αὐτάς, ἐκεῖνός ἐστιν ὁ ἀγαπῶν με· ὁ δὲ ἀγαπῶν με

And so He adds, " because I live, you also shall live "; not
ye *do* live (in the present), for He was not yet risen from the
dead, and His quickening power was not yet set free in those
who " believed on Him."

20. ἐν ἐκείνῃ τῇ ἡμέρᾳ, *i.e.* in the new Dispensation of
the Spirit, which will begin with the Resurrection. See on
16²³.

γνώσεσθε ὑμεῖς κτλ., "*you* will know " (ὑμεῖς being emphatic)
"that I am in my Father, etc." At v. 10 (where see note)
Jesus had indicated that the disciples ought to have reached
as far as *faith* in His ineffable union with the Father; but He
now promises that they shall *know* it, and recognise it as true,
when the illumination of the Spirit has been granted to their
minds.

καὶ ὑμεῖς ἐν ἐμοὶ κἀγὼ ἐν ὑμῖν. He had given this to them
as a precept of life (15⁴, where see note); but the assurance
that they might indeed reckon themselves as "in Him" could
not be complete until the realisation that they shared His Life
(v. 19) was confirmed by the Spirit's internal witness. This
assurance is the highest point in Christian experience. Cf.
17²¹· ²³· ²⁶ ; and see especially the note on 17¹⁸.

The loving disciple is loved by God, and to him Jesus will
manifest Himself (v. 21)

21. What has heretofore been said in terms primarily
applicable to the listening disciples is now said more generally.
The teaching of v. 21 is for all future believers. Not only for
the apostles, but for every disciple, the sequence of spiritual
experience is Obedience, Love, Life, Vision.

ἔχων τὰς ἐντολάς (the phrase does not occur again) is to
have them in one's heart, to *know* them and apprehend their
meaning; but τηρεῖν τὰς ἐντολάς is to *keep* them, which is a
harder thing. See on v. 15 above, where (as at v. 23) it is said
that love issues in obedience; here the point is, that obedience
is the proof of love.

ἐκεῖνος : *he* it is (and no other) who loves me.

ὁ δὲ ἀγαπῶν με ἀγαπηθήσεται ὑπὸ τοῦ πατρός μου. This has
been said before at 16²⁷, where φιλεῖν was used instead of
ἀγαπᾶν (but see on 21¹⁵), and where, in accordance with Jn.'s
usual style, the *active* voice (ὁ πατὴρ φιλεῖ ὑμᾶς) was preferred
to the passive. Abbott (*Diat.* 1885*j*) notes that in this verse

ἀγαπηθήσεται ὑπὸ τοῦ Πατρός μου, κἀγὼ ἀγαπήσω αὐτὸν καὶ ἐμφανίσω αὐτῷ ἐμαυτόν.

22. Λέγει αὐτῷ Ἰούδας, οὐχ ὁ Ἰσκαριώτης, Κύριε, καὶ τί γέγονεν ὅτι ἡμῖν μέλλεις ἐμφανίζειν σεαυτὸν καὶ οὐχὶ τῷ κόσμῳ; 23. ἀπε-

is the only instance in Jn. of ὑπό followed by a genitive of the agent.

κἀγὼ ἀγαπήσω αὐτόν. Cf. Prov. 8¹⁷.

καὶ ἐμφανίσω αὐτῷ ἐμαυτόν. ἐμφανίζειν (in Jn. only here and at v. 22) is used as in Ex. 33¹³· ¹⁸ of a special manifestation of the Divine; cf. also Wisd. 1² 17⁴, Mt. 27⁵³. The reference is to that fuller revelation of Christ which will be made through the Spirit's illumination: cf. 16¹⁴.

Jude asks why Jesus will not manifest Himself to the world ; no direct answer is given, the former teaching being repeated (vv. 22–24)

22. λέγει αὐτῷ Ἰούδας κτλ. This is the *fourth* interruption of the discourse by an apostle anxious to understand what was being said (cf. 13³⁷ 14⁵· ⁸); this time the speaker is Judas the son of James (Lk. 6¹⁶, Acts 1¹³, who is also called Thaddeus Mk. 3¹⁸, Mt. 10³; see on 2¹² above). Syr. sin. reads " Thomas" here for " Judas," and Syr. cur. has " Judas Thomas," which apparently was the personal name (Judas the Twin) of the doubting apostle. The Syriac vss. have confused the un-distinguished apostle, Judas the son of James, with the better known Judas Thomas.

οὐχ ὁ Ἰσκαριώτης. Judas Iscariot had left the company some time before (13³⁰), but Jn. is anxious that the name " Judas " shall not mislead. For " the Iscariot," the man of Kerioth, see on 6⁷¹.

καὶ τί γέγονεν κτλ., " What, then, has happened that, etc." For the initial καί, which is retained by ℵ, see on 9³⁶. It is omitted by ABDLΘ, but its omission is probably due to a mistaken correction of the text by scribes who did not under-stand the initial καί.

Jude catches at the word ἐμφανίζειν. This is what he has been waiting for. For this verb seemed to suggest (see Ex. 33¹³· ¹⁸) a visible manifestation of Jesus in glory, which had been the hope of the Twelve. They clung to the thought of a Messianic theophany which should convince the world. There was a truth behind this Jewish expectation, as Jesus had said on former occasions (5²⁷· ²⁸). But the promise to the faithful in these Last Discourses was not that of any speedy return of the Son of Man in the clouds, although it was mis-

κρίθη Ἰησοῦς καὶ εἶπεν αὐτῷ Ἐάν τις ἀγαπᾷ με, τὸν λόγον μου τηρήσει, καὶ ὁ Πατήρ μου ἀγαπήσει αὐτόν, καὶ πρὸς αὐτὸν ἐλευσόμεθα

interpreted thus by some. The ἐμφανισμός which Jesus promised was the illumination of the heart of the individual disciple: " I will manifest myself *to him*," not to the world. Judas is perplexed by such a limitation, as it seems to him, of the Messianic hope. What, then, about your manifestation of your glory to the world ? See on v. 8 for similar perplexity exhibited by his brother apostle Philip. Both of them desired the same kind of public vindication by Jesus of Himself as His incredulous " brethren " had demanded when they said φανέρωσον σεαυτὸν τῷ κόσμῳ (7⁴).

Such vindication, however, was not given. Even after He had risen, Jesus was not seen by those who hated Him or were sceptical as to His claims. ὁ θεὸς . . . ἔδωκεν αὐτὸν ἐμφανῆ γενέσθαι (Acts 10⁴⁰), not to everybody, but only to the select few. And the only answer that Jesus gives to Jude is to repeat the assurance that He will, in truth, manifest Himself to every loving and obedient disciple : a promise which points forward to the illumination which the Spirit is to give.

No direct answer is given as to the manifestation in glory of Jesus to the world at large. This is in complete correspondence with the habit of Jesus when problems were put to Him by questioners as to the destiny or the duty of other people. He rebuked Peter for asking about John's future career (21²²). " Are there few that be saved ? " another asked Him (Lk. 13²³). But His answer was to bid the man look to his own salvation: " Strive to enter in at the strait gate." And so here, it is said (in effect) to Jude: " If you love and obey me, I will come and abide with you; that is enough for you to know."

23. ἀπεκρ. Ἰησοῦς καὶ κτλ. The rec. inserts ὁ before Ἰησοῦς, but om. אABDLWΓΔΘ: see on 1²⁹.

ἐάν τις ἀγαπᾷ με κτλ. The answer of Jesus to Jude is indirect, and begins by repeating what He had said before v. 15 (cf. v. 21) as to the necessity of obedience for a true disciple.

τὸν λόγον μου τηρήσει. For τὰς ἐντολάς of v. 21, the specific commandments of Jesus, is substituted here τὸν λόγον, the message of Jesus as a whole. For the phrase τὸν λόγον τηρεῖν, see on 8⁵¹ 17⁶. Jn., as has been pointed out before, is fond of changing slightly the form of a great saying, when he repeats it (see on 3¹⁷).

καὶ ὁ πατήρ μου ἀγαπήσει αὐτόν. Cf. 17²³. This must be taken to mean something more than the fundamental Johannine doctrine that " God loved *the world* " (3¹⁶), although

καὶ μονὴν παρ' αὐτῷ ποιησόμεθα. 24. ὁ μὴ ἀγαπῶν με τοὺς λόγους μου οὐ τηρεῖ· καὶ ὁ λόγος ὃν ἀκούετε οὐκ ἔστιν ἐμὸς ἀλλὰ τοῦ πέμψαντός με Πατρός.

this tremendous fact is prior to, and at the root of, every special manifestation of God's love to individual disciples.

καὶ πρὸς αὐτὸν ἐλευσόμεθα. Here the singular ἔρχομαι πρὸς ὑμᾶς (v. 18) is replaced by the plural ἐλευσόμεθα, marking the claim of equality with the Father which is prominent throughout the Fourth Gospel. Cf. 10³⁰ ἕν ἐσμεν. In both passages the reference is to that Divine Advent in the disciple's heart which is mediated by the Spirit. Cf. Rev. 3²⁰ εἰσελεύσομαι πρὸς αὐτόν.

καὶ μονὴν παρ' αὐτῷ ποιησόμεθα. The Spirit παρ' ὑμῖν μένει (v. 17), and the same must be true of the Father and the Son. "In the coming of the Spirit, the Son too was to come; in the coming of the Son, also the Father." [1] In v. 2 (where see note) the μοναί where man shall dwell with God in the future are promised; here we have the promise of a greater thing, the dwelling of God with man in the present. The main thought associated with the sanctuary in the Pentateuch was that there Yahweh dwelt with His people (Ex. 25⁸ 29⁴⁵, Lev. 26¹¹· ¹²; cf. 2 Cor. 6¹⁶); but the indwelling promised here is associated with no special sanctuary or holy place. It is a Presence, real although invisible, in the disciple's heart (Mt. 28²⁰) : the peculiar benediction of the kingdom which does not come "by observation" (Lk. 17²⁰). So Jn. writes later of the disciple who "keeps His commandments," that Christ "abides in him," adding "this we know by the Spirit which He gave us" (1 Jn. 3²⁴; cf. 1 Jn. 4¹³).

ποιησόμεθα. So אBLW fam. 13; but AΘ have ποιήσομεν μονὴν ποιούμενος occurs in Thucydides (i. 131), the phrase being good classical Greek.

24. The implied argument of this verse is that the "world," which does not love Jesus and does not "keep His commandments," is spiritually incapable of apprehending such spiritual manifestations of God and Christ as those which have been promised to faithful disciples. Nothing is said of a manifestation in glory, such as that which Jude and his fellow-disciples longed to see (cf. v. 22).

ὁ μὴ ἀγαπῶν με κτλ., "he that does not love me" (sc. the world) "does not keep my sayings" (λόγοι as distinct from λόγος, His full message). λόγοι here is practically equivalent to ἐντολαί (v. 21).

καὶ ὁ λόγος ὃν ἀκούετε. καί is for καίτοι, in accordance with

[1] Gore, Bampton Lectures, p. 132.

25. Ταῦτα λελάληκα ὑμῖν παρ' ὑμῖν μένων· 26. ὁ δὲ Παράκλητος,
τὸ Πνεῦμα τὸ Ἅγιον ὃ πέμψει ὁ Πατὴρ ἐν τῷ ὀνόματί μου, ἐκεῖνος

Jn.'s usage (see on 3¹¹): "and yet, the word which ye
hear," *i.e.* which the world hears without understanding what
it implies. The phrase ἀκούειν τὸν λόγον τὸν ἐμόν has appeared
before at 8⁴³, where see note.

οὐκ ἔστιν ἐμός κτλ. Cf. 7¹⁶ ἡ ἐμὴ διδαχὴ οὐκ ἔστιν ἐμή, ἀλλὰ
τοῦ πέμψαντός με. See also 8²⁸ 12⁴⁹; and for the thought of
Christ being " sent " by God, see on 3¹⁷.

Parting words : a summary of the Last Discourse (vv. 25-31)

25. ταῦτα λελάληκα ὑμῖν. This is the seventh time that
this solemn refrain (see on 15¹¹) appears in the Last Discourse.
Here ταῦτα may embrace all that has been said throughout the
evening, and not only the sentences immediately preceding.
" These things have I spoken to you, while abiding with you,"
sc. in the flesh. But this temporary companionship in the
body is now to be replaced by a permanent spiritual abiding,
in the Person of the Paraclete.

26. This is the fifth (and last) time that the Paraclete ıs
mentioned (see on 15²⁶ for the meaning of the word). Here
ὁ παράκλητος is for the first time identified with τὸ πνεῦμα τὸ
ἅγιον, an august title familiar to every Jew (cf. Ps. 51¹¹, Isa.
63¹⁰). The complete title does not occur again in Jn. (but
cf. 20²²). We have it, however, in Mk. 3²⁹ 13¹¹, Mt. 12³²; cf.
Lk. 12¹⁰· ¹².

ὃ πέμψει. For ὅ, אᶜL have ὅν. The Old Syriac treats the
Spirit as feminine, but the Peshitta does not follow this Semitic
doctrine.

ὃ πέμψει ὁ πατήρ. This is the Lucan doctrine, that the
Father sends the Spirit (Lk. 24⁴⁹, Acts 2³³), and we have had it
already at v. 16; but at 15²⁶ 16⁷ the Spirit is sent by the Son
(see also 20²²). This is only an additional illustration of the
Johannine doctrine that what the Father does, the Son does
(see note on v. 13 above).

ἐν τῷ ὀνόματί μου. " In my stead " does not convey the
meaning adequately. At 5⁴³ Jesus said that He had come " in
the Name " of the Father, and at 10²⁵ that He wrought His
works in the same Name; the meaning in both cases (see notes
in loc.) being not only that He came as the Father's representative, but as One to whom " the Name," *i.e.* the providential power of the Father, had been given, and who was to
reveal the Father's character and purpose. So here it is said
that the Spirit will be sent " in the Name " of Christ, to explain

ὑμᾶς διδάξει πάντα καὶ ὑπομνήσει ὑμᾶς πάντα ἃ εἶπον ὑμῖν ἐγώ.

His mission and to reveal its consequences. As the Son was sent in the Name of the Father (5⁴³), so the Holy Spirit will be sent in future " in the Name " of the Son. This does not imply that the Holy Spirit was not operative before the Incarnation, but rather that after the Passion and Resurrection (see on 16²³; and cf. 7³⁹) He will come with the more effective quickening power of the new revelation of God in Christ.

ἐκεῖνος. It is He, the Spirit, whose twofold work is now described in relation primarily to the listening apostles, but probably what is said may apply in some measure to all Christian disciples of succeeding generations.

ὑμᾶς διδάξει πάντα. This has already been said at 16¹³ ὁδηγήσει ὑμᾶς εἰς πᾶσαν τὴν ἀλήθειαν. The two phrases are treated as identical at Ps. 25⁵: ὁδήγησόν με ἐπὶ τὴν ἀλήθειάν σου, καὶ δίδαξόν με. Cf. also Ps. 25⁹:

> ὁδηγήσει πραεῖς ἐν κρίσει,
> διδάξει πραεῖς ὁδοὺς αὐτοῦ.

See, for other apparent reminiscences of the Psalter, on 16¹³.

πάντα in this verse corresponds to εἰς πᾶσαν τὴν ἀλήθειαν of 16¹³, and stands in contrast to ταῦτα of v. 25, sc. the things that have already been taught by Jesus. For πάντα, cf. 1 Jn. 2²⁷ τὸ αὐτοῦ χρίσμα διδάσκει ὑμᾶς περὶ πάντων. The reference is only (see again on 16¹³) to religious doctrines (cf. 1 Cor. 2¹⁰ πνεῦμα πάντα ἐρευνᾷ, καὶ τὰ βάθη τοῦ θεοῦ), but of these Divine truths the Spirit is to teach new things as time goes on.

καὶ ὑπομνήσει ὑμᾶς πάντα ἃ εἶπον ὑμῖν. BL add ἐγώ after ὑμῖν, and this would bring out the emphasis well; but it is omitted by most authorities. " And He will bring to your remembrance all that I said to you," the aor. εἶπον indicating that the personal oral teaching of Jesus was ended. This is the second side of the work of the Spirit, who not only was to reveal what was new, but was to recall to the memory of the apostles the old truths that Jesus had taught. Cf. 2²² 12¹⁶, Acts 11¹⁶, for illustrations of the fact that after His Resurrection the apostles entered more fully into the meaning of His words than they had done at the time they were spoken. Here, however, the promise is that their memory of them shall be stimulated. Bengel says pregnantly, " Exemplum praebet haec ipsa homilia."

ὑπομνήσει ὑμᾶς πάντα. ὑπομιμνήσκειν does not occur again in Jn.; but cf. Lk. 22⁶¹, where Peter " remembered " the words of Jesus. There is a literary parallel (but no more) in *Jubilees*

27. Εἰρήνην ἀφίημι ὑμῖν, εἰρήνην τὴν ἐμὴν δίδωμι ὑμῖν· οὐ καθὼς ὁ κόσμος δίδωσιν ἐγὼ δίδωμι ὑμῖν. μὴ ταρασσέσθω ὑμῶν ἡ καρδία μηδὲ δειλιάτω. 28. ἠκούσατε ὅτι ἐγὼ εἶπον ὑμῖν Ὑπάγω καὶ ἔρχομαι

xxxii. 25, where God says to Jacob after his vision, "I will bring all things to thy remembrance."

27. εἰρήνη, i.e. שׁלום "peace," the ordinary salutation and the ordinary word of farewell in the East. The words παρ' ὑμῖν μένων in v. 25 are suggestive of His departure, and He is not forgetful of the parting word of peace. Except in salutations (20^19. 21. 26, 2 Jn.^3, 3 Jn.^14), εἰρήνη is used by Jn. only here and at 16^33; and in both cases it refers to the spiritual peace which Christ gives. Just as in the Priestly Blessing (Num. 6^26) the meaning of the familiar שׁלום is transfigured, "The Lord . . . give thee peace," so here εἰρήνην τὴν ἐμὴν δίδωμι ὑμῖν conveys more than the customary "Go in peace." The peace which Jesus bequeaths (ἀφίημι ὑμῖν) is His to give as a permanent possession (cf. 16^33), and is given, not by way of hope or assurance of good will only, as the world (i.e. the ordinary run of mankind; see on 1^9) gives it in fare-wells, but in the plenitude of Divine power. εἰρήνην δίδωμι ὑμῖν is no less absolute a gift than that other ζωὴν αἰώνιον δίδωμι αὐτοῖς (10^28).

It is noteworthy that in the Apocalypse εἰρήνη is used only of earthly peace (6^4; cf. 1^4), while in Jn. it is used only of spiritual peace. Paul has it in both senses, but more frequently in the latter (cf. Col. 3^15, 2 Thess. 3^16).

μὴ ταρασσέσθω ὑμῶν ἡ καρδία. This is repeated from v. 1 (see note on 3^17), and now is added μηδὲ δειλιάτω. This is the only occurrence of the verb δειλιᾶν in the N.T.; although we find δειλός (Mk. 4^40, Mt. 8^26, Rev. 21^8) and δειλία (2 Tim. 1^7). μηδὲ δειλία is the parting counsel of Moses (Deut. 31^8): so also μηδὲ δειλιάσῃς is the counsel of Joshua to his warriors (Josh. 10^25), as it was the word of Yahweh to him (Josh. 1^9 8^1). μηδὲ δειλιάτω, "let not your heart be dismayed," is, in like manner, the parting word of Christ. There is no place for cowards in the ranks of His army; and the seer of the Apocalypse ranks them with "the unbelieving . . . and murderers . . . and liars," who, in his vision, have their portion in hell (Rev. 21^8).

28. Jesus has told them that they must not be cowards; now He tells them that they must not be selfish. His departure means for Him the resumption of the Divine glory.

ἠκούσατε ὅτι ἐγὼ εἶπον ὑμῖν (sc. at vv. 2-4) Ὑπάγω (see for this verb on 7^33) καὶ ἔρχομαι πρὸς ὑμᾶς (vv. 3, 18). His departure is the condition of His return through the Spirit. This has

πρὸς ὑμᾶς. εἰ ἠγαπᾶτέ με, ἐχάρητε ἂν ὅτι πορεύομαι πρὸς τὸν Πατέρα, ὅτι ὁ Πατὴρ μείζων μού ἐστιν. 29. καὶ νῦν εἴρηκα ὑμῖν πρὶν γενέσθαι, ἵνα ὅταν γένηται πιστεύσητε. 30. οὐκέτι πολλὰ λαλήσω

all been said before. He now makes a new appeal to them, based on their love for Him.

εἰ ἠγαπᾶτέ με (see on 3¹⁶ for ἀγαπᾶν used of the love of His disciples for Jesus; and cf. v. 15 above), "if ye loved me." It is a tender, half-playful appeal. He does not really question their love for Him, but He reminds them of it.

ἐχάρητε ἄν (cf. 16²²), "you would have rejoiced."

ὅτι πορεύομαι πρὸς τὸν πατέρα (repeated from v. 12). His return to the Father is His elevation to His true glory. No precise distinction can be drawn between ὑπάγειν and πορεύεσθαι in such phrases (see on 16⁷).

The rec. inserts εἶπον after ὅτι, but om. ℵABDLΘ. Fam. 13 add μου after πατέρα.

ὅτι ὁ πατὴρ μείζων μού ἐστιν. To this sentence theologians devoted close attention in the fourth century, but it would be out of place in a commentary on the Fourth Gospel to review the Arian controversy. It suffices to note that the *filial* relationship, upon which so much stress is laid in Jn., implies of itself that the Son is from the Father, not the Father from the Son. There is no question here of theological subtleties about what a later age called the "subordination" of the Son, or of any distinction between His οὐσία and that of the Father. But, for Jn., the Father *sent* the Son (see on 3¹⁷), and *gave* Him all things (see on 3³⁵). Cf. Mk. 13³², Phil. 2⁶, 1 Cor. 15²⁷, for other phrases which suggest that ὁ πατὴρ μείζων μού ἐστιν is a necessary condition of the Incarnation. It is the same Person that says "I and my Father are one thing" (10³⁰), who speaks of Himself as "a man who hath told you the truth which I have heard from God" (8⁴⁰).[1] See on 5¹⁸. ³².

The rec. text has μου after πατήρ, with ℵ*D²ΓΔΘ; but om. ℵᶜᵃABD*L.

29. καὶ νῦν, "And now," *sc.* "to make an end" (cf. 17⁵, 1 Jn. 2²⁸, for καὶ νῦν used thus; and see on 11²²), "I have told you before it come to pass, that when it is come to pass ye may believe." See note on 13¹⁹.

πιστεύειν may be used here absolutely (see 1⁷); or the meaning may be governed by 13¹⁹, where the words are ἵνα πιστεύσητε . . . ὅτι ἐγώ εἰμι, "that I (am) He."

In vv. 26 ff., Jesus had told the disciples of His approaching departure, which as yet they had hardly brought themselves

[1] For the patristic comments on this text, see Westcott *in loc.*; and cf. Gore, *Dissertations*, p. 164 f.

μεθ᾽ ὑμῶν, ἔρχεται γὰρ ὁ τοῦ κόσμου ἄρχων, καὶ ἐν ἐμοὶ οὐκ ἔχει
οὐδέν. 31. ἀλλ᾽ ἵνα γνῷ ὁ κόσμος ὅτι ἀγαπῶ τὸν Πατέρα, καὶ καθὼς
ἐνετείλατό μοι ὁ Πατήρ, οὕτως ποιῶ. Ἐγείρεσθε, ἄγωμεν ἐντεῦθεν.

to believe, and of the coming of the Holy Spirit which would
ensue. The experience of this heavenly illumination would
convince them of His superhuman foreknowledge. Cf. 2²².

30. οὐκέτι πολλὰ λαλήσω μεθ᾽ ὑμῶν. If cc. 15 and 16 follow
c. 14, this is difficult to understand, for then sixty verses of
exhortation must be supposed to have been added before the
discourse came to an end. But, in our arrangement of the text,
the discourse has come to its conclusion. See Introd., p. xx.

ἔρχεται γὰρ ὁ τοῦ κόσμου ἄρχων. The rec. inserts τούτου
after κόσμου, as at 12³¹ 16¹¹, but אABDLX omit. For the
phrase "the prince of this world," see on 12³¹. It means
Satan, not merely Satan in the form of Judas (cf. 13²⁷), but
Satan himself, to meet whose last assault (cf. Lk. 4¹³ 22⁵³)
Jesus now prepared.

καὶ ἐν ἐμοὶ οὐκ ἔχει οὐδέν " and has nothing in me," *i.e.* has
no point in my personality on which he can fasten. Twice
in the last hours, Jesus said that He Himself was not "of
this world" (cf. 17¹¹ 18³⁶) ; and thus "the prince of this world"
had no power over Him. This was to claim in serene confidence
that He was sinless (cf. Heb. 4¹⁵). But, although thus superior
to the forces of evil, He must go to meet them in the agony of
conflict, for this was the predestined purpose of God.

31. ἀλλ᾽ ἵνα γνῷ ὁ κόσμος κτλ. We must supply something before ἵνα, "but *I do these things* that the world may
recognise" my love for, and obedience to, the Father. For
similar elliptical constructions with ἵνα, see 9³ 13¹⁸ 15²⁵, 1 Jn.
2¹⁹. Otherwise we are obliged to take the whole clause as
subordinate to "Arise, let us go hence," which is very harsh.
Whichever constr. is adopted, the meaning is the same. Jesus
assures His apostles once more that what He does at this
critical hour is done voluntarily and in obedience to the Divine
purpose. Having made this declaration, He offers His Prayer
(c. 17) before He leaves the house to face arrest and death.

ἵνα γνῷ ὁ κόσμος . . . cf. 17²³ for this ideal of the future;
and cf. 1 Cor. 1²¹ for the reality of the present.

ὅτι ἀγαπῶ τὸν πατέρα. This is the only place in the N.T.
where the "love" of the Son for the Father is mentioned
explicitly. The love of the Father for the Son is mentioned
often in Jn. (see on 3³⁵, where ἀγαπᾶν is the verb employed,
and 5²⁰, where we find φιλεῖν); but it is remarkable that Jn.
never again speaks of Jesus as "loving" God. See on 3¹⁶
for ἀγαπᾶν in Jn.

ἐνετείλατο. So אADΓΔΘ; but BL have ἐντολὴν δέδωκεν, from the parallel saying at 12⁴⁹, where see the exegetical note. For the obedience of Christ to the commandment of the Father, see 4³⁴ 8⁵⁵, and cf. Phil. 2⁸, Heb. 5⁸. This obedience was perfect throughout His life on earth, but here the allusion is rather to the last act of self-surrender in going to meet the Passion. Here is the last word of Jesus to the Eleven : " As the Father commanded me, so I do."

ἐγείρεσθε, ἄγωμεν. According to Mk. 14⁴², Mt. 26⁴⁶, these were the words with which Jesus summoned the sleeping disciples at Gethsemane, just before His arrest. Jn. adds ἐντεῦθεν, and puts the words in a slightly different context; *i.e.* they mark the conclusion of the Discourse in the Upper Room, which was followed by a short pause for prayer, the solemn prayer of c. 17 being said standing, before Jesus and His disciples left the house for Gethsemane and the arrest (18¹).

For those who accept the traditional order of chapters, the sharp finality of ἐγείρεσθε, ἄγωμεν ἐντεῦθεν is not easy of explanation. The allegory of the Vine (c. 15) comes in strangely after such words,[1] which must mark a break in, or the termination of, the Last Discourse of Jesus. Several exegetes suppose that, after He had said " Arise, let us go hence," Jesus and His eleven disciples left the house, the rest of the discourse being spoken as they were walking to Gethsemane. It is difficult to suppose that teaching so profound and so novel was given under such conditions, or that Jn. intends thus to represent the course of events. Westcott suggested that before the little party crossed the Kidron they halted for a time in the Temple precincts, where quiet opportunity could be found for the delivery of cc. 15, 16 and for the great prayer of c. 17. But there is no evidence for such an hypothesis. The simplicity of the exegesis which emerges from placing the text in the order that is here adopted is a strong argument in its favour.

ἄγωμεν, it may be noted, is used thrice in c. 11 of a going forth to meet death (see on 11⁷).

XVII. 1 ff. Of the Prayer of Jesus which is now recorded, it would be too much to suppose that we have the exact words, or even an exact translation of the Aramaic words which He used. We have not here a shorthand report, taken down at the time, but rather the substance of sacred intercessions preserved for half a century in the memory of a disciple. On the other hand, the occasion must have

---

[1] Cf. Introd., p. xxi.

been felt by all who were present to be specially momentous, and the words used of extraordinary significance. They would be remembered when other things were forgotten, as the Last Prayer of Jesus, said in the hearing of His disciples, when the Last Discourse was ended, before He went to meet the Cross. The topics upon which He dwelt—His coming glorification, His committal of His chosen friends to the compassionate protection of the Father while they were in the world with its trials, His intercession for those other disciples who were to receive the Gospel through the ministry of the Eleven, His prayer that the mutual love of Christian for Christian might at last convince the hostile world of the truth of His claims—these things could never pass from the memory of one who heard Him speak of them at the last. Phrase after phrase is repeated, and more than once, as is characteristic of the style of Jn.; but Jn. is drawing all the while upon the tenacious memory of an old man recalling the greatest days of his life. This, at any rate, seems more probable than the hypothesis that the Prayer is a free composition of the evangelist himself. To take such a view would be to ascribe the deepest thoughts in the Fourth Gospel to the disciple rather than to the Master. As Harnack says, the confidence with which Jn. makes Jesus address the Father, "Thou lovedst me before the foundation of the world" (v. 24), "is undoubtedly the direct reflection of the certainty with which Jesus Himself spoke." [1]

No other long prayer of Jesus is recorded. His habit of prayer at crises or great moments is often mentioned (Mk. 1^{35} 6^{46}, Lk. 3^{21} 5^{16} 6^{12} $9^{18. \, 28}$ 11^{1}), but these prayers were usually (as it seems) offered in private, and were overheard by none. Something, however, of His methods of prayer may be gathered from the Synoptists. Two, at any rate, of His ejaculations from the Cross were verses of the Psalms (Ps. 22^{1} 31^{5}), hallowed by long and venerable use. That they should come to His lips in the agony of death, shows that they were familiarly used by Him in life. Again, it was His habit to begin with the word "Father" (cf. Lk. 22^{42} $23^{34. \, 46}$, Mt. 11^{25}, and Jn. 11^{41} 12^{27}), as this great Prayer begins (17^{1}). He prayed, at the end at least, for His own needs, when distressed in spirit (Lk. 22^{43}, Jn. 12^{27}), and the prayer of c. 17 begins with intercession for Himself. He prayed for His disciples (Lk. 22^{32}), and He is represented as doing so in 17^{9-19}. The solemn note of thanksgiving at the beginning of His Prayer of Consecration ($17^{1. \, 2}$) has a parallel at Jn. 11^{41}, and also in Mt. $11^{25f.}$, a passage which recalls the manner of Jn. 17^{1-3} more than any other

[1] *What is Christianity ?*, Eng. Tr., p. 132.

XVII. 1. Ταῦτα ἐλάλησεν Ἰησοῦς, καὶ ἐπάρας τοὺς ὀφθαλμοὺς

passage in the Gospels: " I thank thee, O Father, Lord of heaven and earth, that Thou didst hide these things from the wise and understanding, and didst reveal them unto babes; yea, Father, for so it was well pleasing in Thy sight. All things have been delivered unto me of my Father, etc."

It has been pointed out [1] that several of the thoughts underlying the Lord's Prayer, which Jesus prescribed for the use of His disciples, appear also in the great Prayer of Intercession in c. 17. With the opening address, "Our Father," cf. 17[1. 5. 11. 21. 24. 25] where " Father " is used in the special and personal sense in which Jesus was accustomed to use it. " Hallowed be Thy *Name* " is recalled, vv. 6, 11, 12, 26. Perhaps " Thy kingdom come " is the form in which we may express something of what Christ expressed when He said " Glorify Thy Son " (vv. 1, 5). " As in heaven, so in earth," has echoes in vv. 4, 5. With " lead us not into temptation " cf. " I kept them . . . I guarded them " (v. 12). And " deliver us from evil " is almost verbally reproduced (v. 15).

None of these coincidences or parallels is likely to have been invented by one setting himself to compose a prayer for the lips of Christ on the eve of His Passion; but, when taken together, they show that the spirit which breathes throughout c. 17 is similar to that with which we have been made familiar when reading Jesus' words as recorded by the Synoptists and elsewhere in Jn.

The prayer of c. 17 falls naturally into three divisions. First, Jesus prays for Himself (vv. 1–8); then, for the eleven apostles, His intimate friends (vv. 9–19); and lastly, for the disciples of future generations, who were to be evangelised through the ministry begun by the apostles (vv. 20–26). That is, the prayer begins with what is immediate, intimate, and urgent, and only gradually passes into intercession for that which is distant and of universal import.

The prayer of Jesus for Himself, and His thanksgiving
(XVII. 1–8)

XVII. 1. ταῦτα ἐλάλησεν Ἰησοῦς, " these things said Jesus," viz. the discourse ending 14[31]. The rec. has ὁ before Ἰησ. but אBΘ om. See on 1[29].

καὶ ἐπάρας τοὺς ὀφθαλμούς κτλ. See on 11[41]. The rec. text has ἐπῆρε . . . καὶ εἶπε with AC[3]NΓΔ; but ἐπάρας . . . εἶπεν is found in אBC*DLWΘ

[1] See Chase, *The Lord's Prayer in the Early Church*, p. 111.

αὐτοῦ εἰς τὸν οὐρανὸν εἶπεν Πάτερ, ἐλήλυθεν ἡ ὥρα· δόξασόν σου τὸν
Υἱόν, ἵνα ὁ Υἱὸς δοξάσῃ σέ, 2. καθὼς ἔδωκας αὐτῷ ἐξουσίαν πάσης

πάτερ. For this beginning of the prayers of Jesus, see
on 11⁴¹; πάτερ is repeated, vv. 5, 11, 21, 24, 25.

ἐλήλυθεν ἡ ὥρα, sc. the hour of His "glorification," as
He had already told them (13³¹· ³² and 12²³), had come. The
same prescience is ascribed to Him at Gethsemane in Mk. 14⁴¹.
The idea that the whole course of His Ministry and Passion
was predetermined runs through the Gospel, e.g. 7³⁰ 8²⁰ 13¹;
see on 2⁴.

δόξασόν σου τὸν υἱόν. Here is the only *personal* intercession
throughout this Prayer of Consecration. He cared nothing
for the "glory" which men can bestow (cf. 8⁵⁰, ἐγὼ οὐ ζητῶ
τὴν δόξαν μου), but He prays that the Father may "glorify"
Him in His impending Passion (cf. 12¹⁶· ²³ 13³¹· ³², and see
on 7³⁹ for this use of δοξαζω). This goes deeper than a prayer
for support in the hour of death. A martyr might pray for
such signal measures of grace to be bestowed in the day of
trial, that all who perceived his courage and faith might recognise that he was honoured of God. The "glorification" of
Jesus included this. The centurion, standing by the Cross, was
constrained to say, as he watched the bearing of the Crucified,
"Truly this man was the Son of God" (Mk. 15³⁹, Mt. 27⁵⁴;
cf. Lk. 23⁴⁷). But there was more than this. The "glorification" of Jesus in the Passion was the Divine acceptance
of His Sacrifice by the Father, the sealing of His Mission as
complete. Cf. Phil. 2⁹, "Wherefore God highly exalted Him
(ὑπερύψωσεν) and gave Him the Name that is above every
name."

ἵνα ὁ υἱὸς δοξάσῃ σέ. The redemption of mankind through
the Crucified is a glorification of the Father. The final cause
of the Passion, viewed *sub specie æternitatis*, is "ad majorem
dei gloriam," as was every incident in the ministry of Jesus.
See on 11⁴ and cf. 1 Pet. 4¹¹.

2. The constr. ἵνα . . . καθὼς . . . ἵνα, which we have
here, appears also 13³⁴ 17²¹, in each case the clause introduced
by καθώς being parenthetical, and the second ἵνα being re-
iterative, the clause following it being identical in meaning
with that introduced by the first ἵνα. Consequently ἵνα πᾶν ὁ
δέδωκας αὐτῷ κτλ. in this verse is only another way of saying
ἵνα ὁ υἱὸς δοξάσῃ σέ of v. 1.

καθὼς ἔδωκας αὐτῷ ἐξουσίαν κτλ. To the Son, the Father
gave authority to determine the final destinies of mankind
(see on 5²⁷). His ἐξουσία is over "all flesh" (although not
fully acknowledged by the world), πᾶσα σάρξ being the render-

σαρκός, ἵνα πᾶν ὃ δέδωκας αὐτῷ δώσῃ αὐτοῖς ζωὴν αἰώνιον. 3. αὕτη δέ ἐστιν ἡ αἰώνιος ζωή, ἵνα γινώσκωσιν σὲ τὸν μόνον ἀληθινὸν Θεὸν

ing of the phrase כָּל־בָּשָׂר, very common in the O.T., repre-senting all humanity in its weakness (see Hort on 1 Pet. 1[24]), but infrequent in the N.T. except in quotations (cf. Mt. 24[22], Rom. 3[20], 1 Cor. 1[29], Gal. 2[16]).

ἵνα πᾶν ὃ δέδωκας αὐτῷ κτλ. The meaning is "that He may give eternal life to all whom thou hast given to Him" (see on 6[37]), the latter clause limiting the πᾶσα σάρξ which has pre-ceded. This consummation of His redemptive work is the "glorification" of the Father by the Son.

πᾶν ὃ δέδωκας αὐτῷ. The constr. with a *nom.-pendens* is like πᾶν ὃ δέδωκέν μοι of 6[39], where see the note on the collective use of the neuter singular, which perhaps is here a forecast of ἵνα . . . ἓν ὦσιν of v. 21. πᾶν ὃ δέδωκας αὐτῷ is the Universal Church (cf. v. 24).

There are many variants for δώσῃ (ℵ[c]AC). Westcott adopts δώσει (with BNΓΔΘ), but ἵνα with the future is infrequent in Jn. ℵ* has δώσω, and D avoids all difficulty of construction by reading ἔχῃ, and omitting αὐτοῖς. See Abbott (*Diat.* 2422, 2690, 2740).

ἵνα . . . δώσῃ αὐτοῖς ζωὴν αἰώνιον. Cf. 10[28], 1 Jn. 2[25], Rom. 6[23], and see on 6[39, 40]; and for the conception of ζωὴ αἰωνίος, see on 4[14].

αὐτοῖς refers to all who are included in πᾶν ὃ δέδωκας αὐτῷ, with disregard of formal grammar. As Blass notes (*Gram.* p. 166), this is a usage with classical precedent.

3. This verse seems to be an explanatory comment on the phrase "eternal life," which the evangelist says that Jesus used in His prayer. Jn. often supplies such comments (see Introd., p. cxvi), and this is quite in his manner. To suppose that he means to represent Jesus as introducing a definition of "eternal life" into His prayer, and as calling Himself "Jesus Christ" when speaking to His Father, is not a probable hypothesis. Further, the sequence of thought from v. 2 to v. 4 is direct, and the interposition of a parenthesis in a prayer is unlikely.

αὕτη δέ ἐστιν . . . ἵνα . . . For this Johannine construc-tion, cf. 1 Jn. 3[11] 5[3] (also 15[12]).

ℵBCΘ have γινώσκωσιν, but ADLNWΔ read γινώσκουσιν.

For the possibility of "knowing" the Father, see on 14[7]: the present tense (γινώσκωσιν) marking that continual growth in the knowledge of God which is a characteristic of spiritual life, as physical growth is a characteristic of bodily life. The prophet's ideal was, "We will *follow on* to know

καὶ ὃν ἀπέστειλας Ἰησοῦν Χριστόν.   4. ἐγώ σε ἐδόξασα ἐπὶ τῆς γῆς,

the Lord," διώξομεν τοῦ γνῶναι τὸν κύριον (Hos. 6³).   Cf. Jer. 9²⁴.

τὸν μόνον ἀληθινὸν θεόν.   For μόνος as applied to God, see on 5⁴⁴ above.   He is described as ἀληθινός, Ex. 34⁶, Num. 14¹⁸, I Esd. 8³⁹, Ps. 86¹⁵, 1 Thess. 1⁹, Rev. 6¹⁰; and cf. especially 1 Jn. 5²⁰, οὗτός ἐστιν ὁ ἀληθινὸς θεὸς καὶ ζωὴ αἰώνιος.   For ἀληθινός, see on 1⁹.   The adjectives μόνος and ἀληθινός express the central truth of Monotheism.

Wetstein quotes a verbal parallel from Athenæus (vi. p. 523c): describing the flattery of the Athenians in their reception of Demetrius, he says, ἐπᾴδοντες, ὡς εἴη μόνος θεὸς ἀληθινός.   This shows how natural is the combination of μόνος and ἀληθινός.   Cf. Philo, *Leg. All.* ii. 17, μὰ τὸν ἀληθῆ μόνον θεόν.

That to know God is, itself, eternal life, is a doctrine which has its roots in Jewish sapiential literature.   Wisdom "is a tree of life to them that lay hold on her" (Prov. 3¹⁸).   Again, περίσσεια γνώσεως τῆς σοφίας ζωοποιήσει τὸν παρ᾽ αὐτῆς (Eccles. 7¹²).   An even nearer parallel to Jn.'s definition of eternal life is: εἰδέναι σου τὸ κράτος ῥίζα ἀθανασίας (Wisd. 15³).

Alford appositely cites the words of Irenæus: ἡ δὲ ὕπαρξις τῆς ζωῆς ἐκ τῆς τοῦ θεοῦ παραγίνεται μετοχῆς· μετοχὴ δὲ θεοῦ ἐστὶ τὸ γινώσκειν θεόν, καὶ ἀπολαύειν τῆς χρηστότητος αὐτοῦ (*Hær.* iv. 20. 5).   A little lower down (§ 5, where the Greek is deficient) Irenæus combines with wonderful insight the two thoughts that the giving of eternal life by the Son is a glorification of the Father (v. 2), and that eternal life is the knowledge of God (v. 3), although he does not cite the present passage.   "Gloria enim dei uiuens homo; uita autem hominis uisio deï."   It would not be easy to express these profound thoughts more succinctly.

The writer of the last paragraphs of the Epistle to Diognetus (whom Lightfoot identifies with Pantænus [1]), commenting on the presence in Paradise of both the Tree of Knowledge and the Tree of Life, says: οὐδὲ γὰρ ζωὴ ἄνευ γνώσεως, οὐδὲ γνῶσις ἀσφαλὴς ἄνευ ζωῆς ἀληθοῦς (§ 12. 4).

καὶ ὃν ἀπέστειλας Ἰη. Χρ.   To "know" Jesus Christ is eternal life; cf. 6⁶⁸.   Jn. treats this knowledge as on a par with the knowledge of "the only true God."   So the apostles were bidden to "believe" not only in God, but in Christ (14¹).

For the thought of Jesus as "sent" by God (cf. vv. 8, 18, 21, 23, 25), see on 3¹⁷ above.

The only other place in the Fourth Gospel where the historical name "Jesus Christ" occurs is 1¹⁷ (see note, *in loc.*)

---

[1] *Apostolic Fathers*, p. 489.

τὸ ἔργον τελειώσας ὃ δέδωκάς μοι ἵνα ποιήσω· 5. καὶ νῦν δόξασόν με
σύ, Πάτερ, παρὰ σεαυτῷ τῇ δόξῃ ᾗ εἶχον πρὸ τοῦ τὸν κόσμον εἶναι

4. ἐγώ σε ἐδόξασα ἐπὶ τῆς γῆς. This is in direct sequence
with v. 2 (v. 3 being parenthetical). He had spoken of the
" glorification " of the Father by Him, which was to be consummated in the gift of eternal life through His ministry to those
whom the Father had given Him. This " glorification " had
been His aim throughout His earthly sojourn. " I glorified
Thee on earth " (the aorist ἐδόξασα being the aorist of historical
retrospect) by making known as never before the nature of God.

τὸ ἔργον τελειώσας ὃ δέδωκάς μοι ἵνα ποιήσω. This had
been His purpose throughout (see on 4³⁴), from the day when
He asked οὐκ ᾔδειτε ὅτι ἐν τοῖς τοῦ πατρός μου δεῖ εἶναί με;
(Lk. 2⁴⁹). His " works " had been " given " Him by the
Father to accomplish (3³⁵ 5³⁶). They had now been accom-
plished, and presently He would say τετέλεσται (19³⁰).

For τελειώσας (אABCLNW) the rec. (with ⊙) has
ἐτελείωσα, and for δέδωκας (אABLN⊙) CDW have ἔδωκας.
The variants δέδωκα, ἔδωκα frequently occur (cf. vv. 6, 8, 24,
etc.) in similar contexts throughout the Gospel. Abbott
(*Diat.* 2454) holds that " the aorist usually describes gifts
regarded as given by the Father to the Son on His coming into
the world to proclaim the Gospel; the perfect describes gifts
regarded as having been given to the Son and as now belonging
to Him." But we cannot always press this distinction.

5. καὶ νῦν, " and now," that this earthly ministry is ended
(cf. 14²⁹ for καὶ νῦν).

δόξασόν με. There is emphasis on νῦν. The glorification
prayed for here transcends the glorification in the Passion
prayed for in v. 1. Here the thought is of a heavenly glorification already predicted, 13³², ὁ θεὸς δοξάσει αὐτὸν ἐν αὐτῷ.
For Jesus asks now, with lofty assurance (σύ, πάτερ), that the
eternal glory which was His before the Incarnation (cf. 1¹)
may be resumed in fellowship with the Father (παρὰ σεαυτῷ
. . . παρὰ σοί). Cf. Prov. 8³⁰, Jn. 6⁶², and Rev. 3²¹. The glory
of the Eternal Word is distinguishable from the glory of the
Incarnate Word (see on 1¹⁴); the spheres of life are different,
ἐπὶ τῆς γῆς (v. 4) implying the Incarnate Life, but παρὰ σεαυτῷ
implying life in the bosom of the Godhead.

As He had said, " Before Abraham was, I am " (8⁵⁸),
so here He expresses His sure conviction that He was in
eternal relation with God. τῇ δόξῃ ᾗ εἶχον . . . παρὰ σοί
indicates a real, and not only an ideal, pre-existence.

πρὸ τοῦ τὸν κόσμον εἶναι. See 1¹, v. 24, and cf. Prov.
8²³. For κόσμος, see on 1⁹.

παρὰ σοί. 6. Ἐφανέρωσά σου τὸ ὄνομα τοῖς ἀνθρώποις οὓς ἔδωκάς μοι ἐκ τοῦ κόσμου. σοὶ ἦσαν κἀμοὶ αὐτοὺς ἔδωκας, καὶ τὸν λόγον σου τετήρηκαν. 7. νῦν ἔγνωκαν ὅτι πάντα ὅσα δέδωκάς μοι παρὰ

6. ἐφανέρωσά σου τὸ ὄνομα. This means the same thing as ἐγώ σε ἐδόξασα ἐπὶ τῆς γῆς of v. 4, and as ἐγνώρισα τὸ ὄνομά σου of v. 26, although different phrases are used to bring out the full meaning. For the "Name" of God as indicating His true nature, see on 12²⁸ and especially on v. 11 below.

For the verb φανεροῦν, see on 1³¹.

One of the Messianic Psalms has the aspiration, διηγήσομαι τὸ ὄνομά σου τοῖς ἀδελφοῖς μου (Ps. 22²²), and in the apostolic age the words were interpreted of Christ (Heb. 2¹²). As He looks back on His ministry, He can say that this has been accomplished : ἐφανέρωσά σου τὸ ὄνομα. Although the disciples had not appreciated all of His teaching, they had learnt, through Him, something more of the nature of God than any Jew had learnt before.

τοῖς ἀνθρώποις οὓς ἔδωκάς μοι ἐκ τοῦ κόσμου. See on 6³⁷ for the thought of disciples being " given " to the Son by the Father, which recurs throughout the Priestly Prayer of Jesus (vv. 2, 9, 12, 24).

σοὶ ἦσαν, "they were thine," and **σοί εἰσιν,** "they *are* thine " (v. 9). This means more than that they were " Israelites indeed " (1⁴⁷); it is rather that they were among the men ἐκ τοῦ θεοῦ of whom He spoke before (8⁴⁷).

καὶ τὸν λόγον σου τετήρηκαν. This was some of the fruit of His ministry; the chosen disciples (except Judas) had " kept " the Divine word revealed to them through Jesus. Cf. 8⁵¹ 14²³ for the phrase τὸν λόγον τηρεῖν, and see on 5³⁸.

ἔδωκας (אABDWΘ) is the true reading in this verse, in both places where it occurs, as against the rec. δέδωκας. The reference is to the definite " gift " of the faithful disciples chosen ἐκ τοῦ κόσμου. See on v. 4 above.

There is a passage in the *Odes of Solomon* (xxxi. 4, 5) which recalls the thought of this verse: " He offered to Him the sons that were in His hands. And His face was justified, for thus His holy Father had given to Him." Cf. also v. 11.

7. νῦν ἔγνωκαν κτλ. The disciples had said (16³⁰) νῦν οἴδαμεν ὅτι οἶδας πάντα κτλ., but their confidence was not so deep-rooted as they had supposed. Yet they had come to recognise (ἔγνωκαν expressing the gradual growth of their spiritual insight) that His words were divine (v. 8), or (as it is expressed in this verse) that " all things which Thou hast given me are from Thee " (see on 3³⁵).

σοῦ εἰσίν· 8. ὅτι τὰ ῥήματα ἃ ἔδωκάς μοι δέδωκα αὐτοῖς, καὶ αὐτοὶ ἔλαβον, καὶ ἔγνωσαν ἀληθῶς ὅτι παρὰ σοῦ ἐξῆλθον, καὶ ἐπίστευσαν ὅτι σύ με ἀπέστειλας.

Godet calls attention to the apparent scantiness of the spiritual harvest for which Jesus gives thanks in these verses. " Eleven Galilæan peasants after three years' labour ! But it is enough for Jesus, for in these eleven He beholds the pledge of the continuance of God's work upon earth."

For ἔγνωκαν, there is a Western variant, ἔγνων (א *latt. syrr.*), the mistaken correction of a scribe who returns to the first person of v. 6.

For δέδωκας (see on v. 4), AB have ἔδωκας. And for εἰσίν (אBCLNW) the rec. has ἐστίν, with ΑΔΓΔΘ.

8. ὅτι τὰ ῥήματα κτλ., " that the words which Thou gavest me I have given unto them." For ῥήματα, see on 3³⁴: cf. 5⁴⁷ 6⁶³. ⁶⁸.

These " words " of Jesus were " given " Him by the Father, as has been said before. See on 12⁴⁹, and cf. 15¹⁵ 17¹⁴.

καὶ αὐτοὶ ἔλαβον. The chosen disciples had received and appropriated His words, which " abode " in them (cf. 15⁷). Here was the token that the disciples were, indeed, ἐκ τοῦ θεοῦ (cf. 8⁴⁷).

The rec. has δέδωκας (so אLNΓΔΘ) for ἔδωκας (ABCDW), but the sense requires the aorist here (see on v. 4). The ῥήματα of Jesus were " given " to Him by the Father, when He entered on His mission (see on 3³⁵).

καὶ ἔγνωσαν . . . καὶ ἐπίστευσαν. Here, again, we have the aorist tense. The disciples *recognised*, " knew of a truth," *i.e.* inferred from what they saw and heard, that Jesus had come from God (cf. 3²); and, further, they *believed* (for this was not a matter of merely intellectual inference) that God had sent Him. But perhaps we must not lay stress on the distinction between ἔγνωσαν and ἐπίστευσαν here; for at 16²⁷ Jesus has already said to the Eleven, πεπιστεύκατε ὅτι ἐγὼ παρὰ τοῦ πατρὸς ἐξῆλθον. And at 8⁴² οὐδὲ γὰρ ἀπ' ἐμαυτοῦ ἐλήλυθα, ἀλλ' ἐκεῖνός με ἀπέστειλεν is a single sentence, the " sending " by the Father being the only possible alternative to Jesus having come " of Himself." Cf. 11⁴² ἵνα πιστεύσωσιν ὅτι σύ με ἀπέστειλας, and for the " sending " of the Son by the Father, see on 3¹⁷. For the combination of πεπιστεύκαμεν and ἐγνώκαμεν, see on 6⁶⁹.

σύ με ἀπέστειλας is found five times in this Prayer of Christ (cf. vv. 18, 21, 23, 25), the phrase being repeated like a kind of solemn refrain (see on 15²¹)

9. Ἐγὼ περὶ αὐτῶν ἐρωτῶ· οὐ περὶ τοῦ κόσμου ἐρωτῶ, ἀλλὰ περὶ
ὧν δέδωκάς μοι, ὅτι σοί εἰσιν, 10. καὶ τὰ ἐμὰ πάντα σά ἐστιν καὶ τὰ
σὰ ἐμά, καὶ δεδόξασμαι ἐν αὐτοῖς. 11. καὶ οὐκέτι εἰμὶ ἐν τῷ κόσμῳ,

The prayer of Jesus for the Eleven—(1) *that they may be
    divinely guarded* (vv. 9–16) *and* (2) *that they may be
    consecrated men* (vv. 17–19)

9. ἐγὼ περὶ αὐτῶν ἐρωτῶ. From v. 9 to v. 19, we have
the prayer of Jesus for His chosen disciples, that the Father
may guard them from evil, and that He may sanctify them in
the truth. He had prayed for Peter that his faith should not
fail (Lk. 22³²), but *this* prayer does not contemplate any failure
of faith among the Eleven, in the days to come when their
Master had returned to His glory. For ἐρωτᾶν, which is the
verb generally used by Jesus of His own prayers, see on 11²²,
16²³, and cf. 16²⁶ 14¹⁶.

οὐ περὶ τοῦ κόσμου ἐρωτῶ, *i.e.* "I am not praying for the
world *now*"; the prayers which follow were for those who loved
Him, not for those who rejected Him. But this is not to be
interpreted as indicating that Jesus never prayed for His
enemies (cf. Lk. 23³⁴ and His own precept Mt. 5⁴⁴). The
κόσμος (see on 1⁹) was hostile to Him, but God loved it (3¹⁶);
and even this Prayer of c. 17, which was primarily a prayer
for Himself and His own disciples, present and future, does not
exclude the thought of the world's acceptance of Him at last
(v. 21).

The language of 1 Jn. 5¹⁶, "there is a sin unto death: I
do not say that he should pray (ἐρωτήσῃ) for that," is verbally
similar, but the thought there is different, viz. of the propriety
or duty of praying for a *fellow-Christian* whose sin is πρὸς
θάνατον.

ἀλλὰ περὶ ὧν δέδωκάς μοι, ὅτι σοί εἰσιν, *sc.* because they are
God's. See on v. 6, from which verse this clause is repeated.

Only in this chap. (cf. vv. 15, 20) is ἐρωτᾶν used by Jn.
absolutely or intransitively, being generally followed by the
account of the person who is asked either to give something
or to reply. See on [8]⁷.

10. καὶ τὰ ἐμὰ πάντα σά ἐστιν. So He had said before; see
on 16¹⁵.

καὶ τὰ σὰ ἐμά. This goes further than the preceding clause.
Meyer cites Luther's comment: "This no creature can say
in reference to God."

καὶ δεδόξασμαι ἐν αὐτοῖς. The apostles were Jesus' own
men, not only because the Father "gave" them to Him, when
they were chosen, not only because all that belonged to the

καὶ αὐτοὶ ἐν τῷ κόσμῳ εἰσίν, κἀγὼ πρὸς σὲ ἔρχομαι. Πάτερ ἅγιε,

Father belonged to Him, but for the additional reason that He had been "glorified" in them. He was "glorified" in the physical miracle of the Raising of Lazarus (11⁴), much more in the spiritual miracle of the faith of the Eleven. They exhibited and continued to exhibit (note the perfect tense δεδόξασμαι) the power of the message which He brought. So Paul said of his Thessalonian converts ὑμεῖς γάρ ἐστε ἡ δόξα ἡμῶν (1 Thess. 2²⁰). Cf. 2 Thess. 1¹⁰ of the future "glorification" of Christ in His saints.

Through misunderstanding of the meaning, for δεδόξασμαι D has ἐδόξασάς με (cf. v. 1).

11. The occasion and ground of the prayer are now more distinctly stated. He is going away from the disciples whom He had trained and guarded; henceforth the relations between Him and them will be different from those of the days of His ministry in the flesh. He had told them about this, but they had hardly understood it (13³³. ³⁶; cf. 16¹⁰. ¹⁶). They will need a special measure of the Father's care. Swinburne has finely paraphrased some of the thoughts behind vv. 11, 12:

> "Who shall keep Thy sheep,
> Lord, and lose not one?
> Who save one shall keep,
> Lest the shepherd sleep?
> Who beside the Son?"

οὐκέτι εἰμὶ ἐν τῷ κόσμῳ. Cf. v. 14. His visible ministry in the world of men is over. Meyer cites Calvin's comment: "nunc quasi provincia sua defunctus."

The rec. text has οὗτοι, but אB have αὐτοί.

αὐτοὶ ἐν τῷ κόσμῳ εἰσίν: the disciples are still in the world and have their service and ministry to fulfil.

κἀγὼ πρὸς σὲ ἔρχομαι, repeated v. 13; cf. 13³ 14¹².

After ἔρχομαι D adds οὐκέτι εἰμὶ ἐν τῷ κόσμῳ καὶ ἐν τῷ κόσμῳ εἰμί, a Western gloss, which has some support from a c e, and which evidently was added because the scribe stumbled at the words, "I am no longer in the world."

πάτερ. B reads πατήρ (with N), as it also does at v. 21 (with D), at vv. 24, 25 (with A), and (teste Abbott, Diat. 2053) at 12²⁸. But, although the nom. with the article sometimes takes the place of the voc. (e.g. Mt. 11²⁶, Lk. 10²¹), πατήρ without the article is not easy to defend. At v. 5 D, in like manner, has πατήρ for πάτερ.

πάτερ ἅγιε. The holiness of God is fundamental in the Hebrew religion. This is a characteristically Jewish mode of address in prayer; cf. 2 Macc. 14³⁶, ἅγιε παντὸς ἁγιασμοῦ

τήρησον αὐτοὺς ἐν τῷ ὀνόματί σου ᾧ δέδωκάς μοι, ἵνα ὦσιν ἓν καθὼς

Κύριε, and 3 Macc. 2², ἅγιε ἐν ἁγίοις, μόναρχε, παντοκράτωρ. The conception goes back to Lev. 11⁴⁴ (quoted 1 Pet. 1¹⁶); cf. Isa. 6³, Ps. 71²², and esp. Lk. 1⁴⁹, ἅγιον τὸ ὄνομα αὐτοῦ (Ps. 111⁹). See also 6⁶⁹, ὁ ἅγιος τοῦ θεοῦ, as used of Christ, and 20²², λάβετε πνεῦμα ἅγιον, of the Spirit. We find πάτερ δίκαιε in v. 25, but πάτερ ἅγιε does not appear again in the N.T. A remarkable parallel, which may be a reminiscence of the language of this verse, occurs in the Post-Communion Thanksgiving in the *Didache* (§ 10), εὐχαριστοῦμέν σοι, πάτερ ἅγιε, ὑπὲρ τοῦ ἁγίου ὀνόματός σου, οὗ κατεσκήνωσας ἐν ταῖς καρδίαις ἡμῶν, καὶ ὑπὲρ τῆς γνώσεως καὶ πίστεως καὶ ἀθανασίας, ἧς ἐγνώρισας (cf. v. 26) ἡμῖν διὰ Ἰησοῦ τοῦ παιδός σου.

τήρησον αὐτούς, "keep them," as now specially needing care. For τηρεῖν, of keeping persons safe, cf. vv. 12, 15, Acts 16²³ 24²³ 25⁴· ²¹, and esp. Jude¹, "kept for Jesus Christ," Ἰησοῦ Χριστῷ τετηρημένοις. For τηρεῖν, of keeping or observing commandments, see on 8⁵¹.

ἐν τῷ ὀνόματί σου, "in Thy Name," *i.e.* under Thy Fatherly protection. The Name of God expresses (see on 5⁴³) the revelation of His Being, especially as exhibited in His help in time of need. Cf. Ps. 44⁶, ἐν τῷ ὀνόματί σου ἐξουθενώσομεν τοὺς ἐπανιστανομένους ἡμῖν, Ps. 54¹, ὁ θεός, ἐν τῷ ὀνόματί σου σῶσόν με, and Ps. 124⁸, ἡ βοήθεια ἡμῶν ἐν ὀνόματι κυρίου. In such contexts the "Name" of God is equivalent to what a modern writer would call His "Providence"; and this, in the N.T. and especially in Jn., is associated with the doctrine of God as *Father*.

ᾧ δέδωκάς μοι. The reading here and in v. 12 presents difficulty, and the variants are important.

(1) The rec. text has οὓς δέδωκάς μοι, but this is poorly attested (D², 69 *f g q* vg. cop.), and οὓς may have come from 18⁹, or from v. 6. It gives an excellent sense; that His disciples were "given" to Jesus by the Father is said five times elsewhere in this chapter (vv. 2, 6, 9, 12, 24; see on 6³⁷ for other references).

(2) ὃ δέδωκάς μοι is read by D² *ful.* This might have the same meaning as οὓς, and ὃ δέδωκας is the right reading at vv. 2, 24. For this collective use of the neuter sing., see on 6³⁷. Field, whose opinion is always weighty, prefers ὅ.

(3) But the harder reading, ᾧ, has such strong attestation that it must be accepted. It is supported by the great bulk of MSS and vss., including אABCLWΘ. ᾧ must refer to ὀνόματι, so that "in Thy Name, which Thou hast given me" is the only possible rendering. This is accepted by most

modern editors, including Westcott and Abbott (*Diat.* 2408*f*).
Burney (*Aramaic Origin, etc.*, p. 103), while recognising that
ᾧ is the reading best attested, holds that οὕς must have been
intended by the evangelist, and he traces the variants to the
ambiguity of the relative particle ךּ‎, which might stand for
either οὕς, ὅ, or ᾧ. But this does not explain the superior
attestation of ᾧ, even if an Aramaic origin for the Fourth Gospel
were accepted.

We have seen (on 3³⁵) that it is a favourite thought with Jn.
that the Father gave all things to the Incarnate Son; but it is
only here and at v. 12 that the idea is expressed that the Father
has given His " Name " to Christ, and that it is in this " Name "
that Jesus guarded His disciples. This does not mean only
that the Son was " sent " by the Father (see on 3¹⁷), and that
therefore His ministry was accomplished " in the Name of the
Father " (see on 5⁴³ 10²⁵) as His delegate and representative;
but that in Christ God was revealed in His providential love
and care, His " Name," that is, His essential nature as Father,
being exhibited in the Incarnate Son. Thus that " the Name "
of the Father was " given " to Christ is yet another way of
expressing the essential unity of the Father and the Son (see
on 10³⁰). This transcends any such idea as that of Num. 6²⁷,
where the " Name " of Yahweh is " put " upon Israel by the
priestly blessing; or of Ex. 23²¹, where it is said of the guardian
angel of the people, " My Name is in him "; or of Jer. 23⁶,
where the " Name " of the Messianic King is " Yahweh our
Righteousness." The nearest parallel is Phil. 2⁹, ἐχαρίσατο
αὐτῷ τὸ ὄνομα τὸ ὑπὲρ πᾶν ὄνομα (cf. Rev. 19¹²); but in no
N.T. passage except Jn. 17¹¹· ¹² is found the conception of the
Father giving His " Name," in the sense of His revealed
character as Fatherly Providence, to Christ. See on v. 22 for
the δόξα which the Father had given to the Son.

This interpretation (demanded by the reading, ᾧ δέδωκας),
viz. that the Father gave His " Name " to the Son, is in con-
sonance with the thanksgiving quoted above from the *Didache*,
according to which the Father causes His " Name " to taber-
nacle in the hearts of believers, *i.e.* His Fatherly protection
rests upon them.

ἔδωκας is read by אLNW, but the true reading is δέδωκας
(see on v. 4), the perfect indicating not merely one act of giving
at a definite moment in time, but a continuous " giving " of
the Father to the Son, throughout His earthly ministry.

ἵνα ὦσιν ἐν καθὼς ἡμεῖς, *sc.* that the apostles might be
united in will and purpose and spiritual fellowship even as
the Father and the Son are united (see on 10³⁰). They had
been given a " new " commandment, enjoining all disciples

ἡμεῖς. 12. ὅτε ἤμην μετ᾽ αὐτῶν, ἐγὼ ἐτήρουν αὐτοὺς ἐν τῷ ὀνόματί σου ᾧ δέδωκάς μοι, καὶ ἐφύλαξα, καὶ οὐδεὶς ἐξ αὐτῶν ἀπώλετο εἰ μὴ

to love one another (see on 13³⁴), and the Fatherly protection of God is now invoked for them, that they may be kept of one mind in their sacred fellowship. At v. 21 the thought is no longer of the apostles only, but of all future generations of Christian disciples, for whom again the prayer is ἵνα πάντες ἓν ὦσιν.

The petition ἵνα ὦσιν ἕν, as applied to the apostles, was fulfilled in their case, for otherwise the earliest apostolic preaching could not have achieved its wonderful success; but it was not fulfilled in such fashion that no differences of opinion as to method were observed among the apostolic body, or that they were always right, as compared, e.g., with Paul (cf. Acts 11², Gal. 2¹¹, etc.) See further on v. 21.

It is probably due to its difficulty that the whole clause, ᾧ δέδωκάς μοι, ἵνα ὦσιν ἓν καθὼς ἡμεῖς, is omitted in the O.L. texts a b c e ff² and by the Coptic Q.

12. After ὅτε ἤμην μετ᾽ αὐτῶν, the rec. with AC³NΓΔΘ inserts the explanatory gloss ἐν τῷ κόσμῳ, but om. אBC*DLW.

ἐγὼ ἐτήρουν αὐτούς κτλ., "I (ἐγώ being emphatic) used to keep them," ἐτήρουν marking the continual training of disciples that was so great a feature of the ministry of Jesus.

ἐν τῷ ὀνόματί σου ᾧ δέδωκάς μοι, repeated from v. 11 (where see note) in the Johannine manner. It is "in the Name," that is, in the sure protection of the Father's providence and love, that Jesus guarded (and guards) His disciples.

καὶ ἐφύλαξα κτλ., "and I guarded them (sc. while I was with them in the flesh), and none perished." For φυλάττειν, cf. 2 Thess. 3³, Jude²⁴; and see Wisd. 10⁵, where τηρεῖν and φυλάττειν are both used of the Divine guardianship of Abraham.

The rec. text, as in v. 11, has οὕς for ᾧ, and omits καί before ἐφύλαξα, making the latter govern οὕς directly; אBC*LW ins. καί.

καὶ οὐδεὶς ἐξ αὐτῶν (cf. for constr. 7¹⁹) ἀπώλετο κτλ., "and not one of them perished, except the son of perdition." The falling away of Judas has already been described (13²⁷); ἀπολλύναι is used of the final "perishing," as at 3¹⁶ (where see note) 10²⁸. Jesus is represented as speaking of the fate of Judas as if it were already in the past (see 6⁶⁴· ⁷⁰). Cf. 6³⁹ 10²⁸, where his exceptional case is not in view; and see note on 18⁹, where is quoted this saying of Jesus that He lost none of those whom the Father had "given" to Him. It has often been discussed by theologians whether Judas had really been pre-

ὁ υἱὸς τῆς ἀπωλείας, ἵνα ἡ γραφὴ πληρωθῇ. 13. νῦν δὲ πρὸς σὲ

destined to destruction, or whether his fall from faithfulness was of his free choice. Such questions are foreign to the philosophy of the first century. For Jn., all that happened to Judas was, indeed, predestined, but that this involves any difficulty as to his guilt does not suggest itself to the evangelist.

εἰ μὴ ὁ υἱὸς τῆς ἀπωλείας. The play on words ἀπώλετο . . . ἀπωλείας can hardly be reproduced in English. The constr. υἱός τινος (see on 12³⁶) is not exclusively Hebraic, but it is frequent in Eastern literature. Antichrist is called ὁ υἱὸς τῆς ἀπωλείας (2 Thess. 2³), the same expression being applied to those who perished in the Flood (*Jubilees*, x. 3), and to Satan (*Evang. Nicodemi*, xx.). It signifies one whose end will be perdition, not necessarily that this is inevitable but that it will be so because of his own acts. He is one of whom it may be said, " good were it for him if he had not been born" (Mk. 14²¹). Cf. υἱὸς γεέννης (Mt. 23¹⁵), υἱὸς θανάτου (2 Sam. 12⁵), and τέκνα ἀπωλείας (Isa. 57⁴). Judas was "the son of loss," although Jesus came to save the lost. For him Jesus did not pray (cf. 1 Jn. 5¹⁶).

ἀπώλεια is generally used in the N.T. for the final " loss " of a man (it does not occur again in Jn.); but at Mk. 14⁴ it is the word for the " waste " of the ointment, of which (as Jn. tells, 12⁴) it was Judas that complained. It has been suggested that possibly this incident was in mind when Judas was called ὁ υἱὸς τῆς ἀπωλείας, "the son of loss," the man who really wasted what was precious.[1] But the ordinary interpretation is simpler and more probable.

ἵνα ἡ γραφὴ πληρωθῇ. It is not quite certain whether this is a comment of Jn. on the words of Jesus which he has just narrated, or whether he means to place it in the mouth of Jesus Himself.[2] It is to be observed that in 18⁹, where the words, " of those whom Thou hast given me, I lost not one," are cited from the present passage, there is no appeal to the O.T., but Jn. applies ἵνα πληρωθῇ ὁ λόγος κτλ. to the saying of Jesus as carrying with it the certainty of its fulfilment. Probably here ἵνα ἡ γραφὴ πλ. is a reflective gloss or comment added by the evangelist or an early editor.

ἡ γραφή always refers in Jn. to a definite passage of the O.T. (see on 2²²), and the Scripture here indicated was probably Ps. 41⁹, which was cited before (13¹⁸) as foreshadowing the treachery of Judas. Pss. 69²⁵ and 109⁸ are cited in Acts 1²⁰ in reference to his miserable and execrated end, and

[1] See *D.C.G.* i. 909.   [2] See Introd., p. cxli.

ἔρχομαι, καὶ ταῦτα λαλῶ ἐν τῷ κόσμῳ ἵνα ἔχωσιν τὴν χαρὰν τὴν
ἐμὴν πεπληρωμένην ἐν ἑαυτοῖς. 14. ἐγὼ δέδωκα αὐτοῖς τὸν λόγον
σου, καὶ ὁ κόσμος ἐμίσησεν αὐτούς, ὅτι οὐκ εἰσὶν ἐκ τοῦ κόσμου
καθὼς ἐγὼ οὐκ εἰμὶ ἐκ τοῦ κόσμου. 15. οὐκ ἐρωτῶ ἵνα ἄρῃς αὐτοὺς

his replacement by Matthias, but Ps. 41⁹ is more in place
here.

13. νῦν δὲ πρὸς σὲ ἔρχομαι, repeated from v. 11 ; cf. 14¹².

καὶ ταῦτα λαλῶ, "And I say these things," viz. "I say
them *aloud,*" for λαλῶ implies this.

ἐν τῷ κόσμῳ, *sc.* before my departure.

ἵνα ἔχωσιν κτλ. The prayer was spoken aloud, so that the
apostles might overhear His intercessions for them, and hearing
might rejoice. See on 11⁴², where Jesus is represented, in
the rec. text, as having said explicitly that some words of His
thanksgiving were uttered διὰ τὸν ὄχλον.

τὴν χαρὰν τὴν ἐμὴν πεπληρωμένην ἐν ἑαυτοῖς. This is a
phrase several times repeated in Jn.; see on 15¹¹ 16²⁴. To
hear Jesus rejoice when speaking in prayer of the faithfulness
of His chosen friends would awaken in them feelings of joy,
which would be His joy "fulfilled in them."

For ἑαυτοῖς (אABNW), the rec. has αὐτοῖς (probably from
the next line).

14. ἐγὼ δέδωκα αὐτοῖς τὸν λόγον σου, repeated from v. 8,
τὸν λόγον being substituted for τὰ ῥήματα (see on 5³⁸), the
perfect δέδωκα in both cases implying that Jesus had continued
to give to the disciples the revelation of the Father, and was
still giving it.

καὶ ὁ κόσμος ἐμίσησεν αὐτούς. This was the badge of a
disciple (15¹⁸· ¹⁹, where the verb is in the present tense, μισεῖ,
which D substitutes here for the harder ἐμίσησεν). We should
expect the perf. μεμίσηκεν as in 15²⁴, if not μισεῖ ; this is one
of the cases in which Jn. uses the aorist as if it were a perfect
(cf. 12²⁸ 13³⁴ 15¹⁵ ; and see Abbott, *Diat.* 2441).

ὅτι οὐκ εἰσὶν ἐκ τοῦ κόσμου. A fine and eloquent exposition
of the thought that Christian disciples generally, and not the
apostles only, are *in* the world but not *of* the world is given
in the second-century *Ep. to Diognetus* (vi. 3), with a probable allusion to vv. 11, 14. See on 3¹⁶.

καθὼς ἐγὼ οὐκ εἰμὶ ἐκ τοῦ κόσμου. So He had said at 8²³,
where see note.

15. οὐκ ἐρωτῶ ἵνα ἄρῃς αὐτούς κτλ. The question as to
how far Christians were to separate themselves from the company of non-Christians, from the Jewish and heathen world,
was urgent and difficult in the apostolic age. In 1 Cor. 5¹⁰,
Paul explains, in terms similar to those of this passage, that

ἐκ τοῦ κόσμου, ἀλλ' ἵνα τηρήσῃς αὐτοὺς ἐκ τοῦ πονηροῦ.   16. ἐκ τοῦ κόσμου οὐκ εἰσὶν καθὼς ἐγὼ οὐκ εἰμὶ ἐκ τοῦ κόσμου.   17. ἁγίασον

for a complete dissociation from heathen of evil lives, a Christian disciple would have to "go out of the world." On the other hand, he is equally explicit in his statement (Gal. 1⁴) that the purpose of the sacrifice of Christ was that He might deliver us from the present evil age (αἰῶνος). These two principles are tersely enunciated in the present verse. The apostles would have to live in the world, for that was to be the theatre of their evangelical ministry; but they would need the special grace of God to keep them from its evil influences.

ἀλλ' ἵνα τηρήσῃς αὐτοὺς ἐκ τοῦ πονηροῦ. This is the first petition of Jesus for the Eleven, viz. for their *protection* and deliverance. τηρεῖν ἐκ is found again in N.T. only at Rev. 3¹⁰, a passage very similar to the present : ὅτι ἐτήρησας τὸν λόγον (cf. v. 6, τὸν λόγον σου τετήρηκαν) . . . κἀγώ σε τηρήσω ἐκ τῆς ὥρας τοῦ πειρασμοῦ (cf. v. 11, τήρησον αὐτούς). A nearer parallel is in 1 Jn. 5¹⁸, where it is said of a child of God, that Christ τηρεῖ αὐτόν, καὶ ὁ πονηρὸς οὐκ ἅπτεται αὐτοῦ.

ὁ πονηρός appears again 1 Jn. 2¹⁴ 5¹⁹ (ὁ κόσμος ὅλος ἐν τῷ πονηρῷ κεῖται). The agency of the personal devil, Satan, is not doubted by Jn.; cf. 13²⁷, and the references to ὁ ἄρχων τοῦ κόσμου τούτου (12³¹ 14³⁰ 16¹¹).

In the words ἵνα τηρήσῃς αὐτοὺς ἐκ τοῦ πονηροῦ, we probably have an echo of the clause in the Lord's Prayer, ῥῦσαι ἡμᾶς ἀπὸ τοῦ πονηροῦ (Mt. 6¹³ ; see above on v. 1).[1] Some commentators have endeavoured to distinguish the meaning of ἀπό from that of ἐκ in constructions like this (see on 1⁴⁴), but this is over subtle. Cf. the parallelism in Ps. 140¹:

> ἐξελοῦ με ἐξ ἀνθρώπου πονηροῦ
> ἀπὸ ἀνδρὸς ἀδίκου ῥῦσαί με.

16. This verse is repeated from v. 14, οὐκ εἰμί here preceding ἐκ τοῦ κόσμου, according to אABᶜDLW.

17. Here is the second petition for the Eleven (cf. v. 15), viz. for their *consecration*. ἁγιάζειν (see on 10³⁶) connotes not so much the selection of a man for an important work as the equipping and fitting him for its due discharge. It is applied to the divine separation of Jeremiah for the work of a prophet (Jer. 1⁵); and also to Aaron and his sons for their priestly office, Ex. 28⁴¹, where the Divine command to Moses is ἁγιάσεις αὐτούς, ἵνα ἱερατεύωσίν μοι. (See Additional Note on 18¹⁵.)

ἁγιάζειν is not equivalent to καθαρίζειν; one who is not

---

[1] See Chase, *The Lord's Prayer in the Early Church*, p. 109, for the arguments in favour of τοῦ πονηροῦ being taken as masculine rather than neuter.

αὐτοὺς ἐν τῇ ἀληθείᾳ· ὁ λόγος ὁ σὸς ἀλήθειά ἐστιν. 18. καθὼς ἐμὲ

ἡγιασμένος is not necessarily *impure*. Of the apostles it had already been said ἤδη ὑμεῖς καθαροί ἐστε, and the effective instrument of their *purification* was the λόγος which Jesus had spoken to them (15³), as the Divine λόγος is said here also to be the medium of their *consecration*. But the two ideas of ἁγιασμός and καθαρισμός are not identical. Just because the Eleven were already, in a sense, *pure*, being not " of the world " even as their Master was not " of the world " (v. 16), is their consecration for their future task a fitting boon to be asked in prayer of God who is Himself ἅγιος (v. 11). Cf. Paul's prayer for his Thessalonian converts that God would consecrate them wholly (ἁγιάσαι ὑμᾶς ὁλοτελεῖς, 1 Thess. 5²³).

ἐν τῇ ἀληθείᾳ. Truth would be the medium of their consecration, as (although this is not expressed in the present passage) the " Spirit of Truth " would be the Agent (cf. 16¹³). See also 8³². So Paul said of his Thessalonian converts that God had chosen them εἰς σωτηρίαν ἐν ἁγιασμῷ πνεύματος καὶ πίστει ἀληθείας (2 Thess. 2¹³). Westcott makes the pregnant comment that " the end of the Truth is not wisdom . . . but holiness."

After ἀληθείᾳ the rec. text adds σου, but om. א*ABC*DLWΘ. What is meant by ἀληθείᾳ is explained in the next clause.

ὁ λόγος ὁ σὸς ἀλήθειά ἐστιν. It is not always noticed that this is a quotation from the LXX of Ps. 119¹⁴², ὁ λόγος σου ἀλήθεια (cf. 2 Sam. 7²⁸). Jesus had already said of the disciples, τὸν λόγον σου τετήρηκαν (v. 6, where see note); and thus they were in the way of consecration, which is in truth (cf. 14⁶). Such consecration is not an isolated event in the life-history of a disciple, but is a continuous process (cf. οἱ ἁγιαζόμενοι, Heb. 2¹¹).

Westcott quotes an interesting parallel from a Jewish prayer for the new year: " Purify our hearts to serve Thee in truth. Thou, O God, art Truth, and Thy word is truth, and standeth for ever."

18. καθὼς ἐμὲ ἀπέστειλας. For this thought, five times expressed in this chapter, cf. v. 8 and see on 3¹⁷.

That the relation between Jesus and His disciples is comparable with that between the Son and the Father is several times stated in the discourses of Jesus as reported by Jn. As is the love of the Father to the Son, so is the love of Jesus for His disciples (15⁹). The glory which the Father gave to the Son was given by Jesus to His disciples (17²²). As the Son lives by the Father (διὰ τὸν πατέρα), so His disciples live by Jesus (δι' ἐμέ, 6⁵⁷). As the Father knows the Son, and the Son the

ἀπέστειλας εἰς τὸν κόσμον, κἀγὼ ἀπέστειλα αὐτοὺς εἰς τὸν κόσμον·
19. καὶ ὑπὲρ αὐτῶν ἐγὼ ἁγιάζω ἐμαυτόν, ἵνα ὦσιν καὶ αὐτοὶ ἡγιασμένοι ἐν ἀληθείᾳ.

Father, so does Jesus know His sheep, and they know Him
(10¹⁴· ¹⁵). As the Son is "in" the Father, so are His disciples
"in" Jesus (14²⁰). These are amazing teachings, but they
are deep-rooted in the Fourth Gospel. And, corresponding to
them, we have the saying of this verse that as the Father sent
the Son into the world, so Jesus sent His apostles into the
world.

The comparison καθὼς . . . καί in such passages can never
be exact or definite (see on 6⁵⁷), but at the same time it points
in each case to something more than a superficial analogy.

κἀγὼ ἀπέστειλα αὐτοὺς εἰς τὸν κόσμον. The words carry a
reference not only to the original choice of the Twelve, ἵνα
ἀποστέλλῃ αὐτοὺς κηρύσσειν (Mk. 3¹⁴; cf. Lk. 9²), but to their
future mission, the aorist being used because of the *certainty*
of this predetermined future in store for them. The actual
commission is recorded at 20²¹· ²²: καθὼς ἀπέσταλκέν με ὁ πατήρ,
κἀγὼ πέμπω ὑμᾶς . . . λάβετε πνεῦμα ἅγιον. (No distinction can
be drawn between ἀποστέλλω and πέμπω in such passages; see
on 3¹⁷.) Cf. also 4³⁸.

19. καὶ ὑπὲρ αὐτῶν ἐγὼ ἁγιάζω ἐμαυτόν. ἐγώ is om. by אW,
but ins. BCDLNΘ rightly: it is here *emphatic*.

ὑπέρ is a favourite prep. with Jn., who always uses it as
meaning "on behalf of." See on 1³⁰, and cf. 6⁵¹.

ἐγὼ ἁγιάζω ἐμαυτόν. At 10³⁶ He had spoken of Himself
as One ὃν ὁ πατὴρ ἡγίασεν. But there is no inconsistency. The
Father "consecrated" Jesus for His mission to the world;
and now that His mission is about to be consummated in
death, Jesus "consecrates" Himself, as He enters upon the
Passion. So He had said before of His life, "I lay it down of
myself" (10¹⁸). In His death He was both Priest and Victim.

The two petitions for the disciples were for their *deliverance*
from the Evil One (v. 15), and for their *consecration* (v. 17).
These are the two purposes of the Atonement, as set out Tit. 2¹⁴,
"Who gave Himself for us, in order that He might (1) redeem
us from all iniquity, and (2) purify to Himself a peculiar people
zealous of good works." So here the "consecration" of
Himself to the Cross by Jesus was not only that (ἵνα) His
chosen apostles might in their turn be guarded and consecrated,
but that the same consecration might be the portion of all future
disciples (v. 20). There is a special emphasis on ἐγώ. No one
else could say, "I consecrate myself." It is only through
His consecration that His disciples can be consecrated; and

20. Οὐ περὶ τουτων δὲ ἐρωτῶ μόνον, ἀλλὰ καὶ περὶ τῶν πιστευόντων διὰ τοῦ λόγου αὐτῶν εἰς ἐμέ, 21. ἵνα πάντες ἓν ὦσιν, καθὼς σύ,

so in Heb. 10¹⁰ we find the confession, " We have been consecrated through the offering of the Body of Jesus Christ." In
a sense, He is the consecrator of all such : " He that consecrates
and they that are being consecrated are all of one " (ἐξ ἑνός,
Heb. 2¹¹), a thoroughly Johannine statement, although it does
not appear in Jn.

ἵνα ὦσιν καὶ αὐτοὶ ἡγιασμένοι ἐν ἀληθείᾳ. Cf. v. 17 for truth,
the Divine λόγος, the full revelation of the Father, as the
medium of consecration to the Christian life.

The prayer of Jesus for all future disciples (vv. 20-26)

20. We now reach the third division of the Prayer of Jesus,
which passes from the thought of the apostles to the thought of
all those who should reach discipleship through their ministry.

ἀλλὰ καὶ περὶ τῶν πιστευόντων κτλ. πιστευόντων is a proleptic
or anticipatory present participle, with the force of a future,
qui credituri sunt (Vulg.). Some minuscules, which the
rec. text follows, through misunderstanding, have adopted
πιστευσόντων.

διὰ τοῦ λόγου αὐτῶν. The " word " of the evangelical
preachers was the message of God in Christ which they brought,
such preaching being an essential preliminary to faith. Cf.
Rom. 10¹⁴.

εἰς ἐμέ. For πιστεύειν εἰς . . ., see on 1¹².

21. As the Church grew, so would the risk of disunion
among its members be intensified. Jesus had already prayed
that His apostles might be united in will and purpose even as
the Father and the Son are united (v. 11, ἵνα ὦσιν ἓν καθὼς
ἡμεῖς). He now repeats this petition for all future disciples,
ἵνα πάντες ἓν ὦσιν, stating more fully what the nature of this
ideal unity was to be.

There is no suggestion of a unity of *organisation*, such as
that which appears in Paul's conception of the Church as one
body with many members, each performing its appropriate
function (Rom. 12⁴ᶠ·, 1 Cor. 12¹²ᶠ·). No biological analogy
is offered here to assist us in comprehending the sense in which
Christians are intended to be *one*. Jesus had said already that
His sheep would ultimately be One Flock, even as they had One
Shepherd (10¹⁶). But the mystical phrases used in this passage
transcend even that thought. For He prays that the unity of
His disciples may be realised in the spiritual life, after the
pattern of that highest form of unity, in which the Father is

Πάτερ, ἐν ἐμοὶ κἀγὼ ἐν σοί, ἵνα καὶ αὐτοὶ ἐν ἡμῖν ὦσιν, ἵνα ὁ κόσμος πιστεύῃ ὅτι σύ με ἀπέστειλας. 22. κἀγὼ τὴν δόξαν ἣν δέδωκάς μοι

" in " the Son and the Son " in " the Father. This unity, however, as appertaining to Christian discipleship, is not invisible; it is to be such as will convince the world of the Divine mission of the common Master of Christians. And He has already explained that the badge of this unity is love, the love of Christian for Christian which all men may see (13³⁵).

ἵνα πάντες ἓν ὦσιν. For the use of the neuter singular here, see on 10³⁰; and cf. ἵνα τὰ τέκνα τοῦ θεοῦ . . . συναγάγῃ εἰς ἕν (11⁵²).

καθὼς σύ, Πάτερ, ἐν ἐμοὶ (cf. 14¹⁰· ²⁰) κἀγὼ ἐν σοί (cf. 14¹¹). That men might come to acknowledge this central assertion of His claim had been the immediate object of His mission (see on 10³⁸).

Jn. always expresses the voc. by πάτερ. In this passage πατήρ is read by BDW, and by AB at vv. 24, 25. See Abbott, *Diat.* 2052, and cf. note on [8]¹⁰.

ἵνα καὶ αὐτοὶ ἐν ἡμῖν ὦσιν. Before ὦσιν the rec. text inserts ἕν, with אAC³LNΘ, but BC*DW *a b c e* om. ἕν. It has probably come in from the earlier clause ἵνα πάντες ἓν ὦσιν.

The ideal is that all Christians may be ἐν ἡμῖν. " Abide in *me* " was the counsel of 15⁴ (cf. 1 Jn. 3²⁴ 5²⁰), but rightly obeyed this implies abiding in God; the use of the plural ἡμῖν here, recalling the plural verbs at 14²³. Cf. 1 Jn. 1³, ἡ κοινωνία ἡ ἡμετέρα μετὰ τοῦ πατρὸς καὶ μετὰ τοῦ υἱοῦ αὐτοῦ Ἰησοῦ Χριστοῦ. To be " in Christ " is to be " in God." Those who are thus " in God " share the Divine life in common, and are therefore *one*, ἓν καθὼς ἡμεῖς (v. 11); it being always remembered that καθώς in such passages is only suggestive of a partial, not a complete, analogy (see on v. 18 above, and cf. 6⁵⁷).

Ignatius has some sentences reminiscent of these thoughts, where he approves the Ephesian Christians for being closely joined with the bishop: " *as the Church is with Jesus Christ, and as Jesus Christ is with the Father,* that all things may be harmonious in *unity* (ἵνα πάντα ἐν ἑνότητι σύμφωνα ᾖ, *Eph.* 5).

ἵνα ὁ κόσμος πιστεύῃ ὅτι σύ με ἀπέστειλας. The consequence of the spiritual unity of Christians, as indicated by their common love for each other, is that the world will be at last convinced (cf. 16⁸) that the mission of Jesus was divine, and that He is " the Saviour of the world " (4⁴²). For such forecasts of universal homage, cf. Rev. 3⁹ and 1 Cor. 15²⁸. See v. 23 below.

πιστεύῃ. So א*BC*W, but the rec., with אᶜADLNΘ,

δέδωκα αὐτοῖς, ἵνα ὦσιν ἓν καθὼς ἡμεῖς ἕν· 23. ἐγὼ ἐν αὐτοῖς καὶ σὺ ἐν ἐμοί, ἵνα ὦσιν τετελειωμένοι εἰς ἕν, ἵνα γινώσκῃ ὁ κόσμος ὅτι σύ με

has the inferior reading πιστεύσῃ. πιστεύῃ indicates the gradual growth of faith, "may come to believe."

22. κἀγὼ τὴν δόξαν κτλ. "And I, even I, have given to them the glory which Thou hast given to me." *Quanta maiestas Christianorum!* is Bengel's penetrating comment. But what is this δόξα? It is not the glory of the *Eternal* Word, spoken of in v. 24. *That* a faithful disciple may hope to *see*, but not to *share* (although 1 Pet. 5¹ seems to claim more than is suggested in Jn.). It is rather the glory of the *Incarnate* Word (see on 1¹⁴), which Jesus exhibited in His earthly ministry (2¹¹), the manifestation of the Divine Nature in man. His disciples were the branches of which He was the Vine (15⁵), or, as it is expressed in 2 Pet. 1⁴, they had become θείας κοινωνοὶ φύσεως, "partakers of the Divine Nature." See on 8⁵⁴ for the "glorification" of the Son by the Father; and for the "glorification" of believers, cf. Rom. 8³⁰.

For **δέδωκας** (אBCLΓΔ), ADNW⊙ have ἔδωκας; and for **δέδωκα** (BCDLWΓΔ), אAN⊙ have ἔδωκα. See on v. 4 for similar variants.

ἵνα ὦσιν ἓν καθὼς ἡμεῖς ἕν. The rec. (⊙) adds ἐσμεν, but om. BC*DLW. The consequence of the imparting of His Incarnate δόξα to His disciples by Jesus would be that, sharing this in common with Him and with each other, they would be spiritually united, and thus be *one*, even as the Father and the Son are *one*.

23. ἐγὼ ἐν αὐτοῖς καὶ σὺ ἐν ἐμοί, the nature of the unity of believers being once again illustrated by that highest pattern of Unity, the Unity of the Godhead. "I in them"; so He had spoken before (14²⁰), and the idea of Christ being "in" the believer is as familiar a thought to Paul as it is to Jn.; cf. Rom. 8¹⁰, 2 Cor. 13⁵, Gal. 2²⁰ 4¹⁹.

ἵνα ὦσιν τετελειωμένοι εἰς ἕν. The imparting of His δόξα to the disciples of Jesus would not only tend to unite them, but it would at last completely unite them, "that they may be perfected (cf. for τελειοῦσθαι used thus, 1 Jn. 2⁵ 4¹²· ¹⁷· ¹⁸; cf. Phil. 3¹²) into one." With τετ. εἰς ἕν, cf. συναγάγῃ εἰς ἕν (11⁵²).

ἵνα γινώσκῃ ὁ κόσμος ὅτι σύ με ἀπέστειλας. Here is the final consequence of the impartation of the "glory" of Jesus to His disciples, viz. that the world might come to be assured of His Divine mission; the phrase being repeated from v. 21, γινώσκῃ being substituted for πιστεύῃ. Cf. the concluding words of the Farewell Discourse, ἵνα γνῷ ὁ κόσμος . . . (14³¹). This is Jesus' ideal of the world's future.

ἀπέστειλας καὶ ἠγάπησας αὐτοὺς καθὼς ἐμὲ ἠγάπησας. 24. Πάτερ,
ὃ δέδωκάς μοι, θέλω ἵνα ὅπου εἰμὶ ἐγὼ κἀκεῖνοι ὦσιν μετ᾽ ἐμοῦ, ἵνα
θεωρῶσιν τὴν δόξαν τὴν ἐμήν, ἣν δέδωκάς μοι ὅτι ἠγάπησάς με πρὸ

καὶ ἠγάπησας αὐτοὺς καθώς κτλ. For thus will the world
be led to the knowledge that God loved it (αὐτούς) with the
same kind of love as that with which He loved His Son (5²⁰);
and that therefore He had sent His Son. These are the thoughts
of the " comfortable word " of 3¹⁶, which are here expressed
as a prayer.

For ἠγάπησας there is a Western reading, ἠγάπησα (D a b,
etc.), which is a mistaken correction (introduced from 15⁹), the
connexion of the passage with 3¹⁶ having been missed.

24. There follows the thought of those who have been
" perfected into one " on earth, sharing the fellowship of their
common Lord in heaven, as they behold His eternal glory.

πάτερ. See on v. 11.

ὃ δέδωκάς μοι. ὅ is for οὕς (cf. v. 12), the neuter singular
suggesting their unity, as at 6³⁷, ³⁹, where see note.

θέλω. He does not now say ἐρωτῶ (v. 20 and see on 11²²),
but θέλω, " I wish." He has said repeatedly that He did not
come to do His own will (θέλημα), but the will of the Father
(4³⁴ 5³⁰ 6³⁸⁻⁴⁰); and in the Agony at Gethsemane He distinguishes His human will from the Father's (οὐ τί ἐγὼ θέλω, ἀλλὰ
τί σύ, Mk. 14³⁶). But at this moment of spiritual exaltation,
the climax of His consecration of Himself to death, He realises
the perfect coincidence of His will with the Father's, and so
can say θέλω (cf. ὁ υἱὸς οὓς θέλει ζωοποιεῖ, 5²¹). The use of
θέλω at 21²² is different, for there it is the θέλω of authority
which the master may address to a disciple.

ἵνα ὅπου εἰμὶ ἐγὼ κἀκεῖνοι ὦσιν μετ᾽ ἐμοῦ, sc. hereafter in glory.
See 12²⁶ 13³⁶ 14³ for the thought of the spiritual fellowship of
His disciples with Christ continuing after death. Cf. 2 Tim.
2¹¹· ¹², Rom. 8¹⁷.

ἵνα θεωρῶσιν τὴν δόξαν τὴν ἐμήν. This is not the glory of the
Incarnate Christ. That they had been permitted to see with
the eyes of the body, ἐθεασάμεθα τὴν δόξαν αὐτοῦ (see on 1¹⁴).
θεωρεῖν is used here of spiritual perception (cf. 12⁴⁵, and see
on 2²³). The δόξα, of which the vision is to be the portion of
the saints, is the glory of the Eternal Logos, which He had with
the Father "before the world was " (v. 5). They are to see
Him " as He is " (1 Jn. 3²).

ἣν δέδωκάς μοι. The rec. has ἔδωκας with BNΓΔΘ, but
אACDLW have δέδωκας (see on v. 4), which is accepted by
Westcott-Hort against the testimony of B.

Against the interpretation of δόξα here as referring to the

καταβολῆς κόσμου.   25. Πάτερ δίκαιε, καὶ ὁ κόσμος σε οὐκ ἔγνω,
ἐγὼ δέ σε ἔγνων, καὶ οὗτοι ἔγνωσαν ὅτι σύ με ἀπέστειλας· 26. καὶ

glory of the *Eternal* Word, several exegetes have urged that
a "giving" of glory by the Father to the Son *before* the Incarnation is not explicitly mentioned elsewhere in the N.T.
But there is no other passage which refers to the eternal relationships inherent in Deity with the same boldness and
confidence of vision that appear in this Last Prayer of Christ.
These are unique utterances (cf. also v. 5); and a clear distinction seems to be indicated between the δόξα of v. 22 which
had been given to the disciples, and the δόξα of v. 24 which
they might hope to contemplate hereafter, but which was given
only to Christ.

ὅτι ἠγάπησάς με πρὸ καταβολῆς κόσμου.   This, in fact, is the
δόξα of the Eternal Word.   Eternal Love *is* Eternal Glory;
even as Eternal *Love* and Eternal *Glory* may be regarded as
respectively the subjective and objective aspects of Eternal *Life*.

πρὸ καταβολῆς κόσμου.   καταβολή occurs only once in the
LXX (2 Macc. 2[29], of the *foundation* of a house), and eleven
times in the N.T., in nine of which it is followed by κόσμου
(ἀπὸ κατ. κόσμ., Mt. 25[34], Lk. 11[50], Heb. 4[3] 9[26], Rev. 13[8] 17[8]).
We find πρὸ καταβολῆς κόσμου, as here, at Eph. 1[4], 1 Pet. 1[20].
The phrase also occurs in the *Assumption of Moses*, a first-
century work, in a passage of which the Greek has been preserved (i. 13, 14, ed. Charles).   The sentence "in that Thou
hast loved me before the foundation of the world," suggests
the idea of *predestination*, so frequently appearing in Jn.
(see on 2[4]).

25. Πάτερ δίκαιε.   That God is *righteous* is fundamental
in the Jewish religion (cf. Jer. 12[1], Ps. 116[5] 119[137]), and fundamental, too, in Christianity (Rom. 3[26], Rev. 16[5], 1 Jn. 1[9]).   The
appeal at this point of the Prayer is to the *justice* of God, that
He may distinguish between those who accept the Divine
mission of Jesus, and the hostile world which rejects Him.
For the former, Jesus has made the request that they may be
with Him, hereafter (v. 24).

καί, before ὁ κόσμος, "is intended to keep the reader in
suspense, aware that the meaning is incomplete" (Abbott,
Diat. 2164).   It is omitted by D

ὁ κόσμος σε οὐκ ἔγνω.   See on 8[55].

ἐγὼ δέ σε ἔγνων.   This is a parenthetical sentence, the real
antithesis to "the world knew Thee not" being "but these
knew," which follows.   Jesus, as Incarnate, habitually claims
a unique knowledge of God (7[29] 8[55] 10[15]).

καὶ οὗτοι ἔγνωσαν κτλ.   "But these knew that Thou didst

ἐγνώρισα αὐτοῖς τὸ ὄνομά σου καὶ γνωρίσω, ἵνα ἡ ἀγάπη ἣν ἠγάπησάς με ἐν αὐτοῖς ᾖ κἀγὼ ἐν αὐτοῖς.

send me," this being the important thing to be assured of, viz. that God had sent Jesus, this refrain occurring for the last time (see on v. 8). The thought of Jesus returns from the Church of the future to the disciples in whose company He offered a last prayer. Its final clauses have to do with them. οὗτοι, *these*, knew this much at least, that the mission of Jesus was divine.

The contrast with the failure of "the world" to recognise Him is brought up by καί, used here adversatively, as often in Jn. (see on 3¹¹): "*but* these knew."

26. καὶ ἐγνώρισα αὐτοῖς τὸ ὄνομά σου, repeated in slightly different form from v. 6, where see note. For γνωρίζειν, cf. 15¹⁵.

καὶ γνωρίσω, *sc.* in the Church of the future, by the Spirit which is to come (16¹². ²⁵).

ἵνα ἡ ἀγάπη ἣν ἠγάπησάς με ἐν αὐτοῖς ᾖ. This is not a prayer that God may love Christian disciples with the same kind of love as that with which He loved Christ. Already, at v. 23, we have seen that even "the world"—in its alienation and hostility—was thus loved by God, although the world did not recognise it. But the prayer is that the love of God for all Christian disciples, similar as it is to the love of God for Christ, may be "in them," that is, their sense of it may become vivid and efficacious ; so that they may recognise, in Paul's words, "that the love of God has been shed abroad in their hearts, through the Holy Spirit " (Rom. 5⁵).

For ἥν after ἀγάπη D substitutes the more usual ᾗ, *qua*; but there is an exact parallel to the true reading at Eph. 2⁴: διὰ τὴν πολλὴν ἀγάπην αὐτοῦ ἣν ἠγάπησεν ἡμᾶς (cf. 7³⁹ for a similar constr.).

κἀγὼ ἐν αὐτοῖς. "I in them." This has already been proclaimed as the ideal condition of the disciples of Christ (v. 23, where see note). Here the thought is, as in the preceding clause, of a growing sense of Christ's presence in the believer's heart. It is this for which the last petition is offered, " ut cor ipsorum theatrum sit et palaestra huius amoris " (Bengel). *Ego in ipsis* is the last aspiration of Jesus for His own, before He goes forth to meet death.

The arrest of Jesus in the garden (XVIII. 1–11)

XVIII. 1. ταῦτα εἰπών. As soon as the Prayer of Consecration was ended (see Introd., p. xx), Jesus and His disciples

XVIII. 1. Ταῦτα εἰπὼν Ἰησοῦς ἐξῆλθεν σὺν τοῖς μαθηταῖς αὐτοῦ πέραν τοῦ χειμάρρου τοῦ Κέδρων, ὅπου ἦν κῆπος, εἰς ὃν

left the upper room, and went out, ἐξῆλθεν perhaps implying (as was in fact the case) that they went outside the *city*.

σὺν τοῖς μαθηταῖς αὐτοῦ, *sc.* with the faithful Eleven (see on 2²). This is one of the very rare occurrences of σύν in Jn. (see on 12²), and it is exchanged for μετά within a couple of lines, μετὰ τῶν μαθητῶν αὐτοῦ (v. 2).

πέραν τοῦ χειμάρρου τοῦ Κέδρων. The Kedron gorge between Jerusalem and the Mount of Olives rarely has any water in it. It is called χείμαρρος by Josephus as well as in the LXX (Neh. 2¹⁵, 1 Macc. 12³⁷), but it is nearly always dry, except after very heavy rain.[1]   The modern name is *Wādy Sitti Maryam*.

The majority of texts (א*BCLNΘ) give τῶν κέδρων; א*DW have τοῦ κέδρου; and AΔ *c e f g q* vg. give τοῦ κέδρων   This last, despite the weakness of the MS. support, we take to be the true reading (as the Syriac vss. suggest), and that from which both the others have originated, owing to misunderstanding on the part of scribes. For κέδρων is the transliteration of the Hebrew קִדְרוֹן, *dark*, the name as applied to a torrent being perhaps equivalent to our *Blackwater*.   Josephus treats it as a declinable noun in the nom. case.   Twice in the LXX (2 Sam. 15²³, 1 Kings 15¹³) we find τῶν κέδρων after χείμαρρος, the word being taken as a gen. pl., and the rendering of the phrase being "the ravine (or torrent) of the cedar trees." It is said that at the time cedars grew on the Mount of Olives, and some may have been as low as the *wādy* at its base.   But it is not likely that the ravine was called *Kidron* on that account. A Greek scribe, finding τοῦ κέδρων in his exemplar, would naturally take κέδρων as the gen. pl. of κέδρος, and would correct it either to τοῦ κέδρου or to τῶν κέδρων.[2]

The reading has been much discussed, because assuming τῶν κέδρων to have been the original reading, it has been argued that the evangelist was but ill acquainted with Hebrew names, if he supposed that *Kidron* meant "of the cedars." But, as the LXX shows in the passages cited above, χείμαρρος τῶν κέδρων was treated as a correct rendering of נַחַל קִדְרוֹן, and it *might* have been adopted by Jn. as the title familiar to Greek ears. We hold, however, that it is not the original reading in this verse, so that the argument based on it is worthless.

ὅπου ἦν κῆπος.   Jn. does not give the name *Gethsemane*,[3]

[1] See G. A. Smith, *Jerusalem*, i. 80 f.
[2] Cf. Lightfoot (*Bibl. Essays*, p. 173), Westcott *in loc.*, and Abbott (*Diat.* 2671–4).
[3] Probably גַּת שְׁמָנִים = "oil press" at the foot of the Mount of Olives.

εἰσῆλθεν αὐτὸς καὶ οἱ μαθηταὶ αὐτοῦ.   2. ᾔδει δὲ καὶ Ἰούδας ὁ παραδιδοὺς αὐτὸν τὸν τόπον, ὅτι πολλάκις συνήχθη Ἰησοῦς ἐκεῖ μετὰ τῶν

nor does Lk.; Mk. 14³², Mt. 26³⁶ have χωρίον (*i.e.* a farm or small
property) οὗ τὸ ὄνομα Γεθσημανεί. Jn. alone speaks of it as
κῆπος, *i.e.* it was one of the private gardens in the eastern out-
skirts of Jerusalem (cf. 19⁴¹ for the garden of Joseph). The
word κῆπος is common in the LXX, but in the N.T. is found
only here, at v. 26, 19⁴¹ (cf. 20¹⁵), and Lk. 13¹⁹. For ἦν, see
on 11¹⁸.

εἰς ὃν εἰσῆλθεν, the verb showing that it was an enclosed
place. The site that is now shown was recognised as the
Garden of the Agony in the fourth century at any rate, and
it is quite possible that tradition accurately preserved its position from the beginning.

Jn. does not insert at this point any account of the Agony
in Gethsemane, as the Synoptists do (Mk. 14³²ᶠ·, Mt. 26³⁶ᶠ·,
Lk. 22³⁹ᶠ·); but the allusion to "the cup which the Father
gave" (v. 11, where see note) indicates that the omission was
not due to ignorance. We have seen (on 12²⁷) that the prayer
there recorded is virtually the prayer of anguish at Gethsemane.

It has been suggested, indeed, that the Prayer of the Agony,
if it followed here, would be inconsistent with the Prayer of
Consecration and Farewell that Jn. has just placed on record;
so different are the sublime calm and dignity of c. 17 from the
sadness and shrinking of "remove this cup from me—yet not
what I will, but what Thou wilt" (Mk. 14³⁶). But such a
criticism would be at variance with the facts of human experience, in which the moments of greatest spiritual depression
and trial often follow close on moods of the highest spiritual
exaltation. And it may have been so with the Son of Man
Himself.

2. ᾔδει δὲ καὶ Ἰούδας. The garden was a favourite resort
of Jesus and His disciples (πολλάκις συνήχθη), and probably
belonged to a friend. It is specially mentioned by Jn. that
Judas knew the place. Jesus was not now trying to escape
arrest (cf. 10⁴⁰), for Jn. is anxious to indicate that His surrender
to His captors was voluntary. Jesus had told Judas to delay
no longer the execution of his purpose (13²⁷), and He proceeded
the same night to a place where Judas knew that He was
accustomed to resort.

ὁ παραδιδοὺς αὐτόν, the pres. tense indicating that Judas
was then engaged in the business of the betrayal. Cf. 13¹¹.

τὸν τόπον. Cf. Lk. 22⁴⁰.

πολλάκις, only here in Jn. Jesus went to the garden, as
His custom was (κατὰ τὸ ἔθος, Lk. 22³⁹), and probably not

μαθητῶν αὐτοῦ.   3. ὁ οὖν Ἰούδας λαβὼν τὴν σπεῖραν καὶ ἐκ τῶν
ἀρχιερέων καὶ ἐκ τῶν Φαρισαίων ὑπηρέτας ἔρχεται ἐκεῖ μετὰ φανῶν

only on this last visit to Jerusalem. συνήχθη tells only that this
was a place of habitual resort of Jesus and His disciples, but
possibly they may have slept there occasionally. (Cf. Lk.
21³⁷, τὰς δὲ νύκτας ἐξερχόμενος ηὐλίζετο εἰς τὸ ὄρος τὸ καλούμενον
Ἐλαιῶν.) If this be so, the sleep of the apostles in the garden
during the hour preceding the arrest was natural indeed,
although they had been bidden to keep awake.

3. The Synoptists say nothing about soldiers taking part in
the arrest of Jesus, and mention only the emissaries of the
Sanhedrim (Mk. 14⁴³, Lk. 22⁵² stating that members of the
Sanhedrim were themselves in the crowd). Jn. mentions these
latter (ἐκ τῶν ἀρχιερέων καὶ ἐκ τῶν Φαρισαίων ὑπηρέτας) in the same
terms that he has done before when telling of a projected arrest
(7³², where see the note for the constitution and authority of the
Sanhedrim) ; but he adds here that Judas had brought with
him also a detachment of soldiers (τὴν σπεῖραν).

Troops were always quartered in Fort Antonia, at festival
seasons when the city was crowded, to be ready in case of a
riot; and a representation from the Sanhedrim to the military
authorities that soldiers might be needed to help the Temple
guard (ὑπηρέτας: cf. 7³²) would naturally have been acted on.
Pilate, the procurator, seems to have known that something
important was taking place that night, for he was ready at an
early hour in the morning to hear the case (v. 28; cf. Mt. 27¹⁹,
for the dream of Pilate's wife). There is nothing improbable
in Jn.'s statement that soldiers were present at the arrest.

The term σπεῖρα (if the soldiers were legionaries) was
generally equivalent to the Latin *cohors*, which numbered 600
men. Polybius, indeed, uses it (xi. 23. 1) for *manipulus*, which
is only one-third of a cohort. But here (if, as is probable, they
were auxiliaries) and in the N.T. elsewhere (see esp. Acts 21³¹)
it numbered 1000 men (240 horse and 760 foot), commanded
by a chiliarch (cf. v. 12 below), a *tribunus militum*. It is
not, however, to be supposed that Jn. means that the whole
strength of the regiment (cf. Mk. 15¹⁶) was turned out to aid
in the arrest of Jesus; the words λαβὼν τὴν σπεῖραν indicate
no more than that Judas had got the help of "the cohort,"
i.e. a detachment, with whom the commanding officer of the
garrison came (v. 12), in view of possible developments.

Fam. 13 insert ὅλην before τὴν σπεῖραν (probably from
Mk. 15¹⁶), which shows that the scribe of the common exemplar
thought that τὴν σπεῖραν was not sufficiently definite.

καὶ ἐκ τῶν ἀρχιερέων καὶ ἐκ τῶν Φαρισαίων ὑπηρέτας, *i.e.* officers

καὶ λαμπάδων καὶ ὅπλων. 4. Ἰησοῦς οὖν εἰδὼς πάντα τὰ ἐρχόμενα
ἐπ' αὐτὸν ἐξῆλθεν καὶ λέγει αὐτοῖς Τίνα ζητεῖτε; 5. ἀπεκρίθησαν

of the Sanhedrim (see on 7³² for οἱ ἀρχ. καὶ οἱ Φαρισ., as indicating
the Sanhedrim in its official capacity).   For ὑπηρέτας, cf. 18¹². ²²
19⁶ and Mt. 26⁵⁸; they were the Temple police, under the control
of the Sanhedrim.

μετὰ φανῶν καὶ λαμπάδων. It was the time of the Paschal
full moon, but lights were brought, nevertheless, to search out
the dark recesses of the garden, in case Jesus should attempt to
hide Himself.

φανός (ἅπ. λεγ. in N.T.) is a "link" or "torch," made of
strips of wood fastened together, and λαμπάς is an ordinary
torch-light, the word being used in later Greek for a lantern.
Both were carried by Roman soldiers on duty; cf. Dion. Hal.
xi. 5, ἐξέτρεχον ἅπαντες ἐκ τῶν σκηνῶν ἀθρόοι, φανοὺς ἔχοντες καὶ
λαμπάδας.¹ Lights also were carried, when necessary, by the
Temple guard; thus Lightfoot (on Lk. 22⁴) quotes: "The ruler
of the mountain of the Temple takes his walks through every
watch with torches lighted before him" (*Middoth* i. 2).

καὶ ὅπλων. The Temple guard was not always armed
(Joseph. *B.J.*, iv. 4. 6), but on this occasion they probably
carried weapons as well as the soldiers.   Mk. 14⁴³ speaks of a
crowd with swords and staves (ὄχλος μετὰ μαχαιρῶν καὶ ξύλων)
who had been sent by the Sanhedrim.

4. Ἰησοῦς οὖν. אDLW have δέ for οὖν.

εἰδώς. Cf. 13¹. Jn. is at every point careful to insist that
Jesus foreknew the issues of His ministry, πάντα τὰ ἐρχόμενα ἐπ'
αὐτόν, "everything that was coming upon Him."

ἐξῆλθεν, "went out," *sc.* of the garden into which He had
entered, εἰσῆλθεν (v. 1). The rec. text with אAC³LNΘ has
ἐξελθὼν εἶπεν, but ἐξῆλθεν καὶ λέγει (BC*D) is more in the style
of Jn. (see on 1⁵⁰).

καὶ λέγει αὐτοῖς. He does not address Himself directly to
Judas, but to those who had come, armed, to arrest Him, and
He asks Τίνα ζητεῖτε; Cf. 1³⁸ 20¹⁵.

In the Synoptic narratives (Mk. 14⁴⁵, Mt. 26⁴⁹, Lk. 22⁴⁷)
Judas comes forward and identifies Jesus by a kiss, that is,
by kissing His hand, the recognised salutation from a disciple
to His Master (not by kissing His cheek, as Western painters
have been accustomed to depict the act).   Jn. does not mention
this treacherous sign, and his omission to do so is a difficulty in
the way of critics who think that Jn. displays special animus
against Judas (see on 12⁶).   His reason for the omission is

---

¹ Quoted by Wetstein ; cf. Trench, *Synonyms of N.T.*, p. 162, for
the meaning of λαμπάς in the N.T.

αὐτῷ Ἰησοῦν τὸν Ναζωραῖον. λέγει αὐτοῖς Ἐγώ εἰμι. εἱστήκει δὲ
καὶ Ἰούδας ὁ παραδιδοὺς αὐτὸν μετ' αὐτῶν. 6. ὡς οὖν εἶπεν αὐτοῖς

probably that he is laying stress throughout on the *voluntariness*
of Jesus' acceptance of arrest. Jesus does not wait to be
identified by any one, for He at once announces who He is.
Jn.'s narrative seems to suggest that He had not been recognised
in the uncertain light, even after He came out of the garden
and asked, " Whom seek ye ? " Tatian places the kiss of
Judas immediately *before* v. 4, *i.e.* before Jesus came out of the
garden; and if it is sought to bring the evangelical narratives
into exact correspondence, Tatian's solution may be the right
one.[1]

Jn. says (v. 5) that " Judas, who was in the act of delivering
Him up " (ὁ παραδιδοὺς αὐτόν, cf. 13²), was standing (εἱστήκει)
with those who were making the arrest. Judas had done his
part when he had guided the emissaries of the Sanhedrim to
the place where Jesus was. The scene is described very
vividly.

5. ἀπεκρ. αὐτῷ Ἰησοῦν τὸν Ναζωραῖον. " Jesus the Nazarene,"
or " Jesus of Nazareth," was the name by which He had been
popularly known. The blind man was told that it was " Jesus
of Nazareth " who was passing by (Mk. 10⁴⁷, Lk. 18³⁷). The
man with the unclean devil addressed Him as " Thou Jesus
of Nazareth " (Lk. 4³⁴). The two disciples on the way to
Emmaus spoke of Him thus (Lk. 24¹⁹). So did Peter in his
sermon at Pentecost (Acts 2²²). In Mk.'s account of the Resurrection, the young man at the sepulchre says to the women,
" Ye seek Jesus of Nazareth " (Mk. 16⁶). After His arrest,
He was familiarly described in this way by the maid in the
court of the high priest (Mk. 14⁶⁷, Mt. 26⁷¹). It is clear that
the instructions given to those sent to apprehend Him were
that they should take " Jesus of Nazareth." They inquired
for Him by the designation by which He was best known.
See 19¹⁹.

Jn.'s narrative indicates, as has been said above, that Jesus
identified Himself voluntarily, by saying, " I am He," in
answer to the request for " Jesus of Nazareth." And ἐγώ
εἰμι in v. 5 may mean simply, " I am He of whom you are in
search " (cf. 4²⁶ 9⁹). The reading of B ἐγώ εἰμι Ἰησοῦς *must*
carry this meaning.

6. The words which follow, "they retired and fell to the
ground," then, imply no more than that the men who came
to make the arrest (some of whom at least did not previously

[1] For a curious speculation as to a possible corruption of the text
here, see Abbott (*Diat.* 1365).

Ἐγώ εἰμι, ἀπῆλθαν εἰς τὰ ὀπίσω καὶ ἔπεσαν χαμαί. 7. πάλιν οὖν ἐπηρώτησεν αὐτούς Τίνα ζητεῖτε; οἱ δὲ εἶπαν Ἰησοῦν τὸν Ναζωραῖον. 8. ἀπεκρίθη Ἰησοῦς Εἶπον ὑμῖν ὅτι ἐγώ εἰμι· εἰ οὖν ἐμὲ ζητεῖτε, ἄφετε τούτους ὑπάγειν· 9. ἵνα πληρωθῇ ὁ λόγος ὃν εἶπεν, ὅτι Οὓς δέδωκάς

know Jesus even by sight) were so overcome by His moral ascendancy that they recoiled in fear. (For the Johannine ὡς οὖν, see on 4⁴⁰.) On a previous occasion (7⁴⁴), when some wished to arrest Him, they had faltered and failed to do so. It may have been a similar shrinking which caused some now to recoil from their distasteful task, and in the confusion they, or some of the crowd, stumbled and fell. Indeed, ἔπεσαν χαμαί might be taken figuratively, as expressing discomfiture only. Thus in Ps. 27², Isa. 8¹⁵, Jer. 46⁶, " stumbled and fell " means no more than that enemies were " overthrown " ; and ἔπεσαν χαμαί might be rendered in colloquial English " were floored."

There is no hint in the Synoptists of any hesitancy on the part of those sent to make the arrest   The phrases ἀπῆλθαν εἰς τὰ ὀπίσω (cf. 6⁶⁶) and ἔπεσαν χαμαί (χαμαί is only found again in the N.T. at 9⁶) are peculiar to Jn. And it has been suggested (e.g. by W. Bauer) that Jn. means us to understand that ἐγώ εἰμι, as used by Jesus on this occasion, is the equivalent of the mysterious אֲנִי־הוּא, I (am) He, which is the self-designation of Yahweh in the prophetical books (cf. 8⁵⁸ 13¹⁹ above, and Introd., pp. cxxvii ff.); and that so awful a claim overwhelmed with terror those who heard it made (cf. Dan. 10⁹, Rev. 1¹⁷). But this is too subtle a rendering of the Johannine narrative of the arrest. Cf. Rev. 1¹⁷.

In the *Gospel of Peter*, § 5, where the darkness at the Crucifixion is described, we have περιήρχοντο δὲ πολλοὶ μετὰ λύχνων, νομίζοντες ὅτι νὺξ ἐστιν. [τινὲς δὲ] ἐπέσαντο. This seems to be a reminiscence of Jn. 18³˙⁶; cf. also *Acta Thomæ*, § 157.

7. The question and answer are repeated: " Whom seek ye ? . . . Jesus the Nazarene." This time, those who had come to arrest Him knew to whom they were speaking, but they were so much overawed that they could only repeat what they had said before.

The rec. has αὐτοὺς ἐπηρώτησεν, with אDNΘ ; but ABCL give the more usual order ἐπηρώτησεν αὐτούς.

8. The reply is stern and authoritative. He repeats ἐγώ εἰμι (see on v. 5).

εἰ οὖν ἐμὲ ζητ. κτλ. " If, then, it is I (emphatic) whom you seek, let these (*sc.* the Eleven) go their way," or " go home," for ὑπάγειν has a suggestion of this meaning (see on 7³³). His solicitude for His faithful disciples is characteristic of the Good Shepherd (cf. 10¹², and see on v. 19).

μοι, οὐκ ἀπώλεσα ἐξ αὐτῶν οὐδένα. 10. Σίμων οὖν Πέτρος ἔχων

9. ἵνα πληρωθῇ ὁ λόγος κτλ. For the phrase ἵνα πληρ., introducing a saying of Jesus, see Introd., p. cxliii f. Another example is in v. 32. For Jn., the words of Jesus were possessed of authority, and inspired, like the language of the O.T., by foreknowledge of future events. The λόγος, or "saying" (see on 2²²), to which reference is here made is that of 17¹² loosely quoted. ὅτι is *recitantis*, but it does not introduce the exact words previously ascribed to Jesus.

The comment of Jn. (ἵνα πλ. ὁ λόγος κτλ.) would seem to limit the application of "I lost none of those whom thou gavest me" to the fact that the disciples were let go free when Jesus was arrested. Some at least of Jn.'s explanations of the words of Jesus are of doubtful accuracy (see on 2¹⁹· ²¹); but it is hard to believe that he could have missed here the larger and more spiritual meaning of 17¹², which is already indicated at 6³⁹ 10²⁸.

οὓς δέδωκάς μοι, οὐκ ἀπώλεσα ἐξ αὐτῶν οὐδένα. The close verbal parallel in 2 Esd. 2²⁶ is interesting: "servos quos tibi dedi, nemo ex eis interiet, ego enim eos requiram de numero tuo," words which are addressed by God to the personified nation. Chapters i. and ii. of 2 Esdras are Christian, and probably belong to the second century. The passage quoted above may be a reminiscence of Jn. 18³ or Jn. 17¹² or Jn. 6³⁷. See on 3³¹ above for other parallels between 2 Esdras and Jn.

10. The incident of one of the Twelve attacking the high priest's slave is in all the Gospels (Mk. 14⁴⁷, Mt. 26⁵¹, Lk. 22⁵⁰), although the names, Peter and Malchus, are given by Jn. only.

It appears from Lk. 22³⁸, that the apostles had two swords or knives in their possession; and Lk. also tells that, when they understood that the salutation of Judas was the signal for the arrest of Jesus, they exclaimed, "Lord, shall we smite with the sword?" It would seem that Peter, always hasty and impulsive, struck a blow without waiting for permission from Jesus. He had been forward in declaring that he would give his life for his Master, if there was need (13³⁷). He did not generally carry a sword; ἔχων μάχαιραν implies that he happened to have one with him at the time, presumably because he and others had learnt from what Jesus had said previously that their Master was in danger. It was unlawful to carry arms on a feast-day, and—although at such a crisis, an eager disciple like Peter would probably have had no scruple in breaking the law if the safety of his Master was at stake— the fact that two of the company had knives with them earlier in the evening tends to show that the Last Supper was not

μάχαιραν εἵλκυσεν αὐτὴν καὶ ἔπαισεν τὸν τοῦ ἀρχιερέως δοῦλον καὶ ἀπέκοψεν αὐτοῦ τὸ ὠτάριον τὸ δεξιόν· ἦν δὲ ὄνομα τῷ δούλῳ Μάλχος.

the Passover, and that the Johannine rather than the Synoptic tradition of the day of the Crucifixion is to be followed (see Introd., p. cvi f.).

Peter drew (see on 6⁴⁴ for ἑλκύειν) the sword, καὶ ἔπαισεν τὸν τοῦ ἀρχιερέως δοῦλον, "and struck the high priest's slave." This man was one of the crowd which had gathered; he was not one of the Temple guard (ὑπηρέτας, v. 3). There was something of a scuffle, and Peter hit out.

καὶ ἀπέκοψεν αὐτοῦ τὸ ὠτάριον τὸ δεξιόν, "and cut off his right ear," the blow missing the slave's head, as he swerved to his left to avoid it. That it was the *right* ear is a detail only found in Lk. and Jn. ὠτάριον, the true reading here (אBC*LW), is the word used by Mk. (14⁴⁷); ὠτίον, of the rec. text (AC³DNΘ), is the word in Mt. 26⁵¹ and in Lk. 22⁵¹.

We have here, without doubt, a tradition of an historical incident. If it be asked why Peter was not immediately arrested by the Temple guard or the soldiers who were standing by, the answer may be that it was not observed in the scuffle who had dealt the blow. The earlier Gospels do not disclose Peter's name, although by the time that Jn. wrote, there would be no risk in giving it. Again, an injury to a slave would not excite much interest; had Peter struck one of the officials, it would have been a different matter. Lk. tells, indeed, that Jesus healed the wound (Lk. 22⁵¹), apparently suggesting that the ear had not been wholly severed from the man's head.

ἦν δὲ ὄνομα τῷ δούλῳ Μάλχος. Here, again, is a detail that comes from first-hand knowledge. No evangelist has it except Jn. The name *Malchus* is found five times in Josephus, and probably goes back to the root מלך or "king." Cf. Neh. 10⁴.

11. Jesus forbids the use of arms in resisting His arrest. The Synoptists represent Him as expostulating against it, and especially against the violent way in which it was effected (Mk. 14⁴⁸, Mt. 26⁵⁵, Lk. 22⁵²); but in Jn.'s narrative there is none of this. He moves voluntarily towards the predestined end.

Βάλε τὴν μάχαιραν εἰς τὴν θήκην, "put back the sword into the sheath." Mt., alone of the Synoptists, tells of this saying, which he gives in a more diffuse form: ἀπόστρεψόν σου τὴν μάχαιραν εἰς τὸν τόπον αὐτῆς· πάντες γὰρ οἱ λαβόντες μάχαιραν ἐν μαχαίρᾳ ἀπολοῦνται (Mt. 26⁵²), the latter clause suggesting the hand of an editor. According to Jn., Jesus gave no reason for the quiet command, "Put up your sword." See on v. 36 below.

11. εἶπεν οὖν ὁ Ἰησοῦς τῷ Πέτρῳ Βάλε τὴν μάχαιραν εἰς τὴν θήκην· τὸ ποτήριον ὃ δέδωκέν μοι ὁ Πατήρ, οὐ μὴ πίω αὐτό; 12. Ἡ οὖν σπεῖρα καὶ ὁ χιλίαρχος καὶ οἱ ὑπηρέται τῶν Ἰουδαίων συνέλαβον τὸν Ἰησοῦν καὶ ἔδησαν αὐτόν, 13. καὶ ἤγαγον πρὸς Ἄνναν

After **μάχαιραν** the rec. adds σου (from Mt. 26⁵²), but om. אABCDLNWΘ.

θήκη does not occur again in the N.T.

τὸ ποτήριον ὃ δέδωκέν μοι ὁ πατήρ, οὐ μὴ πίω αὐτό; This recalls the prayer of Jesus at Gethsemane, as recorded by the Synoptists (Mk. 14³⁶, Mt. 26³⁹, Lk. 22⁴²). See on v. 1 above and on 12²⁷.

οὐ μὴ πίω αὐτό is probably to be taken as an interrogative. Abbott, however (*Diat.* 934 *f*, 2232), prefers to take it as an exclamation, " I am, of course, not to drink it ! " [*sc.* according to your desire], comparing οὐ μὴ πίω of Mk. 14²⁵, Mt. 26²⁹, Lk. 22¹⁸. See on 6³⁷.

Jesus is bound and brought to the house of Annas (vv. 12-14)

12. Jn. does not record explicitly that His disciples fled in fear after Jesus had been arrested (Mk. 14⁵⁰, Mt. 26⁵⁶), although he has told that Jesus earlier in the night had predicted that they would abandon Him (16³²). Jn. implies, however (see on v. 15), that Jesus was abandoned at this point by His friends.

The arrest was effected by the Roman soldiers (see on v. 3 for σπεῖρα), with their commanding officer (cf. Acts 21³¹ for χιλίαρχος), acting in co-operation with the Temple police (οἱ ὑπηρέται τῶν Ἰουδαίων). συνλαμβάνειν does not occur again in Jn., but it is the verb used by the Synoptists in this context.

καὶ ἔδησαν αὐτόν. That was a matter of course; probably His hands were fastened behind His back. The Synoptists do not mention this detail until a later point in the narrative (Mk. 15¹, Mt. 27¹; cf. v. 24). It was a patristic fancy that the binding of Jesus was foreshadowed in the binding of Isaac at the altar (Gen. 22⁹); see on 19¹⁷ below.

13. **ἤγαγον.** So אBDW (and Lk. 22⁵⁴); the rec. has ἀπήγαγον (with AC³LNΓΘ, as at Mk. 14⁵³, Mt. 26⁵⁷).

πρὸς Ἄνναν πρῶτον. Annas was not, at this time, *the* high priest, but he had held the office before and was a personage of such influence that he was often *called* " high priest " in a loose way (cf. Lk. 3², Acts 4⁶, and see on 7³²), although that great office was now held by his son-in-law Caiaphas (see on 11⁴⁹ above).¹ It was to his house that Jesus was brought after

¹ The title ἀρχιερεῖς included all ex-high priests (see Schürer, *Hist. of Jewish People*, Eng. Tr., II. i. p. 203).

πρῶτον· ἦν γὰρ πενθερὸς τοῦ Καϊάφα, ὃς ἦν ἀρχιερεὺς τοῦ ἐνιαυτοῦ

His arrest, and there an informal and extra-judicial questioning
of Him went on during the night hours (Mk. 14⁵³ᶠ·, Mt. 26⁵⁷).
Mk. does not give any name : he only says, "they led Jesus
away to the high priest"; but Mt. inserts the name *Caiaphas*
at this point, in which he seems to have been mistaken.
Caiaphas presided at the formal meeting of the Sanhedrim
(Mk. 15¹, Mt. 27¹, Lk. 22⁶⁶, Jn. 18²⁴), held the next morning
as early as possible, when the sentence of death, already agreed
on (Mk. 14⁶⁴), was ratified, and submitted to Pilate, who alone
had authority to order it to be carried out.

It was during the night, at the house of Annas (not the
house of Caiaphas, or the formal place of meeting for the
Sanhedrim, which could legally meet only by day), that the
evidence, such as it was, was prepared, and that the Prisoner
was treated with insult and contumely. Such irregular proceedings would not have been countenanced at a *formal*
meeting of the Sanhedrim, but they were winked at in the courtyard of Annas' private house, which was the scene of Peter's
denial and the reproachful look which Jesus bestowed on him
(Lk. 22⁶¹). Probably some of the evidence as to blasphemy
was repeated in due form at the official sitting of the Sanhedrim,
at which Luke (who says nothing of the preliminary hearing
before Annas) states that Jesus admitted His claim to be
Messiah (Lk. 22⁷⁰), in similar words to those which Mk. 14⁶²,
Mt. 26⁶⁴ ascribe to Him at the earlier cross-examination.

Such seems to have been the course of events on the night of
the arrest and the next morning; but it is not possible to
reconcile precisely all the evangelical accounts.[1] The narrative
of Jn. seems at certain points (vv. 13, 19–23, 26) to be based
on first-hand knowledge, to which the other evangelists had not
access.

ἦν γὰρ πενθερὸς τοῦ Καϊάφα. This piece of information is not
given in the other Gospels, nor does the word πενθερός occur
again in the N.T.

ὃς ἦν ἀρχιερεὺς τοῦ ἐνιαυτοῦ ἐκείνου. This is repeated from
11⁴⁹· ⁵¹. Caiaphas was the official high priest, and that a man
of his principles should have held the position in that fateful
year had grave and awful consequences. See on 11⁴⁹.

The Sinai Syriac places v. 24 at this point after v. 13. The
marginal texts of the Jerusalem and Philoxenian Syriac also
have here "Annas sent Jesus (bound) to Caiaphas," although
v. 24 is retained in its traditional place. Similarly the cursive

---

[1] See, for careful discussions, Schmiedel in *E.B.* 4580 f., and
Moffatt in *D.C.G.* ii. 750 f.

ἐκείνου· 14. ἦν δὲ Καϊάφας ὁ συμβουλεύσας τοῖς Ἰουδαίοις ὅτι συμφέρει ἕνα ἄνθρωπον ἀποθανεῖν ὑπὲρ τοῦ λαοῦ.

15. Ἠκολούθει δὲ τῷ Ἰησοῦ Σίμων Πέτρος καὶ ἄλλος μαθητής.

225 and Cyril Alex. add after πρῶτον, ἀπέστειλεν οὖν αὐτὸν ὁ Ἀννας δεδεμένον πρὸς Καϊάφαν τὸν ἀρχιερέα.

These additions or transpositions are due probably to a desire to bring Jn.'s narrative of the examinations of Jesus by the Jewish authorities into line with the narrative of the Synoptists, who say nothing of the part played by Annas. If v. 24 is moved to a point between v. 13 and v. 14, then all that happens takes place in the house of Caiaphas (as is explicitly said by Mt.), and Annas really does nothing, although Jesus in the Johannine narrative is brought to his house in the first instance.

But, if this were the original position of the words " Annas sent Him bound unto the high priest," it is difficult to find a reason for their being moved by a scribe to their traditional place, after v. 23. See, further, Introd., p. xxvii.

14. The reference is to 11⁵⁰, the unconscious prophecy (as Jn. deems it) made by Caiaphas, which expressed his deliberate conviction that Jesus must be brought to His death. For ἀποθανεῖν (אBC*DWΘ), the rec. here has ἀπολέσθαι (with AC²N), which may be the original reading, corrected by scribes to bring the words into verbal correspondence with 11⁵⁰.

At 11⁵⁰ we had συμφέρει . . . ἵνα εἷς ἄνθρωπος ἀποθάνῃ, but here συμφέρει ἕνα ἄνθρωπον ἀποθανεῖν, a more correct constr.

Peter's first denial of Jesus (vv. 15-18)

15. ἠκολούθει, a descriptive impf. The Synoptists say that Peter was following (ἀπὸ μακρόθεν) at a safe distance (Mk. 14⁵⁴, Mt. 26⁵⁸, Lk. 22⁵⁴), but they do not mention a companion.

Σίμων Πέτρος. Jn. likes to use the double name (see on 1⁴²) when Peter has been absent from the picture for some little time, but he generally relapses into the simple " Peter " as the story proceeds ; see, e.g., 13²⁴. ³⁶ 18¹⁰. ¹¹ 20². ³. ⁴ 21³. ⁷. ¹⁵. ¹⁷. ²⁰. ²¹. Jn. never gives the short title " Peter " to this apostle at the beginning of an incident in which he is concerned. In the present passage we have Simon Peter (v. 15), followed by Peter (vv. 16, 17, 18); then there is an interval, and so when the courtyard scene is resumed, we have Simon Peter again (v. 25), followed by Peter (vv. 26, 27).

καὶ ἄλλος μαθητής. So א*ABDˢᵘᵖᵖW. The rec. has ὁ ἄλλος

ὁ δὲ μαθητὴς ἐκεῖνος ἦν γνωστὸς τῷ ἀρχιερεῖ, καὶ συνεισῆλθεν τῷ

(from v. 16) with אᶜᵇCLNOΓΔΘ, thus identifying Peter's companion here with " the Beloved Disciple."

This " other disciple " was " known to the high priest," and so was admitted into the courtyard or αὐλή of the house where Jesus had been brought. He was sufficiently well known to the portress, at any rate, to persuade her to admit his companion. It does not follow that he was a personal friend of Annas or of Caiaphas, or of the same social class, although this is possible. As Sanday put it: " The account of what happened to Peter might well seem to be told from the point of view of the servants' hall." [1] The word γνωστός as applied to persons is uncommon, as Abbott points out (*Diat.* x. ii. p. 351 f.), but it is to press it too far to interpret it here as meaning " a familiar friend," with an allusion to Ps. 55¹³. Abbott adopts the curious view that the " other disciple " was Judas Iscariot, whose face would have been familiar to the portress, because of his previous visit or visits to the high priest in pursuance of his scheme of betrayal. But that Judas should *wish* to introduce Peter, or that Peter would have tolerated any advances from him or accepted his good offices, is difficult to believe.

The view most generally taken [2] as to the personality of this ἄλλος μαθητής is that he was John the Beloved Disciple, whose reminiscences are behind the Gospel, and whose identity is veiled in some degree (see on 13²³ ; and cf. 1²⁷ 21²⁴). This agrees with the close association elsewhere of Peter and John (see Introd., p. xxxvi). Indeed, John the son of Zebedee had priestly connexions. His mother was Salome, the sister of the Virgin Mary (see pp. 73, 84 f., and note on 19³⁵); and Mary was a kinswoman (συγγενίς, Lk. 1³⁶) of Elisabeth, who was " of the daughters of Aaron " (Lk. 1⁵). Hence John was connected with a priestly family on his mother's side, and there is no improbability in his being " known to the high priest." [3]

But the available evidence does not permit us securely to identify the ἄλλος μαθητής, as Augustine saw (*Tract.* cxiii. 2), saying that it is not plain who he was. This unnamed disciple was probably some one of influence and social importance; if

---

[1] *Criticism of Fourth Gospel*, p. 101.

[2] It was taken by Chrysostom and Jerome (*Epist.* cxxvii. 5), both of whom regard John the son of Zebedee as the Beloved Disciple.

[3] Nonnus, in his paraphrase, explains the phrase by saying that it was because of John's fishing business, ἰχθυοβόλου παρὰ τέχνης, which apparently means that the high priest bought fish from him; but this is not convincing.

Ἰησοῦ εἰς τὴν αὐλὴν τοῦ ἀρχιερέως, 16. ὁ δὲ Πέτρος εἰστήκει πρὸς τῇ

we were to guess, the names of Nicodemus and Joseph of Arimathæa suggest themselves at once. There were disciples outside the circle of the Twelve, some of them men of rank, members of the Sanhedrim itself (see 12⁴²); and it is quite likely that Peter was known, by sight at least, to one of these who had attended at the house of Annas.[1] It is probable that it is to this unnamed disciple (whether John or another) that the details given in vv. 19–23 about the private examination of Jesus at night by the high priest, and also perhaps about the private examination before Pilate (vv. 33 f.), are ultimately due. There are also traces of first-hand information in the statements that "it was cold" (v. 18), and that a kinsman of the slave Malchus identified Peter (v. 26).

εἰς τὴν αὐλὴν κτλ., "into the courtyard." All the evangelists represent this courtyard as the scene of Peter's denial. He was not admitted even so far, until his unnamed friend intervened, but was standing outside at the door. See on 10¹ for αὐλή and θύρα. The examination of Jesus was not conducted in the outer court where all the servants were, but in a chamber of the house of Annas. Mk. implies that this chamber was not on the ground floor, as he says that Peter was κάτω ἐν τῇ αὐλῇ, "below, in the court" (Mk. 14⁶⁶).

Additional Note on XVIII. 15

Delff identified the ἄλλος μαθητής of v. 15 with the Beloved Disciple, whom he distinguished from John the son of Zebedee. In connexion with the remark that he was "known to the high priest," Delff cited the statement of Polycrates (see Introd., p. l) that the Beloved Disciple wore the priestly frontlet; and inferred that he belonged to an aristocratic priestly family in Jerusalem, it being thus easy for him to obtain access to the high priest's house.[2] We have already treated the problem of the ἄλλος μαθητής.

But a larger question is raised by the words of Polycrates, to which some reference may be made at this point. Polycrates says of the Beloved Disciple ἐγενήθη ἱερεὺς τὸ πέταλον πεφορεκώς, an observation difficult to explain. This πέταλον was a golden plate attached in front to the turban or mitre of Aaron (Ex. 28³⁶ᶠ· 29⁶ 39³⁰ᶠ·, Lev. 8⁹), and in later times was

---

[1] So Stanton, *The Gospels as Historical Documents*, iii. p. 143.

[2] *Studien und Kritiken*, 1892, p. 83 ; cf. Sanday, *Criticism of Fourth Gospel*, p. 100.

part of the official dress of the high priest (cf. Josephus, *Antt.* III. vii. 6).[1]

Similar statements are made about James the Just, and about Mark.[2]

Of James the Just, Epiphanius says: τὸ πέταλον ἐπὶ τῆς κεφαλῆς ἐξῆν αὐτῷ φορεῖν (*Hær.* xxix. 4). He adds that his authority was the ὑπομνηματισμοί of former writers of repute; and Lawlor[3] has shown that he is alluding to the ὑπομνήματα of Hegesippus. Hegesippus, as quoted by Eusebius (*H.E.* ii. 23), said that to James alone was it allowed to enter εἰς τὰ ἅγια of the Temple, which he used to frequent in prayer for the people, and that his custom was to wear not woollen but linen garments.[4] Epiphanius may be reproducing other words of Hegesippus when he tells (*Hær.* xxix. 4) that James exercised the priestly office according to the old priesthood (ἱερατεύσαντα κατὰ τὴν παλαίαν ἱερωσύνην) ; but he is probably in error when he says that James alone was permitted to enter the Holy of Holies once a year, as the high priest did, διὰ τὸ Ναζωραῖον αὐτὸν εἶναι καὶ μεμίχθαι τῇ ἱερωσύνῃ (*Hær.* lxxviii. 13). He adds explicitly, ὁ Ἰάκωβος διέφερε τῇ ἱερωσύνῃ, and πέταλον ἐπὶ τῆς κεφαλῆς ἐφόρεσε.

Of Mark, Valois quoted a legend as a note on Eus. *H.E.* v. 24, as follows: "beatum Marcum iuxta ritum carnalis sacrificii pontificalis apicis petalum in populo gestasse Iudaeorum . . . ex quo manifeste datur intelligi de stirpe eum Leuitica, imo pontificis Aaron sacrae successionis originem habuisse."[5] Mark was probably of Levite race (compare Acts 4[36] with Col. 4[10]), and the Vulgate Preface to his Gospel speaks of him as "sacerdotium in Israhel agens,"[6] so that it is quite possible that he was one of the Jewish priests who accepted Christ (Acts 6[7]; cf. Acts 21[20]).

The language of Polycrates, then, about John ἐγενήθη ἱερεὺς τὸ πέταλον πεφορεκώς is almost identical with what is

---

[1] The word is used in *Proteuangelium* 5 as if it meant the λογεῖον or oracle of the *Urim and Thummim*, from which it was clearly distinguished.

[2] Bingham (*Antt.* II. ix. 5) and Routh (*Reliquiæ Sacræ*, ii. 27) give the facts. A special treatise, *De lamina pontificali apostolorum Ioannis Iacobi et Marci* (Tübingen, 1755), was written by J. F. Cotta—a scarce book, as to which I am indebted to Dr. Wieland, the University Library at Tübingen, for information. It does not seem to add anything to what was known before.

[3] *Eusebiana*, pp. 10–14, 99.

[4] The priests wore linen only (Ex. 28[42] 40[13. 14]) ; but according to Josephus (*Antt.* xx. ix. 6), the Levites in the time of Agrippa obtained permission to do the same.

[5] The Passional from which Valois derived this is not known.

[6] See Wordsworth and White, *Nou. Test. Lat.*, p. 171.

told about James and Mark. If the πέταλον were worn by the high priest only on great occasions, it is impossible to suppose that John, James, or Mark ever wore it. But if it was (even occasionally) worn by the ordinary Jewish priest in N.T. times, Mark may have worn it. And if John and James were eligible for the priesthood, they too might have had the privilege. But while James and John were certainly akin to the priestly race on their mother's side, the argument of Epiphanius to prove that James also was "mingled with the priesthood " by blood is not convincing. Yet we know so little of the insistence upon hereditary qualifications for the Jewish priesthood in the first century, that it is not easy to reject the explicit statements made about John and James as well as about Mark.[1]

Jerome, when discussing the statement of Polycrates about John, understands ἱερεύς to mean a Christian priest, and translates: " qui supra pectus domini recubuit, et *pontifex eius* fuit, auream laminam in fronte portans " (*de script. eccl.* 45). This explanation will not apply to the parallel traditions about James and Mark, upon the *Jewish* character of whose priesthood stress is laid. It is conceivable (although improbable) that the Beloved Disciple might have been allowed by his Christian brethren to wear the insignia of a Jewish priest at Ephesus, where he was so greatly venerated. But neither James nor Mark would ever have been allowed such a distinction as *Christian* priests at Jerusalem while the Temple was yet standing. Further, it would be strange that Polycrates should call John a Christian ἱερεύς, while studiously avoiding in his case the title ἐπίσκοπος, which he gives to others of repute.[2] And, finally, that the mitre or πέταλον should have been used as an ornament of Christian bishops in the first century, but never heard of again until three centuries later at least, is highly improbable.

Others interpret the wearing of the πέταλον by John and the others as metaphorical only.[3] The dress of the high priest is used in Rev. 2[17] as the symbol of the investment of the true

---

[1] The legend is that Mark was κολοβοδάκτυλος, which would have made him ineligible as a Jewish priest, being blemished ; but the Vulgate Preface says that he mutilated his thumb after he became a Christian, precisely that he might be counted *sacerdotio reprobus.*

[2] The title ἱερεύς (*sacerdos*) for a Christian minister is used by Tertullian, Cyprian, and Origen (see my essay on Cyprian in *Early Hist. of Church and Ministry*, pp. 223, 228). It might therefore have been used by Polycrates ; but the context makes it improbable that he did use it thus.

[3] So Routh (*Rel. Sacr.* ii. 28), Stanley (*Apostolic Age*, p. 275) ; and cf. Lightfoot (*Galatians*, p. 362).

Christian with the sacerdotal character; cf. Ex. 28³¹· ³⁶ with the "white stone" and the "new name" of Rev. 2¹⁷. This idea is worked out in detail by Origen (*in Lev.* Hom. vi.), who treats the πέταλον as symbolic of the knowledge of divine things by all baptized persons; cf. Clem. Alex. *Strom.* v. 6. If we pursue this line of thought, we recall that engraved on the πέταλον were the words "Holy to Yahweh," ἁγίασμα κυρίου (Ex. 28³⁶), and the command to Moses was ἁγιάσεις αὐτούς, ἵνα ἱερατεύωσίν μοι (Ex. 28⁴¹). The πέταλον, in short, was the symbol of *consecration*, which was the topic of Christ's intercession for His apostles (Jn. 17²). John, James,[1] and Mark were all ἡγιασμένοι (Jn. 17¹⁹) ; and the tradition of wearing the πέταλον in their case might have grown out of a metaphorical statement as to their personal holiness. But this view does not explain why the πέταλον symbol should have been used only of John, James, and Mark among the saints of the apostolic age.

We are inclined to accept the tradition that James, John, and Mark literally wore the πέταλον, at least occasionally, in virtue of their service as Jewish priests. It is to be remembered that James, John, and Peter were the "pillars" of the Jerusalem Church (Gal. 2⁹); they were the heads of the conservative or Judaising party as contrasted with Paul. Of these, Peter was suspect by the more rigid Jews (Acts 11³). But his disciple Mark was under no such suspicion, for he had actually separated himself from Paul because of the latter's liberal policy (Acts 13¹³ 15³⁷). John had, indeed, incurred the hostility of the Temple authorities in early days (Acts 4³· ¹³); but there is no later indication of opposition to him by them, or *any* trace of distrust of him by his fellow-disciples. James was thoroughly respected by all. James, John, and Mark were, then, the three Christian leaders who were most fully trusted by the conservatives at Jerusalem.[2] While whole-hearted disciples of Jesus, they were Jews who were understood to have pride in their Jewish heritage. Provided that they were qualified for the priesthood, there would be nothing surprising in their occasional discharge of priestly offices ; for by the first disciples the Christian faith was not regarded as inconsistent with Judaism. Thus the tradition that they had been privileged to wear the priestly πέταλον is less improbable in their case than it would be in that of any other early leader of the Church of whom we have information.

---

[1] Epiphanius (*Hær.* xxix. 4) applies the word ἡγιασμένος to James.
[2] Barnabas had been too warm a supporter of Paul to be free from suspicion in Jewish circles (Acts 9²⁷).

θύρᾳ ἔξω. ἐξῆλθεν οὖν ὁ μαθητὴς ὁ ἄλλος ὁ γνωστὸς τοῦ ἀρχιερέως καὶ εἶπεν τῇ θυρωρῷ, καὶ εἰσήγαγεν τὸν Πέτρον. 17. λέγει οὖν τῷ Πέτρῳ ἡ παιδίσκη ἡ θυρωρός Μὴ καὶ σὺ ἐκ τῶν μαθητῶν εἶ τοῦ ἀνθρώπου τούτου; λέγει ἐκεῖνος Οὐκ εἰμί. 18. εἱστήκεισαν δὲ οἱ

16. For ἄλλος, *fam.* 13 have ἐκεῖνος, *ille* occurs in some O.L. codices.

καὶ εἶπεν τῇ θυρωρῷ, καὶ εἰσήγαγεν τὸν Πέτρον, *i.e.*, apparently, the friend spoke to the portress and brought Peter in ; but the rendering " and *she* brought Peter in " is defensible.

The θυρωρός was a maid-servant (παιδίσκη), as at Acts 12[13] and 2 Sam. 4[6] (LXX), a custom which Moulton-Milligan illustrate from papyri.

17. μὴ καὶ σὺ ἐκ τῶν μαθητῶν κτλ. The form of the question μὴ καὶ . . . shows that the portress expected a negative answer: " You are not another of His disciples, are you ? " See on 6[67]; and cf. v. 25. That is, she knew that the person who had already been admitted as γνωστὸς τῷ ἀρχιερεῖ was a disciple of Jesus, although not necessarily of the inner circle.

τοῦ ἀνθρώπου τούτου, " of this person," a contemptuous way of speaking.

According to the Johannine account, the first challenge to Peter and his first denial of his Master occurred as he was being admitted to the courtyard. The Synoptists put it later, after he had been admitted and was warming himself at the fire, when he was recognised by a slave girl who saw his face lit up by the flames (Lk. 22[56]). Mk. says that after Peter repudiated any knowledge of Jesus he went outside into the vestibule or porch (προαύλιον, Mk. 14[68] ; cf. εἰς τὸν πυλῶνα, Mt. 26[71]), and that the second interrogation of him (this time apparently by the maid who was portress) took place there.

18. The soldiers had now gone back to barracks, the Temple police (ὑπηρέται) being sufficient guard. The police-men and the slaves lit a fire in the courtyard, as it was a cold night. ὅτι ψῦχος ἦν is a touch peculiar to Jn., and suggests that the story has come from one who was present, and who shivers as he recalls how cold it was in the open court. Jeru-salem is 2400 feet above sea-level, and it is chilly at midnight in spring-time.[1]

ἀνθρακιά occurs again in the N.T. only at 21[9] (cf. Ecclus. 11[32], 4 Macc. 9[20]): it means " a heap of charcoal," probably burnt in a brazier. True coal was not known in Palestine until the nineteenth century. Lk. mentions the lighting of a fire, using the words ἀψάντων πῦρ ἐν μέσῳ τῆς αὐλῆς, and says

---

[1] Aphrahaṭ finds here a fulfilment of Zech. 14[6], " There shall be cold and frost " (in the LXX and Peshitta). (*Select. Dom.* xvii. 10.)

δοῦλοι καὶ οἱ ὑπηρέται ἀνθρακιὰν πεποιηκότες, ὅτι ψῦχος ἦν, καὶ ἐθερμαίνοντο· ἦν δὲ καὶ ὁ Πέτρος μετ᾽ αὐτῶν ἑστὼς καὶ θερμαινόμενος.

19. Ὁ οὖν ἀρχιερεὺς ἠρώτησεν τὸν Ἰησοῦν περὶ τῶν μαθητῶν

that they were all sitting round it. Mk. says that Peter was warming himself in the light (θερμαινόμενος πρὸς τὸ φῶς, Mk. 14⁵⁴), *i.e.* leaning towards the dim flame of the fire. Mt. does not say anything about a fire in the courtyard.

For ἀνθρακιὰν πεποιηκότες the Vulgate has only *ad prunas*, several O.L. codices giving *ad carbones*. This is a rendering which, as Wordsworth-White point out, seems to represent a reading πρὸς τὴν ἀνθρακιάν, for which there is no Greek authority extant.

ὁ Πέτρος μετ᾽ αὐτῶν. So אBCLW, the rec. giving the order of words as μετ᾽ αὐτῶν ὁ Πέτρ. Θ omits Πέτρος. It was necessary for Peter to mingle with the slaves and the police in the courtyard ; to have kept to himself would have made him an object of suspicion. The Synoptists represent him as *sitting* near the fire, with the others; Jn. alone says that he was *standing*, ἑστώς.

Jn. follows Mk. (14⁵⁴· ⁶⁷) in telling that Peter was warming himself (θερμαινόμενος) ; and, like Mk., he tells it twice (see v. 25). Jn.'s narrative of Peter's denials is interrupted by an account of the examination of Jesus which was taking place in the house of Annas (vv. 19–23). After the examination has been described, the story of Peter is resumed. Evidently it was while he was waiting in the outer court that he denied his Master for the second and third times (vv. 25–27).[1] This is consistent with Mk.'s order of events.

Examination of Jesus before Annas (vv. 19–23) ; He is sent on to Caiaphas (v. 24)

19. ὁ . . . ἀρχιερεύς. The "high priest" who conducted the informal examination at the house of Annas was most probably Annas himself (see v. 24). Caiaphas, however, may have been present, and it is *possible* that he was the ἀρχιερεύς of v. 19 and v. 22. But the real leader was Annas (see on 11⁴⁹), and it was probably by his orders that Jesus was brought to his house in the first instance (see on v. 13). Jn. does not tell, as the Synoptists do, of the cross-examination by which the hostile priests and scribes tried to make Jesus incriminate Himself, when they found it difficult to get legal evidence as to His alleged blasphemy about the destruction of the Temple (Mk. 14⁵⁵ᶠ·, Mt. 26⁵⁹ᶠ·). The episode of the

---
[1] Cf. Introd., p. xcviii.

αὐτοῦ καὶ περὶ τῆς διδαχῆς αὐτοῦ. 20. ἀπεκρίθη αὐτῷ Ἰησοῦς Ἐγὼ παρρησίᾳ λελάληκα τῷ κόσμῳ· ἐγὼ πάντοτε ἐδίδαξα ἐν συναγωγῇ καὶ ἐν τῷ ἱερῷ, ὅπου πάντες οἱ Ἰουδαῖοι συνέρχονται, καὶ ἐν κρυπτῷ

Cleansing of the Temple, and the words " Destroy this Temple and I will raise it up in three days," have been given by Jn. in another context (2¹³⁻¹⁹, where see note). Jn. merely says here that the high priest questioned Jesus about His disciples, probably as to who they were and as to their reasons for attaching themselves to Him, and about His doctrine (διδαχή, cf. 7¹⁶). This latter inquiry would cover everything. But the details given here of the reply of Jesus to the high priest are found only in Jn. (See also on v. 32.)

20. ἀπεκρίθη αὐτῳ Ἰησοῦς. See on 1²⁹ for the omission of ὁ before Ἰησοῦς.

Jesus, in His reply, ignores the question as to His disciples and does not mention them. As to His teaching, He declares that it was always available for, and open to, every one, and that there was nothing secret about it. The reply of Socrates to his judges has often been quoted as a parallel: " If any one says that he has ever learnt or heard anything from me in private, which all others could not have heard, know ye that he does not speak the truth " (Plato, *Apol.* 33 B).

ἐγὼ παρρησίᾳ λελάληκα (not ἐλάλησα, as the rec. text has it) τῷ κόσμῳ, " I have spoken openly to the world," *i.e.* to all and sundry. ἐγώ is emphatic: it was *His* teaching that was challenged. For παρρησίᾳ see on 7⁴, and for κόσμος see on 1⁹; cf. ταῦτα λαλῶ εἰς τὸν κόσμον (8²⁶), where, however, the meaning is slightly different. The Jews had said of Him παρρησίᾳ λαλεῖ (7²⁶); and when they had challenged Him on another occasion to speak plainly (εἰπὲ ἡμῖν παρρησίᾳ, 10²⁴) He had done so, with such openness that they had sought to arrest Him (10³⁹). When His own disciples had found difficulty in understanding His mysterious teaching about His approaching departure, He proceeded to make it quite plain (16²⁵· ²⁹).

ἐγὼ πάντοτε ἐδίδαξα ἐν συναγωγῇ (the true text has no article before συναγωγῇ) καὶ ἐν τῷ ἱερῷ, " I always taught in synagogue and in the temple "; *i.e.* it was His custom to teach in these public places, not that He *never* gave any private teaching to an inquirer like Nicodemus (3²). The discourse about the Bread of Life was given in the synagogue at Capernaum, according to the Johannine narrative (6⁵⁹), and the Synoptists frequently speak of His practice of teaching in the synagogues of Galilee. Jn. tells of His teaching in the Temple several times (2¹⁹ 7¹⁴· ²⁸ 8²⁰ 10²³). Cf. Mk. 14⁴⁹, καθ᾿ ἡμέραν ἤμην πρὸς ὑμᾶς ἐν τῷ ἱερῷ διδάσκων. The fact of His public teaching was

ἐλάλησα οὐδέι.   21. τί με ἐρωτᾳς; ἐρώτησον τοὺς ἀκηκοότας τί ἐλάλησα αὐτοῖς· ἴδε οὗτοι οἴδασιν ἃ εἶπον ἐγώ.   22. ταῦτα δὲ αὐτοῦ εἰπόντος εἷς παρεστηκὼς τῶν ὑπηρετῶν ἔδωκεν ῥάπισμα τῷ Ἰησοῦ εἰπών Οὗτως ἀποκρίνῃ τῷ ἀρχιερεῖ;   23. ἀπεκρίθη αὐτῷ Ἰησοῦς Εἰ

notorious. It had been given ἐν τῷ ἱερῷ, ὅπου πάντες (not πάντοτε with the rec. text) οἱ Ἰουδαῖοι συνέρχονται, "where all the Jews come together."

καὶ ἐν κρυπτῷ ἐλάλησα οὐδέν. This is like the utterance of Messiah at Isa. 48¹⁶, οὐκ ἀπ' ἀρχῆς ἐν κρυφῇ λελάληκα (cf. Isa. 45¹⁹). But we have had the contrast between ἐν κρυπτῷ and ἐν παρρησίᾳ before (see 7⁴); and it is not necessary to suppose that there is here a veiled allusion to the Isaiah passage, although it is possible.

See on 3¹¹ for Jn.'s use of λαλεῖν as signifying frank and unreserved speech. It is noteworthy that the strongest repudiation in the Gospels of cryptic or esoteric teaching in the words of Jesus is found in Jn.

21. For ἐρωτᾳς, ἐρώτησον, the rec., with some lesser uncials, has the stronger ἐπερωτᾳς, ἐπερώτησον (cf. v. 7).

τί με ἐρωτᾳς; It was a recognised principle of law that a man's evidence about himself was suspect. See on 5³¹.

τί ἐλάλησα αὐτοῖς . . . ἃ εἶπον ἐγώ. The two verbs have the same meaning (see on 3¹¹).

22. εἷς παρεστηκὼς τῶν ὑπηρετῶν. So ℵ*BW a ff, but AC²DˢᵘᵖᵖNΓΔΘ syrr. have the order εἷς τῶν ὑπηρ. παρεστ. For the constr. εἷς τῶν . . . cf. 12⁴ 19³⁴.

This ὑπηρέτης was one of the Temple policemen, who have been mentioned vv. 3, 12 as having taken part in the arrest of Jesus; he was standing by to guard the prisoner.

ῥάπισμα is also used by Mk. (14⁶⁵) in the same context, and is applied again, 19³, to the insults offered to Jesus by the Roman soldiers. As Field has shown (in loc.), it means a slap on the cheek, given with the open hand by way of insulting rebuke rather than with the intention of inflicting bodily injury. Cf. Isa. 50⁶, τὸν νῶτόν μου ἔδωκα εἰς μάστιγας, τὰς δὲ σιαγόνας μου εἰς ῥαπίσματα. ῥαπίζειν was used by the older Greek writers for ῥαβδίζειν, "to strike with a stick," but it came to be reserved for "to slap." Cf. Hos. 11⁴, Mt. 5³⁹ 26⁶⁷. Abbott (Diat. 493) cites 1 Esd. 4³⁰, where one of the king's favourite women slaps him playfully.

Οὗτως ἀποκρίνῃ τῷ ἀρχιερεῖ; "Answerest Thou the high priest," i.e. probably Annas, "so unbecomingly?"

It is obvious that conduct of this kind on the part of an underling would not have been permitted at a formal judicial sitting of the Sanhedrim.

κακῶς ἐλάλησα, μαρτύρησον περὶ τοῦ κακοῦ· εἰ δὲ καλῶς, τί με δέρεις; 24. ἀπέστειλεν οὖν αὐτὸν ὁ Ἄννας δεδεμένον πρὸς Καϊάφαν τὸν ἀρχιερέα.

23. ἀπεκρ. αὐτῷ ’Ιησοῦς. See on 1²⁹ for the omission of ὁ before ’Ιησ.

μαρτύρησον, *i.e.* give your testimony in legal fashion.

εἰ δὲ καλῶς, τί με δέρεις; δέρειν, " to beat," is the word used in the same context at Lk. 22⁶³. It is used of an insulting blow in the face, as here, at 2 Cor. 11²⁰.

This dignified reply shows that the precept of Mt. 5³⁹ is not always to be obeyed in the letter.

24. ἀπέστειλεν cannot be treated as a pluperfect, as the A.V. treats it : " had sent," in order to escape the difficulties that arise if Caiaphas is supposed to have been the high priest of vv. 19, 23 (see on v. 13). ἀπέστειλεν οὖν κτλ., means, " So Annas sent Him to Caiaphas," *sc.* when his preliminary inquiry was over. οὖν is read by BC*LNWΘ and must be retained; א has δέ, and the rec. text omits any conjunctive particle, an omission which obscures the sense. See p. 37 f.

δεδεμένον. He had been unbound, no doubt, during the inquiry (cf. v. 12); but He was bound again, on being sent off to the official place of meeting of the Sanhedrim, where Caiaphas would preside, in order to ratify the sentence that had already been informally arranged. This official hall was not the palace of the high priest, but was situated on the western side of the Temple mount.[1]

Peter's second and third denials of Jesus (vv. 25–27)

25. The courtyard scene is now taken up again from v. 18, where see note. We had there ὁ Πέτρος ἑστὼς καὶ θερμαινόμενος, and the phrase is repeated to bring us back to what has been said before, but with the characteristic substitution of Σίμων Πέτρος for ὁ Πέτρος of v. 18, as the apostle has been out of the narrative for some paragraphs (see on v. 15 above).

That there was some interval between the first denial of Peter and the third is apparent from the Synoptists, although they do not agree in small details. Mk. and Mt. suggest that the second interrogation of Peter followed hard upon the first, but this is told explicitly only by Lk. (μετὰ βραχύ, Lk. 22⁵⁸). Then Mk. 14⁷⁰ and Mt. 26⁷³ say that the third interrogation was μετὰ μικρόν after the second, but Lk. allows an hour

[1] See Schürer, *Hist. of Jewish People*, II. i. p. 190 f. Schürer holds, however, that on this occasion the Sanhedrim *did* meet in Caiaphas' house, referring to Mt. 26⁵⁷.

25. Ἦν δὲ Σίμων Πέτρος ἑστὼς καὶ θερμαινόμενος. εἶπον οὖν αὐτῷ Μὴ καὶ σὺ ἐκ τῶν μαθητῶν αὐτοῦ εἶ; ἠρνήσατο ἐκεῖνος καὶ εἶπεν Οὐκ εἰμί. 26. λέγει εἷς ἐκ τῶν δούλων τοῦ ἀρχιερέως, συγγενὴς ὢν οὗ ἀπέκοψεν Πέτρος τὸ ὠτίον Οὐκ ἐγώ σε εἶδον ἐν τῷ κήπῳ

to elapse (διαστάσης ὡσεὶ ὥρας μιᾶς, Lk. 22⁵⁹). Jn. brings the second denial nearer to the third than Lk. does; but that there was more than an hour's interval between the first denial and the third, as Lk. records, is quite in agreement with the Johannine account.

εἶπον οὖν αὐτῷ. The speakers are not defined: *on lui dit.*

Μὴ καὶ σύ ἐκ τῶν μαθ. αὐτ. κτλ. The question and answer are almost the same as those of v. 17; and the question is again expressed as if a negative answer were expected (see on v. 17). This is a point peculiar to Jn.'s narrative; he describes the first two interrogatories as put in a form which almost *suggested* that Peter should say "No!" In this (see also on v. 27), Jn. gives a less severe account of Peter's lapse from courage and faithfulness than the Synoptists do.

26. The slaves of the high priest have been mentioned as present in the courtyard (v 18). One of them is here described as a kinsman of Malchus (v. 10), a remark which has been thought to imply some acquaintance with the high priest's household (see on v. 16). The reason for the slave's insistent identification, viz. that he had seen Peter with Jesus at Gethsemane, is not found elsewhere; the Synoptists telling that Peter was suspected because of his Galilæan accent. "Did not *I* see thee in the garden with Him?" ἐγώ is emphatic, "I, with my own eyes." But the slave apparently was not able to satisfy the bystanders that he was right, for Peter's denial was accepted. The temptation to say "No" was even greater this time than before, for the mention of the blow struck at Malchus suggests that Malchus' kinsman suspected Peter of having been the assailant. Had Peter been arrested on this count, he would have been dealt with very severely. To be a "disciple" of Jesus was not a legal offence, although the confession of it might lead to trouble; but to have drawn a weapon and assaulted one of the high priest's household was another matter.

27. πάλιν οὖν ἠρνήσατο. No words are given; only the fact of the denial is recorded. This is in strong contrast to the denial with curses and oaths which is described by Mk. 14⁷¹ (followed by Mt. 26⁷⁴, but not by Lk.).

According to the Lucan narrative, at this point, "the Lord turned and looked upon Peter" (Lk. 22⁶¹). Accordingly, we must suppose Jesus to have come down from the chamber

μετ᾽ αὐτοῦ; 27. πάλιν οὖν ἠρνήσατο Πέτρος, καὶ εὐθέως ἀλέκτωρ
ἐφώνησεν.

28. Ἄγουσιν οὖν τὸν Ἰησοῦν ἀπὸ τοῦ Καϊάφα εἰς τὸ πραιτώριον.

where He had been informally examined, and to have been
passing through the courtyard on His way to Caiaphas for
formal trial and sentence, when Peter again denied his discipleship, and was overheard by his Master. Jn. hurries over this
scene of painful memories.

εὐθέως ἀλέκτωρ ἐφώνησεν, "immediately a cock crew."
Lk. 22⁶⁰ has παραχρῆμα, but Mt. 26⁷⁴ has εὐθέως as here. In Jn.
εὐθέως always connotes *immediate* consecutiveness (see on 5⁹).

All the evangelists speak of the actual crowing of a cock
(Mk. speaks of *two* crowings, 14⁶⁸· ⁷²) within the precincts of
the palace, and find in it the literal fulfilment of the prediction
made by Jesus (13³⁸). Salmon[1] held that this prediction
"meant no more than that Peter should deny Him thrice before
the hour of cockcrow, viz. that hour of early morning which was
technically known as ἡ ἀλεκτοροφωνία" (cf. Mk. 13³⁵). C. H.
Mayo made a further suggestion; viz. that the signal heard by
Peter was "the *gallicinium*, the signal given on the *buccina*
at the close of the third night watch, and the change of guard."[2]
This is probably what happened. "Before a cock shall
crow" (13³⁸) would be a vague note of time, for cocks are apt
to crow at uncertain hours during the night. But "before
the ἀλεκτοροφωνία" is precise; and the hour of ἀλεκτοροφωνία
was made public by a military signal.

On this interpretation, the word πρωΐ in v. 28 is peculiarly
appropriate, for, according to Roman reckoning, the four
watches of the night were ὀψέ, μεσονύκτιον, ἀλεκτοροφωνία,
and πρωΐ. As soon as the signal had sounded at the close of
ἀλεκτοροφωνία, it would be πρωΐ.

Jn. says nothing about Peter's bitter tears of repentance
for his failure. Every one knew, when the Fourth Gospel was
written, that Peter had repented, and his return to his Master's
favour is specially recorded in the Appendix (21¹⁵). It is quite
in the manner of Jn. to omit something which no Christian
needed to be told.

Jesus is brought before Pilate and accused by the Jews
(*vv.* 28–32)

28. ἄγουσιν οὖν τὸν Ἰησοῦν ἀπὸ τοῦ Καϊάφα κτλ. We have
in v. 24 the statement that Jesus was "sent to Caiaphas,"

[1] *Human Element in the Gospels*, p. 509.
[2] *J.T.S.*, July 1921, p. 367.

i.e. to the formal meeting of the Sanhedrim, not necessarily or probably held in the house of Caiaphas, over which Caiaphas would preside. Nothing is told here of the proceedings (see on v. 13, and cf. Mk. 15¹, Mt. 27¹), which were only formal, as the decision had been already reached at the irregular meeting in the house of Annas. But as the Sanhedrim could not execute the sentence of death (see v. 31) without the sanction of the Roman authorities, they had now to bring Jesus before Pilate, that he might give the necessary orders.

ἀπὸ τοῦ Καϊάφα need not mean " from the house of Caiaphas " (cf. Mk. 5³⁵, Acts 16⁴⁰), but more naturally means " from Caiaphas," *i.e.* from the ecclesiastical court over which he presided. Some O.L. codices, e.g. *e ff₂ g*, etc., have *ad Caiphan*, a reading due to a misunderstanding of the sequence of events. See Introd., pp. xxvi–xxviii.

εἰς τὸ πραιτώριον. πραιτώριον signified a prætor's or general's quarters in a camp, and the word came to be used of the official residence of a governor (cf. τὸ πραιτώριον of Herod at Cæsarea, Acts 23³⁵). It is not certain where the *prætorium* at Jerusalem, that is, Pilate's house, was situated; but it is probably to be identified with Herod's palace on the Hill of Zion in the western part of the upper city. Pilate was certainly lodged there on one occasion, for Philo (*ad Caium*, 38) reports that he hung up golden shields ἐν τοῖς κατὰ τὴν ἱερόπολιν Ἡρώδου βασιλείοις. Further, Gessius Florus, who was procurator of Judæa about thirty-five years after Pilate, had at one time Herod's palace as a residence, for Josephus says so in a passage so illustrative of the Passion narratives that it must be quoted: Φλῶρος δὲ τότε μὲν ἐν τοῖς βασιλείοις αὐλίζεται, τῇ δ' ὑστεραίᾳ βῆμα πρὸ αὐτῶν θέμενος καθέζεται, καὶ προσελθόντες οἵ τε ἀρχιερεῖς . . . παρέστησαν τῷ βήματι (*Bell. Jud.*, ii. 14. 8). And in ii. 15. 5, Josephus explicitly calls the Procurator's residence ἡ βασιλικὴ αὐλή ; cf. Mk. 15¹⁶, ἔσω τῆς αὐλῆς, ὅ ἐστι πραιτώριον. The mention of the βῆμα placed in full view of the high priests and the notables who came before Florus for judgment is noteworthy (cf. 19¹³ below).

The other site suggested for the Prætorium is the Castle of Antonia, to the north of the Temple area, a fourth-century tradition placing Pilate's house in this neighbourhood. That a large part of the garrison lived here is admitted, but that does not favour the idea that it was the Procurator's residence. The course of the Via Dolorosa, as now shown, favours Antonia as the place of condemnation of Jesus; but there is no real authority behind this tradition.[1]

[1] See G. A. Smith, *Jerusalem*, ii. 573 f. ; G. T. Purves in *D.B.*,

ἦν δὲ πρωΐ· καὶ αὐτοὶ οὐκ εἰσῆλθον εἰς τὸ πραιτώριον, ἵνα μὴ μιανθῶσιν ἀλλὰ φάγωσιν τὸ πάσχα. 29. ἐξῆλθεν οὖν ὁ Πειλᾶτος ἔξω

πρωΐ, *i.e.* early in the morning of Friday, 14 Nisan (see on v. 27). Pilate must have known already that Roman soldiers had been sent to arrest Jesus the night before (v. 3), and he may have been warned to be ready at an early hour. The Jewish ecclesiastics who accompanied Jesus to the Prætorium did not enter ἵνα μὴ μιανθῶσιν ἀλλὰ φάγωσιν τὸ πάσχα. See on 11⁵⁵. By going into a house from which the leaven had not been removed (Ex. 12¹⁵), they would have been incapacitated from eating the Passover that evening. Ceremonial uncleanness in many cases lasted until sunset only (Lev. 11²⁴ 14²⁵, Num. 19⁷, Deut. 23¹¹, etc.); but in the case of the Passover one who was unclean had to postpone its observance for a whole month (Num. 9⁶· ¹¹; cf. 2 Chron. 30²· ³). This would have been inconvenient for the priests, and so they remained outside the house, Pilate having to come out to ask for the charge against Jesus, and to go back again into the Prætorium to question Him as to His defence.

For ἀλλὰ φάγωσιν (אABC*DNWΘ), the rec. has ἀλλ' ἵνα φάγωσι. For φαγεῖν τὸ πάσχα, which must mean the eating of the Passover meal itself, cf. Mk. 14¹², Mt. 26¹⁷.

The scruple of the priests about entering the Prætorium is recorded by Jn. only. It is an instance of his " irony " (see on 1⁴⁵) that he does not comment upon it. These men were about to pollute their souls by unscrupulous testimony which was to bring Jesus to a horrible death, yet were unwilling to incur technical or ceremonial uncleanness while giving that testimony. There is no perversion so sinister as that of the human conscience.

29. The narrative of Pilate's action in regard to Jesus is told with more fulness in Jn. than in the Synoptists (cf. Mk. 15²ᶠ·, Mt. 27¹¹ᶠ·, Lk. 23²ᶠ·).

ἐξῆλθεν οὖν ὁ Πειλᾶτος ἔξω. As the Jews would not enter the Prætorium, Pilate came outside. This is the force of οὖν, " therefore " . . . The redundant ἐξῆλθεν . . . ἔξω is for the sake of explicitness " he came out, outside "; cf. 19⁴· ⁵ and see on 4³⁰. The rec. text, with AC³Dˢᵘᵖᵖ om. ἔξω, but ins. אBC*LNW.

Abbott points out (*Diat.* 1969) that Jn.'s habit is to introduce a personal name *without* the article; but here we have ὁ Πειλᾶτος, as at Lk. 23¹.

For **φησίν** (אBC*L), the rec. has εἶπε.

s.v. " Prætorium "; Sanday, *Sacred Sites*, p. 52 f. Westcott and Swete favour Antonia.

πρὸς αὐτοὺς καὶ φησίν Τίνα κατηγορίαν φέρετε τοῦ ἀνθρώπου τούτου;
30. ἀπεκρίθησαν καὶ εἶπαν αὐτῷ Εἰ μὴ ἦν οὗτος κακὸν ποιῶν, οὐκ ἄν
σοι παρεδώκαμεν αὐτόν.   31. εἶπεν οὖν αὐτοῖς ὁ Πειλᾶτος Λάβετε
αὐτὸν ὑμεῖς, καὶ κατὰ τὸν νόμον ὑμῶν κρίνατε αὐτόν.   εἶπον αὐτῷ οἱ

Τίνα κατηγορίαν φέρετε κτλ. Pilate (see on v. 28) knew
something of the case already; but it was necessary for him
to be notified formally of the nature of the accusation brought
against the prisoner.

The rec. has κατὰ τοῦ ἀνθρώπου τούτου, with אᵃACDˢᵘᵖᵖLNWΘ,
but א*Be om. κατά.   Cf. Lk. 6⁷, ἵνα εὕρωσιν κατηγορίαν αὐτοῦ.

30. The Jews are not sure of their case, and so they hesitate
to specify the charge in explicit terms. They say, in effect,
" That is our business; we would not have brought the prisoner
for sentence, if we were not satisfied with His guilt."

Εἰ μὴ ἦν οὗτος κακὸν ποιῶν κτλ.   " If this person were not
doing wrong, we should not have delivered Him up to thee."
For κακὸν ποιῶν (אᶜBLWe), the rec., with AC³DˢᵘᵖᵖNΓΔΘ,
has κακοποιός, a word found in N.T. only in 1 Pet. 2¹². ¹⁴
3¹⁶ 4¹⁵.   Perhaps ἦν followed by the pres. part. suggests a
habitual evil-doer (cf. Abbott, *Diat.* 2277).

οὐκ ἄν σοι παρεδώκαμεν αὐτόν.   σοι *may* be emphatic, " we
should not have delivered Him up to *thee* " (cf. Abbott, *Diat.*
2566b).   In any case, the reply of the Jews is an insolent one.

31. Pilate, however, knew how to deal with insolence of
this kind: " Very well ; take Him yourselves (ὑμεῖς being
emphatic) and judge Him according to your own law," an
answer not unlike that of Gallio in Acts 18¹⁴.   Pilate repeats
this Λάβετε αὐτὸν ὑμεῖς at 19⁶ ; throughout he is unwilling to
take any responsibility, and he knows that if the Jews take over
the case for final settlement, they cannot inflict the death
penalty.   On the other hand, if they wish *him* to send Jesus to
death, they must satisfy him that their sentence was a just one.

This rejoinder disconcerts the Jewish accusers of Jesus, who
are bent upon His death, although they are not sure of their
legal position as regards evidence; so they can only say, " It
is not lawful *for us* to put any one to death."

This was, in fact, the law from the time that Judaea became
a Roman province. The *jus gladii* was reserved to the procurator (Josephus, *B.J.* ii. viii. 1).   Josephus tells of a case
in which the high priest had sentenced some persons to death
by stoning, a sentence against which some citizens successfully
protested as *ultra vires*, the high priest being deposed for his
presumption (*Antt.* xx. 9. 1).   No doubt, violent and high-
handed action on the part of the Sanhedrim may have been
occasionally winked at by the Roman authorities, for political

Ἰουδαῖοι Ἡμῖν οὐκ ἔξεστιν ἀποκτεῖναι οὐδένα· 32. ἵνα ὁ λόγος τοῦ
Ἰησοῦ πληρωθῇ ὃν εἶπεν σημαίνων ποίῳ θανάτῳ ἤμελλεν ἀποθνήσκειν.

33. Εἰσῆλθεν οὖν εἰς τὸ πραιτώριον πάλιν ὁ Πειλᾶτος καὶ

reasons. If Jesus had been killed by the agents of the Sanhedrim before He had gained the ear of the Jerusalem populace
(cf., *e.g.*, 7¹· ²⁵), it might have been overlooked by the procurator ; but the chief priests were not sure now that they had
the people with them, and their only safe course was, having
examined Jesus themselves, to bring Him to Pilate for sentence.

32. In this, the evangelist, as is his wont, sees the fulfilment
of a saying of Jesus. If the Jews had put Jesus to death by
stoning, His death by crucifixion, of which He had already
spoken (12³³), would not have taken place; and stoning was the
Jewish penalty for blasphemy, of which the Sanhedrim had
found Him guilty. Jn. has told nothing as yet of the charge
of blasphemy, and he gives no particulars of it, merely indicating at a later point in the narrative (19⁷) that it was reported to
Pilate (see on v. 19 above).

ἵνα ὁ λόγος τοῦ Ἰησοῦ πληρωθῇ. Cf. v. 9 for the phrase
ἵνα πληρωθῇ, introducing another saying of Jesus, and see
Introd., p. clv, for Jn.'s doctrine that the words of Jesus were
predestined to fulfilment, even as the words of the O.T. Scriptures. The saying to which allusion is made here is, " I, if I
be *lifted up* from the earth, etc." (12³², where see note). There,
as here, Jn. adds the comment σημαίνων ποίῳ θανάτῳ ἤμελλεν
(see on 6⁷¹ for this verb) ἀποθνήσκειν. See Introd., p. clv,
for the comments which Jn. is accustomed to make on his
narrative; and cf. 3¹⁴ for the predictions by Jesus of His death.

The first examination of Jesus by Pilate (vv. 33-37)

33. The Roman soldiers, at this point, took charge of
Jesus. Pilate retired from the open court, where he had met
the Jewish leaders, and went back into his palace, summoning
Jesus to come before him for private examination.

εἰσῆλθεν οὖν εἰς τό πραιτώριον πάλιν. So אΑΓΔΘ (cf. 19⁹),
but BC*DˢᵘᵖᵖLW support πάλιν εἰς τὸ πραιτ. For πάλιν, which
here signifies " back " to the place where Pilate was before,
see on 1³⁵.

For ἐφώνησεν, see on 1⁴⁸. The disciple who seems to have
been present at the examination of Jesus by Annas (see on
v. 15) may also have been a witness of the scene in Pilate's
palace which is here told so vividly. The priestly accusers of
Jesus could not follow Him inside the house, because of their

ἐφώνησεν τὸν Ἰησοῦν καὶ εἶπεν αὐτῷ Σὺ εἶ ὁ βασιλεὺς τῶν Ἰουδαίων;
34. ἀπεκρίθη Ἰησοῦς Ἀπὸ σεαυτοῦ σὺ τοῦτο λέγεις, ἢ ἄλλοι εἶπόν σοι
περὶ ἐμοῦ; 35. ἀπεκρίθη ὁ Πειλᾶτος Μήτι ἐγὼ Ἰουδαῖός εἰμι; τὸ
ἔθνος τὸ σὸν καὶ οἱ ἀρχιερεῖς παρέδωκάν σε ἐμοί· τί ἐποίησας:

scruples about ceremonial uncleanness (v. 28); but it is not
likely that admission to the chamber of inquiry was forbidden
to others duly introduced who wished to hear what was going on.

Σὺ εἶ ὁ βασιλεὺς τῶν Ἰουδαίων; This question was immediately put to Jesus by Pilate,[1] as all the evangelists tell
(Mk. 15^2, Mt. 27^1, Lk. 23^3); but it is only Lk. who explains
that Jesus had first been accused *to* Pilate of claiming to be a
King (Lk. 23^2). Pilate fixes upon this point as one which it
was necessary for him as procurator to examine, and he puts
his question in a form which suggests that he expected a
negative answer. "Thou! (σύ is emphatic) art *Thou* the King
of the Jews?" Evidently, Pilate did not believe that Jesus was
a revolutionary leader, as he had been informed (Lk. 23^2).
There was nothing in His appearance or His demeanour to
make such a charge plausible.

34. ἀπεκρίθη Ἰησοῦς. The rec. has ἀπεκρ. αὐτῷ ὁ Ἰησ.,
but αὐτῷ is om. by ABC*D^{supp}L and ὁ by BL. ἀπεκρ. Ἰησοῦς
is a frequent Johannine opening (see on 1^{29}, but cf. v. 37 and
19^{11}). WΘ have ἀπεκρίνατο (see on 5^{17}).

Ἀπὸ σεαυτοῦ is the better reading (אBC*LN) as against the
rec. Ἀφ᾽ ἑαυτοῦ (Θ).

The answer cf Jesus is to put another question, viz. whether
Pilate has any reason of his own, apart from the accusation
just now made by the Jewish leaders (ἢ ἄλλοι εἶπόν σοι περὶ
ἐμοῦ;), for supposing that Jesus had claimed to be "King of
the Jews."

35. But Pilate will not bandy words with an accused
prisoner. What could he know about Jesus except what he
had been told? "Am *I* a Jew?"

For the form of the question Μήτι ἐγὼ . . .; see on 4^{29}.

"Thy nation (for ἔθνος, cf. 11^{48-52}) and the chief priests
have delivered Thee to me," the chief priests representing the
leaders of the Sanhedrim (cf. 11^{57} 12^{10}).

τί ἐποίησας; "What did you *do*?" That was the point
which Pilate wished to find out. What action of Jesus had
provoked this fierce hostility? Was it an action which ought
to be punished, from Pilate's point of view, with death?

---

[1] The language in which the conversation with Pilate was carried
on was probably Greek ; but it is, of course, possible that Pilate was
able to speak the vernacular Aramaic sufficiently for the purposes of a
judicial inquiry.

36. ἀπεκρίθη Ἰησοῦς Ἡ βασιλεία ἡ ἐμὴ οὐκ ἔστιν ἐκ τοῦ κόσμου
τούτου· εἰ ἐκ τοῦ κόσμου τούτου ἦν ἡ βασιλεία ἡ ἐμή, οἱ ὑπηρέται οἱ

36. But Jesus does not answer this question. He goes back
to the charge that He had claimed to be " King of the Jews."
He had refused such a title already (6¹⁵), but He had often
spoken of a coming kingdom. It was the kingdom of which
Daniel had written (Dan. 2⁴⁴ 7¹⁴· ²⁷), a spiritual kingdom of
which the saints were to be citizens. And this He states before
Pilate, that there may be no ambiguity in His position. When
cross-examined by the priests, as the Synoptists tell, He had
accepted their statement that He claimed to be Messiah (Mk.
14⁶², Mt. 26⁶⁴, Lk. 22⁷⁰), and so far there was some plausi-
bility in their accusation of Him before Pilate. But He did
not interpret the title of Messiah as implying earthly domina-
tion and national leadership against the suzerainty of Rome;
and this was the gravamen of the charge brought against
Him, so far as Pilate was concerned. Hence He tells the
procurator that His kingdom is not " of this world " (cf., for
the phrase ὁ κόσμος οὗτος, 8²³ 14³⁰). He does not claim to
be " King of the Jews " in any sense that was treasonable to
Rome.

εἰ ἐκ τοῦ κόσμου τούτου κτλ., " If my kingdom were of this
world, then would my officers (ὑπηρέται) be striving, so that
I should not be delivered to the Jews," *i.e.* the hostile Jews,
as regularly in Jn. (see on 5¹⁰).

Except in this passage, ὑπηρέται in Jn. is always used of
the Temple police, the " officers " of the Sanhedrim. ὑπηρέτης
occurs only 4 times in the LXX (Prov. 14³⁵, Wisd. 6⁴, Isa.
32⁵, Dan. 3⁴⁶), and always means the minister or officer of a
king, as here. Jesus tells Pilate that He, too, has His ὑπηρέται,
as well as the high priests, but that just because His kingdom
is of the spirit they are not defending Him by force.

Who are meant here by the ὑπηρέται of Jesus ? Certainly
not the small and timid company of His disciples, who made
no attempt to prevent His arrest, with the sole exception of
Peter, whose action only showed the uselessness of trying to
resist the police and the soldiers. Jesus, indeed, according
to Mt. (26⁵²) as well as Jn. (18¹¹), forbade Peter to employ force;
but He did not suggest that the resort to arms by the disciples
would have been of any practical use. Pilate knew very well
that the followers of Jesus were not numerous enough to resist
by force the carrying out of any sentence of his.

The ὑπηρέται of Jesus upon whom He might call, if He
would, were mentioned by Him, according to Mt. 26⁵³, at the
moment of His arrest : " Thinkest thou that I cannot beseech

ἐμοὶ ἂν ἠγωνίζοντο, ἵνα μὴ παραδοθῶ τοῖς Ἰουδαίοις· νῦν δὲ ἡ βασιλεία ἡ ἐμὴ οὐκ ἔστιν ἐντεῦθεν. 37. εἶπεν οὖν αὐτῷ ὁ Πειλᾶτος Οὐκοῦν βασιλεὺς εἶ σύ; ἀπεκρίθη ὁ Ἰησοῦς Σὺ λέγεις ὅτι βασιλεύς

my Father, and He shall even now send me more than twelve legions of angels?" These were the ὑπηρέται of the kingdom which Jesus had come to establish.

ἠγωνίζοντο. The verb does not occur again in Jn.; cf. 1 Tim. 6^{12}.

νῦν δέ κτλ., "but now, as things are, my kingdom is not from hence," *sc.* of this world. For νῦν δέ, cf. 8^{40} 9^{41} 15^{22}.

37. Οὐκοῦν βασιλεὺς εἶ σύ; Pilate fastens on this mention of Jesus' kingdom: "Well then, are you a king?" The concluding σύ is incredulous in its emphasis: "*you* poor prisoner." οὐκοῦν is found again in the Greek Bible only in the A text of 2 Kings 5^{23}.

ἀπεκρίθη ὁ Ἰησοῦς. The art. is omitted, according to Jn.'s usual habit when using this phrase (see on $1^{29.\,50}$), by LWΓΔ; but it must be retained here, being read by ℵABD^{supp}N.

Σὺ λέγεις ὅτι βασιλεύς εἰμι. Westcott-Hort note in the margin that this might be taken as a question: "Do you say that I am a king?" But the Synoptists agree in giving as the reply of Jesus to the question "Art thou the King of the Jews?" the words σὺ λέγεις (Mk. 15^2, Mt. 27^{11}, Lk. 23^3), which is neither a clear affirmation nor a denial, but an assent given as a concession. But cf. the answer ὑμεῖς λέγετε ὅτι ἐγώ εἰμι to the question of the priests, "Art thou the Son of God?" in Lk. 22^{70}. Here, in like manner, we must translate, "Thou sayest that I am a king." This is the point on which Pilate has been insisting, that Jesus' claim seemed to be one of kingship, and Jesus admits it again (cf. v. 36), but adds some explanatory words.

The R.V. margin offers the alternative rendering, "Thou sayest it, because I am a king," but the Synoptic parallels do not support this.

It has been alleged that σὺ λέγεις or σὺ εἶπας was a Rabbinic formula of solemn affirmation (Schöttgen on Mt. 26^{25}), but Dalman has shown that this cannot be sustained. Where "thou hast said" appears in the Talmud, it is merely equivalent to "you are right."[1] In any case, we have here not an ellipse such as σὺ λέγεις, with nothing added, but a complete sentence, "Thou sayest that I am a king."

After εἰμι the rec. adds ἐγώ (repeating it again in the next sentence, ἐγὼ εἰς τοῦτο κτλ.) with ΑΓΔΝΘ, but ℵBD^{supp}L omit the first ἐγώ. If it were genuine, it might carry a reference

[1] Cf. Dalman, *Words of Jesus*, Eng. Tr., pp. 309–312.

εἰμι. ἐγὼ εἰς τοῦτο γεγέννημαι καὶ εἰς τοῦτο ἐλήλυθα εἰς τὸν κόσμον, ἵνα μαρτυρήσω τῇ ἀληθείᾳ· πᾶς ὁ ὢν ἐκ τῆς ἀληθείας ἀκούει μου τῆς φωνῆς.

38. λέγει αὐτῷ ὁ Πειλᾶτος Τί ἐστιν ἀλήθεια; Καὶ τοῦτο εἰπὼν πάλιν ἐξῆλθεν πρὸς τοὺς Ἰουδαίους, καὶ λέγει αὐτοῖς Ἐγὼ οὐδεμίαν

to the contemptuous σύ in Pilate's question; but the answer is more dignified, without any emphasis on the "*I*": "Thou sayest that I am a king."

ἐγὼ εἰς τοῦτο γεγέννημαι. Here the ἐγώ is impressive: "To this end I have been born." [1] See note on 1[13]; and cf. Lk. 1[35] τὸ γεννώμενον ἅγιον, Jn. 16[21] ἐγεννήθη. The reference is to the Nativity, not to the Incarnation; cf. also Rom. 14[9].

καὶ εἰς τοῦτο ἐλήλυθα εἰς τὸν κόσμον, a favourite Johannine phrase, *e.g.* 9[39] 16[28]; see on 11[27].

ἵνα μαρτυρήσω τῇ ἀληθείᾳ. Truth is one of the keywords of the Fourth Gospel (see on 1[14]). It was John the Baptist's privilege to bear witness to the truth (5[33]), but in a deeper and fuller measure was this the purpose of Jesus' mission. His witness to the truth was not confined to this " good confession " before Pilate (1 Tim. 6[13]), but was continuous throughout His ministry (3[11. 32] 7[7] 8[14]). Cf Rev. 1[5].

πᾶς ὁ ὢν ἐκ τῆς ἀληθείας (for this description of a candid mind, cf. 1 Jn. 3[19]) ἀκούει μου τῆς φωνῆς, " heareth my voice," *i.e.* hears with appreciation and obedience, for such is the force of ἀκούειν followed by the gen. (see on 3[8]). The sheep hear the voice of the Shepherd (10[16. 27]); and the spiritual deafness which does not hear it is blameworthy (see on 8[47], and cf. 1 Jn. 4[6]). No such claim on man's allegiance was ever made by any other master: "*Every one* who is of the truth heareth my voice."

Pilate suggests to the Jews, unavailingly, that Jesus should be released (vv. 38-40)

38. Pilate is now convinced that Jesus' " kingdom " is not a temporal one, and that He is innocent of revolutionary designs. His rejoinder is perhaps wistful rather than cynical or careless: " What *is* truth ? " But to this, the greatest of questions, he does not wait for an answer. He goes outside again (πάλιν, see v. 29) to the Jews assembled in the courtyard, and roundly tells them that he can find no reason why Jesus should be put to death.

ἐγὼ οὐδεμίαν εὑρίσκω ἐν αὐτῷ αἰτίαν. This is the order of

[1] The phrase is reproduced by Justin of Christ : εἰς τοῦτο γεννηθέντα (*Apol.* i. 13).

εὑρίσκω ἐν αὐτῷ αἰτίαν. 39. ἔστιν δὲ συνήθεια ὑμῖν ἵνα ἕνα ἀπολύσω ὑμῖν ἐν τῷ πάσχα· βούλεσθε οὖν ἀπολύσω ὑμῖν τὸν βασιλέα

words in BL, but the rec., with אANWΓΔΘ, puts αἰτίαν after
οὐδεμίαν. According to Jn., Pilate says this three times to the
Jewish accusers (19⁴·⁶); as also does Lk. 23⁴·¹⁴·²², who has
αἴτιον for αἰτίαν. The αἰτία is the *crimen*, the thing charged
against the prisoner; cf. Mk. 15²⁶, Mt. 27³⁷, and see on 19¹⁹.
For this use of αἰτία, cf. Gen. 4¹³, Prov. 28¹⁷.

At this point in the narrative, Luke gives an incident unrecorded by the other evangelists (Lk. 23⁷⁻¹²). He says that
Pilate caught at the word " Galilæan " which had been used
by the accusers of Jesus, and, anxious to evade responsibility,
sent Jesus to Herod, the tetrarch of Galilee, who was then at
Jerusalem. According to this story, which has every mark
of genuineness and which no one was likely to invent, Jesus
kept silence before Herod, and having been mocked by the
soldiers was sent back to Pilate. Herod was not anxious
to involve himself in any question of treason against the imperial
authority

Pilate's next effort to save Jesus, or to save himself from
the shame of condemning one whom he believed to be innocent,
was to appeal to a Passover custom of releasing a prisoner from
custody. Of this custom we know nothing beyond what
is told in the Gospels, but there is nothing improbable in
the statement that it prevailed at Jerusalem. Livy tells of
something similar at the Roman *Lectisternia* (Livy, v. xiii. 8),
and there is an allusion to it in Dion. Halicar. (xii. 9).[1]

39. This συνήθεια (cf. 1 Cor. 8⁷ 11¹⁶) is alluded to by the
other evangelists (see Mk. 15⁶, Mt. 27¹⁵) ; Lk. (23¹⁷) even makes
it an ἀνάγκη.

βούλεσθε οὖν ἀπολύσω ὑμῖν τὸν βασιλέα τῶν Ἰουδαίων; Mk. 15⁹
has the question in the same words, Jesus being described as
" the King of the Jews " by Pilate, with a contemptuous
allusion to the charge made against Him by the chief priests.

At this stage in the narrative, Mt. 27¹⁹ tells that a dream of
Pilate's wife was reported to him, warning him not to condemn
Jesus. There is nothing of this in the other Gospels, but the
incident, if genuine, would fully account for Pilate's hesitancy
in signing the death warrant.

40. ἐκραύγασαν (see on 11⁴³ for this verb) οὖν πάλιν κτλ.,
" Then they yelled again, etc." Jn. condenses the story; he
has not told before of the wild shouts of the crowd. After
πάλιν, the rec. inserts πάντες, but om. אBLW. For πάλιν, א
substitutes πάντες.

---

[1] See *E.B.* 476 for these passages.

τῶν Ἰουδαίων; 40. ἐκραύγασαν οὖν πάλιν λέγοντες Μὴ τοῦτον,
ἀλλὰ τὸν Βαραββᾶν. ἦν δὲ ὁ Βαραββᾶς λῃστής.

XIX. 1. Τότε οὖν ἔλαβεν ὁ Πειλᾶτος τὸν Ἰησοῦν καὶ ἐμαστί-
γωσεν. 2. καὶ οἱ στρατιῶται πλέξαντες στέφανον ἐξ ἀκανθῶν

Μὴ τοῦτον, ἀλλὰ τὸν Βαραββᾶν. Mk. 15¹¹ (followed by Mt.
27²⁰) tells that the priests had suggested this to the mob. Mt.
alone says that Pilate had *offered* the alternative " Jesus, or
Barabbas " (Mt. 27¹⁷, where a famous variant gives Jesus as
the name also of the robber, whose patronymic was Barabbas).
Lk. 23¹⁹· ²⁵ says that Barabbas was an insurgent and a murderer (cf. Acts 3¹⁴); Mk. 15⁷ saying that he was an associate
of such. Mt. 27¹⁶ only says that he was a " notable " prisoner
(δέσμιον ἐπίσημον), and the article here, τὸν Βαρ., would agree
with this, " the well-known Barabbas."

ἦν δὲ ὁ Βαραββᾶς λῃστής. Jn.'s description of him is powerful
in its brevity, and provides a good illustration of his " irony "
(see on 1⁴⁵). For λῃστής, cf. 10¹· ⁸.

The release of Barabbas, which must have followed here,
is not explicitly related. Probably Pilate ascended his βῆμα
(cf. 19¹³) to pronounce the formal sentence which would free
the prisoner.

*Jesus is scourged and mocked by the soldiers (XIX. 1–5).
Pilate makes another unavailing attempt to save Him
(vv. 6, 7)*

XIX. 1. Pilate went back into the palace, where Jesus was,
and ordered Him to be scourged, in the hope (apparently) that
this sufficiently terrible punishment would satisfy the chief
priests (cf. Lk. 23¹⁶). Mk. 15¹⁵, Mt. 27²⁶ connect the scourging
and the mock coronation with the death sentence (see on v. 16
below), but Jn.'s narrative is very explicit and is to be followed
here. The " Pillar of the Scourging " is now shown in the
Church of the Holy Sepulchre, but in the fourth century it was
shown to the Bordeaux Pilgrim in the traditional house of
Caiaphas. The original pillar to which the Lord was bound
was, no doubt, inside the Prætorium. Cf. Mt. 20¹⁹, Lk. 18³³.

2. In the account of the mockery of Jesus by the soldiers of
Pilate, Jn. follows Mk. 15¹⁷, or, at any rate, uses phrases which
recall Mk. There is no probability that he uses Mt. Lk. 23¹¹
ascribes this cruel indignity to the soldiers of *Herod*. The
soldiers were amused by the idea that the poor prisoner claimed
to be a king, and their rough jests were directed rather against
the Jews than against Jesus personally. " This, then, is the
King of the *Jews* ! "

πλέξαντες στέφανον ἐξ ἀκανθῶν. Verbally identical with Mt.

ἐπέθηκαν αὐτοῦ τῇ κεφαλῇ, καὶ ἱμάτιον πορφυροῦν περιέβαλον αὐτόν,
3. καὶ ἤρχοντο πρὸς αὐτὸν καὶ ἔλεγον Χαῖρε, ὁ βασιλεὺς τῶν Ἰου-
δαίων· καὶ ἐδίδοσαν αὐτῷ ῥαπίσματα. 4. Καὶ ἐξῆλθεν πάλιν ἔξω

27²⁸; Mk. 15¹⁷ has πλέξαντες ἀκάνθινον στέφανον. Lk. does not
mention the mock coronation. Pseudo-Peter (§ 3) attributes
the jest to an individual; τις αὐτῶν ἐνεγκὼν στέφανον ἀκάνθινον
ἔθηκεν ἐπὶ τῆς κεφαλῆς τοῦ κυρίου.

The soldiers plaited the twigs of some thorny plant into a
crown or wreath (cf. ὁ στέφανος . . . ὁ πλεκείς, Isa. 28⁵).

ἐπέθηκαν αὐτοῦ τῇ κεφαλῇ. This phrase, too, might be
thought to come from Mt. 27²⁹ ἐπέθηκαν ἐπὶ τὴν κεφαλὴν αὐτοῦ,
for Mk. 15¹⁷ has only περιτιθέασιν αὐτῷ. But Jn. says nothing
of the mock sceptre which Mt. mentions, a detail which is not
in Mk. It would be precarious to infer that Jn. is using Mt.'s
narrative.

καὶ ἱμάτιον πορφυροῦν περιέβαλον αὐτόν. This is reminiscent
of Mk. 15¹⁷, ἐνδύουσιν αὐτὸν πορφύραν, rather than of Mt. 27²⁸
or Lk. 23¹¹ (where, however, we find περιβαλὼν αὐτὸν ἐσθῆτα
λαμπράν).[1] The substitute for the regal purple (cf. 1 Macc.
8¹⁴, etc.) may have been the scarlet cloak of one of the legionaries (χλαμύδα κοκκίνην, Mt. 27²⁸). Jesus had first been stripped
of His own outer clothing (ἐκδύσαντες αὐτόν, Mt. 27²⁸). For
ἱμάτιον, see on v. 23.

3. καὶ ἤρχοντο πρὸς αὐτόν. This clause is omitted in the
rec. text, following ADˢᵘᵖᵖΓΔ, but is retained in אBLNWΘ.
It is descriptive of the soldiers approaching Jesus with mock
reverence. Philo has a story of the mock coronation of a half-
witted man called Carabas by the mob at Alexandria, which
illustrates this. "They approached, some as if to salute him,
others as if pleading a cause, others as though making petition
about public matters " (in Flacc. 6).

καὶ ἔλεγον Χαῖρε, ὁ βασιλεὺς τῶν Ἰουδαίων. This is verbally
identical with the pretended salutation as given in Mt. 27²⁹.
The soldiers cried Ave! as they would to Cæsar. The art. ὁ
before βασιλεὺς τ. Ἰ. suggests their derision.

καὶ ἐδίδοσαν αὐτῷ ῥαπίσματα. "They slapped Him" with
the palms of their hands. See on 18²² for ῥάπισμα. ἐδίδοσαν
(אBLNW) is to be preferred to the rec. ἐδίδουν (ADˢᵘᵖᵖΓΔΘ).
They gave Him some slaps in the face, during their cruel
horse-play, but this was not a continuous form of insult, like
the shouting of Ave.

4. Pilate had gone into the Prætorium to order the scourging, and he now comes out again to make another appeal to the
pity of the Jews The exact reading is not certain. ABL give

_____
[1] Cf. Introd., p. xcviii.

ὁ Πειλᾶτος καὶ λέγει αὐτοῖς "Ἴδε ἄγω ὑμῖν αὐτὸν ἔξω, ἵνα γνῶτε ὅτι οὐδεμίαν αἰτίαν εὑρίσκω ἐν αὐτῷ. 5. ἐξῆλθεν οὖν ὁ Ἰησοῦς ἔξω, φορῶν τὸν ἀκάνθινον στέφανον καὶ τὸ πορφυροῦν ἱμάτιον. καὶ λέγει αὐτοῖς Ἰδοὺ ὁ ἄνθρωπος. 6. ὅτε οὖν ἴδον αὐτὸν οἱ ἀρχιερεῖς καὶ οἱ

καὶ ἐξῆλθεν, אDsuppΓ omit καί; and NWΘ have ἐξῆλθεν οὖν (as at 18²⁹: see 18³⁸ and cf. v. 5).

Pilate says to the Jews that He is bringing Jesus out to them, that they may understand that, as he said before (18³⁸), he can find no fault in Him. Up to this Jesus had been inside the Prætorium, and the scourging and mockery were probably not visible to the waiting Jews.

Ἴδε, a favourite word in Jn.; see on 1²⁹.

ὅτι οὐδεμίαν αἰτίαν εὑρίσκω ἐν αὐτῷ. א* has the shorter form ὅτι αἰτίαν οὐκ εὑρίσκω. The phrase has occurred 18³⁸, and appears again 19⁶, in slightly different forms.

5. Jesus was brought out, no doubt weak and faint after the scourging, still wearing the mocking insignia of royalty. These He probably continued to wear until He was brought out for the last time for formal sentence (v. 15; cf. Mt. 27³¹).

φορῶν. This is the regular word for "wearing" clothes; cf. Mt. 11⁸, Jas. 2³.

καὶ λέγει αὐτοῖς (sc. Pilate) Ἰδοὺ ὁ ἄνθρωπος. For ἰδού (אBL), the rec. has Jn.'s favourite ἴδε (cf. vv. 4, 14). In this verse B omits ὁ before Ἰησοῦς (see on 1²⁹), and also before ἄνθρωπος (cf. Zech. 6¹² ἰδοὺ ἀνήρ, referring to "the Man whose name is the Branch," the future Builder of the Temple). For Ἰησοῦς N has Πειλᾶτος by mistake

Ἰδοὺ ὁ ἄνθρωπος, Ecce homo! This, on Pilate's lips, meant, "See the poor fellow!" ὁ ἄνθρωπος, expressing pity. This is a classical use (cf. Dem. de falsa leg. 402, § 198, and Meid. 543, § 91); see also Mt. 26⁷⁴. Pilate thought to move the priests to compassion by exhibiting Jesus to them, who had been scourged by his orders, and whom the soldiers had treated as an object of mockery and rude jesting.

Jn. may mean to represent Pilate, like Caiaphas (11⁵¹), as an unconscious prophet, his words, "Behold the Man!" pointing to the Ideal Man of all succeeding Christian generations. Abbott (Diat. 1960c) recalls some passages from Epictetus, in which ὁ ἄνθρωπος is thus used of the ideal of humanity. But such an interpretation of Pilate's famous words is probably a Christian afterthought.

The whole clause λέγει . . . ἄνθρωπος is omitted in the O.L. texts a e ff² r, and also by the Coptic Q, an interesting combination.

6. ὅτε οὖν ἴδον αὐτὸν οἱ ἀρχιερεῖς κτλ. The common people

ὑπηρέται, ἐκραύγασαν λέγοντες Σταύρωσον σταύρωσον. λέγει αὐτοῖς
ὁ Πειλᾶτος Λάβετε αὐτὸν ὑμεῖς καὶ σταυρώσατε· ἐγὼ γὰρ οὐχ εὑρίσκω
ἐν αὐτῷ αἰτίαν. 7. ἀπεκρίθησαν αὐτῷ οἱ Ἰουδαῖοι Ἡμεῖς νόμον
ἔχομεν, καὶ κατὰ τὸν νόμον ὀφείλει ἀποθανεῖν, ὅτι Υἱὸν Θεοῦ ἑαυτὸν
ἐποίησεν.

are not mentioned; the chief priests were the important persons
whom Pilate wished to move from their purpose. But the
sight of Jesus only angered them; and they, with their satellites
(οἱ ὑπηρέται), raised the shout of "Crucify!" It has been
implied throughout that this was the death which they had
designed for Jesus, but the word σταύρωσον is used now for the
first time. Cf. Mt. 27²².

For ἴδον (אADˢᵘᵖᵖLNW) the rec. with BΘ has εἶδον. After
ἐκραύγασαν (cf. 18⁴⁰), the rec. adds λέγοντες with ABDˢᵘᵖᵖNWΘ
(cf. 7³⁷); but om. א. Again, after σταύρωσον *bis* אABDˢᵘᵖᵖNΘ
add αὐτόν (as at v. 15); but om. BL.

Λάβετε αὐτὸν ὑμεῖς καί κτλ. "Take Him yourselves, etc."
Pilate repeats this suggestion, which had disconcerted the priests
when he made it before (18³¹, where see note). He now adds
"and crucify Him," although he and they both knew that
the Sanhedrim could not legally do this. He also says for
the third time that he can find no just cause for a death
sentence (cf. 18³⁸ and v. 4). Jn., like Lk. (23⁴· ¹⁴· ²²), is careful
to record that Pilate three times affirmed his conviction of
Jesus' innocence.

7. The chief priests, however, make an unexpected rejoinder. They tell Pilate that, according to Jewish law, Jesus
ought to be put to death as a blasphemer, and they warn him
by implication that he must not set aside their law in such a
matter. It was the Roman practice to respect the laws and
customs of Judæa, as of other distant provinces of the empire;
and of this the accusers of Jesus remind Pilate.

Ἡμεῖς νόμον ἔχομεν, viz. Lev. 24¹⁶, which enacted that a
blasphemer should be stoned to death. The chief priests knew
that this could not be put into operation (see on 18³¹). In
any case, the witnesses had to cast the first stone (Deut. 17⁷),
and those who bore witness as to the blasphemy of Jesus
were not in agreement with each other (Mk. 14⁵⁶). The
Sanhedrim, therefore, were content, in this particular case,
that the responsibility lay with Pilate.

κατὰ τὸν νόμον (the rec. adds ἡμῶν with AΓΔΘ, but om.
אBDˢᵘᵖᵖLNWΔ) ὀφείλει ἀποθανεῖν. For the verb ὀφείλειν, see
on 13¹⁴.

ὅτι υἱὸν θεοῦ ἑαυτὸν ἐποίησεν. This charge was better
founded than the charge of treason, alleged to be inherent in

8. Ὅτε οὖν ἤκουσεν ὁ Πειλᾶτος τοῦτον τὸν λόγον, μᾶλλον
ἐφοβήθη, 9. καὶ εἰσῆλθεν εἰς τὸ πραιτώριον πάλιν καὶ λέγει τῷ Ἰησοῦ

Jesus' claim to be a king. "Son of God" was a recognised
title of Messiah (see on 1³⁴); and in his examination before the
chief priests Jesus had admitted that He was the Messiah
(Mk. 14⁶², Mt. 26⁶⁴, Lk. 22⁷⁰, in the last passage the phrase
ὁ υἱὸς τοῦ θεοῦ being explicitly used). But He had been
suspected of, and charged with, blasphemy on several occasions
before this, according to Jn. See 5¹⁸ 10³³· ³⁶. To the question
τίνα σεαυτὸν σὺ ποιεῖς; (8⁵³), the Jews had good ground for
believing that υἱὸς θεοῦ would be His answer.

The omission of the def. articles in υἱὸς θεοῦ is probably
due to the tendency to drop the article before familiar titles
rather than to the phrase being used in any sense less exalted
than the highest, as may be the case at Mt. 14³³. But in this,
the Messianic sense, Pilate could not have understood it, any
more than the centurion at the Cross (Mt. 27⁵⁴). It must have
suggested to Pilate a vague, mysterious claim on the part of
Jesus to be more than human; and hearing of it awakened
in his mind a superstitious fear. υἱὸς θεοῦ is frequently used
in inscriptions as a title of the Emperor.[1]

The second examination of Jesus by Pilate (vv. 8–11)

8. ὅτε οὖν ἤκουσεν ὁ Πειλᾶτος τοῦτον τὸν λόγον κτλ.   Observe
that ἀκούειν followed by the acc. does not connote an
intelligent hearing (see on 3⁸); as Abbott says (*Diat.* 2586),
"the hearing does not produce (upon Pilate) any result beyond
emotion."

μᾶλλον ἐφοβήθη, "he was more alarmed than he had been
before" (see on 18³⁹).

9. The first questioning of Jesus by Pilate has been described, 18³³⁻³⁸.

καὶ εἰσῆλθεν εἰς τὸ πραιτώριον πάλιν : cf. 18³³.

Pilate's question, Πόθεν εἶ σύ; is no formal interrogatory
as to the birthplace or domicile of Jesus. He had learnt
already that He was of Galilee (Lk. 23⁶· ⁷). But Pilate has
been moved by the dignified bearing of the prisoner, and is
uneasy because of the strange claim which He was said to have
made for Himself, that He was υἱὸς θεοῦ (v. 7). The question
recalls the similar question Σὺ τίς εἶ; which was put by the
Jews who were impressed, despite their incredulity, by His
words (8²⁵).

ὁ δὲ Ἰη. ἀπόκρισιν (cf. 1²², Lk. 2⁴⁷ 20²⁶) οὐκ ἔδωκεν αὐτῷ.

[1] Deissman, *Bible Studies*, Eng. Tr., 167.

Πόθεν εἶ σύ; ὁ δὲ Ἰησοῦς ἀπόκρισιν οὐκ ἔδωκεν αὐτῷ. 10. λέγει οὖν αὐτῷ ὁ Πειλᾶτος Ἐμοὶ οὐ λαλεῖς; οὐκ οἶδας ὅτι ἐξουσίαν ἔχω ἀπολῦσαί σε καὶ ἐξουσίαν ἔχω σταυρῶσαί σε; 11. ἀπεκρίθη αὐτῷ

The silence of Jesus under cross-examination is mentioned in all the Gospels. Mk. 14⁶¹, Mt. 26⁶³ note His silence before the high priest; Lk. 23⁹ says that He did not answer Herod at all; Mk. 15⁵, Mt. 27¹⁴ state that He would not reply to the accusations which the Sanhedrim put before Pilate; and in the present passage His silence is irritating to the dignity of Pilate, who in this repeated inquiry was trying to elicit something that would save Him. Salmon suggested[1] that the silence of Jesus is sufficiently explained by bodily fatigue and exhaustion; and so far as this last examination by Pilate is concerned, it may well be that His exhaustion after being scourged was such that speech was difficult for Him. After the scourging Jn. ascribes only one sentence to Jesus (v. 11) before He was crucified. But bodily fatigue would not, by itself, explain His silence when cross-examined by the high priest (Mk. 14⁶¹) or before Herod (Lk. 23⁹); and His refusal to answer questions which were not asked in sincerity, but out of mere curiosity or with intent to betray Him into some dangerous admission, is explicable on moral grounds. Indeed, the dignity of His silence before His accusers does not need exposition. He was moving to a pre-destined end, and He knew it.

Many commentators, following Chrysostom and Augustine, find in the silence of Jesus before His judges a fulfilment of Isa. 53⁷.

10. Pilate's dignity is offended by receiving no answer to his question. The silence of Jesus amounts to contempt of court. Ἐμοὶ οὐ λαλεῖς; "Do you not speak *to me* ?" ἐμοί being placed first for emphasis. "I have power (ἐξουσία) to release you, and I have power to crucify you" (the rec. text interchanges the order of these clauses).

ἐξουσία (see on 1¹²) is "authority," rather than "power." Pilate had both, but he is reminded by Jesus that his authority, like all human authority, is *delegated*; its source is Divine, and therefore it is not arbitrary power which can be exercised capriciously without moral blame.

11. ἀπεκρ. αὐτῷ Ἰησοῦς. ΑΝΓΔΘ om. αὐτῷ, which is retained by אBDˢᵘᵖᵖW ; and אALNWΘ ins. ὁ before Ἰησ., but om. BDˢᵘᵖᵖ. Cf. for similar variants, 18³⁴.

Οὐκ εἶχες ἐξουσίαν κτλ. So BWΓΔΘ, but אADˢᵘᵖᵖL have ἔχεις.

---

[1] *Human Element in the Gospels*, p. 512 ; cf. *contra*, Moffatt, *D.C.G.* ii. 754.

Ἰησοῦς Οὐκ εἶχες ἐξουσίαν κατ' ἐμοῦ οὐδεμίαν εἰ μὴ ἦν δεδομένον σοι ἄνωθεν· διὰ τοῦτο ὁ παραδούς μέ σοι μείζονα ἁμαρτίαν ἔχει.

εἰ μὴ ἦν δεδομένον σοι ἄνωθεν. This doctrine of authority is expressed by Paul in other words (Rom. 13¹· ²). For ἄνωθεν, see on 3³. It must mean " from God " ; the suggestion that it means " from the ecclesiastical authority " is untenable. Pilate's ἐξουσία was not, in fact, delegated to him by the Sanhedrim.

ὁ παραδούς μέ σοι κτλ. So אBΔΘ ; the rec., with ADˢᵘᵖᵖLNW, has παραδιδούς. Judas is repeatedly described in Jn. as the person who was to deliver Jesus up (cf. 6⁶⁴· ⁷¹ 12⁴ 13²· ²¹ 18²· ⁵), but he is not indicated in this passage. He did not deliver Jesus up to *Pilate*; and he disappears from the Johannine narrative after the scene of the betrayal in the garden (18⁵). In Mt. 27³ᶠ· he is represented as repenting, after the priests brought Jesus before Pilate; but the other evangelists say nothing as to this. It is remarkable that it is not told anywhere that Judas bore " witness " to what Jesus had said or done. His part was finished when he identified Jesus at Gethsemane.

Those who delivered Jesus to Pilate were the members of the Sanhedrim (18³⁰· ³⁵; cf. Mt. 27², Acts 3¹³), with Caiaphas as their official chief. ὁ παραδούς μέ σοι is Caiaphas, as representing those who were ultimately responsible for the guilt of putting Jesus to death.

μείζονα ἁμαρτίαν ἔχει. These words are commonly taken to mean " has greater sin " than *you*; *i.e.* that Caiaphas was more guilty than Pilate; and this was, no doubt, true. But such an interpretation will not suit the context, or explain διὰ τοῦτο at the beginning of the sentence. " Your power and authority are delegated to you from God, *therefore* Caiaphas, who brought me before you for sentence, is more guilty than you." That is not easy to understand; for the ἐξουσία of Caiaphas was a trust from God, equally with that of Pilate. Wetstein suggested a better explanation: " Your power and authority are delegated to you from God, therefore Caiaphas is more guilty than he would be if you were only an irresponsible executioner, for he has used this God-given authority of yours to further his own wicked projects." μείζονα ἁμαρτίαν ἔχει, " he has greater sin," not than *you* (which is not in question), but than he would have had if Pilate had not been a power ordained of God. " Therefore his sin is the greater " is the meaning.

For the Johannine phrase ἔχειν ἁμαρτίαν, cf. 9⁴¹.

12. Ἐκ τούτου ὁ Πειλᾶτος ἐζήτει ἀπολῦσαι αὐτόν· οἱ δὲ Ἰουδαῖοι
ἐκραύγασαν λέγοντες Ἐὰν τοῦτον ἀπολύσῃς, οὐκ εἶ φίλος τοῦ
Καίσαρος· πᾶς ὁ βασιλέα ἑαυτὸν ποιῶν ἀντιλέγει τῷ Καίσαρι.
13. ὁ οὖν Πειλᾶτος ἀκούσας τῶν λόγων τούτων ἤγαγεν ἔξω τὸν

*Pilate again fails to obtain the consent of the Jews to acquit
Jesus ; and pronounces the formal sentence of death by
crucifixion (vv. 12–16).*

12. ἐκ τούτου, " thenceforth." See on 6⁶⁶.

οἱ δὲ Ἰουδαῖοι ἐκραύγασαν λέγοντες κτλ. ἐκραύγασαν (BDˢᵘᵖᵖ)
represents the yell of fury with which the Jews received
Pilate's last attempt to set Jesus free. The rec., with אᶜ, has
ἔκραζον, and ALNΘ have ἐκραύγαζον, but the impf. does not
represent the meaning so well as the aor. does. Mt. 27²⁴ᶠ·
relates that after Pilate's failure to persuade the Jews he
ostentatiously washed his hands, thereby endeavouring to shift
his responsibility.

The last argument which the chief priests used, and which
was effective, although their former overtures to Pilate (18³⁰
19⁷) had failed, was an appeal to his fears. " If you release
Him, you are no friend of Cæsar." There is no need to
limit the term φίλος τοῦ Καίσαρος, as if it were an official title
(cf. 15¹⁵); the expression is used generally. The official title
is probably not found before Vespasian.

πᾶς ὁ βασιλέα ἑαυτὸν ποιῶν κτλ., " every one who makes
himself a king," which was the charge brought in the first
instance against Jesus (see on 18³³), ἀντιλέγει (only here in Jn.),
" opposes Cæsar." Here was a veiled threat. If Pilate were
reported at Rome to have set free a man making pretension
to the title " King of the Jews," it might go badly with him.
Treason to the emperor was the cardinal offence for a viceroy
or procurator.

13. We must read τῶν λόγων τούτων, with אABW, rather
than τοῦτον τὸν λόγον of the rec. text, which has come in
from v. 8. Pilate not only heard what the Jews said, but he
appreciated its force (see on 3⁸ for ἀκούειν followed by the
gen.). The reference is to the threat of v. 12. Pilate could
not afford to have it reported to the emperor that he had
acquitted a prisoner who was accused of setting himself up
as a king. His position would be safe only if the Jews *asked*
for an acquittal; for then he could always say that the charge
had broken down.

ἤγαγεν ἔξω τὸν Ἰη., " he led Jesus out," sc. from the
Prætorium, where He had been under examination (v. 9).

ἐκάθισεν ἐπὶ βήματος must be rendered " he sat down on

Ἰησοῦν, καὶ ἐκάθισεν ἐπὶ βήματος εἰς τόπον λεγόμενον Λιθόστρωτον,

the judgment seat," *i.e.* Pilate sat down, the examination being over, intending now to give judgment with full dignity. Before he finally passed sentence, he gave the priests another opportunity of claiming, or acquiescing in, the release of Jesus. This (intransitive) rendering of ἐκάθισεν agrees with Mt.'s report καθημένου δὲ αὐτοῦ ἐπὶ τοῦ βήματος (Mt. 27[19]), as well as with the only other place where ἐκάθισεν occurs in Jn. (12[14]). We have καθίσας ἐπὶ τοῦ βήματος used of Herod and of Festus in Acts 12[21] 25[6. 17].

καθίζειν, however, is used transitively in 1 Cor. 6[4], Eph. 1[20] (cf. Hermas, *Vis.* III. ii. 4), and Archbishop Whately maintained [1] that ἐκάθισεν should be rendered transitively here, the meaning being that Pilate did not sit on the βῆμα himself, but *set* Jesus on it in derision. It is worthy of note that there was a tradition current in the second century that Jesus had thus been placed by the Jews on the judgment seat. It appears in the *Gospel of Peter* (§ 3): ἐκάθισαν αὐτὸν ἐπὶ καθέδραν κρίσεως, λέγοντες, Δικαίως κρῖνε, βασιλεῦ τοῦ Ἰσραήλ   Justin (whencesoever he obtained the tradition) has it also: διασύροντες αὐτὸν (referring to Isa. 58[2]) ἐκάθισαν ἐπὶ βήματος, καὶ εἶπον Κρῖνον ἡμῖν (*Apol.* i. 35). Perhaps it came from a misunderstanding of Jn. 19[13], attributing this derisive action to Pilate, not to the Jews. But a misunderstanding it must be, for, apart from the intransitive use of καθίζειν being always found elsewhere in the Gospels, it is inconceivable that a Roman procurator should be so regardless of his dignity, when about to pronounce sentence of death, as to make a jest of the matter.[2]

ἐπὶ βήματος, " upon *a* judgment seat," *sc.* perhaps upon one improvised for the occasion, as the Jews would not enter the Prætorium, and judgment had to be given in public.

The rec. text has ἐπὶ τοῦ βήματος, but τοῦ is omitted by אABD[supp]LN, and it probably came in from such passages as Acts 12[21] 25[6. 17].

Josephus (*Bell. Jud.* II. ix. 3), when telling of another sentence pronounced by Pilate, has ὁ Πιλᾶτος καθίσας ἐπὶ βήματος ἐν τῷ μεγάλῳ σταδίῳ, judgment in this case also being delivered in the open air. Here we have ἐπὶ βήματος εἰς τόπον κτλ., instead of ἐν τόπῳ. Perhaps εἰς is used because of the verb at the beginning of the sentence (see on 9[7]); but it is possible that it is used for ἐν here, as it often is in Mk.[3] and in Lk. and Acts. See on 1[18] 9[7]

---

[1] See Salmon, *Introd. to N.T.*, p. 67 *n.*
[2] See Zahn, *Einleitung in N.T.*, § 69, and Abbott, *Diat.* 2537.
[3] See Turner in *J.T.S.*, Oct. 1924, p. 14.

Ἐβραϊστὶ δὲ Γαββαθά.   14. ἦν δὲ Παρασκευὴ τοῦ πάσχα, ὥρα ἦν

εἰς τόπον λεγόμενον Λιθόστρωτον, Ἑβραϊστὶ (see on 5²) δὲ Γαββαθά. Λιθόστρωτον is not the *interpretation* of the name Gabbatha (see on 4²⁵); Jn. gives the two names, Greek and Aramaic, of distinct derivation, by which the place was known. The word Λιθόστρωτον does not occur again in the N.T., and in the LXX it is found only at Esth. 1⁶, Cant. 3¹⁰, 2 Chron. 7³; in the last-mentioned passage being applied to the pavement of Solomon's temple. (cf. Josephus, *Antt.* VIII. iii. 2).

The situation of the Prætorium has been already discussed (see on 18²⁸), and we have identified it with Herod's Palace, which was to the south of the Temple area. But the name *Gabbatha* is not known elsewhere. Its derivation is probably from the root נבה " to be high," so that נַּבְּתָא would mean " an elevated place." ¹ G. A. Smith (*Jerusalem*, ii. 575) suggests that it is derived from גבב, " to pack closely," so that *Gabbatha* would be equivalent to "a mosaic."

It was customary to place the βῆμα or judgment seat on a dais of tesselated or mosaic pavement, in order that the judge might be seen and heard conveniently; and Julius Cæsar is said to have carried about with him *tessellata et sectilia pavimenta*, to be laid down wherever he encamped (Suet. *Jul.* 46). A portable dais of this kind could not, however, have given its name to a locality; Λιθόστρωτον was probably one of the names by which the elevated place of judgment came to be known, because of the mosaic pavement which was laid down for the sake of dignity

14. ἦν δὲ Παρασκευὴ τοῦ πάσχα, *i.e.* " Friday of the Passover week." Elsewhere (Mk. 15⁴², Lk. 23⁵⁴, Mt. 27⁶², and Jn. 19³¹) παρασκευή means the day of preparation for the Sabbath, as here (see on 19⁴² for a possible exception). Thus Josephus has ἐν σάββασιν ἢ τῇ πρὸ αὐτῆς παρασκευῇ (*Antt.* xvi. 6. 2); and in the *Didache* (§ 8) παρασκευή again means Friday (cf. Clem. Alex. *Strom.*, § 75).

In the year of the Passion, the Passover, *i.e.* Nisan 14, fell on a Friday (v. 31). Had the meaning of παρασκευὴ τοῦ πάσχα here meant " It was the Preparation day of the *Passover*," *i.e.* the day before the Passover, we should have had ἡ παρασκευή with the def. article. See on v. 42.

ὥρα ἦν ὡς ἕκτη. So אABNW and vss. For ἕκτη, א°DˢᵘᵖᵖLΔ read τρίτη, thus harmonising the text with Mk. 15²⁵. Eusebius (as quoted by Severus) explains the variant by ascribing it

---

¹ See Nestle in Hastings' *D.B.*, *s.v.* " Gabbatha," for the difficulties of the etymology.

ὡς ἕκτη· καὶ λέγει τοῖς Ἰουδαίοις Ἴδε, ὁ βασιλεὺς ὑμῶν. 15. ἐκραύγασαν οὖν ἐκεῖνοι Ἆρον ἆρον, σταύρωσον αὐτόν. λέγει αὐτοῖς ὁ Πειλᾶτος Τὸν βασιλέα ὑμῶν σταυρώσω; ἀπεκρίθησαν οἱ ἀρχιερεῖς

to the confusion between Γ (3) and F (6).[1] But the textual evidence for ἕκτη is overwhelming.

In Mk. 15[25] Jesus is said to have been crucified at "the third hour," the darkness beginning at "the sixth hour " and continuing until "the ninth hour," when He died. This is corrected by Jn.,[2] who tells that the Crucifixion did not begin until after "the sixth hour," *i.e.* after noon. The hypothesis that Jn.'s method of reckoning time was different from that of the Synoptists is inadmissible (see on 1[39]). That a discrepancy should exist as to the actual hour will not surprise any one who reflects on the loose way in which time intervals are often reported by quite honest witnesses.[3] Jn. is specially careful to fix the time at which things happened, and he is here followed by the *Acts of John* (§ 97), in which it is distinctly said "at the sixth hour." Indeed it is difficult to believe that all that happened on the day of the Passion before Jesus was actually crucified was over by 9 a.m., as Mk.'s report indicates.

For ἴδε "behold," a favourite word with Jn., see on 1[29] ; and cf. v. 14 above for the derisive Ἴδε, ὁ βασιλεὺς ὑμῶν. The sarcasm of Pilate is directed against the Jews, not against Jesus.

15. ἐκραύγασαν οὖν ἐκεῖνοι. So ℵ[c]BL, ἐκεῖνοι being emphatic : the rec. text has οἱ δὲ ἐκραύγασαν. W has ἔλεγον. For κραυγάζειν, see on 11[43] (cf. v. 6).

Ἆρον ἆρον. Cf. Lk. 23[18] αἶρε τοῦτον, and Acts 21[36]. Moulton-Milligan illustrate this usage of αἴρω from a second-century papyrus letter in which a mother says of her son: "He upsets me; away with him ! " (ἆρρον αὐτόν).

Τὸν βασιλέα ὑμῶν σταυρώσω; Pilate's ironical question is made specially incisive by the prominence in the sentence of τ. βασιλέα ὑμ.

οἱ ἀρχιερεῖς, who have been the prime movers throughout (cf. vv. 6, 21, and 12[10]), in their eagerness to answer Pilate, not only deny that Jesus was their King, but repudiate the idea that they have any king but Cæsar, thus formally denying the first principle of the Jewish theocracy that "Yahweh was their King " (1 Sam. 12[12]). Implicitly, they denied the ideal of the Messianic King, in order to conciliate a heathen power; and thus, by saying "We have no king but Cæsar," they abandoned that which was most distinctive of the religion of Judaism. In words, they not only rejected Jesus; they re-

[1] See *E.B.*, 1773.   [2] See Introd., p. cvii f.
[3] See *D.B.*, Extr. v. 478.

Οὐκ ἔχομεν βασιλέα εἰ μὴ Καίσαρα.   16. τότε οὖν παρέδωκεν αὐτὸν
αὐτοῖς ἵνα σταυρωθῇ.

pudiated the claims of the Christ, to whose Advent they professed to look forward. So, at least, the Johannine narrative
implies.

To be sure, they did not mean as much as this; they were
so anxious to gain their point that they did not measure their
words. By the time the Fourth Gospel was written, the Jewish
state had been overthrown by Titus; and some of those who
avowed before Pilate their unreserved loyalty to Cæsar had
doubtless fallen, fighting against Cæsar's legions.

16. τότε οὖν παρέδωκεν κτλ. Pilate's efforts to save Jesus
had failed. The people had taken up the cry, " Crucify Him ! "
The priests had just announced their loyalty to Cæsar in
extravagant terms, and Pilate was afraid of their innuendo
(v. 12) that he was not overzealous in Cæsar's cause. *Therefore*, afraid of the popular clamour, and not specially interested
in the fate of an unpopular fanatic (as he deemed Jesus to be),
" he delivered Him to them," *i.e.* to the Jews (cf. 18³⁶ ἵνα μὴ
παραδοθῶ τοῖς Ἰουδαίοις), " that He might be crucified."

The usual form of sentence in such cases was " ibis ad
crucem," but the Gospels do not record that it was formally
pronounced. This may have been done, but in any case Pilate's
attitude was rather that he acquiesced in the capital penalty
being inflicted than that he approved it. According to Roman
custom, after the death sentence was pronounced, the criminal
was first scourged, and then led off to execution without delay.
So Josephus says of crucifixions under the procurator Florus :
μαστιγῶσαί τε πρὸ τοῦ βήματος καὶ σταυρῷ προσηλῶσαι (*Bell.
Jud.* ii. 14. 9). Mk. (followed by Mt.) represents the scourging
of Jesus as taking place at this point, that is, after His sentence.
According to Jn. (19¹), He had already been scourged by Pilate's
order, in the hope that the Jews would be satisfied with this
sufficiently terrible punishment (cf. Lk. 23²²). It is probable
that Jn.'s report is the more accurate here; and it is not likely
that Pilate would have permitted a *second* scourging.

The Crucifixion and the title on the Cross (vv. 17–22)

17. παρέλαβον οὖν τὸν Ἰη., " So they received Jesus," *sc.* at
the hands of Pilate (cf. 1¹¹, 14³, the only other places where
Jn. used παραλαμβάνειν).

AW add καὶ ἀπήγαγον after Ἰησοῦν, and D^suppΓΔΘ read
καὶ ἤγαγον ; but BL 33 *a b c e ff* add nothing (cf. Mk. 15²⁰

626 THE GOSPEL ACCORDING TO ST. JOHN [XIX. 17.

17. Παρέλαβον οὖν τὸν Ἰησοῦν· καὶ βαστάζων ἑαυτῷ τὸν
σταυρὸν ἐξῆλθεν εἰς τὸν λεγόμενον Κρανίου τόπον, ὃ λέγεται

Lk. 23²⁶, Mt. 27³¹, from a reminiscence of which passages
ἀπήγαγον has crept into the Johannine text).

βαστάζων ἑαυτῷ τὸν σταυρόν. So ℵ; the rec. has βαστάζων
τὸν στ. αὐτοῦ. B has αὐτῷ. For βαστάζειν, see on 12⁶.

A criminal condemned to be crucified was required to carry
his own cross; cf. Plutarch (de sera numinis vindicta, 9),
ἕκαστος κακούργων ἐκφέρει τὸν αὐτοῦ σταυρόν, and Artemidorus
(Oneir. ii. 56), ὁ μέλλων σταυρῷ προσηλοῦσθαι πρότερον αὐτὸν
βαστάζει, a custom which gives special point to the exhortation, Mk. 8³⁴. The Synoptists speak of the Cross being
borne by Simon of Cyrene, and do not mention that Jesus
carried it Himself; however, the ancient explanation is
sufficient, viz. that Jesus carried it as they were leaving the
Prætorium, but that when He was found to be overborne by its
weight, Simon was compelled to carry it for Him. The
patristic idea that Jesus bearing His Cross was typified by
Isaac, upon whom τὰ ξύλα (Gen. 22⁶) were laid, as he went to
the place of sacrifice, goes back to Melito¹ and Tertullian.²
See on 18¹².

ἐξῆλθεν, "He went out," for executions were not allowed
within the city walls. See on v. 20.

εἰς τὸν λεγ. Κρανίου τόπον κτλ. Γολγοθά is the transliteration of the Aramaic גֻּלְגָּלְתָּא, Hebrew גֻּלְגֹּלֶת which is
transl. by κρανίον in Judg. 9⁵³, 2 Kings 9³⁵. For Ἑβραϊστί,
see on 5²; and for Jn.'s habit of giving Aramaic names with
their Greek equivalents, see on 1³⁸. Mk. 15²² and Mt. 27³³ give
the Greek name as Κρανίου, Lk. 23³³ giving Κρανίου, while Mt.
and Mk. as well as Jn. supply also the Aramaic designation.

We do not know why this place was called "the Place of a
Skull" (Calvaria). Origen is the first to mention a tradition,
afterwards widely prevalent, that Adam was believed to be
buried on this site (Comm. in Mt. 27³³); but no evidence has
been found to show that this was a pre-Christian tradition, and
the idea may have grown out of a passage like 1 Cor. 15²².
It has been suggested in modern times that this place-name was
given because of the shape of the knoll or little hill where the
Crucifixion was carried out. But there is no tradition whatever in favour of this, nor is there any evidence in the Gospel
narratives to support the popular idea that Calvary was on a
hill or rising ground. Yet another explanation of the name
"Golgotha" is that it means "the place of skulls," i.e. a
public place of execution, where the bodies of the victims were

¹ Cf. Routh, Rel. Sacr. i. 122.   ² Respons. ad Iudaeos, x.

Ἑβραϊστὶ Γολγοθά, 18. ὅπου αὐτὸν ἐσταύρωσαν, καὶ μετ' αὐτοῦ ἄλλους δύο ἐντεῦθεν καὶ ἐντεῦθεν, μέσον δὲ τὸν Ἰησοῦν. 19. ἔγραψεν

left. This would require κρανίων not κρανίου, not to speak of the facts that bodies were never left unburied in this way near a town, and that Joseph of Arimathea's "new tomb" (19⁴¹) would certainly not have been built near a place so abhorrent to a Jew. The tradition reproduced by Origen *may* be pre-Christian; and if so it gives an explanation of the name *Golgotha*, but no other explanation is, in any case, forthcoming. See on v. 20.

18. ὅπου αὐτὸν ἐσταύρωσαν, "where they crucified Him," *i.e.* the soldiers [1] (see v. 23), who were told off for the purpose.

μετ' αὐτοῦ ἄλλους δύο. Mt. and Mk. call them λῃσταί (such as Barabbas was, 18⁴⁰); Lk. says κακοῦργοι; Jn. does not apply any epithet to them. All the evangelists note that the Cross of Jesus was placed between the other two. Mediæval fancy gave names to the robbers, Dismas or Titus or πιστός to the penitent (who is generally represented as on the right side of the Cross of Jesus), Gestas or Dumachus or θεομάχος being the impenitent one.

ἐντεῦθεν καὶ ἐντεῦθεν. Cf. Dan. 12⁵ (Theodotion); the LXX has the more usual ἔνθεν καὶ ἔνθεν : cf. 1 Macc. 6³⁸ 9⁴⁵.

19. τίτλον. The title or *titulus*, the technical name for the board bearing the name of the condemned or his crime or both, is only so called by Jn. In Mk. it is called ἡ ἐπιγραφή. Also it is only Jn. who tells that Pilate wrote it. As it appears in Jn. it included both the Name (Ἰησοῦς ὁ Ναζωραῖος ; see 18⁵) and an indication of the crime, conveyed in words of mockery (ὁ βασιλεὺς τῶν Ἰουδαίων). In Mk. and Lk. only the αἰτία is given, the name being absent, while Mt. has οὗτός ἐστιν Ἰησοῦς ὁ βασιλεὺς τῶν Ἰουδαίων.[2] It is not possible to determine which form is verbally correct, but probably it was considered sufficient to give the αἰτία only. In Suetonius (*Domit.* 10) the terms of a similar *titulus* are preserved: "impie locutus parmularius," *i.e.* "a parmularian (the name by which the adherents of a gladiatorial party were known) who has spoken impiously."

---

[1] Le Blant argued that soldiers would not have been put to work of this kind, and that executions were entrusted not to the legionaries, but to civil police or apparitors attached to the court of the procurator. But his arguments are taken from the conditions of a later age. See the art. "Bourreau" in Cabrol's *Dict. d'archéologie chrétienne* for a full discussion. Cf. Acts 22²⁴⁻²⁵ : the scourging of Paul was about to be entrusted to *soldiers* under the command of a centurion.

[2] The Gospel of Peter gives it in the form οὗτός ἐστιν ὁ βασιλεὺς τοῦ Ισραήλ.

δὲ καὶ τίτλον ὁ Πειλᾶτος καὶ ἔθηκεν ἐπὶ τοῦ σταυροῦ· ἦν δὲ γεγραμ-
μένον ΙΗΣΟΥΣ Ο ΝΑΖΩΡΑΙΟΣ Ο ΒΑΣΙΛΕΥΣ ΤΩΝ ΙΟΥ-
ΔΑΙΩΝ. 20. τοῦτον οὖν τὸν τίτλον πολλοὶ ἀνέγνωσαν τῶν
Ἰουδαίων, ὅτι ἐγγὺς ἦν ὁ τόπος τῆς πόλεως ὅπου ἐσταυρώθη ὁ
Ἰησοῦς· καὶ ἦν γεγραμμένον Ἑβραϊστί, Ῥωμαϊστί, Ἑλληνιστί.
21. ἔλεγον οὖν τῷ Πειλάτῳ οἱ ἀρχιερεῖς τῶν Ἰουδαίων Μὴ γράφε
Ὁ βασιλεὺς τῶν Ἰουδαίων, ἀλλ' ὅτι ἐκεῖνος εἶπεν βασιλεύς εἰμι τῶν
Ἰουδαίων. 22. ἀπεκρίθη ὁ Πειλᾶτος Ὃ γέγραφα γέγραφα.

ἔθηκεν ἐπὶ τοῦ σταυροῦ: in Mt. 27³⁷ we have ἐπέθηκαι
ἐπάνω τῆς κεφαλῆς αὐτοῦ, which suggests that the cross was of
the shape called *crux immissa*, with a cross-bar for the arms,
as painters have generally represented it to be.

20. τοῦτον οὖν τὸν τίτλον κτλ. " This title, then (οὖν being
a favourite conjunction with Jn. ; see on 1²²), many of the
Jews read," as they would have opportunity of doing, the
place being near the city, and as they would be able to do,
because it was written in Aramaic as well as in Latin (the
official language) and Greek (a detail peculiar to Jn.). That
" many of the Jews " read the title placed in mockery above
the cross, " the King of the Jews," is not explicitly stated by
any other evangelist, and Jn. makes no comment on it. But
the irony of the statement is plain enough, and it is probably
intentional. See on 1⁴⁵.

ἐγγὺς ἦν κτλ. We may translate this either by " the place
where Jesus was crucified was near to the city," or " the place
of the city where Jesus was crucified was near " ; but the former
rendering is to be preferred. He suffered, not within the city
walls, but " without the gate " (Heb. 13¹²); cf. Mt. 27³²,
Num. 15³⁵, Acts 7⁵⁸. The traditional site of Golgotha may
not be the true one, but it has better claims to recognition than
any other.[1] Although within the present walls of Jerusalem,
it may have been outside the walls as they existed in the first
century.

21. οἱ ἀρχιερεῖς τῶν Ἰουδαίων. That the " chief priests "
were " of the Jews " seems superfluous to mention, but Jn.
writes for Greek readers. See on 2⁶, and cf. 6⁴.

They were uneasy about the title, lest any should fail to
understand that it was written in mockery, and so they appealed
to Pilate to change it. None of this is told by the Synoptists.

ἐκεῖνος, *ipse*, is used for clearness. See on 1⁸.

22. ὃ γέγραφα γέγραφα. Pilate was a true Roman in his
respect for an official document   He was himself responsible
for the phrasing of the *titulus*; and, once written and affixed

[1] Cf. Sir C. W. Wilson, *Golgotha and the Holy Sepulchre* (1907), the
fullest and best discussion of the site of Calvary.

23. Οἱ οὖν στρατιῶται, ὅτε ἐσταύρωσαν τὸν Ἰησοῦν, ἔλαβον τὰ ἱμάτια αὐτοῦ καὶ ἐποίησαν τέσσερα μέρη, ἑκάστῳ στρατιώτῃ μέρος, καὶ τὸν χιτῶνα. ἦν δὲ ὁ χιτὼν ἄρραφος, ἐκ τῶν ἄνωθεν ὑφαντὸς δι'

to the cross, it was the expression of a legal decision. From the legal point of view he was right in refusing to alter its terms. *Litera scripta manet.*

To the form of expression, " What I have written, I have written," Lightfoot (*Hor. Hebr.* iii. 432) gives some Rabbinic parallels (cf. also Gen. 43¹⁴, Esth. 4¹⁶); but they are hardly apposite, as Pilate was not a Jew. Cf., however, ὅσα ἐστήσαμεν πρὸς ὑμᾶς ἔστηκεν (1 Macc. 13³⁸). The perf. tense γέγραφα marks the permanence and abiding character of his act. Jn. uses the perfect as distinct from the aorist, with strict linguistic propriety.

The distribution among the soldiers of Jesus' garments
(vv. 23, 24)

23. ἔλαβον τὰ ἱμάτια αὐτοῦ. Nothing is said of the clothes of the crucified robbers. It was customary to remove the clothes before a condemned person was nailed to the cross, and by Roman law they were the perquisites of the soldiers who acted as executioners.[1] But, presumably, the clothes of the malefactors were not worth anything, and so are not mentioned.

Of the soldiers there was the usual quaternion (τετράδιον, Acts 12⁴); and according to the Synoptists (Mk. 15³⁹, Mt. 27⁵⁴, Lk. 23⁴⁷) a centurion was also present. The Synoptists do not give any detailed account of the doings of the soldiers; they merely say, paraphrasing the words of Ps 22¹⁸ (which was no doubt in their minds), that the soldiers divided the clothes, casting lots. But throughout the Johannine account of the Crucifixion (vv. 23-37), the fuller testimony of an eye-witness (see v. 35) reveals itself. This account is due to one who was near the Cross all the time. And so Jn. tells that it was for the χίτων or long cassock-shaped coat (as distinguished from the ἱμάτιον or outer cloak : cf. v. 2 and Mt. 5⁴⁰, Lk. 6²⁹), which was woven in one piece, that lots were cast; and he adds that this was ἵνα ἡ γραφὴ πληρωθῇ, quoting Ps. 22¹⁸ from the LXX :

διεμερίσαντο τὰ ἱμάτιά μου ἑαυτοῖς
καὶ ἐπὶ τὸν ἱματισμόν μου ἔβαλον κλῆρον.[2]

In this verse ἱμάτια and ἱματισμός represent distinct Hebrew

---

[1] See art. " Bourreau " cited above.
[2] Barnabas (§ 6) quotes from this verse, ἐπὶ τὸν ἱμ. μου ἔβ. κλῆρον, of the Crucifixion in like manner.

ὅλου. 24. εἶπαν οὖν πρὸς ἀλλήλους Μὴ σχίσωμεν αὐτόν, ἀλλὰ λάχωμεν περὶ αὐτοῦ τίνος ἔσται· ἵνα ἡ γραφὴ πληρωθῇ Διεμερίσαντο words, בְּנַד and לִבְוּשׁ, but it is not always possible to distinguish the meanings of these. In the original context, we have the ordinary parallelism of Hebrew poetry; but Jn. finds in the words an inspired forecast of that which was witnessed at the Crucifixion, viz. the division of some garments, and the drawing of lots for one in particular. "These things, *therefore*, the soldiers did." Jn. sees in all the incidents of the Passion the fulfilment of the Divine purpose disclosed in the O.T., and so he says that these things happened ἵνα ἡ γραφὴ πληρωθῇ.[1]

The χίτων was ἄρραφος (this word does not occur elsewhere in the Greek Bible), "without seam," as was the robe of the high priest's ephod (a long garment, ὑποδύτης ποδήρης, Ex. 28[32]). Josephus (*Ant.* III. vii. 4) calls this robe of the high priest a χίτων, and (following the directions given in Exodus) he explains elaborately that it was woven in one piece.[2] But this is only a verbal coincidence; the idea of a high-priestly robe does not enter here.[3] χίτων is the ordinary word for the long coat worn in the East under the cloak. It was of some value, and Jn. records that the soldiers said (the witness was near enough to hear the words) Μὴ σχίσωμεν αὐτόν, ἀλλὰ λάχωμεν περὶ αὐτοῦ τίνος ἔσται.

Field (*in loc.*) urges that λαγχάνειν is unprecedented in the sense of "to cast lots," its usual meaning being "to obtain by lot." But Symmachus translated יַפִּילוּ גּוֹרָל in Ps. 22[18] by ἐλάγχανον.

The account of this incident in the second-century *Gospel of Peter* is as follows: τεθεικότες τὰ ἐνδύματα ἔμπροσθεν αὐτοῦ διεμερίσαντο, καὶ λαχμὸν ἔβαλον ἐπ’ αὐτοῖς, "having set His garments before Him, they parted them among them and cast a lot for them." It is not stated by Pseudo-Peter that this was the act of the *soldiers*, who appear a little later as a body of eight men, with a centurion, guarding the tomb, while Jn. is explicit that there were only four : τέσσερα μέρη, ἑκάστῳ στρατιώτῃ μέρος. The unusual word λαχμός, for κλῆρος, in Pseudo-Peter may have been suggested by Jn.'s λάχωμεν. It is reproduced by Justin (*Tryph.* 97), who quotes Ps. 22[15-18] from

[1] Cf. Introd., pp. 153 ff.

[2] Philo (*de Prof.* 20) says that the high priest in Leviticus represents the Divine Word, and that he is forbidden to "rend his clothes" (Lev. 21[10]), because the Word is the bond of all things. But this has no bearing on the text here.

[3] Ingenious computers have discovered that by applying *Gematria*, χίτων = 87 = Ἰησοῦς. Cyprian (*de unit.* 7) found in the seamless robe a symbol of the Unity of the Church.

τὰ ἱμάτιά μου ἑαυτοῖς καὶ ἐπὶ τὸν ἱματισμόν μου ἔβαλον κλῆρον. Οἱ μὲν οὖν στρατιῶται ταῦτα ἐποίησαν.

25. Εἱστήκεισαν δὲ παρὰ τῷ σταυρῷ τοῦ Ἰησοῦ ἡ μήτηρ αὐτοῦ, καὶ ἡ ἀδελφὴ τῆς μητρὸς αὐτοῦ, Μαρία ἡ τοῦ Κλωπᾶ, καὶ Μαριάμ

the LXX, and adds: ὅτε γὰρ ἐσταύρωσαν αὐτόν, ἐμπήσσοντες τοὺς ἥλους τὰς χεῖρας καὶ τοὺς πόδας αὐτοῦ ὤρυξαν, καὶ οἱ σταυρώσαντες αὐτὸν ἐμέρισαν τὰ ἱμάτια αὐτοῦ ἑαυτοῖς, λαχμὸν βάλλοντες ἕκαστος κατὰ τὴν τοῦ κλήρου ἐπιβολὴν ὃ ἐκλέξεσθαι ἐβεβούλητο.

οἱ μὲν οὖν στρατ. κτλ. μέν, recalling what the soldiers did, corresponds to δέ in v. 25 introducing the fact that the women were present. μὲν οὖν occurs again in Jn. only at 20[30], where also it is followed by a corresponding δέ.

Three sayings of Jesus from the Cross, before His death
(vv. 25-30)

25. εἱστήκεισαν δὲ παρὰ τῷ σταυρῷ κτλ. From the Synoptic parallels (Mk. 15[40], Mt. 27[56]; cf. Lk. 24[10]) we gather that Mary Magdalene, Mary the mother of James and Joseph, and Salome the wife of Zebedee and mother of the apostles James and John, were present at the Cross. Jn. enumerates Mary the mother of Jesus (whose presence the Synoptists do not mention), her sister, Mary the wife of Clopas, and Mary Magdalene, *i.e. four* persons and not *three* as one reading of the text might suggest. Not only does the Peshitta make this clear by putting " and " before " Mary the wife of Clopas "; but the balance of the sentence, if four persons are indicated, is thoroughly Johannine. If we compare this with the Synoptic parallels we reach two important conclusions: (1) Salome was the sister of Mary the mother of Jesus, and therefore John the son of Zebedee and Salome was a maternal cousin of Jesus. (2) Mary the wife of Clopas is the same person as Mary the mother of James and Joseph (cf. Mt. 27[56], Mk. 15[40. 47] 16[1], Lk. 24[10]). It would be impossible to equate the Synoptic " Mary, the mother of James and Joseph " with the Lord's mother, for no one can suppose that the Synoptists, when telling the names of the women at the Cross, would have described the mother of Jesus in so circuitous a manner. This James is called by Mk. ὁ Ἰάκωβος ὁ μικρός or " James the Little," the adjective not relating to his dignity, but to his stature. Of him we know nothing more.

Attempts have been made to identify Clopas with Alphæus, who was father of one of the Twelve (James the son of Alphæus, Mk. 3[18], Mt. 10[3], Lk. 6[15], Acts 1[13]); but philological considerations will not permit us to reduce *Clopas* and

ἡ Μαγδαληνή.　26. Ἰησοῦς οὖν ἰδὼν τὴν μητέρα καὶ τὸν μαθητὴν παρεστῶτα ὃν ἠγάπα, λέγει τῇ μητρί Γύναι, ἴδε ὁ υἱός σου.　27. εἶτα

Alphæus to the same Hebrew original.[1]　The N.T. tells us no more of Clopas (Cleopas of Lk. 24[18] is a different name); but Hegesippus [2] (*fl. circa* 150 A.D.), states that he was the brother of Joseph, the Lord's foster-father, and so " the Lord's uncle." Hegesippus also says that he had a son, Symeon or Simon, who became second bishop of Jerusalem, " being a cousin of the Lord," succeeding James the Just, " the Lord's brother," who was the first bishop. See, further, Additional Note on 2[12].

The MSS. vary as to the spelling of Mary Magdalene's name (Μαριάμ or Μαρία), but Mary of Clopas seems to be always Μαρία. As we have seen (on 11[2. 20]), B 33 always describe Mary of Bethany as Μαριάμ, while א always has Μαρία. But when Mary Magdalene (whom we take to be the same person) is mentioned the usage is different. In 19[25] 20[1. 11] B gives Μαρία, and א 33 give Μαριάμ. At 20[16. 18] אB 33 agree in reading Μαριάμ. Probably the Hebrew form Μαριάμ should be adopted throughout (this is the spelling in Pseudo-Peter).[3]

26. Ἰησοῦς κτλ. For the omission the article before Ἰησοῦς when followed by οὖν, see on 6[15].

τῇ μητρί. So אBL. AD[supp]NLΓΔΘ, some O.L. texts, and the Coptic Q add αὐτοῦ, as in the rec. text.

The true reading both here and in v. 27, seems to be ἴδε (a favourite word with Jn.; see on 1[29]), and not ἰδού which occurs only 16[32] 19[5]. In v 26 אAΘ give ἰδού, but BD[supp]N have ἴδε. In v. 27 ἰδού is read by AD[supp], ἴδε being read by אBLNΘ.

The Coptic Q and the O.L. *e* omit the introductory γύναι, perhaps feeling it to be harsh.

The reasons for identifying " the disciple whom Jesus loved " with John the son of Zebedee and Salome, the maternal cousin of Jesus, have been given in the Introduction, p. xxxvi f. We now find John at the Cross, with the women, including the Virgin Mother and his own mother Salome.

It was natural that the Virgin should be commended to his care, rather than to the care of " the brethren," James and Simon and Joseph and Jude, with whom she had been so intimately associated in the past, and whose home she had probably shared (see on 2[12]), because they were not yet disciples; they had not accepted the claims of Jesus or believed in His mission. As we have seen, John was nephew to Mary,

---

[1] See *E.B., s.v.* " Clopas," and Deissmann, *Bible Studies*, p. 315 *n.*
[2] As reported by Eusebius (*H.E.* iii. 11, iv. 22).
[3] For the spelling, see Westcott-Hort, *Appendix*, 156.

and in sympathy he was nearer to her than these stepsons. And so Jesus bade His mother look to John, His beloved friend and cousin, to be her " son." He is going from her, but John will take His place in such measure as is possible

The words " Woman, behold thy son . . . behold thy mother " are more than a mere commendation [1] or suggestion from a dying friend. They convey a command from Him who was, to Mary, as well as to John, Master and Lord. He did not address her as " Mother," even while He shows tender solicitude for her future. " Mother," as a title of address by Jesus, was abandoned long since, and for it " Woman," a usual title of respect, has been substituted. See on 2^4.

When Jesus said to John " Behold thy mother," John's own mother, Salome, was present and may have overheard the words. But the Virgin was her sister, broken-hearted and desolate, with whom she was in complete sympathy, for she too had accepted Jesus as Master. She was not necessarily set aside or superseded by the charge to her son to regard her sister Mary as a second mother, and treat her with filial care.

The place which this farewell charge occupies among the Words from the Cross is noteworthy, as will be seen if they are read in their probable sequence.

ADDITIONAL NOTE ON THE WORDS FROM THE CROSS

The evangelical narratives of the Passion reflect at least three distinct lines of tradition. The Marcan tradition (which according to Papias goes back to Peter, whose disciple Mark was) is followed with amplifications of a later date by Matthew. It is also followed by Luke, who seems, however, to have had some additional source of information. His account of the trial before Herod (23^{8-12}), e.g., has no parallel in the other Gospels; and it has been often observed that Luke alone mentions Joanna, the wife of Chuza, Herod's steward, as one of the women who accompanied Jesus in His public ministry (Lk. 8^3) and were present at the Crucifixion (Lk. 23^{49}) and heralds of the Resurrection (Lk. 23^{55} 24^{10}). To this Joanna, Luke's special information as to the Passion may possibly be due. The third distinct tradition of the Passion is that of Jn., which goes back for details to the personal witness of the Beloved Disciple (19^{35}).

The Marcan tradition reports one Word from the Cross, the Lucan tradition three, and the Johannine tradition yet

---

[1] Wetstein cites a parallel from Lucian (*Toxaris*, 22). The bequest of Eudamidas was, " I leave to Aretæus my mother, to cherish and support in her old age."

another three.   There is nothing surprising in this variation.
Independent witnesses may honestly and truthfully give
different, although not inconsistent, reports of the same events.
They report only what they have personally observed, and only
such part of that as has specially impressed them or is suitable
for the purposes of their narrative, if they are writing one.   It
may not be possible to harmonise precisely the various accounts
of the Passion, or to place the Words from the Cross in exact
chronological sequence.   But there is no critical objection
to the order which has generally commended itself to students
of the Gospels, as being suggested by the sacred text.   It may
be set out as follows :

1. Πάτερ, ἄφες αὐτοῖς· οὐ γὰρ οἴδασιν τί ποιοῦσιν (Lk. 23³⁴).
This comes in the Lucan narrative, according to the received
text, immediately after the statement that Jesus had been
crucified between the two thieves.   But that it is part of the
original text of Lk. is uncertain; it is omitted by אᵃBD* and
other authorities, and Westcott-Hort " cannot doubt that it
comes from an extraneous source." [1]   Wherever it comes from,
whether the knowledge of it came to Lk. from some eye-witness,
such as Joanna, or whether it found its way into the text of Lk.,
after his narrative was completed, it has an unmistakable note
of genuineness.

2. Ἀμὴν λέγω σοι, σήμερον μετ᾿ ἐμοῦ ἔσῃ ἐν τῷ παραδείσῳ
(Lk. 23⁴³).   This was addressed to the penitent thief, and, like
the First Word, must have been said at the beginning of the
awful scene.   " It was now about the sixth hour," is Lk.'s
comment (Lk. 23⁴⁴); i.e. it was about noon.   See on Jn. 19¹⁴.
The report of this saying must have come from some one who
stood near the Cross, and so was able to hear what was said.

3. Γύναι, ἴδε ὁ υἱός σου . . . Ἴδε ἡ μήτηρ σου (Jn. 19²⁶, ²⁷).
There is no difficulty in understanding why this saying should
have been specially treasured in memory by the Beloved
Disciple, and thus recorded at last in the Fourth Gospel.   It
was specially addressed to him, and to her whom he was to
cherish henceforth as a mother; there is no reason to suppose
that other bystanders were unable to hear the words.

If we examine the sequence of these first three Words from
the Cross, in the order seemingly suggested in the Gospel
texts, we cannot fail to notice the narrowing of the circle of
interest, as death draws near.   That always happens.   When
death is at a distance, men are still concerned with the wider
interests of life; then it draws closer, and it is only the nearer
and more intimate interests that appeal; and the time comes
when the energies of thought are taxed to the full by the

[1] *Notes on Select Readings*, p. 68.

messages of farewell to those who have been best beloved. So it was with the Son of Man. In the hour of death, the first movement of the heart of Jesus is towards those who had brought Him to the Cross. "Father, forgive them." His mission of Redemption is still in His thoughts. Then, as strength ebbs away, the cry of the penitent thief by His side reaches Him, and the response to the individual pleading does not fail. "This day shalt thou be with me." But the circle is narrowing fast. His dying eyes are fixed upon those who have been dearest. The forgiveness of enemies; the consolation of the fellow-sufferer; these give place to the thought of mother and of friend. "Behold thy son . . . behold thy mother." These are the stages of the approach of death, for the Perfect Man.

4. *Eli, Eli, lama sabachthani?* θεέ μου, θεέ μου, ἱνατί με ἐγκατέλιπες; (Mt. 27⁴⁶, Mk. 15³⁴). This is the only Word from the Cross which rests upon the Marcan tradition, and may be taken as due to Peter. It was uttered "with a loud voice," and so could be heard even by those standing at a distance, as Peter probably was. (Cf. Mt. 27⁵⁵, ἦσαν δὲ ἐκεῖ γυναῖκες πολλαὶ ἀπὸ μακρόθεν θεωροῦσαι.) There is no hint in any Gospel that he was one of the little circle who stood near the cross. This cry was misunderstood by the crowd, who thought that Jesus was calling for succour upon Elijah the prophet, an observation (Mk. 15³⁵) which shows that we have here to do with words actually used, and not with words afterwards placed in the mouth of Jesus, being thought appropriate as the opening phrase of a Messianic Psalm (Ps. 22¹). Indeed, the difficulty that interpreters have always felt in explaining these words of seeming despair as spoken by One who was Himself Divine, proves that they are not likely to have been the invention of pious fancy dwelling afterwards on the Agony of Calvary. They were reproduced later in a Docetic form in the apocryphal *Gospel of Peter* : Ἡ δύναμίς μου, ἡ δύναμις, κατέλειψάς με. Why they are not recorded by Lk. or Jn. it is idle to conjecture.

5. Διψῶ (Jn. 19²⁸). This was spoken near the end. Although the actual word διψῶ is recorded only by Jn., yet the incident of the Lord's thirst being assuaged is given in Mk. 15³⁶ (Mt. 27⁴⁸). "I thirst" would naturally have been said in a low voice, so that it could be heard only by those near the Cross.

That Jn. should have specially recorded this word is in keeping with the emphasis laid, throughout the Fourth Gospel, on the *humanity* of Jesus. As He asked the Samaritan woman for water when He was thirsty (4⁷), so now. Jn. is anxious to

expel Docetic doctrine (1 Jn. 4²), and both here and at 19³⁴
he brings out recollections of the Beloved Disciple which
forbid any theory of Christ's Person that does not recognise
His manhood. Jesus was *thirsty* at the Cross.

6. Τετέλεσται (Jn. 19³⁰). That after He had assuaged
His thirst, Jesus uttered a loud cry, just before the end, is
recorded Mk. 15³⁷, Mt. 27⁵⁰; cf. also Lk. 23⁴⁶. But the spec-
tator upon whose testimony Jn. is dependent not only heard
the cry, but identified the word spoken. This, for Jn., who
sees all through the Passion the predestined march of events to
the fulfilment of God's purposes,¹ is the Great Word. Everything had happened as it did happen, in order that the Divine
purpose, as foreshadowed in the O.T., might be accomplished
(τελειωθῇ 19²⁸). And τετέλεσται marks this Consummation.

7. Πάτερ, εἰς χεῖράς σου παρατίθεμαι τὸ πνεῦμά μου (Lk. 23⁴⁶).
Lk. specially notes that this was after the Great Cry (φωνήσας
φωνῇ μεγάλῃ), and that this was the last word spoken.
To the utterance of faithful confidence from the ancient
Psalm (31⁵), the one word " Father " was prefixed, which
charged it for future generations with a deeper meaning.   In
the Psalm, it is the trustful prayer of life; on the lips of Jesus
(and thereafter; cf. Acts 7⁵⁹), it became a prayer of the dying.
It is noteworthy that the two personal cries of Jesus from the
Cross (Nos. 4 and 7) are old and familiar verses from the Psalter.

Jn. does not record this, but we cannot know his reason.
If it was indeed the last word spoken, the Beloved Disciple
must have heard it, as well as the witness, Joanna or another,
from whom it was transmitted to Lk.   It is just possible that
the words of Jn. 19³⁰, παρέδωκεν τὸ πνεῦμα, contain a reminiscence of Lk.'s παρατίθεμαι τὸ πνεῦμά μου.   But in any case
Jn. never attempts to tell *all* that had happened, or all that
he knew; his method is to select and arrange the sayings and
acts of Jesus which best bring out the main thesis of his Gospel
(20³¹).   And τετέλεσται is, in his scheme, the final word of
the Cross.

Of other arrangements of the Seven Words, that of Tatian,
our earliest harmonist, is the most noteworthy.   It differs in
one particular only from that which has been set out here.
Tatian in his *Diatessaron* puts " Father, forgive them . . . "
immediately before " Father, into thy hands . . . "; thus
contradicting the order in which Lk. (who alone records
them both) places the two sayings, " Father, forgive them "
and " This day shalt thou be with me in Paradise."   Bishop
Andrewes in his *Litania* places our No. 3 before our No. 2, an
arrangement adopted also in some German hymns.   Certainty

¹ Cf. Introd., pp. cliii ff.

λέγει τῷ μαθητῇ Ἴδε ἡ μήτηρ σου. καὶ ἀπ' ἐκείνης τῆς ὥρας ἔλαβεν ὁ μαθητὴς αὐτὴν εἰς τὰ ἴδια. 28. Μετὰ τοῦτο εἰδὼς ὁ Ἰησοῦς

cannot be reached, but a clearer insight into the significance of these Words is gained by any honest attempt to reach the order in which they were spoken.

27. ἀπ' ἐκείνης τῆς ὥρας, "from that hour." It has been thought that this implies that Mary did not wait for the end, but that John led her away at once. It may have been so, but in that case John returned soon, for he is present at the Cross later (vv. 28–35). Cf. 11⁵³.

That Jn. does not mention the cry *Eli, Eli, lama sabach-thani?* which is reported by Mk. (15³⁴) followed by Mt. (27⁴⁶) as having been uttered "with a loud voice," may perhaps be explained as due to the absence of the eye-witness at this point. The aged disciple recalls only his own personal experiences. Another possible explanation is that Jn. has omitted this saying, because he wishes to emphasise the voluntary character of Christ's death. See on v. 30.

εἰς τὰ ἴδια, "to his own home." The phrase is used thus Esth. 5¹⁰, 3 Macc. 6²⁷· ³⁷ 7⁸, Acts 21⁶, and it is the most natural meaning. It occurs twice elsewhere in Jn. (1¹¹ 16³²), where the sense is probably the same, but is not quite so clear as it is here (see note on 1¹¹). John brought the Virgin Mother to his own lodging [1] (see on 20¹⁰), and she lived with him thereafter; but we cannot build on the phrase εἰς τὰ ἴδια a theory which would give him a house of residence at Jerusalem (see on 18¹⁵).

28. μετὰ τοῦτο. The phrase does not convey that the incident of vv. 28–30 *immediately* followed on that of vv. 25–27. In fact, there was interposed the long interval of darkness and of silence, of which all the Synoptists speak as lasting for some three hours (Mk. 15³³, Mt. 27⁴⁵, Lk. 23⁴⁴). But it means, as it does elsewhere in Jn.[2] that the second incident was later than the first; whereas the phrase μετὰ ταῦτα does not carry the sense of strict chronological sequence so explicitly.

εἰδὼς ὁ Ἰησοῦς κτλ. The same phrase occurs in 13¹, where in like manner it leads up to the statement that the appointed hour had come. He knew that "all things had now been finished," ἤδη πάντα τετέλεσται. Jn. never allows

---

[1] Latham, *The Risen Master*, p. 216, suggests that John brought her to Bethany, and thinks that she could not have been in Jerusalem on the day of the Resurrection, or she would have been sent for when the tomb was found empty.

[2] Cf. Introd., p. cviii.

ὅτι ἤδη πάντα τετέλεσται, ἵνα τελειωθῇ ἡ γραφή, λέγει Διψῶ.

his readers to forget that events which he records were eternally fore-ordained, and that Jesus was conscious of this. Primarily ἤδη πάντα τετέλεσται may have reference to the details of the Passion, and the Lord's word τετέλεσται may be taken to mean that the Passion with its anguish and its sordid accompaniments was now over. And so " that the Scripture might be accomplished, Jesus said, I thirst."

28, 29, 30. ἵνα τελειωθῇ ἡ γραφή. So ABLNWΓ. ﬡDsuppΘ and *fam.* 13 have the more usual πληρωθῇ. Some have found a more complete consummation expressed by τελειωθῇ than πληρωθῇ would convey, but this is over subtle. If a reason is sought for the choice of the word τελειωθῇ, it may be found in the preceding τετέλεσται; τελεῖν suggesting τελειοῦν.

ἵνα τελ. ἡ γρ. probably refers to what follows, not to what precedes.[1] Jn. held that every incident of the Crucifixion took place as foreshadowed in the O.T. Scriptures, and that the Divine purpose as expressed therein might be accomplished. For him, the thirst of Jesus and its relief were foretold and fore-ordained in Ps. 69²¹: εἰς τὴν δίψαν μου ἐπότισάν με ὄξος. That this is the passage in Jn.'s mind appears from the mention of ὄξος after the word διψῶ. The phrasing of the parallel narrative (Mk. 15³⁶), σπόγγον ὄξους περιθεὶς καλάμῳ ἐπότιζεν αὐτόν, shows that Mk. (followed by Mt. 27⁴⁸) had the same passage from the Psalter in his thought. The ὄξος, or *posca*, was the sour wine which was the usual drink of the legionaries, some of which, according to Lk. (23³⁶), had already been offered by the soldiers to Jesus in mockery, as if it were a coronation cup.

It is not doubtful, however, that Jn. intends τετέλεσται to have a deeper significance than that the various incidents of the Passion were now finished. τετέλεσται is not a cry of relief that all is over; it is a shout of Victory. The mission of Redemption has now been perfected. See on 4³⁴. According to the Synoptists (see Additional Note on v. 26) τετέλεσται was cried " with a loud voice." This may have some bearing on the request suggested in the preceding word διψῶ. Jesus may have desired that those who were present, the idle spectators and the soldiers as well as the faithful disciples, should understand that He counted His Death as a Victory. He may have wished to announce this publicly, so that all could hear. But if He was to speak now, after the long torture of

[1] Abbott (*Diat.* 2115) connects πάντα τετέλεσται with ἵνα τελειωθῇ ἡ γραφή.

the Cross, "with a loud voice," His parched throat must be cooled. It was necessary that He should ask for drink. And so, ὅτε οὖν ἔλαβεν τὸ ὄξος, "when He had therefore taken the wine," He cried Τετέλεσται, that all might know that great fact of which He was Himself assured, ἤδη πάντα τετέλεσται. It was this majestic word which seems specially to have impressed the centurion who was there. "When the centurion, which stood by over against Him, saw that He so gave up the ghost, he said, Truly this man was a Son of God" (Mk. 15³⁹), "Certainly this was a righteous man" (Lk. 23⁴⁷). At any rate, Jn. regards it as the Final Word, and will add nothing to it.

But whether this connexion between the two words διψῶ and τετέλεσται be suggested by Jn. or no (and it may be thought over subtle), διψῶ must be taken in its plain meaning of *physical* thirst. This Jesus felt, and a merciful bystander relieved Him.

We are not to confuse this incident with the refusal by Jesus, before He was crucified, of the drugged wine which it was customary to offer criminals who were condemned to the Cross (Mk. 15²³, Mt. 27³⁴). The Talmudists say of this kindly custom "they gave them to drink a little frankincense in a cup of wine . . . that their understanding might be disordered." [1] This Jesus refused because He willed to endure the Cross with full and unimpaired consciousness. But now all is finished. The work of redemption has been completed. It is no part of Christ's revelation that the enduring of *purposeless* pain is meritorious. The pains of thirst were terrible to one exposed to the scorching heat of midday, while hanging naked on the Cross. And so Jesus said, "I thirst," in His death-agony.

It would seem that some provision had been made for relieving the thirst of the dying men.

σκεῦος ἔκειτο ὄξους μεστόν, "a vessel full of vinegar was set there"; it was quite ready. Some have imagined that this also was a drugged potion, such as that of Mt. 27³⁴ (οἶνον μετὰ χολῆς), given with the view of hastening the death of the sufferers. But there is no ground for this in the evangelical narratives. Mt., who follows the words of Ps. 69²¹, takes the word χολή from thence, this being the only place where χολή is mentioned in the Gospels, viz. in connexion with the draught offered to Jesus *before* He was crucified. Neither Mt. (see 27⁴⁸) nor any other evangelist mentions χολή in connexion with the final draught accepted by Jesus at the end. Barnabas (§ 7) says, indeed, σταυρωθεὶς ἐποτίζετο ὄξει καὶ χολῇ, but he probably

---

[1] Lightfoot, *Hor. Hebr.* iii. 434, quotes this from *Sanhedr.* fol. 43. I.

29. σκεῦος ἔκειτο ὄξους μεστόν· σπόγγον οὖν μεστὸν τοῦ ὄξους ὑσσώπῳ περιθέντες προσήνεγκαν αὐτοῦ τῷ στόματι. 30. ὅτε οὖν

had Mt. 27³⁴ rather than Mt. 27⁴⁸ in his mind. In any case, he is a confused writer, as is also the author of the *Gospel of Peter* who writes thus (§ 5): καί τις αὐτῶν εἶπεν Ποτίσατε αὐτὸν χολὴν μετὰ ὄξους· καὶ κεράσαντες ἐπότισαν. καὶ ἐπλήρωσαν πάντα, καὶ ἐτελείωσαν κατὰ τῆς κεφαλῆς αὐτῶν τὰ ἁμαρτήματα. Nonnus (fifth cent.) suggests that Jesus *asked* for the draught in order that the end might come more quickly: νοήσας | ὅττι θοῶς τετέλεστο, θοώτερον ἤθελεν εἶναι. But there is no hint of such a motive in the canonical Gospels.

29. σκεῦος ἔκειτο ὄξους μεστόν. So ABLW 33, but the rec., with DˢᵘᵖᵖNΓΔΘ, adds οὖν after σκεῦος. For the next clause, σπόγγον οὖν μέστον τοῦ ὄξους (אᶜBLW 33), the rec., with ADˢᵘᵖᵖNΓΔΘ, substitutes οἱ δὲ πλήσαντες σπόγγον ὄξους, καὶ . . . Θ *fam.* 13 interpolate μετὰ χολῆς καὶ ὑσσώπου after ὄξους, and Θ proceeds καὶ περιθέντες καλάμῳ προσήνεγκαν κτλ., these variants in the rec. text being derived from Mk. 15³⁶, Mt. 27³⁴·⁴⁸. The change in Θ of ὑσσώπῳ to καλάμῳ is evidently due to the difficulty felt by the scribe in the words ὑσσώπῳ περιθέντες.

ὑσσώπῳ περιθέντες. This would mean that the sponge filled with vinegar or sour wine was placed " on hyssop " and so conveyed to the mouth of Jesus as He hung on the Cross. But hyssop is not a plant which commonly provides sticks or reeds (if at all); bunches of it were used for sprinkling purposes (Ex. 12²², Heb. 9¹⁹), but while a sponge could be attached to a bunch of hyssop, some rod or stick would yet be needed to raise it up to the Cross. The Synoptists say nothing about hyssop, but both in Mt. 27⁴⁹ and Mk. 15³⁶ (cf. Lk. 23³⁷) we read σπόγγον ὄξους περιθεὶς καλάμῳ, *i.e.* they say that a bystander put the sponge on a reed or cane or stick, as it was natural to do

Now in the eleventh century cursive No. 476 we find ὕσσῳ περιθέντες, the corruption of υσσωπεριθεντες into υσσωπωπερι-θεντες being due to the repetition by the scribe of two letters ωπ. ὕσσος is the Latin *pilum*, of which each Roman soldier carried two; and the meaning of ὕσσῳ περιθέντες is that the bystanders put the sponge on the end of a soldier's javelin or *pilum*, several of which were ready to hand (see on v. 34). This not only brings Jn. into correspondence with the περιθεὶς καλάμῳ of the Synoptists, but it reveals the personal observer. The man behind the story knew, for he had seen, to what kind of a stick the sponge was fastened ; it was a ὕσσος, a soldier's javelin.[1]

[1] See Field (*Notes on the Trans. of the N.T.*, p. 106), who accepted the emendation (which was a conjecture of Camerarius) while unaware of the actual reading of the cursive 476.

ἔλαβεν τὸ ὄξος ὁ Ἰησοῦς εἶπεν Τετέλεσται, καὶ κλίνας τὴν κεφαλὴν παρέδωκεν τὸ πνεῦμα.

30. κλίνας τὴν κεφαλήν, "having bowed His head." This detail is given only by Jn., and suggests that the account depends on the testimony of an eye-witness. κλίνειν τὴν κεφαλήν occurs again in N.T. only at Mt. 8²⁰, Lk. 9⁵⁸, "The Son of Man hath not where to lay His head." The only resting-place for Him was the Cross. Abbott¹ argues that Jn. *means* here to imply that Jesus in death rested His head on the bosom of the Father. But this is to apply the allegorical method of Origen, and is quite unnecessary here.

παρέδωκεν τὸ πνεῦμα, "He gave up His spirit." Mk. 15³⁷ and Lk. 23⁴⁶ have simply ἐξέπνευσεν, while Mt. 27⁵⁰ has ἀφῆκεν τὸ πνεῦμα. παραδιδόναι is "to give up voluntarily" (see note on 6⁶⁴), and it may be that the verb is chosen deliberately, to emphasise the unique manner of the Lord's death; cf. 10¹⁸, "I have power to lay it down, and I have power to take it up."

Or, the expression παρέδωκεν τὸ πνεῦμα may carry a reminiscence of the Lord's last words according to Lk. 23⁴⁶ παρατίθεμαι τὸ πνεῦμά μου. See Additional Note on p. 636.

Or, we may have here a covert allusion to Isa. 53¹² : "He poured out His soul unto death," which the LXX turns into the passive form παρεδόθη εἰς θάνατον ἡ ψυχὴ αὐτοῦ, but which would more literally be rendered παρέδωκεν εἰς θάνατον τὴν ψυχὴν αὐτοῦ. When it is remembered that the next clause of Isa. 53¹² is "and He was numbered among the transgressors" (which is quoted as predictive of the Passion in Lk. 22³⁷), it is not improbable that Jn. is here translating directly from the Hebrew of Isa. 53¹², and that his intention is to describe the death of Jesus in the same words as those used by the prophet of the death of the Servant of Yahweh.² Isa. 53 is for Jn. a Messianic prophecy. See on 12³⁸.

In any case, the verb παραδιδόναι expresses a voluntary act, and is thus in contrast with the ἐξέπνευσεν of Mk. and Lk.

For the use of πνεῦμα, see on 11³³. It is not legitimate to lay any special emphasis on the employment here of πνεῦμα, as distinct from ψυχή, even if the suggestion made above that Isaiah's "poured out His soul" suggested Jn.'s παρέδωκεν τὸ πνεῦμα be not adopted. Indeed in the second century *Acts of John* (§ 115) παρέδωκεν τὸ πνεῦμα is used of Jn.'s own death.

¹ *Diat.* 1456, 2644.
² Abbott (*Paradosis*, passim) has much to say about παραδιδόναι in Isa. 53¹², but his treatment is very speculative and is not followed here.

So of the death of Agathonice by martyrdom it is said οὕτως ἀπέδωκεν τὸ πνεῦμα καὶ ἐτελειώθη σὺν τοῖς ἁγίοις;[1] and the same phrase is used of the martyrdom of Peter.[2]

The piercing of the Lord's side, and the fulfilment of Scripture (vv. 31–37)

31. The statement that the "Jews," i.e. the Sanhedrists who had brought about the condemnation of Jesus, approached Pilate with the request that the death of those who had been crucified should be hastened, and their bodies removed, is peculiar to Jn. (see on v. 38). It has every mark of truth. Criminals crucified on a Friday might linger until the Sabbath, when they could not be buried, so that they would remain hanging on the Cross. But it was contrary to the Deuteronomic law that the dead bodies of criminals should remain on the cross after sunset (cf. Deut. 21[23], Josh. 8[29] 10[27]). Accordingly, Josephus (B.J. iv. v. 2) tells us that the Jews of his time were careful to bury before sundown the bodies of those who had been crucified. Thus it was urgent, from the Sanhedrist's point of view, that those crucified on a Friday should die on that day, and that their bodies should be removed forthwith. But this could be arranged only by an order from the Roman governor.

Now the usual Roman practice was to leave a corpse on its cross (cf. Horace, Epistles, i. xvi. 48), as in England the bodies of criminals used to be left hanging in chains. But there was no Roman law forbidding burial. Wetstein quotes Quintilian, Declam. vi., "omnes succiduntur, percussos sepeliri carnifex non uetat." And Philo mentions that he had known of bodies being taken down from the cross and handed over to the relatives of the condemned for burial, on the occasion of the emperor's birthday or the like (in Flacc. 10). Hence, although Pilate, in ordinary circumstances, might have refused the request of the Sanhedrists, there was nothing to prevent him from granting it if he wished. And, in this case, apart from his evident unwillingness to condemn Jesus, there was the further consideration that Jerusalem, at the moment, was crowded with pilgrims who had come for the Passover, and that it was desirable to avoid a conflict between the Jews and the Roman authorities.[3]

For Παρασκευή, see on v. 14 above. It was " Preparation "

[1] See von Gebhardt's Ausgewählte Märtyreracten (Berlin, 1902), p. 17.
[2] Acta Petri et Pauli, § 83.
[3] See C. H. Turner in Ch. Quarterly Review, July, 1912, p. 294.

31. Οἱ οὖν Ἰουδαῖοι, ἐπεὶ Παρασκευὴ ἦν, ἵνα μὴ μείνῃ ἐπὶ τοῦ σταυροῦ τὰ σώματα ἐν τῷ σαββάτῳ, ἦν γὰρ μεγάλη ἡ ἡμέρα ἐκείνου τοῦ σαββάτου, ἠρώτησαν τὸν Πειλᾶτον ἵνα κατεαγῶσιν αὐτῶν τὰ σκέλη καὶ ἀρθῶσιν. 32. ἦλθον οὖν οἱ στρατιῶται, καὶ τοῦ μὲν πρώτου κατέαξαν τὰ σκέλη καὶ τοῦ ἄλλου τοῦ συνσταυρωθέντος αὐτῷ· 33. ἐπὶ δὲ τὸν Ἰησοῦν ἐλθόντες, ὡς εἶδον ἤδη αὐτὸν τεθνηκότα, οὐ

or " Friday," doubly a day of preparation this year, because the Sabbath day following synchronised with " the first day of unleavened bread," which was a " great " day. It is called a " holy " day in the LXX of Ex. 12¹⁶, ἡ ἡμέρα ἡ πρώτη κληθήσεται ἁγία.

ἦν γὰρ μεγ. κτλ., " for the day of *that* sabbath was a great day," ἐκείνου being emphatic. AD^suppO transfer the words ἐπεὶ παρασκευὴ ἦν to a position after σαββάτῳ, but ℵBLW *fam.* 13 support their more natural place at the beginning of the sentence after Ἰουδαῖοι. The Peshitta gives the paraphrase: " Because it was Preparation, they say, these bodies shall not remain on the Cross, because the sabbath dawneth." ἐπεί is " because," exactly as in the parallel passage Mk. 15⁴² ἐπεὶ ἦν παρασκευή.

The *crurifragium*, or breaking of the limbs, was done by a heavy mallet; and terrible as such blows would be, if inflicted on a man in health and strength, they were merciful if they ended quickly the torture of a lingering death by crucifixion.

32. ἦλθον οὖν οἱ στρ. " Therefore," *sc.* in obedience to the orders they received, " the soldiers came," and broke the legs of the two robbers, who were not yet dead. The *Gospel of Peter* (which betrays knowledge of the Johannine narrative of the Passion) gives a curious turn to this incident. It represents the Jews as indignant with the penitent thief, because of his defence of Jesus' innocence (cf. Lk. 23⁴¹), and as commanding " that his bones should not be broken to the end that he might die in torment " (§ 4). This is inconsistent with what Pseudo-Peter says in § 3 about the illegality of allowing the bodies to remain on the crosses after sundown; but its interest is that it shows the freedom with which this apocryphal writer treats the Gospel narrative.

33. ὡς εἶδον ἤδη αὐτὸν τεθνηκότα. Jesus died before the robbers did. According to Mk. 15⁴⁴, Pilate was surprised that He had died so soon; for in the case of a crucified person, death sometimes did not ensue for two or three days. A highly strung nature is less able to endure physical agony than one of coarser fibre; and Jesus was the Perfect Man. See above on v. 10.

34. This verse was introduced into St. Matthew's Gospel at an early period. אBCLΓ, with some cursives, the Ethiopic vs., and several " mixed " Latin texts of the British and Irish type, supply at the end of Mt. 27⁴⁹ the words ἄλλος δὲ λαβὼν λόγχην ἔνυξεν αὐτοῦ τὴν πλευράν, καὶ ἐξῆλθεν ὕδωρ καὶ αἷμα. Mt. represents one of the bystanders (εἶς ἐξ αὐτῶν) as offering Jesus the sponge of vinegar, while others were for waiting to see if Elijah would come to save Him. Then he adds the incident about the piercing of the Lord's side, the apparent inference being that it was to render fruitless any intervention on the part of Elijah. As the verse occurs in Mt., it represents Jesus as *alive*, His death following with a loud cry immediately *after* the piercing. It has been held that Chrysostom supports this view; but an examination of his homily on Mt. 27⁴⁹ will show that it is not so, despite some confusion in the order of his comments. For although he mentions the piercing immediately after the giving of the vinegar, he adds: " What could be more brutal than these men, who carried their madness so far as to insult a dead body "; a comment which he briefly repeats on Jn. 19³⁴. Tatian has also been cited in support of the interpolation at Mt. 27⁴⁹, but there is no trace of it in the *Diatessaron*. The probability is that εἶς ἐξ αὐτῶν of Mt. 27⁴⁸ recalled to a copyist εἶς τῶν στρατιωτῶν of Jn. 19³⁴ and suggested the interpolation. Perhaps Jn.'s ἀλλ' εἶς was read as ἄλλος by the scribe of Mt. The theory that the passage was part of the original Mt.[1] (being omitted by the Syriac and O.L. vss. because of its inconsistency with Jn.), and that Jn. here silently corrects Mt. by placing the incident in its true context, is improbable, for there is no evidence to prove that Jn. knew Mt. at all.[2]

The rendering of the Latin Vulgate *aperuit* in this verse depends on a corruption of the Greek text. The true Greek reading is ἔνυξεν " pricked," which is the basis of most of the O.L. vss., *pupugit, perfodit, inseruit*, etc. But the O.L. codices *f* and *r* have *aperuit*, which presumably indicates a Greek variant ἤνοιξεν " opened." This was adopted by Jerome, and is supported by the Peshitta and the Jerusalem Syriac. But for the Greek ἤνοιξεν there is no MS. authority. Cod. 56 has ἤνυξε; Cod. 58 has ἔμυξε (corr. to ἔνυξε by a second hand); Cod. 68, the Evangelisteria 257, 259, and (according to Tischendorf) Cod. 225 have ἔνοιξε, all of which

---

[1] Cf. Westcott-Hort, *Select Readings*, p. 22 ; Nestle, *Textual Criticism*, p. 227 ; Salmon, *Human Element in the Gospels*, p. 524 ; Abbott, *Diat.* 1756 ; and esp. Tischendorf's critical note on Mt. 27⁴⁹.

[2] Cf. Introd., p. xcvi.

κατέαξαν αὐτοῦ τὰ σκέλη, 34. ἀλλ' εἰς τῶν στρατιωτῶν λόγχῃ αὐτοῦ

are natural corruptions of ἔνυξε, and it is plain that ἤνοιξεν was another corruption of the same kind.[1]

εἰς τῶν στρατιωτῶν. Jn.'s general usage is to write εἰς ἐκ τῶν . . . (see on 1⁴⁰), but at 12⁴ 18²² as well as here ἐκ is omitted. Tradition gives the name Longinus to this soldier, probably because of the λόγχη (ἅπ. λεγ. in N.T.) or *lancea* which he carried.

νύσσειν (ἅπ. λεγ. in N.T.) is "to prod," and is generally used of a light touch (*e.g.* Ecclus. 22¹⁹ of pricking the eye, and 3 Macc. 5¹⁴ of "prodding" a sleeping person to awake him). Field quotes a passage from Plutarch (*Cleom.* 37) where it is used of touching a man with a dagger to ascertain if he were dead, and he suggests that it is used similarly here.

On the other hand, νύσσειν is used of a spear wound which kills a man (*e.g.* Josephus, *Bell. Jud.* III. vii. 35; cf. *Acta Thomæ*, § 165), and 20²⁵ indicates that the wound made in Jesus' side was a large one. Origen (in Mt. 27⁵⁴) seems to say that a lance thrust was sometimes given as a *coup de grâce* to hasten the death of those who had been crucified. The language of the text suggests that the soldier was determined to make sure that Jesus was dead.

The λόγχη was a long slender spear, not so heavy as the ὕσσος (see v. 29) or *pilum* which was the usual weapon of the Roman legionaries. The ὕσσος had a barbed iron head, which would inflict a wide and deep wound. If we are to press the use of λόγχη here, it would fall in with the idea, which has been put forward, that the soldier's act was a mere gesture as he passed; that he perceived Jesus to be dead, and so, without any special purpose, prodded the Body with his lance, the touch being possibly a light one.

The Ethiopic version (sæc. vi.) says that it was the *right* side of the Body that was pierced. This was widely accepted in ancient times (see e.g. *Acta Pilati*, B. xi.), and the incident is frequently represented thus in art, *e.g.* in the sixth-century Syriac Evangeliarium of Rabula at Florence.[2] The verse Jn. 19³⁴ is recited at the mixing of the chalice in several Eastern liturgies; and in the Liturgy of St. Chrysostom the rubric preceding its recitation has the words, νύττων δὲ αὐτὸν ἐν τῷ δεξίῳ μέρει μετὰ τῆς λόγχης κτλ.[3]

---

[1] That the readings of Codd. 56, 58, and 68 are respectively ἤνυξε, ἔνυξε, and ἔνοιξε, I have determined by personal inspection. See "The Vulgate of St. John," in *Hermathena*, xxi. 188.

[2] This is figured in Cabrol's *Dict. d'archéol. chrétienne*, s.v. "Croix."

[3] See Brightman, *Eastern Liturgies*, p. 357; cf. also pp. 71, 97, 251.

τὴν πλευρὰν ἔνυξεν, καὶ ἐξῆλθεν εὐθὺς αἷμα καὶ ὕδωρ. 35. καὶ

ἐξῆλθεν εὐθύς. So אBLNW (cf. 13³⁰); the rec. has εὐθὺς ἐξῆλθεν. There is emphasis on εὐθύς ; the "blood and water" flowed immediately. See on 5⁹, and on 1²².

That there should be a flow of blood from a *dead* body, when pierced with a spear, is abnormal; and various physical explanations have been offered. W. Stroud [1] suggested that the death of Jesus had been caused by rupture of the heart (which explains why it came so soon after His Crucifixion), and that the " blood and water " were the separated clot and serum of the escaped blood in the pericardial sac, which the lance had pierced. This assumes that the wound was on the left side, of which there is no evidence, tradition (whatever it be worth) indicating the right side.

Stroud's arguments have not approved themselves to all physicians. It is objected, *e.g.* by Dr. C. Creighton,[2] that " the blood escaping into a serum cavity from rupture of a great organ " does not show any tendency to separate into clot and serum, " but remains thick dark-red blood." Creighton suggests that the stroke of the spear may have been only a light touch (see above), directed to " something on the surface of the body, perhaps a discoloured wheal or exudation, such as the scourging might have left"; and that it " was a thoughtless rather than a brutal act," Jesus already being dead. " Water not un-mixed with blood from some such superficial source is conceivable, but blood and water from an internal source are a mystery."

We have hardly sufficient data to reach an exact conclusion as to the cause of the gushing forth of blood and water from the wound; or as to the time—possibly a very short interval—which had elapsed since the Death of Jesus; but that blood and water were observed to flow is not doubtful.

It has, however, been frequently urged (*e.g.* by Westcott and Godet) that we must not expect a complete physical explanation of this incident; inasmuch as, according to the apostolic teaching, the Body of Christ did not suffer corruption after His Death (cf. Acts 2³¹). He truly died (see on v. 30), but the physical changes which succeed death in our experience did not necessarily follow in His case. We may not assume that the Death of Christ was exactly like the death of an ordinary human being. This view of the matter was put forward by Origen. In dead bodies, he says, blood is clotted and water does not flow; but from the dead Body of Christ blood and water issued, and here was a miracle.[3]

---

[1] *Physical Cause of the Death of Christ* (1847).
[2] See *E.B.* 960.   [3] *c. Celsum,* ii. 36.

The language of Jn. is compatible with this interpretation. In that case, the solemn attestation of v. 35 was added because Jn. regarded the incident as so extraordinary as to be difficult of credence. It had not been narrated by earlier evangelists, and exceptionally good testimony would be necessary if it were to be believed.

But it is more probable that Jn. regards the flow of blood and water from the pierced side of Jesus as a natural phenomenon, which he specially notes because he wishes to refute the Docetic doctrines prevalent when the Gospel was composed.[1] Alike in the Gospel and in the First Epistle he is anxious to lay stress on the true humanity of Christ (see on 1[14]); and when telling of the Passion he would guard against the Docetism which treated the Body of Jesus as a mere phantom. We know from the second-century *Acts of John*, as well as from other sources, something of the curious teaching which denied humanity to Christ and explained His Crucifixion as an illusion. In this Docetic work (§ 101), Jesus is actually represented as saying that there was no real flow of blood from His Body; αἷμα ἐξ ἐμοῦ ῥεύσαντα καὶ οὐκ ἔρευσεν. In opposition to teaching of this kind, which goes back to the first century, Jn. is earnest in explaining that the Death of Jesus was a human death; His Body bled when it was pierced; it was no phantom.

In like manner, the language of the First Epistle is strongly anti-Docetic. " Every spirit which confesseth that Jesus Christ is come *in the flesh* is of God," the spirit which denies this being the spirit of antichrist (1 Jn. 4[2, 3]). That the language of 1 Jn. 5[6], " This is He who came by water and blood, even Jesus Christ; not with the water only, but with the water and the blood," carries a direct allusion to Jn. 19[34] is doubtful. Perhaps the words are sufficiently explained of the historic Baptism of Jesus and of His historic Crucifixion. But the whole passage is strikingly similar to Jn. 19[34, 35] in its insistence on the true humanity of Christ in the circumstances, alike, of His Life and His Death. This was what Jn. was most anxious to teach, viz. that the Man Jesus is the Christ, the Son of God (20[31]); and the incident recorded in Jn. 19[34] is so apposite in this connexion, as opposed to Docetic mysticism, that he calls attention to it by an emphatic and special attestation (v. 35).

One of the earliest extant comments on Jn. 19[34], is that of Irenæus, who takes this view of the evangelist's purpose. To show the true humanity of Christ, Irenæus calls attention to His being hungry at the Temptation, to His being tired (Jn. 4[6]), to His tears (Jn. 11[35]), to His bloody sweat (Lk. 22[44]), and

---

[1] Cf. Burkitt, *Two Lectures on the Gospels*, p. 64.

lastly to the piercing of His side, when blood and water flowed forth. He concludes ταῦτα γὰρ πάντα σύμβολα σαρκός, τῆς ἀπὸ γῆς εἰλημμένης (c. Hær. III. xxii. 2; cf. IV. xxxiii. 2). It will be observed that Irenæus has no thought of a miracle here, nor does he proceed to find any mystical meaning in the incident.

All later fathers are concerned with the symbolism. Among them may be named Claudius Apollinaris, bishop of Hierapolis about 171, a contemporary of Irenæus. A fragment ascribed to him [1] runs as follows : ὁ τὴν ἁγίαν πλευρὰν ἐκκεντθεὶς (cf. v. 37), ὁ ἐκχέας ἐκ τῆς πλευρᾶς αὐτοῦ τὰ δύο πάλιν καθάρσια, ὕδωρ καὶ αἷμα, λόγον καὶ πνεῦμα. Here the Water and the Blood seem to correspond respectively to the Word and the Spirit (for it is arbitrary to suppose that the order is to be reversed), as they do in the famous Comma Johanneum about the Three Heavenly Witnesses; and this suggests a doubt as to the genuineness of the alleged quotation from Claudius Apollinaris. In any case, the writer holds that the Water and the Blood at the Crucifixion are " the two things that again purify," [2] πάλιν probably referring to the purifications under the Old Covenant. He may have had in mind the dedication of the Covenant with Israel (Ex. 24[6f.]), which in Heb. 9[19] is said to have been with the blood of the victims and with water (water is not mentioned in Ex. 24). The elder Lightfoot [3] suggested that this was in the thought of the evangelist here, but there is no hint of anything of the kind in his words.

Tertullian finds in the water and the blood, symbols of the two kinds of baptism, that of the martyr being a baptism with blood (de Pud. 22). In another place, he suggests that there is a prefigurement of the two sacraments, which is the favourite comment of later theologians. The passage (de Bapt. 16) is the first which indicates a connexion with 1 Jn. 5[6], and must therefore be quoted in full: " Venerat enim per aquam et sanguinem, sicut Joannes scripsit, ut aqua tingerentur, sanguine glorificarentur, proinde nos faceret aqua vocatos, sanguine electos. Hos duos baptismos de vulnere perfossi lateris emisit, quatenus qui in sanguinem eius crederent, aqua lavarentur, qui aqua lavissent, etiam sanguinem potarent." [4]

---

[1] See Routh, Rel. Sacr. i. 161.

[2] Cf. Toplady's hymn, " Rock of Ages " :

> " Let the water and the blood,
> From Thy riven side which flowed,
> Be of sin the double cure,
> Cleanse me from its guilt and power."

[3] Hor. Hebr. iii. 440.

[4] The author of the curious treatise Pistis Sophia (circa 280 A.D.) brings into juxtaposition (c. 141) the Water of Jn. 4[14], the Blood of

ὁ ἑωρακὼς μεμαρτύρηκεν, καὶ ἀληθινὴ αὐτοῦ ἐστὶν ἡ μαρτυρία, καὶ

We need not pursue the patristic interpretations further.

35. This verse is omitted in *e* (Cod. Palatinus of the fifth century), nor does it appear in the rearrangement of the Gospel texts called *fu* (Cod. Fuldensis of the sixth century). From this slender evidence Blass [1] concluded that the verse was of doubtful genuineness, and must be treated as a later gloss. But such a conclusion is perverse in the face of the overwhelming mass of MSS and vss. which contain the passage, not to speak of its characteristically Johannine style.

ὁ ἑωρακὼς μεμαρτύρηκεν. Jn. lays much stress on "witness" (see Introd., pp. xc–xciii); and here the witness of the incident that has just been recorded is John the Beloved Disciple, who has been mentioned in v. 26 as having been present at the Cross. This is strictly parallel to 21²⁴, οὗτός ἐστιν ὁ μαθητὴς ὁ μαρτυρῶν περὶ τούτων, where also the Beloved Disciple is the witness to whom appeal is made.

καὶ ἀληθινὴ αὐτοῦ ἐστὶν ἡ μαρτυρία. This is (as again at 21²⁴) the attestation of Jn. that the evidence of the Beloved Disciple is genuine and trustworthy (see on 1¹⁰ for ἀληθινός).

καὶ ἐκεῖνος οἶδεν ὅτι ἀληθῆ λέγει. Here, once more, we have a parallel at 21²⁴, οἴδαμεν ὅτι ἀληθὴς αὐτοῦ ἡ μαρτυρία ἐστίν. Nonnus is so certain of the parallelism that he alters οἶδεν into ἴδμεν, *i.e.* οἴδαμεν as at 21²⁴. But the reference of ἐκεῖνος must be more closely examined.

It has been thought that ἐκεῖνος here designates the actual writer of the Gospel,[2] including this verse. ἐκεῖνος is used at Jn. 9³⁷ by the Speaker of Himself. A closer parallel is provided by Josephus. He writes of his doings in the third person, and says that once he had thoughts of escaping from the city, but that the people begged him to remain : οὐ φθόνῳ τῆς ἐκείνου σωτηρίας, ἔμοιγε δοκεῖν, ἀλλ' ἐλπίδι τῆς ἑαυτῶν· οὐδὲν γὰρ ἠξιοῦν πείσεσθαι δεινὸν 'Ιωσήπου μένοντος (*Bell. Jud.* iii. 7, 16). Here ἐκεῖνος is the author ; and to those who accept the view that the Beloved Disciple was the writer of the Fourth Gospel as well as the witness to whom he appeals, the language of Josephus helps to justify the use of ἐκεῖνος in Jn. 19³⁵, although in Josephus it is markedly contrasted with ἑαυτῶν. Nevertheless, such a way of speaking would be curiously

the New Covenant (Mk. 14²⁴), and the Water and Blood of Jn. 19³⁴, but he does not say what the connexion is.

[1] *Theol. St. u. Kritiken* (1902), p. 128 ; cf. also *Philology of the Gospels*, p. 227, and Blass, *Euang. sec. Iohannem*, p. liii.

[2] Drummond, *Character and Authorship, etc.*, p. 389 f., takes this view.

indirect here. If the writer is the eye-witness, he has already said of himself that his witness is trustworthy, and he does not strengthen his affirmation by repeating it in so awkward a fashion.

Grammatically, ἐκεῖνος is, indeed, resumptive of αὐτοῦ in the the preceding clause, being used for the sake of emphasis; cf. 7²⁹ ἐγὼ οἶδα αὐτόν, ὅτι παρ' αὐτοῦ εἰμι, κἀκεῖνός με ἀπέστειλεν (see also 10¹· ⁶). As we take the words καὶ ἐκεῖνος οἶδεν ὅτι ἀληθῆ λέγει, they are the words of the evangelist, but not of the witness; and the repetition is not meaningless. "He," sc. the Beloved Disciple himself, "knows," for he is yet alive, "that he is telling true things." The evangelist's tribute is his own, and so is not exactly like the certificate of 21²⁴ which is that of the elders of the Church. Jn. assures his readers that the aged apostle knows exactly what he is saying: ἐκεῖνος οἶδεν. The alteration by Nonnus of οἶδεν into ἴδμεν is a paraphrase which alters the sense.

A quite different explanation of ἐκεῖνος has been held by some critics [1] since the days of Erasmus. It is said to apply to Christ Himself, who may be appealed to as the Witness here, ἐκεῖνος being used absolutely of Him as it is in 1 Jn. 3⁵· ¹⁶, where He has not been named in the immediate context. In 19³⁵, on this showing, ἐκεῖνος οἶδεν ὅτι ἀληθῆ λέγει is a parenthetical observation, claiming the support of Christ for the testimony borne by the Beloved Disciple: "Jesus knows that he is telling the truth." This is very unlike the manner of the author of the Fourth Gospel (although Paul has a similar asseveration, 2 Cor. 11³¹). The same may be said of the attempt to refer ἐκεῖνος here to God the Father, as at 1³³ 5¹⁹· ³⁷ 6²⁹ 8⁴², where ἐκεῖνος is undoubtedly used of Him. It might be thought more plausible to hold that ἐκεῖνος οἶδεν was an allusion here to the witness of the Paraclete (of whom ἐκεῖνος is used 14²⁶ 15²⁶ 16¹³· ¹⁴); the words ἀλήθεια, μαρτυρεῖν, ὕδωρ, αἷμα being associated with the witness of the Spirit in 1 Jn. 5⁶· ⁷. But we have seen already that the exegesis which refers 1 Jn. 5⁶· ⁷ to Jn. 19³⁴ is improbable.

The fact is that there is nothing distinctive of Deity in the use of ἐκεῖνος by Jn. (see on 1⁸). In the Fourth Gospel ἐκεῖνος stands in the same way for John the Baptist (5³⁵), or Moses (5⁴⁶), or the blind man (9¹⁰), or Mary of Bethany (11²⁹ 20¹⁵· ¹⁶), or Peter (18¹⁷· ²⁵), or the Beloved Disciple himself (13²⁵ 21⁷· ²³). The pronoun is a favourite one with Jn., and he uses it to express emphasis or for clearness irrespectively of the person to whom it is applied. Here we hold it to refer

[1] E.g. in our day by Zahn (Einheit. ii. 474), Sanday (Criticism of Fourth Gospel, 78), and Abbott (Diat. 2384, 2731).

ἐκεῖνος οἶδεν ὅτι ἀληθῆ λέγει, ἵνα καὶ ὑμεῖς πιστεύητε. 36. ἐγένετο γὰρ ταῦτα ἵνα ἡ γραφὴ πληρωθῇ Ὀστοῦν οὐ συντριβήσεται αὐτοῦ. 37. καὶ πάλιν ἑτέρα γραφὴ λέγει Ὄψονται εἰς ὃν ἐξεκέντησαν.

emphatically to the Beloved Disciple, whom we identify with the son of Zebedee.

ἵνα καὶ ὑμεῖς πιστεύητε. The rec. omits καί, but ins. אABD^suppLNWΘ. Again the rec., with א^aAD^suppNWΘ, has ἵνα . . . πιστεύσητε, but א*B have ἵνα . . . πιστεύητε as at 20³¹. The witness has borne his testimony about the blood and water, "in order that you also," sc. the readers of the Gospel, "may believe," not being misled by Docetic mysticism.

36. ἵνα ἡ γρ. πληρωθῇ . . . See Introd., pp. cxlix ff., for the significance of this formula, introducing a testimonium from the O.T. Here there is a free quotation of Ex. 12⁴⁶, "neither shall ye break a bone thereof," sc. of the Passover lamb. Cf. also Num. 9¹². The passage Ps. 34²⁰, "He keepeth all his bones: not one of them is broken," although there are verbal similarities, is not apposite to the context.

The Passover lamb of the ancient ritual was not only slain to provide a commemorative meal; it was an "oblation" (Num. 9¹²), and it was not fitting that it should be mutilated. The offering must be perfect. This, to Jn., was a prophetic ordinance, and pointed forward to the manner of the death of Him who was the true Paschal Lamb. In this identification of Jesus with the Paschal Lamb, Paul is in agreement with Jn. "Christ our Passover is sacrificed for us" (1 Cor. 5⁷).[1]

37. καὶ πάλιν ἑτέρα γραφὴ λέγει. ἕτερος "different" does not appear again in Jn.

The manner of the Lord's death was, according to Jn., in fulfilment both of type and prophecy; negatively, because His legs were not broken as the usual custom was in the case of crucified persons, so that the type of the Paschal Lamb might be fulfilled in Him; and positively, by the piercing of His side, as had been prophesied in Zech. 12¹⁰ ὄψονται εἰς ὃν ἐξεκέντησαν, "they shall look on Him whom they pierced."

The LXX, reading רקדו for דקרו, by an erroneous transposition of ר and ד, has the curious κατωρχήσαντο, "they danced insultingly," instead of ἐξεκέντησαν, "they pierced," which is the natural rendering of the Hebrew and is followed by Theodotion and Aquila, Symmachus having ἐπεξεκέντησαν. The same rendering is found in Rev. 1⁷, where the prophecy is given a different turn and referred to the Second Advent, ὄψεται αὐτὸν πᾶς ὀφθαλμός, καὶ οἵτινες αὐτὸν ἐξεκέντησαν. Justin uses similar words (with ἐκκεντεῖν) of the Second Advent

[1] Cf. Introd., p. clv.

38. Μετὰ δὲ ταῦτα ἠρώτησεν τὸν Πειλᾶτον Ἰωσὴφ ἀπὸ Ἀριμαθαίας, ὢν μαθητὴς τοῦ Ἰησοῦ κεκρυμμένος δὲ διὰ τὸν φόβον τῶν

(*Apol.* i. 52, *Tryph.* 64), and in *Tryph.* 32 distinguishes the two
Advents, thus: δυὸ παρουσίας αὐτοῦ γενήσεσθαι ἐξηγησάμην, μιὰν
μὲν ἐν ᾗ ἐξεκεντήθη ὑφ᾽ ὑμῶν, δευτέραν δὲ ὅτε ἐπιγνώσεσθε εἰς ὃν
ἐξεκεντήσατε.

It is clear that Jn. did not use the LXX here, and while he
may have translated independently from the Hebrew, it is
more probable that he has adopted a version current in his
time.

Abbott (*Diat.* 2318) suggests that Jn. means the prophecy
to apply to the four soldiers (whom he fantastically supposes to
represent the four quarters of the globe) : "*they* shall look on
Him whom they pierced." But Zech. 12¹⁰ refers in its original
context to " the inhabitants of Jerusalem "; and it is more
natural to take the Jews for the subject of " they shall look."
It was to the Jews that Jesus was delivered to be crucified (v. 16),
and the "piercing" was, indirectly, their act.

The burial of the Body of Jesus (vv. 38–42)

38. μετὰ ταῦτα is the phrase by which Jn. introduces new
sections of the narrative. See Introd., p. cviii.

Ἰωσὴφ ἀπὸ Ἀριμαθαίας. Arimathæa is probably to be
identified with the O.T. *Ramathaim-Zophim* (1 Sam. 1¹ ;
cf. 1 Macc. 11³⁴), a place about 13 miles E.N.E. of Lydda, and
about 60 miles from Jerusalem. Joseph was a member of the
Sanhedrim, εὐσχήμων βουλευτής (Mk. 15⁴³), and rich (according
to Mt. 27⁵⁷), Lk. 23⁵⁰ adding the information that he was a
good and just man, who had not consented to the proceedings
of his colleagues in the condemnation of Jesus. He was a
disciple of Jesus, in the wider sense of μαθητής (cf. Mt. 27⁵⁷),
although a secret one, κεκρυμμένος δὲ διὰ τὸν φόβον τῶν Ἰουδαίων
(cf. 7¹³, 9²²). Mk. only says of him that he was " looking for the
kingdom of God." Pseudo-Peter alleges that he was " a friend
of Pilate and of the Lord." But he was not a familiar figure
among the disciples of Jesus, for the Galilæan women do not
seem to have been acquainted with him: they only watched
what he and his servants did at the tomb (Mk. 15⁴⁷). It was
only after the Crucifixion that Joseph and Nicodemus avowed
their discipleship by their solicitude for reverent treatment of
the body of Jesus. Mk. notes that Joseph went to make his
request to Pilate, τολμήσας " having plucked up his courage "
(Mk. 15⁴³).

Joseph's request and his subsequent action are narrated in

Ἰουδαίων, ἵνα ἄρῃ τὸ σῶμα τοῦ Ἰησοῦ· καὶ ἐπέτρεψεν ὁ Πειλᾶτος. ἦλθεν οὖν καὶ ἦρεν τὸ σῶμα αὐτοῦ. 39. ἦλθεν δὲ καὶ Νικόδημος, ὁ ἐλθὼν πρὸς αὐτὸν νυκτὸς τὸ πρῶτον, φέρων μίγμα σμύρνης καὶ

all the Gospels (Mt. 27⁵⁷, Mk. 15⁴², Lk. 23⁵⁰); in Pseudo-Peter (§ 2) the request is made in advance before the Crucifixion, and is referred to Herod before it is granted.

Turner has suggested [1] that Joseph's petition to Pilate was made at the time when the deputation from the Sanhedrim asked that the death of the crucified persons should be hastened (see above on v. 31); and, although Jn. introduces v. 38 with μετὰ ταῦτα, this is more probable than the alternative that Pilate gave two separate audiences on the subject of the death of Jesus and the subsequent disposal of His body.

At any rate, Pilate acceded to the request of Joseph that the body of Jesus should be given him for burial, and made no difficulty about it. ἐδωρήσατο τὸ πτῶμα is Mk.'s phrase (Mk. 15⁴⁴): he gave the corpse freely. (Cf. Mk. 6²⁹ Mt. 14¹².)

ἦρεν τὸ σῶμα αὐτοῦ. So ℵᶜBL; the rec., with DˢᵘᵖᵖΝΓΔΘ, has τὸ σῶμα τοῦ Ἰησοῦ. W has αὐτόν. Jn. uses the word σῶμα only of a *dead* body (see Introd., p. clxx). Joseph arrived at the Cross before the soldiers had finished their task; cf. ἀρθῶσιν, v. 31.

39. For πρὸς αὐτόν (ABL) the rec. has the explanatory πρὸς τὸν Ἰησοῦν, with ℵDˢᵘᵖᵖΝΓΔΘ.

ℵ*BW read ἕλιγμα, "a roll," but this is probably a corruption of μίγμα, "a mixture" or "confection" (cf. Ecclus. 38⁸), which all other MS. authorities support, two cursives giving σμίγμα or σμήγμα. Probably the original was ϹΜΙΓΜΑ which could easily be corrupted into ΕΛΙΓΜΑ. Neither word occurs elsewhere in N.T.

ὡς, with ℵBDˢᵘᵖᵖLΘ, is to be preferred to ὡσεί of rec. text.

For Nicodemus see on 3¹: he is described here as ὁ ἐλθὼν πρὸς αὐτὸν νυκτὸς τὸ πρῶτον, recalling his former interview with Jesus (see on 7⁵⁰). It has been suggested that he is to be identified with Joseph of Arimathæa,[2] which has no more probability than the fancy that he is only an ideal character invented by Jn. (see on 3¹). In this passage he is represented as assisting Joseph of Arimathæa in the preparation of the Body of Jesus for burial, after Pilate had given his permission; but with that timid caution which was a characteristic (see on 7⁵⁰) he does not seem himself to have approached Pilate in the first instance. Nicodemus was probably a rich man, for a hundred pounds weight of spicery was a costly gift It is not

---

[1] *Ch. Quarterly Review*, July 1912, p. 297.
[2] Cf. *E.B.* 3408, and *D.B.* iii. 543.

ἀλόης ὡς λίτρας ἑκατόν.   40. ἔλαβον οὖν τὸ σῶμα τοῦ Ἰησοῦ καὶ
ἔδησαν αὐτὸ ὀθονίοις μετὰ τῶν ἀρωμάτων, καθὼς ἔθος ἐστὶν τοῖς

said that Nicodemus bought the spices for this special purpose
(there would have been little time for that); probably he
brought them from his own house.

The myrrh was a sweet-smelling gum which was mixed
with the powdered aromatic wood of aloes. Myrrh and aloes
are mentioned together as forming a fragrant mixture or
confection several times in the O.T. (Ps. 45[8], Prov. 7[17], Cant.
4[14]). The use of such spices, when a dead body was placed
with honour in its sepulchre, is mentioned in connexion with
the burial of King Asa (2 Chron. 16[14]). They appear also to
have been used for embalming, but nothing is said of such an
intention in this case.

There was little time before the Sabbath came on, and no
final disposition of the Body in its resting-place was attempted.
Pseudo-Peter says that it was washed, which may be only an
imaginative addition to the narrative. It was not anointed;
the anointing (cf. Mk. 14[8], Mt. 26[12]) was postponed until the
day after the Sabbath, when the women came to do it, having
bought spices on their own account (Mk. 16[1], Lk. 24[1]).

40. ἔλαβον οὖν κτλ. "Then they took the body of Jesus,"
i.e. Joseph and Nicodemus. Mk., followed by Mt., tells that
Mary Magdalene and Mary the wife of Clopas were present
at the burial; they had been at the Cross (as Jn. has told
already, v. 25), and they waited until the end. Salome was
also at the Cross (see on v. 25), but she may have accompanied
her sister Mary the Mother of Jesus when she left the scene
(v. 27); at any rate, she is not mentioned by name as having
been at the burial (cf. Lk. 23[55]).

ἔδησαν αὐτὸ ὀθονίοις μετὰ τῶν ἀρωμάτων, "they bound it with
strips of cloth, with the spices"; apparently the spices were
scattered freely between the folds of the cloths, and the body
was embedded in them.[1] It was the custom of the Jews (as
distinct from that of the Egyptians) to bury (ἐνταφιάζειν; cf.
Gen. 50[2] where this word is used of the embalming of Jacob) in
this way. Cf. Jn. 11[44] for the "swathes" (κειρίαι) with which
Lazarus had been bound.

The word ὀθόνιον, "linen cloth," occurs again only
20[5. 6. 7] and Lk. 24[12] (cf. Judg. 14[13]). The Synoptists in their
accounts of the burial have the word σινδών. Milligan (*s.v.*)
cites the use of ὀθόνιον in papyri for burial linen, or for the
wrappings of a mummy.

[1] See Latham, *The Risen Master*, p. 36 f., for a suggestive study of
what was done.

Ἰουδαίοις ἐνταφιάζειν.   41. ἦν δὲ ἐν τῷ τόπῳ ὅπου ἐσταυρώθη κῆπος,
καὶ ἐν τῷ κήπῳ μνημεῖον καινόν, ἐν ᾧ οὐδέπω οὐδεὶς ἦν τεθειμένος·
42. ἐκεῖ οὖν διὰ τὴν Παρασκευὴν τῶν Ἰουδαίων, ὅτι ἐγγὺς ἦν τὸ
μνημεῖον, ἔθηκαν τὸν Ἰησοῦν.

41. ἦν δὲ ἐν τῷ τόπῳ ὅπου ἐσταυρώθη κῆπος. None of the
Synoptists mention a garden (see for κῆπος on 18[1]) as the place
of burial. This, with the detail that it was " in " the place of
Crucifixion, is peculiar to Jn.   (For the use of the impf. ἦν,
see on 11[18].)   There was no time to lose, and this garden was
near Golgotha.   Mt. 27[60] adds that the tomb in the garden
belonged to Joseph of Arimathæa, but this is not in Mk., Lk.,
or Jn., although it may have been the case.   Pseudo-Peter
explicitly says that the garden bore the name κῆπος Ἰωσήφ.
Two instances of royal tombs in gardens are given 2 Kings
21[18, 26], and the LXX of Neh. 3[16] makes mention of κῆπος τάφου
Δανειδ.   Milligan (s.v.) cites κηποτάφιον " a tomb in a garden,"
from a papyrus of 5 B.C.

ἐν τῷ κήπῳ μνημεῖον καινόν (D[supp]N 69 give κενόν), ἐν ᾧ
οὐδέπω οὐδεὶς ἦν τεθειμένος.   Mk. 15[46] has " a tomb which
had been hewn out of a rock," which Mt. 27[60] follows: adding
(as Jn. does) that the tomb was καινόν.   Lk. also says (23[53])
that the tomb was λαξευτόν, adding οὗ οὐκ ἦν οὐδεὶς οὔπω
κείμενος.   Thus Jn. agrees with Lk. in saying that the tomb
had not been used before, and he uses almost the same words,
substituting οὐδέπω for οὔπω (cf. 20[9]).

42. ἐκεῖ οὖν κτλ., " there then, because the tomb was near,
they laid Him."

διὰ τὴν Παρασκευὴν τῶν Ἰουδαίων.   This was the reason that
made delay impossible.   The " Preparation " was at hand.
This may mean either "the Preparation for the Sabbath," i.e.
Friday, or " the Preparation for the Passover."   It has been
pointed out on 19[14] that elsewhere in the N.T. παρασκευή always
means *Friday* ; and this gives a good sense here.   But inasmuch
as in this passage the words τῶν Ἰουδαίων follow, an addition
which Jn. always makes when speaking of the Passover festivals
(see 2[13] 6[4] 11[55]), it may be that we are to lay stress on τήν which
precedes παρασκευήν (see on 19[14]) and understand him here
to say " the Preparation of the Passover."   The meaning of
the passage is not altered in any case, for both on account of
the impending Sabbath and of the impending Passover Feast,
it was necessary that the burial should be hastened.

Field rightly calls attention to the solemn and stately cadences
of the rendering of this verse in the R.V.: " There then because
of the Jews' Preparation (for the tomb was nigh at hand) they
laid Jesus."

XX. 1. Τῇ δὲ μιᾷ τῶν σαββάτων Μαριάμ ἡ Μαγδαληνὴ ἔρχεται πρωί, σκοτίας ἔτι οὔσης, εἰς τὸ μνημεῖον, καὶ βλέπει τὸν λίθον ἠρμένον

XX. 1 ff. The narrative in Jn. 20 of the appearances of Christ after His Resurrection, like the narrative in Lk. 24 and the Marcan Appendix, tells only of appearances in Jerusalem or its immediate neighbourhood. On the other hand, the narrative of Mt. 28[16f.] tells of an appearance in Galilee, and in this it probably follows the Lost Conclusion of Mk. The Appendix to Jn. (c. 21) also lays the scene of a manifestation of Christ in Galilee. There are thus two traditions as to the appearances of the Risen Lord: one which places them in Jerusalem, and another which places them in Galilee. It may be impossible, from the evidence at our disposal, to construct a complete table which shall indicate the order in which they occurred; but there is no inherent difficulty in the circumstance that they were not all observed in the same locality. If it be accepted that Jesus Christ rose from the dead, it was as easy for Him to manifest Himself to His disciples in Jerusalem and in Galilee, as in Jerusalem only or in Galilee only. The Jerusalem tradition is followed in c. 20, with the addition of particulars which no other authority gives, and which may plausibly be referred to the eye-witness whose testimony is behind the narrative. In c. 21 we have a version of the Galilæan tradition (see p. 690 f.).

The Sepulchre found empty by Mary Magdalene, and by Peter and John (XX. 1–10)

1. τῇ δὲ μιᾷ τῶν σαββάτων . . . πρωί, σκοτίας ἔτι οὔσης. Mk. 16[2] says in like manner, λίαν πρωὶ τῆς μιᾶς σαββάτων. For πρωί, see on 18[28]. Lk. 24[1] and Mt. 28[1] agree in mentioning "the first day of the week," and in describing the visit to the tomb as being made in the half-light just before dawn.

Jn. names Mary Magdalene only as visiting the tomb, but the plur. οἴδαμεν of v. 2 suggests that she was not alone, and that her perplexity as to how the Lord's body had been disposed of was shared by others. It is unlikely that a woman would have ventured by herself outside the city walls before daylight, and the Synoptists agree in telling that she was accompanied by others. Mk. 16[1] names as her companions Mary the mother of James (*i.e.* the wife of Clopas; see on 2[12]) and Salome, the Virgin's sister, who were also present at the Crucifixion with her (19[25]). Mt. 28[1] only names "Mary Magdalene and the other Mary." Lk. 24[10] mentions "Mary Magdalene and Joanna and Mary the mother of James and the other women."

ἐκ τοῦ μνημείου. **2.** τρέχει οὖν καὶ ἔρχεται πρὸς Σίμωνα Πέτρον καὶ

Pseudo-Peter (§ 11) also notes that Mary Magdalene was accompanied by other women.

Jn. does not say what the purpose of this visit to the tomb was; and in this he is in agreement with Mt. 28¹, where it is merely told that they went "to see the sepulchre." But Mk. 16¹ and Lk. 23⁵⁶ 24¹ explain that the purpose of the women was to anoint the body of Jesus. In Jn.'s narrative (see 19³⁹) the body was hastily laid in spices on the Day of Crucifixion by Joseph and Nicodemus, but there was no time for any anointing then, or final disposition of the body. Nothing further could be done on the Sabbath, and the women came as early as possible the next morning, with the spices and unguents that they had provided for themselves (Mk. 16¹, Lk. 23⁵⁶).¹

We hold that Mary Magdalene is the same person as Mary of Bethany (see Additional Note on 12¹⁻⁸); and her desire to anoint the body of her Master is thus significant in connexion with His words to her when she anointed His feet at Bethany (12⁷). She had kept the ointment "against the day of His burying." Jn., however, does not introduce this point expressly. He narrates Mary's visit to the tomb briefly, because what he is anxious to describe is the subsequent visit of Peter and the Beloved Disciple, which was suggested by her report.

Both Mk. and Lk. agree with Jn. in the statement that Mary (and the other women) found the stone taken away from the tomb. For τὸν λίθον ἠρμένον ἐκ τοῦ μνημείου, see on 11³⁸·³⁹.

According to the Johannine narrative, Mary does not suspect as yet that anything out of the ordinary course of nature has happened. She sees that the stone which sealed the sepulchre has been removed, and (seemingly) she looks in to assure herself that the tomb is empty ² (v. 2); but her inference is only that the body has been removed to some other resting-place.

2. τρέχει οὖν κτλ. The haste with which the women ran back from the tomb is mentioned also Mk. 16⁸, Mt. 28⁸.

ἔρχεται πρὸς Σίμωνα Πέτρον. Peter was still, despite his denial of Jesus, reckoned as the leader, or at any rate as one of the leaders, of the disciples; and so it is naturally to him that the surprising news of the tomb being empty is carried first. He has not been mentioned since 18²⁷; and so on his reappearance in the narrative, Jn., according to his habit (see on 18¹⁵), gives his full name *Simon Peter*. The names of the

---

¹ See Latham, *The Risen Master*, p. 37, and cf. p. 225.
² Latham supposes that the other women looked into the tomb and reported its emptiness to Mary (*l.c.* p. 40).

πρὸς τὸν ἄλλον μαθητὴν ὃν ἐφίλει ὁ Ἰησοῦς, καὶ λέγει αὐτοῖς, Ἦραν
τὸν Κύριον ἐκ τοῦ μνημείου, καὶ οὐκ οἴδαμεν ποῦ ἔθηκαν αὐτόν.
3. Ἐξῆλθεν οὖν ὁ Πέτρος καὶ ὁ ἄλλος μαθητής, καὶ ἤρχοντο εἰς τὸ
μνημεῖον. 4. ἔτρεχον δὲ οἱ δύο ὁμοῦ· καὶ ὁ ἄλλος μαθητὴς προέ-
δραμεν τάχιον τοῦ Πέτρου καὶ ἦλθεν πρῶτος εἰς τὸ μνημεῖον, 5. καὶ
παρακύψας βλέπει κείμενα τὰ ὀθόνια, οὐ μέντοι εἰσῆλθεν. 6. ἔρχεται

disciples to whom the women brought the news are not specified
in Mt. 28⁸; but cf. Lk. 24¹².

καὶ πρὸς τὸν ἄλλον μαθητήν κτλ. As Bengel observes, the
repetition of πρός indicates that Peter and "the other disciple"
were not lodging in the same house. The women had to visit
them separately. Cf. πρὸς αὐτούς of v. 10, and see 19²⁷.

ὃν ἐφίλει ὁ Ἰησοῦς. See 13²³, and cf. 21¹⁷. This association
of Peter and the "Beloved Disciple" is significant, in view of
the identification of the Beloved Disciple with John, the son of
Zebedee. See Introd., pp. xxxiv ff.

Ἦραν τὸν κύριον κτλ., "they have taken away the Lord from
the tomb, and we do not know where they have laid Him."
The subject of ἦραν is indefinite; Mary and her companions
did not know who they were. For the designation of Jesus
as "the Lord," see the note on 4¹.

The plur. οἴδαμεν, as has been noted on v. 1, suggests that
Mary was speaking for her companions as well as for herself.

3. Peter takes the lead, more suo. ἐξῆλθεν οὖν ὁ Πέτρος καὶ
ὁ ἄλλος μαθητής. For the singular verb ἐξῆλθεν, see Mt. 28¹.

καὶ ἤρχοντο κτλ., "and they set out for the tomb."

In the Musée du Luxembourg at Paris there is a remarkable
picture by E. Burnand of Peter and his young companion
hastening to the sepulchre, which will repay examination.

4. ἔτρεχον δέ κτλ., "So they began to run, the two together, and the other disciple ran on in front more quickly than
Peter." προτρέχειν occurs again in N.T. only at Lk. 19⁴. Cf.
1 Macc. 16²¹.

καὶ ἦλθεν πρῶτος κτλ. The Beloved Disciple was probably
the younger man of the two.

5. καὶ παρακύψας βλέπει κείμενα τὰ ὀθόνια. This sentence
invites comparison with the parallel passage Lk. 24¹² in the
rec. text, viz.: ὁ δὲ Πέτρος ἀναστὰς ἔδραμεν ἐπὶ τὸ μνημεῖον καὶ
παρακύψας βλέπει τὰ ὀθόνια κείμενα μόνα· καὶ ἀπῆλθε πρὸς
αὐτόν, θαυμάζων τὸ γεγονός. With ἀπῆλθε πρὸς αὐτόν cf. Jn. 20¹⁰,
ἀπῆλθον οὖν πάλιν πρὸς αὐτοὺς οἱ μαθηταί.

The verse Lk. 24¹² is found in אABLΓΔΘ, the old and
the Pesh. Syriac, and in c f ff₂, a strong combination. It is
omitted in D a b e l r ful etc., and on that account Westcott-Hort
place it in double brackets, treating it as a "Western non-

interpolation." They regard it as " condensed and simplified "
from Jn. 20⁵⁻⁹, θαυμάζων τὸ γεγονός being added to the
Johannine account. Yet Hort's view of what he calls
" Western non-interpolations " is not universally accepted ;[1]
and, in this instance, it is hard to believe that a scribe would be
bold enough to alter so materially a statement made in the
Fourth Gospel after it had received general acceptance,[2] and
thus to omit all mention of the Beloved Disciple as Peter's
companion. On the contrary, the evidence for Lk. 24¹² being
part of the original text of Lk. is too strong to be set aside by
the authority of D, an admittedly eccentric manuscript; and
the true inference from the verbal similarities between Lk. 24¹²
and Jn. 20⁵ seems to be that Jn., here as often elsewhere (see
Introd., p. xcix), is using Lk.'s words for the purpose of correcting him. It was not Peter, he says, who peeped into the tomb
and saw the linen wrappings lying on the ground, but it was the
Beloved Disciple, who had arrived at the tomb before Peter did.
He retains the words of Lk. so as to make it clear that he is
dealing with the same incident, but he corrects the narrative
of Lk. in so far as Peter is represented as being alone. Thus
" he went home " in Lk. 24¹² becomes " the disciples went
home " in Jn. 20¹⁰.

The difference between Lk. and Jn. is that between a man
who is reproducing a generally accepted tradition, and that of
an author relying on and reproducing what he has been told
by an eye-witness of, and a participator in, the events narrated.
Lk., indeed, implies at 24²⁴ that he had heard that more than
one disciple had gone to the tomb to verify the women's report
that it was empty; but there is no reason to think that he
alludes there to the visit of Peter and John. Pseudo-Peter
says there were many visitors to the sepulchre.

παρακύψας βλέπει. παρακύπτειν, in its primary and etymological meaning, would suggest " to *stoop down* for the purpose
of looking." [3]   But in this sense the verb is seldom used, and
in the LXX it *always* means " to peep " through a door or a
window (cf. Gen. 26⁸, Judg. 5²⁸, 1 Kings 6⁴, 1 Chron. 15²⁹,
Prov. 7⁶, Cant. 2⁹, Ecclus. 14²³ 21²³), without any stooping
being implied [4] Cf. also Jas. 1²⁵, 1 Pet. 1¹². Nor does the word
imply an earnest or searching gaze.[5] The Beloved Disciple
" peeped in and saw " is the rendering which best gives the sense.

---

[1] See, *e.g.*, Chase, *Syro-Latin Text of the Gospels*, p. 130 n., and
Salmon, *Some Criticism of the Text of N.T.*, p. 150.
[2] See Abbott, *Diat.*, 1803.
[3] So the Vulgate has here " cum se inclinasset, uidet."
[4] Tatian makes no mention of *stooping*.
[5] Cf. Abbott, *Diat.* 1804, and Field on Lk. 24¹².

οὖν καὶ Σίμων Πέτρος ἀκολουθῶν αὐτῷ, καὶ εἰσῆλθεν εἰς τὸ μνημεῖον· καὶ θεωρεῖ τὰ ὀθόνια κείμενα, 7. καὶ τὸ σουδάριον, ὃ ἦν ἐπὶ τῆς κεφαλῆς αὐτοῦ, οὐ μετὰ τῶν ὀθονίων κείμενον ἀλλὰ χωρὶς ἐντετυ-

κειμενα τὰ ὀθόνια (see on 19⁴⁰ for ὀθόνια). The participle κείμενα is put first for emphasis. What startled the disciple was that he saw the grave-cloths lying on the ground. If the body had been removed to some other resting-place, as Mary had suggested, it would presumably have been removed as it had been originally prepared for burial. The cloths would also have disappeared.[1]

οὐ μέντοι (for μέντοι, see on 12⁴²) εἰσῆλθεν. That the first disciple to note the presence of the grave-cloths in the tomb did not actually go into it first is not a matter that would seem worth noting, to any one except the man who himself refrained from entering. This strongly suggests that we are dealing with the narrative of an eye-witness. As to why John (for we believe the disciple to have been John) waited for Peter to go in first, we do not know. He may have been afraid, or overcome with emotion. Peter was a man of coarser fibre, more hasty, and more ready to put himself forward. That may be the whole explanation.

6. Peter's part in what happened is now resumed, and so he is given his full name Σίμων Πέτρος (cf. v. 2, and see on 18¹⁵). He did not hesitate, but entered the tomb at once.

καὶ θεωρεῖ τὰ ὀθόνια κείμενα, "and notices (he did not merely glance in: see on 2²³ 9⁸ for θεωρεῖν) the linen cloths lying." In the parallel passage, Lk. 24¹², we have βλέπει τὰ ὀθόνια κείμενα μόνα. Jn. leaves out μόνα, but explains carefully in v. 7 what it means in this context.

7. τὸ σουδάριον. See on 11⁴⁴. The napkin for the head was not lying with the grave-cloths for the body.

ἀλλὰ χωρὶς ἐντετυλιγμένον εἰς ἕνα τόπον. ἐντυλίσσειν is a rare verb, not found in the LXX; and in the parallels Mt. 27⁵⁹, Lk. 23⁵³ (not again in N.T.) it is used of wrapping the body of Jesus in a cloth, ἐνετύλιξεν αὐτὸ σινδόνι. Here it is the head-covering itself or "napkin" that is "rolled up." Latham believes that the language in vv. 6, 7 implies that the body had withdrawn from the grave-cloths, the swathes, and the turban-like napkin ; the body-cloths being thus not scattered about, but lying flat, and the napkin, retaining the shape into which it had been wound (so as to cover the head), lying where the head had been. This is reverently and suggestively worked out in *The Risen Master* (pp. 39, 89); but it cannot be regarded as certain.

[1] Chrysostom calls attention to this point.

λιγμένον εἰς ἕνα τόπον. 8. τότε οὖν εἰσῆλθεν καὶ ὁ ἄλλος μαθητὴς ὁ ἐλθὼν πρῶτος εἰς τὸ μνημεῖον, καὶ εἶδεν καὶ ἐπίστευσεν· 9. οὐδέπω

Milligan (*s.v.* ἐντυλίσσω) cites a remarkable verbal parallel from a third-century magical papyrus, ἐντύλισσε τὰ φύλλα ἐν σουδαρίῳ καινῷ.

8. τότε οὖν εἰσῆλθεν κτλ. Peter may have told John what he saw; at any rate, John no longer refrained from entering the tomb, "and he saw and believed" (εἶδεν καὶ ἐπίστευσεν). He had no vision of the Risen Christ, but the sight of the abandoned grave-cloths was sufficient to assure him that Jesus had risen from the dead. Jn. (16¹⁶) and the Synoptists (Mk. 8³¹ 9⁹· ³¹ 10³⁴ with parallels) agree in telling that Jesus had, on one occasion or another, assured the disciples that He would rise from the grave, and that they would see Him again. They had not understood or appreciated what He meant. But when John, the Beloved Disciple, saw the grave-cloths and the napkin in the tomb, the meaning of the strange predictions to which he had listened came to him with a flash of insight. "He saw and believed." This was a moment in his inner life, which was so charged with consequence, that he could never forget it, and the incident is recorded here as explaining how and when it was that he reached the fulness of Christian faith. That he "believed" without "seeing" his Risen Lord was in marked contrast to the attitude of Thomas, to whom it was said, "Blessed are they that have not seen and yet have believed" (v. 29).

ἐπίστευσεν. Syr. sin. has "*they* believed," and 69, 124 give ἐπίστευσαν, a mistaken correction due to a desire to include Peter as also "believing." For, although Peter "believed," it seems to have been after the Risen Christ had appeared to him (Lk. 24³⁴, 1 Cor. 15⁵), and not after his first glance at the tomb. He went away, according to Lk. 24¹², "wondering at that which was come to pass."

Dˢᵘᵖᵖ has the eccentric reading οὐκ ἐπίστευσεν, the scribe being misled by the words which follow.

For πιστεύειν used absolutely, without the object of belief being specified, see on 1⁷.

9. οὐδέπω (cf. 19⁴¹) γὰρ ᾔδεισαν τὴν γραφήν. γάρ is often used by Jn. to introduce a comment on incidents or words which have been recorded (cf. *e.g.* 3¹⁶ and 5²¹). Here γάρ does not introduce the reason for, or explanation of, the faith of John. Its meaning is, "You must remember that," etc. Jn. is thinking of his readers, who may be surprised that Peter and the Beloved Disciple were not more quick to recognise what had happened. "You must remember that they did not

γὰρ ᾔδεισαν τὴν γραφήν, ὅτι δεῖ αὐτὸν ἐκ νεκρῶν ἀναστῆναι.
10 ἀπῆλθον οὖν πάλιν πρὸς αὐτοὺς οἱ μαθηταί.

11. Μαριάμ δὲ εἱστήκει πρὸς τῷ μνημείῳ ἔξω κλαίουσα. ὡς οὖν

yet know (*i.e.* understand) the scripture which had foretold
the Resurrection of Christ."

ᾔδεισαν is used as in Mk. 12²⁴ μὴ εἰδότες τὰς γραφάς, "not
appreciating the meaning of the scriptures."

The γραφή, or particular passage of Scripture in the evangelist's mind, was probably Ps. 16¹⁰ (see on 2²²).

ὅτι δεῖ αὐτὸν ἐκ νεκρῶν ἀναστῆναι. The Divine necessity
which determined the course of Christ's Ministry, Passion, and
Resurrection has been often indicated by Jn.; see on 3¹⁴ for
Jn.'s use of δεῖ in this connexion, and cf. 2⁴. That the Scriptures must be "fulfilled" is fundamental in Jn.'s thought;
see Introd., pp. cxlix-clvi.

10. ἀπῆλθον οὖν πάλιν κτλ. "Dans un trouble extrême"
is Renan's description of their state of mind. But for this
there is no evidence. Lk. 24¹² describes Peter as bewildered
rather than troubled, while Jn. 20⁸ records that the Beloved
Disciple's faith in the Risen Christ was already assured.

πρὸς αὐτούς, i.e. *chez eux*, "to their lodgings." John had
brought the Virgin Mother εἰς τὰ ἴδια (19²⁷), and nothing could
be more probable than that he should bring the wonderful news
to her without any delay, as it is here recorded that he did.

πρὸς αὐτούς is used in a similar way by Josephus (*Antt.*
VIII. iv. 6), πρὸς αὐτοὺς . . . ἀπῄεσαν, "they returned home."

οἱ μαθηταί, *sc.* the disciples Peter and John. See on 2².

The Appearance of Christ to Mary and her report to the disciples (*vv.* 11–18)

11. Μαριάμ δὲ εἱστήκει κτλ. For the spelling Μαριάμ (here
supported by אO 1, 33), see on 19²⁵; and for εἱστήκει, see on 1³⁵

Mary, according to Jn., had returned to the tomb, after
she had told Peter and John that it had been found empty.
She "was standing by the tomb outside, weeping." πρὸς
τῷ μνημείῳ ἔξω κλαίουσα is read by ABD^suppLNW, as against
πρὸς τὸ μνημεῖον κλαίουσα ἔξω of the rec. text. א has ἐν τῷ
μνημείῳ, which is inconsistent with ἔξω. Mary is not represented
by Jn. as having entered the tomb at all.

For the introductory ὡς οὖν . . . see on 4⁴⁰.

For κλαίειν, see above on 11³¹, where it is the verb used
of Mary's weeping at the tomb of Lazarus; an interesting
correspondence in connexion with the identity of Mary Magdalene with Mary of Bethany (see Introductory Note on 12¹⁻⁸)

ἔκλαιεν, παρέκυψεν εἰς τὸ μνημεῖον, 12. καὶ θεωρεῖ δύο ἀγγέλους ἐν

As she wept, she " peeped " into the tomb. For παρακύπτω
see on v. 5.

12. καὶ θεωρεῖ δύο ἀγγέλους κτλ., "and she notices (see on
2²³ and esp. v. 14 below) two angels in white " (ἐν λευκοῖς,
ἱματίοις being understood, the Greek idiom being the same
as the English) " sitting, one at the head, and one at the feet,
where the body of Jesus had lain."

All four Gospels agree in telling of an angelic appearance to
the women at the tomb, but there are discrepancies in the
various accounts. In Mk. 16⁵ the women " entering into the
tomb, saw a young man sitting on the right side, arrayed in a
white robe "; in Mt. 28²ᶠ· the women (apparently) see an
angel descending from heaven who rolls away the stone from
the tomb and sits upon it   As in Mk., he tells the women that
Jesus is risen, and has gone into Galilee.   In Lk. 24⁴, after the
women have entered the tomb and found it empty, " *two* men
stood by them in dazzling apparel," who remind them that
when Jesus " was yet in Galilee " He had predicted that He
would rise on the third day.   The Marcan saying about the
risen Lord having gone to Galilee is thus altered by Lk., who
mentions no Galilæan appearance, and follows a Jerusalem tradition.   It is noteworthy that " two men in white apparel "
are mentioned again by Lk. in Acts 1¹⁰, as appearing to the
apostles at the Ascension.   In Jn. we have " two angels in
white," who only ask Mary why she is weeping.   They do not
give any message or counsel, for Jesus Himself is immediately
seen by Mary.

It was a common belief that angels or celestial visitants
were clad in white.   Cf. Dan. 10⁵ εἷς ἐνδεδυμένος βύσσινα, and
Ezek. 9²; Rev. 15⁶ ἄγγελοι . . . ἐνδεδυμένοι λίνον καθαρὸν καὶ
λαμπρόν.   In *Enoch* lxxxvii. 2 mention is made of beings
coming forth from heaven " who were like white men."   Mk.
and Mt. only mention *one* angel, but Lk. and Jn. mention *two*.
The appearance of a *pair* of angels seems to be a not unusual
feature of what were believed to be heavenly visitations; *e.g.*
in 2 Macc. 3²⁶ *two* young men appeared to Heliodorus, " splen-
did in their apparel " (διαπρεπεῖς τὴν περιβολήν).   So, too, in
the *Apocalypse of Peter* (§ 3) *two* men suddenly appeared, καὶ
φωτεινὸν ἦν αὐτῶν ὅλον τὸ ἔνδυμα.   The development of legend
is well illustrated by the fanciful narrative which is found
in the *Gospel of Peter* of the appearances at the sepulchre.
First (§ 9) the soldiers saw " three men coming out of the
tomb, two of them supporting the other," *i.e.* two angels supporting Christ.   Then (§ 10) the heavens are opened and " a

λευκοῖς καθεζομένους, ἕνα πρὸς τῇ κεφαλῇ καὶ ἕνα πρὸς τοῖς ποσίν,
ὅπου ἔκειτο τὸ σῶμα τοῦ Ἰησοῦ. 13. καὶ λέγουσιν αὐτῇ ἐκεῖνοι
Γύναι, τί κλαίεις; λέγει αὐτοῖς ὅτι Ἦραν τὸν Κύριόν μου, καὶ οὐκ
οἶδα ποῦ ἔθηκαν αὐτόν. 14. ταῦτα εἰποῦσα ἐστράφη εἰς τὰ ὀπίσω,

man descended and entered the sepulchre "; and (§ 11) when
Mary and her companions look into the tomb "they see there
a young man sitting in the midst of the tomb, fair and clothed
with an exceeding bright robe," who speaks to them as in Mk.

That Mary reported having seen and addressed two persons
at the tomb, whom the evangelist calls " angels," is all that
is involved in the Johannine narrative. Lk. also tells of two
men, but Mk. of one man only. What really happened is not
possible now to determine. That the women saw some person
or persons at the tomb can hardly be doubted; and that they
were heavenly or angelic visitants was evidently the belief of
Mt. and, probably also, of Lk. and Jn. Latham supposes them
to have been members of the Essene sect who were accustomed
to wear white clothing, or " young men of the priestly school." [1]
But there is no sufficient evidence of this.

ἕνα πρὸς τῇ κεφαλῇ καὶ ἕνα πρὸς τοῖς ποσίν. Wetstein observes
that as the body of Jesus had hung between two thieves on
the Cross, so the place where His body had lain was guarded
between two angels; and he recalls the cherubim on the mercy-
seat (Ex. 25²², 1 Sam. 4⁴, Ps. 80¹, etc.). But there is no evidence
of such thoughts being those of the evangelist

13. καὶ (א a b d f g sah om. καί) λέγουσιν κτλ. All they say
is " Woman, why are you weeping ? " There is nothing in
the Johannine narrative of any counsel given by the watchers
at the tomb, or (except the use of the word " angels ") any hint
that they were not ordinary men. In the other Gospels, the
women are represented as being terrified when addressed by
the angels at the tomb; but in Jn. Mary shows no fear, nor
does she indicate by her demeanour that she has seen anything
unusual. She answers her questioners quite simply, by telling
them why she is in grief. The story, so far, has nothing of
the miraculous about it; and it probably represents a tradition
more primitive than that of the other Gospels, in that it may go
back to Mary herself

For γύναι as a mode of address, see on 2⁴.

Ἦραν τὸν κύριον κτλ., repeated from v. 2 with the significant
addition of μοῦ after κύριον.

οὐκ οἶδα, not οἴδαμεν as in v. 2, for the other women were
not with Mary on this, her second, visit to the tomb.

14. ταῦτα εἰποῦσα κτλ. So אABDNW⊖, but the rec. prefixes

[1] The Risen Master, pp. 417, 418.

καὶ θεωρεῖ τὸν Ἰησοῦν ἑστῶτα, καὶ οὐκ ᾔδει ὅτι Ἰησοῦς ἐστίν.

καί. The absence of connecting particles in vv. 14–18 is noteworthy.

For εἰς τὰ ὀπίσω cf. 6⁶⁶ 18⁶. Mary turned round, perhaps being half-conscious (as often happens) that some one was behind her.

καὶ θεωρεῖ τὸν Ἰησοῦν ἑστῶτα, "and notices Jesus standing." The two watchers in the tomb had been seated. θεωρεῖν (cf. v. 12, and see on 2²³) is the verb used in the promise to the disciples ὑμεῖς θεωρεῖτέ με (14¹⁹). Such "seeing" would be impossible for unbelievers; it was a vision possible only for faith.

καὶ οὐκ ᾔδει ὅτι Ἰησοῦς ἐστίν. She did not recognise Him. A similar thing in like words is told of the disciples on the lake (21⁴); and of the two on the way to Emmaus (Lk. 24¹⁶). The Marcan Appendix says of this latter incident that He was "manifested in another form" (ἐν ἑτέρᾳ μορφῇ, Mk. 16¹²). Cf. Mt. 28¹⁷, where "some doubted." See further on 21⁴.

This appearance of the Risen Lord to Mary is not mentioned by Lk., but the Marcan Appendix (Mk. 16⁹) agrees with the Fourth Gospel in mentioning it as the *first* manifestation of Jesus after His Resurrection. Cf. Mt. 28⁹· ¹⁰.

An essential difference between the Gospel stories of visions of the Risen Lord, and the stories widespread in all countries and in all times of visions of departed friends after death, is that all the Gospels lay stress on the empty tomb.[1] It was the actual body that had been buried which was revivified, although (as it seems) transfigured, and, so to speak, spiritualised. This must be borne in mind when the evangelical narratives of the Risen Jesus *speaking*, and *eating* (Lk. 24⁴³; cf. Jn. 21¹³ ¹⁵), and being *touched* (Lk 24³⁹, and perhaps Jn. 20²⁷) as well as *seen*, are examined critically. Such statements are difficult of credence, for no parallel cases are reported in ordinary human experience; but they must be taken in connexion with the repeated affirmations of the Gospels that the tomb of Jesus was empty, and that it was His *Body* and not only His *Spirit* which was manifested to the disciples. See also on v. 20.

The question has been asked, how did the evangelists believe the Risen Lord to have been *clothed*, not only when Mary saw Him in the garden, but when He manifested Himself to the assembled disciples (vv. 19, 26)? It is difficult to suppose (with Tholuck and others) that He appeared only in the loin-

---

[1] I have endeavoured to draw out this distinction in *Studia Sacra*, p. 122 f.

15. λέγει αὐτῇ Ἰησοῦς Γύναι, τί κλαίεις; τίνα ζητεῖς; ἐκείνη δοκοῦσα ὅτι ὁ κηπουρός ἐστιν, λέγει αὐτῷ Κύριε, εἰ σὺ ἐβάστασας αὐτόν, εἰπέ μοι ποῦ ἔθηκας αὐτόν, κἀγὼ αὐτὸν ἀρῶ. 16. λέγει αὐτῇ

cloth in which He had been crucified and buried. His appearances after death were more intense, indeed, than the appearances of dead men to their friends (for which there is some evidence); but just as in the latter case the eye of love clothes the vision in familiar garments, so it may have been in the more objective and more significant manifestations of the risen body of Jesus.

15. λέγει αὐτῇ Ἰησοῦς. ℵBLW om. the rec. ὁ before Ἰησοῦς (see on 1²⁹· ⁵⁰).

Γύναι, τί κλαίεις; This is a repetition of the question put to Mary (v. 13) by the watchers at the tomb. In like manner, in Mt. 28⁷· ¹⁰ the message given by the angel to the women is repeated by the risen Jesus, when they see Him. But, whether this be only a coincidence or no, in the Johannine story Jesus adds τίνα ζητεῖς; He knew whom she was seeking, and what was the cause of her grief, whereas there is nothing in vv. 11–13 to show that the watchers at the tomb understood her tears, or knew that she was a disciple of Jesus.

Mary does not recognise Jesus at once, nor do His first words tell her who He was. She thinks He may be the gardener, probably because at so early an hour the gardener was the most likely person to be met in the garden (see 19⁴¹). It is plain, however, that she does not find anything abnormal in the appearance or dress or voice of Him who speaks to her.

ὁ κηπουρός. The word does not occur again in the Greek Bible, but is common in the papyri (see Milligan *s.v.*).[1]

Κύριε (an ordinary title of respect), εἰ σὺ ἐβάστασας αὐτόν. "Sir, if *you* have stolen Him away." Her mind is so full of her quest, that she does not answer the question "For whom are you looking?" She assumes that every one must know who it is For βαστάζειν in the sense of "to steal," see on 12⁶.

εἰπέ μοι ποῦ ἔθηκας αὐτόν κτλ., "tell me where you have laid Him, and I will take Him away." She does not stay to consider if she would have strength by herself to remove the body to a fitting resting-place.

---

[1] E. C. Hoskyns finds a mystical meaning in the whole story: "The risen Lord is ὁ κηπουρός, for He is the Lord of the Garden, and once more He walks in His garden in the cool of the day, the early morning, and converses not with the fallen, but with the redeemed." Cf. Gen. 3⁸ (*J.T.S.*, April 1920, p. 215). The idea is worthy of Origen, but is too subtle to be convincing.

Ἰησοῦς Μαριάμ. στραφεῖσα ἐκείνη λέγει αὐτῷ Ἑβραϊστί Ῥαββουνεί (ὃ λέγεται Διδάσκαλε). 17. λέγει αὐτῇ Ἰησοῦς Μή μου ἅπτου,

16. λέγει αὐτῇ Ἰησοῦς. Here (see on v. 15) BD om ὁ before Ἰησοῦς, but ins. ℵANWΓΔ.

Μαριάμ So ℵBNW 1 33; but the rec., with ADΓΔΘ, has Μαρία. See on 19²⁵ for the spelling of the name.

Apparently Mary had turned her face away from Jesus towards the tomb, taking no interest in the gardener who gave her no help in her quest; for when she hears her name, she turns round again (στραφεῖσα) in amazement. Who is this that calls her "Mary"? The personal name, addressed to her directly, in well remembered tones, reveals to her in a flash who the speaker is.

λέγει αὐτῷ Ἑβραϊστί. So ℵBDNWΘ, although the rec., with AΓ, om. Ἑβραϊστί. Mary addresses Jesus in the Aramaic dialect which they were accustomed to use. See on 5² for Ἑβραϊστί.

Ῥαββουνεί (ὃ λέγεται Διδάσκαλε). The form *Rabboni*, "my Teacher," is found in N.T. here only and at Mk. 10⁵¹, but it is hardly distinguishable in meaning from *Rabbi*, the pronominal affix having no special force.[1] Jn. interprets it here for his Greek readers, as he interprets "Rabbi" (see on 1³⁸). It will be remembered that Martha and Mary were accustomed to speak of Jesus as *the Rabbi* ὁ διδάσκαλος (see 11²⁸), when talking to each other

An interpretative gloss is added here by ℵᶜᵃΘ and *fam.* 13, viz. καὶ προσέδραμεν ἅψασθαι αὐτοῦ, which appears also in Syr. sin. in the form "and she ran forward unto Him that she might draw near to (*or* to touch) Him." So also the Jerusalem Syriac. The gloss "et occurrit ut tangeret eum" is found in several Latin texts with Irish affinities; *e.g.* in the Book of Armagh, the Egerton MS. (*mm*), Cant., Stowe, and Rawl. G. 167. The idea behind the gloss is probably that Mary approached to clasp the Lord's feet in respect and homage; cf. Mt. 28⁹ where it is said of the women that "they took hold of His feet, and worshipped Him."

17. This verse must be compared with Mt. 28⁹· ¹⁰ where, again, the Risen Lord is seen by Mary Magdalene and speaks to her and her companion. In that passage the women, returning from the tomb to tell the disciples of the angel's message, are at once in fear and joy. Jesus greets them by saying Χαίρετε. They clasp His feet in worship. He then tells them not to fear, Μὴ φοβεῖσθε, and adds ὑπάγετε ἀπαγγείλατε

[1] Burkitt observes (*Christian Beginnings*, p. 45) that Jael said *Ribboni* to Sisera, according to the Aramaic Targum (Judg. 4¹⁸).

τοῖς ἀδελφοῖς μου ἵνα ἀπέλθωσιν εἰς τὴν Γαλιλαίαν, κἀκεῖ με ὄψονται. This almost reproduces the words of the angel in v. 7, with the significant change of μαθηταῖς into ἀδελφοῖς. Only here in the Gospels (Jn. 20¹⁷, Mt. 28¹⁰) is Jesus represented as speaking of His disciples as " my brethren." Cf. Heb. 2¹¹· ¹² (quoting Ps. 22²²).

It is likely that the account in Mt. 28⁹· ¹⁰ of the appearance of Jesus to the Maries was based on the lost conclusion of Mk.; for Mt. 28¹⁻⁸ is plainly an amplified version of the simpler Mk. 16¹⁻⁸. The phrase " tell to my brethren " was probably in Mk.'s story, and we have already seen that Jn. knew Mk.¹, whose narrative he corrects, when he thinks it necessary. In this instance, the message sent to the disciples is not, as in Mk. and Mt., that they should go to Galilee, where they would see their Risen Master. Jn. represents the message quite differently. It is : " Say to them, I go up to my Father."

This expression ἀναβαίνω πρὸς τὸν πατέρα μου is only another form of the words spoken so often by Jesus, ὑπάγω πρὸς τὸν πάτερα (16¹⁰ ; cf. 7³³ 16⁵), or πορεύομαι πρὸς τὸν πατέρα (14¹²· ²⁸ 16²⁸). He had warned the disciples repeatedly that He would return to the Father who had sent Him. The time for this had not been reached on the day of the Resurrection, οὔπω γὰρ ἀναβέβηκα πρὸς τὸν πατέρα, but it was near. ἀναβαίνω πρὸς τὸν πατέρα. It is said for the last time.

The term " Ascension " *for us* indicates the climax of the earthly life of Christ, but ἀναβαίνειν, ἀνάβασις, are common Greek words, which at first were not always used of the Ascension of Christ, still less appropriated to it. They are not used of the Ascension in the Synoptists (Lk. 24⁵¹ has ἀνεφέρετο, while [Mk.] 16¹⁹ has ἀνελήφθη). ἀναβαίνειν is thus used in Eph. 4⁸, which is a quotation from Ps. 68¹⁸, but Paul does not use the verb again of the ascending Christ. In Acts 2³⁴ we have οὐ γὰρ Δαβὶδ ἀνέβη εἰς τοὺς οὐρανούς, which contains an allusion to the fact that Christ did thus " go up." But, apart from these, the only other places in N.T. where ἀναβαίνειν is thus used, are Jn. 6⁶² (see note, *in loc.*) and the present passage. Barnabas (§ 15) employs the verb thus, and so does Justin (*Tryph.* 38) ; but Justin also uses ἀνέλευσις (*Apol.* i. 26) and ἄνοδος (*Tryph.* 82) of the Ascension of Christ. It was not until the days of Creed-making that the Church settled down to ἀναβαίνειν, ἀνάβασις, as the technical terms for Christ's ascending. We miss the point of the employment of ἀναβαίνειν in the present verse if we do not treat it as an ordinary verb for " going up," which would be recognised by the disciples

¹ Introd., pp. xcvi ff.

as practically equivalent to ὑπάγειν or πορεύεσθαι often used by Jesus when predicting His departure.[1]

Thus the message which Mary was bidden to give to the disciples would recall to them words such as those of 14[2, 3]. Jesus was going to the Father's house, where He would prepare a place for them. It is remarkable that the form of the message is like that of Mt. 28[10] (probably based on the lost conclusion of Mk.), although there the place where He is to see His disciples again is not heaven but Galilee (cf. Mk. 14[28]). Lk. 24[6], as has been already said, alters the Marcan and Matthæan tradition here, by substituting for the promise of a meeting in Galilee, the words μνήσθητε ὡς ἐλάλησεν ὑμῖν ἔτι ὢν ἐν τῇ Γαλιλαίᾳ, λέγων, that the Son of Man must die and rise again, etc. Abbott's inference from this comparison is that " an expression mis-understood by Mk. and Mt. as meaning *Galilee,* and omitted by Lk. because he could not understand it at all, was under-stood by Jn. to mean *My Father's place, i e.* Paradise."[2] This is precarious reasoning, but at any rate it is certain that Jn. (*a*) was aware of the Matthæan (? Marcan) tradition and (*b*) that he corrected it, bringing the message into corre-spondence with a saying of Jesus which he has previously recorded more than once.

Attention must now be directed to the words Μή μου ἅπτου, which (according to all extant texts) Jesus addressed to Mary, His reason being " for I have not yet ascended to My Father." It is not said explicitly in this chapter that Jesus was ever *touched* by His disciples after He was risen, although it is suggested both in v. 22 and in v. 27. In the latter passage, Thomas is actually invited to touch the Lord's wounded side (although it is not said that he did so), just as in Lk. 24[39], Jesus says ψηλαφήσατέ με to the assembled disciples. The only *explicit* statement in the Gospels of the Risen Christ being touched is Mt. 28[9]. Nevertheless Lk. 24[39] and Jn. 20[27] sufficiently indicate that, in the judgment of the evangelists, it was possible to touch Him, and that He invited such experi-ment to be made. (See further on v. 20.)

Hence " Touch me not, *for* I have not yet ascended," is difficult of interpretation, inasmuch as within a week at any rate, and before His final manifestation at His departure, Jesus had challenged the test of touch. We can hardly suppose that Jn. means us to believe that in the interval between v. 17 and v. 27 the conditions of the Risen Life of Jesus had so changed that what was unsuitable on the first occasion became suitable

---

[1] Origen, twice at least (*Comm.* 285, 357), substitutes πορεύομαι for ἀναβαίνω when quoting Jn. 20[17].

[2] *E.B.* 1770.

on the second. And there is the further difficulty, that as the words μή μου ἅπτου οὔπω γὰρ κτλ. stand, it is implied that to "touch" Jesus would be easier *after* His Ascension than before. The gloss *et occurrit ut tangeret eum*, which is inserted before *noli me tangere* in some texts (see on v. 16), shows that the primitive interpretation of the words implied a physical *touching*, and not merely a spiritual *drawing near*. The parallel Mt. 28[10] confirms this. Accordingly, to give to the repulse, "Touch me not," a spiritual meaning, as if it meant that freedom of access between the disciple and the Master would not be complete until the Resurrection had been consummated in the Ascension and the Holy Spirit had been sent, seems over-subtle. Yet this is what the words must mean if μή μου ἅπτου is part of the genuine text of Jn.

Meyer cited a conjectural emendation of these words (by Gersdorf and Schulthess) which he dismissed without discussion, but for which nevertheless there is a good deal to be said. We have drawn attention already to the parallel passage, Mt. 28[10], but there is yet another point to be noted. By all the Synoptists the *fear* of the women at the tomb is emphasised. ἐφοβοῦντο γάρ (Mk. 16[8]), although the νεανίσκος had said μὴ ἐκθαμβεῖσθε (Mk. 16[6]). They were ἔμφοβοι (Lk 24[5]). And in Mt. 28[5, 10] not only the angel, but Jesus Himself prefaced His message to the disciples by saying to the women (after they had clasped His feet) μὴ φοβεῖσθε. Now in our texts of Jn. there is no hint that Mary Magdalene (who is the only woman mentioned here by this evangelist) was frightened at all. She is without fear, apparently, when she recognises the Lord. The parallel passage, Mt. 28[9], would suggest (as the gloss here does) that she cast herself at His feet in awestruck homage. We should expect here (as in Mk., Mt.) that Jesus would encourage her by forbidding her to be afraid. Instead of this, we find the enigmatic words μή μου ἅπτου. But if these words are a corruption of μὴ πτόου, as might very well be the case, "be not affrighted," all is clear This is the verb used of the fright of the disciples in Lk. 24[37] (πτοηθέντες), caused as Lk. says by their idea that they saw a spirit. And μὴ πτόου would come exactly where μὴ φοβεῖσθε comes in Mt. 28[10], viz. after the Lord's feet have been clasped in homage and fear. The sequence, then, is easy "Be not affrighted, for I have not get gone up to my Father ": I am still with you, as you knew me on earth; I have not yet resumed the awful majesty of heaven. Do not fear: carry my message to the disciples, as in the old days.

The best supported reading is μή μου ἅπτου, but B has μὴ ἅπτου μου, and two cursives (47[ev] and *d*[scr]) omit μου alto-

οὔπω γὰρ ἀναβέβηκα πρὸς τὸν Πατέρα· πορεύου δὲ πρὸς τοὺς ἀδελφούς μου καὶ εἰπὲ αὐτοῖς Ἀναβαίνω πρὸς τὸν Πατέρα μου καὶ Πατέρα
ὑμῶν καὶ Θεόν μου καὶ Θεὸν ὑμῶν. 18. ἔρχεται Μαριὰμ ἡ Μαγδαληνὴ ἀγγέλλουσα τοῖς μαθηταῖς ὅτι Ἑώρακα τὸν Κύριον, καὶ ταῦτα
εἶπεν αὐτῇ.

gether. If the text were originally μὴ πτόον, an easy corruption
would be μὴ ἅπτου, and then μου would naturally be added
either before or after ἅπτου to make the sense clear.

οὔπω γὰρ ἀναβέβηκα, "for I have not yet gone up . . ."
i.e. taken my final departure. For Jn., a week at the least
(v. 27, and see on 21[1]) elapsed between the Resurrection and
that last of the manifestations of the Risen Christ which we
call the Ascension. He says nothing of the interval of forty
days for which our only authority is Acts 1[3]. But Jn., nevertheless, uses language (6[62]) which implies not only that the final
departure of Christ was a startling and wonderful incident,
but that it was visible, in this agreeing with Lk. 24[50-52], Acts
1[9]; cf. Appx. to Mk. (16[19]).

Ἀναβαίνω πρὸς τὸν πατέρα μου. That was what He had said
often before (in effect); but now He adds καὶ πατέρα ὑμῶν. His
Father was their Father too, although there was a difference
in the relation (see on 2[16]); and of this He would remind them
now. Observe He does not say "*Our* Father."

καὶ θεόν μου. So He said "My God" on the Cross (Mk.
15[34]); cf. Rev. 3[2]. He is still Man, and so Paul repeatedly has
the expression "the God and Father of our Lord Jesus Christ"
(Rom. 15[6], etc.). And His God is the God also of His disciples
—the only God.

18. ἔρχεται Μαριὰμ ἡ Μαγδ. ἀγγέλλουσα κτλ. אAB have
ἀγγέλλουσα, as against the rec. ἀπαγγελλουσα (NΘ). W has
ἀναγγέλλουσα.

Lk. 24[11] and [Mk.] 16[11] say that the disciples did not believe
the report of the women. Mt. does not tell whether the message
to the disciples was delivered or no.

ὅτι (*recitantis*) Ἑώρακα τὸν κύριον. This was the first thing
Mary said before she gave her message (cf. v. 25). אBN *a g*
support ἑώρακα, as against the rec. ἑώρακε (with ADLΔΘ).

For ὁ κύριος as a title used by Mary, see on 4[1].

The appearance to Mary is not mentioned by Paul in his
summary of the visions of the Risen Christ (1 Cor. 15[5-7]). It is
the appearances to the leaders of the future Church (Peter and
James), and to the assembled disciples, that were regarded as
the basis for the Church's faith in the Resurrection.

19. Οὔσης οὖν ὀψίας τῇ ἡμέρᾳ ἐκείνῃ τῇ μιᾷ σαββάτων, καὶ τῶν
θυρῶν κεκλεισμένων ὅπου ἦσαν οἱ μαθηταὶ διὰ τὸν φόβον τῶν

First appearance of the Risen Christ to the disciples: their commission and their authority (vv. 19–23)

19. οὔσης οὖν ὀψίας. This appearance is described also in
Lk. 24³⁶f·. Lk. places it after the return of the two from
Emmaus, who reported to the apostles their meeting with the
Risen Jesus; this would necessarily be late in the evening
(cf. Lk. 24²⁹), probably about 8 p m. (see for ὀψία on 6¹⁶).
The Appendix to Mark (16¹⁴) states that He appeared to the
Eleven " while they sat at meat." It is not improbable that
they were assembled in the room where the Last Supper was
eaten (cf. also Acts 1¹³), and where Jesus had spoken the
discourses of farewell (Jn. 14–16).

It would appear from Lk. 24³⁶ that the two Emmaus disciples were present, as well as the apostles, and probably
some others also (Lk. 24³³). This is not necessarily inconsistent with Jn., although He speaks only of " the disciples,"
for μαθηταί often includes others besides the inner circle of
apostles (see on 2²). But in the later chapters of Jn. οἱ μαθηταί
generally stands for the Eleven, and the Lord's manifestation of
Himself to them in particular, as had been promised (16¹⁶), is
mentioned as fundamentally important in 1 Cor. 15⁵. Whether
others were present or not, it is His appearance to the apostles
on this occasion that is treated as of special significance; and
the words of His commission in v. 21 are most naturally limited
to those who were commissioned by Him as " apostles " at
the beginning of His ministry.[1]

τῇ ἡμέρᾳ ἐκείνῃ, a favourite phrase in Jn.; cf. 1³⁹ 5⁹ 11⁵³
14²⁰ 16²³· ²⁶, and see on 1²⁹ for Jn.'s precision in noting dates.
He adds here, accordingly, τῇ μιᾷ σαββάτων. The rec. text
has τῶν before σαββάτων as in v. 1, but אABIL om. τῶν here.

τῶν θυρῶν κεκλεισμένων . . . διὰ τὸν φόβον τῶν Ἰουδαίων. The
rumour that the tomb was empty had spread (as is indicated in
Mt. 28¹¹), and the Jewish leaders were doubtless suspicious
of any gathering of the disciples of Jesus For the phrase
τὸν φόβον τῶν Ἰουδ., cf. 7¹³. It is repeated at v. 26 that the
doors of the room were shut at the time of the meeting a week
later.

ὅπου ἦσαν οἱ μαθηταί. Only ten of the original Twelve were
present (v. 24); Lk. 24³³ has οἱ ἕνδεκα. See on 2² for οἱ μαθηταί
used absolutely.

[1] The final commission, as described in Mt. 28¹⁶, would seem to be
addressed to the Eleven only ; cf. also Mt. 16¹⁴ -¹⁶.

Ἰουδαίων, ἦλθεν ὁ Ἰησοῦς καὶ ἔστη εἰς τὸ μέσον, καὶ λέγει αὐτοῖς

The rec. adds συνηγμένοι (NΘ), but אABDW om. Perhaps it was inserted by scribes because of its occurrence in the words of the promise, Mt. 18²⁰.

ἦλθεν ὁ Ἰησοῦς. No attempt is made to explain *how* He came.

καὶ ἔστη εἰς τὸ μέσον (repeated v. 26). Lk. 24³⁶ has the more usual ἐν μέσῳ αὐτῶν; but εἰς τὸ μέσον after a verb of motion is quite correct (cf. Mk. 3³, Lk. 6⁸), and has classical authority (*e.g.* Xenophon, *Cyropæd.* IV i. 1, στὰς εἰς τὸ μέσον).

Justin (*Tryph.* 106) finds in Jesus standing in the midst of His brethren (cf. v. 17) a fulfilment of Ps. 22²² (quoted Heb. 2¹²),

> διηγήσομαι τὸ ὄνομά σου τοῖς ἀδελφοῖς μου,
> ἐν μέσῳ ἐκκλησίας ὑμνήσω σε.

καὶ λέγει αὐτοῖς Εἰρήνη ὑμῖν. These words are found also in most texts of Lk. 24³⁶, but being omitted there by D *a b e ff₂ l r* are described by Hort as a "Western non-interpolation" in that place. If that judgment is correct, scribes have brought the words into Lk.'s text from Jn., where there is no doubt of their genuineness. It is, however, possible that the words are part of the original text of Lk.; and in that case they furnish an additional illustration of the use of Lk.'s tradition by Jn. at this point (see v. 20). Throughout their accounts of the appearance of the Risen Jesus to the apostles, it is clear that Jn. and Lk. are following the same tradition, while Jn. does not hesitate to correct and amplify or reduce the current version of it (as found in Lk.) at several points.

Εἰρήνη ὑμῖν is the ordinary Eastern salutation on entering a room, and is so used (Lk. 24³⁶, Jn 20¹⁹· ²⁶). But in v. 21 εἰρήνη ὑμῖν is solemnly repeated before the apostles receive their commission, and may carry an allusion to the parting gift of peace in 14²⁷.

20. Here, again, we must compare Lk. 24⁴⁰ καὶ τοῦτο εἰπὼν ἔδειξεν αὐτοῖς τὰς χεῖρας καὶ τοὺς πόδας, which also Hort regards as a "Western non-interpolation," for these words in Lk. are omitted by D *a b e ff l r* Syr. cur. They are identical with the words in Jn. 20²⁰, except that in Jn. we have τὴν πλευράν, while in Lk. we have τοὺς πόδας. Jn. being the only evangelist who mentions the piercing of the Lord's side (19³⁴), it is natural that τὴν πλευράν should not appear in Lk.; but if (as Hort supposes) the scribes of Lk. took over the words in question from Jn., they must have deliberately substituted τοὺς πόδας for τὴν πλευράν.

The words τοὺς πόδας in Lk. 24³⁹· ⁴⁰ provide the only

Εἰρήνη ὑμῖν. 20. καὶ τοῦτο εἰπὼν ἔδειξεν καὶ τὰς χεῖρας καὶ τὴν

Biblical evidence for the belief that the Lord's feet as well as His hands were nailed to the Cross. In the narratives of the Crucifixion all that is said is " they crucified Him ": but it is not specified whether His hands and feet were *tied* or *nailed* to the Cross (both methods being common). Both Lk. and Jn. agree that His *hands* were marked, and Jn. speaks of " the print of the nails " in them (v. 25); but Jn. says nothing of the feet having been nailed. Pseudo-Peter, in like manner, speaks of drawing out the nails from the hands of Jesus, after He had died (§ 6), but does not mention the feet. So also Cyril of Jerusalem says nothing of the nailing of the feet, while he finds a symbolic meaning in the nailing of the hands (*Cat.* xiii. 38). The earliest reference (excepting Lk. 24[39, 40]) to the piercing of the feet is in Justin's *Trypho* (§ 97), who claims Ps. 22[16-18] as a literal prophecy of the Crucifixion. Having regard to the language of Jn. 20[20, 25], as well as to the second-century tradition of Pseudo-Peter, it would seem as if the tradition of Lk. 24[39] [[40]] rests on the early application of " they pierced my hands and my feet " (Ps. 22[16]) to the Crucifixion of Jesus rather than on the testimony of an eye-witness. Such testimony we believe to lie behind the narrative of the Fourth Gospel (cf. 19[35]); and hence it is probable that the Lord's feet were *not* marked by the print of nails. Jn. in 20[20] is (in our view) deliberately correcting the account given in Lk. 24[39, 40] (for we take Lk. 24[40] to be as original as Lk. 24[39]), so as to bring it into correspondence with the facts.

τὰς χεῖρας καὶ τὴν πλευρὰν αὐτοῖς is the best attested reading (אABD) as against the rec. αὐτοῖς τὰς χεῖρας καὶ τὴν πλευρὰν αὐτοῦ.

Jn. says only that Jesus *showed* them His hands and His side; Lk. goes further and says that He invited them to dispel their doubts by handling and touching Him (ψηλαφήσατέ με, Lk. 24[39]); representing the disciples as disturbed and terrified by His sudden appearance. Jn. does not say that they touched Him, or that they were asked to do so; this omission being probably designed, so as to correct an over-statement in Lk.

A later tradition as to this incident, preserved in Ignatius (*Smyrn.* 3) must now be cited. Ignatius writes: " I know and believe that He was in the flesh even after the Resurrection, and when He came to Peter and his company (πρὸς τοὺς περὶ Πέτρον), He said to them, *Take, handle me, and see that I am not a bodiless demon* (λάβετε ψηλαφήσατέ με, καὶ ἴδετε ὅτι οὐκ εἰμὶ δαιμόνιον ἀσώματον). And straightway they touched Him (αὐτοῦ ἥψαντο), and they believed, being mixed with

πλευρὰν αὐτοῖς. ἐχάρησαν οὖν οἱ μαθηταὶ ἰδόντες τὸν Κύριον.
21. εἶπεν οὖν αὐτοῖς ὁ Ἰησοῦς πάλιν Εἰρήνη ὑμῖν· καθὼς ἀπέσταλκέν

(κραθέντες) His flesh and blood. . . . And after His Resurrection, He ate and drank with them as one in the flesh, although
spiritually He was united with the Father." Jerome states
that this version of the story of the appearance of Jesus comes
from the apocryphal Gospel to the Hebrews (see *Catal. Script.
Eccl.* § 16), and it may be so (see Lightfoot on Ignat. *Smyrn.* 3).
In any case, it is dependent on Lk. 24³⁹⁻⁴³, and amplifies Lk.'s
account in particular by stating explicitly that Jesus was
touched (see on v. 17 above), and by adding that He drank as
well as ate with the disciples.

The simplicity and restraint of Jn.'s account of this incident
are not only in marked contrast with the story as Ignatius
has it, but are also a feature of Jn.'s narrative as compared with
Lk.'s. Jn. does not speak in the Gospel itself of the Risen
Lord *eating* (but cf. the Appendix 21¹³ and the note there), or
explicitly of His being touched (see above on vv. 14, 17).

ἐχάρησαν οὖν οἱ μαθηταὶ ἰδόντες τὸν κύριον. This was the
fulfilment of the promise to the apostles, πάλιν δὲ ὄψομαι
ὑμᾶς καὶ χαρήσεται ὑμῶν ἡ καρδία (16²²). Lk. 24⁴¹ says that
the disciples " disbelieved for joy," but he states at v. 37 that
they were terrified when they saw Jesus standing in their midst.
Of their *fear*, there is no hint in Jn. This is the first occurrence
in Jn. of ὁ κύριος being used of Jesus in the direct narrative
(see on 4¹, where the apparent exceptions are mentioned). The
evangelist is thinking of his Master, not as He moved about
in the days of His earthly ministry, but as risen and about to
ascend to His glory, *i.e.* as "the LORD."

21. εἶπεν οὖν αὐτοῖς. The rec. adds ὁ Ἰησοῦς with ΑΒΝΓΔΘ,
but om. אDW.

For πάλιν, see on 1³⁵. For the repeated εἰρήνη ὑμῖν, see on
v. 19.

καθὼς . . . κἀγώ. For this constr., see on 6⁵⁷ (cf. 10¹⁵).
Here there can be no doubt that the sentence means " As the
Father hath sent me, so I send you." When He commissioned
His disciples for their ministry before His final departure, He
reproduced the words of the great Prayer which had been said
in their hearing : καθὼς ἐμὲ ἀπέστειλας εἰς τὸν κόσμον, κἀγὼ
ἀπέστειλα αὐτοὺς εἰς τὸν κόσμον (17¹⁸). These words primarily
had reference to the original choice of the twelve " apostles "
(see note on 17¹⁸), viz. ἐποίησεν δώδεκα . . . ἵνα ἀποστέλλῃ
αὐτοὺς κηρύσσειν κτλ. (Mk. 3¹⁴), but they had a forward
reference also to their final commission.

The constr. καθὼς . . . κἀγώ at 15⁹ and 17¹⁸ (which are

parallel in form to the present passage) has to do in both cases
with a comparison of the Father's relation to Christ and Christ's
relation to the *apostles*, not to the general body of disciples.
It is natural to interpret the καθὼς . . . κἀγώ here as involving
the same comparison, and therefore to take the commission
here as entrusted to the *apostles*. Others may have been
present (see on v. 19), but the final commission was not
specifically given to any but the inner circle, who had been
long since selected as those who were to be " sent forth."

καθὼς ἀπέσταλκέν με ὁ πατήρ. This is the constant theme
of the Johannine Christ when speaking of His authority. He
is, pre-eminently, ὁ ἀπόστολος (Heb. 3¹); for God the Father
has sent Him (cf. 3¹⁷).

κἀγὼ πέμπω ὑμᾶς. So אᶜᵇABD²ΝΓΔΘ against אᶜᵃD*L 33
ἀποστέλλω, but no distinction can be drawn between πέμπω
and ἀποστέλλω (see on 3¹⁷ above).

The sending of the apostles by Christ was (in a deep sense,
although not with exact correspondence; see on 6⁵⁷) like the
sending of Christ by the Father. He had told them at the
Last Supper that whoever received those whom He sent received *Him*, while those who received *Him* received the Father
that sent Him (13²⁰). Language of this kind is addressed in
the Fourth Gospel to the apostles *alone*; and it is difficult,
in the face of the parallel passages that have been cited, to
suppose that in this verse, and here only, the evangelist means
us to understand that the great commission was given to all
the disciples who were present, alike and in the same degree.
It is quite just to describe this verse as "the Charter
of the Christian Church " (Westcott), but the Charter was
addressed in the first instance to the leaders of the Church,
and not to all its members, present and future, without
discrimination.

The question as to who were the first recipients of the gift
and the authority conferred by Jesus in vv. 22, 23, has been
much debated in connexion with modern controversies as to
Confession and Absolution;[1] but the exegete must ask one
question only, viz., "What did the evangelist intend his readers
to believe ? " We must not assume, because Lk. 24³³ tells
that others were with the Eleven on the evening of the Resurrection just before the Lord manifested Himself, that therefore
Jn. in his report of the same incident implies either (*a*) that
others beside the apostles were present when Jesus began to
speak, or (*b*) that His commission was not addressed exclusively
to the apostles even if others were there. On the contrary, the

[1] See Report of Fulham Conference on *Confession and Absolution*,
pp. vii, 109.

μὲ ὁ Πατήρ, κἀγὼ πέμπω ὑμᾶς. 22. καὶ τοῦτο εἰπὼν ἐνεφύσησεν

language used by Jn. seems, as has been said, distinctly to
imply that the commission was given to apostles alone.

This was the interpretation put upon Jn. 20²⁰⁻²³ by the
earliest Christian writers who allude to these verses. Justin
(*Tryph.* 106) ignores the presence of any but apostles. Origen
(*de princip.* i. iii. 2 and *Comm. in Jn.* 388) and Cyprian (*de
unit.* 4, *Epist.* lxxiii. 6) say explicitly that *Accipe spiritum
sanctum,* etc., was addressed to the apostles. The Liturgy of
St. Mark (which may be as early as the second century) is
equally explicit.[1] I do not know, indeed, of any early writer
who takes a different view. The words of Cyprian (*Epist.*
lxxv. 16) *in solos apostolos insufflauit Christus,* etc., express the
accepted view as to the persons to whom the Lord said " Take
the Holy Spirit." It would be going much further to claim
that Cyprian's subsequent *inference* was justified, for he proceeds
to say: " potestas ergo peccatorum remittendorum apostolis
data est, *et ecclesiis quas illi a Christo missi constiterunt, et
episcopis qui eis ordinatione uicaria successerunt.*" The words
which are italicised need not necessarily be accepted by those
who recognise that Jn.'s narrative is a narrative of a commission
given in the first instance to the apostles alone.

22. καὶ τοῦτο εἰπὼν ἐνεφύσησεν κτλ. " He breathed upon
them." ἐμφυσᾶν does not occur again in N.T., but it is the
verb used Gen. 2⁷ (cf. Wisd. 15¹¹) of God " breathing " into
Adam's nostrils the breath of life. So in Ezek. 37⁹ " breathe
on these slain that they may live " is addressed to the life-
giving Spirit. Milligan quotes a parallel from a second or
third-century papyrus, ὁ ἐνφυσήσας πνεῦμα ἀνθρώποις εἰς ζωήν.

The language of this verse goes back to Gen. 2⁷, it being
implied that as the life of Adam was due to the " breath " of
God, so the gift of spiritual life to the apostles was imparted
by the " breath " of Christ. (Cf. 1 Cor. 15⁴⁵.) The Johannine
doctrine is that this quickening power of His spirit could
not be released until the " glorification," *i.e.* the death, of
Jesus (see on 7³⁷⁻³⁹); and in strict accordance with this, Jn.
represents the Spirit as given and received on the day of His
Resurrection. It is not that we have here a foretaste, as it
were, of a fuller outpouring of the Spirit which was manifested
at Pentecost (*arrha Pentecostes,* as Bengel calls it); but that,
for Jn., the action and the words of Jesus here are a complete
fulfilment of the promise of the Paraclete. As has been said
on 16²³ (where see note), there is nothing in the Fourth Gospel
inconsistent with the story of the Pentecostal effusion (Acts 2¹ᶠ·);

[1] See Brightman, *Eastern Liturgies,* p. 116.

καὶ λέγει αὐτοῖς Λάβετε Πνεῦμα Ἅγιον. 23. ἄν τινων ἀφῆτε τὰς
ἀμαρτίας ἀφέωνται αὐτοῖς· ἄν τινων κρατῆτε κεκράτηνται.

but for Jn. the critical day, when the Spirit was not only
promised, but given, is not Pentecost (as with Lk.) but the day
of the Resurrection.   We cannot distinguish here, any more
than at 7³⁹, between πνεῦμα and τὸ πνεῦμα.

Λάβετε πνεῦμα ἅγιον. The gift is freely offered, but that it
may be " received " demands a responsive effort on the part
of him to whom it is offered. Cf. τὸ πνεῦμα . . . ὃ ὁ κόσμος
οὐ δύναται λαβεῖν (14¹⁷). An unspiritual man could not
assimilate the gift. Λάβετε, τοῦτό ἐστιν τὸ σῶμά μου (Mk.
14²²) does not mean that the sacramental gift can operate
automatically, but that it is offered freely. So in the Acts
(8¹⁵. ¹⁷. ¹⁹ 10⁴⁷) λαμβάνειν πνεῦμα ἅγιον occurs several times, but
always the "taking" implies a certain disposition on the part
of him who takes.

For πνεῦμα ἅγιον, see on 14²⁶.

23. ἄν τινων ἀφῆτε τὰς ἀμαρτίας ἀφέωνται αὐτοῖς. ἄν is used,
as often, for ἐάν. ἀφέωνται is the reading of ℵᶜADL, as
against the rec. ἀφίενται. B* has ἀφείονται. ἀφιέναι in the
sense of " forgive " (sin) does not appear elsewhere in the
Fourth Gospel, but cf. 1 Jn. 2¹² ἀφέωνται ὑμῖν αἱ ἁμαρτίαι.
In the Synoptists, Jesus declares to individuals " thy sins are
forgiven " (Mk. 2⁵ and parallels, Lk. 7⁴⁸) ; but here He
seemingly commits, to those to whom He had imparted His
Spirit, authority to use the like words.

" Whose soever sins you forgive, they are forgiven unto
them."   The meaning of this passage *in its context* must be
sought quite apart from the inferences that have been drawn
from it in later ages.   As it stands, it is the parting commission
of Jesus to the apostles, to whom He had previously promised
the Holy Spirit, and to whom He had now imparted that
Divine gift.   Jn. says nothing about the authority of those who
received it to impart the Spirit in their turn to others.   That
may be a legitimate inference, but it is an *inference* for the
validity of which we must seek evidence elsewhere.

That the apostles interpreted their evangelical mission as
giving them authority to hand it on is, indeed, not doubtful.
The terms of their commission as described in Mt. 28¹⁹. ²⁰
(cf. [Mk.] 16¹⁵) imply that it was to last " to the end of the
world," the apostolate being established in permanence.
Clement of Rome, whose Epistle is contemporary with the
Fourth Gospel, expresses the accepted view: " Jesus Christ
was sent forth from God . . . the apostles are from Christ
. . . preaching everywhere, they appointed their firstfruits,

when they had proved them by the Spirit, to be bishops and
deacons to them that should believe" (*Clem. Rom.* 42). And
it would appear in like manner that, as early as the time of
Origen [1] at any rate, the bishops were regarded as having
succeeded to the powers of binding and loosing committed to
the apostles in Mt. 18¹⁸.

But, whether these developments were legitimate or not,
we are here concerned only with the meaning of the commission
to the apostles as recorded in vv. 22, 23; and confining our-
selves strictly to this, we start from the presupposition—common
to Jews and Christians—that no one can "forgive" sin but
God (Mk. 2⁷). But God is always ready to forgive (1 Jn. 1⁹);
and the assurance of God's forgiveness can always be given
confidently to repentant sinners. This assurance may be
given by any one; it needs no authority to give it, for it is a
fundamental principle of the Gospel. But, then, no one can
give this assurance in an individual case, without being certain
that this individual sinner is, indeed, repentant in his heart.
And to be sure of this, he who says "thy sins *are* forgiven"
must be able to read men's hearts. Jesus claimed that *He*
could do this : "the Son of Man hath power on earth to forgive
sins" (Mk. 2¹⁰). Of this the explanation is found in Jn. 3³⁴,
"He whom God hath sent speaketh the words of God, for
He giveth not the Spirit by measure." To Jesus, and to Him
alone, was the Spirit given in its fulness, and so He alone could
infallibly discern the secrets of the human heart (Jn. 2²⁵). He
could say, therefore, "thy sins are forgiven thee" (Mk. 2⁵)
with a complete authority.

Now a main theme of the Fourth Gospel is that Jesus
promised that He would send (14¹⁶ 16⁷⁻¹³), and did in fact impart (20²²), the Spirit to the apostles. It was not confined to
them, but was for every believing disciple (7³⁸) But it was
more largely promised, and more explicitly bestowed, on them
than on any one else. And it was in the power of this Spirit of
God that they were authorised not only to proclaim universally
the message of God's forgiveness (Acts 10⁴³), but to say in
individual cases "thy sins are forgiven." Among the gifts
of the Spirit was the gift of insight (cf. διακρίσεις πνευμάτων,
1 Cor. 12¹⁰ and see Jn. 16⁸). Hence the words λάβετε πνεῦμα
ἅγιον govern the words giving the apostles authority to forgive
or not to forgive. In so far as the Spirit was theirs, so far was
their judgment of men's hearts a true judgment.

Lk. does not tell of so explicit an authority being conferred
upon the apostles; but the parting commission for him too is
"that repentance and remission of sins should be preached to

---

[1] *Comm. in Mt.* xii. 14 (Lommatzsch, iii. 156).

all the nations "; and the authority is described as "the promise of the Father " which is presently to be granted (Lk. 24⁴⁷·⁴⁹). The parting commission to the Eleven in Mt. 28¹⁸f. has one point of similarity with Jn. 20²³, viz. that it rests the command to make disciples upon the universal authority of Christ. " All authority hath been given to me in heaven and on earth. Go ye *therefore*," etc. Their power as evangelists would rest upon their being *His* disciples; just as in Jn. 22²³ their power of absolving is made dependent upon their assimilation of *His* Spirit. It is to be observed that Jn. makes no mention of any commission to *baptize*.

The passages in Mt., however, which are specially recalled by Jn. 22²³ are Mt. 16¹⁹ 18¹⁸, in both of which we find " What things soever you shall bind (δήσητε) on earth shall be bound in heaven ; and what things soever you shall loose (λύσητε) on earth shall be loosed in heaven." In Mt. 16¹⁹ these words are addressed to Peter, as having the keys of the kingdom of heaven; in Mt. 18¹⁸ they are (seemingly) addressed to the Twelve. To " bind " and to " loose " are Rabbinical expressions signifying to " prohibit " and to " permit " (many illustrations are given in Lightfoot's *Hor. Hebr.* on Mt. 16¹⁹) [1]; and the use of these verbs would suggest to Jews a form of ecclesiastical discipline (cf. 1 Cor. 5⁴, and esp. Acts 15²⁹ 16⁴). In Mt. 18¹⁸ the context shows that something of this sort is indicated; the Divine ratification being promised of the Church's action. The words refer to the " loosing " of " sin," and may imply forgiveness as well as discipline. To forgive sins is to *loose* ; cf. τῷ λύσαντι ἡμᾶς ἐκ τῶν ἁμαρτιῶν ἡμῶν (Rev. 1⁵; see also Job 42⁹, LXX).

Mt. 16¹⁹ and Mt. 18¹⁸ are passages which have marks of lateness; they are, *e.g.*, the only two passages in the Gospels where the word " Church " is found; and the tradition preserved in them of the Lord's commission to the Apostles is more likely to be dependent on that of Jn. 22²³ than *vice versa*. Indeed Jn.'s brief narrative here is clearly an original statement, and does not betray any acquaintance with Mt. 16¹⁹ 18¹⁸.

ἄν τινων κρατῆτε κεκράτηνται. The Sinai Syriac renders "whom ye shall shut *your door* against, it shall be shut " ; *i.e.* it takes κρατῆτε as governing τινῶν, rather than τὰς ἁμαρτίας. κρατεῖν does not occur elsewhere in Jn., but it generally takes the accusative, and the parallelism of the sentence would suggest that ἀφῆτε and κρατῆτε both govern τὰς ἁμαρτίας here. The two verbs are contrasted similarly in Mk. 7⁸, ἀφέντες τὴν ἐντολὴν τοῦ θεοῦ, κρατεῖτε τὴν παράδοσιν τῶν ἀνθρώπων.

The broad, unqualified form of this great assurance to the

[1] Cf. also Dalman, *Words of Jesus*, pp. 215–217.

24. Θωμᾶς δὲ εἷς ἐκ τῶν δώδεκα, ὁ λεγόμενος Δίδυμος, οὐκ ἦν μετ᾽ αὐτῶν ὅτε ἦλθεν Ἰησοῦς. 25. ἔλεγον οὖν αὐτῷ οἱ ἄλλοι μαθηταί Ἑωράκαμεν τὸν Κύριον. ὁ δὲ εἶπεν αὐτοῖς Ἐὰν μὴ ἴδω ἐν ταῖς χερσὶν αὐτοῦ τὸν τύπον τῶν ἥλων καὶ βάλω τὸν δάκτυλόν μου εἰς τὸν τύπον τῶν ἥλων καὶ βάλω μου τὴν χεῖρα εἰς τὴν πλευρὰν αὐτοῦ, οὐ

apostles is characteristic of many of the sayings of Jesus as recorded in the Gospels, e.g. " Whatsoever you shall ask of the Father in my name, He will give it you " (15¹⁶). He did not stay to explain the limitations or conditions of such a promise. It is a mark of every great teacher, confident in himself, that he does not weaken the force of his teaching by pointing out, at every stage, possible exceptions to the maxims which he has enunciated; and it was a mark of the greatest Teacher of all.

The incredulity of Thomas (vv. 24, 25) and its removal
(vv. 26–29)

24. This section is peculiar to Jn., who is specially interested in Thomas (11¹⁶ 14⁵). See on v. 28.

Θωμᾶς . . . ὁ λεγόμενος Δίδυμος. See on 11¹⁶ for this expression. As has been noted there, Thomas was the pessimist of the apostolic band. We can imagine his saying " I told you so," when the Cross seemed to be the end of all their hopes. His absence from the meeting of the disciples on the Resurrection day may have been due to a feeling that such gatherings were futile, henceforth. But he came to the second meeting a week later, although unconvinced by what the others had told him, just as Lk. tells that the others were unconvinced by the report of the women (Lk. 24¹¹).

εἷς ἐκ τῶν δώδεκα. See on 6⁷¹ for this phrase. The apostolic company are still described as " the Twelve " (cf. 6⁶⁷), although one had failed in his allegiance and was now separated from them. " The Twelve " remained a convenient title for the inner circle of disciples; cf. 1 Cor. 15⁵, *Pseudo-Peter*, § 12, and *Acta Thaddæi*, 6.

25. Ἑωράκαμεν τὸν κύριον. So Mary had said (v. 18). But Thomas was not satisfied. He claimed that he must test the matter by his sense of touch (a test which according to Jn. had not been offered to the other disciples, see v. 20), and not by sight only.

τὸν τύπον. AΘ have τὸν τόπον at the second occurrence of this word, a very natural mistake. The Vulgate has *fixuram clauorum*, followed by *in locum clauorum*: *fixuram* is the rendering of τύπον by *g*, but *b c d e* give *figuram*.

μὴ πιστεύσω. 26. Καὶ μεθ' ἡμέρας ὀκτὼ πάλιν ἦσαν ἔσω οἱ μαθηταὶ
αὐτοῦ, καὶ Θωμᾶς μετ' αὐτῶν. ἔρχεται ὁ Ἰησοῦς τῶν θυρῶν κεκλεισμένων, καὶ ἔστη εἰς τὸ μέσον, καὶ εἶπεν Εἰρήνη ὑμῖν. 27. εἶτα λέγει
τῷ Θωμᾷ Φέρε τὸν δάκτυλόν σου ὧδε καὶ ἴδε τὰς χεῖράς μου, καὶ
φέρε τὴν χεῖρά σου καὶ βάλε εἰς τὴν πλευράν μου, καὶ μὴ γίνου

Thomas is represented as knowing of the lance-thrust in
Jesus' side, which suggests that he was a witness of the Crucifixion. As has been pointed out on v. 20, no mention is made
of any nailing of the *feet*.

26 μεθ' ἡμέρας ὀκτώ. The disciples seem to have remained
in Jerusalem for the whole of Passover week, either because
they had made arrangements to do so before the feast began,
or (more probably) because they had some reason to believe
that Jesus would manifest Himself to them again. This
second manifestation was seemingly in the same room (ἔσω)
where He had shown Himself to them on the evening of the
Resurrection day; there is no evidence that any manifestation
of the Risen Lord was granted during the week. Jn. follows
his usual habit (see on 1[29]) of giving *dates* for the incidents of
his narrative.

This time Thomas was with his ten comrades (οἱ μαθηταὶ
αὐτοῦ instead of οἱ μαθηταί as at v. 19 ; see on 2[2]), the doors
again being shut, perhaps because they were still afraid of the
Sanhedrim. Jn. writes here ἔρχεται ὁ Ἰησοῦς, a solemn phrase
which (unlike ἦλθεν ὁ Ἰησοῦς of v. 19) may be intended
to express that He was expected to come. The narrative
proceeds exactly as in v. 19 (where see note) καὶ ἔστη εἰς τὸ
μέσον, καὶ εἶπεν Εἰρήνη ὑμῖν, Jesus giving them the customary
salutation of *Peace*, as before.

27. εἶτα λέγει τῷ Θωμᾷ. Jn. tells the story, as if Jesus
immediately addressed Himself to Thomas, and as if it were
on his account that He had come among them again.

Jesus offers to Thomas at once the test which he had declared
would be essential if he were to credit the story that the Lord
had risen, and suggests it in almost the same words that Thomas
had used (v. 25). He thus shows to Thomas that He knows
what has been in his mind and how he had expressed it. And
His words, revealing that this was He who could read men's
hearts (2[25]), proved sufficient to sweep away all doubt from the
mind of His incredulous disciple. There is no suggestion in
the text that Thomas took advantage of the proferred test, or
that he touched the body of the Risen Jesus at all (see on v. 20
above).

ἴδε τὰς χεῖράς μου, "look at my hands," which were probably uncovered. This is perhaps in contrast with . . . βάλε

ἄπιστος ἀλλὰ πιστός.   28. ἀπεκρίθη Θωμᾶς καὶ εἶπεν αὐτῷ Ὁ Κύριός

εἰς τὴν πλευράν μου, " put your hand into my side," as if the invitation were to put his hand under the *garments* of Jesus, to assure himself. But, perhaps, all that is implied is that the test of touch was offered to Thomas, while the other disciples had been content with *seeing* the Lord's hands and side (v. 20).[1]

καὶ μὴ γίνου ἄπιστος ἀλλὰ πιστός, "and become not faithless, but believing." As Meyer points out, Thomas was not faithless, but he was on the way to such a state of mind. If the Lord's words to him are behind [Mk.] 16¹⁴, where it is said that " He upbraided them with their unbelief and hardness of heart, because they believed not them which had seen Him after He was risen," the author of the Marcan Appendix must have regarded the quiet exhortation of Jesus as conveying a more severe rebuke than is suggested by Jn. See on v. 29.

28. ἀπεκρίθη Θωμᾶς. The rec. prefixes καί, but om. אBC*DWLΘ ; it also has ὁ before Θωμᾶς, with אL 33, but om. ABCDWΓΔΘ.

καὶ εἶπεν αὐτῷ κτλ. Thomas did not apply the test which he had said was essential. Once he had seen and heard his Master, it seemed to him unnecessary. He breaks out into joyful words of recognition and adoration, ὁ κύριός μου καὶ ὁ θεός μου. Like Mary, who exclaimed *Rabboni,* when she recognised Jesus (v. 16), Thomas exclaims " my Lord " (see on 4¹ for κύριος). But he goes beyond this, for he now, in a flash, perceives that Jesus was his Lord in a deeper sense than he had understood before; he may henceforth be called ὁ θεός μου. This, indeed (as the Jewish ecclesiastics had vaguely suspected, 5¹⁸), was involved in the claims that Jesus had made for Himself, but He had not expressed them so explicitly.

The Confession of Thomas goes far beyond the Confession of Nathanael (1⁴⁹), which had drawn forth the praise of Jesus at the beginning of His ministry. It expresses the deepest of Christian truths, which Jn. had placed in the forefront of his Gospel as governing and explaining all that he is about to narrate, Θεὸς ἦν ὁ Λόγος (1¹). But Jn. does not represent any disciple as having recognised its truth before the eager and enthusiastic Thomas perceived it at this moment of spiritual exaltation.

For the use of ὁ with a nominative case for a vocative, cf. Mk. 14³⁶, Pss. 63¹ 65¹ 71¹⁷, and especially Ps. 35²³, ὁ θεός μου

---

[1] In the second-century *Epistle of the Apostles* (c. 11), Peter and Andrew as well as Thomas are invited by Jesus to apply the test of touch, and were convinced by it.

μου καὶ ὁ Θεός μου. 29. λέγει αὐτῷ ὁ Ἰησοῦς Ὅτι ἑώρακάς με, πεπίστευκας; μακάριοι οἱ μὴ ἰδόντες καὶ πιστεύσαντες.

καὶ ὁ κύριός μου. Milligan (s.v. κύριος) cites, for the combination of θεός and κύριος, a Fayûm inscription of B.C. 24 on a building at Socnopæi, τῷ θεῷ καὶ κυρίῳ Σοκνοπαίῳ. Cf. Abbott, Diat. 2682.

29. λέγει αὐτῷ ὁ Ἰησ. B omits ὁ, as usual (see on 1²⁹).

ὅτι ἑώρακάς με. The rec. adds Θωμᾶ, but om. אABCDWΘ.

πεπίστευκας; We should probably treat this as interrogative, "Hast thou believed, because thou hast seen Me?" (cf. 16³¹). It was sight, not touch, that convinced Thomas. Jesus does not say, "Hast thou believed, because thou hast touched Me?" Thomas was convinced, just as the other disciples were, by seeing the Lord (v. 20). The faith which is generated thus is precious (cf. on 2¹¹ for the faith which rests on "signs"); but it was possible for Jesus' contemporaries alone to see Him as the disciples saw Him. By the time the Fourth Gospel was written, the first generation of Christian believers had passed away, and the path to faith for all future disciples could not be the path of sight (cf. 2 Cor. 5⁷, 1 Pet. 1⁸). So Jn. adds here as the last word of Jesus in the Gospel as originally planned, "Blessed are they that have not seen, and yet have believed." [1]

This Beatitude has been sometimes supposed to contain an implied rebuke to Thomas. But it can be no more a rebuke to him than to the other disciples ([Mk.] 16¹⁴), who, equally, saw before they believed. If Thomas is rebuked at all, it is in the words μὴ γίνου ἄπιστος (v. 27, where see note). It is never taught in the Gospel that a facile credulity is a Christian virtue; and Thomas was not wrong in wishing for some better proof of his Master's Resurrection than hearsay could give. Indeed, Jesus had warned His disciples not to give credence to every tale that they heard about Him: "If any man shall say, Lo, here is the Christ . . . believe it not" (Mk. 13²¹).[2] But cf. 4⁵⁰ for an illustration of the faith that does not require to "see."

For μακάριοι, see on 13¹⁷, and cf. Lk. 1⁴⁵.

After ἰδόντες, א with 346, 556, supported by the Syriac vss. and some Latin texts with Irish affinities, add με, an explanatory gloss.

---

[1] Cf. 2 Esd. 1³⁷, "I take to witness the grace of the people that shall come, whose little ones rejoice with gladness; and though they see me not with bodily eyes, yet in spirit they shall believe the thing that I say."

[2] Cf. Latham, The Risen Master, pp. 186 ff., for the mental attitude of Thomas, as depicted by Jn.

30. Πολλὰ μὲν οὖν καὶ ἄλλα σημεῖα ἐποίησεν ὁ Ἰησοῦς ἐνώπιον τῶν μαθητῶν, ἃ οὐκ ἔστιν γεγραμμένα ἐν τῷ βιβλίῳ τούτῳ· 31. ταῦτα δὲ γέγραπται ἵνα πιστεύητε ὅτι Ἰησοῦς ἐστιν ὁ Χριστὸς ὁ Υἱὸς τοῦ Θεοῦ, καὶ ἵνα πιστεύοντες ζωὴν ἔχητε ἐν τῷ ὀνόματι αὐτοῦ.

Scope and purpose of the Gospel (vv. 30, 31)

30. These verses form the conclusion (*clausula*, as Tertullian calls v. 31, *adv. Prax.* 25) of the Gospel as originally planned, c. 21 being a supplement added before the book was issued (see p. 687).

πολλὰ μὲν οὖν καὶ ἄλλα σημεῖα . . . For μὲν οὖν, cf. 19²⁴. Jn. explains that it was not his purpose to write a complete narrative of Jesus' ministry. Other "signs" were done by Him (cf. 2²³ 4⁴⁵ 12³⁷) which he does not stay to record, although they were done in the presence of the disciples, who were the witnesses of His wonderful works, chosen by Jesus Himself (15²⁷; cf. Acts 1²¹ 10⁴¹). Such were, *e.g.*, the healings of lepers and demoniacs, of which none is described in the Fourth Gospel. They were not written " in this book," although some of them were written in other books, such as the Synoptic Gospels, of which Jn. knew Mk. and probably Lk. also.

After μαθητῶν the rec. with אCDLWΘ adds αὐτοῦ, but om. ABΔ. The witnesses of the " signs " were not only the Twelve, but disciples generally. See on 2² for the omission of αὐτοῦ.

ἐνώπιον. This prep. occurs only once again in Jn. (1 Jn. 3²²). It is frequent in Lk., but is not found in Mk. Mt. (see Abbott, *Diat.* 2335).

31. ταῦτα δὲ γέγραπται, δέ corresponding to μέν of v. 30. But the signs which have been chosen by Jn. for record were recorded with the aim of inspiring in his readers the conviction that Jesus is divine, so that with this belief they may have life in His name. The Gospel, like the First Epistle, was written with a definite purpose. Cf. ταῦτα ἔγραψα ὑμῖν, ἵνα εἰδῆτε ὅτι ζωὴν ἔχετε αἰώνιον, τοῖς πιστεύουσιν εἰς τὸ ὄνομα τοῦ υἱοῦ τοῦ θεοῦ (1 Jn. 5¹³).

ἵνα πιστεύητε. So א*BΘ (as at 19³⁵), as against the rec. πιστεύσητε (אACDNW).

ὅτι Ἰησοῦς ἐστιν ὁ Χριστὸς ὁ υἱὸς τοῦ θεοῦ. This reproduces the terms of Martha's confession of faith (11²⁷), *before* Lazarus had been restored to her. But whereas, on her lips, ὁ υἱὸς τοῦ θεοῦ was probably used only as a title of Messiah, as Jn. uses it here it appears to have a deeper significance (see on 1³⁴). The faith of future believers is to be not only a faith in Jesus as the Christ (cf. 1⁴¹ and Mk. 8²⁹), but a faith in Him as the Son of God in the higher sense which has been suggested many times in the Gospel (1¹⁸ 3¹⁸ 5²⁵ 19⁷), and which is made explicit in the Confession of Thomas at its close (v. 28).

καὶ ἵνα πιστεύοντες κτλ. This is the central message of the Fourth Gospel, that belief in Jesus Christ is the path to life. See 3¹⁵. ¹⁶. ³⁶, 1 Jn. 5¹³. " In Him was life " is proclaimed in the Prologue (1⁴), and the purpose of His coming was that men might have life; cf. 5⁴⁰ 6⁵³ 10¹⁰.

The order of words suggests as the natural rendering " that, believing, ye may have life in His Name." The sequence " life in His Name " (ἐν τῷ ὀνόματι αὐτοῦ) does not occur elsewhere; but the prayer of Christ was that His faithful disciples might be " kept in His Name " by the Father (17¹¹. ¹²), and this perhaps provides a sufficient parallel. Cf. Acts 10⁴³ " to receive forgiveness of sins through His Name," and 1 Cor. 6¹¹.

On the other hand, in the closely similar passage quoted above (1 Jn. 5¹³) it is those " who believe in the name (εἰς τὸ ὄνομα) of the Son of God " that have eternal life. And at 1¹² (where see note) the authority to become children of God is for those who " believe in His Name." It would thus be more explicitly in accordance with Johannine teaching if we disregarded the natural order of the words here, and rendered " that believing in His Name, ye may have life " (see on 3¹⁵). It would seem from 16²³ (where see note) that to take ἐν τῷ ὀνόματι αὐτοῦ with πιστεύοντες, despite the intervention of ζωὴν ἔχητε, would be consistent with Johannine style.

After ζωήν ℵC*DL and fam. 13 add αἰώνιον, probably through reminiscence of 1 Jn. 5¹³, but om. ABNWΔΘ. For ζωή and ζωὴ αἰώνιος, see on 3¹⁵.

THE APPENDIX (CHAPTER XXI)

THE Fourth Gospel was plainly intended to end with 20³¹.
Anything following this is of the nature of an anticlimax. No
copy, however, of the Gospel, so far as we know, was ever issued
without the addition of c. 21, which is quoted by Tertullian
(*Scorp.* 15) and is treated by Origen in his Commentary as
on a par with cc. 1–20. It is probable that the Appendix was
added as an afterthought, before the Gospel was published,
and various opinions have been held as to its authorship,
purpose, and source.

We have first to ask if c. 21 is by the same hand as cc.
1–20. The only evidence by which such a question can be
determined is the evidence of vocabulary and style; and it is
hardly possible within the brief compass of twenty-five verses
to collect sufficient data. δίκτυον (v. 6) does not occur in
cc. 1–20, nor does πιάζειν (v. 3) in the sense of catching fish;
but then there is no fishing anecdote in the body of the Gospel.
Similarly no stress can be laid on unusual words such as
προσφάγιον (v. 5), or ἐπενδύτης (v. 7). τολμᾶν and ἐξετάζειν
(v. 12) do not appear elsewhere in Jn., and this must be noted,
for they might very naturally have been used. So too in v. 4
we find πρωΐα, while πρωΐ is the form adopted in 18²⁸ 20¹.
In 1⁴² we have Σίμων ὁ υἱὸς Ἰωάνου, while at 21¹⁵ we have
the shorter Σίμων Ἰωάνου. But against these differences may
be set remarkable agreements in style between cc. 1–20
and c. 21. The use of ἀμὴν ἀμήν at v. 18; the evangelistic
comment at v. 23; the verbal correspondence between v. 19
and 12³³, are among the more obvious. Such similarities
might possibly be due to conscious imitation of the mannerisms
of Jn. by the author of the Appendix, but there are others, more
subtle, which can hardly be thus explained. ἀπό in v. 8 is
used exactly as at 11¹⁸; ὁμοίως in v. 13 just as at 6¹¹; σύν (v. 3)
is rare in Jn., but it is found 12² 18¹; μέντοι (v. 4) is thoroughly
Johannine (cf. 12⁴²); and so is ὡς οὖν (v. 9; see on 4⁴⁰).[1]

---

[1] Further arguments may be found in Lightfoot (*Biblical Essays*,
p. 194), who accepts the Johannine authorship of the Appendix, as
do Harnack (*Chron.* i. 676), Sanday (*Criticism of Fourth Gospel*,
p. 81), and W. Bauer in his *Handbuch* ; Pfleiderer (*Primitive Christianity*, iii. 79), Moffatt (*Introd. to N.T.*, p. 572), and Stanton (*The
Gospels as Historical Documents*, iii. p. 28) take the other side.

The view taken in this commentary is that the author of c. 21 is the person whom we designate as Jn. But, whereas throughout cc. 1–20 Jn. is accustomed to reproduce the reminiscences of John the son of Zebedee, often in the form in which the aged disciple dictated them, this cannot be affirmed with confidence of the earlier part of c. 21, although it is true of vv. 15–22.

The correspondence between 21¹⁻¹³ and Lk. 5¹⁰⁻¹¹ are so close that they demand investigation; and it is necessary also to take account of the Synoptic parallels to the Lucan passage. The story of the Call of Peter and Andrew, and also of James and John (Mk. 1¹⁶ᶠ·, Mt. 4¹⁸ᶠ·, Lk. 5¹ᶠ·) is not given by Jn., who reports instead an earlier incident, when these four disciples were attracted to Jesus for the first time (1³⁵ᶠ·). The Lucan narrative differs from that of Mk., Mt. in significant particulars:

(*a*) Lk. does not tell explicitly of any *call* of the fishermen, as Mk., Mt. do; while he ends his story by saying that the four left all and followed Jesus (Lk. 5¹¹), *sc.* that James and John followed as well as Peter and Andrew. Cf. Jn. 21¹⁹· ²⁰ where John (who has not been invited to do so) follows as well as Peter, to whom alone the call " Follow me " is addressed.

(*b*) In Mk., Mt. the promise, " I will make you fishers of men," is explicitly given to Peter and Andrew, while the story suggests that it was intended for James and John as well. But in Lk. it is confined to Peter *alone*: " Fear not, from henceforth *thou* shalt catch men." This is in remarkable correspondence with the giving of the commission, *Pasce oues meas*, to Peter alone, in Jn. 21¹⁷.

(*c*) Lk. interpolates the incident, which Mk., Mt. do not report, of Peter's allegiance having been stimulated by a great catch of fish which he regarded as due to supernatural knowledge on the part of Jesus. So too in Jn. 21 it is Peter who is specially moved by the great success of the fishing due, again, to the direction of Jesus, and he alone plunges into the water to greet Jesus before the others (cf. at this point the story, peculiar to Mt. 14²⁸⁻³¹, of Peter walking on the waters).

(*d*) That the vocabulary of Jn. 21 should recall that of Lk. 5 is not in itself remarkable, for in stories relating to successful catches by fishermen the same words would naturally occur; *e.g.* ἐμβαίνειν " to embark " (Lk. 5³, Jn. 21³), ἀποβαίνειν " to disembark " (Lk. 5², Jn. 21⁹), δίκτυον (Lk. 5⁴, Jn. 21⁶). But the correspondence is not only one of vocabulary. In Lk. 5⁵ the fishermen say δι᾽ ὅλης νυκτὸς κοπιάσαντες οὐδὲν ἐλάβομεν: cf. Jn. 21³ ἐν ἐκείνῃ τῇ νυκτὶ ἐπίασαν οὐδέν. In both cases, it is by the direction of Jesus that they cast the net into deeper water (Lk. 5⁴, Jn. 21⁶, where see note); and in both

cases they make a great catch. In Lk. 5[6] the nets were beginning to break (διερήσσετο), but they did not actually break,
for the fishermen managed to secure them full of fish; so in
Jn. 21[11] it is noted that the nets were not broken. That this
should be mentioned shows that there was danger of them
breaking, as in Lk. 5[6].

These correspondences between the stories in Lk. 5 and
Jn. 21 of a great draught of fishes are so close that they cannot
reasonably be accounted for on the hypothesis that they represent distinct traditions of two distinct incidents. Accordingly,
two alternative explanations offer themselves.

(1) The author of Jn. 21 may have taken his story directly
from Lk. 5, putting it in a different context (Wellhausen,
Pfleiderer). Pfleiderer [1] regards Lk. 5[4-11] as itself only an
" allegorical " narrative, and if this were the aspect under
which it was viewed by Jn., his transference of the Lucan
passage from one point to another would hardly call for comment. But that Lk. intended his story of the miraculous
draught of fishes to be taken as an account of an incident that
actually happened is not doubtful; nor is there any reason
for thinking that Jn. understood it differently. Jn., however,
corrects Synoptic narratives sometimes; [2] and it is conceivable
that he has deliberately retold this Lucan story, and ascribed it,
not to the early days of our Lord's ministry, but to the period
after His Resurrection.

(2) A more probable explanation, however, is that Lk. 5[1-11]
and Jn. 21 are derived, in part, from the same source, viz.,
a Galilæan tradition (see on 20[1]) about the Lord's appearance to
Peter after His Resurrection, and the restoration of Peter
to his apostolic office.

(a) First, as to Lk. 5. We have seen that Mk. (followed
by Mt.) tells that when Peter, Andrew, James, and John abandoned their fishing and followed Jesus, He promised two of
them (if not all four) that He would make them " fishers of
men." Lk. seems to have confused this promise with the
commission afterwards given to Peter to feed the sheep of
Christ; and accordingly in his account of the call of the disciples
he has interpolated the tradition of a miraculous draught of
fishes followed by a special charge to Peter. In Lk., the
promise " henceforth thou shalt catch men " is for Peter alone.

Further, the words which Lk. ascribes to Peter, " Depart
from me, for I am a sinful man," (Lk. 5[8]) are not adequately
explained by saying that Peter was moved to confess his sin-
fulness because of an extraordinary take of fish. But if such
words were spoken when he met his Master for the first time

[1] *Primitive Christianity*, iii. 79.   [2] See Introd., p. xcix.

after he had denied Him, they are very appropriate. This sentence in Lk.'s narrative suggests of itself that the narrative belongs to the period after Jesus had risen.

(*b*) Next, in Jn. 21 there are indications that the story was originally current as a tradition, not of the *third* appearance of the risen Jesus to the disciples, but of His *first* manifestation of Himself after His Resurrection.

It is difficult to understand how disciples who already had *twice* conversed with the Risen Christ (20¹⁹· ²⁶) should fail to recognise Him when He presented Himself by the lake-side (but see note on 21⁴). That they should have gone back to their fishing after the extraordinary communication to them recorded in 20²²· ²³ is strange enough (Chrysostom can only suggest that they had gone back to Galilee through fear of the Jews); but it would be stranger still if they were not sensitive, after such an experience, to every slightest indication of the presence of Jesus.

Again, the story, as narrated, suggests that this was the first occasion on which Peter met and conversed with Jesus since the night when he denied Him. Vv. 15–19 relate how he was questioned by his Master, and finally reinstated, with a new and great charge, in his apostolic office. Is it likely that the person who first wrote down this story believed that Peter had seen the Risen Lord at least twice before, and had, along with his companions, been already granted the gift of the Holy Spirit and a commission to forgive sins ? The inference that 21¹⁵⁻¹⁹ must not be taken as posterior to 20²³ is difficult to evade.

It must not be overlooked, in this connexion, that the genuineness of πάλιν in 21¹ is doubtful. Different MSS. place πάλιν at different points in this verse (see note *in loc.*), and one uncial, at least, omits it altogether. It is probable that the adverb πάλιν in v. 1 and the whole of v. 14 (τοῦτο ἤδη τρίτον ἐφανερώθη κτλ.) have been added by Jn. to his source to bring the tradition of an appearance in Galilee into harmony with those which he has already described at Jerusalem. V. 14 is obviously a parenthesis, for the narrative runs smoothly and consecutively from v. 13 to v. 15.

These considerations lead to the conclusion that Lk. 5¹⁻¹¹ and Jn. 21 both go back to a current story that the first manifestation of the Risen Jesus to Peter (at any rate) was by the Sea of Galilee. According to Mk 16⁷ (followed by Mt. 28⁷), the disciples had been told that Jesus would meet them in Galilee, and Mt. 28¹⁶ states that He actually did so (see on 20¹ 21¹). Another instance of the survival of such a tradition is provided by the *Gospel of Peter* (second century), the extant fragment ending as follows: " It was the last day of unleavened bread, and many went forth, returning to their homes, as the feast was ended. But we, the Twelve (see on 20²⁴) disciples of the Lord, wept and were grieved; and each one, grieving for that which was come to pass, departed to his home. But I, Simon Peter, and Andrew my brother, took our nets and went away to the sea, and there was with us Levi the son of Alphæus, whom the Lord . .'' That is to say, Pseudo-Peter makes the apostles remain at Jerusalem until the Passover Feast was over, but makes no mention of any appearances of the Risen Lord to them there. Instead, he represents them as returning to their homes, the Galilæan fishermen going back to the Sea of Galilee. When the fragment ends, it seems as if an incident like that of Jn. 21¹⁻¹⁴ was being led up to.

Harnack holds ¹ that this tradition, the source of Jn. 21¹⁻¹³ as of Lk. 5¹⁻¹¹, was narrated in the Lost Conclusion of Mark. It may be so—the evidence is insufficient for certainty; but it seems more probable that Mt. 28¹⁶ᶠ· gives us part of what was in the original Marcan narrative.

However that may be, we have reached the conclusion that Jn. 21 and Lk. 5 point back to a common source, viz. a Galilæan tradition about the Risen Lord. The question then arises, *why* did Jn. add c. 21 to the already completed Gospel ?

(1) It has been suggested that c. 21 was added as a kind of postscript, because it was thought important that the rehabilitation of Peter should be placed on record. Of this there is no account in the Synoptists or in Jn. cc. 1–20. His denial is narrated in detail by all the evangelists, but his forgiveness and restoration to apostolic leadership is assumed without any explanation. That at some moment after the Resurrection he regained his old position of leader is manifest from the narrative of Acts. How were the other apostles reassured as to his stability ? The beautiful story of 21¹⁵⁻¹⁹ is the only explanation that has been preserved, whatever be its source; and it is easy to realise that the Church at the end of the first century would be anxious to have it placed on record, more especially after Peter's career had been ended by a martyr's death. The statement in v. 24 that the story was certified by the Beloved Disciple, *i.e.* in our view by John the son of Zebedee, who at the time of its being added to the Fourth Gospel was the only living person who could bear witness to its truth, is in no way improbable. How Peter came to be restored to his apostolic office would not seem to the first generation of Christians to be a question of sufficient importance for inclusion in a Gospel, but when the second generation began to look back it was recognised as of peculiar interest.

¹ *Luke the Physician* (Eng. Tr.) p. 227.

(2) But the principal motive for the addition of c. 21 was, no doubt, that misapprehensions as to the meaning of some words of Jesus might be removed.

The enigmatical promise (Mk. 9[1] and parallels) that there were some among the disciples of Jesus who would not die until " the kingdom of God came with power " must have made a profound impression (see on 1[51]). *Maran Atha* was the watchword of apostolic Christianity (1 Cor. 16[22]), and at first it was expected that the Parousia (cf. 14[3] and 1 Jn. 2[28]) would come soon. Paul at one time thought that some of his contemporaries would live to see it (1 Thess. 4[15], 1 Cor. 15[51]). By the time that the Fourth Gospel was written, the hope of the *speedy* return of Christ was dying out; but it was still believed by some that the Lord had promised (either in the words preserved in 21[22], or in similar words such as Mk. 9[1]) that it would come to pass before all the apostles died. Accordingly, when the last survivor, John the son of Zebedee, was manifestly approaching the end of his course, there must have been some at least who were disconcerted. It was probably to reassure them that the story of the promise made by Jesus to John was added to the Gospel which was based on his reminiscences, and attention directed to its exact phrasing. Vv. 21–23 *may* have been written down after the death of John; but it seems more probable that the true account of this incident was gathered from his lips during the last days of his long life.

The Appendix, then, embodies a tradition that was current as to an appearance of the Risen Christ in Galilee, which is also used (but misplaced) by Lk. In c. 21, it appears in a version for some deatils of which the authority of the Beloved Disciple is expressly claimed (v. 24); but it would seem that it has been edited (vv. 1, 14) by Jn. so as to bring it into harmony with c. 20. The Gospel proper contained only such incidents and sayings of Jesus as would serve the special purpose of the writer (20[30, 31]); but before it was issued to the Christian community it was thought desirable to add an Appendix embodying traditions about Peter and John of which incorrect versions were current.

For vv. 24, 25, see notes *in loc.*

An appearance of the Risen Christ by the Sea of Galilee (XXI. 1–14)

XXI. 1. μετὰ ταῦτα. This introductory phrase does not connote strict sequence.[1] It is used by Jn. to introduce a

[1] See Introd., p. cviii.

XXI. 1. Μετὰ ταῦτα ἐφανέρωσεν ἑαυτὸν πάλιν ὁ Ἰησοῦς τοῖς μαθηταῖς ἐπὶ τῆς θαλάσσης τῆς Τιβεριάδος· ἐφανέρωσεν δὲ οὕτως.

fresh section of his narrative, and hardly means more than "another time."

ἐφανέρωσεν ἑαυτόν. For φανερόω (cf. v. 14) and its use in Jn., see on 1³¹. It is the verb used in the Appendix to Mk. (16¹². ¹⁴) of the manifestations of the Risen Jesus to the two at Emmaus, and to the Eleven. He was not visible *continuously* between His Resurrection and final Departure.

ὁ Ἰησοῦς. BC om. ὁ, but ins. אACNΓΔ (see on 1²⁹· ⁵⁰).

τοῖς μαθηταῖς. Not to the Eleven, but to some of them only. οἱ μαθηταί might stand for "disciples" in the wider sense (see on 2²), but that is not probable at this point, as we shall see.

ἐπὶ τῆς θαλάσσης τῆς Τιβεριάδος, "by the Sea of Tiberias." For this description of the Sea of Galilee, see on 6¹. According to the Marcan tradition (Mk. 16⁷, Mt. 28⁷), Jesus was to manifest Himself in Galilee (cf. Mt. 28¹⁶). Of any appearances there, the Gospels of Lk. and Jn. tell nothing, but in this Appendix to the Fourth Gospel one such manifestation is described in detail, implying (as the story is told by Jn.) that, after the three appearances at Jerusalem described in c. 20, some of the Eleven (at least) returned to Galilee, where Jesus met them. But see note above, p. 656.

πάλιν (a favourite Johannine word, cf. 1³⁵) is placed before ἑαυτόν by א* and before ἐφανέρωσεν by D. It is omitted by some cursives.

ἐφανέρωσεν δὲ οὕτως. This brusque constr. does not appear again in exactly this form in Jn.; but cf. 4⁶, ἐκαθέζετο οὕτως ἐπὶ τῇ πηγῇ.

2. According to Pseudo-Peter (see p. 691 above), the disciples remained in Jerusalem until the end of the Passover Feast, when some returned to their homes in Galilee. This falls in with c. 21.

Peter and the sons of Zebedee were fishermen, who took up their work in partnership, as they had been accustomed to do (Mk. 1¹⁶). ἦσαν ὁμοῦ, "they were *together*," and with them were Nathanael and also Thomas. The words ἄλλοι ἐκ τῶν μαθητῶν αὐτοῦ δύο suggest that all seven who were present were of the Twelve, for οἱ μαθηταὶ αὐτοῦ generally represents the Twelve in the Fourth Gospel. οἱ μαθηταί (without αὐτοῦ) in vv. 4, 12 stands for the seven who *have been already mentioned.* See for this usage on 2².

Nonnus, in his paraphrase of Jn., like Pseudo-Peter, says that Andrew was present on this occasion, and he may have

2. ἦσαν ὁμοῦ Σίμων Πέτρος καὶ Θωμᾶς ὁ λεγόμενος Δίδυμος καὶ Ναθαναὴλ ὁ ἀπὸ Κανᾶ τῆς Γαλιλαίας καὶ οἱ τοῦ Ζεβεδαίου καὶ ἄλλοι ἐκ τῶν μαθητῶν αὐτοῦ δύο. 3. λέγει αὐτοῖς Σίμων Πέτρος Ὑπάγω ἁλιεύειν. λέγουσιν αὐτῷ Ἐρχόμεθα καὶ ἡμεῖς σὺν σοί. ἐξῆλθον καὶ ἐνέβησαν εἰς τὸ πλοῖον, καὶ ἐν ἐκείνῃ τῇ νυκτὶ ἐπίασαν οὐδέν.

been one of the two *innominati*; it would be natural that he would, as formerly, accompany Peter in his fishing. Pseudo-Peter represents " Levi the son of Alphæus " as one of the company, and it is possible that this is a true tradition and that he was the second unnamed disciple, although we should hardly expect that a former tax-gatherer (Mk. 2¹⁴) would be of use in a fishing-boat. If we had to guess at the second *innominatus*, the name of Philip would naturally suggest itself. He was of Bethsaida, as were Peter and Andrew (1⁴⁴); and in the lists of the apostles he always appears among the first five, with Peter, Andrew, and the sons of Zebedee (Mk. 3¹⁸, Mt. 10², Lk. 6¹⁴, Acts 1¹³). He is also associated with Peter, Andrew, and John, and with Nathanael in 1³⁷⁻⁴⁶. The seven disciples present on the occasion now to be described would then be the seven most prominent in the Fourth Gospel and the seven who are named first in Acts 1¹³. But the evidence as to the two *innominati* is not sufficient for certainty.

Σίμων Πέτρος. See on 18¹⁵ for the full name being used at the beginning of a new section, as is the habit of Jn.

Θωμᾶς ὁ λεγόμενος Δίδυμος. So he is described 11¹⁶, where see note; cf. 20²⁴.

καὶ Ναθαναὴλ ὁ ἀπὸ Κανᾶ τῆς Γαλ. There is no reason for supposing (with Schmiedel) that this description is made up from a comparison of 1⁴⁵ and 2¹, or that it does not represent a genuine tradition as to Nathanael's home. See on 1⁴⁵.

οἱ τοῦ Ζεβεδαίου. Zebedee's name is not mentioned elsewhere in the Fourth Gospel. " The sons of Zebedee," their names not being stated, is a phrase occurring Mt. 20²⁰ 26³⁷ 27⁵⁶.

3. λέγει αὐτοῖς Σίμων Πέτρος. He characteristically takes the lead, saying, " I am off to fish." For ὑπάγω, see on 7³³. The verb ἁλιεύειν occurs in the Greek Bible only once elsewhere, at Jer. 16¹⁶.

To repeat the full name Σίμων Πέτρος is not in accordance with Jn.'s habit (see on 18¹⁵); cf. vv. 7, 11, 15.

καὶ ἡμεῖς σὺν σοί. σύν is not a favourite Johannine word, occurring only twice in Jn. (see on 12², 18¹).

ἐξῆλθον, "they went out," not necessarily from the same house, but from the place where they were all gathered.

ἐνέβησαν εἰς τὸ πλοῖον. For this phrase, see on 6¹⁷. The rec. has ἀνέβησαν. Probably τὸ πλοῖον was the large boat

4. πρωίας δὲ ἤδη γινομένης ἔστη Ἰησοῦς ἐπὶ τὸν αἰγιαλόν· οὐ μέντοι ᾔδεισαν οἱ μαθηταὶ ὅτι Ἰησοῦς ἐστίν.   5. λέγει οὖν αὐτοῖς Ἰησοῦς

which they were accustomed to use as they went about the lake with Jesus (see on 6¹).

The rec. adds εὐθύς, but om. אBC*DLNWΔΘ.

ἐν ἐκείνῃ τῇ νυκτὶ ἐπίασαν οὐδέν. This recalls Lk. 5⁵; the night is the best time for fishing, and yet they caught nothing. πιάζειν is used several times by Jn. (see on 7³⁰) of " arresting " or " taking " Jesus; but to use it of the catching of fish, as here and at v. 10, is curious. Cf. Cant. 2¹⁵, Rev. 19²⁰.

4. πρωίας δὲ ἤδη γινομένης, " when dawn was now breaking," and the light not yet good. Jn. never has πρωία in the body of the Gospel, while πρωΐ occurs 18²⁸ 20¹ (see also on 1⁴¹). Mt. has πρωία (Mt. 27¹).

For γινομένης (ABC*LΘ), the rec. has γενομένης (אDNWΓΔΘ).

ἔστη Ἰησοῦς ἐπὶ τὸν αἰγιαλόν. ἐπί is read by אADLΘ (cf. Mt. 13². ⁴⁸, Acts 21⁵ ἐπὶ τὸν αἰγιαλόν); but BCNW have εἰς (cf. Acts 27⁴⁰ εἰς τὸν αἰγιαλόν " towards the beach "). Perhaps εἰς has come in here through assimilation to ἔστη εἰς τὸ μέσον (20¹⁹. ²⁶, where see note).

μέντοι is a Johannine word; see on 12⁴².

For ᾔδεισαν followed by the historic present ἐστίν, see on 1³⁹. That disciples, who had so recently seen the Risen Lord *twice*, according to the Johannine tradition (20¹⁹. ²⁶), should not recognise Him, even after He had spoken to them, might, perhaps, be accounted for by their distance from the shore and the dimness of the early morning light. Again, the failure of the two disciples at Emmaus to identify Him at first (Lk. 24³¹); and the failure of Mary Magdalene to recognise Him when she saw Him (20¹⁴ οὐκ ᾔδει ὅτι Ἰησοῦς ἐστίν, words identical with those used here) may be taken as showing that the Risen Lord was not recognisable, unless He chose " to manifest Himself." The latter may be the true explanation.[1] But the present instance of the disciples' failure to recognise Him is perplexing, for (according to Jn.) they had already seen Him; even if we do not lay stress on the Marcan tradition according to which they had been told that they might expect to see Him in Galilee.

5. λέγει . . . Ἰησοῦς. The rec. inserts ὁ before Ἰησ. with A²CDLNΘ, but om. אB.

παιδία is not put into the mouth of Jesus in any other

---

[1] On this cf. Sparrow-Simpson, *The Resurrection and Modern Thought*, p. 86 : " Recognition, in some cases, instead of becoming easier, [became] increasingly difficult."

Παιδία, μή τι προσφάγιον ἔχετε; ἀπεκρίθησαν αὐτῷ Οὔ. 6. ὁ δὲ εἶπεν αὐτοῖς Βάλετε εἰς τὰ δεξιὰ μέρη τοῦ πλοίου τὸ δίκτυον, καὶ

Gospel passage, when He is addressing His disciples. It is a colloquial form of address, as we might say " My boys," or " lads," if calling to a knot of strangers of a lower social class. παιδίον is thus used in Aristophanes (*Nub.* 137, *Ran.* 33). The use of παιδία in 1 Jn. 2¹³· ¹⁸ is different.

Jesus says τεκνία to the disciples at 13³³, but to have employed a tender term of this kind would at once have betrayed His identity by the lake-side.

μή τι προσφάγιον ἔχετε; *i.e.* " have you caught any fish ? " Wetstein (approved by Field) quotes a scholium on Aristoph. *Clouds*, 731, viz. ἔχεις τι; schol. χαριέντως τὸ · ἔχεις τι τῇ τῶν ἀγρευτῶν λέξει χρώμενος · τοῖς γὰρ ἁλιεῦσιν ἢ ὀρνιθαγρευταῖς οὕτω φασίν· ἔχεις τι; That is to say, ἔχεις τι is the phrase in which a bystander would say to a fisherman or fowler, " Have you had any sport ? " προσφάγιον, lit. a " relish," something to season food, is a Hellenistic word like ὄψον or ὀψάριον for " fish," which was the relish in common use. See on v. 10 below. προσφάγιον is not found elsewhere in the Greek Bible.

The form of the question, beginning with μή, suggests that a negative answer is expected (see on 6⁶⁷),[1] so that we may render " Boys, you have not had any catch, have you ? " And, accordingly, they answered, " No." See on 4²⁹.

6. Then Jesus, perhaps having noticed from the shore that a shoal of fish was gathering at the farther side of the boat, calls to the fishermen, " Cast your net towards the right of the boat, and you will have a take."

εις τα δεξια μερη τοῦ πλοίου is a cumbrous phrase for which no linguistic parallel seems to be forthcoming. In Lk. 5⁴ the advice of Jesus was similar, although expressed differently, viz. to let down the nets in deeper water. As the story is told, it would seem that Peter jumped into the water on the side of the boat nearest the land, being unimpeded by the net which now was on the other (the *right*) side, farther from the shore.[2]

δίκτυον does not occur again in Jn., and is the word used Lk. 5². ⁴. ⁵; but nothing can be inferred from this, as it is the common word for a fishing-net.

After εὑρήσετε, אᶜᵃ and several Latin texts mostly of the Irish school (*e.g.*, ardmach, dim., stowe, corp., and Rawl. 167 [3])

[1] See Abbott, *Diat.* 2701.

[2] Trench, with others, suggests that the " right " side is symbolic of the auspicious side ; cf. Ezek. 4⁴· ⁶, etc.

[3] Cf. Wordsworth-White *in loc.*, and Berger, *La Vulgate*, p. 45, for other Latin MSS. with this interpolation.

εὑρήσετε. ἔβαλον οὖν, καὶ οὐκέτι αὐτὸ ἑλκύσαι ἴσχυον ἀπὸ τοῦ
πλήθους τῶν ἰχθύων. 7. λέγει οὖν ὁ μαθητὴς ἐκεῖνος ὃν ἠγάπα
ὁ Ἰησοῦς τῷ Πέτρῳ Ὁ Κύριός ἐστιν. Σίμων οὖν Πέτρος, ἀκούσας ὅτι
ὁ Κύριός ἐστιν, τὸν ἐπενδύτην διεζώσατο, ἦν γὰρ γυμνός, καὶ ἔβαλεν

interpolate Lk. 5⁵, "but they said, Master, we toiled all
night and took nothing; but at Thy word we will let down
the net." This interpolation shows that the similarity
between the two narratives of a great draught of fishes in Lk.
and Jn. had been observed long before the dawn of modern
criticism.

καὶ οὐκέτι αὐτὸ ἑλκύσαι ἴσχυον. The rec. has ἴσχυσαν but
the more vivid ἴσχυον is read by אBCDLN. For the verb
ἑλκύειν see on 6⁴⁴. ἰσχύειν is not found in the body of the
Gospel.

ἀπὸ τοῦ πλήθους τῶν ἰχθύων. For the same constr cf.
2 Chron. 5⁶ of the animals that "could not be numbered for
multitude," οἳ οὐ λογισθήσονται ἀπὸ τοῦ πλήθους. Nothing is
said here of the breaking of the net, which Simon and Andrew
feared in the parallel story (Lk. 5⁶).

The Sea of Galilee still swarms with fish;[1] and it is noteworthy that this great catch is not described as a σημεῖον, nor
is it suggested that it was miraculous.

7. We have identified the Beloved Disciple with John the
son of Zebedee (see on 13²³, and Introd., pp. xxxv ff.). This
identification agrees well with the statement of v. 2 that the
sons of Zebedee were present on this occasion; although v. 2
does not by itself *prove* this, for the Beloved Disciple might
be one of the two *innominati*.

The Beloved Disciple is the first to recognise Jesus, while
Peter is the first to act on the knowledge that the stranger on
the beach is He. This is entirely congruous with all that the
Gospels tell of the two men, the one a spiritual genius, the
other an eager, impulsive, warm-hearted leader.

ὁ κύριός ἐστιν. See on 4¹.

Σίμων οὖν Πέτρος. See on v. 3.

Peter, while working the boat and the nets, was γύμνος, *i.e.*
he was naked except for a waist-cloth; but before leaping into
the water, he threw on his upper garment, and fastened it
with a belt. ἐπενδύτης is not found elsewhere in the N.T.,
but cf. 1 Sam. 18⁴ where Jonathan presents David with his
ἐπενδύτης as a personal gift. Meyer says that the Talmud
takes over the word in the form אפונדתא, using it to describe
a labourer's frock.

The verb διεζώσατο signifies that Peter tucked the garment

---

[1] Cf. G. A. Smith, *Hist. Geogr.*, p. 462 n.

ἑαυτὸν εἰς τὴν θάλασσαν· 8. οἱ δὲ ἄλλοι μαθηταὶ τῷ πλοιαρίῳ ἦλθον, οὐ γὰρ ἦσαν μακρὰν ἀπὸ τῆς γῆς ἀλλὰ ὡς ἀπὸ πηχῶν διακοσίων, σύροντες τὸ δίκτυον τῶν ἰχθύων. 9. ὡς οὖν ἀπέβησαν εἰς τὴν γῆν, βλέπουσιν ἀνθρακιὰν κειμένην καὶ ὀψάριον ἐπικείμενον καὶ ἄρτον.

up into his girdle before he waded ashore in the shallow water (cf. 13⁴).

Syr. sin. adds, after the words " he cast himself into the sea," the gloss "and came swimming." The paraphrase of Nonnus also speaks of Peter swimming; and this may be intended by the Greek, but in fact the ἐπενδύτης or long garment which Peter put on would only have been an impediment if he had to swim ashore.[1]

Nothing is said of any conversation between Peter and the Risen Jesus at this point of the story (cf. *contra*, Lk. 5⁸).

8. The other disciples wished to get to shore as soon as they could, and to bring their catch with them; but the big fishing boat (τὸ πλοῖον, v. 3) could not come closer in the shallow water, so they came (there were only six of them) in the dinghy (τὸ πλοιάριον, cf. 6²² and the note there), the distance being only about 100 yards.

ἀπὸ πηχῶν διακοσίων, " 200 cubits off." For this constr. of ἀπό see on 11¹⁸. πήχεων is contracted into πηχῶν as in Ezek. 40⁷ 41²¹, Rev. 21¹⁷, etc.

σύροντες τὸ δίκτυον κτλ., " towing the net full of fishes," *i.e.* having attached the ropes of the net to the dinghy. σύρειν does not occur again in Jn.; it is used, as here, of dragging towards one a net full of fish by Plutarch, *de sollertia animalium* c. 26.

9. ἀπέβησαν, " they disembarked." ἀποβαίνειν does not occur again in Jn.; and it is noteworthy that the only other place in the Greek Bible where it is found in the sense of " disembark " is Lk. 5² (cf. Abbott, *Diat.* 1763).

For ἀνθρακιάν, see on 18¹⁸. The Vulg. rendering of ἀνθρακιὰν κειμένην is *prunas positas*; but some O.L. texts have *carbones positos*, while others (*a b c ff₂ r*) have *carbones incensos*, as if they read ἀνθρακιὰν καιομένην. It is possible that this is the original reading, for καιομένην would readily be corrupted into κειμένην, more expecially as ἐπικείμενον follows in the next line.

ὡς οὖν ἀπέβησαν. ὡς οὖν is thoroughly Johannine ; see on 4⁴⁰.

ὀψάριον. We have had the word ὀψάρια already at 6⁹, where it probably means " dried fish " (see note *in loc.*).

---

[1] Abbott (*Diat.* 2999, xvii. n.) finds a symbolic meaning in τὸν ἐπενδύτην διεζώσατο, understanding the words to suggest that Peter girded himself with the fine linen of repentance.

10. λέγει αὐτοῖς ὁ Ἰησοῦς Ἐνέγκατε ἀπὸ τῶν ὀψαρίων ὧν ἐπιάσατε
νῦν. 11. ἀνέβη οὖν Σίμων Πέτρος καὶ εἵλκυσεν τὸ δίκτυον εἰς τὴν γῆν
μεστὸν ἰχθύων μεγάλων ἑκατὸν πεντήκοντα τριῶν· καὶ τοσούτων ὄντων

But here the ὀψάρια (v. 10) are the fresh fish which had just
been caught, and in v. 11 the net is said to have been full " of
great fishes." In fact, despite the derivation of the word,
ὀψάριον came to mean " a fish " or " fish " vaguely, whether
fresh caught or dried; just as πᾶν τὸ ὄψος τῆς θαλάσσης in
Num. 11²² means " all the fish of the sea." See on v. 5.

The ὀψάριον which was cooking on the fire was not one of
the fish which had just been caught; for it is only after the
disciples see it that the net is drawn ashore. It was provided,
along with the bread, by Jesus. Some have thought that the
singular forms ὀψάριον, ἄρτον, are significant; and that there
is here an allusion to a sacramental meal—*one* fish, *one* loaf.
But neither ὀψάριον nor ἄρτον necessarily signify one fish or
one loaf only; both may be taken generally as " fish," " bread."
See further, on v. 13.

The story of Lk. 24⁴², where the disciples give Jesus a piece
of broiled fish (ἰχθύος ὀπτοῦ μέρος), presents some likeness
to the present passage, but there the Risen Jesus asks for food
(cf. 21⁵) and eats it. Jn. does not say that He ate anything,
but only that He presided at the meal by the lake-side.

10. Ἐνέγκατε ἀπὸ τῶν ὀψ. κτλ., " bring of the fish which you
caught just now." *Prima facie*, the story suggests that the
fish on the fire was for the breakfast of Jesus Himself, and that
He now invites the fishermen to bring some of the fish that they
had caught, to cook them, and join Him at His meal. But
this is not said directly.

For πιάζειν, see on v. 3. For νῦν, " just now," cf. 11⁸.

11. ἀνέβη οὖν Σ. Π. " So Peter," in obedience to the
authoritative direction of Jesus, " went aboard " the dinghy,
or little boat. Peter is always foremost in action.

καὶ εἵλκυσεν τὸ δίκτυον κτλ., " and drew the net to land,"
which was easier to do than to haul it over the gunwale into
the dinghy.

μεστὸν ἰχθύων μεγάλων κτλ. Cf. Lk. 5⁶ ἰχθύων πλῆθος πολύ.
Unlike the story in Lk., where the net was breaking
(διερρήγνυτο τὸ δίκτυον), it is noted here as remarkable, οὐκ
ἐσχίσθη τὸ δίκτυον.

The simplest explanation of the number of fish, 153, being
recorded, is that (as fishermen are wont to do, because the
catch has to be divided into shares) the fish were counted, and
their great number remembered as a notable thing. But
commentators, both ancient and modern, have not been con-

οὐκ ἐσχίσθη τὸ δίκτυον. 12. λέγει αὐτοῖς ὁ Ἰησοῦς Δεῦτε ἀριστήσατε. οὐδεὶς ἐτόλμα τῶν μαθητῶν ἐξετάσαι αὐτόν Σὺ τίς εἶ; εἰδότες
ὅτι ὁ Κύριός ἐστιν. 13. ἔρχεται Ἰησοῦς καὶ λαμβάνει τὸν ἄρτον καὶ

tent with this, and have sought for a symbolic meaning in the
number 153, which they (in modern times at least) assume was
invented in order to suggest something esoteric. See Introd.,
p. lxxxvii.

12. Jesus calls to the disciples, Δεῦτε ἀριστήσατε, "Come
and break your fast" (cf. for the constr. δεῦτε, ἴδετε κτλ., 4²⁹).
ἄριστον was the morning meal (Mt. 22⁴, Lk. 11³⁸ 14¹²); the
verb ἀριστᾶν occurs again in N.T. only at Lk. 11³⁷ Nothing
is said of the cooking of any of the fish that had been caught,
but the command of v. 10 suggests that it was thus that the
disciples' breakfast was provided.

οὐδεὶς ἐτόλμα κτλ. The intimate familiarity of the old
days had passed ; they knew that it was Jesus who was
speaking to them, but they did not dare to question Him as
to His identity (cf. 4²⁷). Chrysostom says that they sat down
for the meal in silence and trepidation, which *may* be implied.

οὐδεὶς . . . τῶν μαθητῶν. For this constr., without ἐκ before
the gen. plural, as usual in Jn. (see on 1⁴⁰ 7¹⁹), cf. 13²⁸. On
μαθηταί, see 2².

εἰδότες ὅτι ὁ κύριός ἐστιν. It was not as at the Emmaus
supper, where He was not recognised until He blessed and
broke the bread (Lk. 24³⁰); here He was recognised before the
meal began.

τολμᾶν and ἐξετάζειν do not occur in the body of the
Gospel. For ἐξετάζειν, "to cross-examine," cf. Mt. 2⁸,
Ecclus. 11⁷; it is a natural word to use in this context.

13. ἔρχεται has been thought to imply that Jesus was
standing at a distance from the lighted fire, and that He came
to it only when the disciples were gathered for their breakfast.
But ἔρχεται goes with λαμβάνει which follows (cf. ἔρχεται . . .
καὶ λέγει, 12²²), and hardly needs explanation, or a reference
to 20²⁶.

The rec. οὖν (NΘ) after ἔρχεται is om. by ℵBCDLW.

λαμβάνει τὸν ἄρτον καὶ δίδωσιν αὐτοῖς. Syr. sin. and D
insert εὐχαριστήσας before δίδωσιν, this being evidently introduced from 6¹¹, to the language of which v. 13 is closely
similar. No eucharistic meal is implied at 6¹¹ (see note *in
loc.*), and there is here even less suggestion of such a thing.
τὸν ἄρτον and τὸ ὀψάριον do not indicate *one* loaf and *one* fish
(see on v. 9); indeed the command "bring of the fish which
you caught" (v. 10) implies that several fish had been prepared for the disciples' breakfast. That Jesus "took"

διδωσιν αὐτοῖς, καὶ τὸ ὀψάριον ὁμοίως. 14. τοῦτο ἤδη τρίτον ἐφανερώθη
Ἰησοῦς τοῖς μαθηταῖς ἐγερθεὶς ἐκ νεκρῶν.

15. Ὅτε οὖν ἠρίστησαν, λέγει τῷ Σίμωνι Πέτρῳ ὁ Ἰησοῦς Σίμων

and " gave " them bread and fish, as before (cf. Mk. 6⁴¹ 8⁶,
Mt. 14¹⁹ 15³⁶, Lk. 9¹⁶), means only that He presided at the
meal, as His custom had always been.

With τὸ ὀψάριον ὁμοίως, cf. ὁμοίως καὶ ἐκ τῶν ὀψαρίων (6¹¹).

14. With the constr. τοῦτο ἤδη τρίτον, cf. τοῦτο πάλιν
δεύτερον σημεῖον (4⁵⁴), and see 2¹¹. In both these passages
(2¹¹, 4⁵⁴), Jn. implies a *correction* of Mk.'s narrative, and it is
probable that here too a correction of the Galilæan tradition
as to the appearance by the lake-side is intended. Jesus did
not *first* manifest Himself to the apostles in Galilee (Mt. 28¹⁶);
He manifested Himself to them twice at Jerusalem (20¹⁹·²⁶),
and not until after that (τρίτον) did He show Himself in
Galilee. V. 14 seems to be an addition made by Jn. to his
source.

ἐφανερώθη Ἰησοῦς. Cf. v. 1 and see on 1³¹.

After μαθηταῖς the rec. has αὐτοῦ, but om. ℵABCLWΟ.

ἐγερθεὶς ἐκ νεκρῶν. Cf. 2²² 12⁹·¹⁷. ἀναστῆναι was the verb
used 20⁹.

The restoration of Peter to his apostolic office (vv. 15–17)

15. ὅτε οὖν ἠρίστησαν, when the breakfast was over. Jn. is
fond of these notes of time. See on 1²⁹.

Σίμων Ἰωάνου. This is the better reading (ℵ*BCDLW), as
against Σίμων Ἰωνᾶ of the rec. text; and so also at vv. 16, 17.
Note that we have here Σίμων Ἰωάνου three times, instead
of Σίμων ὁ υἱὸς Ἰωάνου, as at 1⁴².

Jesus addresses him by the personal name by which he was
generally known, " Simon, son of John," as He was accustomed to do. See on 1⁴² for the designation *Peter*, which, it
is to be observed, Jesus only uses once (Lk. 22³⁴) in addressing
the apostle. Cf. Mt. 16¹⁷, Lk. 22³¹.

Peter had thrice denied His Master, and the solemn questioning of him, in the company of his fellow-disciples, as the
prelude to his restoration to the Master's favour and the renewal of His confidence, was fittingly repeated thrice. As
Augustine has it, he was questioned " donec trina voce amoris,
solueret trinam uocem negationis." [1] The questioning has
reference to one thing only, and that is Peter's *love* for Jesus.
He is not asked to renew his confession of *faith* (probably that
had never quite left him, his Master having prayed that it

[1] *Enarr.* in Ps. xxxvii. 17.

should not fail, Lk. 22³²), nor is he asked if he is sure that he will be more courageous in the future than in the past. The Lord does not remind him in words of his failure when the great test came. If he *loves*, that is enough. This is the one essential condition of the apostolic office and ministry.

Attention has often been directed to the use of the two verbs ἀγαπᾶν and φιλεῖν in these verses; Jesus asking ἀγαπᾷς με twice, Peter answering φιλῶ σε, and on the third occasion of His query, Jesus changing the verb and saying φιλεῖς με, taking up Peter's own word. This distinction of verbs is not treated as significant by the ancient commentators, Syriac, Greek, or Latin (Ambrose *in Lc. x.* 176 being perhaps an exception); and, when the delight of Origen, *e.g.*, in playing on words is remembered, this is sufficient to show that the patristic expositors did not venture sharply to differentiate ἀγαπᾶν from φιλεῖν. But in modern times, the exegesis of the passage has largely turned on the idea that whereas Peter will say φιλῶ σε, he does not presume to claim that he can say ἀγαπῶ σε, ἀγαπᾶν being the more lofty word.[1] It is necessary, then, to examine the usage of ἀγαπᾶν and φιλεῖν more closely.

ADDITIONAL NOTE ON φιλεῖν AND ἀγαπᾶν

Of these two words it may be said that φιλεῖν is the more comprehensive, and includes every degree and kind of love or liking, while ἀγαπᾶν is the more dignified and restrained. But even so vague a distinction cannot be pressed very far. Both verbs are used in classical Greek to express sexual love (cf. Lucian, *Ver Hist.* ii. 25, and Aristotle, *Topica*, i. 15 [106, *b* 2]).[2] So, in like manner, in the LXX sexual love is indicated by ἀγάπη, ἀγαπᾶν, at 2 Sam. 13⁴, Cant. 2⁵ 7⁶ etc., and by φιλία at Ecclus. 9⁸, Prov. 7¹⁸ (in which latter passage Aquila and Theodotion give ἀγάπη). In Xenophon (*Memorabilia*, II. vii. §§ 9 and 12), φιλεῖν and ἀγαπᾶν are used interchangeably, both indicating in turn *affection* (not sexual) and *esteem*. Cf. Ælian, *Var. Hist.* ix. 4, where it is said of a man's relations with his brothers, πάνυ σφόδρα ἀγαπήσας αὐτοὺς καὶ ὑπ' αὐτῶν φιληθεὶς ἐν τῷ μέρει.

An analysis of the passages in which φιλεῖν and ἀγαπᾶν occur in Jn. shows that they are practically synonyms in the Fourth Gospel.

[1] See, *e.g.*, Trench, *Synonyms of N.T.*, p. 39 f.
[2] These references are given by J. E. Sandys in a careful study of ἀγαπᾶν and φιλεῖν, first printed in the *Journal of Philology*, 1868, pp. 88–93.

Both verbs are used of *God's love for man*: ἀγαπᾶν at 3¹⁶ (where see note) 14²³ 17²³, 1 Jn. 4¹⁰· ¹⁹, etc., but φιλεῖν at 16²⁷ (cf. Rev. 3¹⁹).

Both verbs are used of *the Father's love for the Son*: ἀγαπᾶν at 3³⁵ 10¹⁷ 15⁹ 17²³· ²⁴· ²⁶ (cf. ὁ υἱός μου ὁ ἀγαπητός, Mk. 9⁷), but φιλεῖν at 5²⁰.

Both verbs are used of *Jesus' love for men*: ἀγαπᾶν at 11⁵ 13¹· ²³· ³⁴ 14²¹ 15⁹ 19²⁶ 21⁷· ²⁰, but φιλεῖν at 11³· ³⁶ 20². The last reference is specially noteworthy, as at 20² the beloved disciple is described as he ὃν ἐφίλει ὁ Ἰησοῦς, while we generally have ὃν ἠγάπα (13²³ 19²⁶).

Both verbs are used of the *love of men for other men*: ἀγαπᾶν at 13³⁴ 15¹²· ¹⁷, 1 Jn. 2¹⁰ 3¹⁰· ¹⁴· ²³ 4⁷· ²⁰, but φιλεῖν at 15¹⁹. The noun ἀγάπη is used for the love of men for each other at 13³⁵ 15¹³, 1 Jn. 4⁷; but the word that came to be specially appropriated to the brotherly love of Christian for Christian was not ἀγάπη but φιλαδελφία (see on 13³⁴, and cf. Tit. 3¹⁵).

Both verbs are used of the *love of men for Jesus*: ἀγαπᾶν at 8⁴² 14¹⁵· ²¹· ²³· ²⁴· ²⁸ 21¹⁵· ¹⁶, but φιλεῖν at 16²⁷ 21¹⁵· ¹⁶· ¹⁷ (cf. Mt. 10³⁷, 1 Cor. 16²²).

The *love of men for God* is generally described in the LXX by ἀγαπᾶν (Ex. 20⁶) or ἀγάπη (Wisd. 3⁹); but in Prov. 8¹⁷ we have φιλεῖν (ἐγὼ τοὺς ἐμὲ φιλοῦντας ἀγαπῶ ¹). In this sense we have ἀγάπη at 5⁴², 1 Jn. 2⁵· ¹⁵ 3¹⁷, and ἀγαπᾶν at 1 Jn. 4¹⁹· ²⁰· ²¹ 5² (not in the Gospel).

The *love of Jesus for the Father* is mentioned only once in the N.T., viz. at 14³¹ (where see note), and there the verb is ἀγαπᾶν.

Having regard to these facts, it would be precarious to lay stress on the change of ἀγαπᾷς in vv. 15 and 16 to φιλεῖς in v. 17. And a closer examination gives further reason for treating them as synonymous here.

First, it is clear that the author uses them as synonymous. Jn. purports to give a translation in Greek of Aramaic words spoken by Jesus. He makes Jesus say ἀγαπᾷς με in vv. 15, 16, and φιλεῖς με in v. 17; but by prefixing τὸ τρίτον to φιλεῖς με in the latter passage (cf. δεύτερον in v. 16), he seems to make it plain that the verbs are to be taken as identical in meaning, and to exclude the idea that a *new* thought is introduced by the use of φιλεῖς.

Secondly, Peter is represented as saying " Yes " to the question ἀγαπᾷς με; ναί, φιλῶ σε is his answer. This is fatal to the idea that Peter will not claim that he loves Jesus with the higher form of love called ἀγάπη, but that he ventures only

---

¹ Note that the *same* Hebrew word אָהֵב is variously rendered by ἀγαπᾶν and φιλεῖν in this verse.

Ἰωάνου, ἀγαπᾷς με πλέον τούτων; λέγει αὐτῷ Ναί, Κύριε, σὺ οἶδας

to say that he has φιλία for his Master. For why should he say " Yes," if he means " No " ?

Thirdly, the Syriac versions (both Old Syriac and Peshitta) use the same word to render ἀγαπᾷς and φιλεῖς in this passage, although two Syriac words were at their disposal. And this is the more remarkable because the Curetonian and Peshitta in rendering ἀγαπᾶν at 14²¹, where it occurs 3 times, use *both* the available Syriac words without distinction.[1]

In this connexion it is significant that ἀγαπᾶν and φιλεῖν are indifferently used in the LXX to translate the Hebr. אָהֵב ; this Hebrew root being nearly always behind ἀγαπᾶν, and always behind φιλεῖν except when φιλεῖν means " to kiss," when it represents נָשַׁק.

The Vulgate Latin distinguishes ἀγαπᾷς and φιλεῖς by the respective renderings *diligis* and *amas*;[2] but the O.L. texts *a e* have *amas* throughout, in this agreeing with the Syriac. No distinction is drawn between ἀγαπᾷς and φιλεῖς here in the Arabic version of Tatian's *Diatessaron*.

We conclude that we must treat ἀγαπᾷς and φιλεῖς in vv 15-17 as synonymous, as all the patristic expositors do.

ἀγαπᾷς με πλέον τούτων; πλέον (אBCDL) must be preferred to the rec. πλεῖον.

What is the meaning of πλέον τούτων ? It has been generally understood as meaning " more than your companions, the other apostles, love me "; and this yields a good sense. Peter had claimed that his loyalty surpassed that of the rest (Mk. 14²⁹; and cf. 13³⁷). He had taken precedence of the others, in speech (6⁶⁸) and act (18¹⁰), more than once. And the question of Jesus may mean, " Do you really love me more than the others do, as your forwardness in acting as their leader used to suggest ? " But (*a*) if this be the meaning, the construction is elliptical and ambiguous. We should expect the personal pronoun σύ to be introduced before or after ἀγαπᾷς to mark the emphasis; (*b*) comparisons of this kind, *sc.* between the love which this or that disciple displays or entertains, seem out of place on the lips of Jesus. To ask Peter if his love for his Master exceeds the love which, *e.g.*, the Beloved Disciple cherished for Him, would be a severe test; and the question would be one which Peter could never answer with confidence.

[1] See J. R. Harris, *Odes of Solomon* (ed. 1911), p. 91.
[2] For the distinction between *diligo* and *amo*, cf. Cicero, *ad Brutum*, I. i. 1 : " Clodius . . . ualde me *diligit*, uel, ut ἐμφατικώτερον dicam, ualde me *amat*."

ὅτι φιλῶ σε. λέγει αὐτῷ Βόσκε τὰ ἀρνία μου.   16. λέγει αὐτῷ

Does, then, ἀγαπᾷς με πλέον τούτων; mean "lovest thou me more than these things?" *sc.* the boat and the nets and the fishing, to which Peter had returned after the Passion and the Resurrection of his Master.   This interpretation is, indeed, unattractive; but it may possibly be right, and it is free from some difficulties which beset the usual interpretation.

At any rate, Peter in his reply takes no notice of πλέον τούτων.   If he had ever intended to claim that his affection for his Master was greater than that of his companions, he does so no longer.   Nor does he rest his answer on his own feelings alone.   His fall had taught him humility.   "Yea, Lord, thou knowest (σὺ οἶδας) that I love thee" (φιλῶ σε, with which cf. 16²⁷).   He rests his case on the Master's insight into his heart.

The answer of Jesus accepts Peter's assurance: "Feed my lambs."   The Lord "confides those whom He loves to the man who loves Him" (Luthardt).   At the time of his call, the charge to Peter was that he was to be a "fisher" of men (Mt. 4¹⁹, Mk. 1¹⁷, Lk. 5¹⁰); and such was his work as an apostle, during the days of his Master's visible presence and control. But that would not be sufficient for an apostolic ministry, when Jesus had departed.   Henceforth the ministry consists not only of "catching" men, but of guiding and guarding them in their new spiritual environment.   And so the image now used at Peter's second "call" is not that of the *fisher*, but of the *shepherd*, whose tender devotion must take as its exemplar the life of the Good Shepherd of 10¹¹⁻¹⁶.

φιλῶ σε is all that Peter will say.   But it is enough.

Βόσκε τὰ ἀρνία μου is the charge committed to him by the Chief Pastor in the first instance.   The charge is repeated in varying forms in vv. 16, 17, and it is not easy either to determine the true text in each case or, having determined it, to decide whether the changes of verbs and nouns are significant for Jn.

In vv. 15, 17, the verb is βόσκε; in v. 16 it is ποίμαινε.   In the Synoptists βόσκειν is always used of feeding swine; but it is regularly used in the LXX of feeding sheep (*e.g.* Gen. 29⁷ 37¹²), and in Ezek. 34² in a metaphorical sense (as here) of a pastor feeding his flock with spiritual food.

ποιμαίνειν is, etymologically, a verb of wider connotation, covering all duties that pertain to a ποιμήν or shepherd, guiding and guarding, as well as feeding the flock.   It occurs again Lk. 17⁷, 1 Cor. 9⁷, in its literal sense, and in the spiritual sense of "shepherding" Acts 20²⁸, 1 Pet. 5², Rev. 2²⁷ 7¹⁷ etc.   But it is doubtful if ποίμαινε of v. 16 should be understood as different from βόσκε of vv. 15, 17. ποιμαίνειν is used in the LXX of feeding sheep, exactly as βόσκειν is (e.g. Gen. 30³¹ 37²), and so too in its spiritual significance, e.g. Ps. 23¹ ὁ κύριος ποιμαίνει με, and Ezek. 34¹⁰ τοῦ μὴ ποιμαίνειν τὰ πρόβατα μου.

The Vulgate has in vv. 15, 16, 17, pasce . . . pasce . . . pasce, no attempt being made to distinguish the Greek verbs; and it would be rash to assume that different Aramaic words lie behind βόσκε and ποίμαινε respectively in the present passage, more particularly as in the LXX βόσκειν and ποιμαίνειν are used indifferently to translate רָעָה.

We now turn to the various words used to describe the flock who are to be tended, and here we have to do with conflicting readings:

   In v. 15, ἀρνία is certainly right; C*D giving πρόβατα.
   In v. 16, προβάτια is read by BC as against πρόβατα, which has the support of אADNΓΔ.
   In v. 17, πρόβατα is read by אDNΓΔ, as against ABC, which have προβάτια.

A careful study of the Syriac versions by Burkitt leads him to the conclusion that ἀρνία . . πρόβατια . . . πρόβατα were probably the original Greek words behind the Syriac.[1] With this, the Latin Vulgate agnos . . . agnos . . . oves agrees, for προβάτια as a diminutive may be very well represented by agnos. The O.L. versions, for the most part, do not distinguish, and give oves three times; but there are also traces of a reading oviculas in vv. 16, 17.

These variants indicate, as it seems, that two or three different Aramaic words lie behind the Greek, although such an inference is not certain, having regard to what has been said above in relation to ἀγαπᾶν–φιλεῖν and βόσκειν–ποιμαίνειν. And we incline to adopt the readings ἀρνία . . . προβάτια . . . πρόβατα in vv. 15, 16, 17 respectively, although the uncial evidence for προβάτια in v. 16 is not very strong. Hence the charge to Peter first entrusts to his care the lambs, then the young sheep, and lastly the whole flock, young and old.

With ἀρνία, προβάτια, may be compared τεκνία of 13³³. This use of diminutives indicates a tenderness in the speaker's words. ἀρνίον occurs in the N.T. elsewhere only in the Apocalpyse, where it is used 29 times of the Lamb of God (see on 1²⁹): it is infrequent in the LXX. προβάτιον does not appear again in the Greek Bible.

Some commentators (who find in the delivery of the special charge " Feed my lambs, . . . my sheep " to Peter individually, an indication of his being entrusted with a higher

---

[1] Ev. da Mepharreshê, note in loc.

πάλιν δεύτερον Σίμων Ἰωάνου, ἀγαπᾷς με; λέγει αὐτῷ Ναί, Κύριε, σὺ οἶδας ὅτι φιλῶ σε. λέγει αὐτῷ Ποίμαινε τὰ προβάτιά μου. 17. λέγει αὐτῷ τὸ τρίτον Σίμων Ἰωάνου, φιλεῖς με; ἐλυπήθη ὁ Πέτρος ὅτι εἶπεν αὐτῷ τὸ τρίτον Φιλεῖς με; καὶ εἶπεν αὐτῷ Κύριε, πάντα σὺ

commission than that of the other apostles) interpret the "lambs" the *faithful laity*, while the "sheep" whom Peter was to feed typify *other pastors*. This is anachronistic exegesis, but hardly more so than the interpretation which finds in this passage an anticipation of the primacy of the Roman See. Such thoughts were outside the purview of Christians at the time when the Fourth Gospel was published.[1]

16. λέγει αὐτῷ πάλιν δεύτερον. For this tautological phrase, see on 4⁵⁴.

Σίμων Ἰωάνου, ἀγαπᾷς με; The "more than these" of v. 15 is now dropped. And Peter's answer is the same as before: **ναί, . . . φιλῶ σε.** The reply ποίμαινε τὰ προβάτιά μου is only to be distinguished from βόσκε τὰ ἀρνία μου (v. 15) or βόσκε τὰ πρόβατά μου (v. 17), in so far as it entrusts a *different section* of the flock to the pastoral care of Peter. To distinguish ποιμαίνειν from βόσκειν here is a modern subtlety, unknown to Christian antiquity; and it has been shown above to be without support from the LXX use of these verbs, which consistently represent the same Hebrew root.

17. τὸ τρίτον. Cf. δεύτερον in v. 16. This is the *same* question as before, repeated for the third time, and not a *new* question, as it would be if φιλεῖς με; were different in meaning from ἀγαπᾷς με; of vv. 15, 16.

W has ἀγαπᾷς here, as in vv. 15, 16.

ἐλυπήθη ὁ Πέτρος. He knew that he had given cause for the doubting of his love, and it grieved him that his repeated assurance that it still inspired him was not treated as sufficient by his Master. For ὁ Πέτρος here, see on 18¹⁵.

καὶ εἶπεν αὐτῷ. אBCDΘ prefix καί, which is omitted by A. For εἶπεν (BCΓΔ), אADWΘ have λέγει.

Peter leaves out ναί in this third answer. He appeals to the knowledge of his feelings which he is assured Jesus must have.

πάντα σὺ οἶδας (cf. 16³⁰). Long before this, the chosen companions of Jesus had learnt that His insight into human character and motive was unerring; cf. 2²⁵ αὐτὸς γὰρ ἐγίνωσκεν τί ἦν ἐν τῷ ἀνθρώπῳ, the verb γινώσκειν, of immediate observation, being used there, as here.

Ἰησοῦς : om. אDW, ins. ΑΝΓΔ. BC om. ὁ.

[1] Cf. Trench, *Miracles*, p. 467, and Stanton, *The Gospels as Historical Documents*, iii. 26.

οἶδας, σὺ γινώσκεις ὅτι φιλῶ σε· λέγει αὐτῷ Ἰησοῦς Βόσκε τὰ πρόβατά μου.

18. Ἀμὴν ἀμὴν λέγω σοι, ὅτε ἦς νεώτερος, ἐζώννυες σεαυτὸν καὶ περιεπάτεις ὅπου ἤθελες· ὅταν δὲ γηράσῃς, ἐκτενεῖς τὰς χεῖράς σου,

Βόσκε τὰ πρόβατά μου. This is the final charge, *pasce oues meas*. τὰ πρόβατα includes the whole flock, young and old.

Prediction of Peter's martyrdom (vv. 18, 19); and a misunderstood saying about John (vv. 20-23)

18, 19. ἀμὴν ἀμὴν λέγω σοι. When Jesus warned Peter that he would deny Him, he prefaced the warning by the same impressive phrase (13[38]; see on 1[51]).

There is no *explicit* reference to Peter's death in the words which follow. He has been bidden to feed the Lord's sheep, and he is reminded that, although, when he was young, he was unfettered and able to follow his own wishes, yet when he grew old he would be obliged to yield to the will of others. At this time he was no longer a youth; he had been married for some time (cf. Mt. 8[14]), and was approaching middle life. The words ἐζώννυες σεαυτὸν . . . ἄλλος ζώσει σε may point only to the contrast between the alertness of youth and the helplessness of old age, which cannot always do what it would; and ἐκτενεῖς τὰς χεῖράς σου may refer merely to the old man stretching out his hands that others may help him in putting on his garments, whereas the young man girds himself unassisted, before he sets out to walk (περιπατεῖν).

Further, ζώννυμι (only again at Acts 12[8] in the N.T.) is always used in the LXX, as in Greek generally, of girding on clothes or armour,[1] and no instance is forthcoming of its use in the sense of *binding* a criminal, which must be supposed to be the meaning of ἄλλος ζώσει σε if the Lord's words are taken as predictive of Peter's martyrdom. The order of the clauses in v. 18 is also strange if crucifixion was in the mind of the speaker; for we should expect the extension of the *hands* to be mentioned last.

On the other hand, this feature of death by crucifixion, that the hands were extended upon the cross, is specially mentioned as its characteristic by other writers. Wetstein quotes Artem. *Oniv.* i. 76, κακοῦργος δὲ ὢν σταυρωθήσεται διὰ τὸ ὕψος καὶ τὴν τῶν χειρῶν ἔκτασιν, and Arrian, *Epict.* iii. 26, ἐκτείνας σεαυτὸν ὡς οἱ ἐσταυρωμένοι. Field adds a quotation from Dion. Hal. *Ant.* vii. 69, οἱ δ' ἄγοντες τὸν θεράποντα ἐπὶ τὴν τιμωρίαν, τὰς

---

[1] It is used at 1 Macc. 6[37] of binding wooden " towers " on an elephant's back, but this does not help us here.

χεῖρας ἀποτείνοντες ἀμφοτέρας καὶ ξύλῳ προσδήσαντες παρὰ τὰ στέρνα τε καὶ τοὺς ὤμους.[1]

More significant than these parallels, however, is the fact that several early Christian writers treat ἔκτασις τῶν χειρῶν or a like phrase as a sufficient description by itself of crucifixion. Thus Barnabas (§ 12) finds a τύπος σταυροῦ in the extension of Moses' hands during the battle with Amalek (Ex. 17[12]). Justin has the same idea : Μωυσῆς . . τὰς χεῖρας ἑκατέρως ἐκπετάσας, and again, διὰ τοῦ τύπου τῆς ἐκτάσεως τῶν χειρῶν (*Tryph.* 90, 91). Irenæus reports the same exegesis as that of one of his predecessors, ὡς ἔφη τις τῶν προβεβηκότων, διὰ τῆς (θείας) ἐκτάσεως τῶν χειρῶν (*Hær.* v. 17. 4; cf. *Dem.* 46).[2] Or, again, the words of Isa. 65[2], " I have spread out my hands all the day to a rebellious people," are regarded as a prophecy of the Crucifixion by Barnabas (§ 12), Justin (*Apol.* i. 35), Irenæus (*Dem.* 79), and Cyprian (*Test.* ii. 20). Cyprian in the same passage quotes also Ps. 88[9] and Ps. 141[2] as predictive of the Cross, although there is nothing in either verse suggestive of it, except that the Psalmist speaks of the " spreading out " or the " lifting up " of his hands in prayer. And, finally, the sign of the Cross in the heavens before the Last Judgment [3] is baldly described in the *Didache* (xvi. 6) as σημεῖον ἐκπετάσεως ἐν οὐρανῷ.

It is, then, intelligible that the writer of the Appendix to Jn. should regard the words ἐκτενεῖς τὰς χεῖράς σου in v. 18 as an unmistakable prediction of martyrdom by the cross. But whatever the meaning of v. 18, the text clearly embodies a genuine reminiscence of words spoken by the Lord. If the author of the Appendix is right in his interpretation of them, " this He said, signifying by what death He should glorify God," he must be taken as relying on memory or tradition for his report of the words used; for, if he desired to place sentences of his own making in the mouth of Jesus, which should contain a prophecy of Peter's crucifixion, he would have phrased them with less ambiguity.

It is possible (see on 2[21] and the references there given) that the comment of v. 19 is a mistaken one. But even in that case we have a clear indication that the narrator, at the time of writing, believed that Peter was dead, and that he had died a martyr's death by crucifixion. This became the tradition of the Church. The earliest appearance of it is in Tertullian (*Scorp.* 15, about 211 A.D.); and it is noteworthy that he makes reference to the words of Jn. 21[18]: " Tunc Petrus ab altero

---

[1] Trench gives other parallel passages (*Miracles*, p. 468).
[2] Cf. also Tertullian, *adv. Judæos*, 10, and Cyprian, *Test.* ii. 21.
[3] Cf. Cyr. Hier. *Cat.* xv. 22.

καὶ ἄλλος ζώσει σε καὶ οἴσει ὅπου οὐ θέλεις.   19. τοῦτο δὲ εἶπεν σημαίνων ποίῳ θανάτῳ δοξάσει τὸν Θεόν.   καὶ τοῦτο εἰπὼν λέγει αὐτῷ Ἀκολούθει μοι.   20. ἐπιστραφεὶς ὁ Πέτρος βλέπει τὸν μαθητὴν

cingitur, cum cruci adstringatur," interpreting ἄλλος ζώσει σε of the binding of the martyr to the cross. Origen (ap. Eus. H.E. iii. 1, if indeed the report is Origen's, which is doubtful) is the first to tell that Peter was crucified with his head down-ward, ἀνεσκολοπίσθη κατὰ κεφαλῆς, a statement which appears, embellished with legend, in the *Acta Petri* and in many later writers. The notices of Peter's death are perplexing,[1] and the subject cannot be pursued here; but it is plain that the tradition of his crucifixion goes back to Jn. 21[18. 19].

With the comment τοῦτο δὲ εἶπεν κτλ. should be compared 12[33], τοῦτο δὲ ἔλεγεν σημαίνων ποίῳ θανάτῳ ἤμελλεν ἀποθνήσκειν. For ἤμελλεν ἀποθνήσκειν we have here δοξάσει τὸν θεόν. We should expect ἤμελλεν δοξάζειν . . . , but δοξάσει places the narrator back in the scene described, when the martyrdom of Peter was still in the future. It is characteristic of the style of Jn. (see on 1[45]), that the writer does not stay to tell explicitly that Peter was dead, for this is a fact which the whole Church knew.

The phrase descriptive of a martyr's death, by which he was said to " glorify God " in his sufferings, occurs again in 1 Pet. 4[16], where a man who is threatened with suffering ὡς Χριστιανός is exhorted thus : δοξαζέτω δὲ τὸν θεὸν ἐν τῷ ὀνόματι τούτῳ. The phrase is common in the martyrologies. See on 13[31], where it is pointed out that this thought must be dis-tinguished from the thought that in his death a martyr " is glorified " by God.

Ἀκολούθει μοι.   See 1[43] for the invitation to Philip ex-pressed thus, and the Synoptic references there given. It would seem from v. 20 that ἀκολούθει μοι here signified a literal following of Jesus as He moved away from the assembled disciples, Peter and John alone going with Him. But the words may well have recalled to Peter the invitation extended to him in early days, " Come, and I will make you a fisher of men " (Mt. 4[19], Mk. 1[17], Lk. 5[10]); and he could hardly have failed to remember a recent occasion when his eager offer to follow Jesus was put aside by the Master (Jn. 13[36]). See p. 529 above.

20. With ἐπιστραφεὶς ὁ Πέτρος, cf. 20[14. 16] (see also Mk. 5[30]). אDNΓΔΘ add δέ after ἐπιστρ., but om. ABCW.

Peter obeyed the summons to follow Jesus, and as they moved away from the others John went after them, not doubting

---

[1] See, for a severe cross-examination of the sources, Schmiedel in E.B., s.v. " Simon Peter."

ὃν ἠγάπα ὁ Ἰησοῦς ἀκολουθοῦντα, ὃς καὶ ἀνέπεσεν ἐν τῷ δείπνῳ ἐπὶ
τὸ στῆθος αὐτοῦ καὶ εἶπεν Κύριε, τίς ἐστιν ὁ παραδιδούς σε;
21. τοῦτον οὖν ἰδὼν ὁ Πέτρος λέγει τῷ Ἰησοῦ Κύριε, οὗτος δὲ τί;
22. λέγει αὐτῷ ὁ Ἰησοῦς Ἐὰν αὐτὸν θέλω μένειν ἕως ἔρχομαι, τί
πρὸς σέ; σύ μοι ἀκολούθει. 23. ἐξῆλθεν οὖν οὗτος ὁ λόγος εἰς τοὺς

that he was welcome, whenever Jesus called his close friend
Peter. See Introd., p. xxxvi f.

The "disciple whom Jesus loved" (v. 7, 13²³) is more
closely described by recalling his action, when, at the instigation
of Peter, he asked who the traitor was. ἀνέπεσεν reproduces
ἀναπεσών of 13²⁵ (where see note).

21. τοῦτον οὖν. The rec. om. οὖν with AWΓΔΘ, but ins. אBCD

Peter has been told that he will die by crucifixion, and he
at once asks what is to be the fate of his friend. Latham notes
in his character " a peculiar kind of curiosity, which we find in
people of very active minds," [1] and cites 13²⁴, where Peter is
eager to ascertain at once who is the traitor in the company.

οὗτος δὲ τί; "This man, what?" To this the answer is a
rebuke, such as Jesus gave more than once to people who were
curious about the duty or the destiny of others (see on 14²²).
Dods (*in loc.*) recalls a man sketched by Thomas à Kempis:
"considerat, quod alii facere tenentur, et negligit, quod ipse
tenetur" (*Imit. Chr.* ii. 1)

22. Ἐὰν αὐτὸν θέλω κτλ. "If it is My will (θέλω is here
the θέλω of masterful authority, cf. 17²⁴) that he should tarry
(μένειν is used of survival, as at 1 Cor. 15⁶) until I come, what
is that to thee?"

ἕως ἔρχομαι is literally "while I am coming" (see on 9⁴ for
ἕως with the pres. indic. in Jn.), but it means here, as at 1 Tim.
4¹³, "*until* I come."

The emphasis is on ἐὰν θέλω. Jesus is not represented as
saying that it *is* His will that the Beloved Disciple would
survive; but if it *was* His will, that was no concern of Peter's.

That ἕως ἔρχομαι is meant to be interpreted by the Second
Coming of Christ is not doubtful (cf. 14³). To apply it to the
coming of Christ at a disciple's death is a desperate expedient of
exegesis; and thus interpreted, the saying is meaningless, for
every one "tarries" until Christ comes in *that* sense

σύ μοι ἀκολούθει. "As for you (σύ is very emphatic),
follow me," repeated from v. 19. This is the last precept of
Jesus recorded in the last Gospel; and it is the final and essential
precept of the Christian life. See on v. 19.

23. ἐξῆλθεν οὖν οὗτος ὁ λόγος κτλ. "So this saying went
forth," etc. Cf. Mk. 1²⁸ for a similar use of ἐξῆλθεν.

[1] *The Risen Master*, p. 265.

ἀδελφοὺς ὅτι ὁ μαθητὴς ἐκεῖνος οὐκ ἀποθνήσκει· οὐκ εἶπεν δὲ αὐτῷ ὁ Ἰησοῦς ὅτι οὐκ ἀποθνήσκει, ἀλλ᾽ Ἐὰν αὐτὸν θέλω μένειν ἕως ἔρχομαι, τί πρὸς σέ;

εἰς τοὺς ἀδελφούς. " The brethren " are the Christian community, who were to each other as brothers (see on 13³⁴ for the new commandment which enjoined this). The expression is not used thus in the Gospel narratives, where indeed it would be anachronistic, the sense of Christian brotherhood not being realised until after the Resurrection; but we have it often in the Acts (1¹⁵ 9³⁰ 10²³, etc.), and it appears in Eph. 6²³, 1 Jn. 3¹⁴. ¹⁶, 3 Jn. ³. ⁵.

ὅτι ὁ μαθητὴς ἐκεῖνος οὐκ ἀποθνήσκει. ὅτι is *recitantis*, introducing the words of the reported saying. The use of ἐκεῖνος is Johannine (see on 1⁸).

οὐκ εἶπεν δέ. This is read by אBCW 33, a strong combination; but the position of δέ is unusual, " perhaps without parallel in Johannine Greek " (Abbott, *Diat.* 2075). AD, followed by *a b e f*, have καὶ οὐκ εἶπεν, καί being used for καίτοι, a frequent Johannine usage (see on 3¹¹). If the original were . . . ΑΠΟΘΝΗΣΚΕΙΚΑΙ . . . καί might easily have dropped out by accident, and then δέ would be added to make the sense clear.

The comment of the writer upon the saying which he has recorded is quite in the manner of Jn. (see on 2²¹), as are the repetition of the saying itself (cf. 16¹⁶⁻¹⁹), and the use of the word λόγος for a " saying " of Jesus (see on 2²²).

τί πρὸς σέ; is om. in this verse by א*, but is found in אᵃABCWΔΘ.

Concluding notes of authentication (vv. 24, 25)

24. The Appendix to the Gospel needed a conclusion; it could not have ended with v. 23. V. 24 identifies the Beloved Disciple, of whom vv. 22, 23 tell, with the author (in some sense) of the Gospel; an identification which has not hitherto been made explicitly; and v. 25 adds that much remains unrecorded about the works of Jesus

V. 24 (like 19³⁵), being an explanatory comment on what has gone before, is thoroughly Johannine (see on 2²¹). Jn., *i.e.* the actual writer of the Gospel, explains that the narratives which he has recorded were derived from the " witness " of the Beloved Disciple. For the present participle μαρτυρῶν, the Sinai Syriac has " bare witness," perhaps implying that the μαθητής was dead at the time when the Appendix (or at any rate the postscript) was added. But the language used and

24. Οὗτός ἐστιν ὁ μαθητὴς ὁ μαρτυρῶν περὶ τούτων καὶ ὁ γράψας ταῦτα, καὶ οἴδαμεν ὅτι ἀληθὴς αὐτοῦ ἡ μαρτυρία ἐστίν. 25. Ἔστιν

the tense of μαρτυρῶν rather suggests that he was alive; cf. "he *knoweth*" at 19[35].

περὶ τούτων probably refers to the whole content of the Gospel, and not merely to the episode recorded in c. 21, although it includes at any rate the latter part of this.

καὶ ὁ γράψας ταῦτα. *Prima facie*, this indicates that the Beloved Disciple actually wrote the Gospel with his own hand,[1] including the Appendix, and not only that his reminiscences are behind it. But γράφειν is sometimes used when *dictation* only is intended. *E.g.* "Pilate wrote a title and put it on the cross" (19[19]) means that Pilate was responsible for the wording of the *titulus*, but hardly that he wrote himself on the wooden board. So Paul says, "I write the more boldly to you" (Rom. 15[15]), while it appears from Rom. 16[22] that the scribe of the epistle was one *Tertius*. Cf. Gal. 6[11], and 1 Pet. 5[12]. The employment of scribes was very common. Further, in Judg. 8[14] the LXX has ἔγραψεν πρὸς αὐτόν (*v.l.* ἀπεγράψατο), where the meaning is "he described," *i.e.* "he caused to be written down," not necessarily that the young prisoner wrote down the list of names *sua manu*. This is the meaning which we attach to ἔγραψεν in the present passage. The elders of the Church certified that the Beloved Disciple *caused these things to be written*. They were put into shape by the writer who took them down, and afterwards published them, not as his own, but as "the Gospel according to John." See Introd., p. lxiv.

καὶ οἴδαμεν κτλ. Chrysostom (*in loc.*) seems to have read οἶδα μέν . . . , and this would give a good sense. "I know," that is, the writer whom we call Jn. knew, that the testimony of the aged disciple was truthful; but it was not to be taken as a complete account of all that Jesus did, μέν in v. 24 being balanced by δέ in v. 25. Such an attestation, however, by a writer who conceals his name and identity, would not be so impressive as οἴδαμεν (which all the versions follow), the plural representing the concurrence of the presbyters of the Church at Ephesus where the Gospel was produced. For the early traditions to this effect, see Introd., pp. lvi, lix.

Jn. is prone to use οἴδαμεν when he wishes to express the common belief and assurance of the Christian community, *e.g.* 1 Jn. 3[2, 14] 5[15, 19, 20]; see also on 3[11].

ὅτι ἀληθὴς αὐτοῦ ἡ μαρτυρία ἐστίν. So BC*DW, while the rec. has ἀληθ. ἐστ. ἡ μαρτ. αὐτοῦ, with ℵAC³ΓΔΘ. Cf. 3 Jn.[12],

---

[1] Sanday presses this too far (*Criticism of Fourth Gospel*, p. 63).

δὲ καὶ ἄλλα πολλὰ ἃ ἐποίησεν ὁ Ἰησοῦς, ἅτινα ἐὰν γράφηται καθ' ἕν, οὐδ' αὐτὸν οἶμαι τὸν κόσμον χωρήσειν τὰ γραφόμενα βιβλία.

οἶδας ὅτι ἡ μαρτυρία ἡμῶν ἀληθής ἐστιν, as well as the parallel 19³⁵, where see note. In the paraphrase of Nonnus this attestation clause is omitted at 21²⁴.

For the stress laid by Jn. on " truth " and " witness " see on 1⁷· ¹⁴, and cf. Introd., p. xci.

25. This verse was omitted from his text by Tischendorf, because he had concluded that it was not in the original text of ℵ, but had been added by a corrector. His judgment was challenged by Tregelles, and was finally shown by Gwynn to be untenable.[1]   There is *no* documentary authority for omitting the verse; the only MS. which does not now contain it (cursive 63) has lost a page at the end, as Gwynn demonstrated in 1893.

ἔστιν δέ.   These words do not appear in the Sinai Syriac, nor does Chrysostom betray knowledge of them.

Wetstein cites several passages from the Talmud couched in hyperbolical language similar to that of v. 25.   A remarkable parallel occurs in Philo, *de post. Caini*, 43, where it is said that if God wished to display the riches of His creation, the whole earth, land, and sea would not contain them (χωρῆσαι).   Cf. 1 Macc. 9²², where, however, the figure is not so exaggerated.

For ἃ (ℵBC*) the rec. has ὅσα with AC²DWΘ.

ἅτινα ἐάν κτλ., " whatsoever things may be written," etc. The constr. is irregular, but the meaning is hardly doubtful. Origen, however, interpreted the verse as meaning that the world would not be equal to the record of such great acts as those of Christ, not merely that it could not contain the books which told of them (see Abbott, *Diat.* 2414).

αὐτὸν οἶμαι is omitted by Syr. sin.   οἴεσθαι occurs again in N.T. only at Phil. 1¹⁷, Jas. 1⁷; cf. 4 Macc. 1³³ ἐγὼ μὲν οἶμαι " such is my opinion."

The singular οἶμαι, following the plur. οἴδαμεν of v. 24, has been thought to show that vv. 24 and 25 are separate notes from different hands.   But this is not necessary to suppose. The writer associates others with himself in the attestation of v. 24, but in the editorial reflection or colophon of v. 25 he speaks only for himself.

ἀμήν, with which the rec. ends, is not part of the true text.

[1] *Hermathena*, 1893, pp. 374 ff.

THE "PERICOPE DE ADULTERA"

(VII. 53–VIII. 11)

THE section (περικοπή) of the Fourth Gospel which contains this incident is contained in many late manuscripts and versions, but it cannot be regarded as Johannine or as part of the Gospel text.

It is not found in any of the early Greek uncials, with the single exception of Codex Bezae (D), being omitted without comment in אBNTWθ. L and Δ omit it, while leaving a blank space where it might be inserted, thus indicating that their scribes deliberately rejected it as part of the Johannine text. A and C are defective at this point, but neither could have contained the section, as the missing leaves would not have had room for it.

The section is omitted also in important cursives, *e.g.* 22, 33, 565 (in which minuscule there is a note that the scribe knew of its existence). The Ferrar cursives, i.e. *fam.* 13, do not give it in Jn., but place the section after Lk. 21³⁸, where it would be, indeed, in better agreement with the context than before Jn. 8¹². Cursives 1, 1582, and some American MSS. place the section at the *end* of the Fourth Gospel. Cursive 225 places it after Jn. 7³⁶.

The Old Syriac vss. (whether in Tatian's *Diatessaron*, Syr. sin., or Syr. cur.) betray no knowledge of the passage, nor is it contained in the best MSS. of the Peshitta. In like manner the Coptic vss. omit it, *e.g.* the fourth century Coptic Q (see p. xvi). Some of the O.L. MSS. are also without it, e.g. *a f l* q.*

Even more significant is the absence of any comment on the section by Greek commentators for a thousand years after Christ, including Origen, Chrysostom, and Nonnus (in his metrical paraphrase), who deal with the Gospel verse by verse. The earliest Greek writer (Euthymius Zigabenus or Zygadenus) who comments on it lived about 1118, and even he says that the accurate copies of the Gospel do not contain it.

Further, the evidence of vocabulary and style is conclusive against the Johannine authorship of the section. The notes which follow demonstrate this sufficiently. Nor in its traditional place does it harmonise with the context. It interrupts the sequence of 7⁵² and 8¹²ᶠ·; while 7⁵³ is not in harmony with what goes before, and has no connexion with 8¹²ᶠ·.

The early Greek evidence in favour of the mediæval view that the section is an authentic part of the Fourth Gospel reduces itself to the witness of Codex Bezae (D), a manuscript with many other Western interpolations. The section is found in the great mass of later uncials and cursives, whatever be the reason of this intrusion into the more ancient text. To be borne in mind, however, is the significant fact that in many of the later MSS. which contain it, the *Pericope de adultera* is marked with an obelus *(e.g.* S) or an asterisk *(e.g.* EMΛ).

The Latin evidence in its favour is considerable. The section appears in several O.L. texts, e.g. *b e* (sæc. v.) and *ff₂* (sæc. vii.), as well as in Jerome's Vulgate. Jerome says expressly " in multis graecis et latinis codicibus inuenitur de adultera," etc. (*adv. Pelag.* ii. 17). Augustine (*de conj. adult.* ii. 6) accounts for its omission from some texts, by hinting that the words of Jesus which it records might seem too lenient.

The section is found also in some late Syriac and Coptic texts, while omitted in the earlier and better versions.

These facts show that the authorities on the side of the *Pericope* are almost wholly Western, and do not become numerous in any language until after the acceptance by Jerome of the section as Johannine. Jerome seems to have followed here some Greek MSS. not now extant. This evidence is, however, wholly insufficient to justify the inclusion of the narrative in the Fourth Gospel. The ignoring of it by the early Greek MSS., vss., and commentators is thus left unexplained.

Nevertheless, the story of the adulteress seems to be an authentic fragment of early tradition as to the sayings and actions of Jesus. The story is mentioned (although not referred to the Fourth Gospel) in the *Apostolic Constitutions* (ii. 24), a passage which goes back to the fourth century or perhaps even to the third. It must have been current as a tradition in the third century at any rate. Eusebius probably refers to it when he says of Papias that " he relates another story of a woman who was accused of many sins before the Lord which is contained in the Gospel according to the Hebrews " (Eus. *H.E.* iii. 39). Whether Papias got the story from the extra-canonical " Gospel according to the Hebrews," or from some other source, is not certain. But that the *Pericope de adultera* is the story which Papias told has been accepted by many critics ; and, accordingly, in Lightfoot's *Apostolic Fathers* the passage [Jn.] vii. 53–viii. 11 is printed as one of the surviving fragments of Papias, bishop of Hierapolis.

This is highly probable, but is not certain. All we can assert with confidence is that the passage is very like the Synoptic stories about Jesus ; while its tenderness and gravity commend it as faithfully representing what Jesus said and did when a woman who had sinned unchastely was brought before Him.

No reason for the ready acceptance in the West of the story as evangelical, and of its incorporation in the Latin Gospels as early as the fourth century, can be assigned with certainty. It is perhaps significant that in the *Apostolic Constitutions* (ii. 24), where we find the narrative for the first time, it is cited as a lesson to bishops who are inclined to be too severe to penitents. Now writers like Origen, Tertullian, and Cyprian, who discuss at length the problems of discipline for adultery, never mention this case. Like the rest of the Church, East and West, in the second and third centuries, they held that punishment for fornication ought to be very severe, inasmuch as it seemed essential to mark the divergence of Christian ethics from heathen ethics on this point. But by the time we reach the fourth century, ecclesiastical discipline began to be relaxed and to be less austere ; and a story which had been formerly thought dangerous because of its apparent leniency would naturally be appealed to by canonists and divines as indicating the tenderness with which our Lord Himself rebuked sins of the flesh. It was but a short step from quoting the story as edifying to treating it as suitable for reading in Church. It would thus get into lectionaries, and in the Greek Menology it is the lection for St. Pelagia's day. From its insertion in Evangelistaria, it readily crept into Gospel texts, from which Jerome did not feel it

vii. 53. Καὶ ἐπορεύθησαν ἕκαστος εἰς τὸν οἶκον αὐτοῦ. viii. 1. Ἰησοῦς δὲ
ἐπορεύθη εἰς τὸ Ὄρος τῶν Ἐλαιῶν. 2. Ὄρθρου δὲ πάλιν παρεγένετο εἰς τὸ ἱερόν,
καὶ πᾶς ὁ λαὸς ἤρχετο πρὸς αὐτόν, καὶ καθίσας ἐδίδασκεν αὐτούς. 3. Ἄγουσιν δὲ
οἱ γραμματεῖς καὶ οἱ Φαρισαῖοι γυναῖκα ἐπὶ μοιχείᾳ κατειλημμένην, καὶ στή-

practicable to expel it. Perhaps thus, or somewhat thus, its presence
in the *textus receptus* of the Fourth Gospel is to be explained.

The text of the *Pericope* which is given here is that adopted by
Hort. The various readings are more numerous than in any other
part of the N.T., and a large number of explanatory glosses were
added to the text in ancient times. Hort's analysis of these can
hardly be improved. We have to do here only with the *later* uncials,
and these are cited by the customary letters (EGH, etc.) as explained
by Gregory or Scrivener. We cite the cursive 1071 because of its
remarkable agreement with D in this section. (See K. Lake, *Texts
from Mount Athos*, p. 1481.)

VII. 53. ἐπορεύθησαν. So D, etc., with O.L. and vg.; the rec. has
ἐπορεύθη with minor uncials and *fam.* 13.

πορεύεσθαι εἰς . . . occurs only at 7³⁵ in Jn., who prefers πορ. πρός
(cf. 14²⁸ 16²⁸ 20¹⁷); the constr. is common in the Synoptists.

VIII. 1. τὸ ὄρος τῶν ἐλαιῶν is, again, a Synoptic term, not occurring
again in Jn. When Jn. introduces a place-name for the first time he
is apt to add a word of explanation (4⁵ 11¹), but nothing of the kind
is here.

Mention of the Mount of Olives would fall in with the story referring
to the week before the Passion, when Jesus lodged at Bethany; cf.
Mk. 11¹¹· ¹⁹ 13³.

2. ὄρθρου is Lucan (Lk. 24¹; cf. Acts 5²¹); Jn. does not use it, but
has πρωΐ instead (18²⁸ 20¹ 21⁴).

The frequent use of δέ in this section to the exclusion of Jn.'s
favourite οὖν (see on 1²²) marks the style as non-Johannine.

παρεγένετο. D 1071 have παραγίνεται. The verb occurs in Jn. only
once (3²²). ἦλθεν is read by *fam.* 13.

λαός is found in Jn. only twice (11⁵⁰ 18¹⁴); he prefers ὄχλος,
which some MSS. give here.

The clause **καὶ πᾶς ὁ λαὸς . . . ἐδίδασκεν αὐτούς** is omitted by *fam.*
13; while D om. καὶ καθίσας ἐδίδασκεν αὐτούς.

For **καθίσας**, as describing the attitude of Jesus when teaching, see
on 6³ (cf. Mk. 13³). Jn. generally specifies the nature of Jesus' teaching
in the Temple (cf. 7²⁸ 8²⁰), but at 7¹⁴ he writes simply ἐδίδασκεν as here.

3. For **ἄγουσιν δέ**, *fam.* 13 gives καὶ προσήνεγκαν αὐτῷ.

οἱ γραμματεῖς. There is no mention of scribes in Jn. "Scribes
and Pharisees" is a frequent Synoptic phrase for the opponents of
Jesus, whom Jn. prefers to describe briefly as "the Jews" (see on 1¹⁹).

The woman was not brought before Jesus for formal trial, but in
order to get His expression of opinion on a point of the Mosaic law,
which might afterwards be used against Him (see v. 6), of which other
examples are given by the Snyoptists (cf. Mk. 12¹³· ¹⁸).

Some minor uncials ins. πρὸς αὐτόν before γυναῖκα, but om. D 1071
and *fam.* 13.

ἐπὶ μοιχείᾳ is supported by the uncials MSUΓΛ and *fam.* 13; ἐν
μοιχείᾳ is read by EGHKΠ, and is smoothed down in D 1071 to ἐπὶ
ἁμαρτίᾳ.

κατειλημμένην. καταλαμβάνειν, "to overtake," occurs in Jn. 1⁵ 12³⁵.
Milligan gives from a fourth- or fifth-century papyrus an exact parallel
to the present passage, where it is used of detection in sin, viz.:
γυναῖκα καταλημφθεῖσαν ὑπὸ τοῦ ἠδικημένου μετὰ μοίχου.

σαντες αὐτὴν ἐν μέσῳ, 4. λέγουσιν αὐτῷ Διδάσκαλε, αὕτη ἡ γυνὴ κατείληπται ἐπ'
αὐτοφώρῳ μοιχευομένη· 5. ἐν δὲ τῷ νόμῳ ἡμῖν Μωυσῆς ἐνετείλατο τὰς τοιαύτας
λιθάζειν· σὺ οὖν τί λέγεις; 6. τοῦτο δὲ ἔλεγον πειράζοντες αὐτόν, ἵνα ἔχωσιν

στήσαντες αὐτὴν ἐν μέσῳ (ἐν τῷ μεσῷ, *fam.* 13). Cf. Acts 4[7] for the
phrase descriptive of " setting " people in the midst of bystanders for
the purpose of examining them.

4. After **αὐτῷ**, D adds ἐκπειράζοντες αὐτόν, and EGHK 1071 πειράζοντες
only. The phrase with ἐκπειράζειν is Lucan ; cf. Lk. 10[25].

For **διδάσκαλε**, see on 1[38].

For **κατείληπται** (D 1071), MSΛ and *fam.* 13 have εἴληπται, while
EGHKΓΠ give κατειλήφθη.

ἐπ' αὐτοφώρῳ, " in the act." The phrase does not occur again in
the Greek Bible, but is thoroughly classical. Cf. Philo, *de spec. leg.* iii.
10, μοιχείας δὲ τάς μὲν αὐτοφώρους . . . ἀπέφηνεν ὁ νόμος. Milligan illustrates from a second-century papyrus τοὺς λη's μφθέντας ἐπ' αὐτοφώρῳ
κακούργους.

μοιχεύειν does not occur in Jn., but several times in the Synoptists.

5. ἐν δὲ τῷ νόμῳ κτλ.. In an ordinary case of adultery (*e.g.* Lev.
20[10]) the penalty was death for both parties, but the manner of execution is not specified, the Talmud prescribing death by strangulation.
But in the exceptional and specially heinous case of a betrothed
woman's unchastity, death was to be by stoning (Deut. 22[21]). It was
an unusual case like this that was put before Jesus.

These severe laws were rarely put in force, but nevertheless the
dilemma was neatly framed. If He said that the guilty woman should
be stoned, He would have been subject to the Roman law for inciting
to murder ; and although the Roman authorities were lax on occasion
about such acts of violence (as in the case of Stephen, Acts 7[58]), there
would have been a good pretext for handing Him over to them to deal
with. If, however, He inclined to more merciful treatment, as was
probably expected of Him, He would have been declared by His
critics to be a blasphemous person who did not accept the enactments
of the sacred law. Cf. Mk. 12[14] for the dilemma about the tribute
money ; and Mk. 10[2] for the question about divorce, which, however
puzzling, would not involve difficulty with the Roman authorities.

Augustine, however, puts the dilemma in a simpler way : " Si ut
iuberet occidi perderet mansuetudinis famam ; si autem iuberet
dimitti incurreret, tanquam reprehensor legis, calumniam " (*Enarr.
in Ps.* l. § 8). This may be right, but it does not recall the attempts to
entrap Jesus recorded by the Synoptists.

For the first clause D has Μωυσῆς δὲ ἐν τῷ νόμῳ ἐκέλευσεν. For
λιθάζειν (cf. 10[31]), which is read by DMSU 1071 and *fam.* 13, the rec.
has λιθοβολεῖσθαι (the verb used Deut. 22[21]) with EGHKΠ.

After **λέγεις** ins. περὶ αὐτῆς MSUΛ *fam.* 13 *c ff₂.*

6. From **τοῦτο δέ** to **κατηγ. αὐτοῦ** is om. by DM, the clause appearing in the rec. supported by SUL *fam.* 13 (in the form κατηγορίαν κατ'
αὐτοῦ). Such laying of traps for Jesus is often mentioned in the
Synoptists, *e.g.* Mk. 8[11], Lk. 11[16].

κατά is seldom used by Jn., but cf. κατηγορίαν κατά followed by a
genitive, at 18[29].

κάτω κύψας is read here, but κατακύψας at v. 8, " having stooped
down." κατακύπτειν occurs again in the Greek Bible only at 4 Kings
9[32], in the sense of " peeping out"; see, for παρακύπτειν, on 20[5]. For
κατακύπτειν, " to stoop," Milligan cites Aristeas ix. 1.

κατέγραφεν. So DEGHMS, but KUΓΛ *fam.* 13 have ἔγραφεν.
καταγράφειν does not occur again in N.T., but appears several times

κατηγορεῖν αὐτοῦ. ὁ δὲ Ἰησοῦς κάτω κύψας τῷ δακτύλῳ κατέγραφεν εἰς τὴν
γῆν. 7. ὡς δὲ ἐπέμενον ἐρωτῶντες αὐτόν, ἀνέκυψεν καὶ εἶπεν αὐτοῖς Ὁ

in LXX, often meaning " to register," a sense also found in papyri.
It indicates a record or register of something blameworthy in Job 13²⁶,
1 Esdr. 2¹⁶, Ecclus. 48¹⁰ ; and this meaning is accepted in some ancient
comments, both here and at v. 8.

In a short recension of the story found in an Armenian MS. of the
Gospels of A.D. 989, we have : " He Himself, bowing His head, was
writing with His finger on the earth, to declare their sins ; and they
were seeing their several sins on the stones." [1] And again, after εἰς
τὴν γῆν in v. 8, U and some cursives add ἕνος ἑκάστου αὐτῶν τὰς
ἁμαρτίας, as if Jesus was writing down the names and sins of the
several accusers. Jerome has the same tradition : " Jesus inclinans
digito scribebat in terra, eorum, uidelicet qui accusabant et omnium
peccata mortalium, secundum quod scriptum est in propheta Relin-
quentes autem te in terra scribentur " (adv. Pelagium ii. 17, citing
Jer. 17¹³).

There is, however, no evidence that Jesus was writing anything
by way of record. That He was able to write may be assumed,
although in no other place in the N.T. is He said to have written
anything. But it is probable that on this occasion He was only
scribbling with His finger on the ground, a mechanical action which
would suggest only an unwillingness to speak on the subject brought
before Him, and preoccupation with His own thoughts.[2]

If, however, the meaning of *register* for κατέγραφεν is to be
pressed, the emphasis must be placed on εἰς τὴν γῆν : " He began to
register the accusation *in the dust*," as if He would have no permanent
record.

After γῆν the rec. adds, with EGHK, the gloss μὴ προσποιούμενος,
" affecting that it was not so," sc. " as though He heard them not."
This is a classical use of προσποιεῖσθαι with a neg. (cf. Thucyd. iii. 47) ;
the verb occurs again in the N.T. only at Lk. 24²⁸ (cf. 1 Sam. 21¹³,
προσεποιήσατο, " feigned himself," sc. to be mad).

7. ἐπέμενον ἐρωτῶντες, " they went on asking," as at Acts 12¹⁶
ἐπέμενεν κρούων. ἐπιμένειν does not occur in Jn.

D om. αὐτόν, ἐρωτῶντες then being used absolutely or intransitively,
as in the (unusual) instance of Jn. 17⁹.

ἀνέκυψεν καί. So D 1071. The rec., with EGHK, has ἀνακύψας
(cf. v. 10), while *fam.* 13 give ἀναβλέψας. In the N.T. ἀνακύπτειν is
found again only Lk. 13¹¹ 21²⁸, " to lift oneself up " ; ἀναβλέπειν is in
all the Gospels.

εἶπεν αὐτοῖς. So DSUΓ 1071 *fam.* 13. M om. αὐτοῖς. EGHK
have πρὸς αὐτούς, the rec. reading.

ὁ ἀναμάρτητος κτλ., " Let him that is faultless," etc. This is the
true Synoptic note. ἀναμάρτητος does not indicate only innocence
of overt sins of the flesh, but freedom from sinful desire cherished and

---

[1] See Conybeare, *D.B.* i. 154 ; and Burkitt, *Two Lectures on the
Gospels*, p. 88.
[2] Perhaps Seeley's comment hits on the truth : " He was seized
with an intolerable sense of shame. He could not meet the eye of the
crowd, or of the accusers, and perhaps at that moment least of all of
the woman. . . . In His burning embarrassment and confusion He
stooped down so as to hide His face, and began writing with His
fingers on the ground " (Ecce Homo, c. ix.).

720 THE GOSPEL ACCORDING TO ST. JOHN [VIII. 7–10.

ἀναμάρτητος ὑμῶν πρῶτος ἐπ' αὐτὴν βαλέτω λίθον· 8. καὶ πάλιν κατακύψας
ἔγραφεν εἰς τὴν γῆν. 9. οἱ δὲ ἀκούσαντες ἐξήρχοντο εἰς καθ' εἰς ἀρξάμενοι
ἀπὸ τῶν πρεσβυτέρων, καὶ κατελείφθη μόνος, καὶ ἡ γυνὴ ἐν μέσῳ οὖσα.
10. ἀνακύψας δὲ ὁ Ἰησοῦς εἶπεν αὐτῇ, Γύναι, ποῦ εἰσίν; οὐδείς σε κατέκρινεν;

indulged in. Cf. Mt. 5²⁸. ἀναμάρτητος does not occur again in N.T.,
but is found Deut. 29¹⁹, 2 Macc. 8¹⁴ 12⁴².

For πρῶτος (D 1071), EGH give πρῶτον.

βαλέτω λίθον. So D and *fam.* 13. Other uncials read τὸν λίθον,
to bring out the point that the casting of the *first* stone was the duty
of the witnesses who certified to the crime (Deut. 17⁷). But the
allusion is the same, even if τόν is omitted. The question of Jesus
asks, in fact, who is to be the executioner in this case? (cf. Augustine,
Sermo xiii. § 4).

8. καὶ πάλιν κτλ. Jesus again indicates His unwillingness to
discuss the matter with the Pharisees. He begins to scribble on the
dust for the second time.

τῷ δακτύλῳ is ins. here after κατακύψας by D 28, 74, 1071 *ff₂*; but
om. *fam.* 13.

As at v. 6, *fam.* 13 support ἔγραφεν for κατέγραφεν (so D 28, 31).

9. The rec., following EGHKS, after ἀκούσαντες interpolates the
explanatory gloss καὶ ὑπὸ τῆς συνειδήσεως ἐλεγχόμενοι: om. DMUΓΛ
fam. 13, 1071 and the Lat. vss.

For the whole clause οἱ δὲ ἀκ. . . . καθ' εἰς, D gives only ἔκαστος δὲ
τῶν Ἰουδαίων ἐξήρχετο, while *fam.* 13 have only ἐξῆλθον εἰς καθ' εἰς.

After πρεσβυτέρων the rec. adds, with SUΛ *fam.* 13, ἕως τῶν
ἐσχάτων, while D 1071 add ὥστε πάντας ἐξελθεῖν, but both additions are
om. in EGHKMΓ, etc. Westcott-Hort suggest that πάντες ἀνεχώρησαν
(cf. M 264) originally followed πρεσβυτέρων as an independent clause.

The glosses are unnecessary, although doubtless right in the explanations they offer. The elder men (πρεσβύτεροι, a word not
occurring in Jn.; cf. 2 Jn.¹, 3 Jn.¹) were naturally the first to leave,
having taken the lead in trying to ensnare Jesus, and having been
silenced by His suggestion that they must have felt the power of the
temptation which had overcome the woman. If the scene is to be
placed in the week following the Triumphal Entry, their acquiescence
in the moral authority which Jesus exercised is more readily intelligible.
They dared not press the moral issue before the admiring and awestruck people.

For εἰς καθ' εἰς, cf. Mk. 14¹⁹; it is not a Johannine phrase.

καὶ κατελείφθη μόνος. μόνος is om. by *fam.* 13. Perhaps some
disciples were present, and nothing is said of their going away, but the
words may mean that Jesus and the woman were left quite alone
(as the rec. text indicates), the onlookers feeling the painfulness of
the scene. Augustine says: "Remansit magna miseria et magna
misericordia" (*Enarr. in Ps.* l. § 8). Yet the woman remained ἐν
μέσῳ, which suggests the presence of a little group; and, furthermore,
the words that Jesus said to her were overheard and were preserved.

κατελείφθη. The verb καταλείπειν is not used by Jn.

10. For ἀνακύψας (cf. v. 7), *fam.* 13 with Λ has ἀναβλέψας.
After ὁ Ἰησ. the rec., with EGHK, adds the gloss καὶ μηδένα
θεασάμενος πλὴν τῆς γυναικός, but om. DMS and *fam.* 13. πλήν is
never used by Jn.

D 1071 have εἶπεν τῇ γυναικί, but MSUΓ *fam.* 13 have εἶπεν, Γυναί.
The rec., with cursive support, has εἶπεν αὐτῇ, Ἡ γυνή, the nom. with
the article being used for the vocative, a Hebraic use that occurs
Mk. 14³⁶, Mt. 11²⁶, Lk. 10²¹, but not in Jn. (see on 17²¹).

11. ἡ δὲ εἶπεν Οὐδείς, κύριε.   εἶπεν δὲ ὁ Ἰησοῦς Οὐδὲ ἐγώ σε κατακρίνω·
πορεύου, ἀπὸ τοῦ νῦν μηκέτι ἁμάρτανε.

ποῦ εἰσίν; The rec. adds ἐκεῖνοι οἱ κατήγοροί σου, and *fam.* 13 has
the gloss, omitting ἐκεῖνοι ; but om. DMΓΛ 1071.

οὐδείς σε κατέκρινεν ; The compound κατακρίνειν is not Johannine.

In this verse, Jesus is represented as waiting for a little before He
spoke. " Has no one proceeded to condemn you ? " is His question
at last.

11. Οὐδείς, κύριε. " No one, sir." That is all the woman says
from beginning to end.   Indeed, she has no excuse for her conduct.

Οὐδὲ ἐγώ σε κατακρίνω. The verbal similarity of these words to
ἐγὼ οὐ κρίνω of 8¹⁵ (where see note) may have suggested the position
which the interpolated section occupies in the rec. text, viz. at the
beginning of c. 8.   But κατακρίνειν conveys condemnation in a degree
which the simple verb κρίνειν does not connote.   Jesus does not
say here that He does not pass judgment, even in His own mind,
upon the woman's conduct, but that He does not condemn her judici-
ally or undertake the duty of a judge who had to administer or interpret the Mosaic law (cf. Lk. 12¹⁴).   Still less does His reply convey
forgiveness ; the woman who was forgiven in Lk. 7⁴⁸ was a penitent,
but there is no hint of penitence in this case.

Probably, the apparent leniency of the words οὐδὲ ἐγώ σε κατακρίνω
(which could readily be misunderstood) led to their omission in the
tenth-century Armenian MS. quoted above on v. 6, and also in a
Syriac paraphrase given by Dionysius Barsalibi.[1] The Armenian
codex ends, " Go in peace, and present the offering for sins, as in their
law is written," while the Syriac paraphrase has only, " Go thou also
now and do this sin no more."

The warning μηκέτι ἁμάρτανε is found also at 5¹⁴, where (as here)
the person addressed has not confessed any sin.   The woman had
still time to repent.

ἀπὸ τοῦ νῦν is om. by *fam.* 13, but ins. DMSUΓ 1071.   The phrase
is Lucan (Lk. 1⁴⁸ 5¹⁰ 12⁵² 22⁶⁹) but not Johannine.

---

[1] See Gwynn, *Trans. R.I. Acad.* xvii. p. 292.

I. GENERAL INDEX

II. INDEX OF AUTHORS AND WRITINGS

III. INDEX OF GREEK WORDS

733

PRINTED BY MORRISON AND GIBB LTD., EDINBURGH AND LONDON